THE NATIONAL UNDERWRITER COMPANY

THE TOOLS & TECHNIQUES OF INCOME TAX PLANNING
4TH EDITION

By Stephan R. Leimberg, Randy Gardner, Michael S. Jackson, Martin J. Satinsky, and Jay Katz

Recent legislation has brought numerous alterations to the tax law, but many of these highly impactful tax changes are unique in that they are contained in laws that, at least on the surface, are not tax-related. In short, today you find hidden—but important—tax implications in unexpected places.

This single-volume reference takes you through all the income tax topics your clients may encounter, no matter where they originate, providing easy-to-understand, practical guidance for situations that are often confusing.

The Tools & Techniques of Income Tax Planning, 4th Edition, provides everything you need to put the optimal strategic plan in place, while taking into consideration the tax-related elements of:

- The American Recovery and Reinvestment Act

- The Affordable Care Act

- The American Taxpayer Relief Act

From mastering the fundamentals of income tax law to managing the implications of wealth transfer—and more—this fully revised and enhanced volume puts expert guidance and successful income tax strategies right at your fingertips.

The Tools & Techniques of Income Tax Planning, 4th Edition, contains six entirely new chapters, which were added to fully reflect recent legislative changes as well as other, crucial developments in this area:

- Business and Non-business Losses

- Self-Employment and Social Security Taxes

- Additional Medicare Tax on Earned Income and Net Investment Income Tax

- Withholding and Estimated Tax Requirements

- Income Tax Issues in Wealth Transfer Planning

- Discharge of Debt

Filled with the actual, applicable tools and techniques you need to help clients manage tax issues, this single volume takes you right to the heart of topics affecting individual taxpayers as well as small- and medium-sized business owners. It is intended to help you master the tax issues faced by your clients, today, and confidently advise them on setting proven income tax strategies for tomorrow.

For customer service questions or to place additional orders, please call 1-800-543-0874.

For substantive updates to this product, please visit: pro.nuco.com/booksupplements

4TH EDITION

The Tools & Techniques of
Income Tax Planning

LEIMBERG LIBRARY

Stephan R. Leimberg

Randy Gardner • Michael S. Jackson

Martin J. Satinsky • Jay Katz

ISBN 978-1-939829-55-9

Library of Congress Control Number: 2014949564

THE NATIONAL UNDERWRITER COMPANY
Copyright © 2009, 2015

The National Underwriter Company
4157 Olympic Blvd., Suite 225
Erlanger, KY 41018

Fourth Edition

ABOUT SUMMIT PROFESSIONAL NETWORKS

Summit Professional Networks supports the growth and vitality of the insurance, financial services and legal communities by providing professionals with the knowledge and education they need to succeed at every stage of their careers. We provide face-to-face and digital events, websites, mobile sites and apps, online information services, and magazines giving professionals multi-platform access to our critical resources, including Professional Development; Education & Certification; Prospecting & Data Tools; Industry News & Analysis; Reference Tools and Services; and Community Networking Opportunities.

Using all of our resources across each community we serve, we deliver measurable ROI for our sponsors through a range of turnkey services, including Research, Content Development, Integrated Media, Creative & Design, and Lead Generation.

For more information, go to http://www.SummitProfessionalNetworks.com.

ABOUT THE NATIONAL UNDERWRITER COMPANY

The National Underwriter Company is a Summit Professional Network

For over 110 years, The National Underwriter Company has been the first in line with the targeted tax, insurance, and financial planning information you need to make critical business decisions. Boasting nearly a century of expert experience, our reputable Editors are dedicated to putting accurate and relevant information right at your fingertips. With *Tax Facts*, *Tools & Techniques*, *National Underwriter Advanced Markets*, *Field Guide*, *FC&S®*, *FC&S Legal* and other resources available in print, eBook, CD, and online, you can be assured that as the industry evolves National Underwriter will be at the forefront with the thorough and easy-to-use resources you rely on for success.

The National Underwriter Company
Update Service Notification

This National Underwriter Company publication is regularly updated to include coverage of developments and changes that affect the content. If you did not purchase this publication directly from The National Underwriter Company and you want to receive these important updates sent on a 30-day review basis and billed separately, please contact us at (800) 543-0874. Or you can mail your request with your name, company, address, and the title of the book to:

> The National Underwriter Company
> 4157 Olympic Boulevard, Suite 225
> Erlanger, KY 41018

If you purchased this publication from The National Underwriter Company directly, you have already been registered for the update service.

National Underwriter Company Contact Information

To order any National Underwriter Company title, please

- call 1-800-543-0874, 8-6 ET Monday – Thursday and 8 to 5 ET Friday

- online bookstore at www.nationalunderwriter.com, or

- mail to The National Underwriter Company, Orders Department, 4157 Olympic Blvd., Ste. 225, Erlanger, KY 41018

DEDICATIONS

Stephan R. Leimberg

To My Best Friend in All The World, my Wife Jo-Ann,
To My Daughters, Charlee and Lara,
and To My Grandsons, Max and Aaron

Martin J. Satinsky
To Marcia

Michael S. Jackson
To my extraordinary wife, Maria,
for her constant love, support and encouragement.
To my wonderful children, Jared and Rebecca,
who make me so proud day after day.

Randy Gardner
To Leslie and my children, Bryn, Kara, Creyton, and Hope.

Jay Katz
Dedicated to the memory of my son, Asher Katz.
Although way too short, his life will be forever celebrated and remembered
in the lifetimes of those who knew him.

ACKNOWLEDGMENTS

Mike Jackson would like to thank his partners at Grant Thornton LLP and those individuals in the Private Wealth Services group that helped complete this edition: Jay Bethard, Albert Cordahi, Ladidas Lumpkins, Paula Marchese, Jared Szycther and Justin Wenzelman.

ABOUT THE AUTHORS

Stephan R. Leimberg

Stephan R. Leimberg is CEO of Leimberg and LeClair, Inc., an estate and financial planning software company, CEO of LISI, Leimberg Information Services, Inc., an e-mail newsletter service, and President of Leimberg Associates, Inc., a publishing and software company. He is an Adjunct Professor in the Masters of Taxation Program of Villanova University School of Law and former adjunct at Temple University School of Law. He holds a B.A. from Temple University, and a J.D. from Temple University School of Law. Leimberg is the Editor of the American Society of Financial Service Professionals audio publication, *Keeping Current*.

Leimberg is the author or co-author of numerous books on estate, financial, and employee benefit and retirement planning and a nationally known speaker. Leimberg is the creator and principal author of the entire nine book *Tools & Techniques* series including *The Tools & Techniques of Estate Planning*, *The Tools & Techniques of Financial Planning*, *The Tools & Techniques of Employee Benefit and Retirement Planning*, *The Tools & Techniques of Life Insurance Planning*, *The Tools & Techniques of Charitable Planning*, *The Tools & Techniques of Investment Planning*, *The Tools & Techniques of Risk Management*, *The Tools & Techniques of Practice Management*, and *The Tools & Techniques of Retirement Income Planning*. Leimberg is co-author of *Tax Planning with Life Insurance* with noted attorney Howard Zaritsky, *The Book of Trusts* with attorneys Charles K. Plotnick and Daniel Evans, and *How to Settle an Estate* with Charles K. Plotnick. He was also a contributing author of the American Bar Association's *The Lawyer's Guide to Retirement*.

Leimberg is co-creator of many software packages for the financial services professional including Estate and Financial Planning *NumberCruncher* (estate planning), DeCoupleCruncher (estate planning), *Financial Analyzer II* (financial calculations), *Estate Planning Quickview* (Estate Planning Flow Charts), *Life Settlement NumberCruncher* (life settlement buy-hold analysis), *Planning Ahead for a Secure Retirement* (PowerPoint Client Seminar) and *Toward a Zero Estate Tax* (PowerPoint Client Estate Planning Seminar).

A nationally known speaker, Leimberg has addressed the Miami Tax Institute, the NYU Tax Institute, the Federal Tax Bar, the Notre Dame Law School and Duke University Law School's Estate Planning Conference, the National Association of Estate Planners and Councils, the AICPA's National Estate Planning Forum, the ABA Section on Taxation, and The Annual Meeting of the American Society of Financial Service Professionals. Leimberg has also spoken to the Federal Bureau of Investigation and the National Aeronautics and Space Administration.

Leimberg was awarded the Excellence in Writing Award of the American Bar Association's Probate and Property Section. He has been honored as Estate Planner of the Year by the Montgomery County Estate Planning Council and as Distinguished Estate Planner by the Philadelphia Estate Planning Council. He is also the recipient of the President's Cup of the Philadelphia Life Underwriters, a two time Boris Todorovitch Lecturer, and the First Ben Feldman Lecturer.

Leimberg was named Edward N. Polisher Lecturer of the Dickinson School of Law and 2004 recipient of the National Association of Estate Planners and Councils Distinguished Accredited Estate Planner award,

Leimberg's LISI e-mail newsletter/data base http://www.leimbergservices.com is used daily by thousands of estate, financial, employee benefit, charitable, and retirement planning practitioners.

Martin J. Satinsky

Marty Satinsky, CPA/PFS, J.D., LL.M., AEP, has been providing tax and financial planning services to individuals and businesses for over forty years. He has worked with regional and international accounting firms, including seven years as a tax partner with Coopers & Lybrand. Mr. Satinsky is currently Principal in charge of the tax practice of Crosslin & Associates, P.C., a CPA firm in Nashville, Tennessee.

Throughout his career, Mr. Satinsky specialized in tax consulting for high net worth individuals and closely held businesses. While a partner in the accounting firm of Smart and Associates, LLP, Mr. Satinsky was the Director of Professional Development, responsible for the Firm's training and Continuing Professional Education (CPE) program through Smart University.

An accomplished author on personal financial matters, he has co-authored seven books on income and estate taxes and personal financial planning, including the popular *Tools & Techniques of Financial Planning*. A frequent lecturer, Mr. Satinsky has also been an instructor at the American College, Temple University Law School, Georgetown University Law School, Syracuse University Law School, the University of Pennsylvania, Philadelphia University, and the Owen Graduate School of Management at Vanderbilt University.

Mr. Satinsky was also a founding shareholder of Second Opinion Financial Services, Inc. (SOFS) a company with a focus on educating professionals on the use and mechanics of life insurance. SOFS developed a software program which dynamically illustrated the impact of the variables affecting the performance of life insurance products.

A graduate of the Pennsylvania State University and the Law School of the University of Pennsylvania, Mr. Satinsky also received his Master of Law degree in Taxation from Temple University Law School. He is a Certified Public Accountant in Pennsylvania and Tennessee. He is a member of the American Institute of Certified Public Accountants, and the Pennsylvania Institute of Certified Public Accountants, as well as the Tennessee Society of Certified Public Accountants. He has served as an officer of the Philadelphia Estate Planning Council and as a member of the AICPA

Personal Financial Planning Executive Committee and the PICPA Personal Financial Planning Committee.

Mr. Satinsky has conducted numerous seminars on tax, estate planning and financial planning topics, including many presentations on life insurance issues, for such organizations, as the Pennsylvania Bar Institute, the AICPA, PICPA, FPA NAPFA, Accountants' Continuing Education Network, CLE Options, and several Estate Planning Councils. In 2000, he was honored with the Distinguished Estate Planner Award by the Philadelphia Estate Planning Council and in 2006 he received the Distinguished Accredited Estate Planner Award from the National Association of Estate Planners and Councils. Mr. Satinsky is a member of the National Association of Estate Planners and Councils and the Society of Financial Service Professionals.

Marty is a past Chairman of the Jewish Community Centers of Greater Philadelphia and is an emeritus member of its Board. He has also served as the Treasurer of Hillel of Greater Philadelphia and a member of the Board of Jewish Community Center Association and the Maccabi Continental Games Board. He has been active with the Federation of Jewish Agencies in Philadelphia, Washington, D.C. Syracuse, N.Y. and Nashville, TN, and has most recently served as the Treasurer of Hillel of Vanderbilt University, a member of the Board of the Gordon Jewish Community Center of Nashville, Tennessee, and Treasurer of Temple Sherit Isreal of Nashville.

Michael S. Jackson

Michael S. Jackson, CPA/PFS, M.T., has provided tax compliance and consulting services to closely held businesses and high net worth individual clients for nearly 20 years. Mr. Jackson is currently a Managing Director in the tax department of SMART Business Advisory and Consulting, LLC in Devon, Pennsylvania. Over the last 15 years, he also has consulted with clients as a fee-based personal financial planner and has been certified as a Personal Financial Specialist (PFS) by the American Institute of Certified Public Accountants.

Prior to joining SMART, Mr. Jackson spent three years as a senior tax accountant at Ernst & Young, LLP specializing in S corporation, partnership and individual tax consulting and compliance in the Entrepreneurial Services Group. He left to join Martin J. Satinsky & Associates in 1993 to serve as a tax compliance, consulting and personal financial planning manager. That firm merged with Isdaner & Company, LLC in Bala Cynwyd,

Pennsylvania in 1999. Mr. Jackson joined SMART in 2003 as part of the firm's enhancement of its private client services within the tax department.

Mr. Jackson received his Masters Degree in Taxation from Villanova University School of Law. He graduated Magna Cum Laude from Drexel University with a Bachelor of Science in Business Administration, majoring in accounting and finance. As a student at Drexel, he participated in internships in the tax departments of Fishbein & Company and Arthur Young.

Mr. Jackson is a Certified Public Accountant in Pennsylvania and a member of the American Institute of Certified Public Accountants and Pennsylvania Institute of Certified Public Accountants. He has been a frequent lecturer of tax and financial planning topics for various organizations, authored numerous articles for local and national publications, and has been interviewed several times for Philadelphia news and community television broadcasts. In addition to this title, he is a co-author of *The Tools & Techniques of Financial Planning*, also published by National Underwriter.

Randy Gardner

Mr. Randy Gardner, LLM, MBA, CPA, CFP® is a Professor of Taxation and Director of the Certificate in Financial Planning Program at the University of Missouri - Kansas City. Randy is also the Director of Education for Wealth-Counsel, LLC, a national organization of estate planning attorneys. Coauthor of *101 Tax Saving Ideas* and co-editor of *WealthCounsel Estate Planning Strategies*, Randy is a highly rated discussion leader who was recognized as Educator of the Year by the Missouri Society of CPAs.

In addition to teaching, Randy works as a tax and estate planning consultant for several accounting firms and over 400 individual clients. Randy earned a Bachelor of Arts degree, cum laude, from Harvard University; his Juris Doctorate and Master of Business Administration degrees from the University of Kansas; and a Master of Law in Taxation from the University of Missouri - Kansas City. A member of the AICPA and the Missouri Society of CPAs, Randy serves on the Editorial Board of *The Journal of Financial Planning and formerly served* on the Certified Financial Planner™ Board's Council on Examinations. He lives in Leawood, Kansas with his four children.

Jay Katz

Jay Katz is a tax attorney in Delaware with more than a decade of experience in private practice litigating tax cases and handling audits, collection matters, and offers in compromise for corporate and individual clients. He has earned LLMs in taxation from both the NYU and University of Florida graduate tax programs. During twelve years as a professor at Widener University Law School and Beasley School of Law at Temple University, Jay has taught virtually every tax and estate planning course on the curriculum and was the director of the Widener tax clinic.

In addition to being a coauthor of the 4th Edition of *The Tools & Techniques of Income Tax Planning*, Jay is a contributing editor and member of the Tax Facts Advisory Board at the National Underwriter Company and has penned seven published tax articles, including "An Offer in Compromise You Can't Confuse: It is not the Opening Bid of a Delinquent Taxpayer to Play Let's Make a Tax Deal with the Internal Revenue Service," 81 *Miss. L. J.* 1673 (2012) (lead article); "The William O. Douglas Tax Factor: Where Did the Spin Stop and Who Was He Looking Out For?" 3 *Charlotte Law Review* 133 (2012) (lead article); and "The Untold Story of Crane v. Commissioner Reveals an Inconvenient Tax Truth: Useless Depreciation Deductions Cause Global Basis Erosion to Bait A Hazardous Tax Trap For Unwitting Taxpayers," 30 *Va. Tax Rev.* 559 (2011).

About the Publisher

Kelly B. Maheu, J.D., is Managing Director of the Professional Publishing Division of The National Underwriter Company, a Division of Summit Professional Networks. Kelly has been with The National Underwriter Company since 2006, and served in editorial, content acquisition, and product development roles prior to being named Managing Director.

Prior to joining The National Underwriter Company, Kelly worked in the legal and insurance fields for Lexis-Nexis®, Progressive Insurance, and a Cincinnati insurance defense litigation firm.

Kelly has edited and contributed to numerous books and publications including the *Personal Auto Insurance Policy Coverage Guide, Cyberliability and Insurance, The National Underwriter Sales Essentials Series*, and *The Tools & Techniques of Risk Management for Financial Planners*.

Kelly earned her law degree from The University of Cincinnati College of Law and holds a BA from Miami University, Ohio, with a double major in English/Journalism and Psychology.

About the Editor
Managing Editor – Professional Publishing Division

Christine G. Barlow, CPCU, is Managing Editor of the Professional Publishing Division at the National Underwriter Company, a division of Summit Professional Networks. Christine has fifteen years' experience in the insurance industry, beginning as a claims adjuster then working as an underwriter and underwriting supervisor handling personal lines. Before joining National Underwriter, Christine worked as an Underwriting Supervisor for the Maryland Auto Insurance Fund, and as a Senior Underwriter for Montgomery Mutual, Old American, and Nationwide.

Editor

Jason Gilbert, J.D., M.A., is an assistant editor with the Professional Publishing Division of the National Underwriter Company, a division of Summit Professional Networks. He edits and develops publications related to tax and insurance products, including titles in the *Advisor's Guide* and the *Tools & Techniques* series of investment and planning products. He also develops content for Summit's other financial services publications and online products. He has worked on insurance and tax publications for more than nine years.

Jason has been a practicing attorney for more than a dozen years in the areas of criminal defense, products liability, and regulatory enforcement actions. Prior to joining Summit Professional Networks, his experience in the insurance and tax fields has included work as a Westlaw contributor for Thomson Reuters and a tax advisor and social media contributor for Intuit. He is an honors graduate from Wright State University and holds a J.D. from the University of Cincinnati College of Law as well as a master's degree in Economics from Miami University in Ohio.

Editorial Services

Connie L. Jump, Supervisor, Editorial Services

Patti O'Leary, Editorial Assistant

CONTENTS

Tools of Income Tax Planning

Techniques of Income Tax Planning

Appendices

INCOME TAX LAW FUNDAMENTALS

CHAPTER 1

It's no secret to anyone who has prepared their own (or anyone else's) tax return that the federal income tax laws can be hard to comprehend and difficult to work with. The sheer number of laws, and the complexity of those laws, can be somewhat daunting. Even the Internal Revenue Service (IRS), the nation's tax collection agency, acknowledges that "for anyone not familiar with the inner workings of tax administration, the array of IRS guidance may seem, well, a little puzzling at first glance."[1] Since even Albert Einstein expressed his concern that tax laws were among the most complex of all human tasks, this statement by the IRS could be one of the great understatements of all time!

Yet, the financial planner must have a good general working knowledge of the tax laws in order to effectively assist his or her clients. This chapter explains the sources of federal tax law, the relative importance of each federal tax law source, and how to identify a source by its citation.

There are four general sources of federal tax law:

1. the Internal Revenue Code;

2. the regulations of the Treasury Department;

3. rulings and other guidance of the IRS; and

4. court decisions.[2]

Not all tax law resources have the same value. *Primary authorities* are official pronouncements of the law made by Congress (in the form of statutes), courts (in the form of case decisions), and governmental agencies (in the form of regulations).

Secondary authorities are explanations or interpretations of the law. The Internal Revenue Code is an example of a primary authority. Legislative history is an example of a secondary authority. The relative importance of each of the four general federal tax law sources is explained in more detail below.

In addition to the law, regulations, IRS interpretations, and court decisions, financial planners should keep abreast of what changes may be ahead. Pending legislation, and regulations, and tax litigation awaiting court resolution are key examples of what might change "the rules of the game." In recent years, many of the tax code amendments have been focused on extending existing provisions of the law which are scheduled to expire, as opposed to actual changes in the law itself.

THE INTERNAL REVENUE CODE

Congress derives its power to levy taxes under the Constitution of the United States. Congress exercises this power by enacting tax statutes that are compiled in the *Internal Revenue Code* ("the Code"). The Code is actually a "title" (Title 26) within the larger *United States Code*.[3] All federal tax legislation currently in effect is contained in the Internal Revenue Code of 1986; legislation enacted after 1986 repeals, amends, or adds sections to the 1986 Code.

The Internal Revenue Code is the law. The IRS and all courts are required to follow it. Keep in mind, however, that even though the Code is voluminous, it simply states the basic law. Not all tax questions are answered in the Code. Unanswered questions arise daily as taxpayers attempt to apply the general provisions of the Code to many different factual situations. Thus, in its role in administering the laws enacted by Congress, the IRS is required to take the specifics of those laws and translate them into detailed regulations, rules, and procedures.

The Code is made up of several parts, known as subtitles, chapters, parts, sections, subsections, paragraphs, and subparagraphs. However, *citations* to provisions of the Code refer only to sections, subsections, paragraphs, and subparagraphs.[4] A Code section may be referred to generally as "I.R.C. Section 101." However, when referring to a more specific part, the section should be cited as "I.R.C. §101(a)(2)(B)." Separated into its essential components, this citation refers to:

- Internal Revenue Code Section 101;

- subsection (a);

- paragraph (2);

- subparagraph (B).

TREASURY REGULATIONS

Treasury regulations are issued by the IRS and the Treasury Department to: (1) provide guidance for new legislation; and (2) address issues that arise with respect to existing Internal Revenue Code sections. The purpose of the Treasury regulations is to assist taxpayers and their advisors in interpreting and complying with the law. Through examples and explanatory material, the regulations let taxpayers know how the government will interpret the Code in numerous situations and how to comply with certain Code provisions.

The Internal Revenue Regulations (Title 26) are one of 50 titles in the *Code of Federal Regulations* (CFR).[5] Regulations are initially published in proposed form in the *Federal Register*[6] in what's known as a "Notice of Proposed Rulemaking" (NPRM). After public input has been fully considered by the IRS, through written comments and comments made in person during a public hearing, a final or temporary regulation is published as a "Treasury Decision" (TD) in the *Federal Register*.

Regulations are referred to by section numbers that roughly correspond to the sections of the Internal Revenue Code. Thus, for example, the citation "26 CFR §1.170-1(a)(3)" refers to a regulation found in Title 26 of the *Code of Federal Regulations* that explains Internal Revenue Code Section 170. The parenthetical letter and number pinpoint more precisely the specific subpart of the regulation that is pertinent to answering a question about Internal Revenue Code Section 170.

Relative Importance

There are two kinds of regulations, *legislative* and *interpretative*. *Legislative* regulations are issued under the express direction of Congress. They have the force and effect of law and are generally treated as if they were part of the Code itself. (Note, however, that legislative regulations can be overturned if a court finds them to be unreasonable or inconsistent with the statute.)

Where the statute does not provide instructions to the Secretary of the Treasury, a regulation is considered to be merely *interpretative*. Interpretative regulations are issued pursuant to the Commissioner of Internal Revenue's general rulemaking authority under Code section 7805(a). These regulations provide taxpayers with guidance in order to comply with a statute. Courts are not bound to follow interpretative regulations, but generally will give them great weight. Courts will declare an interpretative regulation invalid only if it is clearly unreasonable or out of keeping with the statute it is supposed to interpret. In dealing with a taxpayer, the IRS and its agents are bound by interpretative regulations.

Proposed regulations are generally considered to be the partisan *opinions* of the IRS, and do not bind the IRS, the courts, or anyone else. However, proposed regulations can serve as authority for purposes of avoiding the penalty for substantial understatement of income tax.[7]

Final Treasury regulations state the interpretation that the IRS will use in enforcing the law and have the effect of law.

Temporary regulations essentially have the same authority as final regulations—that is, they generally have the force and effect of law.[8]

IRS RULINGS AND GUIDANCE
Revenue Rulings

A *revenue ruling* is an official interpretation by the IRS of the Internal Revenue Code, related statutes, and regulations. It is the conclusion of the IRS on how the law is applied to a specific set of facts. Revenue rulings serve as guidance to taxpayers, IRS personnel, and tax professionals.[9] For example, a revenue ruling may hold that taxpayers can deduct certain automobile expenses. Revenue Rulings are issued in response to a problem common to many taxpayers. The purpose of the ruling is to provide a uniform application of the tax laws.

Revenue rulings that are published in the *Internal Revenue Bulletin* do not have the force and effect of law (as with Treasury regulations), but they may be used as precedents. The Service may revoke (or modify) a revenue ruling at any time, but revocation (or modification) is usually not retroactive.

Other taxpayers may count on the IRS to follow a revenue ruling in situations where the *facts are substantially the same* as those in the ruling. The weight given to revenue rulings by courts varies. Courts are not bound by revenue rulings since they are an expression of the opinion relating to only one of the parties before it.[10]

An example of a citation for a revenue ruling is " Rev. Rul. 2003-99, 2003-34 IRB 388," which when separated into its components means:

- the 99th revenue ruling issued by the IRS in 2003;

- published in the 34th issue of the *Internal Revenue Bulletin*;

- beginning on page 388.

Revenue Procedures

A *revenue procedure* is an official statement of a procedure that affects the rights or duties of taxpayers or other members of the public under the Code, related statutes, and regulations, and that should be a matter of public knowledge. For example, a revenue procedure might specify how taxpayers entitled to deduct certain automobile expenses should compute them by applying a certain mileage rate in lieu of calculating actual operating expenses. Revenue procedures published in the *Internal Revenue Bulletin* do not have the force and effect of Treasury regulations, but they may be used as precedents.

An example of a citation for a revenue procedure is "Rev. Proc. 2003-60, 2003-31 IRB 274," which when separated into its components means:

- the 60th revenue procedure issued by the IRS in 2003;

- published in the 31st issue of the *Internal Revenue Bulletin*;

- beginning on page 274.

Private Letter Rulings

A *private letter ruling* (PLR) is a written statement issued to a taxpayer that interprets and applies tax laws to the taxpayer's specific set of facts. A PLR is issued to establish with certainty the federal tax consequences of a particular transaction before the transaction is consummated, or before the taxpayer's return is filed. It is issued in response to a written request submitted by a taxpayer and is binding on the IRS if the taxpayer fully and accurately described the proposed transaction in the request and carries out the transaction as described. Note, however, that a PLR obtained by one party or person may not be relied on as precedent by other taxpayers or IRS personnel.[11] In fact, it may not be used by the same taxpayer in different circumstances. So the protective umbrella of a PLR is very narrowly circumscribed.

There are some areas in which the IRS will not provide taxpayers with a ruling (or a determination letter in the case of a qualified plan). These no-ruling topics are announced by the Service at the beginning of each calendar year.[12]

PLRs are generally made available to the public after all information has been removed that could identify the specific taxpayer to whom it was issued. An example of a private letter ruling citation is "Priv. Ltr. Rul. 201417023," which when separated into its components (2003 - 33 - 028) means – working backwards:

- the 23rd private letter ruling;

- issued by the IRS during the 17th week;

- of 2014.

Technical Advice Memoranda

A technical advice memorandum (TAM) is furnished by the Office of Chief Counsel upon the request of an IRS director (or an area director) in response to technical or procedural questions that develop during a proceeding. A request for a TAM generally stems from an examination of a taxpayer's return, a consideration of a taxpayer's claim for a refund or credit, or any other matter involving a specific taxpayer under the jurisdiction of the territory manager (or the area director).

TAMs are issued for closed transactions, only. They provide the Service's interpretation of the proper application of tax laws, regulations, revenue rulings or other precedents. The advice rendered represents a final determination of the position of the IRS, but only with respect to the specific issue in the specific case in which the advice is issued.

TAMs are generally made public after all information has been removed that could identify the taxpayer whose circumstances triggered the specific memorandum. An example of a citation for a TAM is "TAM 200335032," which when separated into its components (2003 - 35 - 032) means:

- the 32nd technical advice memorandum;

- issued during the 35th week;

- of 2003.

Announcements

An announcement is a public pronouncement that has immediate or short-term value. For example, announcements can be used to summarize the law or regulations without making any substantive interpretation; to state what regulations will say when they are certain to be published in the immediate future; or to notify taxpayers of the existence of an approaching deadline. Announcements are published in the *Internal Revenue Bulletin*. Although it is not clear, it appears that announcements bind the IRS to the same extent as revenue rulings do.

An example of an announcement citation is "Ann. 2012-37, 2012-45 I.R.B 543 ___," which when separated into its components means:

- the 37^h announcement issued by the IRS in 2012;

- published in the 45^h issue of the *Internal Revenue Bulletin*;

- published on page 543___ (the blank space for the page number means that the final page numbering has not been set).

Notices

A notice is also a public pronouncement that may contain guidance that involves substantive interpretations of the Internal Revenue Code or other provisions of the law. For example, notices can be used to relate what regulations will say in situations where the regulations may not be published in the immediate future. Notices are also published in the *Internal Revenue Bulletin*. Although it is not clear, it appears that notices bind the IRS to the same extent as revenue rulings do. An example of a citation is "Notice 2003-33, 2003-23 IRB 990," which when separated into its components means:

- the 33rd revenue ruling issued by the IRS in 2003;

- published in the 23rd issue of the *Internal Revenue Bulletin*;

- beginning on page 990.

THE COURTS

United States Tax Court

The United States Tax Court decides cases of taxpayers from all fifty states. There are no jury trials in the Tax Court. Instead, the Tax Court judges travel throughout the country hearing cases at locations convenient to taxpayers.[13] In most cases, a single judge hears a case and writes an opinion giving the reasons for his/her decision. However, some important cases are reviewed by the entire court (in Washington, D.C.).

The primary advantage in taking a case to the Tax Court is that a taxpayer may bring his case there without paying the deficiency first. On the other hand, if a taxpayer wants to have his tax liability determined in a United States District Court (or by the U.S. Court of Federal Claims), he must pay the tax first.[14]

In order to have a case heard by the Tax Court, a taxpayer must file his petition with the court no later than ninety days after receiving a "deficiency letter" from the IRS (i.e., a letter stating the additional amount of tax the Service claims is due, and why).

The Tax Court is bound by a circuit court of appeals decision in a similar case *if* an appeal from the Tax Court would go to that particular court of appeals (known as the *Golsen* rule). If a court of appeals has *not* ruled on a particular issue, however, the Tax Court may follow its own rule – even if that particular rule has been reversed on appeal in other circuits. A Tax Court decision binds only the Tax Court itself in other decisions (except to the extent where the Tax Court has been reversed by a court of appeals). Except for the case being decided, a Tax Court decision does *not* bind any other court or the IRS.

Tax Court decisions fall into three categories: (1) reported decisions; (2) memorandum decisions; and (3) summary opinions. Reported decisions generally carry more weight than memo decisions or summary opinions. An example of a reported Tax Court citation is *Mayo v. Commissioner*, 136 TC 81 (2011), which means:

- the court decision involving a taxpayer named Mayo versus the IRS Commissioner (sometimes abbreviated as "Comm'r.");

- in volume 136 of the *Tax Court Reports*, at page 81,

- decided by the court in 2011.[15]

An example of a memo opinion citation is *"George B. Douglas, Jr. and Pearl J. Douglas, TC Memo 2014-14,"* which means:

- the court decision involving a taxpayers named George B. and Pearl J. Douglas;

- which was the 14th memorandum decision decided by the Tax Court in 2014.[16]

An example of a citation for a summary opinion is "TC Summary Opinion 2013-44."

A citation to a reported or a memo decision may be followed by "acq." (acquiescence) or by "nonacq." (nonacquiescence). If the IRS Commissioner *acquiesces*, the Service will not appeal the case, and (at least for the time being) the IRS will take the position of the Tax Court on the litigated issue in dealing with other taxpayers. *Nonacquiescence* doesn't mean the IRS will appeal the case; instead, it serves as a warning that the IRS will not follow the Tax Court's ruling in other situations.

The losing party in a Tax Court case (the government or the taxpayer) may appeal the case to the court of appeals for the circuit in which the taxpayer lives.

SMALL TAX CASES

A taxpayer may have his case treated as a *small tax case* if: (1) the amount of the deficiency that the taxpayer disputes *and* (2) the amount he claims was overpaid do not exceed $50,000 (including any additions to the tax and certain penalties) for any one tax year for income taxes.[17]

A case will be tried under the Tax Court's regular procedures *unless* the taxpayer files a petition to have his case treated as a small tax case. The taxpayer may file his petition for small tax case handling *only after* he receives a notice of deficiency from the IRS. The fee for filing a petition is $60 and is payable when the petition is filed.

The Service may object to the request for small tax case treatment on the ground that the case involves an important tax question that should be heard under normal procedures and be subject to appeal, or that the decision should serve as a precedent for other similar matters. At any time before trial, the Tax Court or the taxpayer may remove the small tax case designation and direct that the case be handled as a regular case. After trial, but before the court enters a decision, the Tax Court may order that the small tax case proceeding be discontinued if: (1) the disputed amount or claimed overpayment will exceed $50,000 per year; and (2) the amount of the excess is large enough to justify granting the request.

When there are enough small cases ready for trial, the Tax Court judges move from city to city to try cases at locations convenient to the taxpayers. Generally, small tax case proceedings are less formal and result in speedier dispositions than regular trials. Trials are conducted by one judge, without a jury. Taxpayers may be represented by practitioners admitted to practice before the Tax Court bar, or they may represent themselves if they wish.

Small tax case decisions may not be appealed to any other court by the taxpayer or the government.[18] In other words, once a small tax case is decided, the matter is settled. A small tax case decision cannot serve as *precedent* for any other case – that is, it does not bind the Tax Court, or any other court, or revenue agents in deciding any other similar tax question. However, the decisions of the commissioners may be subject to review by the Tax Court. Small tax cases are not published.

The court of appeals can affirm or reverse the decision of the Tax Court.

United States District Court

There are many federal district courts throughout the United States. To contest a tax deficiency in a district court, a taxpayer must:

(1) pay the tax first;

(2) file a claim for a refund with the IRS;

(3) wait six months (or until the Service denies the refund, if sooner); and then

(4) sue for a refund.

The taxpayer or the government may request a jury trial. Otherwise, one judge will hear the taxpayer's case.

Unless its decision has been appealed, a district court should follow its decision in the case of any other taxpayer in the same district with the same problem. A district court decision does not bind the IRS in its dealings with other taxpayers, nor does it bind any other court. However, federal courts are inclined to follow the decisions of other federal courts.

The losing party in a district court may appeal to the court of appeals for the circuit in which the district court is located. If the decision is reversed on appeal, all the district courts in that circuit must follow the decision of the court of appeals in deciding future cases.

When the Service loses a case in a district court, and decides *not* to appeal the decision, it can announce its "acq." (acquiescence) or its "nonacq." (nonacquiescence) in the decision. The meaning of these terms is the same as when used in Tax Court decisions (see above).

District court decisions are published in the *Federal Supplement* ("F. Supp."). An example of a district court citation is "*May v. McGowan*, 97 F. Supp. 326 (W.D. N.Y. 1950)," which when broken into its components means:

- the taxpayer May sued IRS District Director McGowan;

- the decision may be found in volume 97 of the *Federal Supplement*, on page 326; and

- the case was decided by the district court for the Western District of New York in 1950.

United States Courts of Appeals

There are thirteen United States courts of appeals— one for each of eleven regional circuits, one for the District of Columbia, and one for the Federal Circuit. (See Figure 1.1 for the location of each court and the states and territories in the respective circuits.[19]) In most tax cases, the appeals court usually renders

Figure 1.1

1st Cir.	Boston, Mass. (Me., Mass., N.H., R.I., Puerto Rico)
2nd Cir.	New York City, N.Y. (Conn., N.Y., Vt.)
3rd Cir.	Philadelphia, Pa. (Del., N.J., Pa., Virgin Islands)
4th Cir.	Richmond, Va. (Md., N.C., S.C., Va., W. Va.)
5th Cir.	New Orleans, La. (La., Miss., Texas)
6th Cir.	Cincinnati, Ohio (Ky., Mich., Ohio, Tenn.)
7th Cir.	Chicago, Ill. (Ill., Ind., Wis.)
8th Cir.	St. Louis, Mo. (Ark., Iowa, Minn., Mo., Neb., N. Dak., S. Dak.)
9th Cir.	San Francisco, Calif. (Alaska, Ariz., Calif., Hawaii, Idaho, Mont., Nevada, Oregon, Washington, Guam)
10th Cir.	Denver, Colo. (Colo., Kans., N. Mex., Okla., Utah, Wyo.)
11th Cir.	Atlanta, Ga. (Ala., Fla., Ga.)
D.C. Cir.	Washington, D.C. (District of Columbia)
Federal Circuit	Wash., D.C. (nationwide jurisdiction)

the final word. This is because the only appeal from a court of appeals decision is to the Supreme Court of the United States. Very few tax cases are appealed to the Supreme Court, and fewer still are actually heard.

A decision by a circuit court of appeals binds all district courts in that circuit. However, the decision of a court of appeals for one circuit does not bind the court of appeals, or the district courts, of another circuit. The Tax Court is bound by a court of appeals decision *only if* an appeal from the Tax Court decision could only be made to that particular court of appeals (*Golsen* rule). But if an appeal could be made to another circuit court, the Tax Court is not bound by it. A court of appeals decision does not bind the IRS in dealing with other cases. In fact, the Service has often forced (and may continue to force) taxpayers to litigate an issue, even after having been defeated in several circuits.

The IRS may announce its "acq." (acquiescence) or "nonacq." (nonacquiescence) to decisions of the courts of appeals. The meaning of these terms is generally the same with respect to a court of appeals decision as with a Tax Court or a district court decision (see above).[20]

Decisions of the courts of appeals are published in the *Federal Reporter* ("F.2d.," or "F.3d"). An example of a citation for a circuit court of appeals decision is "*Scott v. United States*, 328 F.3d 132 (4th Cir. 2003)," which when broken down into its parts means:

- the taxpayer Scott versus the United States;

- reported in volume 328, on page 132 of the third series of the *Federal Reporter*;

- decided by the Fourth Circuit Court of Appeals in 2003.

The appeals Fast Track Mediation program provides expedited case resolution for certain types of issues and cases; see Frequently Asked Questions, below.

United States Court of Federal Claims

The court now referred to as the United States Court of Federal Claims (formerly known as the United States Court of Claims before 1982, and as the United States Claims Court from 1982 - 1992) is located in Washington, D.C. The judges of the Federal Claims

Court travel anywhere in the United States and hear cases at times and places established to minimize the citizens' inconvenience and expense.

A taxpayer who wants to challenge a tax deficiency in the Court of Federal Claims must:

(1) pay the tax first;

(2) file a claim for a refund with the IRS;

(3) wait six months (or until the Service denies the refund if sooner); and then

(4) sue for a refund.

A taxpayer who receives an unfavorable decision in the Court of Federal Claims can make an appeal to the United States Court of Appeals for the Federal Circuit. (This appellate court is headquartered in Washington, but it is authorized to hear cases at other designated places throughout the country, too.)

Decisions of the Court of Appeals for the Federal Circuit have nationwide *precedence* – that is, all courts, including the Court of Federal Claims, whose appeals are heard by the Court of Appeals for the Federal Circuit are bound by its decisions. However, a Court of Federal Claims decision does *not* bind the IRS in disposing of other cases. Furthermore, other courts are not bound by a Court of Federal Claims decision (but they may be influenced by it).

If the Service announces its "acq." (acquiescence) in a decision of the Court of Federal Claims, it will follow the decision in disposing of cases with the same controlling facts. On the other hand, if the Service announces its "nonacq." (non-acquiescence) in a decision, it generally will not follow the decision in cases involving other taxpayers.

Citations to the Court of Federal Claims may appear in one of the following forms, depending on when the case was decided:

Pre-1982:

Mississippi River Fuel Co. v. U. S., 314 F.2d 953 (Ct. Cl. 1963), which tells us that the case was decided by the Court of Claims in 1963, and is located in volume 314 of the *Federal Reporter*, 2nd series, starting at page 953.

1982 – 1992:

Wm. T. Thompson Co. v. U.S., 26 Cl.Ct. 17 (Cl.Ct. 1992), which tells us that the case was decided by the United States Claims Court in 1992, and is located in volume 26 of the *United States Claims Court Reporter* starting at page 17.

Transpac Drilling Venture v. U.S., 1992-2 USTC ¶50,486 (Cl.Ct. 1992), which tells us that the case was decided by the United States Claims Court in 1992 and is located in the second of the 1992 volumes of the *U.S. Tax Cases Reporter*, at paragraph 50,486.

Post-1992:

Alexander v. U.S., 28 Fed.Cl. 475 (Fed.Cl. 1993), which tells us that the case was decided by the United States Court of Federal Claims in 1993 and can be found in the 28th volume of the *Federal Claims Reporter* starting at page 475.

Gustafson v. U.S., 1993-1 USTC ¶50,071 (Fed.Cl. 1993), which tells us that the case was decided by the United States Court of Federal Claims in 1993 and can be found in the first of the 1993 volumes of the *U.S. Tax Cases Reporter* at paragraph 50,071.

The Supreme Court of the United States

Very few of the thousands of tax cases arising every year are appealed all the way to the Supreme Court. Even fewer are actually reviewed by the Court. However, if the Supreme Court renders a decision on an issue, the IRS and every court in the United States must follow the decision in dealing with future cases.

The first step in attempting to get a tax case reviewed by the Supreme Court is to file a "writ of certiorari"— which is essentially a petition that is a request to be heard. Whether the Court will, or won't, grant the taxpayer's request is entirely within the Court's discretion. The Supreme Court normally denies over 1,000 petitions every year.

It's important to understand that the Supreme Court's denial of a writ is not an indication of its views on the merits of the case. The denial of a writ simply means that fewer than four justices on the Court deemed it desirable to review a decision of the lower

court as a matter "of sound judicial discretion."[21] Those few tax cases the Court actually consents to review usually involve: (1) a question as to the constitutionality of a provision of the Code; (2) a conflict between decisions of courts of appeals; or (3) an issue of wide public import.

United States Supreme Court decisions are published in the *United States Supreme Court Reports* ("U.S."). An example of a Supreme Court citation is "*Metropolitan Life Ins. Co. v. Massachusetts*, 471 U.S. 724 (1985)," which when separated into its components means:

- the case involving the taxpayer Metropolitan Life Insurance Company;

- reported in volume 471 of the *United States Supreme Court Reports*;

- beginning on page 724; and

- decided by the Supreme Court in 1985.

Legislative History and Other Secondary Authority

Tax problems frequently arise that are not specifically covered in the Code, the regulations, the rulings, or court decisions. Many times the tax adviser must take an educated guess, based on his knowledge of the tax law, as to the probable tax consequences of the transaction. However, the tax adviser may find guidance in the reports of the Congressional tax committees. Although the reports of the Congressional tax committees are not part of the tax law, they can be helpful in interpreting a particular piece of legislation.[22]

The Staff of the Joint Committee on Taxation of the Senate and the House publish a *General Explanation* of the provisions of each new major tax act. Each *General Explanation* is referred to as a *Blue Book*. These "blue books" are generally written within several months after a new piece of legislation has passed. The purpose of the *General Explanation* is to amplify skimpy legislative history of hastily enacted compromise provisions. This information is based on the knowledge of the staff members who generally participated in drafting the provisions of the history of the legislation.

The Blue Book is considered "authority" only for the purposes of avoiding the penalty on the substantial

HOW TAX LAWS ARE MADE

Tax bills originate in the Ways and Means Committee of the House of Representatives. This committee writes the bill and a report explaining the bill to the members of the House. If the bill passes the House, it is sent to the Senate Finance Committee, which may reject the bill, approve it in its entirety, or amend it. If the Senate Finance Committee sends the bill to the Senate for vote, it will also write a committee report explaining its version of the bill.

If the versions of the bills passed by the House and the Senate don't agree, both versions must be sent to a *conference committee*, which is comprised of a few members from both the House and the Senate. The conference committee "irons out" the disputed points, and writes a conference bill and a conference committee report. The conference committee's version of the bill then goes back to the House and the Senate for a vote. If passed by both houses, the tax bill is sent to the President for his approval. When the President signs the bill, it becomes a Public Law and part of the Internal Revenue Code.

understatement of income tax.[23] The *General Explanation* does not technically rise to the level of legislative history because it was authored by a congressional staff and not by Congress. But even the Tax Court has acknowledged that the *General Explanation* can serve as a helpful aid in interpreting tax statutes.[24]

In addition to legislative history and the *Blue Book*, there are also books, tax services, tax magazines, proceedings of tax institutes and articles published in the law reviews of the various law schools. Although these types of literature represent only the authors' personal opinions, the tax adviser may benefit from the research and thinking of other practitioners and legal scholars. Of course, the tax literature does not bind the court or the IRS.

WHERE CAN I FIND OUT MORE?

1. The Internal Revenue Code can be viewed at www.findlaw.com/casecode/uscodes/, and at uscode.house.gov/usc.htm.

2. Treasury regulations can be viewed at www.irs.gov/.

3. Revenue rulings, revenue procedures, announcements, and bulletins are published in the *Internal Revenue Bulletin* (IRB) at www.irs.gov/.

4. Selected cases, rulings, and legislation of importance to tax practitioners are available at www.leimberg-services.com.

FREQUENTLY ASKED QUESTIONS

Question – What is the primary difference between a *revenue ruling* and a *revenue procedure*?

Answer – A revenue ruling generally states an IRS position, whereas a revenue procedure provides return filing or other instructions concerning an IRS position.

Question – What types of tax disputes are best suited for the Tax Court? A District Court?

Answer – In general, complex tax issues may be better suited for the Tax Court because the Tax Court judges have a wealth of tax law knowledge and experience and are accustomed to handling complex tax issues. District courts offer the taxpayer the choice of a judge or a jury trial. If a taxpayer's case might receive a more sympathetic review from a jury of his peers, the district court might be preferable. Of course, the decision may ultimately rest on pure economics. A taxpayer must have sufficient funds to pay the tax up front before he can have his case tried in federal district court. Otherwise, the taxpayer must take his case to Tax Court, where no upfront tax payment is required (but significant interest and penalties may be imposed on tax amounts ultimately due.[25]

Question – What other guidance does the IRS release?

Answer – *Chief Counsel Advice* is written advice or instructions prepared by a national office component of the IRS' Office of Chief Counsel. It is issued to the field (i.e., revenue agents) or to service center employees of the Service to (1) convey a legal interpretation of the Service, or (2) the Service's position or policy relating to a revenue provision, or (3) the assessment of any liability under a revenue provision.

Through *Service Center Advice* the Office of Chief Counsel provides legal advice to the IRS service centers and related IRS functions with regard to their tax administration responsibilities. This advice is distributed and published to provide consistent legal advice to all affected IRS functions and Counsel Office on matters raised by the Service's various functions.

Information letters provide general statements of well-defined law without applying them to a specific set of facts. They are furnished by the IRS National Office in response to requests for general information by taxpayers, by congresspersons on behalf of constituents, or by congresspersons on their own behalf. Information letters have no binding effect on the Service; they are merely advisory. The release of information letters is intended to increase public confidence that the tax system operates fairly and in an even-handed manner with respect to all taxpayers. All three types of guidance can be viewed online at www.irs.gov.

Question – Are any of the Service's internal training materials available for review online by taxpayers and their advisers?

Answer – Yes. *The Internal Revenue Manual* contains the policies, procedures, instructions, guidelines, and delegations of authority, which direct the operation, and administration of the Internal Revenue Service. Topics include, among others, tax administration. The IRS also makes its *Market Segment Specialization Programs* available online. These programs focus on developing examiners for a particular market segment. A market segment may be an industry such as construction, entertainment, or a particular profession (e.g., attorneys, real estate agents), or an issue like passive activity losses. In addition, the Service makes its Continuing Professional Education manuals available annually. The information in these manuals can provide some insight into the issues that revenue agents are being trained to focus on in future audits.

Question – Can a taxpayer rely on the information in an IRS Publication to support his position concerning a particular tax issue?

Answer – Publications provide taxpayers with detailed information on key topics that will assist in the preparation of their tax return. They are designed to supplement forms and instructions by answering typical tax questions and providing helpful examples for a particular topic. They may *not* be

relied on as authority. They are published as explanations that reflect the Service's interpretation of the law, but are not intended to replace the law or change its meaning.

Question – What is Fast Track Mediation?

Answer – Fast Track Mediation gives self-employed taxpayers, small businesses and the IRS the opportunity to mediate disputes through an IRS appeals officer, who acts as a neutral party. In this program, most tax disputes are resolved within forty days compared to several months though the regular appeal process. IRS offers this new service designed to expedite case resolution disputes that arise from examination or collection actions.[26]

CHAPTER ENDNOTES

1. "Understanding IRS Guidance – A Brief Primer," Available at: http://www.irs.gov/uac/Understanding-IRS-Guidance-A-Brief-Primer.
2. Tax treaties are another source of federal tax law affecting the taxation of transactions between the United States and a foreign country.
3. A code is a compilation of individual statutes arranged in a particular order.
4. A citation is a reference to where the law can be found in a reporter (i.e., a book containing court decisions issued by a particular court or group of courts).
5. The Code of Federal Regulations is a compilation of the rules issued by the executive departments and agencies of the federal government.
6. The Federal Register is an official government periodical.
7. I.R.C. §6662.
8. The preamble to a group of final regulations typically lists the changes that have been made by the Treasury in response to written comments and comments received during the public hearing. The Preamble also contains explanations of why the Treasury has not made certain changes suggested or recommended by commentators. The Preamble itself, however, is not the actual regulation.
9. The Internal Revenue Bulletin (I.R.B.) is the authoritative instrument of the IRS for announcing all substantive rulings necessary to promote a uniform application of tax law.
10. However, a federal appeals court has ruled that the IRS and the Tax Court are bound to follow revenue rulings. See *Estate of McClendon v. Comm.*, 135 F.3d 1017 (5th Cir. 1998).
11. As a practical matter, however, tax advisors frequently look to private letter ruling for some indication of how the IRS might rule on a similar issue with similar facts.
12. See e.g., Rev. Proc. 2014-1, 2014 – I.R.B. 1 et seq..
13. For the list of cities in which Tax Court cases are heard, see http://www.ustaxcourt.gov/faq.htm.
14. *Flora v. U.S.*, 362 U.S. 145 (1960).
15. Before 1943, the Tax Court was the Board of Tax Appeals and its reported decisions were published in a series called the Board

of Tax Appeals Reports. A citation to a case in this series was, for example, *Arthur R. Womrath*, 22 BTA 335. Memo decisions of the Board are cited "BTA Memo."

16. To view memorandum opinions (starting from January 1, 1999) and summary opinions (starting from January 1, 2001), go to www.ustaxcourt.gov.

17. I.R.C. §§7463(a), 7463(e).

18. See I.R.C. §§7463(b). See also *Cole v. Comm'r.*, 958 F.2d 288, 1992-1 USTC ¶50,151 (9th Cir. 1992).

19. The types of cases heard by the Court of Appeals for the Federal Circuit are determined by subject matter. Appeals from decisions made by the United States Court of Federal Claims are heard by the Court of Appeals for the Federal Circuit.

20. There is one exception—if he Service does not acquiesce in a court of appeals case, it will recognize the impact on cases that arise within the deciding circuit.

21. Rule 10, Supreme Court Rules; *Maryland v. Baltimore Radio Show, Inc.*, 338 U.S. 912 (1950).

22. In fact, the Treasury Department sometimes takes material from committee reports to include in its regulations.

23. See Treas. Reg. §1.6662-4(d)(3)(iii).

24. See, e.g., *Maria Rivera v. Comm.*, 89 TC 343 (1987).

25. A filing fee of $60 is required for Tax Court.

26. See Rev. Proc. 2003-41, 2003-25 I.R.B. 1047.

COMPLIANCE

CHAPTER 2

INTRODUCTION

Most individuals pay a large portion of their income tax *during* the tax year through employer withholding or by making estimated tax payments. However, an income tax return must still be filed to show the exact amount of tax liability. When the tax return is filed, the taxpayer pays the balance due or makes a claim for any refund payable to him. This chapter explains who is required to file an income tax return, when tax returns must be filed, what to expect if one's income tax return is audited, and what to do if the taxpayer disagrees with the amount of tax the IRS claims is due.

WHO MUST FILE?

Income, filing status, and age generally determine whether an individual must file an income tax return. Generally, an income tax return must be filed by every individual whose *gross income* (i.e., all income received in the form of money, goods, property, and services that is not exempt from tax – see Chapter 3) equals or exceeds the following limits listed below for 2014. These amounts are computed by applying the applicable personal exemption and standard deduction amounts. It should be noted that the personal exemption amount is reduced if Adjusted Gross Income exceeds $152,525 (See Chapter 6).

(1) **Married persons filing jointly**—$20,300 (if one spouse is blind or elderly—$21,500; if both spouses are blind *or* elderly—$22,700; if both spouses are blind *and* elderly—$25,100).

(2) **Surviving spouse**—$16,350 (if elderly or blind—$17,550; if elderly and blind—$18,750).

(3) **Head-of-household**—$13,050 (if blind or elderly—$14,600; if elderly and blind—$16,150).

(4) **Single persons**—$10,150(if blind or elderly—$11,700; if blind and elderly—$13,250).

(5) **Married filing separately**—if neither spouse itemizes, a return must be filed if gross income equals or exceeds $10,150 (if blind or elderly—$11,350; if blind and elderly—$12,550). If either spouse itemizes—$3,950.

(6) **Dependents**—every individual who may be claimed as a dependent of another must file a return for 2014 if he has: unearned income in excess of $1,000 (plus any additional standard deduction if the individual is blind or elderly) *or* total gross income which exceeds the sum of any additional standard deduction if the individual is blind or elderly plus the greater of (a) $1,000 or (b) the lesser of (i) $300 plus earned income or (ii) $6,200.

(7) Taxpayers who are **non-resident aliens** or who are filing a **short year return** because of a change in their annual accounting period—$3,950.[1]

A self-employed taxpayer must file a return if he has net earnings from self-employment of $400 or more.[2]

The dollar requirements apply to *gross* income, and not just taxable income.[3] Thus, a return is required even where the taxpayer's deductions and exemptions exceed his gross income and therefore no tax is due. A taxpayer whose gross income is less than the required amount should file a return to obtain a refund if any income tax was withheld from his salary or wages. All taxpayers should also file a return to begin the running of the statute of limitations on assessment. In addition, if a taxpayer has a loss in one year, resulting in negative Adjusted Gross Income, a tax return should be filed in order to have the loss on record with the IRS for purposes of a Net Operating Loss Carryback or Carryforward.

Low-income taxpayers who do not have to file a return should be encouraged to file if they are eligible for the *refundable* Earned Income Credit. Any individual who receives advance payments of the earned income credit must file a return.[4]

If a taxpayer dies, his executor, administrator, or legal representative must file a final return for the decedent on or before the fifteenth day of the fourth month following the close of the deceased taxpayer's normal tax year.[5]

"Kiddie Tax." Earnings of a minor are taxable to the minor, and he may be required to file his own return. The so-called "kiddie tax" applies to net *unearned* income (i.e., income from sources *other than* wages, salaries, and other amounts received as compensation for services actually rendered) of children: (1) who have not attained certain ages before the close of the taxable year; (2) who have at least one parent alive at the close of the taxable year; and (3) who have over $2,000 (in 2014) of unearned income. Age-wise, the kiddie tax applies to:

(1) a child under age eighteen; *or*

(2) a child who has attained the age of eighteen if: (a) the child has not attained the age of nineteen (twenty-four in the case of a full-time student) before the close of the taxable year; and (b) the earned income of the child does not exceed one-half of the amount of the child's support for the year.

Unearned income is determined as follows:

Level One: The first $1,000 of a minor child's unearned income is generally exempt from tax because of the child's standard deduction.[6]

Level Two: The next $1,000 of unearned income is taxed at the child's tax rate.

Level Three: The amount of unearned income that exceeds $2,000 is taxed to the child at the parent's tax rate.

Certain parents whose children are required to file a return may *elect* to include the child's unearned income

over $2,000 (in 2014) on their own return using Form 8814, thus avoiding the necessity of the child filing a return. The election is available if the child has income of more than $1,000, but less than $10,000 (ten times the child's minimum basic standard deduction), all of which comes from interest and dividends.[7]

One additional area of concern for those with family businesses is that interests in S corporations or other flow-through entities that have been given to the child will also be producing unearned income unless the child's activities are producing earned income. For most children, this is unlikely.

FILING STATUS

Joint returns. Married persons may elect to file a joint return upon which they report their combined income and deductions. They may file a joint return even though one spouse has no income.[8]

Married persons may not, however, file a joint return if (1) either spouse is a nonresident alien, or (2) they have different taxable years (unless the difference is due solely as the result of the death of the other spouse).[9]

Married persons who file separately may, under certain circumstances, amend their returns to file jointly after the due date of the return.[10] However, if a couple files jointly they are precluded, after the due date for the return, from amending their return to file separately.[11]

If the spouses file a joint return, each is generally liable for the entire amount of the tax, not merely the amount of tax on his own income.[12]

A special schedule of tax rates applies to joint returns. (See Appendix E.) In most cases, the rates provided for joint returns will result in a much lower tax than if the couple had filed separate returns.

Married filing separate returns. Married persons may file separate returns upon which they report their separate income and deductions. The tax benefits available for married persons filing separate returns are often less favorable than those for married persons filing a joint return. Nevertheless, it is sometimes more favorable for married persons to file separate returns. Also, as noted above, some married persons do not qualify to file a joint return. More often than not, separate returns are filed by married couples for non-tax reasons, such as separation without a legal divorce or separation order or unknown tax exposure of the other spouse from flow-through entities.

Return of a surviving spouse. A surviving spouse (widow or widower) may use joint return rates for the first two tax years after the year in which his or her spouse died provided that:

- a *dependent* child or stepchild lives with the taxpayer; *and*

- the surviving spouse is entitled to claim a dependency exemption for the child.[13]

However, the deceased spouse's personal exemption may be claimed *only* in the year of death. The surviving spouse must contribute over one-half the cost of maintaining the home.[14] A surviving spouse will not be considered as such if either of the following applies:

- the surviving spouse remarries; or

- the surviving spouse would not have been permitted to file a joint return (e.g., because the deceased spouse was a nonresident alien).[15]

Head-of-household return. A special schedule of tax rates applies to unmarried heads of households (see Appendix E). The tax liability that results from using the "head-of-household" table is lower than that for other unmarried persons. In order to qualify for head of household filing status, the taxpayer must meet all of the following conditions:

(1) The individual must be: (a) either (i) unmarried; (ii) legally separated from his spouse under a decree of divorce or of separate maintenance; or (iii) married, living apart from his spouse during the last six months of the taxable year; *and* (b) maintain as his home a household which constitutes the principal place of abode for *a qualifying child* (see below) with respect to whom the individual is entitled to claim a deduction, and with respect to whom the taxpayer furnishes over one-half the cost of maintaining such household during the taxable year.

(2) The individual must maintain as his home a household in which one or more of the following persons lives: (a) a *qualifying child* [See below. If the child is unmarried, it is not necessary that the child have less than $3,950 (in 2014, as

indexed) of income, or that the head-of-household furnish more than one-half of the child's support. If the child is married, he must qualify as a dependent of the parent claiming head-of-household status or would qualify except for the waiver of the exemption by the custodial parent.], *or* (b) any other person for whom the taxpayer can claim a dependency exemption except a cousin or unrelated person living in the household. An exception to this rule is made with respect to a taxpayer's dependent mother or father; so long as the taxpayer maintains the household in which the dependent parent lives, it need not be his home.

Qualifying child means an individual who: (1) is the taxpayer's "child" (i.e., the taxpayer's son, daughter, stepson, stepdaughter, or eligible foster child); (2) has the same principal place of abode as the taxpayer for more than one-half of the year; (3) has not attained the age of nineteen by the close of the calendar year in which the tax year begins, *or* is a student who has not attained the age of twenty-four as of the close of the calendar year; *and* (4) has not provided over one-half of the individual's own support for the calendar year in which the taxpayer's taxable year begins.

(3) The taxpayer must not be a nonresident alien.[16]

Single return. An unmarried person who is not a head of household files a single return.

WHEN TO FILE

The basic period for determining an individual's income tax liability is one year, or *the taxable year*.[17] Most individuals use the *calendar year* as their taxable year.[18] Individuals using the calendar year must file their returns on or before April 15 of the following year.[19]

Certain individuals, however, may decide to use a *fiscal year* as the basis for reporting their income tax liability. (A *fiscal year* is a period of twelve months ending on the last day of a month *other than* December.)[20] Individuals who use a fiscal year must file their returns on or before the fifteenth day of the fourth month after the close of the fiscal year.[21]

A paper return is filed on time if it is mailed in an envelope that is:

- properly addressed, and

- postmarked no later than the due date.[22]

    However, paper filings are becoming increasingly less common as electronic filing over the internet becomes the standard for tax professionals and is equally available for individuals preparing their own tax returns. While paper filing has become the exception rather than the rule, it is still an important tool that can be useful if the taxpayer is concerned about tax-related identity theft.

An income tax return must also be signed by the taxpayer (and his spouse if married filing jointly) to be considered a valid return.[23] Tax returns electronically filed by tax professionals require the signature of the taxpayers on a Form 8879. Individuals filing their own returns online effectively sign their returns electronically.

If the individual uses one of the private delivery services designated by the IRS (i.e., DHL Express, Federal Express, United Parcel Service), the postmark date is generally the date that the private delivery service records in the database or marks on the mailing label. An electronically filed return (IRS e-file) is considered filed on time if the authorized electronic return transmitter postmarks the transmission by the due date.[24]

If the due date for filing a return or paying taxes falls on a weekend (Saturday or Sunday), or on a legal holiday, the due date is delayed until the next business day.[25] The legal holidays are: January 1 – New Year's Day; third Monday in January – Martin Luther King Jr. Day; January 20 – Inauguration Day (every fourth year); third Monday in February – George Washington's Birthday; the last Monday in May – Memorial Day; July 4 – Independence Day; the first Monday in September – Labor Day; the second Monday in October – Columbus Day; November 11 – Veteran's Day; 4th Thursday in November – Thanksgiving Day; and December 25 – Christmas Day.

Paying the tax. If the individual taxpayer owes additional tax (i.e., in addition to the taxes that have been paid through the year through withholding or estimated tax payments; for details on withholding and estimated taxes, see Chapter 12), the tax due should be paid with the individual's return. Online payment of taxes have become more common, using a transfer from a bank account or a credit card (for a fee).

If the individual cannot pay the full amount of tax that is due at that point, he can ask the Service for permission to make monthly installment payments on Form 9465. However, the individual will be charged with interest, may be subject to a late payment penalty, and must pay a fee (see Frequently Asked Questions, below).[26]

Filing extensions – automatic six-month filing extension: If an individual's income tax return is not filed by the due date (April 15), an automatic six-month extension (October 15) may be available. There are two ways to file for an automatic six-month extension:

(1) File a paper Form 4868 (Application for Automatic Extension of Time to File U.S. Individual Income Tax Return) and mail it to the appropriate address; *or*

(2) File an e-file extension request.

Using either method, the extension request must be filed on or before the due date for the return (April 15). Even though an individual may file his tax return late, any tax due must be paid by the regular due date to avoid interest and penalties.[27]

Individuals serving in combat zones and U.S. citizens living outside the United States are also eligible for automatic extensions. Service personnel serving in combat zones are generally eligible for extensions for the period of service in the zone plus 180 days.

AUDITS

Generally, the IRS has three years from the date the individual filed his return (or the date the return was due, if later) to assess any additional tax.[28] In cases of substantial understatement, the statute of limitations is extended to six years.[29] If the taxpayer's return is fraudulent, the limitation period is extended to six years for criminal evasion and can be assessed at any time under the civil rules. If there is a failure to file a return, the tax can be assessed at any time.[30]

An individual's return may be examined or "audited" for a variety of reasons, and the examination may take place in several different ways. After the examination, the individual can agree with the proposed changes to his individual tax and agree to pay any additional tax, or disagree with the proposed changes and appeal the decision.

A tax return can be audited on the basis of computer scoring.[31] A return can also be selected for examination on the basis of information received from third-party documentation (e.g., Forms 1099 and W-2) that does not match the information reported on the individual's tax return. Or a return can be selected to address the questionable treatment of an item.

In examining or collecting an individual's tax liability, the IRS may contact third parties (e.g., neighbors, banks, employers, or employees). However, the Service must give the individual reasonable notice before contacting other persons, and must provide notice of specific contacts by providing the individual with a record of persons contacted. (Note that the notice rule does not apply to any pending criminal investigation.)

Some audits are handled entirely by mail. Other audits (so-called "office audits") may take place in the individual's home, place of business, an IRS office, or the office of the individual's attorney, accountant, or an enrolled agent.[32]

If the taxpayer thinks he will owe additional tax at the end of the audit, he can stop further accrual of interest on the amount he thinks he might owe by sending a deposit or a payment to the IRS to cover all, or part, of that amount. A deposit is different from a payment in that (1) a deposit can be returned to the taxpayer without filing for a refund, and (2) a deposit does not earn interest.

If the individual agrees with the Service's proposed changes, he can sign an agreement form and pay any additional tax that is due; the individual must also pay interest on any additional tax.[33] If an individual doesn't agree with the Service's proposed changes, and the audit takes place in an IRS office, the taxpayer can request an immediate meeting with the examiner's supervisor to explain his position. If an agreement is reached at that point, the case will be closed.

However, if the taxpayer and the Service cannot reach an agreement with the supervisor at this meeting (or if the examination took place outside of an IRS office), the examiner will write up the case, explaining the positions of the taxpayer and the IRS. The case will then be forwarded to the district office for processing.

Within a few weeks after the closing conference with the examiner (or his supervisor), the individual will receive a package containing:

Fast Track Mediation

The IRS now offers fast track mediation services to help taxpayers resolve many disputes resulting from:

- Examinations (audits),

- Offers in compromise, and

- Other collection actions.

Most cases that are *not* docketed in any court qualify for fast track mediation. Mediation can take place as early as a conference is requested by the individual taxpayer with the examiner's supervisor. The process involves an IRS Appeals Officer who has been trained in mediation. The individual taxpayer may represent himself at the mediation session, or someone else can act as his representative.[34]

- a "thirty-day letter" notifying him of his right to appeal the proposed changes within thirty days;

- a copy of the audit report explaining the examiner's proposed changes;

- an agreement or waiver form; and

- a copy of Publication 5 (Appeal Rights).

The thirty-day period begins to run on the date of the letter. The letter will explain what steps to take depending on whether the taxpayer decides to accept or appeal. It is important that the instructions be followed very carefully. The taxpayer should take great care not to miss any deadlines.

If the individual doesn't respond to the thirty-day letter, the IRS will send the taxpayer a "ninety-day letter," which is also known as a "notice of deficiency." The taxpayer has ninety days from the date of this notice to file a petition with the Tax Court (see Chapter 1). If the taxpayer has been working with a non-attorney preparer, upon receipt of the ninety-day letter it is important that the taxpayer gets in contact with an attorney to ensure that the filing in Tax Court is done properly.

APPEALS

A taxpayer can appeal an IRS decision to the local Appeals Office (which is separate and independent of the taxpayer's local IRS office). The Appeals Office is the only level of appeal within the IRS. Appeals conferences are conducted in an informal manner by correspondence, telephone, or at a personal conference. To file an appeal, the taxpayer must follow the instructions he receives in the letter (see above). Most differences are settled at the appeals level. However, if agreement isn't reached, the taxpayer can take his case to court (see Chapter 1). In addition, the IRS now includes an office called the Taxpayer Advocate, which may be contacted if the taxpayer believes the agent is abusing his or her authority.

Representing Clients before the IRS

Any of the following persons may represent taxpayers before the IRS so long as they are not currently under suspension or disbarment from practice before the Internal Revenue Service:

- attorneys;

- certified public accountants;

- enrolled agents,

- enroll retirement plan agents; and

- enrolled actuaries who meet certain requirements.[35]

WHERE CAN I FIND OUT MORE?

Tax Facts on Insurance & Employee Benefits (National Underwriter Company).[36]

FREQUENTLY ASKED QUESTIONS

Question – How long does an individual taxpayer have to file a claim for a refund (or credit) before the claim period expires?

Answer – An individual must file a claim for a refund (or credit) within the later of the following periods:

- three years from the date the taxpayer filed the original return; or

- two years from the date he paid the tax.[37]

If the individual does not file a claim within this period, he generally is no longer entitled to a refund or credit.[38]

Question – What penalties might apply to a taxpayer who fails to file a return or pay taxes on time?

Answer – **Failure-to-file penalty**. If the individual taxpayer doesn't file his return by the due date (including extensions), the penalty for failure to file a tax return is usually 5 percent of the amount of tax not paid by the due date (without regard to extensions) for each month, or part of a month, that the return is late. However, the penalty cannot exceed 25 percent.[39] An exception applies if the taxpayer can show that he failed to file on time because of reasonable cause and not neglect. A $135 fee will also be imposed if the return is filed more than sixty days after the due date (or extended due date).[40]

Failure-to-pay penalty. The penalty for failure to pay tax on time is 0.50 percent of the unpaid taxes for each month, or part of a month, after the due date that the tax is not paid.[41] This penalty does not apply: during the automatic six-month extension (see above) of time to file period if the taxpayer paid at least 90 percent of his actual tax liability on or before the due date of his return, and pays the balance when he files the return. Underpayment of estimated taxes results in imposition of an interest penalty (compounded daily) at an annual rate that is adjusted quarterly to three percentage points over the short-term applicable federal rate (see Chapter 12 for more details).[42]

Question – What penalties might apply to a taxpayer who underpays his taxes or understates his income?

Answer – **Accuracy-related penalty.** If the taxpayer underpays his tax due to negligence or disregard of the rules, he will generally have to pay a penalty equal to 20 percent of the underpayment.[43]

Substantial understatement of income tax penalty. An individual understates his tax if the tax shown on the return is less than the correct tax. The understatement is considered to be *substantial* if it is more than the larger of the following: (1) 10 percent of the correct tax, or (2) $5,000.[44] The amount of the understatement will be reduced to the extent that it is due to: (1) substantial authority for the position (e.g., Treasury regulations, revenue rulings, revenue procedures, notice and announcements issued by the IRS), or (2) adequate disclosure and a reasonable basis.[45]

Question – What criminal penalties can be pursued against a noncompliant taxpayer?

Answer – A taxpayer or return preparer may be subject to criminal prosecution for such actions as: tax evasion; willful failure to file a return, supply information, or pay any tax due; fraud and false statements; or preparing and filing a fraudulent return.[46]

Question – How does the bankruptcy law change debtors' responsibilities?

Answer – The Bankruptcy Abuse Prevention and Consumer Protection Act of 2005 (BAPCPA 2005) amends the United States Bankruptcy Code by adding new responsibilities for debtors. In general, the new law requires that debtors comply with their tax-filing responsibilities, make available previously-filed tax returns, and in many cases, seek credit counseling services. Under the new law, if debtors fail to file a return that becomes due after the date of their bankruptcy petition, or fail to file an extension, the Service may request the court to order a conversion (e.g., change the bankruptcy type from Chapter 7 to Chapter 11 or from Chapter 11 to Chapter 13) or dismissal of the case. Most BAPCPA 2005 provisions apply to cases filed on or after Oct. 17, 2005.[47]

Guidance released by the Service in 2006 clarifies that under the Bankruptcy Code, the bankruptcy estate—rather than the debtor—must include in its gross income: (1) the debtor's "gross earnings" from his performance of services after the commencement of the case, and (2) the gross income from property acquired by the debtor after the commencement of the case. "Gross earnings" includes wages and other compensation earned by a debtor who is an employee, as well as self-employment income earned by an individual who is self-employed. However, for bankruptcy cases filed before October 17, 2005, post-petition property and earnings from post-petition services generally are *not* includable in the bankruptcy estate's gross income. Instead, such income and earnings are generally includable in the *debtor's* gross income. The individual debtor must continue to file his own individual tax returns during the bankruptcy proceedings, as stated above.[48]

CHAPTER ENDNOTES

1. I.R.C. §§6012(a), 63(c), 151; Rev. Proc. 2013-35 IRB 537.

2. I.R.C. §6017.

3. I.R.C. §6012(a)(1)(A).

4. I.R.C. §6012(a)(8).

5. I.R.C. §§6012(a), 6012(b).

6. The standard deduction of a child claimed as a dependent is the greater of: (1) $950 (in 2009); *or* (2) the sum of $300 *plus* the amount of the child's earned income (to the extent it doesn't exceed the regular standard deduction amount, which is $5,700 in 2009). See Chapter 6.

7. I.R.C. §1(g). For each child, there is also a tax of 10 percent of the lesser of: (1) $950; or (2) the excess of the child's gross income over $950.

8. I.R.C. §6013(a).

9. I.R.C. §6013(a).

10. I.R.C. §6013(b)(1).

11. Treas. Reg. §1.6013-1(a)(1).

12. I.R.C. §6015. However, under the "innocent spouse" rules, a spouse may be relieved of the liability under certain circumstances. See Chapter 21, "Marriage and Divorce."

13. I.R.C. §2(a)(1).

14. I.R.C. §2(a).

15. I.R.C. §2(a)(2).

16. See I.R.C. §§2, 152.

17. I.R.C. §441(a).

18. See I.R.C. §441(g).

19. I.R.C. §6072(a).

20. If the taxpayer keeps his book on a fiscal year basis, he *must* also determine his tax liability on a fiscal year basis.

21. I.R.C. §6072(a).

22. I.R.C. §6072(a); Notice 2004-83, 2004-2 CB 1030.

23. I.R.C. §6061.

24. An authorized electronic return transmitter is a participant in the IRS e-file program that transmits electronic tax information directly to the IRS.

25. I.R.C. §7503.

26. The fee for entering into a new installment agreement is $105; but the fee is $52 when the taxpayer pays by way of a direct debit from the taxpayer's bank account. Also, the fee for restructuring or reinstating an installment agreement is $45. See I.R.B. 2006-40. See also IRS News Release IR-2006-176 (Nov. 13, 2006).

27. Previously, the automatic extension was for 4 months only (i.e., until August 15). The second extension (i.e., until October 15) was not automatic, had to be granted by the Service, and taxpayers had to request additional time and provide a reason for the delay.

28. I.R.C. §6501.

29. I.R.C. §6501(e).

30. I.R.C. §§6531(1), 6501(c).

31. The computer scoring is known as the Discriminant Function System (DiF).

32. Paid preparers are also included in this group. Treasury Circular 230; TD 9011, 67 Fed. Reg. 48760 (Jul. 26, 2002).

33. I.R.C. §6601. If the additional tax is paid when the agreement is signed, the interest is generally figured from the due date of the return to the date of the payment. If the additional tax is not paid when the agreement is signed, the individual will receive a bill that includes interest. If the individual pays the amount due within ten business days of the billing date, the taxpayer will not have to pay any extra interest or penalties.

34. Rev. Proc. 2003-41, 2003-25 IRB 1047.

35. Treasury Circular 230.

36. To order, go to: www.nationalunderwriterstore.com, or call 1-800-543-0874.

37. I.R.C. 6511(a).

38. I.R.C. §6511(a). For the detailed explanation of when a refund claim must be filed if the time for filing such refund claim falls on a weekend or a legal holiday, see Rev. Rul. 2003-41, 2003-17 I.R.B. 814.

39. I.R.C. §6651(a).

40. I.R.C. §6651(a).

41. I.R.C. §6651(a).

42. I.R.C. §6621(a)(2).

43. I.R.C. §6662(a).

44. I.R.C. §6662(d).

45. I.R.C. §6662(d)(2)(B).

46. I.R.C. §§7201, 7202, 7203, 7206, 7207.

47. IRS Fact Sheet FS-2005-18 (November 2005).

48. Notice 2006-83, 2006-40 IRB 596.

GROSS INCOME

CHAPTER 3

WHAT IS GROSS INCOME?

Gross income is the starting point in the computation of taxable income. Simply stated, taxable income is gross income minus deductions and personal exemptions for individuals. More fundamentally, taxable income is the difference between inflows of economic benefits and outflows expense items. As defined in Code section 61(a) of the Internal Revenue Code, gross income is essentially any economic benefit "from whatever source"[1] received—or deemed to be received—by the taxpayer. Although fifteen types of gross income are specifically listed, any item that confers an economic benefit to the taxpayer (whether listed or not) is presumed be included in gross income.[2] Only items specifically excluded from gross income pursuant to other Code sections escape taxation.

At first glance, many of the fifteen types of gross income listed under section 61(a) appear to be self-explanatory. However, in some cases, further refinement can be found in other Code sections and Treasury Regulations. Specifically, the fifteen listed types of gross income are as follows:

1. **Compensation for services rendered** includes wages, salaries, fees, commissions, fringe benefits, and similar items that are usually paid to employees. For the most part, this is W-2 income classified as earned income discussed below. In addition, there are special rules that apply to transfers of property from an employer to an employee that are subject to substantial risk of forfeiture, employer retirement plan contributions, and certain stock options discussed later in this chapter;

2. **Gross income derived from business** is generally defined as the gross receipts from sales or services less business expenses, including cost of goods sold.[3] This category also includes payments received as "independent contractors" for those individuals who are not treated as employees and receive a Form 1099 reporting earnings rather than a Form W-2. This type of income is often referred to as "self-employment income," and is classified as earned income, as discussed below;

3. **Gains derived from dealings in property** includes the taxpayer's profit from the sale or exchange of property. In computing the profit, the amount included in gross income is the difference between the economic benefit received (the amount realized from the sale or exchange of the property) and "adjusted basis," which is the cost of the property to the taxpayer, adjusted as appropriate.[4] Moreover, in order for income to be characterized as a capital gain (discussed below), there must be a sale or exchange of a capital asset;[5]

4. **Interest earned from bonds or bond funds** is set forth on a Form 1099-INT that is usually issued by a brokerage company or the like. Banks also issue Forms 1099-INT on interest earned by CDs and other interest-bearing accounts. It also includes interest received or imputed from private loans;[6]

5. **Rents** received;

6. **Royalties** received;

7. **Dividends declared on publicly traded stock** are set forth on a Form 1099 DIV that is usually issued by a brokerage company. Closely held corporations can also make dividend distributions;[7]

8. **Alimony** (and separate maintenance payments) is included in gross income of the payee spouse. Taxable alimony is defined in Code section 71;

9. **Annuities** provide stream of income payable over a term of years or for life, and their income is subject to special taxation rules set forth in Code section 72;

10. **Income from life insurance (and endowment) contracts** generally does not include death benefits received by the beneficiary of a life insurance. However, there are circumstances in which "income" from life insurance may be includible in gross income;[8]

11. **Pensions** cover a broad range of distributions to retirees from a variety of retirement plans such as 401(k) plans, defined benefit plans, and IRAs;[9]

12. **Income from discharge of indebtedness** is a taxable economic benefit to the taxpayer that occurs when a debtor discharges the taxpayer's debt without receiving compensation from the taxpayer. As discussed below, some or all of the discharged debt may be excluded from gross income pursuant to Code section 108, depending on the circumstances of the discharge;

13. **Distributive share of partnership gross income** is included in the gross income of each partner. A partnership is a pass through entity, so for income tax purposes, all partnership income flows through to the partners;[10]

14. **Income in respect of a decedent** is gross income that the decedent was entitled to, but had not yet received at the time of death. Because the decedent had not received the income prior to death, the decedent's last tax return (for a short tax year assuming he or she died sometime during the calendar year) would not include such income. Thus, the taxpayer who ultimately receives the income (the estate or beneficiary of the decedent) after the decedent's death must include it in gross income in the tax year it was received;[11] and

15. **Income from an interest in an estate or trust.** Under rather complicated rules, income generated from an estate or trust may be taxable to the estate, trust and/or beneficiaries.[12]

In addition to the items listed under section 61(a), other sections of the Code specifically identify certain other items as being included in gross income. The reason these items are set forth in their own Code sections is because of special rules that affect their implementation. Those other specifically included gross income items are:

- **Services of a child**. A child's wages (from a part-time job, for example) are included in the gross income of the child rather than the parent. This is to distinguish a child's earned income from a child's investment income. In contrast, a child's investment income in excess of a certain amount ($2,000 in 2014) is treated as if it was the parents' income taxable at the parents' highest tax rate and is often referred to as the Kiddie Tax, as discussed below.[13]

- **Prizes and awards** are included in gross income and include "amounts received from radio and television giveaway shows, door prizes and awards in contests of all types." Employee achievement awards are also included.[14] There is, however, an exception for awards or prizes made in recognition of past achievements in religious, charitable, scientific, educational, artistic, literary or civic fields. Notable examples of this exception are the Nobel Peace Prize and the Pulitzer Prize for journalism.[15]

- **Premiums paid by an employer for group term life insurance** purchased for employees are partially excluded from gross income. The cost of the first $50,000 of group term life insurance paid by an employer on behalf of an employee is excluded from the gross income of the employee.[16] The incremental cost of insurance in excess of the $50,000 threshold is included in the employee's gross income (see Appendix D).

- **Reimbursement for moving expenses** merits further explanation. Certain moving expenses paid by a taxpayer in connection with a job change or transfer are deductible under Code section 217. In lieu of a deduction, if those deductible expenses were paid or reimbursed by the employer, the reimbursement would be excluded from gross income under Code section 132(a)(6), and the employee would not be able to deduct those expenses. An employer's reimbursement for moving expenses that *would not* have been deductible under section 217 must be included in the gross income of the reimbursed employee.[17]

- **Property transferred in connection with performance of services** is includible in gross income under Code section 61(a)(1), just like any other form of compensation. However, this inclusion under Code section 83 has a twist because it provides that the employee does not have to include the property in gross income if it is subject to a substantial risk of forfeiture, i.e., the employee must return the property back to the employee if the employee fails to meet certain conditions such as remaining in the employ of the employer for a number of years. The availability of a "section 83(b) election" presents tax planning opportunities for the employee that will be discussed below.

- **Transfer of appreciated property to a political organization** can be included in gross income. This is a provision that effectively prevents a taxpayer from receiving a tax benefit by making such a contribution to a political organization that is otherwise non-deductible. To illustrate this point, assume a taxpayer has land for which he or she paid $10,000, but is now worth $100,000. The taxpayer could sell the land, pay tax on the $90,000 gain and contribute the net proceeds to a political organization. Alternatively, the taxpayer could simply contribute the land to the political organization. Without this rule, there would be no taxable gain for the taxpayer in the latter instance, and the political organization would receive $100,000 of land. By avoiding the gain, the taxpayer would have effectively enjoyed a $90,000 deduction for a political contribution. To prevent such back-door deductions, the taxpayer is deemed to have sold the property to the political organization for the fair market value of the property. As a result, the contributing taxpayer must include the difference between the fair market value of the property and the cost basis of the property in gross income.[18]

- **Unemployment compensation** in excess of $2,400 is includible in gross income.[19]

- **Social Security and Tier 1 railroad retirement benefits** can be included in gross income.

Depending on the income and filing status of the taxpayer, either 50 or 85 percent of such benefits may be included.[20]

WHAT ARE EXCLUSIONS FROM GROSS INCOME?

As stated above, any economic benefit is presumed to be included in gross income. The only way to overcome that presumption is to find a Code section that specifically excludes an economic benefit from gross income. Because the computation of taxable income begins with a determination of gross income, excluded items are not part of the tax base. Essentially, any item excluded from gross income is tax-free income for the taxpayer.

Items that are specifically *excluded* from gross income under the Code are as follows:

- **Certain death benefits**. In general, life insurance proceeds paid to the beneficiary of the underlying policy are fully excludable from gross income regardless of the amount of the death benefit. So assume that in 2010, brother purchases a $1,000,000 life insurance policy naming his sister as beneficiary. Upon brother's death in 2014, none of the $1,000,000 death benefit would be included in sister's gross income.[21] However, if brother were to transfer the policy to sister for "*any valuable consideration,*" it would essentially convert the $1,000,000 tax-free exclusion from gross income into a highly taxable inclusion in gross income. Known as the so called "transfer for value rule," sister would include in gross income the difference between the gross proceeds ($1,000,000) less the consideration paid including subsequent premiums. So, if the total amount of consideration and subsequent premiums was $50,000, sister would include $950,000 in gross income ($1,000,000 minus $50,000). Moreover, the character of the income would be ordinary meaning that the lion's share of the death benefit would be taxed at the highest ordinary income tax rate (39.6 percent).[22] For a more complete discussion of the "transfer for value rule," including significant exceptions to its application, see Chapter 25 of *The Tools & Techniques of Life Insurance Planning*.

- **Gifts and inheritances**. A gift, bequest, devise, or inheritance of money or property

MUNICIPAL BONDS

Municipal bonds (often referred to as "munis" or "tax-exempts") have traditionally been among the safest investments and, thus, a favorite with conservative, income-seeking investors. The creditworthiness of bond issuers is evaluated and rated (e.g., AAA) by professional rating agencies, such as Moody's or Standard & Poor's.

Higher-income individuals have also favored municipal bonds because they tend to provide a higher "taxable equivalent yield"—meaning that if an investor's tax bracket (including state and local taxes) is high enough, the lower yield of a tax-exempt bond will most likely result in a higher after-tax return than would be produced by a comparable taxable instrument. For example, assuming an investor is in the 28 percent tax bracket, a tax-exempt yield of 6 percent is equivalent to a taxable yield of 8.33 percent. The chart in Appendix A shows the relationship between taxable and tax-free income for individuals in various brackets.

Some municipal bonds are "double" tax-exempt—that is, they are exempt from both federal and state taxes. Others are "triple" tax-exempt—meaning that they are exempt from federal, state, and local taxes (i.e., city, county, etc.). Generally, the income is exempt from taxation only within the state where the bond was issued.

Interest from "private activity" municipal bonds may—or may not—be exempt from federal income taxation. Private activity bonds are bonds used for nongovernmental purposes, including: industrial development bonds; and bonds for which the proceeds are used in the trade or business of persons other than a state or local government (e.g., student loans, qualified mortgages, qualified waste disposal facilities).[27] Receipt of private activity bond interest may trigger alternative minimum tax for some individuals (see Chapter 9).[28]

are excluded from gross income.[23] Conversely, *income* generated from gifts, bequests, devises, or inheritances are included in gross income of the recipient. Similarly, gifts, bequests, devise or inheritances of income from property (i.e., income distributed from a trust) is also included in the gross income of the recipient.[24]

- **Municipal bond interest**. Interest on bonds issued by state and local governments is usually *excluded* from gross income. If an individual receives tax-exempt interest, and that person is required to file an income tax return (see Chapter 2 and Chapter 7), he must report the amount of tax-exempt interest received during the tax year on his return even though tax-exempt interest is not subject to income tax.[25] Furthermore, even though municipal bond interest may be excluded from gross income, it must be taken into account in the calculation when determining whether Social Security payments are includible in gross income.[26] For more information on municipal bonds, see the sidebar, "Municipal Bonds."

- **Compensation for injuries and sickness**. Amounts received on account of personal physical injuries or physical sickness is generally excludable from gross income.[29] For example, a jury award for injuries sustained in an automobile accident would be excludable from gross income. But payments received as compensation for lost income and/or other economic damages must be included in the recipient's gross income. Payments awarded in an emotional distress suit are generally *not* treated as a physical injury or physical sickness and, therefore, are not excludable.[30] Furthermore, punitive damages—where the court is penalizing the wrongdoer for egregious behavior—must generally be included in the injured party's income.[31]

- **Contributions made by employers to health and accident plans**. Pursuant to section 106(a) of the Code, premiums paid through an employer-provided accident or health insurance plan are excluded from the gross income of the employee. Under those circumstances, however, the employee must include in gross income any amount received by virtue of being covered by such plan for personal injury or sickness (i.e., disability payments) that would have been otherwise excluded from gross income.[32] In other words, if the employee receives the tax-free benefit of not including employer-paid accident or health insurance premiums in gross income, there is no tax-free double dipping with regard to the receipt of would have otherwise been excludible personal injury or sickness payments he or she receives through that coverage. On the other hand, an employer's *reimbursement* of an employee under a MERP (Medical Expense Reimbursement Plan) for expenses incurred by the employee for medical care of himself, his spouse, or his dependents may be fully excludable from gross income.[33]

- **Amounts received under health or accident plans**. If an individual has purchased a health insurance policy himself and paid premiums with his or her own funds, the benefits received under that policy are excludable from gross income.[34] If both the employer and the employee share the premium cost, only the amount received by the employee attributable to the employer's premium payments is includible in the employee's gross income.[35]

- **Rental value of a parsonage**. A member of the clergy is permitted to exclude from income the fair rental value of a home (including utilities) or a housing allowance provided as part of his or her compensation. This applies only to ordained, licensed, or commissioned clergy.[36]

- **Income from the discharge of indebtedness**. Although discharge of indebtedness is includible in gross income,[37] under certain circumstances, all of part of the amount discharged may be excluded from gross income. Those circumstances and the extent of the exclusion are as follows:

  (1) a discharge received in a bankruptcy proceeding.[38]

  (2) the discharge of all or part of a student loan specifically providing for such discharge in exchange for the debtor "work[ing] for a certain period of time in certain professions for any of a broad class of employers" (e.g., a doctor who commits to work for a rural hospital or clinic).[39]

  (3) the discharge of any debt where the payment would have been deductible had it actually been made by the debtor. Stated differently, the discharge of debt income and the lost deduction are treated as offsetting resulting in no taxable income. For example, the discharge of interest on a business related loan would be excluded

from gross income because had the taxpayer actually made the payment, it would have been deductible in exactly the same amount.[40]

  (4) if a seller of property financed through purchase money debt reduces a portion of the debt for no consideration, that reduction is treated as a decrease in the purchase price rather than a discharge of the purchase money debt.[41]

  (5) a discharge that occurs when a taxpayer is insolvent, but only to the extent of the taxpayer's insolvency. To illustrate, assume that at the time of the discharge of $120,000 of debt, the taxpayer had assets of $20,000 and no other debt beyond what was discharged. After the discharge, the taxpayer's net worth would be $20,000. In this instance, $100,000 (the amount by which the taxpayer was insolvent) of the $120,000 of discharged debt would be excluded from gross income. The remaining $20,000—the amount of the taxpayer's resulting solvency—would be includible in gross income.[42]

  (6) the discharge of qualified farm indebtedness, which is defined as debt incurred directly in a farming business in which 50 percent or more of the gross receipts for the three preceding tax years prior to the tax year of discharge is attributable to the farming business, subject to certain limitations.[43]

  (7) the discharge of qualified real property business indebtedness, which is defined as secured debt incurred or assumed to acquire, construct, reconstruct, or substantially improve property used in a trade or business, subject to certain limitations.[44]

  (8) the discharge of qualified principal residence indebtedness of up to $2 million pursuant to a short sale or foreclosure.[45] This exclusion ended on January 1, 2014. However, at the time of print legislation is pending in the U.S. House of Representatives that would extend the exclusion until January 1, 2016.[46]

- **Recovery of "tax benefit" items**. Pursuant to the "tax benefit rule," a taxpayer who recovers by refund, reimbursement or collection an amount that in a prior tax year provided a tax benefit in the form of a deduction, refund or credit must essentially pay back that tax benefit by including that amount in gross income in the tax year of recovery. For example, assume in 2010, the taxpayer claimed a bad debt deduction for a loan default. Then, in 2011, the debtor unexpectedly repaid the loan to the taxpayer. Under the tax benefit rule, because the taxpayer recovered the amount of the loan previously deducted as a bad debt, the taxpayer would have to include the amount of the loan repayment. However, the amount included in gross income is limited to the amount by which the deduction or credit taken for the recovered amount resulted in tax savings in the earlier year. To illustrate this point, assume in 2011, the taxpayer received a state income tax refund for taxes paid in the 2010 tax year. In the taxpayer had itemized, the state income tax paid in 2010 could have been claimed as a deduction for Federal income tax purposes, and, thus reduced the taxpayer's tax liability. However, if the taxpayer did not itemize in 2010, the payment of the state income tax would not have conferred any tax benefit to the taxpayer. Thus, the recovery of the state income tax via refund in 2011 would not be included in gross income.[47]

- **Qualified scholarships.** Amounts received as a "qualified scholarship or fellowship" are not includible in gross income. A "qualified scholarship or fellowship" is any amount the individual receives that is for tuition and fees to enroll at or attend an education institution; *or* fees, books, supplies, and equipment required for courses at the educational institution.[48]

- **Meals or lodging furnished for the convenience of the employer.** The value of meals and lodging provided to an employee (and his family) by the individual's employer at no cost to the employee are not includible in gross income if the following conditions are met:

  - Meals must be furnished on the business premises of the employer, *and* must be furnished for the employer's convenience.

  - Lodging must be furnished on the business premises of the employer, for the

convenience of the employer, *and* must be a condition of the individual's employment.[49]

- **Gain from the sale of a principal residence.** Unmarried taxpayers may exclude up to $250,000 of gain from the sale of a principal residence. Married taxpayers filing jointly may exclude up to $500,000. The full exclusion is available if the taxpayer:

  (1) has used and owned the home as a principal residence for two of the five years preceding the date of the sale; *and*

  (2) has *not* claimed the exclusion in the past two years.

  However, even if the taxpayer does not meet the above requirements, a partial exclusion may still be permitted. If the sale of the home is due to a change in place of employment, health problems, or unforeseen circumstances, then a reduced maximum exclusion may be available to the individual. The maximum exclusion is multiplied by the ratio that the "qualifying period" bears to the two-year period.[50]

- **Educational assistance programs.** An individual may exclude up to $5,250 of employer-provided educational assistance from gross income. The exclusion applies to undergraduate and graduate level courses.[51]

- **Dependent care assistance programs.** Dependent care benefits are generally excludable from gross income. Such benefits include amounts the employer pays directly to the employee for the care of certain individuals *and* the fair market value of care in a day care facility provided or sponsored by the individual's employer.

  The amount that can be excluded is limited to the lesser of: (1) the total amount of dependent care benefits the individual received during the year; (2) the total amount of qualified expenses the individual incurred during the year; (3) the individual's earned income; (4) the income of the individual's spouse; or (5) $5,000, or $2,500 if married filing separately.[52]

- **Certain personal injury liability assignments.** This exclusion relates to structured settlements of damages payable in periodic payments that would have otherwise been excluded from the gross income of the injured party (i.e., on account of physical injury or sickness). In operation, the obligation to make future periodic payments to the injured party is assigned by the wrongdoer to a "qualified assignment company." Using funds received from the wrongdoer, the qualified assignment company acquires a "qualified funding asset" such as an annuity or a US treasury obligation held by a trustee. Subsequently, the company issuing the annuity or the trustee makes the periodic payments to the injured party. Under such an arrangement, none of the amounts received by the injured party would be included in gross income.[53]

- **Certain fringe benefits**. Pursuant to Code section 61(a)(1), fringe benefits, a form of compensation, are included in gross income. (See Figure 3.1 for a more comprehensive list.) However, the fringe benefits listed below are specifically excluded from gross income:

  (1) no-additional-cost services;

  (2) qualified employee discounts;

  (3) working condition fringe benefits;

  (4) de minimis fringe benefits;

  (5) qualified transportation fringe benefits;

  (6) qualified moving expense reimbursement;

  (7) qualified retirement planning services; and

  (8) qualified military base realignment and closure benefits.[54]

- **Income from United States savings bonds used to pay higher education expenses**. A taxpayer may exclude interest on United States savings bonds if the bonds are Series EE or Series I savings bonds, and the proceeds must be used to pay *qualified higher education expenses* (i.e., tuition and fees) required for enrollment at an eligible higher education institution for the bond owner or his/her dependents. In addition, for taxable years beginning in 2014, for all filers other than married filing jointly,

the amount of the exclusion begins to phase out for modified adjusted gross income in excess of $76,000, with a complete phase out at $91,000. For married individuals filing jointly, the exclusion begins to phase out for modified adjusted gross income in excess of $113,950, with a complete phase out at $143,950.[55]

- **Adoption assistance programs**. For taxable years beginning in 2014, an employee may exclude $13,190 of expenses paid and then reimbursed by his employer under an adoption assistance program in connection with the employee's adoption of an eligible child. The amount of the exclusion phases out for modified adjusted gross income in excess of $197,880 with a complete phase out at $237,880.[56]

- **Medicare Advantage MSA**. Distributions for "qualified medical expenses" from "Medicare Advantage MSAs" (Medical Savings Accounts) generally are not includible in gross income. Qualified medical expenses are medical and dental expenses that would be deductible under Code section 213.[57] A "Medicare Advantage MSA" is available only to taxpayers who are entitled to benefits under Medicare Part A, and are enrolled under Part B.[58]

- **Disaster relief payments**. Gross income does not include disaster relief payments intended to help victims of natural disasters.[59] Payments made to victims of a "qualified disaster" on or after September 11, 2001 are also excludable from income. "Qualified disaster" generally means a disaster resulting from a terrorist or military action or a catastrophic airline accident.[60]

Other specifically excluded items include: improvements made by a lessee (i.e., tenant) on the lessor's (i.e., landlord's) property;[61] certain types of combat zone compensation for Armed Forces members;[62] capital contributions to a corporation;[63] amounts received under group legal services plans;[64] certain reduced uniformed services retirement pay;[65] amounts received under insurance contracts for certain living expenses;[66] and cafeteria plans.[67]

Other Non-Income Items

Return of capital. Under our income tax system, economic benefits are taxed only once. Thus, the "return

Figure 3.1

FRINGE BENEFITS*	
Type of fringe benefit	Includable in gross income?
Accident or health plan provided by employer	No
Athletic facilities	No
De minimis (minimal value gifts, such as holiday gifts):	
Cash (bonus check, gift certificate)	Yes
Non-cash (holiday ham)	No
Dependent care benefits	No, if less than applicable limit

Educational assistance:
  - Cost is $5,250 or less
  - Cost exceeds $5,250
	
	No
	Yes

Employee discounts	No, unless discount "not qualified"
Financial counseling fees	Yes, but a limited deduction may be available

Group-term life insurance
  - Cost is $50,000 or less
  - Cost is greater than $50,000
	
	No
	Yes

Meals and lodging	No
Moving expense reimbursement	No
No-additional cost service (i.e., services received for free, or at reduced cost to employee that employer offers for sale to the public and that does not have a substantial additional cost)	No
Retirement planning services	No
Transportation	No, if less than applicable limit
Working condition fringe benefit (i.e., an employer provided product or service that the employer would have been able to deduct had he paid for it himself)	No
* The information in this table is based on the general rule governing each type of compensation. It is not intended to cover all exceptions and/or contingencies.	

of capital" or recovery of after-tax dollars is *not* an economic benefit includible in gross income. Money used to buy property is presumed to be after-tax dollars. So, if an individual buys stock for $10,000 and sells it for $10,000, there is no income because the seller merely recovered his or her after-tax purchase price. Conversely, if the individual sells the stock for $10,500, there is a profit or $500 that would be includible in gross income pursuant to Code section 61(a)(3).[68]

Loans. The proceeds from a loan are not gross income to the borrower because the economic benefit of the use of the borrowed funds is offset by a corresponding obligation to repay the loan. Similarly, the repayment of the principal amount of the loan is not gross income to the lender because the lender is merely recouping the after-tax dollars loaned to the borrower. Interest

income is included in gross income pursuant to Code section 61(a)(4).

Income Characterization Has Tax Significance

Once it is determined that an item is included in gross income, and, no exclusion applies, the next step is to determine the character of the income. The character of the income has two significant roles in income taxation. First, the character of the income determines the tax rates at which the income is to be taxed. Second, the deductibility of certain expenses or losses may be limited based upon characterization. Income is characterized as either *ordinary income* or *capital gain*. Ordinary income is essentially any type of gross income with the exception of gain from the sale or exchange of a capital asset or property described in Code section 1231(b).[69] Capital gain is gain from the sale or exchange of a capital asset, and can be short-term (the asset was owned ty the tax payer for no more than one year) or long-term (the asset was owned for more than one year).[70] The tax rates for ordinary income and short-term capital gain are the same, and range from 10 percent to 39.6 percent.[71] The tax rates for long-term capital gain and qualified dividends[72] (ordinary income taxed at the same tax rates as long-term capital gain) are either 15 or 20 percent, depending on the taxpayer's income level.[73]

Long- and Short-term capital losses can be deducted to offset the amount of long- and short-term capital gains plus $3,000 of ordinary income. Any non-deductible capital loss is carried forward indefinitely, subject to the same restriction.[74] In other words, if a taxpayer has a *net* capital loss in any given tax year, no more than $3,000 of that loss would be deductible against other ordinary income. Without any capital gains to be offset, a taxpayer with a net capital loss of $100,000 would need thirty-four years to fully deduct the entire loss at the rate of $3,000 per year.

For a more detailed explanation of capital gains and qualified dividends, see Chapter 4.

Income Classifications Have Tax Significance

In addition to determining the character of taxable gross income, the *classification* of certain types of gross income can have tax significance. As discussed below, the classification of gross income can be relevant to the allowance of a tax credit, an exclusion from gross income, a limitation on certain deductions, and can be the basis for an additional tax.

Earned Income

The classification of certain types of gross income as *earned income* is a prerequisite for qualifying for the earned income tax credit. The earned income tax credit is a refundable credit meaning that even if the amount of the credit exceeds the amount of tax withheld by the taxpayer's employer or otherwise paid by the taxpayer, the taxpayer would nonetheless be entitled to a refund.[75] The credit is available to those taxpayers who have low or moderate earned income. For purposes of this tax credit, earned income includes:

(1) wages, salaries, tips, bonuses, and other employee compensation to the extent it is included in gross income;[76]

(2) net earnings from self-employment;[77] and

(3) gross income received as a "statutory employee" (agent or commission drivers; certain full-time life insurance salespeople; full-time traveling salespeople; and home workers).[78]

In addition to the earned income credit, there is a foreign earned income exclusion available to U.S. citizens and U.S. resident aliens who work in a foreign country. This credit allows taxpayers who are employed overseas to exclude a relatively large amount of their foreign earned income from gross income. The amount of the foreign earned income subject to the exclusion is indexed for inflation. For the 2014 tax year, the exclusion amount was $99,200.[79]

Investment Income

Investment income (sometimes referred to as "unearned income") is another classification of gross income with tax significance. For example, investment interest (interest paid on a loan that was used to purchase investment property) is deductible only to the extent of net investment income.[80] Any excess "loss" is carried over to subsequent years subject to the same rules, and is only deductible to extent of net investment income in those subsequent years. For this purpose, investment income is income from property held for investment, such as stocks, bonds, and investment property. It includes dividends and royalties as well as the gain from the sale of investment property.[81]

In addition to being a limitation on the deductibility of investment interest, net investment income is also subject to the 3.8 percent net investment income tax imposed on high income taxpayers.[82] For this purpose, investment interest also includes annuity payments, rent generated from investment type property, and passive activity income (described below).[83]

A child's investment income in excess of $2,000 is subject to the "kiddie tax." The purpose of the kiddie tax is to prevent parents from shifting investment income taxed at their higher tax rate to their children to be taxed at their much lower tax rate. For example, parents may be tempted to transfer a substantial investment portfolio to a child so that the income generated therefrom would be taxed to the child rather than the parents.

When the kiddie tax applies, the child's investment or unearned income is treated as if it was earned by the parents, and, thus, taxed at the parents' highest tax rate. For this purpose, investment income includes interest, dividends and capital gain distributions. The kiddie tax applies in each of the following circumstances:

1. until the year in which child attains the age of eighteen regardless of the amount of the child's earned income;

2. in the year the child attains the age of eighteen, unless the child's earned income is more than half of his or her overall support; or

3. in any year from the ages of nineteen to twenty-three, if the child is a full-time student during any part of at least five months and earned income is less than half of the child's overall support.[84]

Passive Activity Income

Passive activity income is income generated from any trade or business activity in which the taxpayer does not "materially participate."[85] Generally, a taxpayer is considered to *materially participate* in an activity if he is involved in the operations of the activity on a regular, continuous, and substantial basis. Note that rental activities are considered to be a passive activity even if the taxpayer materially participates in the activity.[86] This classification is important because if a taxpayer has positive non-passive income from Venture A and substantial non-passive business deductions from Venture B, the Venture B business deductions can offset the taxable income from Venture A. This is not the case with passive activity deductions that are only deductible to the extent of passive activity income.[87] So if the income generated in Venture A was non-passive and the business deductions generated in Venture B were passive, the Venture B deductions could not be applied to reduce the Venture A income. However, if the taxpayer generated passive income in subsequent tax years, the leftover Venture B passive deductions from this year could be deducted against such income. For a more detailed explanation of passive activity income, see Chapter 24.[88]

INCOME DEFERAL AND TIMING ISSUES

There is a distinction between an *exclusion* of income and a *deferral* of income. An exclusion provision means that an item that would otherwise be included in gross income is never taxed. A deferral excludes certain economic benefits from gross income based on the taxpayer meeting the qualifications of the relevant Code section. However, the income may be taxable in the future depending on the qualifications of the deferral. For example, although the gain realized by the taxpayer with regard to like-kind exchanges,[89] involuntary conversions[90] and certain exchanges of insurance policies[91] would be excluded from gross income, the inherent gain remains preserved in the replacement property and would be included in gross income if the taxpayer disposed of the property in a taxable transaction at a later date.[92] In addition to those provisions, as discussed below, there are a number of gross income deferrals available to employees.

Selected Employee Compensation Deferrals

Retirement plan contributions. Employer contributions to a qualified retirement plan (such as a pension, profit-sharing, or stock-bonus plan) for an employee are generally not included in the employee's gross income at the time of the contribution. Over time, the income generated by the invested contributions grows tax-free. When the employee retires, the distributions to the employee would be included in gross income. The tax treatment of retirement plan contributions and distributions is discussed in greater detail in Chapter 32 and Appendix A, as well as the companion resource to this volume, *Tools & Techniques of Employee Benefit and Retirement Planning*.

Stock options. Stock options generally come into two varieties: (1) qualified incentive stock options (ISOs); and (2) nonqualified stock options (NQSOs).[93] The tax treatment and timing for each type of option differs significantly and is based on several different factors. For details on the tax treatment of ISOs and NQSOs, see Chapter 30, and our companion resource, *Tools & Techniques of Employee Benefit and Retirement Planning*.

Section 83(b) election. Pursuant to Code section 83(a), the value of property transferred to an employee is not includible in the employee's gross income until it becomes totally vested and not subject to a substantial risk of forfeiture. An example of a substantial risk of forfeiture would the requirement that the employee must return the property if the employee fails to remain employed with the employer for a number of years. Only in the tax year in which the property vests due to the employee satisfying the condition would the then value of the property be included in gross income.

The election provided by Code section 83(b) can provide significant planning opportunities for the employee by allowing the employee the option of including the value of the stock as income in the year the he or she receives it, even if it has not vested. For example, assume that in 2014, the employer transfers stock worth $10,000 to the employee, subject to forfeiture if the employee does not remain in the employ of the employer for the next five years. Further, assume that at the time of vesting in 2019, the stock is worth $25,000. In the absence of a section 83(b) election, the employee would have no income to report in 2014, but be required to include $25,000 (the value of the stock) as compensation income in 2019, taxable at ordinary income rates.[94] In the alternative, if the employee made a section 83(b) election in 2014, he or she would be required to include the stock's value of $10,000 as compensation income, taxable at ordinary income rates. When ownership of the stock vests in 2019, there would be no reportable gross income, even though the stock had appreciated by $15,000. Moreover, as long as the employee simply held the stock, there would be no further income. When the employee sells the stock, the gain (proceeds from the sale minus the initial $10,000 that was included in gross income in 2014) would be treated as a long-term capital gain rather than ordinary income.

The difference between the two options can be significant for the taxpayer. Without a section 83(b) election, although the employee would not report any of the income until 2019, the $25,000 then included in gross income as compensation would be subject to ordinary income rates. With a section 83(b) election, although the employee would report $10,000 of ordinary income in 2014, none of the appreciation would be taxed until the stock was sold. If the stock was sold in 2019 or anytime thereafter, the gain ($15,000 if sold in 2019) would be taxed at the preferential capital gain rates. Under the latter scenario, the employee would effectively convert what would otherwise be ordinary income into a long-term capital gain, and would be able to control when the gain was taxed by deciding when to sell the stock

Advance payment for services. Most taxpayers report income and deductions under the cash method of accounting, meaning that they report compensation in the year it is received without regard to when it was actually earned. For example, if a taxpayer receives his or her 2015 bonus in 2016, it would be includible in gross income in 2016 even though it was earned in

2015. Similarly, if the taxpayer receives part of his or her 2016 compensation in 2015, that amount would be includible in gross income in 2015 even though it was not earned until 2016.[95] Conversely, under the accrual method of accounting, income is reported in the year it is earned without regard to when it is received. An accrual method taxpayer who did not receive his or her 2015 bonus until 2016 would include it in gross income in 2015, the year in which it was earned. In spite of this general rule, an accrual method taxpayer is often treated as a cash method taxpayer with regard to the receipt of income. An accrual method taxpayer must include compensation in gross income on the earliest of:

1. when the payment is received;

2. when the income is due to the taxpayer;

3. when the income is earned; or

4. with respect to property, when title has passed.[96]

For that reason, it would appear that even under the accrual method of accounting, advance payment for services must be included in gross income in the tax year in which it was paid. There is, however, an exception for an advance payment of services to be performed by the end of the following tax year. For example, in 2014, if an accrual method taxpayer receives an advance for services to be performed by the end of 2015, the taxpayer can elect to defer the inclusion of that income until 2015. However, the taxpayer may only extend the deferral one tax year beyond the year of payment. If the taxpayer received an advance payment in 2014 for services to be performed by the end of 2016, the exception would not apply and he or she would be required to include the advance payment in gross income in 2014.[97]

BEWARE OF SEVERAL TAX TRAPS

Constructive Receipt of Income

In order to defer income from one tax year to another, a cash method taxpayer may be tempted to delay the deposit of the last paycheck of the year to the following tax year. In the alternative, he or she might ask his or her employer to hold the check until January. Likewise, knowing that the postal service will attempt to deliver the taxpayer's last payroll check on the last day of the year, the taxpayer might choose not to be home to accept delivery. By doing so, he or she is attempting to delay the receipt of income and, thus, the inclusion of that income until the following tax year. Under the doctrine of *constructive receipt of income*, none of these ploys would work. Under this doctrine, the taxpayer must include all income that is available to him (credited, set apart, or otherwise available), even though it may not actually be in his possession.[98] So in any of the scenarios described above, the taxpayer would have to include those amounts in gross income in the tax year they were constructively received rather than the later tax year.

Imputed Income From a Below Market Loan

Taxpayers with a close relationship (employer/employee, corporation/shareholder or parent/child) are often tempted to make below market or even interest free loans. By doing so, both the lender and the borrower would enjoy substantial economic and tax benefits. For example, in the case of an interest-free loan, the borrower would enjoy the economic benefit of having the use of the borrowed funds without the economic burden of paying interest. In turn, the lender would be able to provide the economic benefit of the use of the loaned money to the borrower without having to include interest payments from the borrower in gross income. Because the scope of gross income is so broad and is designed to capture any economic benefit as taxable income, Code section 7872 treats such "below-market" loans in a way that would trigger "imputed income" and possibly result in adverse tax consequences to the lender and the borrower. For this purpose, a "below-market" loan is a loan on which either no interest is charged, *or* the interest charged is at a rate below the applicable federal rate (AFR), and thus considered as not charging adequate interest.[99] (A complete history and current AFR rates can be found at http://www.leimberg.com).

In the case of a below market loan, section 7872 effectively rewrites the transaction by imputing that the lender took the following actions:

- made a loan to the borrower in exchange for a note (even though no such note really exists) that requires the payment of interest at the AFR; and

- transferred the amount of foregone interest to the borrower (even though nothing was actually transferred). The amount of the foregone interest is the difference between the AFR and the amount actually paid by the borrower. For example, if the lender made an interest-free loan, the entire amount of the AFR would be an imputed transfer to the borrower.

What would the tax consequences be to the borrower who is deemed to have received an amount equal to the foregone interest from the lender? From the borrower's perspective, the classification of the income from the foregone interest is predicated on the borrower's relationship with lender. For example, if the lender was the employer of the borrower, the phantom payment is deemed to be a form of compensation includible in the borrower/employee's gross income. If the lender was a corporation and the borrower was a shareholder, the phantom payment is deemed be a dividend distribution, also includible in the borrower/shareholder's gross income. Finally, if the lender was a parent and the borrower was a child, the phantom payment would be treated as a gift to the borrower/child, and, thus not included in the gross income.

From the lender's perspective, Code Section 7872(a) specifically states that "the forgone interest shall be treated as ... retransferred by the borrower to the lender as interest"—even though no such interest payment was actually made. The lender will have to include the phantom payment as interest income, although under many circumstances the lender will have an offsetting deduction for the income provided to the borrower.

Consider the following example, in which an employer provides an employee with a no-interest loan of $100,000. Assume that the AFR is 6 percent, providing $6,000 in interest. If the employer had simply paid the employee a bonus of $6,000, the employee would have $6,000 of compensation income and the employer would be entitled to a $6,000 compensation deduction. Then, if the employee paid the employer $6,000 of interest, the employer would have $6,000 of interest income. The employee may or may not be entitled to an interest deduction depending on how he or she used the borrowed funds. Code section 7872 simply recasts a below market loan in just that way. When the employer makes an interest free loan of $100,000 to the employee, the Code treats the employer as if it had paid the employee compensation in the amount of the foregone interest ($6,000). Then, it treats the employee as using the phantom compensation to pay the employer the interest that should have been charged on that loan. In both scenarios, the employee has compensation income and the employer has interest income. Here, the employer also gets a deduction for the phantom compensation and the transaction is a wash. From the employee's perspective, whether he or she would be entitled to a deduction depends on how the borrowed funds are used, just as it would in any regular loan.

Although the tax consequences of below market loans can be onerous, there are several de minimis exceptions that may apply.[100] For example, compensation-related loans (often considered wage advances), corporate-shareholder loans, and loans between individuals for non-business and non-investment purposes are generally exempt so long as the balance owed never exceeds $10,000. Finally—as can be seen in the example above—the deduction consequences with respect to such below market loans are complicated, and many of them are beyond the scope of this chapter.

Restoration of Income Previously Taxed

The *claim of right* doctrine applies to the receipt of income that the taxpayer may have a contingent obligation to repay at a later date. In spite of a potential obligation to repay, the taxpayer must nonetheless include it in gross income unless "the individual recognizes his liability under an existing and fixed obligation and makes provisions for repayment."[101] For example, assume an employee receives a bonus that the employer could possibly dispute and compel the employee to repay at some later date. At the time the bonus was received, there was no fixed obligation for repayment, nor had the employee made any provision for its repayment. Under the claim of right doctrine, the taxpayer would be compelled to include the bonus in gross income. However, in the event the taxpayer was subsequently required to repay all or part of such bonus, the taxpayer would be entitled to "a deduction for the amount of the repayment and, in effect, a credit for the amount of tax that would have been saved in the year of inclusion if the repaid amount had been excluded from that year's gross income."[102]

WHERE CAN I FIND OUT MORE?

1. *Tax Facts on Insurance & Employee Benefits* (National Underwriter Company; published annually).

2. *Tools and Techniques of Employee Benefit and Retirement Planning* (National Underwriter Company).

FREQUENTLY ASKED QUESTIONS

Question – What are installment sales? How are installment payments taxed?

Answer – An installment sale is a sale of property in which the seller makes a gain, and provides credit to the buyer under terms that require at least one payment to be made after the close of the taxable year in which the property was sold. There is usually a promissory note that requires the buyer to pay principal and interest over the payment term of the arrangement. As each payment is received, the seller includes the entire interest portion of the payment in gross income. As to the principal portion of the payment, with each yearly installment, a ratable amount of the gain is included in gross income. This allows the selling taxpayer to spread his or her gain over the payment term.[103]

Example: Mary Worth owns land which she purchased four years ago for $20,000. In 2014, Mary sells the land to Betty Buyer for $100,000, payable in five $20,000 annual installments. The sale is evidenced with a promissory note bearing market rate interest and specifying the interest payments to be made in addition to the $20,000 annual payments toward the purchase price.

Viewing the transaction as a whole, Mary would have a total gain of $80,000 (the selling price of $100,000 less her cost basis of $20,000). Thus, under the installment method of reporting, Mary would ratably include her overall gain in gross income over the five-year term. Since each payment is $20,000 (exclusive of interest), Mary would determine her ratable yearly gain by multiplying the payment by the *gross profit ratio*, which is defined as the total gain as a percentage of the selling price. In this case, the gross profit ratio is 80 percent ($80,000 total gain/$100,000 selling price). For each of the five years, Mary would include $16,000 (80 percent) of the annual payment as gross income. The remaining $4,000 of each principal payment is a tax-free recovery of her cost basis over the same five-year period. So, at the end of the five-year term, Mary would have ratably included $80,000 of income ($16,000 each year) and $20,000 of tax-free recovery of her cost basis ($4,000 each year). The interest payment(s) she received each year would be separately included as gross income in the years in which they are received.

Question – Are attorneys' fees includible in the gross income of an injured party?

Answer – It depends. To the extent that the injured party is awarded a non-taxable judgment for physical injuries, attorneys' fees are not included in the gross income of the injured party. For all other taxable judgment awards the winning litigant must include the entire amount of the judgment including the contingent attorneys' fees in gross income according to a 2005 decision by the United States Supreme Court in *Commissioner v. Banks*.[104]

In the years leading up to the Supreme Court's pronouncement, the number of lawsuits filed in this country had steadily increased. It was not surprising that the tax issues triggered by the large judgments being awarded to injured individuals would also attract increased attention from the IRS. With respect to the judgment awards received by an injured party for personal injuries or sickness, there has never been a dispute since none of it is ever included in the injured party's gross income.[105] For that reason, the portion of the settlement paid in attorneys' fees was inconsequential since the entire award would be non-taxable.

But many lawsuits other than personal injury are also handled on a *contingency basis* – meaning that the plaintiff's attorney gets paid only if the case is won. Consequently, until *Banks* was decided in 2005, a major point of contention was whether the injured party must include the attorneys' contingency fees in gross income or simply include the net amount of the judgment actually received in gross income. In *Banks*, the Supreme Court resolved the dispute by holding that the winning litigant must include the entire amount of the judgment in gross income. As discussed below, the aftermath of the decision has created a substantial tax hardship for the winning litigant.

Attorneys' fees are deductible under Code section 212 as an expense incurred in connection with the production of income, and treated as a miscellaneous itemized deduction subject to a 2 percent adjusted gross income floor.[106] To see why this is important, assume that in 2013, a court awarded the taxpayer $300,000 in taxable economic damages.

Of that amount, $100,000 is payable to her attorney as a contingent fee and deductible pursuant to section 212. Assuming the taxpayer had no other deductions and the award was the taxpayer's only income, 2 percent of $300,000 is $6,000, so the itemized deduction would be limited to $94,000. In addition, by virtue of the section 68 phase-out (overall limitation on itemized deductions), the itemized deduction would be further reduced to $92,500. Thus, even though the taxpayer received $200,000, she would be essentially taxed on $207,500 or $7,500 more than she had received. Compounding the taxpayer's tax woes would be the imposition of the alternative minimum tax that is triggered by the large miscellaneous itemized deduction of the attorneys' fees. As a result, the taxpayer's overall tax liability on the net $200,000 award would be $78,800 ($51,834 regular tax plus $26,966 of alternative minimum tax).

Conversely, if the $100,000 of attorneys' fees were simply taken out of the equation since the taxpayer was only entitled to receive an amount equal to two-thirds of the judgment, or $200,000, the tax consequences would be dramatically different, and arguably much fairer. Assuming the $200,000 was the taxpayer's only income, in the absence of adverse tax consequences caused by the miscellaneous itemized deduction of attorneys' fees that were not fully deductible and triggered alternative minimum tax, there would only be a regular tax of $46,831. So in spite of the fact that in both scenarios, the taxpayer's net share of the judgment was $200,000, under current law, the tax difference resulting from the inclusion of the attorneys' fees in gross income would be over $40,000. Ultimately, it will take an act of Congress to change this result.

Question – Are damages received for certain nonphysical personal injuries includible in the gross income of an injured party?

Answer – Marrita Murphy sued in district court to recover income taxes paid on compensatory damages she had been awarded for emotional distress and loss of reputation in an administrative action brought against her former employer. Murphy contended that under Code section 104(a)(2), her award should have been excluded from her gross income because it was compensation received "on account of personal physical injuries or physical sickness." Alternatively, Murphy maintained that section 104(a)(2) is unconstitutional because it fails to exclude from gross income revenue that is not "income" within the meaning of the Sixteenth Amendment to the Constitution of the United States. The district court rejected all of Murphy's claims on the merits and granted summary judgment for the government and the IRS.[107]

The United States Court of Appeals for the District of Columbia concluded (on rehearing) that Murphy's compensatory award was not received on account of personal physical injuries, was not exempt from taxation pursuant to section 104(a)(2), and was therefore part of Murphy's "gross income," as defined by Code section 61. It also decided that the tax was constitutional because it was an excise tax rather than a direct tax and was uniform throughout the United States. Accordingly, the appeals court affirmed the judgment of the district court.[108]

CHAPTER ENDNOTES

1. I.R.C. §61(a).
2. Treas. Reg. §1.61-1(a).
3. *See* Treas. Reg. §1.61-1(c) referencing "manufacturing, merchandising, or mining business," but obviously applicable to all businesses.
4. I.R.C. §1001(a).
5. I.R.C. §1222.
6. For example, §7872 imputes interest on certain below market loans discussed below.
7. See I.R.C. §§301 and 316 for the rules determining whether distributions from a corporation to shareholders are deemed to be taxable dividends.
8. See I.R.C. §101 and Treasury Regulations, thereunder.
9. See I.R.C. §§72, 402 and 403.
10. I.R.C. §702(c).
11. I.R.C. §691(a) and discussed in more detail in Chapter 26.
12. Part 1 (§641 and following), Subchapter J, Chapter 1 of the Code.
13. I.R.C. §73.
14. Treas. Reg. §1.74(a)(1). Also see I.R.C. §74.
15. Treas. Reg. §1.74(b).
16. I.R.C. §79.
17. I.R.C. §82.
18. I.R.C. §84.
19. I.R.C. §85.
20. I.R.C. §86. Rounding out other items specifically included in gross income are as follows: I.R.C. §75 - dealers in tax-exempt securities (adjustment for bond premiums); I.R.C. §77 - commodity credit loans; I.R.C. §78 - dividends received from certain foreign corporations by domestic corporations choosing the foreign tax credit; I.R.C. §80 - restoration of the value of certain securities; I.R.C. §87 - the alcohol fuel credit; I.R.C. §88 - certain amounts with respect to nuclear decommissioning costs; and I.R.C. §89 - illegal federal irrigation subsidies.
21. I.R.C. §101(a).
22. I.R.C. §§61(a)(10) and 101(a)(2); Treas. Reg. §1.101-1. The amount included in gross income may also be deemed to be "investment income" for purposes of the 3.8 percent net investment income tax.
23. I.R.C. §102(a); Treas. Reg. §1.102-1(a).
24. I.R.C. §102(b); Treas. Reg. §1.102-1(b) and (c).
25. I.R.C. §6012(d).
26. I.R.C. §86(b)(2)(B).
27. I.R.C. §141.
28. I.R.C. §57(a)(5).
29. I.R.C. §104(a)(2). This is true whether the damages are received by the injured plaintiff in a lump sum, as periodic payments, or from a lawsuit or a settlement agreement.
30. I.R.C. §104(a).
31. I.R.C. §104(c). However, if punitive damages are awarded in a wrongful death action, and the applicable state law provides that punitive damages, only, may be awarded, then such damages would be excludable from income.
32. I.R.C. §105(a).
33. I.R.C. §105(b). But if an accident or health plan has reimbursed an employee for medical expenses he deducted in an earlier year, the employee may have to include some of the reimbursed amount in the year in which the reimbursement was received.
34. I.R.C. §104(a)(3).
35. I.R.C. §105.
36. I.R.C. §107.
37. I.R.C. §61(a)(12).
38. I.R.C. §§108(a)(1)(A) and (d)(2).
39. I.R.C. §108(f).
40. I.R.C. §108(e)(2).
41. I.R.C. §108(e)(5).
42. I.R.C. §§108(a)(1)(b) and (d)(3).
43. I.R.C. §§108(a)(1)(C) and (g).
44. I.R.C. §108(a)(1)(D) and (c)(1) and (2).
45. I.R.C. §108(a)(1)(E) and (h).
46. H.R.3856 — 113th Cong.
47. I.R.C. §111.
48. I.R.C. §117.
49. I.R.C. §119.
50. I.R.C. §121.
51. I.R.C. §127.
52. I.R.C. §129.
53. I.R.C. §130.
54. I.R.C. §132(a)(1)-(8).
55. I.R.C. §135. Rev. Proc. 2013-35, 2008-47 IRB 167.
56. I.R.C. §§137(a)(2) and (b)(1). Rev. Proc. 2013-35, 2008-45 IRB 167.
57. IRS Publication 969.
58. I.R.C. §138(b). "Medicare Advantage MSA" was formerly known as "Medicare+Choice MSA."

59. Disaster Relief Act of 1974 (P.L. 98-233); 42 USC 408; Rev. Rul. 76-144, 1976-1 CB 144.

60. Victims of Terrorism Tax Relief Act of 2001 (P.L. 107-134); I.R.C. §139.

61. I.R.C. §109.

62. I.R.C. §112.

63. I.R.C. §118.

64. I.R.C. §120.

65. I.R.C. §122.

66. I.R.C. §123.

67. I.R.C. §125.

68. See I.R.C. §1001(a).

69. I.R.C. §1.

70. I.R.C. §1222.

71. I.R.C. §1.

72. I.R.C. §1(h)(11). A qualified dividend is a dividend received from a domestic corporation or a qualified foreign corporation.

73. I.R.C. §1(h). The 20 percent rate kicks in for single taxpayers with taxable income over $400,000 and married taxpayers filing jointly with taxable income over $450,000.

74. I.R.C. §1211(b)(1).

75. I.R.C. Sec 32.

76. I.R.C. §32(2)(A)(i).

77. Ministers are also considered to be self-employed.

78. I.R.C. §32(c)(2). Statutory employees receive Form W-2s on which the "Statutory Employee" box is checked. They report their income and expenses on Schedule C (or Schedule C-EZ).

79. I.R.C. §§ 911(a), 922(b)(2)(A). See also Rev. Proc. 2013-35, IRB 167.

80. I.R.C. §163(d)(1).

81. See IRS Publication 550.

82. I.R.C. §1411.

83. I.R.C. §1411(c)(2).

84. I.R.C. §1(g).

85. I.R.C. §469(c).

86. I.R.C. §469(c)(2).

87. I.R.C. §469(d)(1). It would also be considered "investment income" subject to the 3.8 percent net income tax. See I.R.C. §1411(c).

88. I.R.C. §469(h)(1).

89. I.R.C. §1031. See Chapter 33 for a more extended discussion of like-kind exchanges.

90. I.R.C. §1033.

91. I.R.C. §1035.

92. For example, although a taxpayer does not have to include the gain realized from a like-kind exchange or involuntary conversion in gross income, upon the subsequent sale of the replacement property, any realized gain would be included in gross income.

93. I.R.C. §422.

94. I.R.C. §61(a)(1).

95. Treas. Reg. §1.451-1(a).

96. IRS Publication 538.

97. IRS Publication 538.

98. Treas. Reg. §1.451-1(a).

99. I.R.C. §7872.

100. I.R.C. §7872(c)(2), (c)(1)(B) and (c)(1)(C).

101. I.R.C. §1341(a).

102. *Hamlett v. Comm'r*, T.C.M. (RIA) 2004-78 at 7 n.8 I.R.C.§.

103. I.R.C. §453.

104. *Comm. v. Banks and Comm. v. Banaitis*, 125 S. Ct. 826, rev'g, 345 F.3d 373 (2003).

105. I.R.C. §104(a)(2). See *Comm. v. Schleir*, 515 US 323 (1995). This exclusion from gross income is based on the theory that the injured party has already "suffered enough" without having to pay tax on the amounts intended to compensate him for his injuries.

106. I.R.C. §67(a).

107. *Murphy v. Comm.*, 362 F.Supp.2d 206 (2005); see note 72 and note 74, below, for subsequent appellate case history.

108. *Murphy v. Comm.*, 493 F.3d 170 (D.C. Cir. 2007).

CAPITAL GAINS AND LOSSES AND QUALIFIED DIVIDENDS

CHAPTER 4

INTRODUCTION

When the income tax was originally created in 1913, capital gains were not distinguished from any other type of income. Legislators soon realized that treating capital gains in the same fashion as other sources of income was producing some inequities and moved to correct the problem. For this reason, gains from transactions involving capital assets have been afforded preferential treatment under the tax law for most of its history. Beginning with the 1921 tax year, capital gains have been taxed at a separate, and generally significantly lower, tax rate than other sources of "ordinary" income. In fact, with only a few exceptions, in every tax year since 1921, the capital gains tax rate has been lower than the highest marginal ordinary income tax rate.[1]

The reasoning behind the separate and lower tax rate was fairly simple. Capital gains generally represent appreciation that is earned over time; however, the annual appreciation is not taxed. By waiting until the capital asset is sold to tax the gain, the taxpayer reports a large sum of income in one year that may actually have been "earned" over a number of intervening years. The inclusion of the lump sum amount in the year of sale could force the taxpayer into higher marginal tax brackets and ultimately to a higher tax in the year of sale than would have been paid had the gain in the asset been subjected to tax on an annual basis.

In order to determine if a transaction qualifies for the more favorable capital gains tax rate, the key question to be answered is whether the asset – in the hands of the seller – is a "capital" asset. In characterizing whether an asset is a capital asset, the length of time the taxpayer held the asset is immaterial.[2]

Losses on sales of capital assets are also subject to special rules. Non-corporate taxpayers first offset capital gains with capital losses. However, to the extent capital losses exceed capital gains, non-corporate taxpayers may use up to $3,000 of net capital losses to offset other taxable income.[3] Excess capital losses for a particular year may not be carried back to offset capital gains or ordinary income in earlier years, but, rather, are carried forward to offset capital gains or ordinary income in future years. Non-corporate taxpayers may only carry forward excess capital losses from a given year to offset capital gains in future years and may do so for an unlimited period until the excess is used.[4]

Corporate taxpayers must also net capital losses with capital gains.[5] The excess capital loss may generally be carried back three years and carried forward five years.[6] Note that corporate taxpayers, unlike individuals, do not benefit from a special tax rate for capital gains. The net capital gain is treated as additional income and is taxed accordingly.

The characterization of whether an asset is capital or not is not elective. This is the source of a great deal of litigation. Obviously, non-corporate taxpayers with large gains will argue for treatment as a capital asset to receive the more favorable tax rates. On the other hand, taxpayers with large losses will vehemently fight for ordinary tax treatment since capital losses will likely take years to offset with capital gains and, even then, will be offsetting income at the lower capital gain tax rate.

Capital gains represent one part of an investment's total return. Another part of that return includes dividend payments. When the income tax was established, dividends were exempt from taxation until 1953, aside from a brief 4 year window starting in 1936. Since 1953 dividends have been taxed at various rates with ever changing amounts being exempt from income.

Beginning in 1985, the exemption of a portion of dividend income was removed from the law, resulting in the full double taxation of dividends. In 2003 the concept of a qualified dividend emerged from the Bush tax cut legislation. A qualified dividend analogizes the dividend payment with the total return principal. Since a dividend reduces the market value of the underlying security, the payment of the dividend should be treated in the same manner as if the investor held the security and sold it for a profit and, therefore, be taxed at the more preferential capital gain rate.

WHAT IS – AND WHAT IS NOT – A CAPITAL ASSET?

In order for a transaction to be treated as a capital gain (or loss), the underlying asset must meet the definition as a capital asset. Like so many other parts of the U.S. tax law, a capital asset is defined by what it is not.

A capital asset is any property held by a taxpayer, whether or not connected with a trade or business, excluding the following categories of assets:[7]

1. stock in trade of the taxpayer or other property that would properly be classified as inventory at the end of a taxable year, or property held by the taxpayer for sale to customers in the ordinary course of the trade or business.[8]

2. depreciable or real property used in a trade or business.[9] However, capital gain status may still be given to such assets under Code section 1231.

3. a copyright, a literary, musical or artistic composition, or a letter or memorandum or similar property held by the creator of such work or certain subsequent owners.[10] Note that taxpayers may elect to treat the sale or exchange of musical compositions or copyrights in musical works created by the taxpayer's personal efforts as the sale or exchange of a capital asset.[11]

4. accounts or notes receivable acquired in a trade or business in exchange for services provided or from the sale of inventory.[12]

5. a publication of the U.S. Government which is received from the U.S. Government or its agency at a price which is less than what it is offered for sale to the general public.[13]

6. any commodities derivative financial instrument held by a commodities derivatives dealer.[14]

7. any hedging transaction which is identified as such before the close of the day on which it was acquired, originated, or entered into.[15]

8. supplies of a type regularly used or consumed by the taxpayer in the ordinary course of a trade or business of the taxpayer.[16]

It would seem that, given these exclusions, it would be relatively simple from this point to determine whether an asset should be considered a capital asset. However, judicial interpretations have muddied the waters over the years. If there is any question about whether an asset is capital in nature or not, research should be done to determine if the courts have already addressed the issue.

Once it has been determined that the asset qualifies as a capital asset, the asset must be disposed of in a transaction that will be treated as a "sale or exchange" to obtain the favorable capital gains treatment. Although tax law does not specifically define a "sale or exchange," there are solid interpretations that are very consistent with what one would expect.

A "sale" is defined as a transfer of property for money or a promise to pay money.[17] A contract to sell shows the intent of the parties to enter into a transaction but not an actual transfer. When there is doubt as to whether a sale or transfer of property has occurred, factors that the courts use to make that determination include:

1. whether legal title has passed;

2. whether the purchaser has acquired an equity interest in the property;

3. whether the acquisition creates a present obligation to transfer legal title for an agreed upon consideration;

4. whether legal title is vested in the purchaser; and

5. whether the purchaser bears the risk of loss and has the benefits of ownership.[18]

An "exchange" is a transfer of property for other property.[19]

Example: Broad Street, Inc. owns a car that it wishes to swap for a computer system that is currently owned by Bullies, Inc. Assume these assets qualify as capital assets. The exchange of these dissimilar assets would constitute a taxable exchange of capital assets for which each company would need to determine its capital gain or loss.

With an exchange, taxpayers must take into account the "like-kind exchange" rules of Code section 1031. Although this will be covered in more detail in Chapter 30 – Like-Kind Exchanges, exchanged property that is similar in nature may not result in the current recognition of gain or loss. The like-kind exchange rules require deferral of any gain or loss in these situations.

Certain events will create a statutory sale or exchange of a capital asset. The more common ones that may be encountered by taxpayers include:

1. A nonbusiness debt of a noncorporate taxpayer that becomes worthless within the taxable year is treated as a loss from the sale or exchange of a capital asset held for not more than one year (i.e., a short-term capital loss).[20]

2. A security that becomes worthless during the taxable year and which is considered a capital asset in the hands of the taxpayer is treated as a loss from the sale or exchange of a capital asset on the last day of the taxable year.[21] For this purpose, a security is:

    a. a share of stock in a corporation;[22]

    b. a right to subscribe for or to receive a share of stock in a corporation;[23] or

    c. a bond, debenture, note, or certificate, or other evidence of indebtedness issued by a corporation or government, with interest coupons or in registered form.[24]

3. Distributions of property from a corporation to a shareholder if the distribution exceeds the shareholder's adjusted basis in the corporation's stock.[25]

Example: Bruce Rosen owns 500 shares of Bellyup, Inc., a publicly traded company. He originally purchased the stock three years ago for $6,000. During the current tax year, Bellyup, Inc. ceased operations, filed for bankruptcy, and was delisted from the securities exchange markets. Since there is no market for the stock and operations have ceased, Bruce may treat his $6,000 as a loss from the sale or exchange of the stock as of the last day of the taxable year.

Section 1231 Assets

Although one of the exclusions from the definition of a capital asset is depreciable or real property used in a trade or business, Code section 1231 may characterize the gain realized upon the sale or exchange of these assets as a capital gain. A "Section 1231 asset" is depreciable or real property that is used in a trade or business and is held for more than one year.[26]

If, in a single tax year, the gains from Section 1231 assets exceed the losses from Section 1231 assets, each Section 1231 asset sale is treated as either a long-term capital gain or loss.[27] If the losses from the disposition of Section 1231 assets exceed the gains, each Section 1231 asset sale is treated as ordinary income or loss.[28]

Example: During a tax year, Bermuda Shorts, Inc. sells a machine at a $5,000 gain, a truck at a $500 gain, and a car at a $3,000 loss. All of the assets are used in the trade or business and have been held for more than one year. (Ignore depreciation recapture issues, which will be discussed later in this chapter.) Since the Section 1231 gains exceed the Section 1231 losses, each gain and loss is treated as a separate long-term capital gain and loss.

It would appear that the taxpayer could obtain the best of both worlds under the rules for Section 1231. Properly timed, a taxpayer can create an ordinary loss in one year by selling Section 1231 assets at a loss and in the next year achieve long-term capital gain treatment for gain assets. For this reason, the amount treated as long-term capital gains under Section 1231 must be reduced by the amount of Section 1231 losses for the five previous tax years.[29]

Example: In 2014, Loose Ends, LLC sold a car at a $5,000 loss. The loss was properly identified and reported as an ordinary loss in

2014. In 2015, the company sold a computer at a $2,000 gain. Were it not for the loss recapture rules, the $2,000 gain could be treated as a Section 1231 long-term capital gain in 2015. Instead, the $2,000 is reported as ordinary income in 2014. The remaining $3,000 of "unrecaptured" Section 1231 losses will be carried forward for four more years.

AMOUNT OF GAINS AND LOSSES

The amount of gain or loss that is realized when a capital asset is sold or exchanged is the difference between the amount realized (AR) and the taxpayer's adjusted basis (AB) for the property.[30] As a formula, this is AR – AB = Gain.

The amount realized from a sale or exchange is equal to the sum of (a) money and (b) the fair market value of other property received in consideration for the transfer of the property.[31] The amount of debt assumed by the purchaser of the property is also considered as part of the amount realized by the seller.[32]

The taxpayer's adjusted basis in the property depends upon how the taxpayer acquired the property and whether it was subject to adjustments (either up or down) while owned by the taxpayer. Determining the adjusted basis is fully covered in Chapter 20 – Basis.

Example: Richard Hart sells 500 shares of Alleycat Corp. for $10,000. He originally paid $6,500 for the stock. The amount realized from the sale is $10,000 and his adjusted basis is $6,500. Hart recognizes a gain of $3,500: the difference between the $10,000 Hart received and Hart's adjusted basis of $6,500.

HOLDING PERIODS

In an effort to distinguish between sales of capital assets that are held for long-term appreciation and those which are held for short-term speculation, taxpayers must determine their holding period for each capital asset that is sold. Congress decided that the more favorable capital gain treatment should be reserved for those taxpayers who seek long-term appreciation rather than those who may be attempting to benefit from quick turns in the market.

Under current law, the more favorable capital gains tax rate is applied to net long-term capital gains. A gain or loss is treated as long-term if the capital asset is held for more than one year.[33] If the capital asset is not held for more than one year, the gain or loss is treated as short-term.[34]

Example: John Hatch purchased 200 shares of Webster's, Inc. on July 31, 2013. If John sells the shares on or after August 1, 2014, any gain or loss will be treated as a long-term gain or loss.

The dates on which holding periods begin and end are not always clear. As a result, the IRS and the courts have specified a number of common capital assets and identified what begins and ends the holding period for each of these capital assets.

For transactions involving stocks and bonds traded over the counter or on an exchange, the holding period begins and ends on the "trade date": the date that the taxpayer enters into a binding contract to buy or sell the stock.[35] Most brokerage statements show the settlement date as the date of the transaction. The settlement date actually takes places as many as five dates after the "trade date." As a result, the settlement date is the wrong date to use to determine the holding period.

Example: Assume the same facts as above. John's trade date was July 31, 2013, even if the settlement date was August 3, 2013 (the date that happened to appear on John's brokerage statement). The settlement date is irrelevant in determining the start of John's holding period.

If the taxpayer has different lots of the same stocks or bonds that were acquired at different times, the "first-in, first-out" method applies unless the taxpayer specifically identifies the stock or bond that is to be sold. Taxpayers can identify a specific stock or bond if the taxpayer notifies the broker of the intent to sell a particular block of shares at the time the trade order is placed and, within a reasonable amount of time thereafter, the broker confirms the shares that were specifically identified to be sold in a written document.[36]

The holding period for property that is given in exchange for the performance of services (Section 83 property) begins "just after" the property is substantially vested. The holding period for Section 83 property begins at the earliest time the property is no longer subject to a substantial risk of forfeiture or is freely transferable.[37]

Property acquired from a decedent is treated as being held by the beneficiary for the one year long-term holding period, regardless of the length of time the property was actually held.[38] In order for this rule to apply, the basis of the property must have been determined based upon the fair market value of the property on either the date of the decedent's death or the alternate valuation date.

Holding periods may occasionally "tack." Tacked (sometimes referred to as tacked on) holding periods typically occur when a taxpayer acquires a property in a nonrecognition transaction, such as a like-kind exchange.[39]

A holding period will also tack in the case of property acquired by gift.[40] An exception to this rule applies when the property received by gift is sold at a loss. In this case, the donee's (recipient's) basis is the fair market value of the property on the date of the gift and not the transferor's basis. Since the donee's basis is no longer determined by reference to the transferor's basis, the holding period is deemed to begin on the date of the gift.

Example: Hal Stevens gave 1,000 shares of Stickershock.com to his son, Larry. Hal purchased the stock on October 31, 2013 for $10,000 and gave the stock to Larry on January 2, 2014 when the value had decreased to $6,000. On November 5, 2014, Larry sells the stock for $4,000. Since the stock is sold at less than the fair market value on the date of the gift, the holding period does not tack. As a result, Larry realizes a short-term capital loss of $2,000.

TAX IMPLICATIONS

Categories

Capital gains and losses come in a variety of types. The categorization process is so important that practically an entire Code section is dedicated to it.

Each capital transaction is first divided into one of four types:

1. Short-term capital gain – a gain from a sale or exchange of property held for one year or less.[41]

2. Short-term capital loss – a loss from a sale or exchange of property held for one year or less.[42]

3. Long-term capital gain – a gain from a sale or exchange of property held for more than one year.[43]

4. Long-term capital loss – a loss from a sale or exchange of property held for more than one year.[44]

There are actually more than four categories to consider since there are different tax rates associated with long-term capital gains. Each long-term capital gain or loss that falls within different capital gains tax rates are grouped together in "rate gain baskets." See "Netting Capital Gains and Losses" which follows.

Once each transaction is divided into one of these four categories, the categories are combined as follows:

- Net short-term capital gain – the excess of short-term capital gains over short-term capital losses in a given year.[45]

- Net short-term capital loss – the excess of short-term capital losses over short-term capital gains in a given year.[46]

- Net long-term capital gain – the excess of long-term capital gains over long-term capital losses in a given year.[47]

- Net long-term capital loss – the excess of long-term capital losses over long-term capital gains in a given year.[48]

Obviously, for any given year, a taxpayer can only have two of these net amounts – one for short-term and one for long-term. However, certain taxpayers may have more than one type of long-term capital gain (i.e., more than one "rate gain basket") since there are a number of different long-term capital gains tax rates. If a taxpayer has both net short and long-term capital gains, no further netting is required. A "net capital gain" results if the taxpayer has net long-term capital gains in excess of net short-term capital losses for the year.[49]

Capital Gains Tax Rates

An individual's net capital gain is subject to taxation at a rate not to exceed the maximum capital gains rate.[50] This implies that there is one overall maximum capital gains rate. In reality, there are actually five that apply for tax years after 2012. Each maximum rate applies to different types of gains or is dependent upon the taxpayer's overall tax bracket:

1. Taxpayers in the lowest two ordinary income tax brackets (currently 10 and 15 percent) will pay tax on their net capital gain at a maximum rate of 0 percent.[51]

2. Taxpayers that have gains that are from the sale of Section 1250 assets pay a maximum rate of 25 percent (the "25 percent basket") on the unrecaptured depreciation (Section 1250 recapture is discussed later in this chapter).[52]

3. A maximum rate of 28 percent (the "28 percent basket") applies to sales of collectibles and the unexcluded gain from the sale of small business (Section 1202) stock. A collectible is any work of art, rug, antique, metal, gem, stamp, coin, alcoholic beverage, or any other property designated by the IRS.[53]

4. Taxpayers in all other tax brackets aside from the 39.6 percent ordinary income tax bracket are subject to a capital gains tax rate of 15 percent (the "15 percent basket").[54]

5. After 2012, a capital gains tax rate of 20 percent applies to adjusted net capital gains if the gain would otherwise be subject to the 39.6 percent ordinary income tax bracket.[55]

Example: Christopher and Jennifer White's taxable income for 2014 is $150,000. Of this amount, $50,000 represents net capital gain from stock sold during the year. They will compute their tax by using the ordinary tax rate brackets on the $100,000 of ordinary income and will add $7,500 (15 percent of $50,000) to this amount to determine their tax for the year.

For purposes of the maximum capital gains rate, the net capital gain is reduced by any amount the taxpayer elects to be treated as investment income for purposes of computing deductible investment interest expense.[56]

The capital gains rates apply for both regular tax and alternative minimum tax (AMT) liabilities.[57] However, the net capital gain for AMT purposes must be recomputed using any adjustments or preferences that are attributable to the gain. Beginning in 2013, capital gains may also be subject to the net investment income tax if a taxpayer's adjusted gross income exceeds certain levels, this will be discussed in more detail in Chapter 11.

Netting Capital Gains and Losses

As mentioned above, long-term capital gains are subject to different maximum tax rates based upon the type of gain. Each type of gain must be grouped by tax rate into "rate gain baskets."

Based on the maximum capital gains rates described above, three rate gain baskets must be considered:

- 28 percent gain (collectibles and Section 1202 stock);

- 25 percent gain (unrecaptured Section 1250 gain); or

- 15 percent gain (all other long-term capital gains).

Note that the 0 percent tax rate is simply an application of a lower tax rate to the 15 percent rate gain basket. Likewise, the 20 percent tax rate applies only to those taxpayers that would otherwise be subject to the 39.6 percent tax bracket.

If one rate gain basket has a net loss, the loss is used to offset the net gain in the rate gain basket with the highest rate, then the next highest rate gain basket, etc. Therefore, if there is a loss in the 15 percent rate gain basket, the net loss is used to offset any gains in the 28 percent basket, then the 25 percent basket.

Short-term capital losses, including short-term capital loss carryovers, are first applied to reduce short-term capital gains. This results in a net short-term capital gain or loss for the year which can then be applied against the rate gain baskets starting with the one with the highest rate.

Example: Ryan Alcott had the following capital gains and losses during 2014:

- $5,000 short-term capital loss from the sale of stock;

- $6,000 long-term capital loss from the sale of stock;

- $10,000 unrecaptured Section 1250 gain from the sale of real estate; and

- $4,000 long-term capital gain from the sale of collectibles.

Since Ryan has one amount in each rate gain basket, the netting process is as follows:

- The $6,000 long-term capital loss offsets the $4,000 gain on the sale of collectibles (28 percent basket) and $2,000 of the unrecaptured Section 1250 gain (25 percent basket).

- The $5,000 short-term capital loss offsets $5,000 of the highest rate gain basket, in this case, the unrecaptured Section 1250 gain.

- The netting process leaves a $3,000 unrecaptured Section 1250 gain subject to a maximum tax rate of 25 percent.

Capital Losses

Taxpayers who have capital losses that exceed their capital gains in a given year must follow a special set of rules. For non-corporate taxpayers, losses from the sale of capital assets are allowed to the extent of capital gains plus up to $3,000 ($1,500 for married taxpayers filing separately) of excess losses.[58]

If the net capital loss for the year exceeds $3,000, an individual or other non-corporate taxpayer may carry the excess amount forward to future years until it is completely utilized.[59] Any capital loss that is carried forward to a future year will retain its original short or long-term character in that future year. Thus, a short-term capital loss carryforward will offset future short-term capital gains and a long-term capital loss carryforward will offset future long-term capital gains.

When both a net short-term capital loss and net long-term capital loss exist, the allowable $3,000 net capital loss is treated as an offset to the short-term capital loss first.[60]

Example: During the tax year, Jimmy Johnson incurred a short-term capital loss of $2,000 and a long-term capital loss of $15,000. His total net capital loss for the year is $17,000. Of this amount, only $3,000 is available to offset other income. Since the $3,000 first offsets the short-term capital loss, that loss is fully utilized during the year. He will utilize $1,000 of his current year long-term capital loss and carry forward a $14,000 long-term capital loss to the next taxable year.

The $3,000 limit has been the source of a great deal of controversy in recent history since there is currently no mechanism to adjust this amount for inflation. When the stock market took a dramatic downturn during the "Great Recession" in 2008 and early-2009, the $3,000 net capital loss limit created a large number of taxpayers with sizable capital loss carryforwards. Many taxpayers have been able to begin to utilize those losses by sheltering gains recognized in the recovery from 2009 and into early-2014.

Corporate taxpayers may only utilize capital losses to offset capital gains.[61] If capital losses exceed capital gains in a given year, the excess may be carried back three years and then forward up to five years.[62] The amount which may be carried back to a prior year is limited to an amount that does not create or increase a net operating loss in the carryback year.[63]

Recapture

Section 1245 Gains

A taxpayer who realizes a capital gain on the disposition of depreciable or amortizable (Section 1231) property used in a trade or business or held for investment must "recapture" all or part of the gain as ordinary income.[64] The logic behind depreciation recapture is reasonable. Taxpayers benefit from the deduction for depreciation as an offset to their ordinary income. The corresponding gain that may be created when the asset is sold should not be taxed at the favorable capital gains rate.

The amount that must be recaptured as ordinary income is the lesser of:

1. the total depreciation or amortization deductions allowed or allowable with respect to the property; or

2. the total gain realized.

If the total gain exceeds the amount that must be recaptured as ordinary income, the excess is treated as Section 1231 gain. If the gain is less than the total accumulated depreciation or amortization, the entire gain is recaptured as ordinary income.

The most common type of "Section 1245 property" is tangible or intangible personal property used in a trade or business. Buildings and their structural components (with limited exceptions) are not considered Section 1245 property.[65]

Example 1: Jones, Inc. sells a piece of machinery for $12,000. Jones originally purchased the equipment four years ago for $25,000. Over the four years, the company claimed depreciation deductions totaling $18,000, making the adjusted basis of the property $7,000 at the time of the sale. The company realizes a gain of $5,000 on the sale ($12,000 - $7,000). Since the gain ($5,000) is less than the total depreciation deductions claimed ($18,000), the entire gain is recaptured as ordinary income.

Example 2: Multimedia, Inc. finds a deal on a conference room table and pays $2,000 for it. Over the next two years, the company claims $1,000 of depreciation deductions, lowering the adjusted basis of the table to $1,000. The company then sells the table for $3,500. The gain on the sale of the table is $2,500 ($3,500 - $1,000). Since the gain ($2,500) exceeds the total depreciation deductions claimed ($1,000), the amount to be recaptured is limited to $1,000 and the remaining $1,500 gain is treated as long-term capital gain.

Taxpayers must watch the "allowed or allowable" clause in the tax law. This has been used by the IRS in the past to recapture income on sales of property for which no depreciation was claimed. For instance, if a taxpayer begins to depreciate a tangible property item used in the business but then fails to claim the depreciation deduction over the next few years, the IRS can assert that the amount to be recaptured as ordinary income is based upon the depreciation that was allowable even though not properly claimed or deducted.

Section 1250 Gains

Section 1250 property is generally real property (buildings and structural components) subject to

depreciation.[66] Gains on the disposition of Section 1250 property are taxed as ordinary income to the extent of post-1969 allowances for depreciation that are in excess of what would have been available using the straight-line method for depreciation.

Gain recapture on Section 1250 property is becoming increasingly rare. Ever since the creation of the Modified Accelerated Cost Recovery System (MACRS) in 1987, almost all real property has been depreciated using the straight-line method.

Residential real property depreciated under the Accelerated Cost Recovery System (ACRS) is subject to recapture to the extent of accelerated depreciation claimed in excess of straight-line depreciation.

ACRS nonresidential real property is treated as Section 1245 property if it is not being depreciated using the straight-line method. Therefore, all depreciation on such a property would be subject to recapture.

Recapture on Section 1250 property is required only if a disposition of the property occurs. The following do not represent dispositions that would trigger recapture:

1. gifts[67]

2. transfers at death[68]

3. certain tax-free exchanges[69]

4. like-kind exchanges and involuntary conversions[70]

5. SEC and FCC transactions[71]

6. property distributed by a partnership to its partners[72]

7. transfers to a tax-exempt organization[73]

8. foreclosures[74]

As mentioned earlier, to the extent depreciation deductions are not recaptured under these rules, the unrecaptured gain from the sale of Section 1250 property is subject to a maximum capital gains tax rate of 25 percent.[75]

Example: Realty Plus, L.P. sells a shopping center for $3,000,000. The original purchase price of the property was $1,250,000 and over the years $400,000 of MACRS depreciation deductions have been claimed. The property's adjusted basis is $850,000 ($1,250,000 - $400,000). Of the total gain of $2,150,000 ($3,000,000 - $850,000), $400,000 is unrecaptured Section 1250 gain and will be taxed at a maximum rate of 25 percent. The remaining gain of $1,750,000 will be taxed as a long-term capital gain.

QUALIFIED DIVIDENDS

Dividends are generally treated as ordinary income to a taxpayer. Beginning in 2003, dividends that meet three requirements are treated as "qualified dividends" and are taxed at the more favorable capital gain tax rate.[76] Those requirements are:

1. The dividends are from a domestic corporation or a qualified foreign corporation.

2. the taxpayer held the stock on which the dividend was paid for more than 60 days during the 121 day period that begins 60 days before the ex-dividend date.[77] The ex-dividend date is generally the first day following the declaration of a dividend that a buyer of the stock is not entitled to a dividend payment. Note that the rules are different for preferred stock, which requires a taxpayer hold the stock for 90 days during the 181 day period that begins 90 days before the ex-dividend date.[78]

3. The dividends are not one of the several "special" types of dividends as stated under Code Section 1(h)(11), including, but not limited to, amounts:

    a. Paid on deposits with mutual savings banks, cooperative banks, credit unions, savings and loan associations, building and loan associations and similar financial institutions;

    b. Paid by a corporation on employer securities that are held on the date of record by an employer stock ownership plan (ESOP) maintained by that corporation;

    c. To the extend the taxpayer is obligated (under a short sale or otherwise) to make related payments for positions in substantially similar or related property; or

    d. Paid on restricted stock, which should be treated as wage income unless the individual has made an election under Code Section 83(b).

FREQUENTLY ASKED QUESTIONS

Question – Can losses from capital assets be used to offset Section 1231 gains?

Answer – Yes. Once the Section 1231 gains are identified as such (i.e., the 1231 gains exceed the 1231 losses for the year and all unrecaptured Section 1231 losses are used to recategorize the gain as ordinary income), the gains are treated as long-term capital gains and may be offset by capital losses from the sale or exchange of capital assets defined under Section 1221.

Question – During the year, Buckshot, Inc., a corporation, sold a truck used in the business (Section 1245 property) for $10,000. Buckshot originally paid $50,000 for the property but fully depreciated it over the years. Knowing that they had this gain, the company decided to sell some investments at a loss of $10,000 to offset the gain. Can the truck gain offset the stock loss?

Answer – Unfortunately, this scenario occurs far too often. The gain on the sale of the truck will be treated as ordinary income due to the depreciation recapture rules under Section 1245. The loss on the sale of the investments is a capital loss that can only offset capital gains. The $10,000 capital loss may be carried back three years and forward up to five years – but may still only be used to offset capital gains occurring in those years.

Question – What are the reporting requirements for capital gains and losses?

Answer – Taxpayers report their gains and losses from the sale or exchange of capital assets on Schedule D. Section 1231 property and properties subject to potential Section 1245 or 1250 recapture are reported on Form 4797.

CHAPTER ENDNOTES

1. The only exception occurred between 1988 and 1990 when the capital gains tax rate and the highest marginal ordinary income tax rate were both 28 percent.
2. Treas. Reg. §1.1221-1(a).
3. I.R.C. §1211(b).
4. I.R.C. §1212(b)(1).
5. I.R.C. §1211(a).
6. I.R.C. §1212(a)(1).
7. I.R.C. §1221(a).
8. I.R.C. §1221(a)(1).
9. I.R.C. §1221(a)(2).
10. I.R.C. §1221(a)(3).
11. Section 1221(b)(3).
12. I.R.C. §1221(b)(3).
13. I.R.C. §1221(a)(5).
14. I.R.C. §1221(a)(6).
15. I.R.C. §1221(a)(7).
16. I.R.C. §1221(a)(8).
17. *Rogers v. Comm'r.*, 103 F.2d 790 (9th Cir. 1939).
18. *Grodt & McKay Realty, Inc. v. Comm'r.*, 77 TC 1221 (1981).
19. *Helvering v. William Flaccus Oak Leather Co.*, 313 US 247 (1941).
20. I.R.C. §166(d).
21. I.R.C. §165(g)(1).
22. I.R.C. §165(g)(2)(A).
23. I.R.C. §165(g)(2)(B).
24. I.R.C. §165(g)(2)(C).
25. I.R.C. §301(c)(3)(A).
26. I.R.C. §1231(b)(1).
27. I.R.C. §1231(a)(1).
28. I.R.C. §1231(a)(2).
29. I.R.C. §1231(c).
30. I.R.C. §1001(a).
31. I.R.C. §1001(b).
32. Treas. Reg. §1.1001-2.
33. I.R.C. §§1222(3)-(4).
34. I.R.C. §§1222(1)-(2).
35. Rev. Rul. 66-97, 1966-1 CB 190.
36. Treas. Reg. §1.1012-1(c).
37. I.R.C. §83(f).
38. I.R.C. §1223(11).
39. I.R.C. §§1223(1)-(2).
40. Treas. Reg. §1.1223-1(b).
41. I.R.C. §1222(1).
42. I.R.C. §1222(2).
43. I.R.C. §1222(3).
44. I.R.C. §1222(4).
45. I.R.C. §1222(5).
46. I.R.C. §1222(6).
47. I.R.C. §1222(7).
48. I.R.C. §1222(8).
49. I.R.C. §1222(11).
50. I.R.C. §1(h)(1).
51. I.R.C. §1(h)(1)(B).
52. I.R.C. §1(h)(1)(D).
53. I.R.C. §1(h)(5)(A).
54. I.R.C. §1(h)(1)(C).
55. I.R.C. §1(h)(1)(D).
56. I.R.C. §1(h)(2).
57. I.R.C. §55(b)(3).
58. I.R.C. §1211(b).
59. I.R.C. §1212(b)(1).
60. I.R.C. §1212(b)(2)(A).
61. I.R.C. §1211(a).
62. I.R.C. §1212(a)(1).
63. I.R.C. §1212(a)(1)(A)(ii).
64. I.R.C. §1245(a)(1).
65. I.R.C. §1245(a)(3).
66. I.R.C. §1250(c).
67. I.R.C. §1250(d)(1).
68. I.R.C. §1250(d)(2).
69. I.R.C. §1250(d)(3).
70. I.R.C. §1250(d)(4).
71. I.R.C. §1250(d)(5).
72. I.R.C. §1250(d)(6).
73. I.R.C. §1250(d)(7).
74. I.R.C. §1250(d)(8).
75. I.R.C. §1(h)(1)(D).
76. I.R.C. §1(h)(11).
77. I.R.C. §1(h)(11)(B)(iii)(I).
78. I.R.C. §1(h)(11)(B)(iii)(I).

BUSINESS AND NONBUSINESS LOSSES

CHAPTER 5

INTRODUCTION

A loss is a reduction in the value of property that is owned by a taxpayer. The Code provides that certain types of losses are deductible against taxable income. Like all deductions, loss deductions can only be taken if a Code section specifically allows for it.[1] Deductions that arise from losses can be related to a taxpayer's business or trade, or they can be personal losses that affect the value of a taxpayer's property. Business losses and personal losses are treated differently by the Code, and some losses that seem quite similar may result in very different deductions depending on the specific circumstances of the loss.

WHAT KINDS OF BUSINESS LOSSES CAN BE DEDUCTED?

Business losses can occur in a variety of circumstances. The sale of property at a price that does not recover the owner's investment can result in a loss. Businesses can sustain losses from their operations or find that debt that is owed to them has become uncollectable. And like individuals, businesses can suffer unexpected casualty losses from theft and natural disasters. While unfortunate, all of these types of losses can be taken as deductions that reduce the amount of tax owed by the taxpayer.

Loss from a Sale of Property

A loss can occur when a taxpayer sells or exchanges property for an amount less than his or her basis in such property. Basis (or cost) is an accounting concept that represents a taxpayer's after-tax investment in the acquired property.[2] In a business context, basis is often adjusted over time for various factors (such as depreciation) that are beyond the scope of this chapter.

Basis is important because it is half of the equation that determines whether a property owner realizes a gain or loss from a sale, which may then result in a corresponding item of income or deduction. If a property sells for less than its basis, the seller may be entitled to a deduction for the loss (the difference between the basis and the sale price) under Code section 165.

Example: Several years ago, Ira Investor purchased raw land as an investment for $100,000. After the fair market value of the land decreases to $80,000, Ira sells the land for that amount to Debby Developer. Because Ira recovers only $80,000 of his initial $100,000 original cost, he realizes a $20,000 loss on that investment[3] that is potentially deductible pursuant to section 165.

NET OPERATING LOSS

The net operating loss deduction (NOL) is one of the most favorable deductions available to a taxpayer engaged in a trade or business. In a given tax year, an NOL occurs when business deductions exceed business income. Under Code section 172, the deduction from this type of loss may be taken as a deduction for a prior tax year (carried back) or a subsequent tax year (carried forward). The NOL is only available for net business losses—losses attributable to personal or investment deductions can never be part of an NOL.

The NOL deduction essentially "permit[s] a taxpayer to set off its lean years against its lush years, and to strike something like an average taxable income computed over a period longer than one year."[4] Stated differently, carrying an NOL forward or back provides the taxpayer with an opportunity to take advantage of what was otherwise—in the year in which it was generated—a useless deduction.

In order to have an NOL, a taxpayer with business income and deductions must have negative taxable income. Once the negative taxable income is calculated, all net nonbusiness capital loss and net nonbusiness ordinary loss (the extent to which nonbusiness deductions exceed nonbusiness income) are subtracted from that amount. If taxable income is still negative after making those adjustments, the amount of negative taxable income is the NOL.

Using NOL to Reduce Tax in Other Years

If a taxpayer has an unused portion of an NOL deduction, he or she may apply that unused portion to other tax years. The default rule for applying the NOL is first to carry it back to the second year preceding the NOL year and then to the tax year immediately preceding the NOL year. Thereafter, any remaining NOL is carried forward to subsequent years following the NOL year until it is used up.[5]

Because the NOL is comprised exclusively of business expenses, it is considered an above-the-line deduction.[6] An above-the-line deduction is subtracted from gross income before calculating adjusted gross income, and is generally more favorable to the taxpayer than a below-the-line deduction. (See Chapter 6 for a more detailed discussion of the differences between the two types of deductions.)

Example: In 2014, Barry, a self-employed engineer reporting income and deductions on Schedule C had gross fees of $100,000 and business expenses of $150,000. Other than his engineering fees, Barry had no other income. The entire $150,000 of business expenses are above-the-line deductions,[7] leaving Barry with no taxable income in 2014 and an unused $50,000 NOL. This unused amount of the deduction can be carried forward or back to other tax years and used as an above-the-line deduction against business income in those years.

A decision to carry an NOL back to prior years can be complex and often has more significant consequences than simply reducing the taxpayer's income for that year. Many types of credits and deductions are subject to income-based limitations and reductions. Carrying back unused NOL to reduce income in past years' returns can have significant impacts on those limitations.

For example, up to 85 percent of the amount of a taxpayer's social security payments is potentially taxable depending on the taxpayer's total adjusted gross income. If a carried-back NOL deduction reduces that income on an amended return, the amount of taxable social security payments would also be reduced.

As mentioned above, the default rule for deducting an NOL is to carry it back two years, then one. Thereafter, any remaining unused NOL is carried forward in successive years until it is used up. However, Code section 172(b)(3) allows the taxpayer to waive the carry back period and simply carried the NOL forward for up to twenty years. Figure 5.1 sets forth the pros and the cons for electing or not electing to waive the NOL carry-back.

BAD BUSINESS DEBTS

In the normal course of operating a business, it is not uncommon for a taxpayer to loan out funds or extend credit to a third party. If such a debt becomes wholly or partially worthless, the taxpayer may be entitled to

Figure 5.1

Reasons to Carry Back NOL	Reasons to Not Carry Back NOL
• Immediate refund (the amended returns can be filed along with the current year's return) • Large tax liability in prior two years • Expectation of lower income and/or tax rates in future years	• Lack of tax liability in prior tax years • State does not allow NOL carry-back to reduce state income tax • Expectation of higher future income and/or tax rates • Potential audit issues in prior two years

a business bad debt deduction.[8] Moreover, because a business bad debt deduction is treated as an ordinary business deduction[9] rather than a capital loss, it is an above-the-line deduction with no limitation of its deductibility.

In order for a bad debt to qualify as a business loss, it must meet three conditions:

First, it must be related to the taxpayer's business. This can happen in one of two ways: (1) the debt was made or acquired in the course of the business, or (2) the loss from the debt becoming worthless was incurred in the course of the taxpayer's business.[10]

Example: In 2010, Mary Mover, a sole proprietor, loaned a vendor $10,000 to pay for the delivery of a truck she had purchased as an addition to her moving business fleet. In 2012, Mary sold the moving business to Frederick Express but retained the debt owed by the vendor. In 2013, after Mary was no longer engaged in the moving business, the debt became worthless. Even though Mary was not then engaged in the moving business, Mary would be entitled to a full $10,000 ordinary business bad deduction because it was incurred by her at a time when she was so engaged.[11]

Second, the money that was to be received had the debt been paid must be "after-tax dollars."[12] In the context of bad business debts, this requirement is conceptually identical to cost basis. The deduction may only be taken for the value of the after-tax assets that were actually transferred to the borrower when the loan was made. For instance, the portion of uncollectable accounts receivable that are attributable to "lost profit" would not qualify for the business bad debt deduction.[13]

Example: Connie Contractor (a cash method taxpayer) installed windows on a restaurant owned by Barry Businessman. The total amount billed to Barry was $15,000. Of that amount, Connie's profit would have been $2,500. After the installation, Barry closes the restaurant and files for bankruptcy and the entire $15,000 bill is discharged. Because $2,500 of the loan represented pre-tax lost profit (i.e. Connie has no basis in that amount), the business bad debt deduction for Barry's account is only $12,500.

Third, in order to qualify for the bad business debt deduction, the debt must be worthless or partially worthless. Unfortunately, the Code does not define "worthless." Although the regulations use the term "evidence of worthlessness," the only specific example of worthlessness provided is bankruptcy.[14] More generally, the regulations state that a determination of worthlessness is based on circumstances indicating that a debt is worthless and uncollectable. Pursuing a legal collection action is not required as a prerequisite for the deduction if such action would be unlikely to satisfy the debt.[15] Examples of "evidence of worthlessness" include:

- The debtor going out of business;

- The debtor cannot be located;

- Then debtor dies and leaves an insolvent estate;

- The debtor goes into receivership; and

- The taxpayer determines that a monetary judgment is non-collectable.

Loans to a Taxpayer's Own Corporation

In some instances, a taxpayer may loan money to a corporation in which he is both a shareholder and an employee. In that case, the determination of whether the debt qualifies as a business debt depends on whether the dominant motivation for the loan was to protect the taxpayer's investment as a shareholder, or to protect his job as an employee.[16] If the purpose was to protect his investment, then he is participating as a shareholder, and the debt is not a business debt. If he is trying to protect his job, it is a business debt. In determining the taxpayer's dominant motivation, three factors are considered:

1. The size of the taxpayer's investment the corporation;

2. The size of the taxpayer's salary as an employee; and

3. The other sources of income available to the taxpayer at the time of the loan.

A large investment and ample other sources of income would likely indicate that the taxpayer's dominant motivation for the loan was protection of an investment rather than preservation of a job. As discussed in more detail below, a bad debt that does not qualify as a business bad debt may be deductible as a "nonbusiness bad debt." However, a nonbusiness bad debt is deducted as a short-term capital loss, which is much less favorable to the taxpayer.

Example: Barry Businessman invested $1,000,000 in a corporation that owns a hotel. Many key employees of the hotel earn more than $100,000. On the other hand, although included in the payroll, Barry rarely takes a paycheck. Additionally, Barry has always maintained ample personal financial resources. In 2010, Barry loaned the hotel $100,000. In 2013, due to adverse economic circumstances, the corporation filed for Chapter 7 bankruptcy in which all of its debts—including Barry's loan—were discharged. Based on the three factors listed above, it is clear that Barry's dominant motivation in making the loan was to protect his investment in the corporation. His investment in the corporation was significant when compared to his wages, and at the time of the loan Barry had ample financial resources. Thus, Barry's dominant motivation was to protect his investment as a shareholder and the worthless bad debt would not qualify for the business bad debt deduction.

Guarantors

In a direct loan, the taxpayer transfers available assets to the debtor, and the debtor is supposed to repay the taxpayer. Under certain circumstances, rather than loaning money directly, the taxpayer will be the guarantor of a debt. This means that the taxpayer guarantees that that a loan made by a third party to the debtor will be repaid. If the debtor is unable to pay, the taxpayer, as guarantor of the loan, can be legally compelled to pay the debt. If a guarantor is forced to pay the loan (and is not reimbursed by the original debtor), he or she may be entitled to a business bad debt deduction.

The rules governing whether a worthless debt is a business bad debt are similar to rules that govern loans made to a taxpayer's own corporation. If the guaranty arose out of the guarantor's *business* interest, the underlying debt is considered a business debt. On the other hand, if the guarantor's dominant motivation was to protect his *investment* in the debtor entity, or was

a transaction entered into for profit (independent of his trade or business), the underlying debt would not be a business debt.[17]

In addition to the dominant motivation test, there are three other requirements for the allowance of a guarantor business bad debt deduction:

- The guarantor must be legally obligated to make the payment (although actual legal action against the guarantor is not required);

- The guarantor must have entered into the guaranty agreement before the obligation became worthless; and

- The guarantor must have received reasonable consideration for entering into the agreement.[18]

"Reasonable consideration" is defined broadly, and need not be explicit or direct compensation. If the guarantor entered into the agreement in circumstances that are customary for the industry or the guarantor's position within the company, this is considered to be "reasonable consideration."

Example 1: Amy is a shareholder in a corporation that provides a telephone answering service to professionals. Amy is also the CEO of the corporation, and depends on her salary as her primary source of income. In 2010, the corporation borrows $100,000 from a bank to purchase equipment. The bank insists that Amy personally guaranty the loan. In 2014, the corporation ceases to operate and the bank compels Amy to repay the balance of the loan. Here, Amy would be entitled to a business bad debt deduction because:

- Amy's dominant motivation for the guaranty was to protect her job.

- Amy signed a legally enforceable guaranty agreement.

- Amy executed the guaranty agreement prior to the debt becoming worthless.

- Amy's consideration was the preservation of the corporation so as to maintain her salary as CEO.

Example 2: Assume the same facts as the example above, except Amy is a major shareholder in the corporation with no involvement in its operations. Since Amy's dominant motivation was to preserve her investment in the corporation, she would not be entitled to a business bad deduction with regard to the repayment of the loan.

Finally, guarantors may only take a deduction for money that they actually paid toward the guaranteed debt. If the lender agrees to let the guarantor make payments for a period that covers more than one tax year, the deduction for the bad business debt is limited in each of those years to the amount of actually paid toward the guaranteed debt.

CASUALTY LOSSES

Subject to certain limitations discussed below, a casualty loss of property used in a trade or business (that is not compensated by insurance) can be taken as an ordinary deduction.[19] A "casualty loss" is damage or destruction of property from a sudden, unexpected, or unusual event, including natural disasters, theft, and vandalism.

The amount of the loss is the difference in the fair market value of the property before and after the casualty event.[20] To prevent taxpayers from enjoying a "tax windfall" from a casualty loss, Treas. Reg. §1.165-7(b)(1) limits the loss to the lesser of:

• the decrease in value of the damaged property (the difference between the FMV of the property before and after the casualty); or

• the adjusted basis of the property before the casualty.

Additionally, if insurance coverage is available, no casualty loss is allowed for any damage that was reimbursed by insurance. Moreover, the deduction is not allowed if insurance coverage is available but the taxpayer fails to file a timely claim.[21] Finally, in the event the damaged property is "totaled," a reduction for salvage value is also required.

Example: Larry Laundry, a sole proprietor, owns and operates a dry cleaning business. As the result of a fire, a cleaning press with a fair market value of $20,000 and an adjusted basis of $10,000 was damaged. The cleaning press was unusable after the fire, but has a salvage value of $1,000. Larry's insurance covered $6,000 of his loss. Despite sustaining an economic casualty loss of $14,000, Larry's deduction would be limited to his adjusted basis of $10,000, and further reduced by his insurance payout and the salvage value of the press.

Decrease in FMV	$20,000
Adjusted basis	$10,000
Tentative deductible casualty loss (lesser of the two)	$10,000
Less insurance reimbursement	–$6,000
Less salvage value	–$1,000
Resulting casualty deduction	**$3,000**

WHAT KINDS OF PERSONAL LOSSES CAN BE DEDUCTED?

Several of the business loss deductions—bad debt and casualty losses—have personal loss equivalents that may also result in a deduction for the taxpayer. In addition, the Code includes deductions for several types of personal losses that are unavailable for businesses, such as gambling and hobby losses. Finally, the type of loss that individual tax payers are most likely to experience—loss on investments—is covered in detail in Chapter 4.

Nonbusiness Bad Debt Deduction

There are two significant differences between the deductibility of nonbusiness bad debts and business bad debts: First, a nonbusiness bad debt must be totally worthless for it to be deductible.[22] Second, the deduction is characterized as a short-term capital loss rather than an ordinary deduction.[23] As discussed in Chapter 6, capital losses are deductible only to the extent of capital gains, plus $3,000.[24] Examples of nonbusiness bad debt include:

• Any debt that does not qualify as a business bad debt because the taxpayer's dominant motivation for making the loan was to protect an investment rather than related to a trade or business.

- A loan to a relative or friend with reasonable anticipation that loan would be repaid.

- A lost deposit, such as with a building contractor who later becomes insolvent.

- Funds deposited in a failed bank that does not have deposit insurance.

Example: In 2012, Larry Loser loans his son $10,000 for the purchase of a car, which is documented by a promissory note signed by his son. In 2014, Larry Jr. files for bankruptcy and discharges the debt, which has a balance of $8,000. Larry has a $1,000 capital gain from the sale of a stock in 2014. Here, Larry's nonbusiness bad debt deduction is limited to $4,000—the extent of his capital gain for 2014, plus $3,000.

Personal Casualty Losses

In addition to business casualty losses, Code section 165(c)(3) also allows a deduction for a personal casualty loss. Although the method in determining the amount of the casualty loss is generally the same as for business casualty losses, there are a few key differences.

First, each personal casualty loss is subject to a $100 floor. This means that right off the top, a personal casualty loss must be reduced by $100.[25] Second, personal casualty losses are only deductible to the extent that they exceed 10 percent of adjusted gross income.[26] Effectively, this means that the casualty loss is reduced by 10 percent of a taxpayer's AGI. Finally, casualty losses are limited to the adjusted basis of the property, though typically bases for personal property are not subject to scheduled depreciation as they are for business property.

Example: Harry Homeowner purchased a house in 2010 for $200,000. In 2014, when the FMV value of Harry's house was $250,000, a flood caused a significant amount of damage to the house and reduced its FMV to $125,000. Harry filed a timely insurance claim and received $50,000, the maximum amount of his coverage. For 2014, Harry's adjusted gross income is $200,000.

Decrease in FMV	$125,000
Adjusted basis (original cost)	$200,000
Tentative personal casualty loss (lesser of the two)	$125,000
Less Insurance Reimbursement	−$50,000
Less $100 floor	−$100
Less 10% of AGI	−$20,000
Personal casualty loss deduction	**$54,900**

Finally, the personal casualty loss deduction is a regular itemized deduction not subject to the 2 percent of adjusted gross income floor.[27] There are additional rules that apply when a taxpayer has "insurance gain" (which can occur when the insurance reimbursement exceeds the value of the property), but they are complex and beyond the scope of this chapter.

PONZI SCHEME LOSSES

A *Ponzi scheme* is a fraudulent investment technique employed to recruit investors with promises of above-market-rate returns. The scheme is fraudulent because instead of actually investing an investor's funds, the perpetrator fulfills the promise of high returns by using money it receives from other investors. As long as the flow of funds from new investors continues, the scheme can run indefinitely. Ponzi scheme losses blur the line between investment losses and casualty losses from theft.

The most recent prominent Ponzi scheme was perpetrated by Bernie Madoff. In Rev. Rul. 2009-9,[28] the IRS provided guidance with respect to the deductibility of losses suffered by those who invested with Madoff, as well as in other Ponzi schemes:

- Ponzi scheme losses are theft losses because the perpetrator intended to deprive the investors of money through criminal acts. Thus, the character of the loss is ordinary, not capital.

- In opening up an investment account with a Ponzi perpetrator, investors enter into a transaction for profit. Therefore, none of the section 165(h) deduction limitations apply.[29]

- Although Ponzi scheme losses are itemized deductions, they are not miscellaneous itemized deductions subject to the 2 percent of adjusted gross income floor.[30] The loss would is deductible in the year the theft was discovered.

- The amount of the deduction is the sum of all investments plus any "earnings" reported by the taxpayer as gross income over the period of the scheme, less any distributions received.[31]

- If a business suffered Ponzi scheme losses and is computing an NOL, the Ponzi loss deduction is included in the computation.[32]

- If then investor has a claim for reimbursement that has a reasonable prospect of recovery, the amount deduction must be reduced by the actual or anticipated recovery. If the amount recovered is more than anticipated, the additional recovery is included as income for the year in which it is received.

Example: In 2007, Iris Investor opened an account with Charles & Bernie Investment Advisors (C&B) with an initial deposit of $1000. Unbeknownst to her, C&B was running a Ponzi scheme. Iris maintained her account with C&B through 2013 without incident. During that time she continued to invest more money with C&B, reported income from her investment, and occasionally received distributions from the account. At the beginning of 2014, C&B's Ponzi scheme was revealed, resulting in criminal charges. Iris estimates that she will receive $200 in court-ordered restitution from C&B. Iris receives no restitution in 2014, but receives $250 in restitution in 2015.

	Iris' C&B investments	False C&B earnings included in Iris' gross income	Distributions to Iris
2007	$1000	$0	None
2008	None	$100	None
2009	$200	$100	None
2010	None	$100	None
2011	None	$100	None
2012	None	$100	None
2013	None	$100	$300
2014	None	None	None
Total	**$1,200**	**$600**	**$300**

Iris' 2014 deductible loss is computed as follows:

Total investment	$1,200
False earnings reported as income	$ 600
Subtotal	*$1,800*
Less distributions	−$300
Less anticipated restitution	−$200
Total deductible loss	**$1,300**

Finally, because the restitution that Iris received in 2015 was $50 more than she had estimated in her 2014 loss deduction, Iris must report the $50 as income in 2015.

GAMBLING LOSSES

Although for the most part gambling is viewed as a recreational (and therefore nonbusiness) activity, there are a significant number of professional gamblers. Unlike a casual gambler, a professional gambler is recognized as being engaged in a trade or business.[33] Whether casual or professional, however, section 165(d) limits the deductibility of wagering losses to the amount of wagering gains. This means that *net* wagering losses are not deductible from any other income. In spite of this uniform rule, however, professional gamblers enjoy much more favorable treatment of their losses than casual gamblers in many respects.

Casual Gamblers

A casual gambler is not considered to be engaged in wagering as a trade or business. Therefore, a casual gambler's non-wagering expenses (such as travel to casinos, books, seminars, etc.) are nondeductible personal expenses.[34] Depending on the game and the amount of winnings, gambling establishments may be required to furnish a Form W-2G to the gambler.

Although a casual gambler may deduct gambling losses to the extent of gambling winnings, they are not actually netted. The gambling winnings are reported as other income on Line 21 of Form 1040, but gambling losses are reported on Schedule A as below-the-line (or itemized) deductions. If a taxpayer's itemized deductions do not exceed the amount of the standard deduction, the gambling losses are essentially nondeductible.

Thus, a taxpayer may end up paying tax on the entire amount of gambling winnings unreduced by what might be a substantial amount of gambling losses.

_____

Example: In 2014, Gary and Grace Gamble, married taxpayers, filing jointly, have $12,000 of gambling winnings and $25,000 of gambling losses. The taxpayers' only itemized deduction is the gambling losses.

Because gambling losses are deductible only to the extent of gambling winnings, the excess of Gary and Grace's gambling losses ($13,000) are totally nondeductible. The remaining $12,000 of gambling losses qualifies as an itemized deduction. However, the standard deduction for a married couple filing jointly is $12,400. Since, their gambling losses (the taxpayers' only itemized deduction) do not exceed their standard deduction, Gary and Grace should take the standard deduction for the extra $400. However, doing so means that none of the gambling losses are deductible. Despite the fact that the Gambles lost more than twice as much as they won, they will nonetheless pay tax on their $12,000 of gambling winnings.

_____

Professional Gamblers

As mentioned above, the rule limiting the deductibility of gambling losses to gambling gains applies to both casual and professional gamblers. However, because a professional gambler is in the trade or business of gambling, the gambling losses (to the extent deductible) are deducted on Schedule C as an above-the-line deduction. Consequently, those losses are deductible dollar-for-dollar even if the taxpayer does not itemize.

Additionally, under a 2008 IRS memorandum[35] and a 2011 Tax Court case,[36] the non-wagering expenses of a professional gambler (such as seminars, books, transportation, meals and lodging) incurred to engage in gambling activities are now considered "ordinary and necessary" business expenses, and the deduction of those expenses is not limited by gambling winnings.

The significance of this new method of reporting gambling income and deductions is invaluable to professional gamblers. Under the new more liberal rules, they may now first offset their winnings with their losses, and then use other business expenses to create an NOL.

_____

Example: Gary Gamble is a professional poker player. Throughout the year, Gary traveled to various casinos and other venues to participate in poker tournaments. For that year, Gary had gambling winnings of $75,000, gambling losses of $100,000, and $15,000 of business expenses for transportation, meals and lodging.

On a Schedule C, Gary reports his gambling income and deductions as follows:

Wagering gains	$75,000
Wagering losses	$100,000
Deductible wagering losses	$75,000
Wagering income	-$0-
Deductible non-wagering expenses	$15,000
Business loss (Potentially NOL)	($15,000)

_____

HOBBY LOSSES

Similar to the gambling loss limitation, deductions with respect to hobby activities are deductible only to the extent of income from such activities.[37] However, with regard to the deductibility of hobby losses, there is one significant negative tax difference. Although the deductible gambling losses of a casual gambler are below-the-line itemized deductions, hobby losses are miscellaneous itemized deductions[38] which are deductible only to the extent that they exceed 2 percent of adjusted gross income. Moreover, if that amount plus the taxpayer's other itemized deductions do not exceed the amount of the standard deduction; the hobby loss deduction provides no benefit to the taxpayer.

_____

Example: In 2014, Fred and Francine Farmer, married taxpayers, filing jointly, have combined wage income of $150,000. Fred is employed as a newspaper reporter and Francine is an executive chef. On the side, they grow flowers that they sell to their neighbors and others. From that activity, they generated $10,000 of income and $25,000 of deductions. Their itemized deductions include $6,500 of mortgage interest and $3,000 of property taxes. If the flower activity is treated as a hobby, the hobby deductions do not exceed the Farmers' standard deduction and provide no tax benefit. Despite having a net loss of $15,000, they nonetheless pay tax on $10,000 of flower sale income and have a total income of $160,000.

Flower Sale Income	$10,000
Flower sale expenses	$25,000
Tentative hobby deduction	$10,000
Less 2% of AGI	−$7,500
Total hobby deduction	$2,500
Other Itemized deduction (mortgage interest and property taxes)	$9,500
Total itemized deductions	$12,000
Standard deduction	$12,400

If the Farmers' flower activity was treated as a trade or business, the income would be reported on Schedule C and all of the relevant expenses would be deductible without limitation. As a result, the $15,000 business loss would be deductible from the Farmers' $150,000 wage income, leaving them with a total income of $135,000.

Here, the same set of income and expenses yields a net difference in $25,000 income, depending on whether it is treated as hobby or business.

Is an Activity a Hobby or a Business?

Whether an activity should be treated as a hobby or trade or business is a question of fact, and the IRS and the taxpayer may come to different conclusions on this issue. Often, activities that have a pleasure element are susceptible to classification by the IRS as hobby activities. Code section 183(d) provides a rebuttable presumption that an activity is a business if it produced a profit for at least three of the last five tax years.[39] Additionally, the regulations list the following factors that may be considered to resolve this issue:[40]

1. *The manner in which the taxpayer carries on the activity.* Does the taxpayer participate in the activity with a businesslike approach, including keeping complete and accurate books and records? If so, it is more likely to be perceived as a business, rather than a hobby.

2. *The expertise of the taxpayers or their advisors.* If the skill and techniques employed in the activity are on par with other professionals in that field, it may indicate that the activity should be classified as a trade or business.

3. *The time and effort expended by the taxpayers on the activity.* If a taxpayer devotes a substantial amount of time on a regular basis to the activity, it would strengthen the arguments for treating it as a business.

4. *Expectation that assets used in the activity may appreciate in value.* This factor encompasses the possibility that in addition to the profit from the activity, one of the taxpayer's motives is the appreciation in the value of assets associated with the activity.

5. *The success of the taxpayer in other similar activities.* This factor focuses on a taxpayer's prior track record with respect to operating profitable businesses. Someone who has started profitable businesses before (particularly in similar fields) is more likely to be running a business.

6. *The taxpayer's history of income or losses with respect to the business.* It is common for a legitimate trade or business to sustain a loss in the first few years. However, sustained long-term losses indicate that the activity may be a hobby, rather than a business.

7. *The amount of profits earned.* An activity in which over a number of years, a taxpayer generates a small amount of profits in relation to a large investment is probably not indicative of an activity engaged in for profit.

8. *The financial status of the taxpayer.* If the taxpayer has a significant amount of income from other sources, it is more likely that activity is not engaged in for profit—especially if there are personal and recreational elements involved in that activity.

9. *Elements of personal pleasure or recreation inherent in the activity.* The greater the potential personal pleasure or recreation that an activity involves, the less likely the taxpayer is engaged in it for profit.

Taxpayers who believe that their activity is a trade or business have the option of using Form 5213 to postpone the determination of whether the activity is a hobby or a business. Making this election ensures that the IRS will not challenge the treatment of the activity as a business until the end of the first four years in which the taxpayer is engaged in the activity,[41] and the deduction of all activity-related expenses is allowed. However, if the IRS determines that the activity was not engaged in for profit after the expiration of the presumption period, the hobby loss rules would be applied retroactively, potentially subjecting the taxpayer to a significant disallowance of deductions as well as accuracy-related penalties.[42]

In the end, even after evaluating all the above factors, it may remain unclear whether the activity is a legitimate business or a mere hobby. Moreover, if the taxpayer and IRS disagree, it may be up to the Tax Court to ultimately decide the issue.

FREQUENTLY ASKED QUESTIONS

Question – Does an NOL that is carried back or forward to other years offset self-employment income; and, thus, reduce self-employment tax in those years?

Answer – No. Section 1402(a)(4) specifically excludes the NOL as a deductible item in the computation of self-employment income.

Example: In 2010, Allison Accountant a self-employed CPA generated net fees of $150,000 (self-employment income). Assume for purposes of this example that Allison's adjusted gross income and taxable income was also $150,000. Self-employment income is subject to both regular income tax and self-employment tax.

In 2012, Allison sustained a net operating loss of $70,000 that she carried back to the 2010 tax year. For income tax purposes, the $70,000 NOL reduces her 2010 taxable income to $80,000. On the other hand, pursuant to section 1402(a)(4), there would be no similar adjustment to Allison's $150,000 self-employment income. As a result, the NOL would reduce Allison's 2010 taxable income; and, thus, her income tax liability. However, it would not reduce Allison's 2010 self-employment income, and her self-employment tax liability would remain the same.[43]

Question – If an NOL is carried back to a prior tax year, should the taxpayer file for a refund with a Form 1040X (amended income tax return) or Form 1045 (application for tentative refund)?

Answer – Either form is acceptable. However, there are different rules that apply depending on which form is filed.

Form 1045

• Must be filed within one year after the year in which the NOL arose.

• Must be filed separately and not attached to the Form 1040 for the year in which the NOL was generated.

• The IRS will process the Form 1045 within ninety days of the later of 1) the date it is filed; or 2) the last day of the month that includes the due date (including extensions) for filing the Form 1040 for the year the NOL was generated.

Figure 5.2

DRAWBACKS OF (CASUAL) GAMBLING AND HOBBY LOSSES	Gambling Loss	Hobby Loss
Deductions limited to income?	Yes	Yes
Allowable deductions save taxes only if itemized deductions exceed the standard deduction?	Yes	Yes
Associated income increases AGI, resulting in limitation of other credits and deductions?	Yes	Yes
Miscellaneous itemized deduction potentially triggering or increasing AMT?	No	Yes
Excess losses cannot be carried over to other tax years?	Yes	Yes

Form 1040X

- Must be filed no later than three years after the due date of the return for the applicable tax year.

- The IRS is not required to process the amended return within ninety days. However, if the amended return is not processed within six months from the date it is filed, the taxpayer may file a suit for a refund.

Assuming the taxpayer decides to file within one year after the year in which the NOL arose, Form 1045 would be the better option because unlike Form 1040X, the IRS must process it within a ninety-day period. However, if the taxpayer fails to file a Form 1045 within the one year filing period, her only option would be to file a Form 1040X.

Question – In determining the decrease in the FMV of property as a result of a casualty loss, can the costs of repairs be used as the measure of the decrease in value?

Answer – Yes, subject to the following conditions:

- The repairs are necessary to restore the property to its condition immediately prior to the casualty;

- The cost of the repairs is not excessive;

- The repairs are limited to the damage caused by the casualty; and

- The repairs do not cause the FMV of the property to exceed the value of the property prior to the casualty.

CHAPTER ENDNOTES

1. The Supreme Court has described deductions as a matter of "legislative grace." *INDOPCO, Inc. v. Comm.*, 503 US 79, 84 (1992).
2. I.R.C. §1012.
3. I.R.C. §1001(a)
4. *Libson Shops v. Koehler*, 353 U.S. 382 (1957).
5. I.R.C. §172(b). NOL may be carried forward for a maximum of twenty years.
6. I.R.C. §62(a).
7. I.R.C. §62(a).
8. I.R.C. §166(a).
9. I.R.C. §166(a).
10. Treas. Reg. §1.166-5(b).
11. Treas. Reg. §1.166-5(1)(d), Example 1.
12. I.R.C. §166(b).
13. Calculating the deduction allowed by this requirement is straightforward for cash method taxpayers. The issue becomes more complex for businesses that use an accrual method.
14. Treas. Reg. §1.166-2.
15. Treas. Reg. §1.166-2(b).
16. *Generes v. Comm'r.*, 405 U.S. 93 (1972).
17. Joint Comm. On Taxation, *General Explanation of the Tax Reform Act of 1976 Rep. No. JCS-33-76*, at 158 (1976); Treas. Reg. §1.166-9(a).
18. Treas. Reg. §1.166-9.
19. I.R.C. §166(d).
20. Treas. Reg. §1.165-7(b)(1)(i).
21. I.R.C. §165(h)(4)(E).
22. I.R.C. §166. This means partially worthless nonbusiness loans are not deductible unless and until they become totally worthless.
23. I.R.C. §166(d).
24. I.R.C. §1211(b)(1).
25. I.R.C. §165(h)(1).
26. I.R.C. §165(h)(2).
27. I.R.C. §67(b)(3).
28. IRB 2009-14 (April 6, 2009).
29. Pursuant to IRC sec. 165(h)(1), a deduction for a theft loss is allowable only to the extent it exceeds $100. Pursuant to IRC sec. 165(h)(2), a personal theft loss is deductible only to the extent that it exceeds the sum of all casualty gains (including thefts), plus so much of the excess that exceeds 10% of the taxpayer's adjusted gross income.
30. IRC Sec. 67(b)(3).
31. I.R.C. §67(b)(3).
32. I.R.C. §172(d)(4). Although nonbusiness deductions are excluded from the NOL, casualty losses—including theft—with respect to a transaction entered into for profit are allowable as part of the NOL deduction.
33. *Comm'r. v. Groetzinger*, 480 U.S. 23 (1987).
34. I.R.C. §262.
35. Office of Chief Counsel Internal Revenue Service Memorandum AM2008-013 (December 19, 2008).
36. *Mayo v. Comm'r.*, 136 T.C. 81 (2011).
37. I.R.C. §183(b).
38. I.R.C. §67.
39. In case of an activity which consists in major part of the breeding, training, showing or racing horses, the safe harbor presumption period is 2 or more tax years in a consecutive 7 year period. I.R.C. §183(d).
40. Treas. Reg. §1.183-2(b)(1)-(9).
41. I.R.C. §183(e)(1). If the 7 year period applies, the IRS will not challenge the validity of the business, if at all, until the end of the 6th year in which the taxpayer first engaged in the activity.
42. I.R.C. §6662.
43. *Decrescenzo v. Comm'r.*, T.C. Memo. 2012-51 (2012).

DEACTIONS

CHAPTER 6

INTRODUCTION

The purpose of income taxation is to tax the inflows of economic benefits, so it is only fair that the taxpayer should be entitled to deduct the outflows of money necessary to generate those economic benefits. In a perfect world, the difference between economic inflows and monetary outflows should be the amount subject to income tax, and taxpayers often take the availability of deductions for granted. However, in sharp contrast to the Internal Revenue Code's broad presumption to include any economic benefit in gross income, there is a narrow presumption with regard to allowing deductions for monetary outflows. In fact, no deduction can ever be taken unless a Code section specifically allows for it.[1]

Simply stated, a deduction is an outlay, usually of money, that reduces the taxable income and therefore also lowers the tax liability. The actual tax savings of a deduction is directly correlated with the taxpayer's tax rate. For example, assume that Sam Smith has taxable income of $10,000, a tax rate of 15 percent, and a $200 potential deduction. With no deductions, Sam's tax liability would be $1,500 (15 percent of $10,000). With the $200 deduction, Sam's taxable income would be reduced to $9,800 and, thus, his tax liability would be $1,470 (15 percent of $9,800). The tax savings to Sam from a $200 deduction is $30 (15 percent of $200).

Next, assume the same facts, except now Sam's tax rate is 20 percent. Without the deduction, Sam's tax liability would be $2,000 (20 percent of $10,000). As in the prior fact pattern, the $200 deduction would reduce his taxable income to $9,800. However, due to the higher tax rate, his tax liability would be $1,960 (20 percent of $9,800), resulting in a tax savings of $40. Comparing the two examples, Sam's tax savings were $10 more when his tax rate was twenty percent instead of fifteen percent.

One important conclusion from the above examples is that spending money just to create tax deductions does not make economic sense. No matter how high the tax rate, each dollar of deduction only saves a percentage of that dollar. Even if the taxpayer's tax rate is 39.6 percent, a $1 deduction only saves approximately 40 cents of that dollar. For this reason, many taxpayers fund deductions by using borrowed money (including credit cards) to pay for deductible items. Although in the long run, the taxpayer will ultimately have to repay the loan, in the short run, the deductible items paid for with the borrowed funds reduce the current tax year's tax liability.

Importantly, not all allowable deductions find their way onto to the taxpayer's Form 1040. This is because each specifically identified allowable deduction must survive a gauntlet of other Code sections that, depending on the circumstances, could limit or even completely eliminate the amount of the deduction. Even those deductions that survive are not treated alike; some are designated as "above-the-line" deductions and some as "below-the-line" deductions. Above-the-line deductions are not usually subject to further reduction and, in some cases, may enhance other tax benefits. Below-the-line deductions are often subject to further reduction and may trigger the alternative minimum tax.[2] The differences are discussed in detail below.

HOW DO DEDUCTIONS WORK?

Generally, a taxpayer generates income other than wages through operating a business or investments. The Code allows certain deductions for expenses related to each of these types of income as well as deductions for certain personal expenses that effectively "reward" the taxpayer for engaging in certain activities.

The Code is far more generous in allowing deductions related to trade or business income and designates them, for the most part, as the much more beneficial above-the-line deductions. Conversely, deductions related to investment income are much harder to come by. The Code imposes a more extensive array of limitations or elimination provisions, and, for the most part, those deductions that are allowable are the much less beneficial below-the-line deductions. Finally, the Code is the least generous with personal deductions, with many of them subject to limitations, phase-outs and floors (discussed in detail below) that effectively eliminate their availability to high-income taxpayers. Although some personal deductions are designated as above-the-line deductions, the more common ones are below-the-line deductions.

The steps necessary to determine whether—and to what extent—an expense item will ultimately be deductible and whether it will be an above-the-line or below-the-line deduction are as follows:

> Step 1 – Is the item deductible as a business, investment, or personal expense?

> Step 2 – What limits apply to the deduction?

> Step 3 – Is the deduction is an above-the-line or below-the-line deduction?

Step 1 – Is the Item Deductible as a Business, Investment, or Personal Expense?

Trade or Business Deductions

The term "trade or business" is actually a single term that is interchangeable with the term "business." Although the term appears in many Code sections, it is not defined in the Code or Treasury Regulations. However, in its publications, the IRS has defined "trade or business" to mean "any activity conducted for the production of income from selling goods or performing services."[3] Several trade or business expenses such as interest,[4] the payment of local and state taxes,[5] and unrecoverable bad debts owed by customers[6] are specifically identified as being deductible. However, it would be impractical to enact a separate Code section for every possible business expense. For that reason, Code section 162 serves as a "catch-all" provision by which all other trade or business expenses (office supplies, utilities, repairs, etc.) that meet broad requirements are deductible.[7] Helpfully, Schedule C (a common attachment to Form 1040 used to report business deductions) lists common items deductible under section 162 including rent, insurance, supplies, utilities, and advertising. When considering what types of expenses may qualify as a business deduction, Schedule C can be a good place to start.

In order for an item to be deductible under section 162(a), it must meet the following requirements:

1. it must be "ordinary";

2. it must be "necessary";

3. it must be an "expense," rather than an "expenditure"; and

4. it must be used to carry out a trade or business

The first two requirements, "ordinary" and "necessary," are questions of fact that require a case-by-case analysis. The term "ordinary" means the item is not unusual in the type of business the taxpayer is conducting. For example, newspaper or internet advertising would be an ordinary expense item for an accountant or tax lawyer. On the other hand, buying and maintaining a yacht to display a banner with the words "Form 1040" would not be considered ordinary advertising. For that reason, the cost of the yacht expenses would not be deductible.[8] Next, the term "necessary" means the item is appropriate and helpful to the business and its cost is reasonable. So, although transportation to and from a meeting would be appropriate and helpful to most businesses, with the availability of much less expensive commercial flights, the cost of chartering a private plane would probably not be reasonable.

The third requirement is the item must be an "expense" rather than an "expenditure." An expense is an item of short duration (used up in a year or less)[9] such as labor, rent, supplies, incidental repairs and advertising.[10] The common denominator of expense items is a relatively short shelf life that requires constant replenishment. Conversely, the cost of heavy manufacturing machinery and buildings that have long periods of usefulness spanning many tax years are expenditures. Even though the cost of office supplies and a warehouse are ordinary and necessary, only the former is deductible under section 162(a).

The fourth and fifth requirements of "carrying out" a "trade or business" must be considered together. First, the taxpayer must be actually operating the business in order to deduct any ordinary and necessary expense. For example, when operating a franchise restaurant, the cost of renting a building and utilities would certainly be deductible under section 162(a). However, if a taxpayer had just acquired a franchise and was preparing to open the restaurant and was not yet serving patrons, the taxpayer would not at that time be carrying on a restaurant business. As a result, the rent and utility expenses would not be deductible under section 162(a).[11]

However, all is not lost with respect to the deductibility of expenditures or pre-opening expenses. In the case of an expenditure, if all the other requirements of section 162(a) are otherwise met, instead of being currently deductible, the expenditure would be *depreciable* pursuant to Code sections 167 and 168. An expenditure generates taxable income throughout a useful life that covers multiple tax years. Depreciation matches a portion of the cost of the expenditure with each tax year's income over a recovery period that approximates the expenditure's useful life.[12] For example, the cost of a warehouse would be depreciable over a recovery period of thirty-nine years, so that a portion of its cost would match each tax year's income over that same period.[13]

In the case of the pre-opening costs (referred to as "start-up expenditures"), the taxpayer may elect to amortize those costs over a period of at least sixty months, beginning in the month in which the trade or business actually commenced.[14] So, beginning in the month in which the restaurant opened for business, a pro-rata share of start-up expenditures would be deductible over the tax years spanning the sixty-month amortization period pursuant to Code section 195 rather than section 162. In other words, instead of deducting start-up expenditures all in the year they were incurred, they must instead be amortized over time.

Investment Deductions

Similar to section 162, Code section 212 is the catch-all provision for the deductibility of investment type items—investment counsel fees, clerical help, office rent, etc.[15]—not specifically deductible under some other Code section. The first three requirements of section 212—"ordinary," "necessary," and "expense"—are identical to the section 162 requirements and require no further explanation.[16] Beyond those requirements, investment expenses must be incurred in one of two contexts:

1. the production or collection of income;[17] or

2. the management, conservation or maintenance of property held for the production of income.[18]

These contexts are very broad and may often overlap. Examples of investment expenses include the costs associated with buying and selling investment property, the occasional rental of real property (such as a vacation home), and projects undertaken for profit that do not rise the level of a trade or business, such as a joint venture. Investment activity is more passive than the grinding intensity of a trade or business. Finally, the fees of tax professionals including tax preparation fees or accounting and legal fees related to a Tax Court litigation, audits, or tax collection actions are also deductible under section 212.[19]

Personal Deductions

Although generally deductions are not allowed for personal, living and family expenses, the Code does allow deductions for certain personal expenses. These deductions are designed to provide tax relief for certain situations and encourage taxpayers to engage in certain activities. Those deductible items include the following:

- Alimony payments[20] are deductible as an accounting adjustment for the payor spouse. In a marriage, each spouse's income is taxed one time, either on a joint return or on married-filing-separately returns. For a divorced couple, the alimony payment deduction simply reflects the transfer of income from one ex-spouse to another. Consistent with taxing the income only once, the payee spouse includes the alimony in gross income and the payor spouse deducts it.

- The IRA deduction[21] encourages taxpayers to save for retirement by allowing them to deduct contributions to a retirement plan.

- Deductions for student loan interest[22] and college tuition and fees paid reward taxpayers for pursuing education.

- Moving expenses[23] are a mix of personal and business expenses. This deduction provides tax relief to the taxpayer who is required to move a significant distance away for a job.

- The deduction for one-half of self-employment taxes paid[24] is an attempt to equalize the tax treatment of W-2 employees with those who are self-employed. For W-2 employees, one-half of the FICA tax imposed on the wages of a W-2 employee (7.65 percent) is paid by the employer. Even though that payment is an economic benefit to the employee, it is considered an obligation of the employer, and that amount is not included in the employee's taxable wages. On the other hand, a self-employed taxpayer must pay the entire amount of the FICA (referred to as self-employment tax when paid by a self-employed taxpayer), or 15.3 percent of self-employment income up to a certain limit, which includes the amount that a W-2 employer would be obligated to pay. In an attempt to equalize the tax treatment of a self-employed taxpayer with the W-2 taxpayer, the self-employed taxpayer is allowed a deduction for one-half of the self-employment taxes paid.

- Self-employed health insurance deduction[25] is another attempt to equalize tax treatment of W-2 employees with self-employed taxpayers. Since employer-provided health insurance is excluded from a W-2 employee's gross income, a self-employed taxpayer may deduct his or her health insurance premiums as an equalizer.

- The deduction for contributions to self-employed retirement plans[26] is another equalizer with W-2 employees covered under an employer-sponsored plan.

- The deduction for contributions to Health Savings Accounts encourages taxpayers to use HSAs to pay for health care expenses;[27]

- The deduction for penalties on early withdrawals of retirement savings[28] provides a small measure of assistance to those taxpayers who are compelled to dip into savings prematurely.

- The medical and dental expenses deduction[29] can provide a tax break to those who pay significant out-of-pocket medical and dental expenses. However, the deduction is subject to a 10 percent adjusted gross income floor (discussed below) and is a below-the-line deduction (also discussed below), so its benefit is often illusory. Only taxpayers with high medical expenses in a single tax year would ever be likely to take advantage of this deduction;

- The state income and property tax deduction[30] gives some relief to taxpayers who are taxed by multiple jurisdictions.

- The mortgage interest deduction[31] helps homeowners by allowing them to deduct the interest (not principal) paid on their mortgages.

- The charitable contribution deduction[32] rewards taxpayers for giving donation to charitable causes.

Step 2 – What Limits Apply to the Deduction?

Finding a Code section allowing for the deduction of a certain item is just the first step on the road to using the deduction to reduce tax liability. There is a variety of instances in which another Code section may derail the process by limiting or even eliminating an otherwise allowable deduction.

Trade or Business Deductions

As discussed above, trade or business deductions are by far the most generous allowed by the Code. In fact, as a general rule, "[t]he full amount of the allowable deduction for ordinary and necessary expenses in carrying on a trade or business is deductible, even though such expenses exceed the gross income derived during the taxable year from such business."[33] This means that the net loss from a trade or business (the excess amount of deductions over income) is deductible, and can be applied to reduce income from other sources.

However, the Code imposes some limits on common business expenses. For example, in many businesses, it is common practice to take a client out for a meal or to an event to discuss business. In an attempt to prevent the taxpayer from disguising personal expenses as deductible business expenses, Code section 274 sets forth strict substantiation rules requiring the taxpayer to document the specific business purpose of any such meals or entertainment. If the taxpayer fails to meet these requirements, the deduction would be totally disallowed. Even if the taxpayer adequately meets the substantiation requirements, the deduction for meals and entertainment is limited to 50 percent of the cost.[34]

Perhaps one of the most significant limitations of trade or business deductions relates to *passive activity loss*, which was discussed in Chapter 3. Passive activity losses are restricted such that they may only be deducted to offset passive activity income, not any other types of income (investment, business, or otherwise) that a taxpayer may have. This restriction can significantly impact the amount of tax liability faced by a taxpayer with passive activity loss deductions. For example, assume that in 2014 the taxpayer was a general partner in a music publishing business partnership but had no actual involvement in the operation of the business. A partnership is a pass-through entity from which all income and deductions flow through to the individual partners as "distributive shares." If the passive general partner's distributive share of partnership income was $10,000 and the distributive share of partnership deductions was $20,000, only $10,000 of the $20,000 in expenses would actually be deductible because he or she did not materially participate in the partnership business. Unless the partner had passive activity income from some other activity, the other $10,000 would be not be deductible.[35] For a more detailed explanation of the tax nuances of passive activities, see Chapter 24.

Investment Deductions

The Code does not particularly favor investment deductions, and often imposes restrictions that limit and sometimes eliminate what would otherwise be a deductible expense. For example, Code Section 163(d)(1) limits the deductibility of investment interest to net investment income (defined as investment income less investment related expenses other than interest). Generally investment income includes interest, dividends, royalties as well as the gain from the sale of investment property. Similar to passive activity losses, discussed above, investment interest is deductible only to the extent of a like amount of net investment income. For example, assume in the current year, the taxpayer pays investment interest of $15,000. If his net investment income is $7,000, the current year's investment interest deduction would be limited to $7,000, leaving $8,000 of investment interest that is not deductible in the current tax year. The excess non-deductible invest interest must be carried over to subsequent years, and remains deductible only to the extent of net investment income in those years.

Perhaps, the most significant limitation of investment type deductions relates to capital loss. A capital loss is the loss from the sale or exchange of a capital asset usually held for investment. For example, if a taxpayer purchased ten shares of stock (a capital asset) for $5,000 and then sells the stock for $2,000, there would be a $3,000 capital loss. The deductibility of capital loss is limited to an offsetting amount of capital gain, plus $3,000 that would be deductible against any other type of income. To illustrate the application of these rules, assume that in current tax year, the taxpayer has

$80,000 of capital gain and $150,000 of capital loss. Of the $150,000 of capital loss, $80,000 would be deductible as an offset against the $80,000 of capital gain. As to the remaining $70,000 of net capital loss, only $3,000 would be deductible against other current tax year income. The remaining $67,000 of capital loss would be carried forward to subsequent tax years subject to the same rules. Assuming the taxpayer did not have any capital gains in any subsequent tax year to offset the capital loss carried forward, it would take twenty-three years, at the rate of $3,000 per year, for the taxpayer to fully deduct the remaining $67,000 of capital loss.

Some restrictions completely eliminate the use of an investment expense as a deduction. For example, a taxpayer may borrow funds to finance the purchase of an investment security to generate investment income and/or to hold for potential sale at a gain. The investment interest payable on such borrowing is deductible pursuant to Code section 163(d). However, if the loan proceeds were used to purchase a tax-exempt bond (generating tax-exempt interest), the investment interest payable on the borrowed funds would be disallowed under Code section 265.[36] In fact, section 265 disallows any type of otherwise deductible section 212 expense that is directly related to the acquisition or maintenance of a tax-exempt security.

Another example of potential deductions that are completely eliminated relates to the attendance of investment-themed seminars that cover various investment opportunities and strategies. While these expenses may be directly relevant to a taxpayer's income-generating investment activities, the deduction is specifically disallowed under Code section 274(h)(7).

Personal Deductions

Unlike business and investment deductions that are related to the generation of income, most personal deductions provide taxpayers with a measure of tax relief or encourage them to engage in certain activities. Thus, the Code often limits or eliminates these deductions for high income taxpayers through the use of "phase-outs," "floors" or "ceilings" that are based on a taxpayer's adjusted gross income.

Phase-outs

A "phase-out" of a deduction is a gradual pro-rata reduction of a deduction over a range of adjusted gross income. For example, if the phase-out range is between $70,000 and $80,000 of adjusted gross income, it means that beginning at the threshold adjusted gross income amount of $70,000, the taxpayer will only be able to take a percentage of the deduction. The percentage of the deduction that is available will decrease as the taxpayer's adjusted gross income rises toward the top of the phase-out range ($80,000). The deduction is completely unavailable for taxpayers with adjusted gross incomes above the top of the phase-out range.

An example of a phased-out deduction is found in Code section 219, which allows taxpayers making contributions to traditional IRAs to deduct contributions of $5,500 (plus a $1,000 catch-up amount for taxpayers older than fifty). In 2014, the deduction for single and head of household taxpayers who are covered by a work-place plan begins phasing out at the adjusted gross income threshold amount of $60,000, and is completely phased out at $70,000. For married spouses filing jointly where the spouse covered by a work place plan is the one making the IRA contribution, the deduction phases out between adjusted gross incomes of $96,000 and $116,000. For married taxpayers filing jointly where the non-covered spouse is the one making the distribution, the deduction phases out between adjusted gross incomes of $181,000 and $191,000. Taxpayers with adjusted gross incomes between the two phase-out values for their respective filing status may only deduct a percentage of their IRA contributions. If their adjusted gross incomes are above the top level of the phase-out, they may not deduct any of their contributions.

Floors

An adjusted gross income "floor" means that a deduction is not allowed until the amount of the potential deduction exceeds the floor. For example, assume the deduction for a certain expense is subject to a 7.5 percent adjusted gross income floor. If the taxpayer's adjusted gross income is $100,000, the "floor" would be $7,500. Thus, any amount of the deductible expense that is $7,500 or less would be under the floor and nondeductible. If the amount of the expense was $8,000, only $500—the amount by which the expense exceeds the floor—would be deductible.

For example, Code section 213 makes certain medical and dental expenses of a taxpayer and his or her dependents deductible. However, there is a floor of 10 percent adjusted gross income. This means to get the first dollar of a usable deduction, the medical and dental expenses must exceed 10 percent of the taxpayer's adjusted gross income. So, if a taxpayer with an adjusted gross income of $30,000 spent $4,000 on medical expenses, he or she would be entitled to a deduction of only $1,000 ($4,000 minus 10 percent of $30,000).

Ceilings

A "ceiling" is the opposite of a floor, and means that a deduction is limited to a certain percentage of adjusted gross income. The resulting amount is a ceiling beyond which no deduction would be allowed. For example, assume a taxpayer incurred $45,000 of a potentially deductible expense, and, that the deduction is limited to 15 percent of adjusted gross income. If the taxpayer's adjusted gross income was $200,000, the "ceiling," or the maximum amount deductible for that particular deduction would be $30,000 (15 percent of $200,000). The remaining $15,000 would not be deductible because it exceeds the ceiling. If the taxpayer's adjusted income was $300,000, the entire $45,000 would be deductible, as it would be the exact amount of the ceiling (15 percent of $300,000).

Charitable contribution deductions are subject to two different ceilings depending on the type of charitable organization receiving the contribution. In the case of a contribution of money to a public charity, the amount of the deductible contribution is limited to 50 percent of the taxpayer's "contribution base," which is essentially adjusted gross income. To the extent that the charitable contribution exceeds 50 percent of the taxpayer's contribution base, such amount is not deductible, and must be carried over to the next tax year (with a five-year maximum carry-over period) subject to the same limitation. Charitable contributions to private foundations are limited to 30 percent of the taxpayer's contribution base. Similarly, to the extent the contribution exceeds 30 percent of the taxpayer's contribution base, such amount is carried over to the next year (again, with a five-year maximum carry over-period subject to the same limitation). For a more detailed discussion of Charitable Contribution Planning, see Chapter 31.

With phase-outs and floors, a taxpayer's adjusted gross income is inversely proportionate to the amount of the deduction; the higher the adjusted gross income, the lower the deduction amount. Conversely (although a ceiling essentially establishes a limitation for a deduction), the higher adjusted gross incomes have higher the ceilings, and the amount of the deduction increases as gross adjusted income goes up.

Step 3 – Is the Deduction is an "Above-the-Line" or "Below-the-Line" Deduction?

After determining which deductions have survived the hurdles of step 2, the final step is to determine which of those deductions are "above-the-line" deductions, and which are "below-the-line" deductions. As discussed below, that designation will be a significant factor in the ultimate tax benefit the taxpayer receives from those deductions.

Above-the-Line Deductions

"Above-the-line" deductions are deducted directly from gross income to compute adjusted gross income. Generally, if a deduction is specifically listed in Code section 62(a), it is an above-the-line deduction. If not, by default, it is a below-the-line deduction. An above-the-line business or investment deduction is always more beneficial to the taxpayer than a below the line deductions, because it is subject to no further limitations so that it reduces gross income dollar-for-dollar.[37]

Business Deductions

Consistent with the Code's preference for business-related deductions, section 62(a)(1) is a catch-all section by which all trade or business deductions, with the exception of certain unreimbursed employee business expenses, are designated as above-the-line deductions.[38] This means that all deductions allowable by Code section 162, as well as all other trade or business-related deductions (business interest, depreciation, start-up expenditures, depreciation, etc.) are above-the-line deductions.

Investment Deductions

As a general rule, investment deductions are below-the-line deductions. There are, however, three exceptions. One is for all deductions attributable to rent and royalty income not generated in the context of a trade or business.[39] For example, a taxpayer who occasionally rents a room in his or her home or a vacation home is probably not in a rental trade or business. Notwithstanding this fact, the section 212 deductions related to such rentals (utilities, repairs, commissions, advertising, etc.) are designated as above-the-line deductions.

Another exception relates to capital losses. As discussed above, capital losses are deductible to the extent of capital gains, plus $3,000 that is deductible against any other type of income.[40] Allowable capital loss deductions are designated as above-the-line deductions.[41]

Finally, Code section 165 designates the penalty for an early withdrawal of funds from a retirement savings account as an above-the-line deduction.[42]

Personal Deductions

While many items that taxpayers think of as "personal" deductions are often designated as below-the-line, some are not. The following personal deductions are designated as above-the-line deductions:

- Alimony payments;[43]
- IRA contribution;[44]
- Student loan interest;[45]
- Moving expenses;[46]
- Qualified tuition and fees;[47]
- One-half of self-employment tax;[48]
- Self-employed health insurance;[49]
- Contributions to self-employed retirement plans;[50]
- Contributions to Health Savings Accounts;[51]

Below-the-Line Deductions

As discussed above, above-the-line deductions are deducted from gross income in the computation of adjusted gross income. Therefore, all remaining deductions are by default "below-the-line" deductions (often referred to as "itemized deductions"). For the most part, itemized deductions are comprised of investment and personal deductions. Below-the-line deductions are often subject to phase-outs and floors that limit—and sometimes entirely eliminate—their value to the taxpayer. Once the amount of deductible below-the-line deductions is determined, that amount is deducted from adjusted gross income as the next-to-last step in the computation of taxable income.

Regular vs. Miscellaneous Below-the-Line Deductions

Within the realm of below-the-line deductions or itemized deductions, there are "miscellaneous" and "regular" itemized deductions. Miscellaneous itemize deductions are subject to a 2 percent adjusted gross income floor, and are often the least tax beneficial of all below-the-line deductions. Any itemized deduction not listed under section 67(b) is a miscellaneous itemized deduction. Conversely, any below-the-line deduction that *is* listed under Code section 67(b) is referred to as a "regular itemized deduction." The following are the most common "regular itemized deductions":

- Medical and dental expenses;

- Taxes;

- Interest;

- Charitable contributions; and

- Casualty and theft losses.

USING ABOVE-THE-LINE AND BELOW-THE-LINE DEDUCTIONS TO COMPUTE TAXABLE INCOME

Once all the steps in the identification of above-the-line and below-the-line deductions have been completed, it is then possible to employ them in the computation of taxable income. The computation can be broken into three parts:

- Determination of adjusted gross income

- Deciding whether to use the standard or itemized deductions (including consideration of the "Pease limitation" on itemized deductions)

- Calculation of personal and dependent exemptions

Determining Adjusted Gross Income

The best way to explain how to compute adjusted gross income is to use the 2013 Form 1040 as a model. The bottom of the first page of the form—line 37—contains the entry "adjusted gross income." This means that all items of gross income minus above-the-line deductions are entered above line 37 (hence the term "above-the-line"). What tends to be confusing is that lines 7 through 21 appear to be items of gross income, the total of which is entered on line 22 (total income). The entries for lines 23 through 35 are above-the-line deductions that are specifically identified, but only

include personal deductions. So where are the other above-the-line deductions, including business and investment deductions? They are included in the various forms and schedules that are used to calculate the taxpayer's gross income, as explained in Figure 6.1 below.

As demonstrated by Figure 6.1, various types of non-personal above-the-line deductions are netted against their respective income as computed on separate schedules and forms. The net numbers, positive or negative, are brought over to the first page of Form 1040. Consequently, the net income or loss numbers account for the above-the-line deductions. Next, the personal above-the-line deductions are totaled and subtracted from adjusted gross income.

The Standard Deduction vs. Itemized Deductions

After computing adjusted gross income, the next step is to subtract below-the-line deductions from adjusted gross income. However, in lieu of claiming below-the-line itemized deductions, taxpayers have the option of deducting the standard deduction. For tax year 2014, the standard deductions are as follows: single taxpayer - $6,200; head of household - $9,100; married filing jointly - $12,400; and married filing separately - $6,200.[52] The standard deduction reflects the minimum amount of an unconditional below-the-line deduction allowed to taxpayers based on filing status. This means that the taxpayer may deduct the greater of the standard deduction or the total amount of itemized deductions. If a single taxpayer had $6,000 of itemized deductions, he or she would deduct the higher standard deduction of $6,200. Conversely, if the single taxpayer had $7,000 of itemized deductions, he or she would deduct that amount.

In order to determine whether to claim the standard deduction or itemized deductions, the taxpayer must compute his or her itemized deductions to ascertain which of the two is higher. Itemized deductions are entered on Schedule A of Form 1040. Using the 2013 Schedule A as a model, if the total amount of itemized deductions exceed the standard deduction, such amount is brought over to Form 1040 in line 40 on the second page, where it is deducted from adjusted gross income.

Significantly, in addition to medical and dental expenses, miscellaneous itemized deductions are subject to a 2 percent adjusted gross income floor. Essentially, as discussed above, miscellaneous itemized deductions are

Figure 6.1

ADJUSTED GROSS INCOME: GROSS INCOME MINUS "ABOVE-THE-LINE" DEDUCTIONS	
Gross income received by the taxpayer.	7. Wages and Salaries 8. Taxable Interest 9. Dividends 10. Taxable Refunds 11. Alimony Received 15. IRA Distributions 16. Pensions and Annuities 19. Unemployment Compensation 20. Social Security Benefits 21. Other Income
Items of gross income that are reduced by above-the-line deductions as computed on a separate schedule to be attached to the return.	12. Business income – Schedule C includes gross business income and above-the-line trade or business expenses deductions. The net amount income or loss is brought over to line 12 on Form 1040. 13. Capital Gain – Schedule D includes capital gain offset by capital losses. On the same schedule, the capital losses are netted with capital gains. A net capital gain is brought over to line 13 in its entirety. Alternatively, up to $3,000 of a net capital loss is brought over to line 13. 14. Other Gains or Losses includes Form 4797 entries, in which all losses from sales of property not listed on Schedule D are netted from gains from such sales. The net amount—either a positive or negative number—is brought over to line 14. 17. Rental Real Estate Income – Schedule E includes rental income offset by rental-related expenses (above-the-line deductions). The net amount is brought over to line 17. 18. Farm Income – Schedule F calculates net farm income. The net amount is brought over to line 18.
Total Income – Line 22	Total Income is the sum of lines 7 through 21 and incorporates the above-the-line deductions described above.
Other Above-the-line Deductions – Totaled on Line 36	23. Educator expense (expired at the end of 2013) 24. Certain business expenses of reservists, performing artists, and fee based officials 25. Health savings account deduction 26. Moving expenses 27. Deductible part of self-employment tax 28. Self-employed SEP, SIMPLE and qualified plans 29. Self-employed health insurance deduction 30. Penalty on early withdrawal of retirement savings 31. Alimony paid 32. IRA deduction 33. Student loan deduction 34. Tuition and fees 35. Domestic production activities deduction
Adjusted Gross Income – Line 37	Total Income Minus Line 36.

any itemized deduction other than medical and dental expenses, taxes, interest, charitable contributions and casualty and theft losses. The most common miscellaneous itemized deductions are investment expenses (other than investment interest) and most unreimbursed employee business expenses (i.e., an employee purchases office supplies for work but is not reimbursed by the employer).

To illustrate the computation of itemized deductions, assume that for tax year 2014, a single taxpayer under the age of sixty-five has adjusted gross income of $80,000, medical expenses of $8,100, state income taxes of $430, home mortgage interest of $8,500, unreimbursed employee business expenses of $2,100 and a tax attorney fee of $700 for a tax matter. Figure 6.2 sets forth an analysis of the deductibility of these items.

Based on the computations in Figure 6.2, it is clear that the taxpayer would deduct the higher of the sum of his or her itemized deductions ($10,230) rather than the lower standard deduction ($6,200). However, due to the application of the 10 percent AGI medical expense floor and the 2 percent AGI miscellaneous itemized deduction floor, the taxpayer's otherwise allowable itemized deductions are reduced from $19,830 to $10,230, eliminating $9,500 of otherwise deductible expenses.

In addition to the adjusted gross income floors that limit the amount of an otherwise allowable itemized deduction, taxpayers with relatively high adjusted gross income are subject to a further reduction known as the "Pease limitation." Code section 68(a) requires a single taxpayer with adjusted gross income in excess

of $254,200 (and married taxpayers filing jointly with adjusted gross income in excess of $305,050) to reduce otherwise allowable itemized deductions (other than medical deductions, investment interest deductions and casualty, theft and gambling losses)[53] by the lesser of (a) 3 percent of adjusted gross income in excess of the threshold, or (b) 80 percent of itemized deductions.[54] To illustrate, assume a single taxpayer has an adjusted gross income of $300,000 and itemized deductions of $100,000. Under the Pease limitation the tax payer can either reduce his or her deductions by 3 percent of $45,800 ($300,000 minus $254,200), or 80 percent of $100,000. The first option is clearly better, and so the taxpayer's itemized deductions would be reduced by $1,374 (from $100,000 to $98,626).

Personal and Dependency Exemptions

As a final deduction in the computation of taxable income, a taxpayer is entitled to a personal exemption[55] and possibly one or more dependency exemptions.[56] A personal exemption is a deduction of a certain amount, indexed for inflation, that a taxpayer[57] (and spouse, if filing jointly) can deduct in addition to the standard deduction or itemized deductions from adjusted gross income. A full personal exemption is allowed for the taxpayer, his or her spouse, and their dependents, even if one or more of them died during the tax year.[58] Indexed for inflation, the 2014 personal exemption amount is $3,950[59] for taxpayers, spouses, or dependents. A dependent must be either a "qualifying child" or a "qualifying relative." A "qualifying child" means an individual who:

Figure 6.2

BELOW-THE-LINE ITEMIZED DEDUCTIONS For a single taxpayer with an adjusted gross income of $80,000 (Standard deduction: $6,200)			
Expense Type	**Amount Paid**	**Floor**	**Amount Deductible**
Medical	$8,100	10% of AGI	$ 100
State Income Tax	$ 430	N/A	$ 430
Home Mortgage Interest	$8,500	N/A	$8,500
Unreimbursed Employee Business Expenses (miscellaneous itemized deductions, includes attorney fee)	$2,100 $ 700 $2,800	2% of AGI	$1,200
Total	$22,630		$10,230

(1) is the taxpayer's "child" (including a step-child, legally adopted child or foster child placed by an authorized placement agency or by court order), or a descendant of such a child, or the taxpayer's brother, sister, stepbrother, stepsister or a descendant of any such relative ("the relationship test");

(2) has the same principal place of abode as the taxpayer for more than one-half of the tax year (the "residency test");

(3) is either a citizen or resident of the United States, or resident of a country *contiguous* to the United States (the "citizenship test," though it also includes non-citizens who are residents of Canada and Mexico);

(4) has not attained the age of nineteen as of the close of the calendar year in which the taxable year begins, or is a student who has not attained the age of twenty-four as of the close of the calendar year (the "age test," though individuals who are permanently and totally disabled as defined by Code section 22(e)(3) are deemed to meet the age test regardless of their age);

(5) if married, will not file a joint return (the "marriage test"); *and*

(6) has not provided more than one-half of his or her own support for the calendar year in which the taxpayer's taxable year begins (the "support test").[60]

If an individual could be a qualifying child for more than one taxpayer, and those taxpayers file separately, they can decide among themselves who will claim the qualifying child. In the event, multiple taxpayers claim the same qualifying child, there are tiebreaker rules to determine who was entitled to claim that individual.[61]

Special rule for divorced parents: In the case of divorced parents, who between them provide more than one-half of a child's support for the calendar year, and have custody of the child for more than one-half of the calendar year, the custodial parent (the parent with whom the child resides for the greater number of nights during the calendar year) is generally allowed the dependency exemption. However, the noncustodial parent can claim the exemption if the custodial parent signs a written declaration (Form 8332 or a statement conforming to the substance of Form 8332) agreeing not to claim the child

as a dependent, *and* the noncustodial parent attaches the declaration to his tax return for the calendar year.

The term "qualifying relative" means an individual:

(1) who passes the "relationship or member of the taxpayer's household test" by being:

(i) an individual who would be a qualifying child but for the fact that he or she did not meet the age requirement (such as an adult child living at home);

(ii) sibling or stepsibling of the taxpayer;

(iii) an ancestor of either the taxpayer or taxpayer's spouse;

(iv) son or daughter of a brother or sister of the taxpayer;

(v) brother or sister of the father or mother of the taxpayer;

(vi) an in-law of the taxpayer; or

(vii) a non-relative who has the same principal place of abode as the taxpayer and is a member of the taxpayer's household;

(2) whose gross income for the calendar year in which the taxable year begins is less than the current year's exemption amount (the "gross income test");

(3) who passes the support test, citizenship test, and marriage test used to determine who is a "qualifying child" (as described above).[62]

"Support" includes the cost of food, shelter, clothing, medical and dental expenses (including premiums on medical expense insurance), church contributions, recreation, and child care expenses. If the dependent lives in a location for which the taxpayer is paying rent, or in a house the taxpayer owns, a proportionate part of the *fair rental value* is counted.[63] If two or more persons collectively furnish more than half the support of a dependent, but none of them contributes more than half the support, any member of the group who has furnished more than 10 percent of the support may be designated to take the exemption under what is known as a *multiple support agreement*. Every other member of the group who has furnished more than 10 percent of the support must file a written declaration on Form 2120 stating that he will *not* claim the exemption.[64]

Personal and dependency exemptions claimed by taxpayers with relatively high adjusted gross income are subject to a phase-out. For 2014, the phase-out range of single taxpayers is adjusted gross income between $254,200 and $376,700 and the phase-out range for married taxpayers filing jointly is adjusted gross income between $305,050 and $427,550. Each $2,500 of adjusted gross income (or fraction thereof) over the threshold amount will result in a 2 percent decrease of the taxpayer's aggregate amount of exemptions.[65]

For example, in 2014, assume married taxpayers filing jointly claiming two exemptions ($7,900) have adjusted gross income of $325,050. For purposes of the phase-out, they are $10,000 above the threshold amount of $305.050. Thus, their personal exemptions of $7,900 must be reduced by 8 percent ($10,000 divided into four $2,500 increments). Thus, the amount the taxpayers may deduct as personal exemptions would be $7,268 ($7,900 minus $632).

THE BOTTOM LINE COMPUTATION OF TAXABLE INCOME

The computation of taxable income follows a number of steps:

1. Begin by determining gross income.

2. After determining which allowable deductions are designated as above-the-line deductions and whether or not phase-outs apply, subtract the aggregate amount of the above-the-line deductions from gross income to arrive at adjusted gross income.

3. Next, determine whether to use the standard deduction or the aggregate amount of itemized deductions. To do so, ascertain which itemized deductions are regular and which are miscellaneous. Apply the applicable adjusted gross income floors to determine the bottom-line amount of itemized deductions. Then, determine and use the higher of the standard deduction or the total amount of itemized deductions. Consider whether the Pease limitation applies, and, if it does, make a further adjustment to the amount of itemized deductions. Subtract the

properly adjusted amount of itemized deductions from adjusted gross income.

4. Finally, determine the number of exemptions (personal and dependency) the taxpayer is entitled to take. Check for a potential phase-out of those exemptions, and, if required, make an appropriate adjustment. Subtract the appropriate exemption amount to arrive at taxable income.

WHERE CAN I FIND OUT MORE?

Tax Facts on Insurance & Employee Benefits (National Underwriter Company; published annually).

FREQUENTLY ASKED QUESTIONS

Question – How can a taxpayer maximize his or her deductions in the tax year in which she starts a new business?

Answer – Code Section 162(a) allows taxpayer to deduct business expenses provided they are incurred when the taxpayer is actually operating her business. Thus, pre-opening start-up expenditures are not deductible. However, once the taxpayer actually begins operating his or her trade or business, Code section 195 allows the taxpayer to amortize (deduct over time) the cost of all start-up expenditures over a period of not less than sixty months beginning in the month in which the taxpayer commences the business.

Assume that between January 1 and June 30 of the tax year, the taxpayer incurred the cost of rent, utilities and labor in the aggregate amount of $6,000 in preparing to open an accounting business. On July 1, the taxpayer opened for business, and through the end of the year incurred an additional cost of rent, utilities and labor also in the aggregate amount of $6,000. Although the taxpayer may deduct the entire $6,000 of the post-opening rent expenses under Code section 162(a), the $6,000 "start-up expenditures" would have to be amortized over a sixty-month period beginning in July, the month she opened for business. As a result, only $600 of the $6,000 of start-up expenditures may be deducted in the first year (one-tenth of $6,000). So in the first year, despite spending $12,000 on rent, utilities and labor, her deduction would be limited to $6,600.

Obviously, the taxpayer would prefer to maximize the deductible amount of her calendar year costs. In order to do so, the taxpayer should consider opening for business as soon as possible even if it is in a makeshift office and even is she is not as fully equipped to begin operations as she might desire. If she opened for business on March 1, her section 162(a) deduction would be $10,000 (assuming her expenses were $1,000 per month). Thus, only $2,000, the aggregate amount of start-up expenditures for January and February would be required to be amortized over a sixty month period.

Question – Is a tax credit or deduction more beneficial to the taxpayer?

Answer – Without question, a tax credit is more beneficial to the taxpayer. This is because each dollar of a tax credit saves one dollar of tax. In monetary terms, a taxpayer in the 39.6 percent tax bracket or the 28 percent tax bracket saves an equivalent amount of tax. Conversely, a tax deduction only saves the taxpayer the amount of tax that would have been owed without the deduction. If a taxpayer is in the 28 percent tax bracket, each dollar of a deduction would save the taxpayer 28 cents in tax. On the other hand, if the taxpayer was in the 39.6 percent tax bracket, each dollar of a deduction would save that taxpayer approximately 40 cents in tax.

CHAPTER ENDNOTES

1. The Supreme Court has described deductions as a matter of "legislative grace." *INDOPCO, Inc. v. Comm'r*, 503 US 79, 84 (1992).
2. I.R.C. §56(b). For purposes of computing the alternative minimum tax, many below-the-deductions are essentially disallowed.
3. IRS Publication 598.
4. I.R.C. §163.
5. I.R.C. §164.
6. I.R.C. §165.
7. In addition to being a catch-all section for deductible business expenses, I.R.C. §162(a) also identifies three specific deductible expenses, i.e., compensation (§162(a)(1)), travel expenses while away from home (§162(a)(2)) and rental expenses (§162(a)(3)).
8. See *Henry v. Comm'r*, 36 T.C. 879 (1961).
9. See *United States v. Akin*, 248 F.2d 742 (10th Cir. 1957).
10. Treas. Reg. §1.162-1(a).
11. See I.R.C. §195.
12. See *Liddle v. Comm'r*, 103 T.C. 285 (1994).

13. I.R.C. §168(c). However, as an exception, by taxpayer election, I.R.C. §179 allows a generous deduction of the cost of certain depreciable property in year such property is placed in service. In 2013, the section 179 deduction limit was $500,000. However, for 2014, the deduction limit is to be reduced to $25,000. Additionally, a special 50 percent bonus depreciation deduction expired at the end of 2013. See H.R. 8 "The American Taxpayer Relief Act of 2012," 113th Cong. 2d Sess. (2014).
14. I.R.C. §195(b).
15. *See* Treas. Reg. §1.212-1(g).
16. Treas. Reg. §1.212-1(d).
17. I.R.C. §212(1).
18. I.R.C. §212(2).
19. I.R.C. §212(3).
20. I.R.C. §215.
21. I.R.C. §219.
22. I.R.C. §§221 and 222.
23. I.R.C. §217.
24. I.R.C. §164(f).
25. I.R.C. §162(l).
26. I.R.C. §401(c)(2).
27. I.R.C. §223.
28. I.R.C. §165.
29. I.R.C. §213.
30. I.R.C. §164.
31. I.R.C. §163.
32. I.R.C. §170.
33. Treas. Reg. §1.162-1(a).
34. I.R.C. §§274(k), 274(n).
35. However, the disallowed loss carries over into subsequent tax years subject to the same rules. So, if in year one, the taxpayer has a $1,000 disallowed passive activity loss, but in year two has $1,000 of passive activity income, the loss would be deductible in year two. I.R.C. §469(b).
36. If only a portion of the borrowed funds were used to purchase a tax-exempt bond, then an allocable portion of the investment income would be disallowed pursuant to section 265. The other portion of the borrowed funds used to purchase securities yielding taxable income would be deductible.
37. Conversely, some personal above-the-line deductions such as contributions to a traditional IRA are subject to phase-out.
38. I.R.C. §62(a)(1) and (2). Unreimbursed employee business expenses are out of pocket business expenses paid for by an employee but not reimbursed by the employer. However, there is an exception for unreimbursed educator expenses paid by elementary and secondary school teachers not in excess of $250. This exception was scheduled to expire on December 31, 2013.
39. I.R.C. §62(a)(4).
40. I.R.C. §1211(b).
41. I.R.C. §62(a)(3).
42. I.R.C. §62(a)(9).
43. I.R.C. §62(a)(10).
44. I.R.C. §62(a)(7).
45. I.R.C. §62(a)(17).
46. I.R.C. §62(a)(15).

47. I.R.C. §62(a)(18).

48. I.R.C. §§62(a)(1), 164(f).

49. IRS Publication 535. *See also* Gen. Couns. Mem. 200524001 (May 17, 2005).

50. I.R.C. §62(a)(6).

51. I.R.C. §62(a)(19)

52. I.R.C. §63. There is an additional standard deduction for taxpayers who are blind or age sixty-five or older. For 2014, the additional standard deduction is $1,200. If such taxpayer is unmarried and not a surviving spouse, the additional standard deduction is $1,550 rather than $1,200. *See* Rev. Proc. 2013-35, IRS News Release IR-2013-87 (Oct. 31, 2013). Certain taxpayers have a zero standard deduction, including: (1) married taxpayers filing separately, if either spouse itemizes; (2) non-resident aliens; (3) taxpayers filing a short year return (because of a change in their annual accounting period); *and* (4) estates or trusts, common trust funds, or partnerships.

53. The adjusted gross income threshold is subject to an adjustment for inflation. *See* I.R.C. §63(b). Rev. Proc. 2013-35, IRS News Release IR-2013-87 (Oct. 31, 2013).

54. I.R.C. §§68(c), 68(d). For purposes of certain other calculations (e.g., the limits on charitable contribution deductions and the 2 percent adjusted gross income floor on miscellaneous itemized deductions), the limitations on each separate category of deductions are applied *before* the overall ceiling on itemized deductions is applied.

55. I.R.C. §§151(a), 151(b).

56. I.R.C. §151(c).

57. I.R.C. §151(d)(4).

58. Treas. Reg. §1.152-1(b).

59. Rev. Proc. 2013-35, IRS News Release IR-2013-87 (Oct. 31, 2013).

60. I.R.C. §152.

61. I.R.C. §152(c)(4). *See also* Notice 2006-86, 2006-41 I.R.B. 680.

62. I.R.C. §152.

63. Treas. Reg. §1.152-1(a)(2).

64. I.R.C. §152(e)(5).

65. I.R.C. §152(d)(3) and (4).

CALCULATION OF TAX

CHAPTER 7

INTRODUCTION

The determination of a taxpayer's exact income tax liabilities is complex, but has three primary components. First a taxpayer must determine his or her filing status, which can vary based on a number of different factors related to the taxpayer's personal circumstances. The choice of filing status can have significant effects on the taxpayer's liability.

Second, the taxpayer must report all income received for the year. See Chapter 3 for a discussion of ordinary income reporting, and Chapter 4 for details about reporting capital gains and dividends. More details on the taxability of particular types of income are included below. A series of calculations are used to incorporate allowable deductions and exemptions (see Chapter 6) and arrive at taxable income.

Finally, a taxpayer's taxable income is used to determine his or her tax liability. Liability for ordinary income taxes is determined by using the tax tables published by the IRS annually. Once the tax liability is calculated, tax credits (See Chapter 8) and prepayments (from withholding and/or quarterly payments) are applied against the liability to determine the amount of money that is either owed to the IRS or due to the taxpayer as a refund.

In addition to ordinary income taxes, certain taxpayers may face several types of additional tax liabilities:

- *AMT*. Taxpayers with relatively high incomes may also have to calculate their liabilities under the Alternative Minimum Tax (AMT) See Chapter 25 for details on the AMT.

- *Self-employment taxes*. Self-employment taxes are levied on earned income to cover social security and Medicare taxes. For wage earners, these liabilities are satisfied through employer withholding, and calculation of the liability by the taxpayer is generally not necessary. Self-employed individuals must calculate and pay (indeed, often pre-pay) these amounts themselves. These tax liabilities are collectively known as the "self-employment tax." See Chapter 10 for details on self-employment taxes.

- *Additional Medicare surtax*. Taxpayers with earned income above certain thresholds are subject to an additional 0.9 percent Medicare surtax on income above the relevant threshold. See Chapter 11.

- *Net investment income tax*. The net investment income tax (NIIT) is also an additional surtax that is imposed on investment income that exceeds certain thresholds. See Chapter 11.

DETERMINATION OF FILING STATUS

The first step to filing a federal income tax return is the determination of the taxpayer's correct filing status. In addition to the proper amount of tax, filing status is used to determine a taxpayer's filing requirements, standard deduction, and eligibility for certain credits and deductions. Generally, filing status is determined by marital status on the last day of the year.[1] A tax payer must file under one of five statuses:

Single. Taxpayers are single if they are unmarried and do not qualify for another filing status. Taxpayers are considered unmarried for the whole year if, on the last day of your tax year, they were unmarried or legally separated from a spouse under a divorce or separate maintenance decree.

Married Filing Jointly. A married couple may file a return together using the married filing jointly status. The couple can choose this status if they are considered married (state law governs whether a couple is married) and both agree to file a joint return. On a joint return, both spouses report their combined income and deduct their combined allowable expenses. A couple can file a joint return even if one of the spouses had no income or deductions.

Married Filing Separately. A couple can choose married filing separately as their filing status if they are married. This filing status may benefit a couple if they want to be responsible only for their own tax, or if this status results in less tax than filing a joint return. If both spouses do not agree to file a joint return, they must use the married filing separately status unless one of the spouses qualifies for head of household status.

If a taxpayer qualifies to file as head of household, instead of as married filing separately, his or her tax may be lower, they may be able to claim the earned income credit and certain other credits, and their standard deduction will be higher.

Head of Household. This status generally applies if the taxpayer is not married, or is considered unmarried at the end of the year, and has paid more than half the cost of maintaining a home for him or herself and a qualifying person. A married taxpayer may file as head of household if he or she files a separate return and the spouse did not live in the home during the last six months of the tax year. A qualifying person is either:

- a "qualifying child" for the purposes of the child tax credit; or

- a "qualifying individual" for the purposes of Child and Dependent are Credit.

See Chapter 8 for detailed discussion of which individuals can be a "qualifying child" or "qualifying individual."

Qualifying Widow(er) with Dependent Child. A taxpayer with one or more dependents may be eligible to use qualifying widow(er) with dependent child as their filing status for two years following the death of a spouse. For example, if a taxpayer's spouse died in 2012, and the taxpayer has not remarried, he or she may be able to use this filing status for 2013 and 2014. This status is beneficial because the tax brackets and standard deduction amount are the same as the status for those married filing a joint return.[2]

Note that if the taxpayer has a same-sex spouse whom the taxpayer legally married in a state (or foreign country) that recognizes same-sex marriage, the taxpayer and his or her spouse generally must use the married filing jointly or married filing separately filing status on their return, even if they now live in a state (or foreign country) that does not recognize same-sex marriage.[3]

WHAT TYPES OF INCOME CALCULATIONS ARE REQUIRED?

Gross income is total of all amounts of a taxable income from all sources. (See below for types of taxable income.) *Adjusted gross income* (AGI) is determined by subtracting any above-the-line deductions from gross income. "Above-the-the" line deductions include:[4]

- Business expense deductions attributable to a trade, business, or profession carried on by the individual taxpayer as a self-employed person, not as an employee;[5]

- Deductions related to investment property held for the production of rents and royalties;[6]

- Losses from the sale or exchange of property;[7]

- Educator expenses;[8]

- IRA deduction;[9]

- Student loan interest;[10]

- Tuition and fees (see Chapter 8 for details on education credits);[11]

- Moving expenses;[12]

- One-half of the self-employment tax (as calculated on Schedule SE);[13]

- Self-employed medical savings account contributions;[14]

- Self-employed retirement plans;[15]

- Contributions to Health Savings Accounts;[16]

- Penalties on early withdrawal of savings;[17] and

- Alimony payments.[18]

See Chapter 3 for a more detailed discussion of the rules governing income calculations.

After calculating AGI, the final income calculation is *taxable income*, which is then used to determine a tax liability. "Taxable income" is AGI, less personal exemptions and any below-the-line deductions. Below-the-line deductions vary widely, and are often subject to restrictions and limitation on their use that may be based on a taxpayer's income level and/or filing status. When determining below-the-line deductions, taxpayers may use one of two methods:

- *Standard deduction.* Individuals may subtract from adjusted gross income an amount for each personal exemption allowable to the individual and the standard deduction (which varies with filing status).

- *Itemized deductions.* Individuals may subtract from adjusted gross income an amount for each personal exemption allowable to the individual and the total of their itemized deductions.

Using either method, the resulting figure is "taxable income." The actual amount of tax due is then determined by referring to the tax rate tables.[19] See Chapter 6 for a discussion of the types of above- and below-the-line deductions that are available.

TAXATION OF PARTICULAR TYPES OF INCOME

Code section 61 defines the types of income that may be taxable, subject to certain deductions and credits. These income types include, but are not limited to:

Compensation for services. This category includes fees, commissions, fringe benefits, and similar items. This category of income includes retirement plan contributions, stock options, restricted property (for example, stock with restrictions that affect its value), sick pay, advance commissions, bonuses and back pay awards, as well as tips. In most cases, a taxpayer must also report as income any amount received for personal injury or sickness through an employer-paid accident or health plan.[20]

Gross income derived from business. In a manufacturing, merchandising, or mining business, "gross income" means the total sales, less the cost of goods sold, plus any income from investments and from incidental or outside operations or sources.[21]

Gains derived from dealings in property. Gain realized on the sale or exchange of property is included in gross income, unless otherwise excluded. For this purpose, property includes tangible items (such as a building) and intangible items (such as goodwill). Generally, the gain is the excess of the amount realized over the unrecovered cost or other basis for the property sold or exchanged.[22] The specific rules for computing the amount of gain or loss are contained in Code section 1001 and related regulations.

Interest. Most interest that a taxpayer receives (interest on bank accounts, money market accounts, certificates of deposit, and deposited insurance dividends) is taxable income. Interest from treasury bonds is subject to federal income tax, but is exempt from all state and local income taxes. However, interest on some bonds used to finance government operations and issued by a state or territory, as well as interest in certain municipal bonds, is not taxable at the federal level.[23] Additionally, exempt-interest dividends received from a mutual fund or other regulated investment company, including those received from a qualified fund of funds in any tax year beginning after December 22, 2010, are not included in taxable income. Interest income is generally not subject to regular withholding. However, it may be subject to backup withholding to ensure that income tax is collected on the income.[24]

Rents. Rental income, defined as any payment that a taxpayer receives for the use or occupation of property, is includable in gross income. Rental income also includes amounts paid by a tenant to cancel a lease, any expenses of the taxpayer paid by the tenant, and the fair market value of property or services that the taxpayer receives instead of money.[25]

Royalties. Royalties from copyrights, patents, and oil, gas, and mineral properties are taxable as ordinary income. Royalties from copyrights on literary, musical, or artistic works and similar property, or from patents on inventions, are amounts paid to a taxpayer for the right to use his or her work over a specified period of time. Royalties generally are based on the number of units sold, such as the number of books, tickets to a performance, or machines sold. Royalty income from oil, gas, and mineral properties is the amount a taxpayer receives when natural resources are extracted from his or her property. The royalties are based on units, such as barrels, tons, etc., and are paid to the taxpayer by a person or company who leases the property.[26]

Dividends. Dividends—the most common type of distribution from a corporation—are distributions from a corporation to its shareholders. Most dividends are paid in cash but may be paid as stock of another corporation or any other property. A taxpayer might also receive dividends through their interest in a partnership, an estate, a trust, a subchapter S corporation, or from an association that is taxable as a corporation. A shareholder of a corporation may be deemed to receive a dividend if the corporation pays the debt of its shareholder, the shareholder receives services from the corporation, or the shareholder is allowed the use of the corporation's property. Additionally, a shareholder that provides services to a corporation may be deemed to receive a dividend if the corporation pays the shareholder service-provider in excess of what it would pay a third party for the same services. A shareholder may also receive distributions such as additional stock or stock rights in the distributing corporation; such distributions may or may not qualify as dividends. Dividends can either be classified as ordinary or qualified. Whereas ordinary dividends are taxable as ordinary income, qualified dividends that meet certain requirements are taxed at lower capital gain rates.[27]

Alimony and separate maintenance payments. Alimony is a payment to or for a spouse or former spouse under a divorce or separation order. Alimony must be included in the spouse's or former spouse's income. Amounts paid under divorce or separate maintenance decrees or written separation agreements entered into between the taxpayer and his or her present or former spouse will be considered alimony for federal tax purposes if:

- The taxpayer and spouse or former spouse do not file a joint return with each other;

- The payor of the alimony makes payment in cash (including checks or money orders);

- The payment is received by (or on behalf of) the spouse or former spouse;

- The divorce or separate maintenance decree or written separation agreement does not say that the payment is not alimony;

- If legally separated under a decree of divorce or separate maintenance, the spouses or former spouses are not members of the same household when the alimony payment is made;

- The taxpayer has no liability to make the payment (in cash or property) after the death of their spouse or former spouse; and

- The payment is not treated as child support or a property settlement.[28]

Pensions and Annuities. If a taxpayer receives retirement benefits in the form of pension or annuity payments from a qualified employer retirement plan, all or some portion of the amounts received may be taxable. Even for payments that are taxable at the federal level, some states have special rules that reduce or eliminate state income taxes on pension payments. The payments that the taxpayer receives are fully taxable if the taxpayer has no investment in the contract because any of the following situations apply:

- The taxpayer did not contribute anything— or is not considered to have contributed anything—for the pension or annuity;

- The taxpayer's employer did not withhold contributions from the taxpayer's salary; or

- The taxpayer received all of his or her contributions (the investment in the contract) tax-free in prior years.

If the taxpayer contributed after-tax dollars to his or her pension or annuity, the pension payments are partially taxable. No tax is payable on the part of the payment that represents a return of the after-tax amount the taxpayer paid. This amount is his or her investment in the contract, and includes the amounts the employer contributed that were taxable to the taxpayer when contributed.[29]

Income from life insurance and endowment contracts. Life insurance proceeds paid to a taxpayer beneficiary by reason of the death of the insured person are not taxable unless the policy was turned over to the taxpayer for a price. This is true even if the proceeds were paid under an accident or health insurance policy or an endowment contract. However, interest income received as a result of life insurance proceeds may be taxable. If death benefits are paid to the taxpayer in a lump sum or other than at regular intervals, only the benefits that are more than the amount payable to you at the time of the insured person's death are includable in income. If the benefit payable at death is not specified, benefit payments that are more than the present value of the premium payments at the time of death are included in income.

Life insurance proceeds that are received in installments are partly excludable from the taxpayer beneficiary's income. To determine the excluded part, the total lump sum payable at the death of the insured person is divided by the number of installments to be paid. Anything in excess of this excluded part is includable in income as interest.

If a life insurance policy is surrendered for cash, any proceeds that are more than the cost of the life insurance policy are includable in income. In most cases, the cost of the policy is the total of premiums paid, less any refunded premiums, rebates, dividends, or unrepaid loans that were not included in income.

Proceeds of an endowment contract that are paid in a lump sum on the contract's maturity are taxable only if the proceeds are more than the cost of the policy. The taxable amount is determined by subtracting any untaxed amount previously received under the contract from the total premiums (or other consideration) paid.[30]

Income from discharge of indebtedness. In general, a taxpayer is liable for a debt that is cancelled, forgiven, or discharged, and must include the canceled amount in gross income. Certain types of cancelled debt outlined in Code section 108 qualify for an exclusion from the taxpayer's income. Cancellation of all or part of a debt that is secured by property may occur because of a foreclosure, repossession, voluntary return of the property to the lender, abandonment of the property, or a loan modification. If the debt is secured by property and that property is taken by the lender in full or partial satisfaction of the debt, the taxpayer is treated as having sold that property and may have a taxable gain or loss.[31] See Chapter 32 for a detailed discussion of cancellation of debt issues.

Distributive share of partnership gross income. A partner's gross income includes his or her distributive share of the partnership's gross income. Generally, the partnership agreement determines a partner's distributive share of any item or class of items of income, gain, loss, deduction, or credit. However, the allocations provided for in the partnership agreement or any modification

will be disregarded if they do not have substantial economic effect. If the partnership agreement does not provide for an allocation, or an allocation does not have substantial economic effect, the partner's distributive share of the partnership items is generally determined by the partner's interest in the partnership.[32]

Income in respect of a decedent. All income a decedent would have received had death not occurred and that was not properly includible on the final return, filed by the decedent's personal representative for the year of death, is income in respect of a decedent. Such income must be included in the income of one of the following:

- The decedent's estate, if the estate receives it;

- The beneficiary, if the right to income is passed directly to the beneficiary and the beneficiary receives it; or

- Any person to whom the estate properly distributes the right to receive it.[33]

Income from an interest in an estate or trust. Interest received as a beneficiary of an estate or trust is generally taxable income. The beneficiary should receive a Schedule K-1 (Form 1041), from the fiduciary with information that needs to be reported on a Form 1040.[34]

Social security benefits include monthly retirement, survivor, and disability benefits. They do not include supplemental security income (SSI) payments, which are not taxable. Equivalent tier 1 railroad retirement benefits are the part of tier 1 benefits that a railroad employee or beneficiary would have been entitled to receive under the social security system. They are commonly called the "social security equivalent benefit" (SSEB) portion of tier 1 benefits.

If the taxpayer is married and files a joint return for the year, the taxpayer and his or her spouse must combine their incomes and benefits to figure whether any of their combined benefits are taxable. Even if the spouse did not receive any benefits, the taxpayer must add the spouse's income to figure whether any of the benefits are taxable. If the only income the taxpayer received during the year was his or her social security or the SSEB portion of tier 1 railroad retirement benefits, the benefits he or she received generally are not taxable and the taxpayer probably does not have to file a return. If the taxpayer has income in addition to the social security (or railroad retirement) benefits, he or she may have to file a return even if none of the benefits are taxable.

To determine whether any of a taxpayer's benefits may be taxable, he or she should compare the base amount for his filing status (explained below) with the total of: (1) One-half of his benefits, plus (2) All of his other income, including tax-exempt interest. When making this comparison, the taxpayer's other income is not reduced by any exclusions for: Interest from qualified U.S. savings bonds, Employer-provided adoption benefits, Foreign earned income or foreign housing, or Income earned by bona fide residents of American Samoa or Puerto Rico.

As described above, the base amount is:

- $25,000 if the taxpayer is single, head of household, or qualifying widow(er);

- $25,000 if the taxpayer is married filing separately and lived apart from his or her spouse for all of the year;

- $32,000 if the taxpayer is married filing jointly; or

- $0 if the taxpayer is married filing separately and lived with his or her spouse at any time during the year.[35]

Other income may include such items as income received in barter exchanges, income received at sales parties, certain repayments, etc. For a discussion of other and miscellaneous income, see Chapter 12 of IRS Publication 17, *Your Income Tax.*

WHERE CAN I FIND OUT MORE?

Tax Facts on Insurance & Employee Benefits (National Underwriter Company).

CHAPTER ENDNOTES

1. IRS Publication 17 (2013), chap. 2; Internal Revenue Manual §21.6.1.1-6.
2. I.R.C. §1; IRS Publication 17 (2013), IRS Tax Tip 2013-13 (Feb. 13, 2013).
3. IRS Publication 17 (2013).
4. I.R.C. §62(a).
5. I.R.C. §162.
6. I.R.C. §212.
7. I.R.C. §§1211, 1222.
8. I.R.C. §62(a)(2)(D).
9. I.R.C. §219.
10. I.R.C. §221.
11. I.R.C. §222.
12. I.R.C. §217.
13. I.R.C. §164(f).
14. I.R.C. §220.
15. I.R.C. §404.
16. I.R.C. §223.
17. I.R.C. §62(a)(9)165.
18. I.R.C. §215.
19. Tax tables for individual taxpayers can be found in the instructions for IRS Form 1040.
20. I.R.C. §61(a)(1).
21. I.R.C. §61(a)(2); Treas. Reg. §1.61-3(a).
22. I.R.C. §61(a)(3); Treas. Reg. §1.61-6(a).
23. IRS Tax Topic 403.
24. I.R.C. §61(a)(4); IRS Publication 17, chap. 17.
25. I.R.C. §61(a)(5); IRS Tax Topic 414.
26. I.R.C. §61(a)(6); Treas. Reg. § 1.512(b)-1; IRS Fact Sheet 2013-6 (April 2013).
27. I.R.C. §61(a)(7); IRS Tax Topic 404. See IRS Publication 550 for a definition of qualified dividends.
28. I.R.C. §61(a)(8); IRS Tax Topic 452.
29. I.R.C. §§61(a)(9), (a)(11); IRS Tax Topic 410.
30. I.R.C. §61(a)(10); IRS Publication 17 (2013), chap. 12.
31. I.R.C. §§61(a)(12), 108; Treas. Reg. §1.108-2; IRS Tax Topic 431.
32. I.R.C. §§61(a)(13), 704; Treas. Regs. §§ 1.61-13, 1.704-1(b)(2)(ii).
33. I.R.C. §61(a)(14); IRS Publication 559 (2013).
34. I.R.C. §61(a)(15); IRS Publication 17 (2013).
35. IRS Publication 17 (2013).

CREDITS

CHAPTER 8

INTRODUCTION

After the income tax has been computed by applying the tax rates to taxable income, certain credits and prepayments may be used to reduce the tax that is otherwise due. A *credit* represents a dollar-for dollar reduction of tax.

All tax credits are *refundable* or *nonrefundable*. *Refundable* credits are recoverable regardless of the amount of the taxpayer's tax liability for the taxable year. In other words, the taxpayer might get money back (a "refund") if the amount of the credit is more than the amount of tax due. On the other hand, *nonrefundable* credits may be used only to reduce the taxpayer's tax liability, and are subject to certain other limitations. The *refundable* credits and prepayments include:

- Taxes withheld on wages;

- Payments of estimated tax;

- Earned income credit;[1]

- a credit for health insurance premiums paid by uninsured workers who were displaced by trade competition.[2]

The first two refundable credits are simply refunds of money paid in advance by the taxpayer that was not required to meet his or her tax obligations. The earned income credit is discussed below. Additionally, some nonrefundable credits may become partially refundable under certain circumstances.

EARNED INCOME TAX CREDIT

The Earned Income Tax Credit (EITC) is a refundable tax credit that is designed to help the working poor.

Because it targets household income, it has been called a "remarkably effective anti-poverty program."[3]

To qualify for the EITC, the taxpayer (and spouse if married filing jointly), must meet all of the following requirements:[4]

1. Have a Social Security number that is valid for employment;

2. Have earned income from wages, self-employment, or some other source;

3. Must file jointly if married;

4. Must be either:

    a. a U.S. citizen or resident alien all year, or

    b. a nonresident alien married to a U.S. citizen or resident alien who files a joint return and chooses to be treated as a resident alien;

5. Cannot be the qualifying child of another person;

6. Cannot file Form 2555 or 2555-EZ (related to foreign earned income);

7. Investment income must not exceed $3,350 for the year; and

8. For 2014, earned income and adjusted gross income (AGI) must each be less than:

    a. $46,997 ($52,427 married filing jointly) with three or more qualifying children;

    b. $43,756 ($49,186 married filing jointly) with two qualifying children;

c. $38,511 ($43,941 married filing jointly) with one qualifying child; or

d. $14,590 ($20,020 married filing jointly) with no qualifying child.

If all of the preceding rules are satisfied, the IRS sets out the maximum credit that may be included on a taxpayer's return. These amounts are based on the number of qualifying children in the taxpayer's household. The amounts change every year. For 2014, the maximum credit is:[5]

Three or more qualifying children	$6,143
Two qualifying children	$5,460
One qualifying child	$3,305
No qualifying children	$496

For purposes of the EITC, a qualifying child must have a valid Social Security Number and meet certain relationship, age, residency, and joint return tests[6] outlined in Figure 8.1.

When a child is a qualifying child for more than one person, "tie breaker" rules apply. These rules do not apply to a spouse filing a joint tax return. Under the tie-breaker rules, the child is treated as a qualifying child only by:

- The parents if they file a joint return;

- The parent, if only one of the persons is the child's parent;

- The parent with whom the child lived the longest during the tax year, if two of the persons are the child's parent and they do not file a joint return together;

- The parent with the highest AGI if the child lived with each parent for the same amount of time during the tax year and they do not file a joint return together;

- The person with the highest AGI if no parent can claim the child as a qualifying child; or

Figure 8.1

REQUIREMENTS FOR QUALIFYING CHILDREN UNDER THE EITC	
Relationship Test	• Must be a son, daughter, adopted child, stepchild, foster child, brother, sister, half-brother, half-sister, stepbrother, stepsister or descendant of any of them (i.e. grandchild, niece or nephew). • "Adopted children" include children lawfully placed with the taxpayer who is filing for adoption. • "Foster children" include children placed with the taxpayer by an authorized placement agency or court. • Relationships formed by marriage (stepdaughter, stepson, etc.), do not end when the marriage that formed the relationship ends.
Age Test	• Must be younger than 19 at the end of the year (or 24 if a full-time student), and younger than the taxpayer (or their spouse if filing a joint return); or • Any age if permanently and totally disabled.
Residency Test	• Must live with the taxpayer (or their spouse if filing a joint tax return) for more than half of the year. Time spent temporarily away from home due to special circumstances (school, illness, military service, etc.) is counted as time the child lived with the taxpayer.
Joint Return Test	• The child cannot file a joint return for the tax year unless the child and the child's spouse did not have a separate filing requirement and filed the joint return to claim a refund only. • A taxpayer cannot claim the EITC credit for a child who was married at the end of the year unless the child can be claimed as a dependent. Exceptions are available for children who could have been claimed as a dependent, but for an agreement to not claim the child contained in a Form 8332 or similar statement.

- The person with the higher AGI than any parent who can also claim the child as a qualifying child but does not.

Additionally, IRS Publication 501 outlines special rules for children of divorced or separated parents.

NONREFUNDABLE CREDITS

As mentioned above, nonrefundable credits can only be used to reduce a tax obligation from reported income. If a taxpayer has reduced his or her in come to zero and still has nonrefundable credits available, those excess credits cannot be used. Nonrefundable credits generally fall into two different categories: business and personal. Business credits are complex and technical, and are available in a wide variety of circumstances that are beyond the scope of this chapter.[7]

Personal credits include allow a taxpayer to reduce his or her tax obligations for a variety of reasons, including credits for children and other dependents who reside with the taxpayer, college-related expenses, and a "saver's credit"[8] available for contributions towards retirement savings that are made under certain circumstances. The foreign tax credit is also a personal credit that is available for taxes that were paid to foreign countries, and may apply to both businesses and individual taxpayers.[9]

Child Tax Credit

Eligible taxpayers who meet certain requirements may claim a child tax credit for each "qualifying child." While this credit is generally nonrefundable, a portion of it may be refundable under certain circumstances discussed below.

Through 2017, the amount of the child tax credit is $1,000.[10] Beginning in 2018, the child tax credit will decrease to $500.[11] A qualifying child is an individual who:

- is the taxpayer's son, daughter, stepchild, foster child, brother, sister, stepbrother, or stepsister (or a descendant of any of them);

- is less than seventeen years old;

- has the same principal place of abode as the taxpayer for more than one-half of the taxable year; *and*

- has not provided over one-half of such individual's own support for the calendar year in which the taxpayer's taxable year begins.[12]

A qualifying child must also be a citizen or resident of the United States.[13] Any adopted children are treated the same as natural born children.[14] The taxpayer's return must identify the individual for whom the credit is being claimed by stating the child's name *and* taxpayer identification number (i.e., Social Security number). The child tax credit must generally be claimed for a full taxable year.[15]

Limitations

The basic child tax credit is "phased out" (i.e., reduced) depending on the taxpayer's *modified* adjusted gross income (MAGI).[16] For this purpose, MAGI consists of the taxpayer's adjusted gross income *plus* any income earned from foreign sources or United States possessions.[17] Specifically, the child tax credit is reduced by $50 for every $1000 (or fraction thereof) by which the taxpayer's MAGI exceeds the following threshold amounts:

- $110,000 for married taxpayers filing joint returns;

- $75,000 for single filers; or

- $55,000 for married taxpayers filing separately.[18]

Refundability of the Child Tax Credit

The child tax credit is generally refundable for all taxpayers to the extent of 15 percent of the taxpayer's earned income in excess of $3,000.[19] This refundable amount is also known as the "additional child tax credit." There is an alternative way of computing the additional child tax credit for families with three or more qualifying children that may increase the amount to the credit which is refundable.[20]

Child and Dependent Care Credit

An individual may claim a credit for certain employment-related child and dependent care expenses.[21] The amount of the credit is up to 35 percent of expenses incurred for the care of a "qualifying individual" who is:

- a qualifying child of the taxpayer who is under age thirteen, and for whom the taxpayer is entitled to take a dependency exemption (see Chapter 4);

- a physically or mentally incapacitated dependent (including a spouse);[22] or

- a person who would have been the taxpayer's dependent but for the fact that his or her income was more than $3,900 or the person filed a joint return.[23]

Payments for dependent care services are "employment-related" *if* they are incurred to enable the taxpayer to be employed or to seek employment (full or part-time).[24] Expenses for service outside the taxpayer's household qualify if they are for a qualifying child or a qualifying individual who regularly spends at least eight hours each day in the taxpayer's household.[25] However, no amount of any expenses for an overnight camp will be considered "employment-related."[26] Payments for child or dependent care to a close relative qualify for the credit if:

- neither the taxpayer nor his spouse is entitled to claim the relative as a dependent; *and*

- the relative is not a child of the taxpayer who is younger than age nineteen at the close of the taxable year.[27]

The name, address, and taxpayer identification number of the childcare provider must be stated on the taxpayer's return in order to claim the credit.[28] The Social Security number of the qualifying individual must also be included on the return in order to claim the credit.

Married couples must file a joint return in order to claim the credit. If the child's parents are divorced, and between them they (1) provide more than one-half of the child's support for the calendar year, *and* (2) have custody of the child for more than one-half of the calendar year, the child will be treated as a qualifying individual for the *custodial parent* (i.e., the one having custody for the greater portion of the year).[29]

Limitations

If the individual's adjusted gross income exceeds $15,000, the individual must reduce the 35 percent credit by one percentage point for each $2,000 (or fraction thereof) by which his adjusted gross income for the taxable year

exceeds that amount. However, the reduction cannot exceed fifteen percentage points.[30] Consequently, for taxpayers with adjusted gross incomes of more than $43,000, the credit is 20 percent of qualifying expenses. The credit is also limited by the number of qualifying individuals. The credit taken may not exceed $3,000 for one qualifying individual or $6,000 for two or more qualifying individuals.

Finally, eligible expenses may not exceed the taxpayer's earned income (or the spouse's earned income, if smaller).[31] If an individual's employer provides a dependent care assistance program, the individual must reduce the amount of the allowable credit by any amounts excluded from income under the dependent care assistance program exclusion.[32] In the case of a spouse who is a full time student, the spouse is deemed to earn $250 per month in the case of one individual ($500 per month in the case of two or more individuals).[33]

Generally, the credit for employment-related expenses is allowable only for expenses which are both incurred and actually paid during the taxable year, regardless of the taxpayer's method of accounting.[34]

CREDIT FOR THE ELDERLY AND DISABLED

A nonrefundable credit for the elderly and disabled is available to individuals who are at least sixty-five years old or permanently and totally disabled.[35] An individual may be required to furnish proof of continuing disability.[36] The credit that can be applied is 15 percent of a qualified individual's "section 22 base amount" for the taxable year.[37] The section 22 base amount is:

- $5,000 for a single taxpayer (or married taxpayers filing jointly if only one spouse qualifies for the credit);

- $7,500 for married taxpayers filing jointly if both qualify; and

- $3,750 for married taxpayers filing separately.[38]

Married persons must generally file a joint return in order to claim the credit.[39]

Limitations

The section 22 base amount is subject to limitations. For individuals under age sixty-five, the base figure cannot exceed the amount of disability income received during the taxable year. "Disability income" is the taxable amount an individual receives under an employer plan as wages or payments in lieu of wages for the period he is absent from work on account of permanent and total disability.[40]

If benefits are received under a plan to which the employee has contributed, the portion of the disability income attributable to the *employer's* contribution is taxable, but the portion attributable to the *employee's* contribution is tax-free, and therefore would not limit the section 22 base amount.[41]

For married taxpayers filing jointly, if both are under age sixty-five, the base figure cannot exceed the amount of both spouses' disability income combined. However, if only one spouse is under age sixty-five, the base amount is limited to the sum of $5,000 *plus* the disability income of the spouse who is under age sixty-five for the taxable year.

In addition, the base figure (or the amount of disability income in the case of individuals under age sixty-five if that is less) is reduced by one-half of adjusted gross income in excess of the following amounts:

- $7,500 for single taxpayers;

- $10,000 for married taxpayers filing joint returns; *or*

- $5,000 for married taxpayers filing separately.[42]

A reduction is also made dollar-for-dollar for tax-exempt Social Security and railroad retirement benefits, as well as certain tax-exempt income.[43]

EDUCATION CREDITS

Two types of credits are available if a taxpayer or his or her dependents incurred college expenses: the American Opportunity Tax Credit (which replaced the Hope Scholarship Credit) and the Lifetime Learning Credit.[44] While the credits are generally nonrefundable, under certain circumstances a portion of them may be refundable. These credits, and the applicable limitations and phase-outs, are described below and summarized in Figure 8.2.

American Opportunity Tax Credit

The American Recovery and Reinvestment Act of 2009[45] included the partially refundable American Opportunity Tax Credit (AOTC) to pay for higher education expenses. The AOTC renamed the existing HOPE education tax credit and modified it by making the credit available to a broader range of taxpayers, including many with higher incomes. It also added required course materials to the list of qualifying expenses and allows the credit to be claimed for four post-secondary education years instead of two.

The amount of the American opportunity credit (per eligible student) is the sum of:

(1) 100 percent of the first $2,000 of qualified education expenses paid for the eligible student; and

(2) 25 percent of the next $2,000 of qualified education expenses paid for that student.

The maximum credit amount is $2,500 per eligible student. Additionally, 40 percent of the credit is refundable.[46] To be eligible for the AOTC, a student must:

- be enrolled in a program leading toward a degree, certificate or other recognized post-secondary educational credential;

- have not completed the first four years of post-secondary education as of the beginning of the taxable year;

- carry at least half of the normal full-time work load for the course of study the student is pursuing for at least one academic period; and

- have not been convicted of a felony drug offense.[47]

Limitations

The full credit is available to individuals whose MAGI is $80,000 or less ($160,000 for married couples filing a joint return). The credit is gradually phased out for taxpayers with incomes above these levels, and taxpayers with MAGI exceeding $90,000 ($180,000 for joint filers) cannot claim the credit.

Lifetime Learning Credit

The Lifetime Learning Credit (LLC) provides a nonrefundable tax credit equal to 20 percent of up to $10,000 of qualified tuition and related expenses paid during the taxable year for education furnished to the taxpayer, the taxpayer's spouse, and any claimed dependent. The expenses must be incurred for an academic period beginning in the taxable year (or treated as beginning in the taxable year).[48]

The LLC is a completely nonrefundable credit, meaning that it can reduce tax obligations to zero, but any excess will not be refunded to the taxpayer. Unlike the American Opportunity Tax Credit, there is no limit on the number of years the lifetime learning credit can be claimed for each student. The credit is available for all years of postsecondary education and for courses to acquire or improve job skills.[49]

Generally, the lifetime credit may be claimed by the taxpayer if the taxpayer pays qualified higher education expenses, such expenses are paid for an eligible student, and the eligible student is either the taxpayer, the taxpayer's spouse, or a dependent for whom the taxpayer claims an exemption on the taxpayer's tax return.

An academic period includes a semester, trimester, quarter, or other period of study (such as a summer school session) as reasonably determined by an educational institution. In the case of an educational institution that uses credit hours or clock hours and does not have academic terms, each payment period can be treated as an academic period.[50]

Limitations

The amount of the credit is phased out if the taxpayer's modified adjusted gross income (MAGI) is between $53,000 and $63,000 ($107,000 and $127,000 for joint returns).[51] Additionally, the LLC is unavailable if any of the following apply:

- The taxpayer's filing status is married filing separately.

- The taxpayer is listed as a dependent on another person's tax return (such as the taxpayer's parents').

- The taxpayer (or his or her spouse) was a nonresident alien for any part of the year and did not elect to be treated as a resident alien for tax purposes.

- The taxpayer claims the American Opportunity Credit or a Tuition and Fees Deduction for the same student in 2013.[52]

Example: The taxpayer files a joint return with a MAGI of $112,000. In 2013, he paid $6,600 of qualified education expenses. He calculates the tentative lifetime learning credit to be a $1,320 (20 percent of $6,600).

Because his MAGI is within the range of incomes where the credit must be reduced, taxpayer must reduce his LLC credit proportionally based on the amount by which his MAGI exceeds the lower threshold. The result is that the amount of taxpayer's phased-out lifetime learning credit is $990.

Tentative LLC credit	$1,320
Phase-out fraction	$\dfrac{\$127,000 - \$112,000}{\$20,000} = .75$
Reduced LLC credit	$\$1,320 \times .75 = \$990$

Prohibition on Double Benefits

The Code contains several restrictions on using the education credits in combination with one another. First, the LLC cannot be claimed on education expenses that are paid for with funds from a Coverdell education savings account (ESA), qualified tuition program (QTP), or any type of tax-free educational assistance (such as a scholarship, grant, or assistance provided by an employer).[53]

Additionally, if a taxpayer claims the LLC for particular education expenses, those same expenses cannot be used to claim the following education-related credits and deductions in addition to the LLC:

- A general deduction for higher education expenses (as, for example, a business expense);

- A tuition and fees deduction under Code section 222; and

- The AOTC.

Other Personal Credits

Adoption credit. The adoption credit is available to individuals who pay or incur qualified adoption expenses in connection with the adoption of a child.[54] The maximum amount of the qualified adoption credit is $123,190 in 2014 per child for qualified adoption expenses paid. For 2014, the credit is phased out for taxpayers with MAGI between $194,580 and $234,580.[55]

Figure 8.2

	AOTC	LLC
Limit	$2,500 per student	$2,000
Covers	First 4 years of post-secondary ed.	Unlimited number of years
AGI Phase-out	$80,000–$90,000 single $160,000–$180,000 married	$53,000–$63,000 single $107,000–$127,000 married

Energy credits. For an overview of the energy-related credits for homeowners and car buyers, see Appendix C.

Foreign credit. The taxpayer is allowed a credit (or a deduction) for foreign income taxes paid or accrued.[56] The credit is subject to limitations.[57] Essentially the credit is limited to the United States rate of tax applied to the ratio of the foreign income compared to the taxpayer's worldwide income. In addition, income must be classified into "baskets" based on the type of income generated (passive, general).[58] For most individuals who are not employed overseas, their only foreign income will be from international investments generally included in the passive basket and the taxes will have been withheld in the foreign jurisdiction. Foreign credits not used in the current year are not refundable, but are instead carried back two years and then forward five years.

AMT CREDITS

Under conventional tax law, a taxpayer can use exclusions of certain kinds of income, and deductions and credits for certain expenses to significantly reduce tax liabilities. The alternative minimum tax (AMT) attempts to ensure that individuals and corporations that benefit from certain exclusions, deductions, or credits pay at least a minimum amount of tax. The AMT does so by establishing a completely separate set of calculations from the regular tax. These calculations do not contain a personal exemption, standard deduction, or many itemized deductions. If the tax benefits would reduce total tax below the AMT limit, the taxpayer must pay the higher AMT amount.[59]

To calculate the AMT for an individual, various tax preference items are added back into taxable income. This "grossed up" amount then becomes the tax base for the AMT. Next, the amount of the basic exemption ($52,800 per individual and $82,100 for joint filers in 2014) is subtracted from the AMT tax base. A two-tiered tax rate structure of 26% and 28% is then assessed against the remaining AMT tax base to determine AMT tax liability. The taxpayer then pays whichever is greater: his regular income tax liability or the AMT tax liability.[60] Importantly, many of the tax credits normally used to lower taxable income are reduced or eliminated when calculating the AMT (see Figure 8.3).

Figure 8.3

CREDITS THAT ARE REDUCED OR ELIMINATED FOR AMT INCOME CALCULATIONS

Eliminated Credits	Reduced Credits
Any general business credit (listed in Code section Sec. 38(b) and the instructions to IRS Form 3800, General Business Credit)	Child credit (up to $1,000 per child)[61]
Qualified electric vehicle credit	Energy credit (30% of the cost of certain fuel cell and energy property)[62]
The personal use part of the alternative fuel vehicle refueling property credit	Credit for foreign taxes[63]
The credit for prior year minimum tax[64]	Specified credits under IRC Sec. 38(c)(4) (i.e., alcohol fuel credit)[65]
	Alternative motor vehicle credit, including the tax credit for purchasing hybrid vehicles[66]

In addition to the preceding credits, a special minimum tax credit is allowed if a taxpayer is not liable for AMT in the current year, but paid AMT in one or more previous years. In this case, the taxpayer may be eligible to take the special minimum credit against his or her regular tax in the current year.[67]

Techniques for Reducing or Eliminating the AMT

The best way to reduce the AMT liability is to shift income or deductions in ways that facilitate reduction in regular and AMT taxes. For instance, because real estate and personal property taxes are not deductible for AMT if they are included in itemized deductions, a taxpayer who otherwise qualifies for the home office deduction can deduct part of these taxes on his or her 1040 Schedule C (Profit or Loss from Business), and such taxes will then be allowed to offset to the AMT. The same is true for taxes deductible on rental schedule (Schedule E), or farm schedule (Schedule F or Form 4835).

Additionally, added pre-tax 401(k) contributions and charitable donations reduce both taxable income and AMT. Cafeteria plans and flexible savings accounts—if offered by a taxpayer's employer and used to pay eligible medical or child-care expenses—will also reduce the taxpayer's reportable income.

When these strategies are used in combination with available tax credits the additional tax bite imposed by the AMT can be reduced or eliminated.

WHERE CAN I FIND OUT MORE ?

Tax Facts on Life Insurance & Employee Benefits (National Underwriter Company).[68]

CHAPTER ENDNOTES

1. I.R.C. §32.
2. I.R.C. §35.
3. Michael R. Strain, resident scholar in economic policy studies, American Enterprise Institute.
4. IRS Publication 596 (2013).
5. IRS Preview of 2014 EITC Income Limits, Maximum Credit Amounts and Tax Law Updates.
6. IRS Publication 3211 (Rev. Jan. 2014).
7. I.R.C. §38(b). The general business credit also includes the portion of the alternative motor vehicle credit to which 30B(g)(1) applies and the portion of the alternative fuel vehicle refueling property credit to which I.R.C. Section 30C(d)(1) applies. The general business credits are listed in I.R.C. §38(b) and in the instructions to Form 3800 ("General Business Credits").
8. I.R.C. §§21, 22, 23, 24, 25A, and 25B.
9. I.R.C. §901.
10. Economic Growth and Tax Relief Reconciliation Act, the Tax Relief, Unemployment Insurance Reauthorization and Job Creation Act of 2010, and the American Tax Relief Act.
11. EGTRRA 2001, §901.
12. I.R.C. §§24(c)(1), 152(a), 152(c).
13. I.R.C. §24(c)(2).
14. I.R.C. §152(f)(1)(B).
15. I.R.C. §§24(e), 24(f). An exception applies if the taxable year is cut short by the death of the taxpayer.
16. I.R.C. §24(b).
17. I.R.C. §§911, 931, 933.
18. I.R.C. §24(b)(2).
19. I.R.C. §§24(d)(3), 24(d)(1); I.R.C. §24(d)(4); Rev. Proc. 2008-66, 2008-45 IRB 1107.
20. I.R.C. §24(d)(1); Rev. Proc. 2008-66, 2008-45 IRB 1107.
21. I.R.C. §21(a)(1).
22. I.R.C. §§21(a)(2), 21(b)(1).
23. IRS Publication 503 (2013), p. 3.
24. I.R.C. §21(b)(2); Treas. Reg. §1.44A-1(c).
25. I.R.C. §21(b)(2).
26. I.R.C. §21(b)(2).
27. I.R.C. §21(e)(6).
28. I.R.C. §21(e)(9).
29. I.R.C. §21(e)(5); Treas. Reg. §1.21-1(b)(5). This rule applies even if the noncustodial parent claims the dependency exemption.
30. I.R.C. §21(a)(2).
31. I.R.C. §21(d).
32. I.R.C. §21(c).
33. I.R.C. §21(d)(2).
34. Treas. Reg. § 1.44A-1(a)(3).
35. I.R.C. §22(b).
36. See, e.g., Let. Rul. 8034008; Gen. Couns. Mem. 39269; S. Rep. No. 94938, 94th Cong., 2d Sess. 137 (1976), 1976-3 CB 175. Per I.R.C. §22(e)(3), "Permanent and total disability" means the inability "to engage in any substantial gainful activity by reason of any medically determinable physical or mental impairment which can be expected to result in death or which has lasted or can be expected to last for a continuous period of not less than twelve months."
37. I.R.C. §§22(a), 26.
38. I.R.C. §§22(c)(2)(A), 22(e)(1).
39. I.R.C. §22(e). An exception to the general rule applies if they live apart at all times during the taxable year.
40. I.R.C. §22(c)(2)(B)(iii).
41. I.R.C. §105(a).

42. I.R.C. §22(d).

43. I.R.C. §22(c)(3).

44. I.R.C. §25A.

45. I.R.C. §25A(b). The American Taxpayer Relief Act of 2012 extended the AOTC through December 2017.

46. I.R.C. §25A(h)(5).

47. Treas. Reg. §1.25A-3(d).

48. I.R.C. §25A(c); Treas. Reg. § 1.25A-4(a). The credit is allowed for qualified education expenses paid for an academic period beginning in the tax year or in the first three months of the following tax year (e.g. a "spring" semester beginning in January, which may have expenses that are paid either before or after December 31).

49. IRS Publication 970 "Tax Benefits for Education" (2013).

50. Treas. Reg. § 1.25A-2(c).

51. IRS Publication 970 "Tax Benefits for Education" (2013).

52. *Ibid.*

53. *Ibid.*, p. 21.

54. I.R.C. §23(a)(1).

55. I.R.C. §23(b)(1); Rev. Proc. 2008-66, 2008-45 IRB 1107.

56. I.R.C. §901(a).

57. I.R.C. §904(a).

58. I.R.C. §904(d). The two "baskets" (passive category income and general category income) are effective for tax years beginning after December 31, 2006. Prior to January 1, 2007, there were nine baskets of income.

59. IRS Tax Topic 556 – Alternative Minimum Tax.

60. I.R.C. §55(b). See also Congressional Research Service Report 7-5700 "The Alternative Minimum Tax for Individuals" by Steven Maguire (Sept. 20, 2012).

61. I.R.C. §24.

62. I.R.C. §48.

63. I.R.C. §59.

64. Instructions to Form 6251, "Alternative Minimum Tax – Individuals."

65. I.R.C. §40.

66. I.R.C. §30.

67. I.R.C. §53. Form 8801 determines the amount of the AMT related to deferral items, which generate credit for future years. This credit is available for individuals, trusts, and estates.

68. To order, call 1-800-543-0874, or visit: www.nationalunderwriter.com.

ALTERNATIVE MINIMUM TAX

CHAPTER 9

INTRODUCTION

The alternative minimum tax (AMT) is in essence an income tax system that runs parallel to the "normal" federal income tax system. It is intended to impose a tax on certain taxpayers who have taken advantage of certain tax deductions, such as state and local taxes, or "preferences," which are items the taxpayer is deemed to be receiving special tax treatment.

While many individual taxpayers are able to complete and file their tax returns by simply filling out Form 1040 and a few supporting schedules, an increasing number of taxpayers are unwittingly subject to the AMT. Often, the AMT is levied on taxpayers after the fact – that is, the IRS compiles the necessary information and lets the taxpayer know that he forgot to compute the AMT liability and pay the additional tax.

Individuals can determine if the AMT applies to them in a given year by preparing IRS Form 6251. Corporations are also potentially subject to the AMT and use IRS Form 4626 to see if the tax applies. These forms are generally not required to be included with the filing of the taxpayer's return if the AMT does not result in a higher tax liability.

Trusts and estates filing income tax returns may also be subject to the AMT. These entities complete Schedule I of Form 1041 to compute their exposure. Pass-through entities like partnerships and S corporations are not subject to the AMT. However, they are responsible for reporting the applicable adjustments or preferences to the partners or shareholders on their Schedule K-1s.

Only a handful of people are even aware of the existence of this separate tax system. Far, far fewer understand how it is determined. Awareness of the AMT has been growing as more taxpayers fall under its reach. On the other hand, anyone who advises others must constantly be aware of the potential AMT impact of any recommendations that they make.

For 2013, an estimated 3.9 million taxpayers were subject to the AMT. This represents over four percent of all taxpayers.[1] The American Taxpayer Relief Act of 2012 (ATRA) provides for permanent indexing of the exemptions, brackets, and phase-outs, which protects even larger numbers of taxpayers from being caught in the snare of the AMT.

HOW IS AMT DETERMINED FOR INDIVIDUALS?

The AMT is assessed at a rate of 26 percent of alternative minimum taxable income (AMTI) up to $175,000 ($87,500 for married taxpayers filing separately) and 28 percent of AMTI exceeding that amount.[2] Preferential tax rates for long-term capital gains and qualifying dividends are also used in determining an individual's AMT.[3] Beginning in 2013, the income thresholds are indexed for inflation. The applicable amount for 2014 is $182,500 for all taxpayers except those married filing separately, which is half of this amount.

With a maximum tax rate of 28 percent, many taxpayers automatically (and incorrectly) assume that if they are in the 28 percent tax bracket or above, the AMT could not possibly apply to them. How is it possible that the AMT would apply when my marginal tax rate is higher than the maximum AMT rate? The answer lies in the differences between the computation of regular taxable income and AMTI. A myriad of add-backs and special tax rules mean that a taxpayer may have an AMTI that is significantly higher than his or her regular taxable income.

A taxpayer's AMTI and AMT are computed as follows:

Step 1: Adjust taxable income. First, compute taxable income using Form 1040[4] then add or subtract the adjustments to taxable income (as discussed below).[5]

Step 2: Add the amount of preference items. "Preference items" are specific tax items, discussed below, on which the taxpayer is receiving preferential tax treatment.[6] **The result is the taxpayer's AMTI.**

Step 3: Compute the applicable exemption amount. Like the regular taxable income, the AMTI has exemption amounts that are based on the taxpayer's filing status. Unlike the exemptions for regular taxable income, the AMTI exemptions are phased-out for incomes above certain thresholds.

For 2014, exemption amounts can be up to 82,100 for a married couple filing jointly, $52,800 for a single taxpayer, or $41,040 for a married individual filing separately.[7] The actual allowable exemption is computed by reducing the exemption limits above by 25 percent of the amount by which AMTI exceeds certain levels. Those levels are $156,500 for married taxpayers filing jointly, $117,300 for single taxpayers, and $78,250 for married taxpayers filing separately.[8]

Note that the reduction in AMTI exemption means that taxpayers with income above certain levels effectively have no exemption. In 2014, the exemption is completely phased out for joint filers with AMTI in excess of $482,300, single filers with AMTI over $328,500, and spouses filing separately with AMTI more than $242,410 for married individuals filing separately.

Related to the phase-out of the exemptions is a provision for certain married individuals who file separate returns to increase their AMTI. In 2014, a married individual filing a separate return must increase AMTI by the lesser of (a) 25 percent of the excess of the AMTI over $242,410, or (b) $41,040.[9]

Step 4: Compute the AMT. The tax rates are then applied to the taxpayer's AMTI (less any exemption) to yield the "tentative minimum tax." If the tentative minimum tax computed under this formula does not exceed the taxpayer's regular tax, the AMT does not apply. If the computed tentative minimum tax

exceeds the taxpayer's regular tax, the excess of the tentative minimum tax over the regular tax is the AMT that is added to the tax liability computed in the normal manner.

Example: Assume Dr. and Mrs. Ginsburg file a joint return for 2014. They have two dependent children. Their regular tax was computed to be $25,463.

Joint taxable income:	$135,000
AMT adjustments to taxable income:	30,000
Total of tax preference items:	57,000
Subtotal:	**$222,000**
Tentative AMT exemption:	$82,100
Reduction of AMT exemption:	$16,375 = 25% of ($222,000 – 156,500)
Actual AMT exemption (after reduction:	$65,725
Alternative minimum taxable income (AMTI):	$156,375
Tentative minimum tax:	$40,632

The excess of the Ginsburgs' tentative minimum tax ($40,632) over their regular tax ($25,463) is $15,169. This amount becomes their alternative minimum tax liability and is added to their regular tax. They would therefore pay a total tax of $40,632.

HOW IS AMT DETERMINED FOR CORPORATIONS?

Corporations were first made subject to the AMT with the imposition of the Tax Reform Act of 1986. Only S corporations and certain small corporations that qualify for an exemption are not subject to the AMT. In the case of S corporations, the adjustments and preferences are determined at the corporate level and are passed on to the shareholders on Schedule K-1 each year.

The corporate AMT is assessed at a rate of 20 percent of the "corporate AMTI." If this tentative minimum tax exceeds the regular corporate tax, the excess is the AMT for the year. Figure 9.1 provides detailed instructions for calculating a corporation's AMT.

Figure 9.1

	CALCULATION OF CORPORATE AMT	
Step 1	Calculate taxable income (or loss) before any net operating loss deduction using Form 1120[10]	
Step 2	Add or subtract Adjustments to taxable income[11]	
Step 3	Add the amount of "preference items."[12] The result is the *pre-adjustment AMTI*.	
Step 4	Adjust the pre-adjustment AMTI by either:	
	If the corporation's adjusted current earnings (ACE) exceeds Pre-adjustment AMTI, 75 percent of the excess of ACE over Pre-adjustment AMTI is added to Pre-adjustment AMTI to yield *post-adjustment AMTI*.[13]	If the corporation's ACE is less than pre-adjustment AMTI, the lesser of the following amounts is subtracted from pre-adjustment AMTI to yield *post-adjustment AMTI*: • 75 percent of the excess of Pre-adjustment AMTI over ACE[14] and • the excess aggregate upward ACE adjustments for prior tax years over the aggregate downward ACE adjustments for prior taxable years.[15]
Step 5	Subtract any allowable Alternative Tax Net Operating Loss deduction from post-adjustment AMTI. The result is the *final AMTI*.	
Step 6	Calculate and subtract the applicable exemption, up to $40,000.[16] This exemption is phased-out by 25 cents for every dollar of the amount of the corporation's final AMTI exceeds $150,000.[17] Therefore, at $310,000, the exemption is completely lost. Note that only one $40,000 exemption is allowed per group of controlled corporations.[18] The exemption is allocated evenly among the group members unless an election is submitted with the tax returns of the group.[19] **The result of this calculation is the** *corporate AMTI*.	
Step 7	Calculate the corporate AMT. The AMT tax rate for corporations of 20 percent is then applied to the corporate AMTI to determine the tentative minimum tax. If the tentative minimum tax exceeds the corporation's regular tax, the excess is added to the corporation's regular tax.	

WHAT ARE AMT ADJUSTMENTS?

A common misconception is that adjustments and preferences for AMT purposes are the same thing. In fact, adjustments and preferences are very different. AMT *Adjustments* are defined under Code section 56 and are usually amounts that are determined separately for regular tax and AMT purposes and may be positive or negative.

AMT *preferences* (see below) are defined under Code section 57 and result in add-backs to taxable income because of some "preferential" treatment received for regular tax purposes. Preferences may only result in an increase to taxable income—negative preferences are not permitted.

Adjustments for Individuals and Corporations

Three common types of adjustments to taxable income apply to both individuals and corporations.

These include adjustments related to depreciation, NOLs (see Chapter 5). And gains and/or losses from sales of property.

Depreciation Adjustments

For property placed in service after 1986, depreciation deductions are adjusted to conform to special rules for the AMT.[20] Normally taxpayers follow the MACRS rules for determining their depreciation on fixed assets, which typically results in a 200 percent declining balance method for determining the annual deduction. The applicable recovery period is determined by referring to Rev. Proc. 87-56[21] and referring to the asset class of the property to be depreciated.

For property placed in service prior to 1999, taxpayers were required to re-compute their fixed asset depreciation using the 150 percent declining balance method and, in most cases, a longer recovery period. This led to potentially large positive adjustments for determining AMTI in the earlier years an asset was in service (i.e. higher AMTI) followed by negative adjustments in later years.

Example: ABC Corporation purchased $10,000 worth of furniture in 1998. The furniture has a seven-year life for regular tax purposes using the 200 percent declining balance method and a ten-year life for AMT using the 150 percent declining balance method. ABC's depreciation calculations are:

Year	Regular Depreciation	AMT Depreciation	AMT Adjustment
1998	$ 1,429	$ 750	$ 679
1999	$ 2,449	$ 1,388	$1,061
2000	$ 1,749	$ 1,179	$ 570
2001	$ 1,249	$ 1,002	$ 247
2002	$ 893	$ 874	$ 19
2003	$ 892	$ 874	$ 18
2004	$ 893	$ 874	$ 19
2005	$ 446	$ 874	($ 428)
2006	-	$ 874	($ 874)
2007	-	$ 874	($ 874)
2008	-	$ 437	($ 437)

For property placed in service after 1998, taxpayers may use the same recovery period that is used for determining their regular tax depreciation. However, the depreciation method still may be no faster than the 150 percent declining balance method.[22]

Example: ABC Corporation purchased $10,000 worth of furniture in 1999. The furniture has a seven-year life for regular tax purposes using the 200 percent declining balance method and a seven-year life for AMT using the 150 percent declining balance method. ABC's depreciation calculations are:

Year	Regular Depreciation	AMT Depreciation	AMT Adjustment
1999	$ 1,429	$ 1,071	$ 358
2000	$ 2,449	$ 1,913	$ 536
2001	$ 1,749	$ 1,503	$ 246
2002	$ 1,249	$ 1,225	$ 24
2003	$ 893	$ 1,225	($ 332)
2004	$ 892	$ 1,225	($ 333)
2005	$ 893	$ 1,225	($ 332)
2006	$ 446	$ 613	($ 167)

In 2002 bonus depreciation became available for certain types of property placed into service on or after September 11, 2001. Originally, 30 percent of the cost of qualifying property could be deducted in the year of purchase. This was later increased to 50 percent for qualifying property purchases on or after May 6, 2003. These provisions were effective through the end of 2004.

In 2008 50 percent a bonus depreciation allowance for qualifying property became available once again. This was increased to 100 percent for property placed into service on or after September 9, 2010, through the end of 2011. Bonus depreciation of 50 percent continued to be available for the 2012 and 2013 tax years. Currently bonus depreciation is no longer available beginning in 2014.

Taxpayers may elect to take the bonus depreciation deduction, but it is not required. Bonus depreciation is allowed for both regular tax and AMT purposes.[23] In addition, any remaining basis of the qualifying property is deductible for both regular tax and AMT.[24]

Example: ABC Corporation purchases $10,000 of furniture in June 2008. The furniture has a seven-year life for regular tax purposes using the 200 percent declining balance method and a seven-year life for AMT using the 150 percent declining balance method. The furniture also qualifies for a 50 percent bonus depreciation in the first year. ABC's depreciation calculations are:

Year	Regular Tax Depreciation	AMT Depreciation	AMT Adjustment
2008	$ 5,715	$ 5,715	$ 0
2009	$ 1,224	$ 1,224	$ 0
2010	$ 875	$ 875	$ 0
2011	$ 624	$ 624	$ 0
2012	$ 447	$ 447	$ 0
2013	$ 446	$ 446	$ 0
2014	$ 446	$ 446	$ 0
2015	$ 223	$ 223	$ 0

NOL Adjustments

The net operating loss (NOL) allowed under Code section 172 is added back to taxable income and replaced with the alternative tax net operating loss (ATNOL) deduction.[25]

A taxpayer that has a NOL in a year may also, but not necessarily, have an ATNOL. For this reason, a separate calculation must be performed to determine a taxpayer's ATNOL. This is done by starting with the NOL for regular tax purposes and increasing or decreasing this amount by the AMT adjustments and preferences in the year of the loss.[26]

Example: Jack determined that he had a NOL of $175,000, which was attributable to one year when his business fell on hard times. His only AMT adjustment in that year was a $15,000 positive depreciation adjustment. Since the positive depreciation adjustment increased his AMTI, it reduces his NOL by that amount to yield an ATNOL of $160,000.

The amount of ATNOL that can be claimed as a reduction to AMTI is limited to 90 percent of the taxpayers AMTI determined without regard to the ATNOL.[27]

Adjustments Related to Gains and Losses from the Sale of Property

Gains or losses on the sale of property are adjusted to reflect the special depreciation rules used for AMT purposes.[28] Since the assets are depreciated using potentially different methods or lives, their adjusted basis for AMT purposes may be different than for regular tax purposes. As a result, when an asset is sold or otherwise disposed of, the gain or loss must be recomputed using the asset's adjusted AMT basis.

Example: In 2003, Tire World, Inc. sold a piece of furniture for $3,000. The company originally purchased for $10,000 in 1998. At the time of the sale, their adjusted tax basis in the asset was $1,785 for regular tax purposes and $4,370 for AMT. Tire World correctly computes their regular tax gain as $1,215 ($3,000 - $1,785). For AMT purposes, Tire World realized a loss of $1,370 ($3,000 - $4,370). Tire World would report an "adjusted gain or loss" adjustment of *negative*

$2,585, the difference between the adjusted basis in the asset for regular tax and AMT purposes.

Individual Adjustments

Certain adjustments apply solely to individuals:

1. *Miscellaneous itemized deductions*. When calculating AMTI, adjustments must be made for any miscellaneous itemized deduction as defined in I.R.C. §67(b).[29] Therefore, taxpayers with investment expenses, tax preparation fees, unreimbursed employee business expenses, and other miscellaneous deductions that exceed 2 percent of their adjusted gross income may not receive a benefit from these expenses if the adjustment for AMT purposes causes them to be subject to the tax.

Example: Joe Grant retired in early 2009 and, as a result his AGI was $45,000, much lower than usual. He paid $1,500 to have his 2008 tax return prepared, $10,000 to his investment manager for managing his investment portfolio and incurred $5,000 of unreimbursed employee business expenses. All of these expenses combined exceed 2 percent of his AGI. Joe's itemized deduction schedule for 2009 will show that $7,500 of these expenses are deductible (the total of his expenses less 2 percent of his AGI). However, $7,500 will need to be added to his taxable income to determine his AMTI for 2009.

---

2. *Taxes claimed as itemized deductions*. Any taxes that are claimed as an itemized deduction (such as local property taxes) must be added back for determining AMTI.[30] A tax that is deducted as part of a trade or business (e.g. as a sole proprietor) is not an AMT adjustment. The taxes that must be added back include itemized deductions of state, local and foreign real estate taxes, state and local personal property taxes and state, local and foreign income taxes. If a taxpayer elects to deduct sales taxes instead of state and local income taxes, the full amount of the sales tax deduction must be added back in determining AMTI.

3. *Medical expenses*. Medical expenses that exceed 7.5 percent of a taxpayer's adjusted gross income

are allowed as an itemized deduction if the taxpayer is over age sixty-five.[31] Beginning in 2013, taxpayers under age sixty-five may deduct medical expenses that exceed 10 percent of AGI. For the purpose of determining a taxpayer's AMTI, medical expenses are only deductible if the expenses exceed 10 percent of the taxpayer's AGI as computed for regular tax purposes.[32]

Example 1: Sam Watson is seventy years old in 2014 and has adjusted gross income of $100,000 and medical expenses of $9,000. His deductible medical expense for regular tax purposes is $1,500 ($9,000 less 7.5 percent of $100,000). When computing AMTI, Sam must add back the entire $1,500 deduction since his medical expenses do not exceed 10 percent of his AGI ($10,000).

Example 2: Assume Sam's medical expenses are $12,000 instead of $9,000. His regular tax deduction is $4,500 ($12,000 less 7.5 percent of $100,000). His AMT deduction is $2,000 ($12,000 less ten percent of $100,000). The difference of $2,500 is the positive AMT adjustment that must be made in order to determine his AMTI.

---

4. *Investment interest expenses.* Investment interest expense must be recomputed considering any adjustments or preference items that relate to total investment income or expense.[33]

5. *Mortgage interest.* Home mortgage interest on indebtedness that was not incurred to acquire, construct or substantially improve the taxpayer's principal residence or second home must be added back for computing AMTI.[34] This would include home equity indebtedness if the proceeds of the loan were not used in the manner described above. Refinancing of previously qualifying indebtedness is allowed, but only to the extent of the amount of the qualifying indebtedness immediately before the refinancing.[35]

6. *Refunds of taxes.* Refunds of taxes that were AMT adjustments in previous years reduce AMTI in the year of receipt.[36]

7. *Standard deduction and personal exemptions.* If the taxpayer's taxable income was reduced by either the standard deduction or personal exemptions, these items must be added back for AMT purposes.[37]

8. *Incentive stock options (ISOs).* Taxpayers may defer regular tax on income resulting from the exercise of an incentive stock option (ISO).[38] Unlike nonqualified stock options which are taxed to the extent of the value of the stock over the exercise cost, the taxation of an ISO occurs only when the stock acquired by exercise of the ISO is sold or otherwise disposed. At that time, the difference between the selling price and the amount paid for the stock when the ISO was exercised is taxed as a capital gain.

The deferral of the gain at the time of the exercise of the ISO does not apply if the taxpayer disposes of the stock within two years from the grant date of the ISO or within one year of the exercise date of the option.[39]

For AMT purposes, the ISO does not receive the deferral treatment at the time of exercise. Instead the ISO is treated like a nonqualified stock option.[40] This means that the value of the stock acquired at the time of exercise in excess of the exercise cost creates a positive AMT adjustment in that year. Sizeable ISO exercises are a common reason for taxpayers to be subject to the AMT.

Taxpayers who exercise ISOs must keep accurate records of the basis of their stock. For regular tax purposes, the basis will equal their exercise cost plus any transaction costs. For AMT purposes, the basis will equal the value of the stock on the date of exercise plus any transaction costs. When the stock acquired by ISO is ultimately sold, the taxpayer will reduce the AMTI in that year by the amount of the basis difference.

Example: Ron Gardner exercised 1,000 ISOs of his employer, WWW, Inc. The exercise cost was $10 per option and at the time of the exercise, the stock was trading at $75 per share. Ron pays the company $10,000 and, in return, receives stock valued at $75,000. For regular tax purposes, Ron reports no income. However, he has a positive AMT adjustment of $65,000 ($75,000 - $10,000) in the year of exercise.

Three years later, Ron decides to sell 500 shares when the stock is trading at $100 per share. He will report a long-term capital gain for regular tax purposes of $45,000 ($50,000 in sale proceeds less the $5,000 basis).

For AMT purposes, his gain is only $12,500. While he has $50,000 in cash proceeds, $32,500 (half of the $65,000 AMT adjustment three years ago) of that amount was subject to AMT three years ago. In order to prevent double AMT taxation, the $32,500 will be reported as a negative AMT adjustment (entered as an adjusted gain or loss on Form 6251) in the year of the sale.

9. *AMT adjustments from pass-through entities.* Pass-through entities are required to separately identify amounts that adjustments for AMT purposes for their investors. For this reason, it is very common to find AMT adjustments for depreciation reported on an investor's Schedule K-1.

Passive activity rules are separately applied for AMT purposes. If the net income or loss from passive activities as adjusted by any AMT items is different than the net passive activity income or loss for regular tax purposes, the difference is reported as an adjustment to AMTI.[41]

Corporate Adjustments

The following adjustments must be made to a corporation's taxable income:

1. A corporation must make an adjustment to its taxable income based on its "adjusted current earnings" (ACE).[42] ACE computations are explained in detail below.

2. The charitable contributions limitation for individuals is determined based upon the taxpayer's adjusted gross income for both regular tax and AMT purposes.[43] However, corporations must re-determine their allowable charitable contribution for AMT purposes based upon the corporation's AMTI, without respect to this adjustment.[44] In fact, the instructions to Form 4626 require that this computation and adjustment be made if necessary.

Adjusted Current Earnings (ACE) for Corporations

When calculating AMT, corporations must make an adjustment based on adjusted current earnings ("ACE"). ACE is defined as the AMTI for the taxable year determined with its own set of "ACE adjustments"

and without the alternative tax net operating loss deduction.[45]

The adjustments that must be made to determine a corporation's ACE are:

1. Depreciation must be recomputed for ACE using a special set of rules for allowable method and recovery period.[46] This creates a third set of depreciation calculations on the same assets – one for regular tax, one for AMT and now one for ACE. An asset's placed in service date determines how the asset is treated for ACE.[47] The adjustment applies to assets placed in service after 1989 – however, assets in service as of 1989 also need an ACE calculation.[48]

The following table is a summary of how assets are depreciated under the ACE rules:

Placed in Service Date	ACE Depreciation Treatment
Taxable year beginning before 1990 (MACRS Assets)	Basis for ACE depreciation begins with AMT basis as of the close of the last year before 1990. Depreciate using straight line method over the remainder of the property's recovery period as determined under the alternative depreciation system.[75]
Taxable year beginning before 1990 (ACRS Assets)	Basis for ACE depreciation begins with regular tax basis as of the close of the last year before 1990. Depreciate using straight line method over the remainder of the property's recovery period as determined under the alternative depreciation system.[76]
Taxable year beginning before 1990 (non-MACRS and ACRS Assets)	No adjustments for ACE required.[77]
Taxable year beginning after 1989 And on or before December 31, 1993	Straight-line recovery over the property's recovery period as determined under the alternative depreciation system.[78]
After December 31, 1993	ACE depreciation computed in the same manner as AMT depreciation.[79]

2. The second ACE adjustment is for items that are included in the determination of a corporation's earnings and profits (E&P) but are excluded from AMTI.[49] The amount of any item that is included as an adjustment may be offset by any deduction which would have been allowable in computing AMTI if the amount were included in gross income.[50]

The ACE worksheet included in the instructions to Form 4626 contains a list of the most common E&P adjustments, such as:

Includible Items:

a. Tax-exempt interest excluded under Code Section 103.

b. Death benefits from life insurance contracts excluded under Code Section 101 (adjusted by the corporation's basis in the life insurance contract).

c. Other distributions from life insurance contracts.

d. Income earned on life insurance contracts minus the part of any premium attributable to insurance coverage.

Nondeductible Items:

a. Deduction for dividends received, with certain exceptions for 100 percent dividend received deductions and dividends from a 20 percent owned corporation if the payor is subject to federal income tax on the earnings to which the dividend is attributable.[51]

b. Dividends paid on certain preferred stock of public utilities deductible under Code Section 247.

c. Dividends paid to an ESOP deductible under Code Section 404(k).

d. Nonpatronage dividends that are paid and deductible under Code Section 1382(c).

Special Items:

a. Intangible drilling costs on productive wells of integrated oil companies must be capitalized and amortized over sixty months.[52]

b. Amortization on circulation and organizational expenditures under Code Sections 173 and 248, respectively, is not permitted.[53]

c. For taxpayers that account for inventory on a last-in, first-out (LIFO) basis, the excess of inventory value on a first-in, first out basis over LIFO basis is an adjustment for ACE.[54]

d. The installment sale method is not permitted for ACE.[55] As a result, taxpayers with an installment sale will have a large adjustment in the first year followed by negative adjustments as payments are made on the installment sale in future years.

Adjustments are not required for discharge of indebtedness income under Code Section 108.[56] In addition, the limit on charitable contributions is not recomputed for ACE.[57]

Once the corporation's ACE is determined, the ACE is compared to its pre-adjustment AMTI. If ACE exceeds pre-adjustment AMTI, the corporation must increase its AMTI by 75 percent of the excess.[58]

If ACE is less than pre-adjustment AMTI, the corporation may reduce its AMTI by 75 percent of the difference.[59] However, the potential negative adjustment is limited to the excess of the aggregate positive ACE adjustments made to AMTI in prior years over the aggregate negative ACE adjustments made to AMTI in prior years.[60]

WHAT ARE AMT PREFERENCES?

The following tax preference items must be *added* to a taxpayer's taxable income in computing AMTI. As discussed above, tax preference items may only increase AMTI – negative tax preference items are not permitted.

- *Depletion*. The excess of the deduction for depletion over the adjusted basis of the property at the end of the taxable year.[61]

- *Intangible drilling costs*. The amount by which excess intangible drilling costs are greater than 65 percent of the net income of the taxpayer's oil, gas, and geothermal properties for the tax year.[62]

The excess intangible drilling costs are the excess of the intangible drilling and development costs paid or incurred in connection with oil, gas and geothermal wells over the amount that would have been allowable for the taxable year if such costs had been capitalized and straight line recovery of intangibles (over 120 months) had been used with respect to such costs.[63]

- *Tax-exempt interest on private activity bonds.* Any tax-exempt interest earned on specified private activity bonds must be added to AMTI. The amount of interest to be added back is reduced by any deductions which would have been allowable if the tax-exempt interest was includible in gross income for regular tax purposes.[64]

A "specified private activity bond" is any private activity bond which is issued after August 7, 1986.[65] Private activity bonds are covered by I.R.C. §141 and include any bonds that meet either (1) the "private business use" test and the "private security or payment" test or (2) the "private loan financing" test.

A bond is identified as a private activity bond at the time of its issue. Because of the inclusion of the interest paid on such bonds in the AMTI of its holders, these bonds typically will pay a higher yield than pure tax-exempt municipal bonds.

Investors in mutual funds that earn some tax-exempt interest should watch for the percentage of tax-exempt income that was earned on private activity bonds. The proportionate share of the tax-exempt income earned on such bonds must be added to AMTI.[66]

- *Gains on small business stock.* Gains of certain small business stock that is held for more than five years qualify for a 50 percent exclusion from taxation.[67] Small business stock must meet the following requirements:

    a. It must have been issued after August 10, 1993.[68]

    b. The taxpayer must be the original holder of the stock and the stock must have been acquired in exchange for money or other property (not including stock) or as compensation for services performed.[69]

    c. The corporation must be an active business.[70]

    d. The corporation must be a qualified small business.[71] That is, it must be a domestic C corporation with aggregate gross assets of less than $50,000,000.[72]

The amount of the excluded gain that must be added back to AMTI is 7 percent.[73]

Example: Jack Armstrong realized a gain of $300,000 on the sale of Section 1202 stock on June 1, 2014. Accordingly, Jack excludes $150,000 of the gain for regular tax purposes. Jack must add back $10,500 ($150,000 x 7 percent) as a preference item when determining his AMT.

AMT EXEMPTION FOR SMALL CORPORATIONS

The Taxpayer Relief Act of 1997 created an exemption from the AMT for certain "small" corporations. The exemption applies to qualifying corporations with tax years beginning after 1997.

In order to qualify for the exemption, a corporation must look to its three taxable years prior to the taxable year in question.[74] The average gross receipts for this three-year period must not exceed $7.5 million.[75]

Example: Smallville, Inc. needs to determine if it can qualify for the AMT exemption in 2013. They expanded operations in the prior year and their revenue doubled. The company reviews their prior three years of revenue and find that for 2010, 2011, and 2012 their gross receipts were $6 million, $6 million, and $12 million, respectively. Their average gross receipts for the preceding three-year period is $8 million. Therefore, Smallville no longer qualifies for the small corporation AMT exemption beginning in 2013.

A special exception applies for new corporations. Any first year corporation is automatically exempted from the AMT regardless of the amount of gross receipts derived from operations.[76] For a new corporation's second year, the exemption will only apply if the corporation's gross receipts in the first year were no more than $5 million.[77] After a corporation's second year, the corporation must meet the $7.5 million average gross receipts test. Gross receipts for any taxable period of less than twelve months must be annualized when applying these tests.[78]

If a qualifying small corporation ceases to be a small corporation because its average gross receipts exceed the allowable limits, the corporation will be subject to the AMT for that and all future years. The first day of the taxable year during which the taxpayer ceases to be a small corporation is the "change date."[79] The AMT is then computed with the following modifications:

1. The depreciation adjustment is computed only on property placed in service after the change date.[80]

2. The mining and exploration adjustment is applied only to costs paid or incurred after the change date.[81]

3. The long-term contract adjustment is applied only to contracts entered into after the change date.[82]

4. The adjustment for alternative tax net operating loss deduction must be computed as of the change date.[83]

5. The limitation on the allowance of negative adjustments to AMTI based on adjusted current earnings will apply only to those "prior taxable years" that begin on or after the change date.[84]

6. The depreciation adjustment for computing ACE does not apply.[85]

7. The earnings and profits adjustment and depletion must be computed as of the change date.[86]

FOREIGN TAX CREDIT

A credit for foreign taxes paid or accrued is permitted as a reduction to the tentative minimum tax for individuals and corporations. The credit is computed in the same manner as it is for regular tax purposes except it is based on the tentative minimum tax before the credit. Taxpayers claiming the credit must adjust taxable income by the adjustments and preferences of Code sections 56, 57 and 58.[87]

CREDITS AGAINST REGULAR TAX

There are a number of credits that are available to reduce a taxpayer's regular tax liability. However, a taxpayer may be limited in the amount of credits that may be used to offset their regular tax liability based on the AMT for the year.

Currently, only the adoption credit, child tax credit, retirement savings contribution credit, and certain energy efficiency credits may be used to offset both a taxpayer's regular tax and AMT. Other credits may offset regular tax only.

A taxpayer that has business tax credits may not use the credits to offset their AMT in a given year. The general business credit of a taxpayer is limited to the taxpayer's net regular tax (net of nonrefundable personal credits, foreign tax credit, and certain other rarely used credits) plus AMT, less the larger of (1) tentative minimum tax or (2) 25 percent of the amount by which the net regular tax exceeds $25,000.[88]

Example: Jessica's net regular tax liability for 2014 was $50,000. Her tentative minimum tax was $47,000. She also received a $5,000 general business credit from one of her partnership investments. She is permitted to claim $3,000 of the credit against her 2014 tax liability and thereby reduce her regular tax to $47,000. The remaining $2,000 may be carried forward to future years subject to carryforward limitations.

MINIMUM TAX CREDIT

Taxpayers that are caught by the AMT may have the opportunity to recoup some of that payment in future years through the minimum tax credit (MTC).[89] For individuals, the MTC is created by AMT that is attributable to *deferral* adjustments or preferences. "Deferral adjustments and preferences" are adjustments or preferences that are made merely because of the timing of particular tax item. On the other hand, AMT that is attributable to *exclusion* adjustments and preferences does not create a

MTC. Exclusion adjustments and preferences are ones that would have to be made regardless of timing of the particular tax item.

It is easier to list the exclusion adjustments and preferences, keeping in mind that all other adjustments and preferences are of the deferral type and will add to a taxpayer's MTC:[90]

- Taxes

- Medical expenses

- Certain residential interest expense

- Miscellaneous itemized deductions

- Standard deduction

- Personal exemptions

- Excess depletion

- Tax-exempt interest from private activity bonds

- Applicable add back for the Section 1202 exclusion for gain from the sale of small business stock

For individuals, the MTC amount is the difference between the taxpayer's actual AMT and the AMT that would have been owed if only the exclusion adjustments

and preferences were considered.[91] The MTC is available to reduce a taxpayer's regular tax liability only if the taxpayer is not subject to the AMT. Obviously, an MTC credit will not be available to the taxpayer in the year it is generated. However, any unused MTC is carried forward to offset future regular tax liability in years that the taxpayer is not subject to the AMT. Note that taxpayer's may only use a carried-forward MTC to offset regular tax liability to the extent that their regular tax liability exceeds their AMT tax liability. This restriction means that it can take many years to completely use a significant MTC.

Individuals report the MTC on Form 8801. Figure 9.2 illustrates the calculation and use of a hypothetical MTC credit for an individual.

Unlike what is required for individuals, The MTC for corporations is determined without making any adjustments to the AMT paid in prior years.[92] If a corporation pays the AMT in a prior year, the full amount of the AMT is available as a MTC in subsequent years offset the entity's regular tax liability to the extent that it exceeds the AMT liability. Corporations use Form 8827 to determine the MTC.

Example: Palace Amusements paid $5,000 of AMT in 2013. In 2014, the company's regular tax liability, before the MTC, was $55,000. The company's tentative minimum tax was $47,000. Since the utilization of the

Figure 9.2

EXAMPLE OF MTC CREDIT CALCULATION AND USE

In 2013, Jerry exercised a number of ISOs and, as a result, paid $25,000 of AMT. The only other adjustment he had for AMT purposes was his standard deduction and personal exemption. When preparing his 2014 individual income tax return, Jerry must determine the amount of the MTC available to him. He does this by using Form 8801 to calculate the value of his 2013 deferral adjustments (here, his standard deduction and personal exemption). After completing Form 8801, Jerry realizes that the deferral adjustments increased his 2013 AMT by $22,000. This amount becomes Jerry's MTC. Because Jerry was subject to the AMT in 2013, the entire MTC credit will be carried forward to be used in subsequent years.

Year	MTC available	Regular tax Liability	AMT liability	Amount of MTC used to offset regular tax liability
2014	$22,000	$25,000	$20,000	$5,000
2015	$17,000	$25,000	$24,000	$1,000
2016	$16,000	$30,000	$22,000	$8,000
2017	$8,000	$30,000	$25,000	$5,000
2018	$3,000	$32,000	$28,000	$3,000

MTC against regular tax does not reduce the tax below the company's tentative minimum tax, the full amount of the MTC is allowed in 2014. The company's net tax liability for 2014 is reduced to $50,000.

Refundable MTC. Beginning in 2007 and ending with the 2012 tax year, the Tax Relief and Healthcare Act of 2007 allowed taxpayers with long-term unused minimum tax credits an opportunity to benefit from the minimum tax credit sooner. This "Refundable Minimum Tax Credit" was equal to the greater of $5,000 or 20 percent of the long-term unused MTC for the year. The primary purpose of creating this provision was to give relief to the many taxpayers who exercised incentive stock options in prior years and, for one reason or another, have not benefited from the existing MTC rules. This exception expired is no longer applicable for current tax returns.

CHAPTER ENDNOTES

1. Quick Facts: Alternative Minimum Tax; www.taxpolicy center.org.
2. I.R.C. §55(b)(1)(A).
3. I.R.C. §55(b)(3).
4. I.R.C. §55(b)(2).
5. I.R.C. §55(b)(2)(A).
6. I.R.C. §55(b)(2)(B).
7. I.R.C. §55(d)(1).
8. I.R.C. §55(d)(3).
9. I.R.C. §55(d)(3).
10. I.R.C. §55(b)(2).
11. I.R.C. §55(b)(2)(A).
12. I.R.C. §55(b)(2)(B).
13. I.R.C. §56(g)(1).
14. I.R.C. §56(g)(2).
15. I.R.C. §56(g)(2)(B).
16. I.R.C. §55(d)(2).
17. I.R.C. §55(d)(3).
18. See I.R.C. §1561(a)(3) for groups defined under I.R.C. §1563(a).
19. I.R.C. §1561(a).
20. I.R.C. §56(a)(1).
21. 1987-2 C.B. 674.
22. I.R.C. §56(a)(1)(A).
23. I.R.C. §168(k)(2)(G).
24. Rev. Proc. 2002-33, 2002-1 CB 963.
25. I.R.C. §56(a)(4).
26. I.R.C. §56(d)(2).
27. I.R.C. §56(d)(1)(A).
28. I.R.C. §56(a)(6).
29. I.R.C. §56(b)(1)(A)(i).
30. I.R.C. §56(b)(1)(A)(ii).
31. I.R.C. §213(a).
32. I.R.C. §56(b)(1)(B).
33. I.R.C. §56(b)(1)(C).
34. I.R.C. §56(e)(1)(A).
35. I.R.C. §56(e)(1)(B).
36. I.R.C. §56(b)(1)(D).
37. I.R.C. §56(b)(1)(E).
38. I.R.C. §421(a).
39. I.R.C. §422(a)(1).
40. I.R.C. §56(b)(3).
41. I.R.C. §58(b).
42. I.R.C. §56(c)(1).
43. I.R.C. §170(b)(1).
44. TAM 9320003.
45. I.R.C. §56(g)(3).
46. I.R.C. §56(g)(4)(A)(ii).
47. I.R.C. §56(g)(4)(A)(iii).
48. I.R.C. §56(g)(4)(A)(i).
49. I.R.C. §56(g)(4)(B)(i)(I).
50. I.R.C. §56(g)(4)(B)(i)(II).
51. I.R.C. §56(g)(4)(C)(ii).
52. I.R.C. §56(g)(4)(D)(i).
53. I.R.C. §56(g)(4)(D)(ii).
54. I.R.C. §56(g)(4)(D)(iii).
55. I.R.C. §56(g)(4)(D)(iv).
56. I.R.C. §56(g)(4)(B)(i).
57. I.R.C. §56(g)(4)(I).
58. I.R.C. §56(g)(1).
59. I.R.C. §56(g)(2).
60. I.R.C. §56(g)(2)(B).
61. I.R.C. §57(a)(1).
62. I.R.C. §57(a)(2)(A).
63. I.R.C. §§57(a)(2)(B) and 57(b)(1).
64. I.R.C. §57(a)(5)(A).
65. I.R.C. §57(a)(5)(C)(i).
66. I.R.C. §57(a)(5)(B).
67. I.R.C. §1202(a)(1).
68. I.R.C. §1202(c)(1).
69. I.R.C. §1202(c)(1)(B).
70. I.R.C. §1202(c)(2).
71. I.R.C. §1202(c)(1)(A).
72. I.R.C. §1202(d).
73. I.R.C. §57(a)(7).
74. I.R.C. §55(e)(1)(A).
75. *Ibid.*

76. I.R.C. §55(e)(1)(C).
77. I.R.C. §55(e)(1)(B).
78. I.R.C. §55(e)(1)(D).
79. I.R.C. §55(e)(4).
80. I.R.C. §55(e)(2)(A).
81. I.R.C. §55(e)(2)(B).
82. I.R.C. §55(e)(2)(C).
83. I.R.C. §55(e)(2)(D).
84. I.R.C. §55(e)(2)(E).

85. I.R.C. §55(e)(2)(F).
86. I.R.C. §55(e)(2)(G).
87. I.R.C. §59(a)(1).
88. I.R.C. §38(c).
89. I.R.C. §53(a).
90. I.R.C. §53(d)(1)(B)(ii).
91. I.R.C. §53(d)(1)(B)(i).
92. I.R.C. §53(d)(1)(B)(iii).

SOCIAL SECURITY/ MEDICARE TAXES: WAGE EARNERS AND SELF-EMPLOYED INDIVIDUALS

CHAPTER 10

INTRODUCTION

In addition to regular income tax, the Internal Revenue Code imposes a flat social security tax and a flat Medicare tax on the *earned income* of wage earners (generally defined as taxpayers who work for someone else) and self-employed individuals. While the term "earned income" broadly describes the types of income that are subject to these two flat taxes, the actual calculation of their respective tax bases is significantly different.

Although the tax rate is the same for wage income and self-employment income, the tax base, tax liability computations, payment requirements for the taxes are different. The economic impact of these taxes on a self-employed individual is typically much greater than on a wage earner.

HOW DO THE SOCIAL SECURITY AND MEDICARE TAXES WORK?

The respective social security and the Medicare tax rates are 12.4 percent and 2.9 percent, for a total of 15.3 percent of earned income. The social security tax and the Medicare tax are often referred to as the "payroll tax" for wage earners and the "self-employment tax" for self-employed individuals. Employees are only obligated to pay half of the payroll tax, or 7.65 percent of the 15.3 percent total tax liability. Employers are required to withhold the employees' half of the payroll tax, as well

as pay the other half directly. Because the payroll tax is a flat tax that is paid entirely through withholding, a wage earner will never have an outstanding payroll tax liability to pay out of pocket. Moreover, there is no line item on Form 1040 for employee payroll tax. Because employees do not actually pay the tax directly and do not see it on their regular income tax returns, they often do not realize its full impact.

Conversely, subject to some offsetting tax relief discussed below, self-employed taxpayers are obligated to pay the entire amount of self-employment tax directly to the IRS. Self-employed individuals report the tax on Form 1040 using a Schedule SE. In addition, to avoid penalties, they are obligated to make quarterly payments of estimated tax directly to the IRS to avoid a significant balance owed to the IRS on April 15.

SOCIAL SECURITY AND MEDICARE TAXES FOR WAGE EARNERS

As mentioned above, the social security tax and Medicare tax rates are the same on the wage income of a wage earner and as they are on the self-employment income of a self-employed individual. However, the operative statute for the imposition of payroll taxes on wage earners is the Federal Insurance Contributions Act, and collectively payroll taxes are referred to as the "FICA tax."[1]

Tax Base

Obviously, the tax base of a wage earner is wages (with certain exclusions). "Wages" is defined as compensation for employment in any form, including money, benefits, or property.[2] "Employment" is any service performed by an employee for the person employing him.[3] The term "service performed" goes beyond work actually done and encompasses the entire employee-employer relationship.[4]

Under this broad concept of employee compensation, sick pay, back pay, or vacation pay are treated as wages subject to the FICA tax. Additionally, a recent supreme court decision has expanded the definition of wages to include severance pay. In *U.S. v. Quality Stores, Inc.*,[5] the employer—in the midst of a Chapter 11 bankruptcy—made severance payments to 3,100 terminated employees. Reversing a decision by the Sixth Circuit Court of Appeals, the supreme court held that severance payments were paid in the realm of an employer-employee relationship, and thus were unquestionably wages. Under this ruling, severance payments—like any other type of wages—are subject to the FICA tax.

There are, however, certain types of employee compensation that are specifically exempted from the FICA tax. Figure 10.1 is a non-exclusive list of some of the excluded compensation.[6]

Computation and Payment of FICA Tax

As mentioned above, the liability for the FICA tax is split equally between the employee and the employer.[7] Although the social security tax rate is much higher than the Medicare tax rate, it is capped at a certain (inflation-adjusted) amount of wages. For 2014, the social security tax caps at wages of $117,000.[8] Thus, the maximum amount of social security tax liability for the employee and employee shares would be $14,508 (12.4 percent of $117,000), or $7,254 each.

On the other hand, there is no cap on the Medicare tax. This means the combined employer/employee 2.9 percent tax rate will be imposed on all wages without limit. So, for 2014, although the imposition of social security tax ceases on wages in excess of $117,000, the Medicare tax is imposed on all wages. Moreover, starting 2013 an Additional Medicare Surtax of 0.9 percent is added to the 1.45 percent employee portion of the Medicare tax for wages above certain threshold levels. (For a more detailed discussion of the Additional Medicare Surtax, see Chapter 11.)

Each year, all wage items—including withholding of the employee's portion of the FICA tax—are reported on a Form W-2 that is provided to the employee and the Social Security Administration. However, the employer is actually responsible for the payment of the FICA tax. Essentially, on an ongoing basis, the employer remits both its share of FICA the employee's share of FICA that was withheld from his or her wages in the form of a payroll tax deposit. Additionally, all FICA payments are reported quarterly to the IRS on Form 941.

Refunds or Tax Credits for Overpayment of Social Security Tax

Although the FICA tax withheld from an employee's paycheck is reported on Form W-2, there is no line item for it on Form 1040. A wage earner who never actually makes a FICA tax payment may be oblivious to his or her FICA tax liability—much less its payment through wage withholding. Moreover, a wage earner with two or more jobs who is unaware of the social security wage cap may miss an opportunity to receive a tax credit or refund for an overpayment.

This could occur for a taxpayer with multiple jobs. Each employer only knows the amount that it has paid the employee. If an employee has aggregate wages from multiple jobs that exceed the social security tax cap for the year, it is quite possible that he or she may have paid more in social security taxes than was required. In that instance, the amount of social security tax withheld on wage income above the cap would be an overpayment, and the taxpayer can either apply the overpayment as a credit against income tax liability on From 1040, or apply for a refund by filing Form 843.

Example: In 2014, William Widget was a salaried IT technician earning $100,000. In addition, William earned $50,000 in wages working evenings and weekends as a manager of a computer store. The 2014 social security wage cap was $117,000. Thus, while neither of the jobs paid wages in excess of the cap, the aggregate amount of William's wages exceeded the social security wage cap by $33,000.

William's two employers collectively withheld $9,300 in social security taxes (6.2 percent of $150,000), but his maximum amount of social security tax liability was only $7,254 (6.2 percent of $117,000). Here, William has a $2,046 social security tax overpayment.

Figure 10.1

Type of Compensation Excluded	Requirements for FICA Exclusion
Employee business expense reimbursements	The reimbursements must be part of "accountable plan," in which: • The deductible expense must be incurred by employee while performing employee-type services; • The reimbursement or advance must match actual amount of expense; • Expenses must be substantiated within reasonable period of time; and • Any amounts in excess of substantiated expenses must be returned to employer.
Noncash payments for household work, agricultural labor and services not in the employer's trade or business	• Wages are paid "in-kind" (i.e., goods, lodging, food, clothing and services); and • The services provided are not related to the employer's trade or business.
Reimbursed and employer-paid moving expenses	• Must be an expense that is otherwise deductible by the employee; and • Must be paid under an accountable plan.
Meals and lodging	• Meals must be furnished on employer's premises for the convenience of employer, (e.g., so employee is available during lunch for emergency. • Lodging must be furnished for the convenience of the employer on employer's premises as condition of employment.
Health insurance plans	Includes employer-paid accident or health insurance for employee, employee's spouse and dependents.
Health savings accounts and medical savings accounts	Includes contributions to Health Savings Accounts (HSAs) and Archer Medical Savings Accounts (MSAs).
Medical care reimbursements	Must be paid for employee under the employer's self-insured medical reimbursement plan.
Military differential pay	• Employee is on active duty for more than 30 days. • Payments must represent wages the employee would have received if he or she was performing services for the employer.
Fringe benefits	Must be nontaxable (i.e., excluded from the gross income of the employee).
Family employees	Wages for a child under 18 who works for a parent in a trade or business.
Payments after an employee death or disability retirement	Amounts must be paid under a definite plan or system (i.e. sick pay plan).
Post-mortem sick pay payments	Paid to employee's estate or survivor after calendar year of employee's death.
Payments to employee entitled to disability insurance benefits	Includes payments made when an employee is entitled to disability insurance benefits pursuant to Section 223(a) of the Social Security Act.
Certain types of sick pay	Applies to sick pay payments made more than six calendar months after the last calendar month the employee worked.

SOCIAL SECURITY AND MEDICARE TAXES FOR SELF-EMPLOYED INDIVIDUALS

Analogous to the FICA tax imposed on wage income, social security and Medicare taxes are imposed on self-employment income through the Self-Employment Contributions Act of 1954 (SECA).[9] Unlike the FICA tax which has no line item on Form 1040, the SECA tax is computed on Schedule SE and entered on line 56 of Form 1040.

Tax Base

The SECA tax base (commonly referred to as *self-employment income*) is defined as "net earnings from self-employment,"[10] and includes income generated by:

1. a sole proprietor;

2. a single-member LLC that is treated as a disregarded entity and taxed as a sole proprietor;[11] and

3. a general partner's distributive share of ordinary income from the partnership.[12]

As the word "net" implies, gross self-employment income from the taxpayer's business is reduced by deductible expenses attributable to the business. (See Chapters 5 and 6 for a more detailed discussion of the types of deductions that may be used to reduce business income.)

For a sole proprietor or a single-member LLC, self-employment income is calculated on Schedule C. Specifically, a self-employed individual reports gross receipts less all allowable deductions. In this way, Schedule C serves the dual purpose of determining both business income for regular income tax purposes and net self-employment income for SECA purposes.

Similarly, ordinary income and deductions for a partnership are netted on the partnership level. The distributive share of that net income is allocated to each general partner[13] and recorded on a Schedule K-1 that is provided to each partner. That amount is then used on Schedule SE for SECA tax purposes.

Computation of SECA Tax

Unlike a wage earner whose liability is limited to half of the FICA tax, a self-employed individual is obligated to pay the entire amount of the 15.3 percent SECA tax. Similar to FICA, the social security tax cap for self-employment income is the same dollar amount as the social security wage cap ($117,000 in 2014 and indexed for inflation).[14]

Also like FICA, there is no cap on the amount of self-employment income subject to the Medicare tax, and the 0.9 percent Additional Medicare Surtax is added to the 2.9 percent Medicare tax rate for self-employment income that exceeds certain thresholds.

The first step in the computation of the SECA tax is to determine the amount of net self-employment income from all potential sources. If a taxpayer has more than one source of self-employment income, such as income from multiple Schedules C and/or K-1s, net income and loss from those sources are combined. Obviously, if the combined amount is negative, no SECA tax is owed.

Because a self-employed individual is compelled to pay the entire amount of the SECA tax, the following two types of tax relief are provided to ease the burden:

1. The SECA tax base is only 92.35 percent of net self-employment income earnings;[15] and

2. The self-employed individual is entitled to an above-the-line *income tax deduction* equal to one half of the SECA tax.[16]

The first type of tax relief reduces the SECA tax base by 7.65 percent to lessen the amount of SECA tax a self-employed individual would otherwise owe. The above-the-line income tax deduction of one half of the SECA tax reduces taxable income; and, thus, lessens the amount of regular income tax a self-employed individual would otherwise owe. The purpose of this deduction is to level the playing field with wage earners. For wage earners, the employer is responsible for paying half of FICA taxes, and that amount is not included in the wage earner's taxable income.

Example: In 2014, Betty Business operated an IT business as a sole proprietor. In addition, she was a general partner in a partnership that owned and operated a computer store. Finally, she sold refurbished computers through a single-member LLC that was treated as a disregarded entity. Betty is a single taxpayer with no dependents and does not itemize deductions.

On a Schedule C reporting her IT income and expenses, Betty showed net income of $20,000. On a separate Schedule C reporting her refurbished computer income and expenses, Betty showed a net loss of $40,000. Finally, her income from the LLC—recorded on Schedule K-1—was $80,000.

Betty's net self-employment income and tax liabilities are computed as follows:

Net self-employment income

IT business net income	$20,000
Refurbished computer business net loss	–$40,000
LLC income	$80,000
Net self-employment income	**$60,000**

SECA tax

SECA tax base	$60,000 × 92.35% = $55,410
SECA tax owed	**$55,410 × 15.3% = $8,478**
Above-the line deduction for half of SECA tax	$4,239

Income tax

Total income	**$60,000**
Less above-the-line SECA deduction	–$4,329
AGI	**$55,761**
Less standard deduction ($6,100) and personal exemption($3,900)	–$10,000
Taxable Income	**$45,761**

Total tax liability

Income tax (from tax tables)	$7,373
SECA tax	$8,478
Total tax liability	**$15,851**

Figure 10.2

Are Wages and Self-Employment Income Taxed Equivalently?

If a wage earner and a self-employed individual have exactly the same amount of income, would they face the same tax liability? This is a hard question to answer with complete certainty. The 7.65 percent reduction of the SECA tax base provides only moderate tax relief. In the example from the previous section, the SECA tax on the entire amount of Betty's self-employment income ($60,000) would have been $9,180. With the 7.65 percent reduction of her self-employment income ($55,410), the SECA tax was $8,478. The tax savings of $702 does not appear to be that significant.[17]

On the other hand, the above-the-line deduction of one-half of the SECA tax provides more potent tax relief because it is available to all self-employed individuals, even those who do not itemize. The benefit of this deduction depends on the amount of the deduction and the self-employed individual's marginal tax rate. Obviously, higher deductions and higher marginal rates will increase the tax savings.

Above-the-line deductions that reduce adjusted gross income can potentially save tax in other ways because other tax benefits tend to phase out (and tax detriments tend to phase in) with higher amounts of adjusted gross income. Consequently, this deduction could provide even more benefits to a self-employed individual with tax items that are sensitive to the level of adjusted gross income.

COMPARISON OF TAXES ON EARNED INCOME: WAGES vs. SELF-EMPLOYMENT INCOME

	Wages (FICA)	Self-Employment Income (SECA)
Tax Rate	15.30%	15.30%
Amount Subject to Tax	100% of includible wage income	92.35% of self-employment income and/or general partner's distributive share of ordinary income
Who Is Responsible for Tax?	7.65% employee; 7.65% employer	100% Self-employed individual
Income Tax Deduction	None for the employee	Above the line deduction of half of the SECA Tax
Reporting on Form 1040	None for the employee	On Schedule SE and on line 56 on Form 1040
Social Security Earned Income Cap	$117,000 of wages for 2014 Adjusted annually for inflation	$117,000 (or $126,692 multiplied by 92.35%) Adjusted annually for inflation
Medicare Earned Income Cap	None	None
Subject to Additional Medicare Surtax	Yes	Yes

For instance, such a deduction would be helpful to a self-employed individual with a substantial amount of miscellaneous itemized deductions, which are subject to a floor of 2 percent of adjusted gross income.[18] An above-the-line deduction that reduces adjusted gross income lowers the floor, and allows a greater amount of deductions.

Similarly, higher amounts of adjusted gross income increase the amount of social security benefits that are taxable.[19] For a self-employed individual receiving social security benefit payments, an above-the-line deduction that reduces adjusted gross income would also reduce the taxable amount of those payments.

Because of variations in the amount of the above-the-line SECA tax deduction, the marginal tax rate, and types of income-sensitive tax items that any given self-employed individual may have, there is no easy answer to the question above. What is clear (as illustrated in Figure 10.3), is that a self-employed individual who does not itemize will always pay a substantial greater amount of overall tax than a similarly situated wage earner.

USING AN S CORPORATION TO REDUCE SOCIAL SECURITY AND MEDICARE TAXES

Individuals inclined to go into business for themselves should consider forming an S corporation to lessen the tax burden of being self-employed. S corporations do this by providing two important benefits.

Shareholders can become employees. In an S corporation, the individuals who would otherwise be sole proprietors or partners can be employed by the entity and be subject to the FICA rules rather than the SECA rules. As an employee, only half of the 15.3 percent FICA tax would be withheld from the individual's wages. While the full FICA tax is still paid, the half that is paid by the S corporation is a deductible business expense, and is never realized by the shareholder as income.

Shareholders can take dividend distributions. In lieu of taking strictly wage income, shareholders can take some of their compensation as "dividend distributions." Dividend distributions are considered capital gains rather than wages. This has two advantages: (1)

Figure 10.3

SIDE-BY-SIDE COMPARISON OF A WAGE EARNER AND A SELF-EMPLOYED INDIVIDUAL Both are single with no dependents or itemized deductions in tax year 2013.			
Wages	$100,000	Self-employment income	$100,000
Employee's share of the FICA tax:	$7,650 ($100,000×7.65%)	SECA tax:	$14,130 ($100,000×92.35%×15.3%)
Wages $100,000	$100,000	Self-employment income	$100,000
Less standard deduction ($6,100) and personal exemption ($3,900)	-$10,000	Less half of SECA tax	-$7,650
		Less standard deduction ($6,100) and personal exemption ($3,900)	-$10,000
Taxable income	$90,000	Taxable income	$82,935
Regular income tax	$18,500	Regular income tax	$16,660
FICA tax	$7,650	SECA tax	$14,130
Total FICA and regular income tax	$26,150	Total SECA and regular income tax:	$30,790
Excess amount of total tax paid by self-employed individual as compared to wage earner: $30,790 - $26,150 = $4,640			

they are not subject to the FICA tax;[20] and (2) they are often taxed at a lower rate than ordinary income. A shareholder/employee who is compensated with a combination of wages and dividend distributions could potentially realize a significant savings of FICA tax.

However, the IRS considers disproportionately large dividend distributions to be an inappropriate way to avoid FICA tax. In Revenue Ruling 74-44, two shareholders of an S corporation who provided services to the corporation received dividend distributions but no compensation. Under those circumstances, the IRS recharacterized the amount of the distributions that would have been reasonable compensation for the services provided as wages subject to FICA.[21]

Obviously, the facts of the revenue ruling were egregious because the shareholder/employees received no compensation. If the wages of a shareholder/employee are "reasonable compensation" for the services that were performed, he or she may legitimately receive some compensation in the form of dividend distributions. When determining whether the amount of wages paid constitutes "reasonable compensation" for a shareholder/employee, the IRS will consider a number of factors:[22]

- The shareholder/employee's training and experience

- The duties and responsibilities of the shareholder/employee

- The amount of time and effort devoted to the business

- Compensation of similar employees who are not shareholders

- What comparable businesses pay for similar services

- The use of a formula to determine compensation

These factors are particularly relevant to a professional service corporation. Obviously, a shareholder/employee who provides substantial specialized professional services to the business should command a relatively high salary. On the other hand, a shareholder/employee who, with age, decides to assume a reduced role may be able to justify a lower amount of compensation, and, perhaps a significant amount as a dividend distribution.

An obvious lack of reasonable compensation is evidenced when the salary of a high qualified shareholder/employee is less than the salary of a lesser qualified non-shareholder/employee. Attempts to make up the difference through dividend distributions would not likely pass IRS scrutiny.

Another indication of reasonable compensation is what a comparable business would pay an employee for providing similar services. If the going compensation for a specific type of professional is $250,000, paying a shareholder/employee a salary of $50,000 to perform those same services would likely not be considered reasonable compensation. When deciding on how to distribute compensation between wages and dividend distributions, shareholders should consult independent salary surveys for their specific industries.

Finally, published, businesses can use industry-specific compensation formulas to determine the wages of a shareholder/employee as a percentage of sales or profits. The use of these formulas should allow the compensation decisions to withstand IRS scrutiny.

Example: Kristi is a veterinarian who owns a two-doctor practice. She sees patients five days per week in addition to her management duties. After realizing a $40,000 profit in 2013, in 2014 she incorporates her two-doctor veterinary practice as an S Corporation, Veterinary Medical Center, Inc. (VMC). VMC compensates her with monthly wages in the amount of 23 percent of her billings. Using this formula, her 2014 wages were $100,000, and she paid herself a total of $25,000 in quarterly dividend distributions. She also pays a less-experienced associate veterinarian wages in the amount of 20 percent of his billings, which resulted in $80,000 in wage compensation for 2014.

Although Kristi's wages are subject to both FICA tax and ordinary income tax, the dividend distribution would be subject only to income tax, and taxed as a capital gain. As a result, Kristi would save a total of $3,825 of FICA tax (15.3 percent of $25,000), and likely enjoy a lower tax rate on the dividend income than she would have if the money had been received as wages.

Additionally, she can justify the dividend distributions by clearly showing that her wages were "reasonable compensation" for the services performed:

- She is an experienced and licensed veterinarian.

- Her duties included full-time clinical hours in addition to her management responsibilities.

- She worked in her practice five days per week.

- Her non-shareholder associate was paid similar wages (after accounting for his lower level of experience).

- Her wages were based on a formula that can be reconciled with the accounting records of the business.

- Her dividend distributions are similar to the profit earned by the business the year before.

FREQUENTLY ASKED QUESTIONS

Question – Are below-market or interest-free loans between an employer and employee subject to the FICA tax?

Answer – Yes, for loans greater than $10,000.[23] The amount of imputed "wages" subject to the FICA tax from such a loan is the difference between the interest that would have been payable to the employer using the applicable federal rate, and the amount actually that was paid by the employee.[24]

Example: Gary Gizmo borrows $100,000 from his employer. The loan is an interest-free demand loan. Assuming the applicable federal rate is 3 percent, the amount of Gary's imputed compensation is the foregone interest of $3,000. As a result, $3,000 of imputed wage income is subject to FICA tax.[25]

Question – Are there any additional filing requirements for individuals who form an S corporation rather than operate as sole proprietors or partners?

Answer – Yes. First, the S corporation must file an income tax return using Form 1120S. Unlike Form 1040, the filing deadline for a Form 1120S is March 15. Also, the S corporation must report wages quarterly using Form 941 and make periodic payroll tax deposits.

Question – Are there any other above-the-line deductions available for self-employed individuals?

Answer – Yes, a self-employed individual may be entitled to an above-the-line deduction for premiums paid on medical, dental or long-term care insurance policies that cover himself, his spouse, and his dependents. The deduction is available to sole proprietors, single-member LLCs treated as a disregarded entities, general partners, or a shareholders of an S corporation who own more than 2 percent of the outstanding stock. Since the deduction is personal (not business), it is not entered on Schedule C. Instead, it is taken as an above-the-line deduction on Form 1040.

CHAPTER ENDNOTES

1. Codified as Chapter 21 of the Internal Revenue Code (I.R.C. §§3101-3128).
2. I.R.C. §3121(a).
3. I.R.C. §3121(b).
4. *Social Security Bd. v. Nierotko*, 327 U.S. 358 (1946).
5. *U.S. v. Quality Stores, Inc.*, 572 U.S. ___ (2014).
6. IRS Publication 15 (2014), "Wages and Other Compensation."
7. I.R.C. §§3101(a), 3111(a), 3101(b) and 3111(b).
8. Press Release, Social Security Administration (October 13, 2013).
9. SECA is codified as Chapter 2 of the Internal Revenue Code.
10. I.R.C. §1402(a).
11. Treas. Reg. §301.7702-2(c)(2)(iv)(D), "Example (iii)."
12. I.R.C. §1402(a).
13. I.R.C. §702(a)(8).
14. IRS Publication 517 (2013).
15. Social Security Handbook, "Net Earnings from Self-Employment." Available at http://www.ssa.gov/OP_Home/handbook/handbook.html.
16. I.R.C. §164(f).
17. Expressed as a percentage, the tax savings seem minimal. Based on self-employment income of $60,000, the lesser SECA tax of $8,478 would reduce the overall tax rate to 14.13 percent ($8,478/$60,000), or a savings of 1.17 percent.
18. I.R.C. §67.
19. I.R.C. §86.
20. Rev. Rul. 59-221, 1959-1 C.B. 225.
21. Rev. Rul. 74-44, 1974-1 C.B. 287.
22. IRS Fact Sheet 2008-25 (August 2008).
23. I.R.C. §7872(c)(3). Below-market loans between employers and employees are subject to a $10,000 de minimus exception for the purposes taxation.
24. I.R.C. §7872.
25. IRS Publication 15-A (2014).

ADDITIONAL MEDICARE SURTAX ON EARNED INCOME AND NET INVESTMENT INCOME TAX

CHAPTER 11

INTRODUCTION

There are two basic ways to increase taxes. The most obvious way is to raise the rate brackets. The other way is to impose a surtax. A *surtax* is a "tax levied on top of another tax,"[1] and is generally triggered when certain income levels are exceeded. The Health Care and Education Reconciliation Act of 2010[2] enacted two "flat" surtaxes. The "Additional Medicare Surtax" is a 0.9 percent tax on earned income, and the "Net Investment Income Tax" (NIIT) is a 3.8 percent tax on net investment income.

WHAT IS THE MEDICARE SURTAX?

As the name suggests, the Additional Medicare Surtax is not a new surtax, but instead increases the surtax rate and extends the tax base of the Health Insurance tax. The Health Insurance tax—itself a previously existing surtax—is also known as the Medicare tax, and is part of the Federal Insurance Contributions Act and Railroad Retirement Tax Act Taxes ("FICA").[3] FICA is imposed on all *earned income*, including wage-type income (salaries, commissions, etc.) that are typically reported on a W-2, as well as self-employment income (including income from self-proprietors, single-member LLCs taxed as sole proprietors, and general partners' distributive shares of partnership ordinary income).[4]

Effective for tax years 2013 and later, there is an Additional Medicare Surtax of 0.9 percent added to the FICA wages and/or self-employment income in excess of the applicable thresholds.[5] Once earned income exceeds the applicable threshold, the imposition of the Additional Medicare Surtax increases the overall Medicare tax rate to 3.8 percent (the same percentage as the flat NIIT rate, discussed below). The applicable thresholds for the Medicare surtax are defined in terms of earned income, and vary by filing status:

- $250,000 for a married couple filing jointly;

- $125,000 for a married individual filing separately; and

- $200,000 for all other filing statuses.[6]

Although the Additional Medicare Tax is not imposed on the employer share of the Medicare tax, the employer is nonetheless obligated to withhold 0.9 percent of an employee's wages in excess of $200,000 - without regard to whether such employee is actually subject to the tax.[7]

WHAT IS THE NET INVESTMENT INCOME TAX?

The Net Investment Income Tax ("NIIT") is the other surtax enacted pursuant to The Health Care and

Education Reconciliation Act of 2010.[8] Unlike the Additional Medicare Surtax that is limited to individuals, estates and many trusts are also subject to the tax.[9] For individual taxpayers, the NIIT is a 3.8 percent surtax that is imposed on the lesser of:

- a taxpayer's net investment income; or

- the amount by which the taxpayer's adjusted gross income[10] exceeds the applicable threshold amounts (which are the same as the Medicare surtax threshold amounts discussed above).[11]

The threshold amounts for the NIIT are the same as the Additional Medicare Tax thresholds. But these thresholds are based on the taxpayer's adjusted gross income, not earned income. Additionally, as discussed in more detail later in this Chapter, the threshold amount for trusts and estates is much lower than the thresholds of the individual taxpayers subject to the tax.[12]

In essence, NIIT is a surtax on net investment income that has already been subject to regular federal income tax. In operation, the computation of net investment income is comparable to the computation of taxable income. With regard to regular taxation, items of gross income comprise the tax base. As discussed in Chapter 3, taxable income equals gross income minus deductions for the expenses necessary for generating that income. Similarly, with regard to NIIT, items of investment income that have already been taxed (i.e., were included in gross income) comprise the NIIT tax base. Thus, similar to the computation of taxable income, net *investment* income is gross investment income minus deductible expenses properly allocable to such income.

However, the devil is in the details, and the complexity of NIIT calculations cannot be underestimated.

The process of computing the NIIT obligation requires several steps:

1. First, identify items included in gross income that fit the Code definition of "investment income."

2. Second, identify deductions properly allocable to that income to determine the amount of "net investment income."

3. The final step—assuming the applicable threshold for the imposition of the tax has been crossed—is to multiply the NIIT rate of 3.8 percent by the lesser of:

a. net investment income (as calculated in the second step), or

b. the difference between the taxpayer's adjusted gross income and the applicable threshold.

Important caveat: Any item of income that is Medicare wage income or self-employment income is never considered net investment income, even if it would otherwise meet the Code definition. In that case, such income may be subject to the Additional Medicare Surtax.[13]

WHAT TYPES OF INCOMES ARE SUBJECT TO THE SURTAXES?

Each surtax has its own threshold (listed above) and tax base. The *threshold* is the triggering point of the surtax, and the *tax base* specifies the type of income that is subject to the surtax. The Additional Medicare Surtax threshold is based on the taxpayer's total amount of *earned income* (defined to include Medicare wages and/or self-employment income) in excess of the applicable threshold amount, and its tax base is the taxpayer's earned income.

The NIIT has the same threshold amounts, but it has a different tax base. It is applied to the lesser of either *adjusted gross income*—not earned income as is the case for the Medicare surtax.[14]—or net investment income. In other words, if the amount of net investment income is greater than the excess of adjusted gross income over the threshold amount, the NIIT would be imposed on the excess amount of adjusted gross income, rather than net investment income.

Example: Iris, a single taxpayer has adjusted gross income of $208,000, including a net investment income of $10,000. As a single taxpayer she has a threshold amount of $200,000. In Iris' case, the NIIT would be imposed on the $8,000 in AGI that is beyond the threshold amount—rather than her $10,000 of net investment income—because that is the lesser of the two amounts.

Significantly, any income subject to the Additional Medicare Tax is not also subject to the NIIT.[15] This means that wages and self-employment income are *never* included in the NIIT tax base, and thus are not subject to the NIIT. On the other hand, if the taxpayer has wages and/or self-employment income as well as net investment income, it is possible to be subject to both surtaxes. The Additional Medicare Tax could be imposed on the wage and self-employment income, while the NIIT could be imposed on the investment income. The example below illustrates the following fact pattern in which a taxpayer is subject to the Additional Medicare Surtax and the NIIT on top of the regular income tax.

Example: In 2014, Ira, a single taxpayer has $410,000 of taxable income which includes wages of $300,000 and net investment income of $110,000. After some preliminary calculations, Ira's adjusted gross income is determined to be $350,000.

Ira's regular tax without regard to the surtaxes is $119,476.[16] The Additional Medicare Surtax is also imposed because the taxpayer's earned income of $300,000 exceeds the threshold of $200,000 for a single individual,[17] resulting in $900 of Additional Medicare Surtax on the excess $100,000. Finally, the NIIT is also imposed because Ira's adjusted gross income exceeds the NIIT threshold of $200,000 for a single individual.[18]

Once the threshold is triggered, the tax would be computed on:

- the lesser of net investment income ($110,000); or

- the excess of adjusted gross income over the threshold amount ($150,000).

In Ira's case, the NIIT would be $4,180 (3.8 percent of $110,000).

Taxable Income $410,000
Including:
Wages $300,000
Net Investment Income $110,000 Adjusted Gross Income $350,000

Step 1: Compute Regular Income Tax on $410,000 of taxable income	**$119,476**
Step 2: Compute Additional Medicare Surtax on wages in excess of $200,000.	**0.9% of $100,000 = $900**
Step 3: Compute NIIT on $110,000 (the lesser of NII or AGI in excess of the threshold amount)	**$4,180**

This example demonstrates that the two surtaxes are subject to their own thresholds and their own tax rates that are levied on top of the regular income tax. Based on this illustration, the total tax liability with respect to the three taxes would be $124,556—of which $5,080 would be attributable to the two new surtaxes.

HOW DOES THE ADDITIONAL MEDICARE SURTAX WORK?

Although perhaps not the norm, it is possible for a taxpayer to have W-2 wage income as well as self-employment income from a business outside of his or her employment. As stated above, the Additional Medicare Surtax is imposed on any combination of Medicare wages and self-employment income in excess of the applicable threshold. This is a relatively simple calculation, as demonstrated in the example below.

Example: A single taxpayer has Medicare wages of $275,000 and self-employment income of $100,000. Based on the single filing status, the applicable threshold is $200,000, and the total of Medicare wages and self-employment income exceeds the threshold by $175,000. To compute the Additional Medicare Surtax, multiply that amount by the surtax rate of 0.9 percent.

Medicare wages	$275,000
Self-employment income	$100,000
Total income subject to Additional Medicare Surtax	$275,000 + $100,000 = $375,000
Threshold for single taxpayer	$200,000
Income subject to Additional Medicare Surtax (amount by which Medicare and SE income exceeds threshold)	$375,000 − $200,000 = $175,000
Additional Medicare Surtax rate	0.9%
Additional Medicare Surtax obligation	$175,000 × 0.9% = $1,575

HOW DOES THE NIIT SURTAX WORK?

As stated above, the 3.8 percent NIIT surtax is imposed on "net investment income." In order to compute "net investment income," it is necessary to determine which items of regular gross income are considered "investment income." In the most general terms, Code section 1411(c) defines "investment income" as what would commonly be considered investment income. Beyond that, what else is considered investment income is more complicated. In essence, investment income also includes any passive activity income derived from a trade or business. As discussed in Chapter 3, a passive activity is any trade or business activity in which the taxpayer does not "materially participate."[19] Generally, a taxpayer materially participates in an activity if he is involved in the operations of the activity on a regular, continuous, and substantial basis. By implication, income derived from a trade or business in which a taxpayer materially participates would not be "investment income" for the purposes of the NIIT.

Important caveat: All income of any type generated by a business trading financial instruments or commodities is always treated as investment income, without exception.[20]

WHAT IS INCLUDED IN NET INVESTMENT INCOME?

Net investment income includes items that are specifically enumerated by the Internal Revenue Code, as well as other items that arise from a taxpayer's business activities or ownership of interests in corporate entities. These items are discussed in detail below.

Specifically Enumerated Investment Income Items

Section 1411(c)(1)(A)(i) specifically enumerates what most would consider the "traditional" types of investment income: interest, dividends, annuities, royalties and rents. However, there are exceptions. Such income would *not* be considered investment income if:

1. the income was generated in a trade or business;

2. the income was derived in the ordinary course of that trade or business; and

3. the trade or business activity generating the income is non-passive with respect to the taxpayer.

The term "trade or business" is defined the same way for net investment income as it is for regular income in Code section 162.[21] With regard to the second requirement, income "derived in the ordinary course of a trade or business" means the type of income the trade or business was designed to generate. Finally, the third requirement requires the taxpayer to materially participate in the trade or business that generates such income so that the activity is non-passive with respect to the taxpayer. In addition to this general exception, there are other exceptions set forth in the Code and regulations.

Figure 11.1 sets forth each of the five enumerated items of investment income with examples of circumstances in which they are either included or excluded from the scope of the NIIT. These examples assume that the income is not included in a general partner's distributive share of ordinary income or reportable on Schedule C for a sole proprietor or single-member LLC that is treated as a disregarded entity.

Income from Passive Business Activity

As discussed above, Code section 1411(c)(1)(A)(i) specifically enumerates five types of income treated as investment income. Conversely, Code section 1411(c)(1)(A)(ii) broadly includes all passive activity business income as net investment income.

However, there are exceptions. Passive activity income would *not* be considered investment income if:

1. the income was generated in a trade or business;

2. the income was "earned" in the ordinary course of that trade or business; and

3. the trade or business activity generating the income is non-passive *with respect to the taxpayer.*

An important issue is whether a shareholder of an S corporation must treat his or her distributive share of ordinary income (Line 1 of Schedule K-1 of Form 1120S) as investment income. The exception above can give a curious result. It is possible that the distributive share of the ordinary income of one shareholder may be treated as net investment income whereas the distributive share of another shareholder may be excluded from net investment income because, for an S corporation, the determination of whether an activity is non-passive is made at the shareholder level rather than the entity level.[39]

Figure 11.1

SECTION 1411(c)(1)(A)(i) ITEMS	
Interest	
Included: Interest derived from the investment of working capital set aside for future use by a non-passive trade or business is nonetheless considered investment income.[22]	*Excluded*: Tax-exempt interest from a state or local bond is not investment income. (Because NIIT is a surtax on top of the regular income tax, any item excluded from gross income is also excluded from gross investment income.)[24]
Included: Interest distributed to a beneficiary from a trust or estate to the extent that character of the income would be net investment income.[23]	*Exclude*: "Self-charged interest" is interest charged by a taxpayer for lending money to a business that he or she owns and/or where he or she works. Because such taxpayers are generally not be in the trade or business of loaning money, without a specific exception, such interest income would be investment income. However, the regulations provide an exception if the lending taxpayer materially participates in the business. In that case, the interest income would not be considered investment income.[25]
	Excluded: Interest earned by a banking business with respect to which the taxpayer materially participates (so it is a non-passive activity) would not be investment income because it is derived in the ordinary course of business. (Interest is the type of income that a bank is designed to generate.)[26]
Dividends	
Included: All items defined as "dividends" in the Code.[27]	*None excluded*. Dividends are always considered net investment income.
Included: Dividends derived from the investment of working capital set aside for future use by a non-passive trade or business are nonetheless considered investment income.[28]	
Included: Dividends distributed to a beneficiary from a trust or estate to the extent that character of the income would be net investment income.[29]	
Annuities	
Included: Generally, gross income from annuities as defined by Code sections 72(a), (b) and (e) is considered investment income.[30]	*Excluded*: Gross income from annuities paid by an employer as compensation is not considered investment income.[31]
	Excluded: All distributions from retirement plans, including: qualified pension, profit-sharing and stock bonus plans; qualified annuity plans; annuities for employees of tax-exempt organizations or public schools; IRAs (regular and Roth); and deferred compensation plans of governments and tax-exempt organizations.[32]

Figure 11.1 (cont'd)

SECTION 1411(c)(1)(A)(i) ITEMS	
Royalties	
Included: Gross income from royalties—including mineral, oil, and gas royalties—as well as amounts received for the privilege of using patents, copyrights, secret processes and formulas, goodwill, trademarks, tradebrands, franchises and other like property.[33]	*None excluded*. Royalties are always considered net investment income.
Rents	
Included: Rents distributed to a beneficiary from a trust or estate to the extent that character of the income would be net investment income.[34]	*Excluded*: Rental income from a rental activity of a real estate professional. Generally, all rental income is considered passive, and is treated as investment income even if it was derived in the ordinary course of business. There is a safe harbor for "real estate professionals"[35] who participated in that rental activity for more than 500 hours during that year or more than five of any of the ten years immediately preceding that year.[36]
	Excluded: "Self-charged rent." Similar to self-charged interest, self-charged rent is rental income derived from renting property to a trade or business in which the taxpayer materially participates. According to the passive loss regulations, such income is treated as non-passive.[37] The final regulations extend the same treatment of self-charged rent as being non-passive if it would be treated as non-passive pursuant to the passive loss regulations, or if the taxpayer elects to group such rental activity with other rental trades or business (which is another way to convert rental income from passive to non-passive income).[38]

Example: Hugh Haule and Frederica Expresso are equal shareholders in an S corporation that delivers packages. Whereas Hugh works in the business on a fulltime basis, Frederick has no involvement in the business. In the current year, their S corporation earns $100,000 of ordinary income allocated $50,000 to each shareholder.

Hugh's distributive share of ordinary income is not treated as net investment income because it was earned in the ordinary course of business (meeting the first two requirements listed above), and—because Hugh actively works as a material participant in the business—it is a non-passive activity with respect to him (meeting the third requirement listed above). Conversely, Frederica's distributive share of ordinary income is net investment income to

her. Although the income meets the first two requirements of being earned in a trade or business, as a non-participant in the business, it is a passive activity with respect to her because she does not actively work in the business (and thus it fails the third requirement of the exception).

Income from a Pass-through Entity

As discussed earlier in this chapter, "self-employment income" is never treated as net investment income regardless of whether it would otherwise meet the definition for such under the NIIT.[40] What can cause some confusion is that a taxpayer can receive some items meeting the definition of "net investment income" via an interest in a pass-through entity such as a partnership, LLC, or S corporation.[41] In some instances, the nature of the taxpayer's interest in the pass-through entity would cause such income to be treated as self-employment income.

In addition to the income of a sole proprietor, self-employment income also includes a general partner's distributive share of ordinary income and any item of income reported on Schedule C for a single-member LLC that is treated as a disregarded entity. For that reason, such income would be subject to the Additional Medicare Surtax even if it would otherwise meet the Code definition of net investment income.

On the other hand, with some exceptions, certain types of income, such as dividends, interest, gains from the disposition of property, and rent are generally not treated as self-employment income regardless of the taxpayer's interest in the entity.[42] Consequently, in most of those instances, such income would be subject to NIIT.

Figure 11.2 sets forth the various ownership interests in which the nature of the ownership interest may dictate whether the flow-through income would be characterized as self-employment income or potentially net investment income.

Gain from the Sale of Property Held by a Business

Unlike a general partner's distributive share of ordinary income or the income of a sole proprietor, gains from the disposition of property (other than inventory) are specifically excluded from self-employment income.[49] This provision applies across the board, and includes gains from the disposition of property that the taxpayer owns directly, as well as property that "flows through" to the taxpayer by virtue of an ownership interest in the entity disposing of the property.

Code section 1411(c)(1)(A)(iii) treats net gains from the disposition of property as net investment income if the property is held in a trade or business that is a passive activity with respect to the taxpayer. The word "disposition" is broadly defined as a "sale, exchange, transfer, conversion, cash settlement, cancellation, termination, lapse, expiration, or other disposition."[50] If the gain meets those requirements, it must be included in gross income under Code section 61(a)(3).[51]

Importantly, some "dispositions" can occur over long periods of time, leading to questions about when income from the gain of the disposition is realized by the taxpayer. Deferred or excluded gains such as gain from an installment sale,[52] like-kind exchanges,[53] involuntary conversions[54] and the sale of a principal residence[55] are not considered investment income *unless and until* they are included in regular gross income.[56]

In order for a gain from the disposition of property *not to be treated* as net investment income, the two following requirement must be met:

1. the gains were derived from property held in a trade or business; and

2. the trade or business activity generating the gain is non-passive with respect to the taxpayer.

3. The following two examples demonstrate how gain from the sale of property held by a

Figure 11.2

Ownership Interest	How the Income is Reported	Treated as Self-Employment Income?
General partner interest	Distributive share of partnership ordinary income.[43]	Always self-employment income.[44]
Sole proprietor (not a flow-through entity)	Reported on Schedule C.	Always self-employment income.[45]
Single-member LLC treated as a disregarded entity	Reported on Schedule C as if a sole proprietor.	Always self-employment income.[46]
Limited partner interest	Distributive share of ordinary Income.	Not self-employment income (potentially net investment income.)[47]
Shareholder of S corporation	Distributive share of any type of S corporation Income.	Not treated as self-employment income (potentially net investment income.)[48]

business may (or may not) be excluded from net investment income.

Example 1: Iris owns a boat in her own name and rents it to Ira for $100,000 per year. Iris' rental activity fails to meet both exclusion requirements because her rental activity does not reach the level of a trade or business, and because rental activities are always considered passive. Assume Iris sells the boat to Ira in a subsequent year and recognizes a taxable gain of $500,000. Having failed the requirements for exclusion in the prior year, Iris must include such gain as investment income.[57]

Example 2: Hugh Haule and Frederica Expresso are equal owners of a partnership engaged in the moving business. Hugh is involved in day-to-day operations, Frederica devotes all of her time to another endeavor. In 2014, the business sells a facility it had used to store furniture, recognizing a gain of $200,000 that is evenly allocated to both shareholders. Because the property was used in the S corporation's trade or business, and Hugh materially participates in the business, his share of the gain meets both exclusion requirements, and is not treated as investment income. Because Frederica does not materially participate in the business, she fails the second part of the test, and her allocable share of the gain would be treated as investment income for the purposes of the NIIT.

Gain from the Sale of an S Corporation or a Partnership

To this point in the discussion, the determination of whether income generated by pass-through entities such as S corporations and partnerships was treated as net investment income was based on the taxpayer's participation in the business. If the individual materially participated in the business, the income was not treated as net investment income. If the taxpayer's participation in the business was passive, the income was included as net investment income.

However, the sale of an interest in a pass-through entity to a third party does not generate any income or loss to the underlying entity. Similar to the sale of any individually-owned asset, the sale of an entity interest would generate gain or loss to the selling shareholder or partner. From the entity's perspective this is not a taxable event in and of itself, as one shareholder/partner is merely substituted for another shareholder/partner.

Code section 1411(c)(4) specifically addresses the extent to which the gain from the sale of an interest in a pass-through entity taxed as an S corporation (or a partnership) is to be treated as net investment income. In addition to "conventional" S corporations and partnerships, the section also addresses sales of interests in LLCs electing to be taxed as either one of those entities.[58]

First, section 1411(c)(4) creates a "fictional" pass-through scenario by recasting the transaction as if the entity had sold all of its assets for their fair market value, and the selling shareholder/partner was allocated his or her share of the gain or loss based on his or her ownership interest.

Second—in the same way as determining whether a shareholder/partner's distributive share of real gain from the sale of an entity asset would be excluded from net investment income—the two following requirements must be met in order to exclude the gain from net investment income:

- the gains were derived from property held in a trade or business; and

- the trade or business activity generating the gain is non-passive with respect to the taxpayer.

The application of this test with regard to the sale of an interest in an S corporation or partnership can be problematic. The question of whether a shareholder/partner's distributive share of gain from the sale of a *single* entity asset is to be treated as net investment income depends on whether the asset was used in a trade or business activity that was passive or non-passive with respect to the taxpayer. What about a hypothetical sale of *all* the assets owned by the entity? Moreover, it is possible that any given entity may engage in more than one distinct business activity in which different assets are employed. It is equally possible that a shareholder/partner's participation in those distinct activities may vary.

For these reasons, the proposed regulations take an activity-by-activity approach. Based on the level of a shareholder/partner's participation in the distinct business activities, some of the gain from the hypothetical sale of entity assets may be characterized as net investment income and some may not. The proposed regulations also allow the use of two different formulas to determine a portion of the shareholder/partner's gain from the sale of his or interest would be similarly characterized.[59] Bear in mind that at the time of publication, these were only proposed regulations that were not final and are subject to change.

If the taxpayer does not materially participate in any of the business activities of the entity, the gain from the sale of the entity is all passive with respect to the taxpayer. Under these circumstances, there is no need to apply any formula, and the taxpayer's entire gain from the disposition of the interest would be treated as net investment income.

Equally obvious, if the taxpayer materially participates in all the business activities of the entity, they are all non-passive with respect to the taxpayer. In this instance, the taxpayer's entire gain from the disposition of the interest would not be treated as net investment income.[60]

Finally, if the taxpayer materially participates in only some of the business activities of the entity, one of the two formulas from the proposed regulations would be applied to determine how much of the taxpayer's gain on the sale of the entity interest would be treated as net investment income.

Problematically, the first formula requires the selling shareholder/partner to gather a significant amount of information regarding the underlying assets of the entity that may not be readily accessible. The second formula—the "optional simplified method"—requires much less information, all of which would be found on the taxpayer's Form K-1. However, it is only available to taxpayers who meet certain criteria.

The First Formula

The best way to understand the first formula is to walk through an example that shows the steps required and the information that needs to be gathered to follow those steps.

Example: Iris owns 50 percent of an S corporation engaged in two distinct business activities: a moving business and a telephone answering business. Iris works exclusively in the moving business and has no involvement in the telephone answering business. The S corporation has three assets:

Assets of Iris' S Corporation

Asset	Fair Market Value (FMV)	Basis (amount paid for the assets by Iris' S Corp)
Telephone Answering Equipment	$126,000	$136,000
Storage Warehouse	$150,000	$75,000
Marketable Securities	$50,000	$8,000

Assume that in 2014 Iris sells all of her stock in the S corporation to a third party and recognizes a capital gain of $200,000. The process of calculating Iris' net investment income from the sale using the first formula involves multiple steps.

Step 1 – Identify the different business activities within the entity. As stated above, the S corporation is engaged in a moving business and a telephone answering business.

Step 2 – Determine which business activities are passive and non-passive with respect to the selling taxpayer. Based on Iris' level of participation in the respective businesses, the moving business is non-passive and the telephone answering business is passive.

Step 3 – Identify what the proposed regulations define as "section 1411 property" with respect to the selling taxpayer. "Section 1411 property" includes:

- Property that is associated with a business activity that was passive with respect to the taxpayer; and

- any marketable securities.[61]

By that definition, the telephone answering equipment and the marketable securities are section 1411 property. The storage warehouse is not section 1411 property because it is used in a business activity which is non-passive with respect to Iris.

Step 4 – Determine Iris' distributive share of gain from a hypothetical sale of the section 1411 property at FMV. The hypothetical sale of the telephone answering equipment would generate a $10,000 loss. Because Iris owns 50 percent of the

S corporation, Iris' distributive share of the loss would be $5,000. The hypothetical sale of the marketable securities would yield a $42,000 gain, of which Iris' distributive share would be $21,000. Thus, Iris' net distributive share of the net gain would be $16,000 ($21,000 gain minus $5,000 loss).

Property	FMV	Basis	Gain/ Loss	Iris Share Gain/ Loss
Telephone Answering Equipment	$126,000	$136,000	($10,000)	($5,000)
Marketable Securities	$50,000	$8,000	$42,000	$21,000
Total	$176,000	$144,000	$32,000	$16,000

Step 5 – Determine the amount of gain treated as net investment income. This amount is the lesser of:

- the overall regular income tax gain ($200,000); or

- the shareholder's hypothetical distributive share of the entity gain as computed in Step 4 ($16,000).

Here, Iris' regular income tax gain was $200,000 and her hypothetical distributive share of S corporation gain from the sale of section 1411 assets was $16,000. As a result, Iris' net investment income from the sale using the first formula would be $16,000 with the balance of the gain, $184,000, excluded from net investment income.

Optional Simplified Method

The optional simplified method contained in the proposed regulations allows the taxpayer to compute net investment income from the sale or disposition of an S Corporation by multiplying the gain from the sale by a simple ratio.[62] One definition is key to understating the optional simplified method: the "section 1411 holding period," which is defined as the current year plus the last two years.

Importantly, not all taxpayers may use the optional simplified method. In order to do so, the taxpayer must qualify by satisfying one of two tests.

Test 1: The first test has two requirements:

1. The sum of net investment income, gain, loss and deduction (loss and deduction added as a positive numbers for purposes of this calculation) allocated to the selling taxpayer over the section 1411 holding period is less than 5 percent of the sum of all items of income, gain, loss and deduction (again, with loss and deduction added as positive numbers for purposes of this calculation), allocated to the selling taxpayer during the section 1411 holding period; and

2. the total amount of gain recognized for regular income tax purposes with regard to the sale of the entity interest must be less than $5 million.

Test 2: Test 2 is simpler, and requires only that the total amount of gain recognized on the sale of the interest in the entity be less than $250,000.

Under the optional simplified method, the net investment income is computed by multiplying the gain from the sale of an interest in an S corporation or a partnership by a ratio that must be computed for each sale. The ratio is calculated by dividing the sum of *net* investment income, gain, deduction, or loss allocated to the seller by the sum of *all* items of income, gain, deduction, or loss allocated to the seller. Both values are calculated over the section 1411 holding period.

Multiplying the total gain from the sale by the ratio described above gives the amount of gain from the sale that is treated as net investment income. Stated differently, the amount of gain treated as net investment income is based on the percentage of the shareholder/partner's distributive share of net investment income over all income of the entity during the section 1411 holding period. Again, an example is helpful.

Example: Hugh Haule sells his S corporation stock to a third party and recognizes a gain of $500,000. The S corporation has two distinct businesses, a moving business in which Hugh materially participates, and a telephone answering business in which he does not materially participate.

Total Amounts over Section 1411 Holding Period

Hugh's Distributive Share of Income Attributable from Non-Passive Moving Business	$2,000,000
Hugh's Distributive Share of Dividend Income	$50,000
Hugh's Distributive Share of Loss from Passive Telephone Answering Service	($15,000)

First, Hugh must determine whether he qualifies for the optional simplified method. Hugh's recognized gain of $500,000 clearly fails Test 2, so he must pass Test 1 in order to use the optional simplified method. To do so, the sum of his distributive share of *net* investment income, gain, loss and deduction (all added as a positive numbers) over the section 1411 holding period must be less than 5 percent of the sum of his distributive share of all income, gain, loss and deduction (all added as a positive numbers) over that same period.

Test 2

Sum of *net* investment gain, loss, and deduction	Sum of *all* income, gain, loss, and deduction	Ratio of net investment income over all income must be less than 5%
$50,000 + $15,000 = $65,000	$2,000,000 + $50,000 + $15,000 = $2,065,000	$\dfrac{\$65,000}{\$2,065,000} = 3.15\%$

Here, Hugh passes Test 1 because $65,000 divided by $2,065,000 is approximately 3.15 percent, which is less than 5 percent required for the test. Therefore Hugh may use the optional simplified method.

Next, Hugh must determine the amount of gain that is treated as net investment income. To make that determination, he first calculates the ratio of the total distributive share of net income divided by the total distributive share of all items of income (again, all figures are for the section 1411 holding period). He then multiplies that ratio by the total gain from the sale to determine the amount of the gain that is included in net investment income.

Calculation of Net Investment Income from Sale

Total distributive share of net income (net investment dividend income minus passive loss)	$(\$50,000 - \$15,000) = \$35,000$
Total distributive share of all income (non-passive income plus net investment dividend income, minus passive loss)	$(\$2,000,000 + \$50,000 - \$15,000)$ $= \$2,035,000$
Ratio	$\dfrac{\$35,000}{\$2,035,000} = 1.7\%$
Ratio multiplied by total gain from sale yields net investment income from sale	$1.7\% \times \$500,000 = \$8,600$

In this case, approximately 1.7 percent of all S corporation income allocated to Hugh over the section 1411 holding period was net investment income. Multiplying that percentage by the gain from the sale of his stock ($500,000), Hugh calculates that approximately $8,600 of the gain is *included* in net investment income, and the balance of $491,400 is *excluded* from net investment income.

How Is Net Gain Calculated?

Significantly, Code section 1411(c)(1)(A)(iii) refers to "net gain"—meaning that gains are netted against losses, as both terms are defined in the section. In a taxpayer-friendly provision, the final regulations provide for the treatment of capital gains and losses for net investment income purposes that parallels their treatment for regular income tax purposes. For regular income tax purposes, capital losses are deductible to the extent of capital gains plus $3,000 of any excess being deductible against other income. The unused excess loss is carried over to subsequent tax years subject to being netted against capital gains generated in such years. Similarly, a taxpayer may use the same netting rules to reduce investment income net gain to zero, with $3,000 of any excess reducing other investment income. Any unused excess capital loss is carried over to subsequent years to be re-employed in the same manner.[63]

Example: In 2014, Iris, a single taxpayer has the following items of income and loss: a $40,000 capital loss and a $10,000 capital gain from the sale of publicly traded stock, $300,000 of wage income and $5,000 of interest income. For regular income tax purposes, capital gain and loss are netted resulting in a net capital loss of $30,000, of which $3,000 can be used as a deduction against other income. The balance of the net capital loss, $27,000, would be carried over to subsequent tax years.

Viewing the example from a net investment income perspective, the two items of net investment income are:

1. the interest income of $5,000;[64] and

2. the gain generated from the stock sale of $10,000.[65]

The process of determining the "net gain" for investment income is the same as it is for regular income; the capital gain ($10,000) and capital loss ($40,000) are netted, but only to the extent of zeroing out the capital gain. Of the resulting $30,000 of net capital loss, $3,000 of it can be used reduce the $5,000 of interest income included as net investment income. Thus, Iris' 2014 net investment income would be $2,000, with a $27,000 capital loss to be carried over to subsequent tax years.

Now assume that Iris recognizes a capital gain of $30,000 in 2015 from the sale of publicly traded stock. For regular income tax purposes, the $27,000 capital loss carryover from 2014 is netted against the 2015 capital gain, resulting in a net capital gain of $3,000. Similarly, for purposes of computing net gain under Code section 1411(c)(1)(A)(iii), the same netting occurs to reduce the 2015 net gain included in net investment income to $3,000.[66]

Which Deductions Can Be Applied to Net Investment Income?

Up to this point the terms "net investment income" and "investment income" have been used interchangeably. Inherent in the term "net investment income," however, is the notion that certain deductions be allowed. Indeed, per Code section 1411(c)(1)(B), in arriving at "net investment income," investment income is reduced by "the deductions allowed by this subtitle which are properly allocable to such gross income or net gain." Figure 11.3 sets forth the list of deductions that are taken into account in determining net investment income.

It is important to note that deductions from investment income are subject to the same limitations as deductions for regular income tax. In other words, a taxpayer would not be entitled to a greater deduction from investment income than he or she would be entitled to for regular tax. For that reason, it is important to understand the hierarchy of deductions for regular income tax purposes.

Figure 11.3

AVAILABLE DEDUCTIONS AGAINST NET INVESTMENT INCOME
Deductions allocable to gross income from rents and royalties
Deductions allocable to gross income from trades or business to the extent not taken into account in determining self-employment income
Penalty on early withdrawal of savings
Net operating losses properly allocable to determining net investment income for any taxable year
Investment interest expenses as defined in Code section 163(d)(3)
Investment expenses as defined in Code section 163(d)(4)(c)
Taxes described in Code section 164(a)(3)
Investment expenses described in Code section 212(3)
Amortizable bond premium under Code section 171(a)(1)
In the case of a trust or estate, fiduciary expenses deductible under Code section 212
Losses allowed per Code section 165
Excess losses under Code section 642(h) upon termination of a trust or estate

Above-the-Line Investment Income Deductions

As discussed in Chapter 4, "above-the-line" deductions used to calculate adjusted gross income are usually the most beneficial deductions to the taxpayer. This is because they are not typically subject to restrictions that would otherwise limit their deductibility. Taken "off the top," they reduce the amount of taxable income, dollar-per-dollar. For net investment income purposes, the above-the-line regular income tax deductions properly allocable to rent and royalty income, losses from the sale or exchange of property, net operating losses as well as the deduction for the penalty on early withdrawal of savings provide a similar tax benefit.[67]

Net Operating Losses

The final regulations allow a taxpayer to use a portion of his or her net operating loss (NOL) to reduce net investment income as an above-the-line deduction.[68] This special net operating loss—referred to as a "section 1411 NOL" in the regulations—is the lesser of:

- a NOL for the loss year computed by including only items of investment income gross income less only properly allocable net investment income deductions; or

- the taxpayer's regular income tax NOL for the loss year.

Like regular NOLs, unused section 1411 NOLs can be carried over to subsequent tax years. The example in the final regulations—presented here in a simplified form—is helpful in understanding this technique.

Example: Assume that in 2014, the taxpayer's NOL for regular income tax purposes was $1,000,000 and the section 1411 NOL (taking into account only net investment income and deductions) was $200,000. Because the taxpayer had a net loss (and therefore no income) for 2014, the $1,000,000 NOL and $200,000 section 1411 NOL are available to be carried forward to subsequent tax years.

However, there is a bit of a twist. Although the taxpayer is entitled to an overall section 1411 NOL of $200,000, in subsequent years, when applying the section 1411 NOL to from 2014 to later tax years the taxpayer must multiply his or her regular income tax NOL carried over to that subsequent year by the ratio of the section 1411 NOL generated in 2014 divided by the regular

Figure 11.4

2014: No taxable income		
Regular income tax NOL available for subsequent years	Section 1411 NOL available for subsequent years	2014 ratio of regular NOL to section 1411 NOL
$1,000,000	$200,000	$\left(\dfrac{\$2,000,000}{\$1,000,000}\right) = 0.2$
2015: $540,000 in taxable income		
2014 regular taxable income NOL carried to 2015	Carried over 2014 NOL multiplied by 2014 ratio	2014 section 1411 NOL used to reduce 2015 net investment income
$540,000	$540,000 × 0.2	= $108,000
2016: Taxable income greater than $460,000		
2014 regular taxable income NOL carried to 2016	Carried over 2014 NOL multiplied by 2014 ratio	2014 section 1411 NOL used to reduce 2016 net investment income
$460,000	$460,000 × 0.2	= $92,000
2017: 2014 Regular income tax NOL and section 1411 NOL exhausted		
		$\left(\dfrac{\$2000,000}{\$1,000,000}\right) = 0.2$
	$540,000 × 0.2	= $108,000
	$460,000 × 0.2	= $92,000

income tax NOL generated in 2014. Here, that ratio is 0.2 ($200,000 divided by $1,000,000)

To illustrate this point, assume that in 2015 the taxpayer is has $540,000 in income and elects to use $540,000 of his 2014 NOL to reduce taxable income. For purposes of reducing the taxpayer's *net investment income* for that year, the carried over section 1411 NOL is limited to 20 percent of $540,000, or $108,000. Thus, going into 2016, the taxpayer has a remaining section 1411 NOL of $92,000 ($200,000 minus $108,000).

Subsequently, in 2016, assume the taxpayer is able to use the balance of his 2014 NOL ($460,000) to reduce that year's taxable income. Again, for purposes of reducing the taxpayer's net investment income for that year, the carried over section 1411 NOL is limited to 20 percent of $460,000, or $92,000.

Below-the-Line Investment Income Deductions

Many of the deductions against investment income—such as state and local taxes, investment interest, professional fees and investment advisory fees—are treated for regular income tax as itemized deductions. These are known as "below-the-line" deductions. Unlike above-the-line deductions, below-the-line deductions are subject to limitations that often impact their ultimate deductibility.

For regular income tax purposes, some below-the-line deductions are treated as "miscellaneous itemized deductions"[69]—as opposed to "regular" itemized deductions—and are subject to a "floor" of 2 percent of adjusted gross income. This means that miscellaneous itemized deductions are deductible only to the extent they exceed 2 percent of a taxpayer's AGI.[70]

In addition, for tax year 2014, taxpayers with adjusted gross income in excess of $254,200 for single filers ($305,050 for joint filers) are subject to a reduction of the value of their miscellaneous itemized deductions equal to 3 percent of the amount by which their adjusted gross income exceeds the applicable threshold.[71] This is known as a "section 68 phase-out" reduction.

Both of these limitations apply to the computation of net investment income. The miscellaneous itemized deduction "floor" is applied to the miscellaneous itemized deductions first. The taxpayer must then determine if the section 68 phase-out will further reduce the miscellaneous itemized deductions that apply to the calculation of net investment income.[72]

With regard to the floor for net investment income miscellaneous itemized deductions, the regulations provide that the amount of miscellaneous itemized deductions tentatively deductible against net investment income is the lesser of:

- the amount of miscellaneous itemized deductions; or

- all miscellaneous itemized deductions (including those allocable to net investment income) that exceed the 2 percent of adjusted gross income floor.[73]

The following example illustrates how these rules work.

Example: Iris is a single taxpayer with the following items of income and miscellaneous itemized deductions:

Income

Adjusted Gross Income	$500,000
Investment Income (included in adjusted gross income)	$150,000

Miscellaneous Itemized Deductions

Investor Advisor Fees	$35,000
Other Non-Investment Income Miscellaneous Itemized Deductions	$15,000

Applying the special rule on net investment income miscellaneous itemized deduction rules to Iris, the amount deductible is the lesser of:

- her net investment income miscellaneous itemized deduction unreduced by the 2 percent floor ($35,000); or

- all miscellaneous itemized deduction after the applying the 2 percent floor ($20,000).

Thus, Iris' tentative miscellaneous itemized deduction against net investment income—subject to the potential section 68 phase-out of itemized deductions discussed below—is the $20,000 of investor advisor fees.

After determining the tentative amount of allowable miscellaneous deductions, the next step is to apply the special rules for the section 68 phase-out of itemized deductions. The phase-out reduces *total* miscellaneous itemized deductions against *regular* income by 3 percent of the amount by which the taxpayer's adjusted gross income exceeds the threshold ($254,200 for single taxpayers).

- If the taxpayer's miscellaneous itemized deductions against net investment income (after applying the 2 percent AGI floor discussed in the previous step) are less than the total amount of miscellaneous itemized deductions against regular income permitted under the section 68 phase-out, then the net investment deductions remain unchanged.

- If the net investment income miscellaneous itemized deductions *exceed* what is permissible under the section 68 phase-out, the taxpayer may only take miscellaneous itemized deductions against net investment income up to the section 68 phase-out limit.

For purposes of this example, assume Iris has the following itemized deductions:

State income taxes properly allocable to net investment income (regular itemized deduction)	$40,000
Investment interest expense properly allocable to net investment income (regular itemized deduction)	$50,000
Deductible investor advisor fees (miscellaneous itemized deduction)	$20,000
Total itemized deductions against net investment income	**$110,000**
Additional miscellaneous itemized deductions against regular income	$90,000
Total Itemized Deductions Subject to the section 68 phase-out (including those not properly allocable to net investment income)	$200,000
Section 68 phase-out reduction (3% of difference between threshold and AGI)	($500,000 – $254,200) ×3% = $7,374
Total itemized deductions after section 68 phase-out	**$200,000 – $7,374 = $192,626**

Based on the foregoing itemized deduction scenario, the total of Iris' *net investment income* itemized deductions would be $110,000, and the total of *all* itemized deductions subject to the section 68 phase-out would be $200,000. Applying the section 68 phase-out will reduce Iris' total itemized deductions by an amount equal to 3 percent of the difference between adjusted gross income ($500,000) and the threshold for a single taxpayer ($254,200), or $7,374. Subtracting this number yields $192,626 as the amount of itemized deductions allowed after applying the phase-out. Because Iris' investment income itemized deductions ($110,000) would be less than her regular itemized deductions after applying the phase out ($192,626), she would be entitled to deduct the former amount—meaning there would be no further reduction of Iris' net investment itemized deductions form the section 68 phase-out.

Using Excess Losses to Reduce Net Investment Income

In the discussion regarding the computation of "net gain" pursuant to Code section 1411(c)(1)(A)(iii), it was noted that the deductibility of loss was limited to the amount of gain, so a "net investment loss" would not be allowed for the purposes of the NIIT. In spite of that limitation, the final regulations allow those section 1411(c)(1)(A)(iii) losses to be used to reduce other net investment income provided those losses had been taken as a deduction in the computation of regular income tax.[74]

Example: Iris, a single taxpayer, has the following income sources:

Interest and dividends	$125,000
Ordinary losses from a trade or business trading in financial instruments or commodities	$60,000
Long-term capital gain from the sale of undeveloped land	$50,000

For regular income tax purposes, the $125,000 of interest and dividend income and the $50,000 of long-term capital gain are included in gross income. The $60,000 of ordinary loss is totally deductible without limitation—unlike capital loss, which is deductible to the extent of capital gain plus $3,000.) Ignoring itemized deductions and personal exemptions, Iris' *regular taxable income* would be $115,000 ($175,000 in interest, dividends, and long-term capital gain, minus $60,000 in business losses).

For the purposes of computing *net investment income*, recall that all income, gain, or loss from a business that trades in financial instruments or commodities is treated as net investment income regardless of whether the activity is non-passive with respect to the taxpayer. For Iris, the $125,000 of interest and dividend income and the $50,000 of long-term capital gain are clearly included in net investment income. However, the $60,000 loss is deductible only to the extent of the $50,000 gain. In other words, since the final regulations do not allow a "net" loss under Code section 1411(c)(1)(A)(iii), the regular income tax rule allowing such a loss would appear to be inapplicable. Thus, without further relief, the "net" $10,000 loss would not be allowed, resulting in $125,000 of interest and dividends included in net investment income rather than $115,000.

However, the final regulations allow Iris to use that otherwise useless loss to reduce her other net investment income. This is possible because the net $10,000 loss:

- was deductible for regular income tax purposes; and

- would have been allowed as reduction of net gain under Code section 1411(c)(1)(A)(iii) but for the net loss limitation.

Thus, Iris' investment income of $125,000 would be reduced by the $10,000 excess loss deduction resulting in $115,000 of net investment income.[75]

APPLICATION OF NIIT TO TRUSTS AND ESTATES

To this point in the chapter, the discussion of NIIT has focused exclusively on individual taxpayers. However, unless otherwise specifically excluded, all trusts and estates that are subject to the provisions Subchapter J of the Internal Revenue Code are also subject to NIIT.[76] The impact of NIIT on trusts and estates cannot be understated. Because trusts tend to remain in existence far longer than estates, the overall tax consequences of this surtax on trusts is likely to be even more profound, and the following discussion will focus mainly on trusts.

In operation, the 3.8 percent NIIT surtax is imposed on trusts and estates on the lesser of:

- "undistributed net investment income"; or

- the excess of adjusted gross income over the amount of the highest regular income tax bracket in effect for such taxable year.[77]

Compared to the thresholds for individual taxpayers that are based on adjusted gross income, the threshold for trusts and estates is based on the highest tax bracket of those entities. Though the threshold for trusts and estates is indexed for inflation (unlike the thresholds for individual taxpayers), that is of little comfort to fiduciaries and beneficiaries. The highest regular income tax bracket for trusts and estates (above which the NIIT surtax is imposed) begins at an amount that is significantly lower than the NIIT thresholds for individuals.[78]

For example, for tax year 2014, the highest regular income tax bracket for trusts and estates (39.6 percent) begins with taxable income in excess of $12,150. The unindexed thresholds for individual taxpayers (e.g. $250,000 for married taxpayers who are filing jointly) are much higher. Moreover, by their nature, most trusts and estates are likely to have *only* net investment income. This means that trusts and estates with relatively small amounts of net investment income may nonetheless be in the highest income tax bracket and be subject to the 3.8 percent NIIT.

As mentioned above, The NIIIT tax base of trusts and estates is "undistributed net investment income." In simple terms, undistributed net investment income is any net investment income—as defined by Code section 1411(c)(1)(A)—that is retained by a trust or an estate.[79] Distributions retain their characterization as net investment income when distributed to a beneficiary. If the trust has net investment income that is distributed to a beneficiary, it will be considered net investment income for beneficiary (as opposed to regular income).[80]

The two types of trusts most impacted by NIIT are "simple trusts" and "complex trusts." A simple trust is required to distribute all of its current fiduciary accounting income (FAI) to its beneficiaries.[81] FAI is income derived from principal such as interest and dividends (as opposed to capital gains derived from the sale or disposition of principal). Since a simple trust is required to distribute all of its FAI to its beneficiaries each year, its undistributed net investment income is limited to the capital gain it generates.

A complex trust is not required to make mandatory distributions to its beneficiaries.[82] Instead, complex trusts generally make discretionary distributions of FAI (and sometimes principal) to beneficiaries. A complex trust is likely to have a mix of net investment income that includes dividends, interest and capital gains. This income may or may not be retained by the trust.

In order to understand how to compute the undistributed net investment income of a trust, it is necessary to comprehend the meaning of distributable net income (DNI). Essentially, the DNI of a trust is the taxable income of a trust, with certain modifications.[83] Distributions to beneficiaries are not included in DNI,[84] effectively shifting the obligation to pay tax on the distributed income from the trust to the beneficiaries.

Similarly, for net investment income purposes, DNI that is distributed to a beneficiary is included in the beneficiary's net investment income, and is subject to the NIIT. Conversely, *undistributed* investment income included in DNI—as well undistributed investment income not included in DNI—is included in the net investment income tax base of the trust. The most notable exclusion of income from the computation of DNI is capital gain.

The following example from the regulations[85] demonstrates how to compute net investment income for a complex trust, including calculations of DNI.

Example: Assume that in 2014 the trustee of this complex trust makes a discretionary FAI distribution of $10,000 to Beneficiary A.

Trust Income 2014

Dividend Income	$15,000
Interest Income	$10,000
Capital Gain	$5,000
IRA Distribution	$75,000
Total Trust Income	**$105,000**

Step 1: Determine the DNI of the trust. Code section 643(a) provides that the DNI of a trust is tentative taxable income ($105,000) minus capital gain. Excluding the $5,000 of capital gain, the DNI of the trust is $100,000.

Step 2: Determine the trust's distribution deduction. According to Code section 661(a), the distribution deduction of a complex trust is equal to the amount distributed (here, $10,000).

Step 3: Determine the extent to which the amount distributed is deemed to be net investment income. Code section 661(b) provides that the character of the amount distributed to the beneficiary "shall be treated as consisting of the same proportion of each class of income entering into the computation of distributable net income." In this example, the distribution of $10,000 is equal to 10 percent of $100,000, the total amount of DNI. Thus, the beneficiary is deemed to have received 10 percent of each type of income included in DNI.

Trust Income 2014

Income in DNI	Retained by Trust	Distributed to Beneficiary
Dividend Income	$13,500	$1,500
Interest Income	$9,000	$1,000
IRA Distribution	$67,500	$7,500
Total	**$90,000**	**$10,000**

Step 4: Determine the amount of net investment income in DNI that is retained by the trust. In this case, most of the retained income is net investment income. The only exception is the IRA distribution. Pursuant to Code section 1411(c)(5), distributions from IRAs are excluded from net investment income.

Trust Income 2014

Income in DNI	Retained by Trust	Net Investment Income
Dividend Income	$13,500	$13,500
Interest Income	$9,000	$9,000
IRA Distribution	$67,500	$0
Total	**$90,000**	**$22,500**

Step 5: Determine the total amount of net investment income retained by the trust. This should

include any undistributed item of net investment income not included in DNI. Here, the $5,000 of capital gain excluded from DNI (clearly net investment income) is added to the $22,500 of net investment income retained by the trust. Thus, the total amount of undistributed net investment income is $27,500.

Step 6 – Compute the NIIT. The 3.8 percent NIIT surtax is imposed on the lesser of:

- undistributed Net Investment Income ($27,500): or

- $92,850, which is the excess of the adjusted gross income ($105,000) over the amount of the highest regular income tax bracket ($12,150).

In this example $27,500 is less than $92,850, so the NIIT would be 3.8 percent of $27,500, or $1,045.

HOW CAN INDIVIDUALS MINIMIZE THE NIIT?

1. *Create tax-exempt income.* Any investment type income that is excluded from gross income is also excluded from the NIIT base. Consequently, an investment in state and local bonds would yield income that is exempt from both regular and net investment taxes.

2. *Use life insurance.* A whole life insurance policy has an insurance component and an investment component. The growth of the investment component would depend on the amount of the premium and how it is invested. Investments earnings within the policy grow tax deferred and are therefore do have to be currently included in gross income. Moreover, some insurance policies allow the owner to borrow the "earnings" generated by the policy. Since borrowed funds are generally excluded from gross income, they would not be considered net investment income. Using life insurance in this way allows the owner to enjoy the benefit of policy earnings without being subject to regular income tax or NIIT.

3. *Materially participate in a business activity.* Income from a business in which is the taxpayer materially participates (i.e. "non-passive") would not be included in net investment income. If a taxpayer was to materially participate in a business activity that was otherwise passive to him, he would effectively exclude the income from that business from the NIIT tax base. This strategy only works if materially participating in the business does not convert such income into self-employment income that is subject to the Additional Medicare Surtax. Although this technique would not work for a general partner, it would be effective for the shareholder of an S corporation.

4. *Increase voluntary contributions to a qualified retirement plan.* Many qualified retirement plans, such as a 401(k), allow for deductible voluntary contributions of a participant's wages. Although the amount of such contributions may vary from plan to plan, the regular income tax deductible limit for 2014 is $17,500 ($23,500 for taxpayers over forty-nine years old). Note that voluntary contributions are not deductible from Medicare wages subject to the Additional Medicare Surtax.[86] However, distributions from those plans (presumably upon the taxpayer's retirement) are excluded from net investment income,[87] and the earnings generated in the plan are tax-free until distributed. Compared to investing in vehicles that produce net investment income, investing additional amounts in a qualified retirement plan effectively converts future net investment income into excluded qualified plan distributions.

5. *Consider installment sales of property.* If a taxpayer sells property qualifying for reporting gain on the installment method, his or her gain is reportable on a ratable basis.[88]

Example: Assume in December 2014, Iris—a single taxpayer—has the opportunity to sell undeveloped land with a basis of $100,000 for $300,000. If Iris receives the entire selling price in 2014, her adjusted gross income would be increased by the total amount of the gain ($200,000). Assuming that her taxpayer's adjusted gross income for 2014 apart from the sale was $100,000; the additional $200,000 of adjusted gross income would increase her adjusted gross income to $300,000 and subject her to an additional $3,800 of NIIT (3.8 percent of $100,000).

On the other hand, if she received $150,000 of the sales price in December 2014 and $150,000 of the sales price in January 2015, her $200,000 gain would be spread equally over the two tax years (meaning her adjusted gross income would be increased by the $100,000 of gain reported in each tax year). Thus, in 2014, because her adjusted gross income would not exceed the $200,000 threshold (it would be exactly that amount), there would be no NIIT. Moreover, assuming the same adjusted gross income amount in 2015, she would avoid NIIT for that year as well. By converting an immediate sale into an installment sale that spans two "years," Iris could save $3,800 in NIIT obligations.

HOW CAN TRUSTS MINIMIZE THE NIIT?

1. *Allocate indirect expenses to undistributed net investment income.* The regulations allow for the allocation of the deduction of items indirectly attributable to any particular type of income to be allocated in any way, including the total allocation of the deduction to capital gain.[89] For example, by allocating all or part of trustee fees to capital gain not distributed by the trust, the amount of undistributed net income subject to NIIT would also be reduced.

2. *Make discretionary distributions of net investment income items to beneficiaries who are not subject to the NIIT.* Assuming a trustee is aware of the amounts of adjusted gross income of the trust beneficiaries, discretionary distributions of net investment net income could be made in amounts that would not cause the recipient beneficiary's adjusted gross income to exceed the applicable threshold and thus not be subject to NIIT. By doing so, the trustee could reduce NIIT within the trust without subjecting the beneficiary to the surtax.

However, the trustee must be mindful to not make distributions that would be contrary to the terms of the trust or otherwise be considered a breach of his or her fiduciary obligations. Moreover, even if the distribution would not cause the beneficiary's adjusted gross income to exceed the applicable NIIT threshold, the increase in income may deprive the taxpayer of some other tax benefits.

For example, a higher adjusted gross income would reduce or potentially eliminate the deductibility of miscellaneous itemized deductions subject to the 2 percent of adjusted gross income floor. Also, the taxation of social security benefits could be triggered by an increase in adjusted gross income.[90] There are many other examples of similar adverse tax consequences potentially triggered by an increase in adjusted gross income.[91]

FREQUENTLY ASKED QUESTIONS

Question – Do the regulations provide a means of allocating deductible state and local taxes between net investment income and non-net investment income?

Answer – The final regulations are very vague on this issue, providing that "in the case of a properly allocable deduction [such as state and local taxes] … that is allocable to both net investment income and excluded income, the portion of the deduction that is properly allocable to net investment income may be determined by using any reasonable method."[92]

Without endorsing any one method, the regulations provide examples of "reasonable methods." One method outlined is to allocate the state and local expense to net investment income based on the percentage of the taxpayer's net investment included in the taxpayer's total gross income.[93]

Example: In 2014, Hugh Haule has $600,000 of wages and $400,000 of interest income on which Hugh paid state income taxes of $100,000. Since 40 percent of Hugh's income is net investment income, Hugh could reasonably deduct $40,000 of the state income taxes paid against the $400,000 of net investment income.

Question – Is there another alternative to decrease the undistributed net investment income of a trust other than a distribution of money to a beneficiary?

Answer – Yes. The trustee could make in in-kind distribution of trust assets.

Example: Assume a trust has appreciated stock with a fair market value of $30,000 and a basis of $10,000. If the trustee were to sell the stock for $30,000, there would be taxable capital gain of $20,000. Even if trustee distributed the entire $30,000 to the beneficiary, the $20,000 of gain deemed to be retained by the trust would be treated as undistributed net investment income subject to NIIT.[94]

In the alternative, the trustee could make a discretionary in-kind distribution of the stock. Such a distribution would not trigger taxable capital gain to the trust; and, thus, no undistributed investment income subject to NIIT.

The amount of the distribution to the beneficiary is the lesser of the stock's fair market value or basis in the hands of the trust.[95] In this example, the lesser number is the stock's $10,000 basis.

———————

There is, however, an additional potential downside to the beneficiary. Because the beneficiary would take a carryover basis of $10,000 in the stock,[96] if the beneficiary were to sell the stock for $30,000, he or she would recognize a $20,000 capital gain that would be included as net investment income.

Question – Does the "sixty-five-day rule" apply with regard to a distribution of net investment income to a beneficiary?

Answer – Apparently, yes. Pursuant to Code section 663(b), by making an appropriate election, a trust can make a distribution to a beneficiary within sixty-five days after the end of the tax year and it will be considered to have been made on the last day of the preceding year. If the trustee makes this election, the deemed distribution would reduce the DNI remaining in the trust and shift the income tax consequences from the trust to the beneficiary. This rule allows the trustee to use the benefit of hindsight to determine whether a distribution would be in the best interest of the trust and/or beneficiary in the prior tax year.

Obviously, the use of the sixty-five-day rule would provide a similar benefit to a trustee in determining whether to make a distribution of net investment income effective for the preceding tax year. This would allow the trustee more time to evaluate the relative merits of making a distribution of net investment income to a beneficiary or

retaining the income in the trust effective as of the end of the prior tax year.

Although, the final regulations do not directly acknowledge the application of the sixty-five-day rule with regard to distributions of net investment income, it was applied in Example 3 of Treas. Reg. §1.1411-3(e). In that example, a section 663(b) election was effectively made by the executor of an estate. Since the sixty-five-day rule applies equally to trusts and estates, there is no reason to believe such an election would not be effective if made by a trustee of a trust.

CHAPTER ENDNOTES

1. "Definition of 'Surtax,'" Available at: www.investopedia.com/terms/s/surtax.asp.
2. P.L. 111-152, 124 Stat. 1029.
3. The other "FICA" tax is the old-age, survivors, and disability insurance tax (OASDI) also known as the social security tax.
4. Reported on Schedule SE of Form 1040.
5. Patient Protection and Affordable Care Act. P.L. No. 111-148.
6. I.R.C. §§3101(b)(2)(a), 1401(b)(2)(A).
7. I.R.C. §3102(a).
8. P.L. 111-152, 124 Stat. 1029.
9. Not all trusts are subject to the NIIT. Those not subject to the tax include charitable trusts, qualified retirement plan trust, grantor trusts, real estate investment trusts and common trust funds. Treas. Reg. §1.1411-3(b); I.R.C. §1411(e)(2).
10. The term used in Code section 1411(a)(1)(B) is "modified adjusted gross income" rather than "adjusted gross income." Throughout this Chapter, the term "adjusted gross income" will be utilized because modified adjusted gross income is only relevant to the few taxpayers who claim the foreign earned income exclusion. Pursuant to Code section 1411(d), modified adjusted gross income is computed by adding the amount of the foreign earned income exclusion over the amount of any disallowed deductions or exclusions taken account in computing adjusted gross income pursuant to Code section 991(a)(1). For most taxpayers this modification would not be applicable, and the Code section 1411(a)(1)(B) amount would be adjusted gross income.
11. I.R.C. §1411(b)(1)-(3).
12. See I.R.C. §1411(a)(2).
13. I.R.C. §1411(c)(6).
14. I.R.C. §1411(b).
15. See I.R.C. §1411(c)(6).
16. Rev. Proc. 2013-35, IRB 2013-47. For a single individual, the income tax on $410,000 of taxable income is computed as follows: $118,189 on taxable income of $406,750 plus 39.6 percent of $3,250 ($410,000 - $406,750), or $1,287, for a total tax of $119,476.
17. I.R.C. §3101(b)(2)(C).
18. I.R.C. §1411(b)(3).
19. I.R.C. §469(c).

20. I.R.C. §1411(c)(2).

21. Treas. Reg. §1.1411-1(d)(12). Although trade or business is not defined in Code section 162, it is commonly defined as offering goods or services to customers or clients on a regular basis.

22. I.R.C. §1411(c)(3); Treas. Reg. §1.1411-6(a).

23. Treas. Reg. §1.1411-4(e)(1)(i).

24. Treas. Reg. §1.1411-1(d)(4)(i). All items of income excluded from gross income are also excluded from the investment income tax base. Interest on state or local bonds are excluded from gross income under Code section 103.

25. Treas. Reg. §1.1411-4(g)(5).

26. Treas. Reg. §1.1411-4(b)(3), Example 4.

27. Treas. Reg. §1.1411-1(d)(3).

28. Treas. Reg. §1.1411-6(a).

29. Treas. Reg. §1.1411-4(e)(1)(i).

30. Treas. Reg. §1.1411-1(d)(1). The regulation also provides that in case of a sale of annuity, the amount of gain no in excess of the surrender value would not be treated as investment income. If the sales price of the annuity exceeds its surrender value, the gain equal to the difference between the basis in the annuity and the surrender value would be treated as gross income from an annuity, and, thus, treated as investment income.

31. Treas. Reg. §1.1411-1(d)(1).

32. I.R.C. §1411(c)(5).

33. Treas. Reg. §1.1411-1(d)(11).

34. Treas. Reg. §1.1411-4(e)(1)(i).

35. I.R.C. § 469(c)(7)(B) defines who is a "real estate professional."

36. Treas. Reg. §1.1411-4(g)(7).

37. Treas. Reg. §1.469-2(f)(6). As alluded numerous times in this Chapter, with very limited exceptions, rental income is always treated as passive. The reason for recharacterizing self-charged interest as non-passive income is to prevent taxpayers from creating "passive income" to offset otherwise non-deductible passive loss.

38. Treas. Reg. §1.1411-4(g)(6).

39. Treas. Reg. §1.1411-4(b)(2)(i).

40. I.R.C. §1411(c)(6).

41. See Treas. Reg. §1.1411-4(b)(3), Examples.

42. See generally I.R.C. Sec 1402 (listing certain income items that are excluded from the self-employment income tax base) and I.R.C. §702(a) (listing certain income items that are "separately" listed on a partner's Form K-1 and, thus also excluded from the self-employment income tax base).

43. I.R.C. §702(a)(8).

44. I.R.C. §1402(a).

45. The net income from Schedule C flows to Schedule SE of Form 1040 upon which self-employment tax is calculated.

46. Treas. Reg. §301.7702-2(c)(2)(iv)(D), Example (iii).

47. I.R.C. §1402(a)(13).

48. Rev. Rul. 59-221, 1959-1 C.B. 225 (undistributed S corporation income not considered self-employment income). However, Rev. Rul. 74-44, 1974-1 C.B. 287 provides that S corporation income distributed to a shareholder would be re-characterized as compensation subject to self-employment tax if paid in lieu of reasonable compensation for services performed for the corporation. However, "unrecharacterized" S corporation dividend distributions would not be treated as self-employment income per Code section 1402(a)(2).

49. I.R.C. §1402(a)(3).

50. Treas. Reg. §1.1411-4(d)(1).

51. Treas. Reg. §1.1411-4(d)(3).

52. I.R.C. §453.

53. I.R.C. §1031.

54. I.R.C. §1033.

55. I.R.C. §121.

56. Part 2 of the preamble to the proposed regulations (REG-1030507-11, 77 Fed. Reg. 72612, at 72613 (12/05/2012); Treas. Reg. §1.1411-4(d)(3)(ii), Example 3, Example 4; Treas. Reg. §1.1411-4(d)(4)(i)(C), Example 2.

57. Treas. Reg. §1.1411-4(d)(4)(i)(C), Example 1.

58. Prop. Reg. §1.1411-7 (Dec. 2, 2013).

59. All of the discussion regarding the sale of an interest in an S corporation and partnership is based on Prop. Treas. Reg. §1.1411-7 (Dec. 2, 2013), replacing Prop. Treas. Reg. §1.1411-7 (2012).

60. This also assumes that the entity did not own any marketable securities otherwise known as section 1411 property. Obviously, marketable securities are investment assets not used in a trade or business.

61. The sale of marketable securities would always generate net investment income because they are not used in a trade or business.

62. Prop. Treas. Reg. §1.1411-7(c).

63. Treas. Reg. §1.1411-4(d)(2).

64. I.R.C. §1411(c)(1)(A)(i).

65. I.R.C. §1411(c)(1)(A)(iii).

66. Treas. Reg. §1.1411-4(d)(3)(ii), Example 1.

67. I.R.C. §§62(a)(3),(4) and (9).

68. IRS Publication 536 (2013), Treas. Reg. §1.1411-4(h).

69. I.R.C. §67.

70. See I.R.C. §67(b) in which all below-the-line deductions *not* listed are considered miscellaneous itemized deductions.

71. I.R.C. §68. Rev. Proc. 2013-35, IRB 2013-47.

72. Treas. Reg. §1.1411-4(f)(7).

73. Treas. Reg. §1.1411-4(f)(7)(i).

74. Treas. Reg. §1.1411-4(f)(i). Also, losses from the disposition of property are treated as above the line deductions for regular income tax purposes. I.R.C. §62(a)(3).

75. Treas. Reg. §1.1411-4(h).

76. Treas. Reg. §1.1411-3.

77. I.R.C. §1411(a)(2)(B)(ii).

78. The threshold for trusts and estates is indexed because the regular tax income tax brackets for trusts and estates are indexed for inflation.

79. Treas. Reg. §1.1411-3(a)(1). Subchapter J deals exclusively with the taxation of trusts and estates and their beneficiaries. Treas. Reg. §1.1411-3(b)(1) lists the types of trusts and estates specific excluded from NIIT.

80. I.R.C. §§652(b) and 662(b).

81. I.R.C. §§651(a).
82. I.R.C. §662(a).
83. I.R.C. §643(a).
84. I.R.C. §§651(a) (simple trust) and 661(a) (complex trust).
85. Treas. Reg. §1.1411-3(e)(5), Example 2.
86. I.R.C. §3121(v)(1)(B).
87. I.R.C. §1411(c)(5).
88. I.R.C. §453.
89. Treas. Reg. §1.652(b)-3(c).
90. I.R.C. §86.
91. I.R.C. §219 (deductibility of a traditional IRA contribution).
92. Treas. Reg. §1.1411-4(g).
93. Treas. Reg. §1.1411-4(g).
94. I.R.C. §643(e).
95. I.R.C. §643(e)(2).
96. I.R.C. §643(e)(1).

WITHHOLDING AND ESTIMATED TAX REQUIREMENTS

CHAPTER 12

INTRODUCTION

Federal income tax is collected on a "pay-as-you-go" system. This means that individuals must pay tax on their earned income at the time they receive it.

There are two methods for collecting individual income taxes in the year the income is earned:

1. *withholding* on income earned during the year; and

2. *estimated* tax payments.

Employers are *required* to withhold a portion of each employee's wages. These amounts are subsequently applied toward the employee's tax liability when the employee files his income tax return.[1] After an individual determines tax liability, a credit may be taken against the tax for all amounts that have been withheld or paid as estimated taxes.[2] Any balance due must be paid, or a refund request must be filed for any overpayment.

Self-employed persons (and some employees) are generally required to file an estimated tax return and pay the estimated tax themselves, in either a lump sum or in installments. Actually, any taxpayer is required to make estimated tax payments if failure to pay would result in certain underpayments of tax.[3]

WAGE WITHHOLDING

Employers who pay wages to one or more employees *must* withhold a portion of each employee's wages and turn the withheld amount over to the government. The withheld amount is later applied toward the employee's tax liability on his or her federal income tax return.[4]

Note that only those payments that fall within the definition of "wages" are subject to withholding. "Wages" generally means pay for services rendered by an employee (e.g., salary, fees, bonuses, commissions, and vacation pay).[5]

Payments that are excludable from the employee's gross income (see Chapter 3) are generally not subject to withholding (e.g., employer-paid group term life insurance premiums).[6] Moving expenses are also exempt from withholding if the employer reasonably believes they will be deductible to the employee.[7]

Some types of employment are *specifically excluded* from withholding. For example, no withholding is required on payments made to ministers, priests, rabbis, or other clergypersons for performance of their regular duties. Likewise, no withholding is required on pay to a household worker, even a full-time worker. However, the household worker, even though classified as an employee, must still file an estimated tax return *and* pay the estimated tax currently.[8]

Withholding calculation. An employer may calculate the amount to be withheld by either the *percentage method* or the *wage-bracket table* method.[9] Both methods are based on graduated rates. Both the percentage and the wage-bracket methods take into account the employee's payroll period, marital status, and number of exemptions claimed.

The employee claims his exemptions and "standard deduction allowance" by filing Form W-4 with his employer. Usually, an employee may claim no more exemptions on Form W-4 than the number he is allowed on his return. Individuals may not claim the same exemption with more than one employer. In order to prevent over-withholding in some cases, the law permits an employee who has unusually large excess itemized deductions to claim one or more additional exemptions.[10]

Withholding on Pensions and Annuities

Unless a taxpayer elects otherwise, income tax will be withheld from benefits paid under pension or profit sharing plans and annuities.[11]

- If the payments are *periodic* (e.g., monthly), they are treated similarly to salaries and wages for the purpose of determining the amount of tax to be withheld. Form W-4P is used to indicate the individual's marital status and the number of allowances he is claiming. Individuals may also use Form W-4P to elect not to have any tax withheld.

- If the payments are *nonperiodic*, there is generally a flat withholding rate of 10 percent. Recipients of nonperiodic payments use Form W-4P only if they want to elect out of withholding.[12]

ESTIMATED TAX PAYMENTS

Who Must Make Estimate Tax Payments?

Taxpayers are generally required to pay estimated tax if failure to pay would result in an underpayment of federal income tax.[13] Specifically, taxpayers must make estimated tax payments if they expect to satisfy two criteria:

1. to owe at least $1,000 in tax for 2014, after subtracting withholding and refundable credits; and

2. their withholding and refundable credits to be less than the smaller of:

   a. 90 percent of the tax to be shown on the current year tax return; or

   b. 100 percent of the tax shown on the previous year's tax return (assuming the previous year's return covers a twelve-month period).[14]

In calculating the amount owed (or expected to be owed), taxpayers must include:

- the alternative minimum tax;

- self-employment tax;

- the Net Investment Income Tax (NIIT); and

- the Additional Medicare Surtax.[15]

An underpayment is the amount by which a required installment exceeds the amount, if any, paid on or before the due date of that installment. Taxpayers who anticipate an underpayment that would require estimated payments to be made have the option to increase their withholdings in such an amount that would reduce their underpayment to the point where they would no longer be required to make estimated payments. Obviously, the earlier in the tax year this adjustment is made, the easier it is to avoid estimated payments.

If estimated payments cannot be avoided through withholding adjustments, the due dates for the quarterly payments are April 15, June 15, September 15, and January 15 of the following year.[16]

Example 1: Jane files as head of household claiming her dependent son, takes the standard deduction, and expects no refundable credits for 2014.

Expected adjusted gross income (AGI) for 2014	$82,800
AGI for 2013	$73,700
Total tax on 2013 return (Form 1040, line 61)	$8,746
Total 2014 estimated tax	$11,015
Tax expected to be withheld in 2014	$10,000

Here, Jane expects to owe at least $1,000 for 2014 after subtracting her withholding from her expected total tax ($11,015 – $10,000 = $1,015). However, she expects her income tax withholding ($10,000) to be at least 90 percent of the tax to be shown on her 2014 return ($11,015 × 90 percent = $9,913.50). Jane does not need to pay estimated tax.

Example 2: The facts are the same as in Example 1, except that Jane expects only $8,700 tax to be withheld in 2014. This amount is less than is less than 90 percent of the expected tax owed in 2014. Additionally, she does not expect her income tax withholding ($8,700) to be at least 100 percent of the total tax shown on her 2013 return ($8,746). Here, Jane must increase her withholding or pay estimated tax for 2014.

Example 3: The facts are the same as in Example 2, except that the total tax shown on Jane's 2013 return was $8,600. Because she expects to have more than $8,600 withheld in 2014 ($8,700), Jane does not need to pay estimated tax for 2014.[17]

How Are Additional Payments Calculated?

The required amount for each installment is 25 percent of the required annual payment.[18] Generally, the "required annual payment" is the lower of:

- 90 percent of the tax shown on the return for the taxable year (or, if no return is filed, 90 percent of the tax for the year); or

- 100 percent of the tax shown on the return for the preceding year (but only if the preceding taxable year consisted of twelve months and a return was filed for that year).[19]

However, for an individual whose adjusted gross income for the previous tax year exceeded $150,000 ($75,000 in the case of married individuals filing separately), the required annual payment is the lesser of:

- 90 percent of the current year's tax, as described above, or

- the *applicable percentage* (110 percent) of the tax shown on the return for the preceding year.[20]

Alternatively, individuals can pay estimated tax by paying a specified percentage of the current year's tax, computed by "annualizing" the taxable income for the months in the taxable year ending before the month in which the installment falls due. Under this method, the applicable percentages are as follows:

- 22.5 percent (1st quarter);

- 45 percent (2nd quarter);

- 67.5 percent (3rd quarter); and

- 90 percent (4th quarter).[21]

If an individual underpays estimated taxes, an interest penalty (compounded daily) will be imposed at an annual rate, adjusted quarterly, to 3 percentage points over the short-term AFR (applicable federal rate).[22] However, no interest penalty will be imposed if either of the following applies:

- the tax shown on the return for the taxable year (or, if no return is filed, the tax) after reduction for withholdings is less than $1,000; *or*

- the taxpayer owed no tax for the preceding year (a taxable year consisting of twelve months) and the taxpayer was a U.S. citizen or resident for the entire taxable year.[23]

If the taxpayer elects to apply an overpayment to the succeeding year's estimated taxes, the overpayment will be applied to unpaid installments of estimated tax due on or after the date(s) the overpayment arose in the order in which they are required to be paid to avoid an interest penalty for failure to pay estimated income tax for that particular tax year.

SELF-EMPLOYMENT TAX

An individual whose net earnings from self-employment are $400 or more for the taxable year must pay the self-employment tax.[24] The rate for self-employment tax, as adjusted by an automatic cost-of-living increase in the earnings base, is 15.30 percent (12.40 percent OASDI and 2.90 percent hospital insurance). In 2014, the OASDI tax is imposed on up to $117,000 of self-employment income for a maximum OASDI tax of $13,243. The hospital insurance tax is imposed on all of a taxpayer's self-employment income. However, an above-the-line deduction is permitted for one-half of the self-employment tax paid by an individual and attributable to a trade or business carried on by the individual (not as an employee).[25] See Chapter 10 for more information about the calculation of self-employment taxes.

WHERE CAN I FIND OUT MORE?

Tax Facts on Insurance & Employee Benefits (National Underwriter Company).

CHAPTER ENDNOTES

1. I.R.C. §3401(a).
2. I.R.C. §31(a).
3. I.R.C. §6017.
4. I.R.C. §3402(a).
5. I.R.C. §3401(a).
6. I.R.C. §§3401(a)(12), 3401(a)(14).
7. I.R.C. §§217 and 3401(a)(15); Treas. Reg. §31.3401(a)(15)-1.
8. I.R.C. §§3401(a) and 6017.
9. I.R.C. §§3402(b)-(c).
10. I.R.C. §3402(m).
11. I.R.C. §3405(a).
12. I.R.C. §3405(b).
13. I.R.C. §6654.
14. IRS Publication 505, "Who Must Pay Estimated Tax".
15. I.R.C. §6654(d)(2)(B)(i). See also "Questions and Answers on the Net Investment Income Tax" at: www.irs.gov/uac/Newsroom/Net-Investment-Income-Tax-FAQs; and "Questions and Answers for the Additional Medicare Tax" at: www.irs.gov/Businesses/Small-Businesses-&-Self-Employed/Questions-and-Answers-for-the-Additional-Medicare-Tax. See Chapter 11 for more information on the NIIT and the Additional Medicare surtax.
16. I.R.C. §§6654(b)-(c).
17. IRS Publication 505, "Who Must Pay Estimated Tax," examples.
18. I.R.C. §6654(d)(1)(A).
19. I.R.C. §6654(d)(1)(B).
20. I.R.C. §6654(d)(1)(C).
21. I.R.C. §6654(d)(2).
22. I.R.C. §6621(a)(2). A complete history of AFRs including the present rates can be found at www.leimberg.com.
23. I.R.C. §6654(e).
24. I.R.C. §6017.
25. I.R.C. §164(f).

GRANTOR TRUSTS

CHAPTER 13

INTRODUCTION

A trust is an entity established either through a will or during an individual's life. In creating a trust, assets are placed in the trust by the grantor (also referred to as the settlor, creator, or trustor). These assets, called the corpus of the trust, are then managed by the trustee (sometimes referred to as the fiduciary) for the beneficiaries. The beneficiaries may receive either the income from the trust or the remainder of the trust, which is the corpus at the time the trust ends, or both. The trustee manages and holds legal title to the property while the beneficiaries hold beneficial title.

Trusts take many forms and are established for different reasons, but they are commonly set up for probate avoidance and tax purposes. For example, a revocable trust avoids probate and can serve as a will substitute by governing the distribution of the grantor's property. Because the grantor has not parted with control of the property, the grantor incurs no gift tax when the trust is set up; the grantor is responsible for the income tax on the income from the trust property; and the trust property is included in the grantor's estate for estate tax purposes when he or she dies.

In contrast, irrevocable trusts are often set up to obtain a trustee's management expertise and to avoid estate taxes. Because the grantor has relinquished rights to the property, the transfer is subject to gift tax; income tax on the income from the trust property is paid either by the trustee for the trust or by the beneficiaries (unless the trust is a grantor trust); and the property is not pulled back into the grantor's estate.

Trusts are required to file a Form 1041 (U. S. Income Tax Return for Estates and Trusts) if the trust has any taxable income, or if it has gross income of $600 or more for the year. Trusts are referred to as modified conduit entities because they receive a deduction for income that is distributed from the trust and are taxed on income that is retained by the trust. Trust tax rates are horrendous. Trusts are taxed at the 39.6 percent marginal tax rate when taxable income exceeds $12,150 (in 2014). In comparison, individuals (unless married and filing a separate return) are not taxed at the 39.6 percent rate until their taxable income exceeds $406,750 (in 2014). The beneficiary that receives the income from the trust is liable for the tax on the income. Trusts are also much more likely to be subject to the additional 3.8 percent Net Investment Income Tax (see Chapter 11).

TWO TYPES OF TRUSTS

There are two broad types of trusts – grantor trusts and non-grantor trusts. A grantor trust is a trust in which the grantor retains significant control over the assets in the trust or the income of the trust. For example, a revocable trust is a grantor trust. The consequence of being categorized as a grantor trust is that the trust is ignored for income tax purposes, meaning that the grantor must pay taxes on the trust income. With non-grantor trusts, the grantor does not retain significant control over the assets of the trust, and the trust is treated as a separate taxable entity.

WHAT POWERS LEAD TO GRANTOR TRUST STATUS?

The grantor trust provisions are contained in I.R.C. Sections 671 through 679. One of the keys to understanding the retained powers that lead to grantor trust status is the distinction between adverse and nonadverse parties. An adverse party is any one who has a substantial beneficial interest in the trust (something to lose) that would be adversely affected by the exercise or nonexercise of the power held by such party. A person with a general power of appointment over trust property is deemed to have a beneficial interest in the trust.[1] A nonadverse party is anyone who is not an adverse party.[2] A related or subordinate party means any person who is not adverse, who is the grantor's spouse living with the grantor, and any of the following: the grantor's father, mother, issue, brother or sister; an employee of the grantor; a corporation or any employee of a corporation in which the grantor and the trust have significant stock voting control; or a subordinate employee of a corporation in which the grantor is an executive.[3]

Example: The grantor has the right to revoke the trust but only with the consent of the grantor's child. If the grantor's child is an income beneficiary, remainder beneficiary, or has a power to invade corpus, the child is an adverse party because the child has something to lose if the grantor revokes the trust. If the child has no rights to the trust property, the child is a nonadverse party.

Furthermore, the grantor is treated as holding any power or interest that is held by a person who was the grantor's spouse when the power or interest was created, or anyone who became the grantor's spouse after the power or interest was created.[4]

Section 673 – Reversionary Interests

The grantor is taxed on the income from the trust if, based on IRS valuation tables, the grantor or the grantor's spouse has a reversionary interest in the trust exceeding five percent of the value of the affected portion of the trust.[5] However, if the beneficiary is the lineal descendant of the grantor and holds all the present interests in any portion of the trust, the grantor is not treated as the owner of such portion solely by reason of a reversionary interest that takes effect if the beneficiary dies before reaching age twenty-one.[6]

Example: Grantor establishes a trust with income payable to Grantor's daughter until she reaches age twenty-one. At that time, the trust will terminate and the corpus will be distributed to the daughter. If the daughter dies before reaching age twenty-one, the trust assets will revert to the Grantor. The trust is not a grantor trust because the reversion is contingent on the death of the daughter before age twenty-one.

Section 674 – The Power to Control Beneficial Enjoyment

The grantor is taxed on trust income if the grantor, the grantor's spouse, or a nonadverse party has the power to control others' beneficial enjoyment of the trust corpus or income without the consent of an adverse party. Examples of such powers generally include the power to invade corpus, the power to accumulate income, and the power to sprinkle income among beneficiaries. However, such powers may be retained by an independent trustee or trustees, none of whom is the grantor, and no more than half of whom are related or subordinate parties who are subservient to the wishes of the grantor.

Code section 674 contains a list of exceptions that may be held by anyone and still avoid the grantor being designated the owner of the trust. The list of exceptions includes:

- a power to hold or accumulate income for distribution to the grantor or grantor's spouse that would not be subject to tax under Code section 677(b) (see below).

- a power that can affect beneficial interest only after the period of time to which Code section 673 (see above) would apply if the power were a reversionary interest (i.e., less than 5 percent interest). However, the grantor may be treated as the owner after the period of time expired unless the power is relinquished.

- a power exercisable only by will, but not the power to appoint by will accumulated income that the grantor or a nonadverse party, or both, has had the power to accumulate without the consent of an adverse party;

- the power to allocate the income of the trust or corpus among charitable beneficiaries if that corpus or income is irrevocably allocated to charity;

- the power to distribute corpus to a current income beneficiary, provided that this distribution is chargeable against the proportionate share of corpus held in trust for the payment of income to the beneficiary;

- the power to distribute corpus to a beneficiary or beneficiaries or a class of beneficiaries, whether or not an income beneficiary, as long as that power is limited by a standard set forth in the trust agreement (does not include power to add to beneficiaries unless limited to adding after-born or after-adopted children);

- the power to withhold income temporarily on behalf of a designated beneficiary;

- the ability to retain a beneficiary's income during the beneficiary's minority or disability; and

- the power to allot receipts and disbursements between income and corpus.[7]

Section 675 – Administrative Powers

The grantor is also treated as the owner of the trust if the grantor or grantor's spouse has certain administrative powers over the trust. These powers include:

1. *The power to deal with trust property* – the grantor or a nonadverse party, or both, without the consent of an adverse party, has the power to purchase, exchange, or deal with trust property or income for less than adequate consideration;

2. *The power to borrow* – the grantor or a nonadverse party, or both, has the power to borrow the trust corpus or income without providing adequate security or paying adequate interest except where trustee (other than grantor) is authorized to do so;

3. *Actual borrowing* – the grantor or the grantor's spouse has borrowed corpus or income and has not completely repaid the loan (including interest) by the beginning of the tax year (does not apply to loan which provides for adequate interest and security if loan made by trustee other than the grantor or a related or subservient trustee); and

4. *General powers of administration* – any person in a nonfiduciary capacity can, without approval of a person in a fiduciary capacity:

    - vote trust stock in a corporation in which the grantor and the trust have significant voting control;

    - control trust investments to the extent the trust owns securities in which the grantor and the trust have significant voting control; or

    - reacquire trust assets by substituting other property of an equivalent value.[8]

Section 676 – Power to Revoke

The grantor is considered the owner of any portion of a trust which the grantor, grantor's spouse, or a nonadverse party has the power to revoke. The power to revoke includes the power to terminate the trust, the power to alter or amend the trust, and the power to appoint trust property to beneficiaries. The trust is not a grantor trust if the power cannot be exercised until after the period of time to which Code section 673 (see above) would apply if the power were a reversionary interest (i.e., less than 5 percent interest). However, the grantor would be treated as the owner after the period of time expired unless the power is relinquished.

Section 677 – Income Used For the Benefit of the Grantor

The grantor is treated as the owner of any portion of the trust with respect to which the income, without the consent of an adverse party is, or in the discretion of the grantor, grantor's spouse, or nonadverse party, may be:

- Distributed to the grantor or the grantor's spouse;

- Held or accumulated for distribution to the grantor or grantor's spouse;

- Applied to the payment of premiums on insurance on the life of the grantor or grantor's spouse (unless irrevocably payable to charity); or

- To the extent used, the power to use trust income for the support of the grantor's dependents (the grantor will be taxed on the portion actually used).

This does not apply if the power cannot be exercised until after the period of time to which Code section 673 (see above) would apply if the power were a reversionary interest (i.e., less than 5 percent interest). However, the grantor would be treated as the owner after the period of time expired unless the power is relinquished.

Example: Grantor transfers $100,000 to an irrevocable life insurance trust. The income from the funds is used to buy life insurance on the grantor's life. The trust owns the policy and the grantor's children are the beneficiaries of the trust. The trust earns income of $8,000 on the $100,000. The trustee uses $6,500 of the income to pay the premiums on the life insurance. The $6,500 is treated as income to the grantor, and the remaining $1,500 ($8,000 – 6,500) is income to the trust.

Section 678 - Person Other than the Grantor Treated as the Owner of the Trust

If a person other than the grantor has the power exercisable solely by himself to vest the trust corpus or income in himself, the person holding the power is taxed on the trust income as if he was the owner. This provision also applies if such person has previously partially released or otherwise modified such a power and afterwards retains a power that would cause a grantor holding such a power to be treated as the owner under the grantor trust rules. However, Code section 678 does not apply to a power over income if the grantor is otherwise treated as the owner under the grantor trust rules.

TAX TREATMENT OF TRUSTS

If the grantor is considered the owner of all or a portion of the trust, he must include all of the trust's income, deductions, and credits in computing his taxable income, to the extent that he is the owner.[9] A grantor may deduct a charitable contribution made by a grantor trust, or a grantor may be taxable on a grantor trust's foreign source income. Both of these would be treated as if the transactions had involved the grantor himself.[10]

How does one determine which specific portion of a trust a grantor owns? A grantor generally owns a portion of a trust in one of the following ways:

- ownership of the ordinary income portion or the principal portion only;

- ownership of a fractional or pecuniary share of all items of trust income and principal; or

- ownership of all items attributable to specific trust assets.[11]

Reporting Trust Taxes

Trusts with a gross income of at least $600 during the taxable year must file a tax return. A wholly-owned grantor trust must report its income in the same taxable year as its grantor. A trust that is only partially a grantor trust should file its income tax return for whatever fiscal year is appropriate for the taxable portion, and also file a grantor trust return for the portion owned by the grantor.[12]

If a grantor trust is taxed as owned entirely by the grantor (or the grantor and the grantor's spouse), and the grantor, grantor's spouse, or both are trustees or co-trustees, the grantor trust need not file a tax return. Trust income is then simply reported on the grantor's personal tax return.[13]

HOW ARE GRANTOR TRUSTS USED?

Probate Avoidance

The most common grantor trust is a revocable living trust. Although these trusts do not avoid estate tax or incur gift tax, they can reduce the cost, delay, and publicity of probate. Because the trust is revocable, the income from the trust is taxed to the grantor. In many cases, this treatment is advantageous because the income tax rates otherwise applicable to the trust are higher than the income tax rates applicable to the grantor.

Intentionally Defective Irrevocable Trust (IDIT)

To avoid the high income tax rates applicable to trusts, estate planners will often create an intentionally defective irrevocable trust (IDIT). Because the trust is irrevocable, the grantor may have to pay gift tax when the trust is established, but the property in the trust is removed from the grantor's estate. Under normal cI.R.C.umstances, if the trust is not a grantor trust, the income from the trust is taxed at the trust's income tax rates if the trustee does not distribute the income, or at the beneficiaries' income tax rates if the income is distributed.

By intentionally breaking one of the grantor trust rules discussed above, a defective grantor trust is created. A defective grantor trust can reduce the income tax liability for a grantor who wants to accumulate income in a trust for a minor. Because trusts are taxed at the top tax rate when they have taxable income greater than $12,150 (in 2014), the defective grantor trust can be an effective tool. The grantor sets up a trust that will accumulate income for a child and will purposely give the parent-grantor a right or power that will cause him to be taxed on the trust's income under the grantor trust rules, such as the power to purchase property for less than adequate consideration or the power to borrow from the trust without adequate interest (see "Section 675," above). The power must not be one that would cause the trust property to be included in the grantor's estate. For example, a power to substitute property of an equivalent value might be used.[14] The trust's income is then taxed at the parent-grantor's lower tax rates.

The defective grantor trust is also used when an individual wishes to remove the trust assets from his estate, but continue paying income taxes upon the trust's income. In this way the income can go to the beneficiaries, but because the grantor has paid the income tax he has reduced his estate and avoided making a taxable gift.

The grantor must be careful, however. If the trust must reimburse the grantor for income tax paid on the trust income, the grantor is considered to have retained a right to trust income causing the trust to be included in the grantor's estate.[15]

In selecting which powers to retain over the defective trust, the grantor must be sure not to select powers which will cause the trust to become part of the grantor's taxable estate. Problematic powers include:

- a reversionary interest that is more than 5 percent of the trust corpus;

- personal control over the enjoyment of the trust;

- certain administrative powers, such as the power to vote stock; and

- power to retain the trust income.

Trust-Leasebacks

A grantor who transfers business assets to a trust and then leases them back under a prearranged plan generally cannot deduct the rent paid to the trust. However, if the following conditions are met, the lessor-grantor may deduct the lease payments and the trust may deduct depreciation:

- the grantor does not retain substantially the same controls over the property that the grantor had prior to the transfer;

- the lease is in writing and the rent is reasonable;

- the lease has a bona fide business purpose (whether or not the original transfer had a bona fide business purpose); and

- the grantor does not possess a disqualifying equity interest in the property.

FREQUENTLY ASKED QUESTIONS

Question – Why would someone set up a grantor trust if it is going to be included in the grantor's estate?

Answer – First, trusts are set up for a variety of reasons, including probate avoidance, estate tax avoidance, and the professional management of assets. With some grantor trusts, such as revocable living trusts, the goal is not to avoid estate tax but the costs of probate. Because the grantor is taxed on the income from a revocable living trust rather than the trust, the income on the trust property also avoids the high income tax rates applicable to trusts.

Second, not all grantor trusts are included in the grantor's estate. Intentionally defective irrevocable trusts (referred to as IDITs) and spousal power of appointment trusts are examples of trusts where the income from the trust is included on the grantor's income tax return but not included in the grantor's estate.

CHAPTER ENDNOTES

1. I.R.C. §672(a).
2. I.R.C. §672(b).
3. I.R.C. §672(c).
4. I.R.C. §672 (e).
5. I.R.C. §673(a).
6. I.R.C. §673(b).
7. I.R.C. §675.

8.   I.R.C. §674(b).

9.   Treas. Reg. §1.671-2(a).

10. Treas. Reg. §1.671-2(c).

11. Treas. Reg. §1.671-3.

12. Treas. Reg. §1.671-4.

13. Treas. Reg. §1.671-4.

14. Rev. Rul. 2008-22, 2008-16 IRB 797.

15. Rev. Rul. 2004-64, 2004-2 CB 7.

SIMPLE VS. COMPLEX TRUSTS

CHAPTER 14

WHAT IS THE DIFFERENCE BETWEEN SIMPLE AND COMPLEX TRUSTS?

A non-grantor trust is any trust that is not a grantor trust. Generally, non-grantor trusts are irrevocable and the trustee pays income tax from the trust assets on taxable income retained by the trust.

Non-grantor trusts can be classified as simple trusts or complex trusts. A simple trust has the following characteristics:

- it is required to distribute all trust income annually;

- it does not permit charitable donations; and

- it does not distribute corpus.[1]

Whether a simple trust distributes all its income or not, the beneficiaries are treated as receiving the income and are taxed on the income as if they did receive it.[2] Simple trusts typically retain and pay income tax on capital gains on the trust assets, although the trust document could direct the trustee to distribute this income.

A complex trust differs from a simple trust in that:

- the trustee has the discretion whether to accumulate or retain income;

- the trust may distribute corpus or income accumulated in prior years; or

- the trust may make charitable contributions.[3]

Thus, a trust that distributes income from a prior year is a complex trust. Also, a trust that accumulates part of its income or distributes corpus according to the discretion of the trustee is a complex trust.

COMPUTING TAX ON TRUSTS

Calculating the taxable income of a trust is similar to calculating the taxable income of an individual. Gross income is reduced by deductions to arrive at taxable income. The trust is taxed on this income to the extent it is retained by the trust.

Gross Income

Gross income may include:

- income accumulated in trust for the benefit of unborn or unascertained persons or persons with contingent interests;

- income accumulated or held for future distribution under the terms of the trust;

- income which is to be distributed currently by the fiduciary to the beneficiaries;

- income collected by a guardian of an infant which is to be held or distributed as a court may direct; and

- income which, in the discretion of the fiduciary, may be either distributed to the beneficiaries or accumulated.[4]

Typically, trusts report interest, dividend, and rental income and gains and losses from the sale of property.

Distributable Net Income

In determining the amount of income taxable to the trust and taxable to the beneficiaries, *distributable net income* (DNI) serves three very important purposes:

- DNI limits the deduction allowable to the trust for amounts paid, credited, or required to be distributed to beneficiaries;

- DNI limits the amount includable in the taxable income of the beneficiaries; and

- DNI is used to prorate the character of income distributions among the trust and beneficiaries.[5]

DNI is defined as the taxable income of the trust increased by the following:

- deduction for distributions;

- deduction for personal exemptions;

- capital losses; and

- tax-exempt income.[6]

DNI does not include:

- extraordinary dividends that are not paid to any beneficiary, but are instead allocated to corpus; and

- capital gains – unless they are allocated to income, allocated to corpus and distributed to beneficiaries, utilized to determine the amount of distributions, or allocated for charitable purposes.[7]

To conform with modern portfolio theory, most states have adopted the Uniform Principal and Income Act[8] which allow the trustee to distribute income based on the total income of the trust. If capital gain income is allocated to income, it will be included in DNI.

The amount of taxable income distributed by a trust is deductible by the trust and is income to the beneficiary who received it.

OTHER TRUST DEDUCTIONS

The personal tax exemption for a simple trust is $300, and the exemption for most complex trusts

is $100.[8] Complex trusts are allowed an exemption of $300 if they are required to distribute all of their income each year.[9] A trust may be a simple trust in one year and a complex trust in a different year. If a trust that would otherwise be considered a simple trust distributes corpus, it is treated as a complex trust for the year. However, because simple trusts are required to distribute their income annually, a simple trust distributing corpus in any year still qualifies for the $300 exemption, even though it is treated as a complex trust for that year.

Complex trusts are allowed a deduction for the portion of taxable (not tax-exempt) income that is paid out as a charitable contribution.[10] Simple and complex trusts are allowed a deduction for administration expenses, such as trustee's fees and tax return preparation fees. Investment-related expenses are subject to a floor of 2 percent of adjusted gross income, similar to the miscellaneous itemized deductions of an individual.

Simple and complex trusts are allowed a "distribution deduction" to the extent they distribute the taxable income of the trust. For complex trusts, this deduction is for:

- mandatory distributions - the amount of income for the taxable year which is required to be distributed currently, and

- discretionary distributions - any other amounts paid for the taxable year.[11]

The distribution deduction may not exceed distributable net income.

TAX RATES FOR TRUSTS

The income tax rates for trusts and estates shown in the table below are extremely harsh. While single and married filing jointly filers are taxed at 39.6 percent (the highest marginal tax rate) starting at income of $406,750 in 2014, a trust is taxed at the 39.6 percent rate starting at income of $12,150. Consequently, most trusts distribute ordinary income, such as dividends and interest, to the beneficiaries so that the income will be taxed at the beneficiaries' rates. Capital gain rates for trusts are the same as the capital gain rates for individuals. Thus, there is not as great a need to avoid this type of income at the trust level.

2014 Marginal Tax Rates for Trusts and Estates

Taxable Income

From:	But Not Over:	Tax Rate:
$0	$2,500	15%
$2,501	$5,800	25%
$5,801	$8,900	28%
$8,901	$12,150	33%
Over $12,150		39.6%

The alternative minimum tax (AMT), which insures that high income persons and entities are not able to avoid taxation through the use of certain tax breaks, applies to trusts. Trusts are allowed an exemption deduction of $23,500. For example, the AMT might apply if a trust receives tax-exempt interest from private activity bonds or royalty income from oil wells.

Example (Simple Trust): The Jones Trust has the following income and administrative expenses for 2014:

- Dividend income - $6,000

- Interest income - $8,000

- Capital gain income - $4,000

- Fiduciary fees - $2,000

Under the trust agreement, dividend and interest income are distributed to beneficiaries, and capital gains and fees are allocated to corpus.

Accounting income for the trust is $14,000 ($8,000 + $6,000) and is distributed to the beneficiary. The trust's taxable income is $15,700 before the distribution deduction (dividend, interest, and capital gain income minus the $2,000 of fees and the $300 personal exemption deduction).

To arrive at distributable net income (DNI), the previously subtracted exemption is added back to the trust's taxable income. The capital gains allocated to corpus are not included, so DNI is $12,000 ($15,700 + 300 – 4,000). The distribution deduction is the lesser of the amount distributed ($14,000) or DNI. Hence, in this case, it is $12,000, the amount of DNI.

To determine the trust's taxable income for the year, the distribution deduction is subtracted from

the $15,700 calculated earlier. Thus, the taxable income for the trust is $3,700 ($15,700 – 12,000). This amount is comprised of the $4,000 long-term capital gain less the $300 trust exemption deduction. The trust owes federal income tax of $740 ($3,700 at the capital gain rate of 20 percent).

When DNI is distributed to the beneficiary, it retains its character. Here, the beneficiary receives $14,000 of gross income which consists of $6,000 of dividend income and $8,000 of interest income. The beneficiary receives and is taxed on DNI of only $12,000 ($14,000 - 2,000 of fiduciary fees). Even though fees are allocated and paid from corpus, they reduce the amount of income taxed to the beneficiary. Thus, the beneficiary is treated as receiving dividend income of $5,143 ($6,000/14,000 x 12,000) and interest income of $6,857 ($8,000/14,000 x 12,000).

The above example showed a DNI and taxable income calculation for a simple trust. How would this calculation change for a complex trust?

Example (Complex Trust): The James Trust has the following income and expenses for 2014:

- Interest income - $14,000

- Capital gain income - $4,000

- Fiduciary's fees - $2,000

The trust agreement allocates fiduciary's fees and capital gains to trust corpus. The trust has two beneficiaries: Sue and Dan. The trust is required to distribute half of the trust accounting income ($7,000) to Sue and is allowed to make discretionary distributions to Dan. The trust made a discretionary distribution to Dan of $3,000 during the year.

Taxable income of the trust, before the distribution deduction, is $15,900 (capital gain and interest income minus the fiduciary's fees and the $100 exemption).

DNI is $12,000 ($15,900 + 100 – 4,000). Because expenses were allocated to corpus, the DNI is less than the accounting income.

The distribution deduction is the lesser of the amount actually distributed ($10,000) or DNI

($12,000). After the distribution deduction, the trust's taxable income is $5,900 ($15,900-10,000). The $5,900 is comprised of $1,900 of interest income and $4,000 of capital gain income. The trust's tax is $1,085 ($285 on the $1,900 of interest income plus 20 percent capital gain rate on the $4,000).

Sue received a distribution of $7,000 from the trust. She pays tax on $7,000, which reflects half of the trust's interest income. Dan pays tax on the $3,000 of interest income he received from the trust.

Filing Returns for Trusts

The responsibility for filing the tax return and paying the tax on trust income falls upon the trustee of the trust. If the tax is not paid, this liability may follow the assets distributed to beneficiaries who may have to pay the tax on the share they received.[12]

Trusts are separate taxable entities with their own accounting periods and accounting methods. Generally, trusts must use the calendar year (December 31 as their year-end) as their accounting period. The only trusts exempt from this rule are tax-exempt trusts and wholly charitable trusts.[13] Most trusts use the cash basis method of accounting, although trusts with substantial business and real estate holdings sometimes use the accrual basis.

Because trusts are separate taxable entities, the beneficiaries do not receive the benefit of trust losses until the trust is terminated. Net operating losses can be carried back two years and forward twenty years, while net capital losses may be carried forward indefinitely. When the trust is terminated, losses are allocated to the beneficiaries in proportion to the amount of corpus they receive when the trust is terminated.

SIXTY-FIVE DAY RULE

Trustees who are required to distribute income to beneficiaries often do not know the trust's income on the last day of the year. The tax law gives trustees sixty-five days to determine the income and make the distribution. These amounts are considered paid on the last day of the previous taxable year if the fiduciary of the trust so elects.[14] The election is only effective for the taxable year for which the election is made. The amount this rule applies to cannot be greater than the amount of trust income for that taxable year or the amount of DNI of the trust reduced by any distributions.[15] The fiduciary may elect this treatment on the trust Form 1041.[16]

WHAT HAPPENS WHEN THE TRUST DISTRIBUTES PROPERTY?

When trusts are formed, grantors usually transfer cash or property to the trust. There are generally no income tax consequences either to the grantor or to the trust as a result of this transfer.

The distribution of property, such as stock, from a trust to the beneficiaries does not typically trigger gains or losses to the trust. The distribution is treated as income to the beneficiaries in the amount of the lesser of: the property's basis to the beneficiary; or its fair market value, to the extent of DNI. The trust claims a distribution deduction, and the beneficiary takes a carryover basis in the property.[17]

The trustee may elect to report the gain at the trust level. The gain is calculated as if the trust sold the property to the beneficiary. When this election is made, the trust reports the gain at the trust level, the income reported by the beneficiary is equal to the fair market value of the property to the extent of DNI, the trust's distribution deduction is equal to the fair market value of the property to the extent of DNI rather than its basis, and the beneficiary takes a basis in the property equal to its fair market value. Because losses from sales between related parties, such as the trust and beneficiary, are disallowed, this election is usually not made when the property's basis is greater than its value.[18]

Example: Jane Smith formed the Smith Trust with a transfer of $100,000 of stock with a basis of $25,000. Neither Jane nor the trust recognizes income as a result of this stock transfer.

Ten years later when the stock has a value of $150,000 and the trust has DNI of $15,000, the trust distributes the stock to the beneficiary. The beneficiary reports income of $15,000 (the amount of DNI) and takes a carryover basis in the stock of $25,000. The trust reports no income from the property transfer and receives a distribution deduction of $15,000.

If the trustee elects to treat the trust as selling the stock, the beneficiary reports income of

$15,000 (the amount of DNI) and takes a basis of $150,000 in the stock. The trust reports capital gain income of $125,000 ($150,000 – 25,000) from the property transfer and receives a distribution deduction of $15,000.

WHERE CAN I FIND OUT MORE?

1. FDIC, *Trust Examination Manual*, available at: https://www.fdic.gov/regulations/examinations/trustmanual/index.html.

2. Keene, David, "A Primer on the Uniform Principal and Income Act: How Accounting Affects Trust and Estate Beneficiaries," from Leimberg & LeClair, available at: http://www.leimberg.com/freeresources/truarticles/primeronuniformprincipal.html.

FREQUENTLY ASKED QUESTIONS

Question – Considering the high income tax rates that apply to trusts, how do the parties to trusts use trusts to their advantage?

Answer – The parties to trusts can avoid taxation at the trust's high income tax rates in several ways. First, the trust can distribute all its income. Many trusts, including simple trusts and trusts that qualify for the estate and gift tax marital deduction, are required to distribute their income annually.

Second, the grantor can retain powers over the property that cause the trust to be treated as a grantor trust. Retaining the power to revoke the trust or borrow from the trust with favorable terms are examples of such powers. The income from a grantor trust is taxed to the grantor at the grantor's tax rates rather than the trust rates.

Third, the trust fiduciary can invest in property that pays nontaxable income or appreciates in value rather than paying currently taxable income. Investing in tax-exempt bonds, growth stocks, and land are examples of investments that may be used to pursue this strategy.

CHAPTER ENDNOTES

1. I.R.C. §651(a).
2. I.R.C. §652(a).
3. I.R.C. §661(a).
4. Treas. Reg. §1.641(a)-2.
5. Treas. Reg. §1.643(a)-0.
6. Treas. Reg. §1.643(a).
7. Treas. Reg. §1.643(a).
8. For a list of States that have adopted the Uniform Principal and Income Act, see the FDIC's *Trust Examination Manual*, Appendix C. Available at: https://www.fdic.gov/regulations/examinations/trustmanual/appendix_c/appendix_c.html#_toc497113670.
9. I.R.C. §642 (b)(2).
10. Treas. Reg. §1.642(b)-1.
11. I.R.C. §642 (c)(1).
12. Treas. Reg. §1.661(a)-2.
13. Treas. Reg. §1.641(b)-2.
14. I.R.C. §644.
15. I.R.C. §663 (b)(1).
16. Treas. Reg. §1.663(b)-1.
17. Treas. Reg. §1.663(b)-2.
18. I.R.C. §643(e).

INCOME TAXATION OF ESTATES

CHAPTER 15

INTRODUCTION

When a person (the decedent) dies, the property he or she owned becomes the property of a taxable entity called an estate. The estate holds legal title to the property, but the decedent's heirs (beneficiaries) are entitled to the income from and enjoyment of the property.

An estate generally does not own all the property that is subject to estate tax. Jointly held property and property that is transferred automatically to a designated beneficiary, such as life insurance proceeds and retirement plan assets, are often subject to estate tax, but these amounts do not become part of the estate for income tax purposes. The property included in the income tax estate more closely approximates the property that will pass through probate. This estate exists until the executor or administrator has collected all the assets, paid the debts and taxes, filed the decedent's final income tax return and estate tax return, and distributed the assets to the heirs.

The estate is a separate tax entity that is taxed like a complex trust. Similar to a trust, the estate reports the income from the property it holds on a Form 1041, claims deductions for expenditures it makes, and is subject to the same compressed tax rates. Estates also calculate distributable net income (DNI) for the purpose of allocating income and the related tax burden between the beneficiaries and the estate. An estate may deduct from its taxable income amounts paid or permanently set aside as charitable contributions and may also take deductions for depreciation, depletion, and amortization in the same manner a trust or individual may.[1] An estate receives a larger personal exemption deduction than a trust – $600.[2] If an estate has a net operating loss carryover or a capital loss carryover when it terminates, the heirs may take these deductions on their returns.[3]

2014 Marginal Tax Rates for Trusts and Estates

Taxable Income		
From:	But Not Over:	Tax Rate:
$0	$2,500	15%
$2,501	$5,800	25%
$5,801	$8,900	28%
$8,901	$12,150	33%
Over $12,150		39.6%

Example: The James Miller Estate has the following income and expenses for 2014:

- Interest income - $14,000

- Capital gain income - $4,000

- Executor's fees - $2,000

The estate has two beneficiaries: Sue and Dan. The estate distributes half of its accounting income ($7,000) equally to Sue and Dan.

The taxable income of the trust, before the distribution deduction, is $15,400 (capital gain and interest income minus the fiduciary's fees and the estate's $600 exemption).

DNI is $12,000 ($15,400 + 600 − 4,000). Because expenses were allocated to corpus, the DNI is less than the accounting income.

The distribution deduction is $7,000, the lesser of the amount actually distributed ($7,000) or DNI ($12,000). After the distribution deduction, the estate's taxable income is $8,400

($15,400 – 7,000). The $8,400 is comprised of $4,400 of interest income and $4,000 of capital gain income. The estate's tax is $1,650. This includes $850 on the $4,400 of interest income (from Figure 15.1 above, $2,500 at 15 percent plus $1,900 at 25 percent) as well as $800 in capital gains tax (20 percent capital gain rate on the $4,000).

Sue and Dan received distributions of $3,500 each from the estate. They each pay income tax on the $3,500 of interest income they received at their respective marginal tax rates.

Because of the estate's high tax rates, the executor must constantly balance the benefit of distributing income to the beneficiaries with the benefit of retaining income in the estate. By retaining income in the estate, the decedent's survivors may be able to avoid some personal income taxes, but the executor must be cognizant of a regulation governing the termination of the estate. If the administration of an estate is considered by the IRS to be unduly prolonged, the estate is regarded as terminated for federal income tax purposes after the expiration of a reasonable period for the performance by the executor of all his or her duties.[4]

Estates differ from trusts in a couple of important ways. First, estates do not have to use the calendar year for tax reporting. They can use a fiscal year, such as March 31, as the end of their accounting period. One benefit of this characteristic is that the estate can end its final year shortly after the heir's calendar year ends. In this way, the income to the heir from the estate's final distribution will be postponed to the following year.[5]

Because of the availability of a fiscal year, convenience, and the ability to claim a charitable deduction for amounts set aside for charity, the trustee of a revocable trust that was treated as owned by the decedent under the grantor trust rules may wish to elect to be taxed as part of the estate. This election is irrevocable and must be made by both the executor of the estate and the trustee of the revocable trust. The election is valid for two years from the earlier of the date of the decedent's death or six months after the final determination of estate tax liability.[6]

A second difference from trusts is that estates do not need to make quarterly estimated tax payments from the outset. They can wait until the third tax year following the decedent's death.[7] This rule also applies to the decedent's grantor trust to which the residue of the estate will pass. Furthermore, in the estate's final tax year, the fiduciary may elect to treat any portion of an estimated tax payment made by the estate as a payment made by a beneficiary. If this election is made, the payment will be taxed to the beneficiary as if it were paid on the last day of that taxable year. This amount is not treated as a payment of estimated tax by the estate. Instead it is treated as a payment of estimated tax made by the beneficiary.[8]

Income in Respect of a Decedent

Income in respect of a decedent (IRD) is income the decedent earned before his or her death that is received after death. If the decedent reported income using the cash receipts and disbursement method of accounting, the income is not includable on the decedent's final income tax return because it was not received during the final year. Examples include dividends declared and recorded before death but received after death and salary income that was earned, but not received, before death. Payments from installment sales entered into before death and retirement plan distributions received after death are also IRD.

When IRD is received, it must be included in the gross income, for the taxable year when received, of:

- the decedent's estate;

- the beneficiary who acquires the right to receive the amount; or

- the person who the decedent gives the right to receive the amount by bequest, devise, or inheritance.[9]

IRD income, including possibly the fair market value of property at the time of the transfer, is included in the gross income of the estate or the person.[10] Income amounts received by the estate or any beneficiaries retain the character they had prior to the death of the decedent. In other words, income from an installment sale would continue to be reported as interest income, capital gain income, and return of basis.[11]

Similar in principle to the IRD income that must be reported by the recipients, the estate or heirs may deduct certain expenses that were accrued by the decedent but not paid prior to his or her death. These expenses include: trade or business expenses, interest, taxes, expenses for the production of income, and depletion.[12] If these expenses have not been paid before death, they may also be deductible by the estate as debts, one of the rare instances when the same expense may be deducted on two different returns.

IRD assets and accrued income are subject to estate tax as well as income tax. A retirement plan that the decedent owned at death will be included in the decedent's estate for estate tax purposes. To make matters worse, IRD property does not receive a step up in basis, meaning that the heir will pay income tax on the income that the decedent did not report prior to his death. To alleviate this adverse treatment, the heirs are allowed to deduct a pro rata portion of any estate tax that was paid by the executor on the income they receive.[13]

Example: Assume a decedent owns a $500,000 IRA which is included in his estate and subject to $200,000 of estate tax when he dies. The following year, the heir withdraws $100,000 from the IRA. The heir must pay income tax on the $100,000, but the heir is allowed a deduction of $40,000 ($200,000 x 100,000 / 500,000) because of the estate taxes paid by the executor.

FREQUENTLY ASKED QUESTIONS

Question – A father's will directs that his daughter receive $20,000 of stock from his estate. The estate has income greater than $20,000 from other sources. Is the distribution of the stock in accordance with the will considered a distribution of the income, making it taxable?

Answer – Recipients of gifts and inheritances are not generally subject to income tax.[14] They are subject to income tax on any income from the property they inherit. When an estate distributes property pursuant to a specific bequest, the distribution is treated as a nontaxable distribution of estate assets, not a distribution of income.

CHAPTER ENDNOTES

1. I.R.C. §§642(e), 642(f).
2. I.R.C. §642(b)(1).
3. I.R.C. §642(h)(1).
4. Treas. Reg. §1.641(b)-3(a).
5. I.R.C. §441(a).
6. I.R.C. §645.
7. I.R.C. §6654(l).
8. I.R.C. §643(g).
9. I.R.C. §691(a)(1).
10. I.R.C. §691(a)(2).
11. I.R.C. §691(a)(3).
12. I.R.C. §691(b).
13. I.R.C. §691(c).
14. I.R.C. §102(a).

ACCOUNTING METHODS

CHAPTER 16

INTRODUCTION

An accounting method is a set of rules used to determine when and how income and expenses are reported. Although no single method is required of all taxpayers, each taxpayer must use a system that clearly reflects income and expenses and use that method consistently.

There are two basic accounting methods:

- **Cash Method:** Under the cash method, income is reported in the tax period during which it is received. Expenses are deducted in the tax period during which they are paid. The cash method is simple, and is used by most individual taxpayers. There are restrictions that prevent some taxpayers from using the cash method.

- **Accrual Method:** Under the accrual method, income is reported in the tax period during which it is earned, even if it is not received until later. Expenses are deducted in the tax period during which they are incurred, whether or not they are paid that year. The accrual method does a better job realistically matching income and expenses, but is more complicated.

Taxpayers may also use certain special and hybrid (combination) methods of accounting. In particular, certain long-term contracts (see below) and installment sales (see Chapter 29) require special accounting methods. There are also special uniform capitalization methods of accounting for certain direct and indirect costs allocable to real and tangible personal property produced by the taxpayer. See the discussion of the UNICAP rules, below.

WHEN IS A PARTICULAR METHOD INDICATED?

1. When an individual or a small business desires a simple method of accounting, the cash method may be appropriate. The cash method is relatively straightforward and easy to implement.

2. When a business produces, purchases, or sells merchandise, the accrual method is generally required for sales and purchases of the business inventory. There are, however, exceptions for certain *qualifying taxpayers* and *qualifying small business taxpayers*, as discussed below.

3. When a C corporation or a partnership with a C corporation partner, has *average annual gross receipts* exceeding $5 million, the accrual method is generally required. This is discussed further below.

4. When a *family corporation* has gross receipts of $25 million or less for each prior tax year after 1985, it may still use the cash method. This is discussed further below.

5. When a corporation is a *qualified personal service corporation*, it may use the cash method regardless of its gross receipts. This is discussed further below.

6. When an entity is classified as a *tax shelter*, it must use the accrual method of accounting.[1]

7. When a taxpayer expends amounts to acquire, produce, or improve tangible property, and such amounts are otherwise deductible, the expenditures may have to be capitalized under the Code section 263A unicap rules, which call for a special uniform capitalization method of accounting (see below).

THE CASH METHOD

Advantages

1. The cash method of accounting is relatively straight-forward and easy to implement.

2. Timing of both income and deductions is important. The cash method of accounting provides a limited but useful amount of planning flexibility in postponing income or accelerating deductions. A taxpayer may postpone income by delaying receipt of income, including *constructive receipt*, discussed below, to the following tax period. A taxpayer may likewise accelerate deductions by paying expenses before the close of the tax period.

What Are The Requirements?

1. Under the cash method, the taxpayer must include in gross income all items of income actually or constructively received during the tax year. Income is constructively received when it is credited to a taxpayer's account, set apart, or otherwise made available without restriction, even if the taxpayer does not actually take physical possession of the income until after the close of the tax year.

2. Under the cash method, the taxpayer generally deducts expenses in the tax year in which they are actually paid. An expense paid in advance may generally only be deducted in the tax year to which the expense applies.

3. Any hybrid (combination) method of accounting which includes the cash method is treated as the cash method.

4. The following individuals and entities may generally use the cash method of accounting:

   - individuals and sole proprietorships;

   - S corporations;

   - C corporations and partnerships, other than those engaged in the business of farming, with *average annual gross receipts* not exceeding $5 million;

   - partnerships, other than those engaged in the business of farming, without a C corporation as a partner, regardless of the gross receipts;

   - C corporations and partnerships engaged in the business of farming with *average annual gross receipts* not exceeding $1 million;

   - *family corporations*, including those engaged in the business of farming, with gross receipts of $25 million or less for each prior tax year after 1985; and

   - *qualified personal service corporations*.

5. A C corporation or a partnership meets the *average annual gross receipts* test if it meets the test for every tax year after 1985 (1975 for those engaged in the business of farming).[2] A C corporation or partnership meets the test for a tax year if the average annual gross receipts from the three prior tax years do not exceed $5 million (or $1 million for those engaged in the business of farming).[3]

6. A *family corporation* is a corporation of which at least 50 percent of the combined voting power of all voting stock and at least 50 percent of all classes of non-voting stock are owned directly or indirectly by members of the same family.[4] The members of a family are defined broadly as an individual, such individual's brothers and sisters, the brothers and sisters of such individual's parents and grandparents, the ancestors and lineal descendants of any of the foregoing, a spouse of any of the foregoing, and the estate of any of the foregoing.[5]

7. A *qualified personal service corporation* is a corporation, at least 95 percent of the activities of which are in the performance of services in the fields of health, veterinary services, law, engineering, surveying, architecture, accounting, actuarial science, performing arts, or consulting (the function test).[6] In addition, at least 95 percent of the stock must be owned directly or indirectly by employees performing services for the corporation in one of the fields described above, by retired employees who performed services in those fields, or by the estate of a former employee who performed services in those fields (the ownership test).[7] Ownership by any other person who acquired the stock by reason of the death of a former employee who performed services in one of the fields described above also counts toward the 95 percent, but only for the two-year period beginning on the date of death.

8. A taxpayer must use the accrual method of accounting when the production, purchase, or sale

of merchandise is an income-producing factor in the taxpayer's business,[8] unless the taxpayer is a *qualifying taxpayer*[9] or a *qualifying small business taxpayer*.[10] A taxpayer is a *qualifying taxpayer* if the taxpayer's *average annual gross receipts* do not exceed $1 million for each tax year ending after December 16, 1999.[11] A taxpayer is a qualifying small business taxpayer if the taxpayer's *average annual gross receipts* do not exceed $10 million for each prior tax year ending on or after December 31, 2000 and the principle business activity for the prior tax year was not retailing, wholesaling, manufacturing, mining, publishing, or sound recording.[12]

THE ACCRUAL METHOD
Advantages

1. The accrual method of accounting most accurately matches income and expenses and better reflects the profitability of a business. The cash method may not provide owners, suppliers, lenders, or potential buyers a meaningful picture of business operations.

2. The accrual method is generally required for non-tax reporting purposes, making it possible to use the same accounts for tax purposes. A business may have to keep two sets of accounts in order to use the cash method for income tax purposes. So the accrual method may result in some accounting savings.

WHAT ARE THE REQUIREMENTS?

1. Any taxpayer may use the accrual method of accounting. The purpose of the accrual method is to match income and expenses in the correct year.

2. Under the accrual method, the taxpayer must generally include in gross income any item for which all events that fix the right to receive the income have occurred in the tax year, as long as the amount can be determined with reasonable accuracy. This is commonly referred to as the "all-events" test. If the taxpayer includes a reasonably estimated amount in income, and the actual amount is later determined to be different, the taxpayer must take the difference into account in the later tax year.

3. Under the accrual method, the taxpayer generally deducts expenses when the *all-events test* has been

met and *economic performance* has occurred. The all-events test is met when all events have occurred that fix the fact of liability, and the liability can be determined with reasonable accuracy. Economic performance occurs, for example, when purchased property or services are provided.

Example: Joseph runs a small computer business as a sole proprietorship. Joseph sells two computers on December 30, 2008, one to Jill for $1,000 and a second to Jack for $1,500. Jill's computer is in stock, so she pays for her computer by check and takes it home immediately. Joseph deposits Jill's check for $1,000 on January 2, 2009.

Jack also takes delivery of his computer immediately, but he asks Joseph to bill him. Joseph bills Jack on January 2, 2009, and receives payment back on January 29, 2009. Joseph deposits the check on January 30, 2009.

If Joseph operates his business on the cash basis, he must report the $1,000 from Jill in income in the 2008 tax year. Joseph will report the $1,500 from Jack in income for the 2009 tax year.

If Joseph operates his business on the accrual basis, he must report both the $1,000 from Jill and the $1,500 from Jack in income for the 2008 tax year.

UNIFORM CAPITALIZATION (UNICAP) RULES

The uniform capitalization, or UNICAP rules, were the direct result of—and effectively codified—the U.S. Supreme Court's decision in *Commissioner v. Idaho Power Company*.[13] In the case, Idaho Power claimed a current deduction under Code section 167(a) for depreciation on transportation equipment (cars, trucks, etc.) it owned and used in the construction of its own capital facilities. IRS denied the deduction, ruling the depreciation was a nondeductible capital expenditure under Code section 263. The Supreme Court upheld the IRS position, ruling the construction-related depreciation must be amortized and deducted over the longer life of the capital facilities constructed, as provided in section 263, rather than over the shorter life of the equipment under section 167(a). According to the court, a contrary holding that the depreciation was deductible under section 167(a) would lead to disparate treatment among taxpayers because it would allow the firm with sufficient resources to construct its own facilities and to obtain a current deduction, whereas another firm without such resources would be required to capitalize its entire cost including depreciation charged to it by the contractor.

The Court's findings in the *Idaho Power* case were the origin of Code section 263A, which requires certain producers of tangible property to include in their inventory the indirect (including mixed service) and direct costs of producing that inventory. While this seemed like a simple and uncomplicated concept, the devil was in the details. How could those indirect costs be repeatedly and reliably allocated and subject to capitalization under the new section 263A? This question led some experts to conclude "this is primarily a result of the confusing and ill-defined terminology throughout section 263A and its related regulations."[14]

With a few exceptions (such as taxpayers using the cash method of accounting and resellers with gross receipts less than $10 million for the prior three tax years), the UNICAP rules of section 263A require certain direct and indirect costs—that are customarily expensed—to be capitalized as inventory. These costs include all direct costs and certain indirect costs properly allocable to real property and tangible personal property produced by the taxpayer, as well as real or personal capital assets that are acquired by the taxpayer for resale. For example, a taxpayer would have to capitalize the direct costs of constructing a building, such as labor expenses, as well as indirect costs such as construction-related depreciation (as in the *Idaho Power* case).

For purposes of the UNICAP rules, to "produce" means to construct, build, install, manufacture, develop, improve, create, raise or grow.[15] Self-constructed assets and property built under contract are treated as property "produced" by the taxpayer, and the rules under section 263A(a) govern.

In addition, section 263A(f) requires the capitalization of interest expense when the taxpayer produces certain property. The interest capitalization rules under Treasury regulation 1.263A-8 contain precise definitions of designated property and include inherently permanent structures in the definition of real property.

In summary, for taxpayers who are subject to the UNICAP rules, all real property and certain types of tangible personal property are subject to the interest capitalization rules. Therefore, any change in the allocation of costs between real and tangible personal property may have an impact on the amount of capitalized interest.

CHANGING ACCOUNTING METHODS

A taxpayer may generally choose any permitted accounting method when filing the taxpayer's first tax return. Any method of accounting selected must clearly reflect the taxpayer's income and expenses, but no specific IRS approval is needed when making the initial choice. After the initial choice, a taxpayer must use the selected method consistently from year to year.

In general, a taxpayer may change accounting methods only with the permission of the IRS. A change in accounting method includes not only a change in the taxpayer's overall accounting method, but also a change in the treatment of any material item.

WHEN IS IT INDICATED?

When an existing method of accounting does not provide the most favorable tax treatment, a taxpayer should consider whether a change in accounting method is desirable. A taxpayer may potentially change to any acceptable accounting method, provided the taxpayer obtains approval for the change from the IRS.

WHAT ARE THE REQUIREMENTS?

1. In general, a taxpayer may change accounting methods only with the permission of the IRS. Permission is required whether a taxpayer is changing the taxpayer's overall accounting method or merely changing the accounting treatment of a single item.

2. To request an accounting change, a taxpayer must file IRS Form 3115 during the tax year for which the change is requested, and must generally pay a user fee.[16] The application requires the taxpayer to account for all items that will be duplicated or omitted as a result of the proposed accounting

change, and to calculate the adjustments necessary to prevent the duplications or omissions.[17]

3. The IRS has set up procedures and requirements for a number of specific changes that will be automatically granted by the IRS. These changes still require Form 3115, but require no user fee. Revenue Procedure 2008-52[18] sets out the procedures for obtaining automatic consent, and lists, in the appendix, the areas in which a taxpayer can obtain automatic consent. The list is quite extensive and includes accounting method changes ranging from the commonplace to the obscure. The following are just a few examples of changes that will be granted with automatic consent:

    a. Changing the overall accounting method from cash or hybrid to accrual;

    b. Certain small taxpayers changing to the overall cash method;

    c. Changing from the reserve method to the specific charge-off method of accounting for bad debts;

    d. A restaurant or tavern changing its method of accounting for the cost of restaurant smallwares;

    e. Changing the treatment of timber fertilization costs from capital expenditures to ordinary and necessary business expenses; or

    f. Changing accounting methods to obtain the Liberty Zone bonus depreciation deduction.

4. Taxpayers who have received approval from the IRS for an accounting change, or who have been ordered by the IRS to make an accounting change, must make adjustments to income to account for the net effect of the accounting change. Where the net effect of an accounting change is small, the adjustments must be accounted for in the year of the change. Where the net effect of an accounting change is greater than $3,000, either positive or negative, however, a taxpayer is entitled to use either of two alternative methods: the *three-year method* or the *reconstruction of income method*.[19]

    Under the *three-year method*, the net amount of the adjustment is divided by three. This amount is then added to the taxable income for the current year and for each of the two prior years.[20] Where an accounting change is made voluntarily, the period can be extended to four years.[21]

Under the *reconstruction of income method*, the income for prior years is recomputed using the new method of accounting for all prior years during which the taxpayer used the former accounting method.[22] The adjustment for the current tax year is then limited to the combined net increase for the prior years. For a business that has been operating for a while, reconstructing income for prior years can be cumbersome. For that reason, this method is not often used.

Example: Joseph runs a small computer business as a limited liability company taxed as a sole proprietorship and uses the cash method of accounting. Joseph decides that after ten years in business, his company has grown to a size that he should switch to the accrual method of accounting.

Joseph's business currently has $50,000 in accounts receivable that were not reported in income last year, because he was operating on the cash basis. Likewise, the business has $15,000 in accounts payable that were incurred in the prior year, but were not deductible because they were not paid.

Joseph files Form 3115 requesting a change for which the IRS has granted automatic approval in Revenue Procedure 2008-52. Joseph calculates the adjustments required to include the $50,000 accounts receivable in income and to obtain the $15,000 deduction for the accounts payable. The net adjustment is positive, $35,000, so Joseph elects to take the $35,000 into income evenly over four years, $8,750 per year.

CHANGE OF ACCOUNTING METHOD TO IMPLEMENT UNICAP RULES

The IRS considers any change from deducting to capitalizing an item of cost or expense (or from capitalizing to deducting the item) to be a change in the method of accounting.[23] Revenue Procedure 2014-16 provides rules for changing the accounting method used for costs that are required to be capitalized under UNICAP rules.[24]

Notably the rules waive certain limitations which precluded accounting method changes by taxpayers under IRS examination.[25] However, if the accounting method changes are filed on a single Form 3115.

If the taxpayer is changing any unit(s) of property or the identification of any building structure(s) or system(s) for purposes of determining whether amounts are deducted as repair and maintenance costs, or capitalized as improvement costs, the taxpayer must include with Form 3115 a detailed description of the unit(s) of property, building structure(s), or buildings system(s) used under both its present and proposed method of accounting, together with a citation to the paragraph of the final regulation or temporary regulation under which the unit of property is permitted

WHERE CAN I FIND OUT MORE?

1. IRS Publication 538, Accounting Periods and Methods (Rev. March 2008).

2. IRS Publication 334, Tax Guide for Small Business (Revised Annually).

3. Revenue Procedure 2001-10, 2001-2 IRB 272

4. Revenue Procedure 2002-9, 2002-1 CB 327.

FREQUENTLY ASKED QUESTIONS

Question – Can changing the method of accounting for inventory benefit a taxpayer?

Answer – For taxpayers who maintain inventories for their businesses, the method of accounting for the costs of inventory can have a major impact on taxable income. Inventory methods of accounting are used to match up costs between the purchase or manufacture of inventory and the subsequent sale of that inventory. The First-In-First-Out (FIFO) inventory method matches up the oldest item in inventory with the current sale. The Last-In-First-Out (LIFO) inventory method matches up the newest item in inventory with the current sale.

In most industries, where inventory costs are inflationary, the LIFO inventory method helps taxpayers reduce income by matching up the latest – and more expensive – items in inventory with current sales, leaving older and less expensive items remaining in inventory. These taxpayers, if currently using the FIFO or another inventory method might benefit from a switch to LIFO. In certain industries, such as the computer industry, where costs are constantly declining, LIFO would reduce the cost of goods sold and increased taxable income.

Because inventories are so important, there are special requirements for taxpayers changing to the LIFO accounting method.[26] Advance approval is generally not required to change to the LIFO method, but Form 970 should be filed along with the taxpayer's tax return for the year of the change. Form 970 includes an analysis of the beginning and ending inventories.

Question – Are taxpayers required to use any particular accounting period?

Answer – Taxpayers must use a "tax year" to report taxable income. A tax year is an annual accounting period for keeping records and reporting income and expenses. Depending on the taxpayer, a tax year may be a calendar year or a fiscal year (including a 52-53-week tax year). (Taxpayers who are not in existence for an entire year, or who change their tax year, may be required to report on a short tax year.)

A calendar year is a period of twelve consecutive months that begins on January 1 and runs through December 31. A calendar-year taxpayer must maintain books and record and report income and expenses for that period. Generally, anyone can adopt the calendar year as a tax year; moreover, certain taxpayers are required to use a calendar year by the Internal Revenue Code or Treasury regulations (see below).

A fiscal year is a period of twelve consecutive months that ends on the last day of any month except December 31. Taxpayers who are allowed to adopt a fiscal year must maintain books and records and report income and expenses using that period.

Certain taxpayers may also adopt a 52-53-week tax year. A 52-53-week tax year always ends on the same day of the week. The tax year may end on either (1) the last time that the chosen day falls in a given month or (2) the closest time the chosen day falls to the end of the given month. This definition will result in a tax year that is fifty-two weeks long in most years, but that is fifty-three weeks long in certain years.

Taxpayers who wish to change their tax year must file Form 1128 (*Application To Adopt, Change, or Retain a Tax Year*) to request IRS approval. (S Corporations must use Form 2553 (*Election by a Small Business Corporation*) instead.)

Question – Which taxpayers are required to adopt a particular tax year?

Answer – Generally, individuals must adopt the calendar year as their tax year, but an individual may adopt a fiscal year if the individual maintains his books and records on the basis of the adopted fiscal year.

Partnerships must generally conform its tax year to its partners' tax years (either the tax year used by a majority of partners, the tax year used by all the principal (5 percent) partners, or the year that results in the least aggregate deferral of income to the partners). A partnership may also use a 52-53-week tax year ending with reference to the required tax year. To use any other than the required tax year, a partnership must establish a business purpose for a different tax year or file an election under Code section 444 (see below).

S Corporations and Personal Service Corporations (PSCs) must generally use a calendar year or a 52-53-week tax year ending with reference to the calendar year or must establish a business purpose for a different tax year. An S Corporation may also file an election under section 444.

Question – What is a "section 444 election?"

Answer – Under Code section 444, a partnership, S Corporation, PSC may elect to use a tax year other than its required tax year. Under a section 444 election, an electing entity must make certain required payments or distributions in exchange for adopting a tax year that begins no more than three months later than the required tax year.[27] (A tax year established based on a business purpose does not require a Section 444 election.)

Question – Are taxpayers required to use any particular method to account for long-term contracts?

Answer – Yes. Generally speaking the income from any "long-term contract" must be determined using the "percentage of completion" (POC) method of accounting.[28] A "long-term contract" means any contract for the manufacture, building, installation, or construction of property, if such contract is not completed within the taxable year in which such contract is entered into.[29]

Under the POC method, a taxpayer generally must include in income the portion of the total contract price that corresponds to the percentage of the entire contract that the taxpayer has completed during the taxable year. The percentage of completion is determined by comparing current contract costs incurred with estimated total contract costs. Thus, the taxpayer includes a portion of the total contract price in gross income as the taxpayer incurs allocable contract costs.[30]

The requirement to use the POC does not apply to home construction contracts or to other construction contracts estimated to be completed within the two-year period beginning on the contract commencement date, where the taxpayer's average annual gross receipts for the three taxable years preceding the taxable year in which such contract is entered into do not exceed $10,000,000.[31]

Question – Can a taxpayer operate two businesses using different accounting methods for each?

Answer – A taxpayer operating two or more separate and distinct businesses can use a different accounting method for each. In order to be distinct, each business must maintain a complete and separate set of books and records. Furthermore, a taxpayer may not shift profits or losses between businesses so that income is not clearly reflected.

Question – What happens if a business using the accrual method of accounting incurs a business expense with a related business using the cash method of accounting?

Answer – Where a taxpayer using the accrual method of accounting owes a debt to a *related person* using the cash method of accounting, the taxpayer may not deduct the expense until it is actually paid *and* that amount is includible in the recipient's gross income.[32]

CHAPTER ENDNOTES

1. Treas. Reg. §1446-1(e)(3).

2. I.R.C. §481; Treas. Reg. §1.446-1(e)(3).

3. 2008-36 I.R.B. 587.

4. I.R.C. §481.

5. I.R.C. §481(b)(1).

6. I.R.C. §481(c); Rev. Proc. 97-27, 1997-1 CB 680.

7. I.R.C. §481(b)(2).

8. I.R.C. §472.

9. I.R.C. §448(a)(3).

10. I.R.C. §§448(c), 447(d).

11. I.R.C. §§448(c), 447(d).

12. I.R.C. §447(d)(2)(C).

13. 418 U.S. 1 (1974).

14. Brighenti, William "How to Apply UNICAP: Uniform Capitalization Rule 263A – Simplified Production Method and Simplified Service Cost Method are really simple!" Available at: http://www.cpaconnecticut.com/unicap.html.

15. I.R.C. §263A(g)(1); Treas. Reg. §1.263A-2(a)(1)(i).

16. I.R.C. §447(e).

17. I.R.C. §448(d)(2)(A).

18. I.R.C. §448(d)(2)(B).

19. I.R.C. §§446, 471.

20. Rev. Proc. 2001-10, 2001-2 I.R.B. 272.

21. Notice 2001-76, 2001-52 I.R.B. 613.

22. Rev. Proc. 2001-10, 2001-2 I.R.B. 272.

23. Internal Revenue Manual §4.11.6.2 (05-13-2005).

24. 2014-9 I.R.B. 606.

25. 2011-4 I.R.B. 330.

26. Notice 2001-76, 2001-52 I.R.B. 613.

27. I.R.C. §§280H, 444, 7519.

28. I.R.C. §460(a).

29. I.R.C. §460(f).

30. Treas. Reg. §1.460-4(b)(1).

31. I.R.C. §460(e)(1).

32. I.R.C. §267(a)(2). For the definition of "related person," see I.R.C. §267(b).

CHOICE OF ENTITY

CHAPTER 17

INTRODUCTION

When establishing a new business, the owner(s) must decide which business entity best supports the objectives of the business. When making this choice, owners should consider the tax implications, protection from liability, flexibility in ownership, and state business laws as they relate to each option. Given the multitude of the factors to be considered by a new business owner, this chapter focuses mainly on the federal tax implications of such a decision.

New owners of a business have several entities to choose from, and the best choice depends on the business owner's goals and intent. The following is a list of some of the most commonly used entity types.

1. Sole Proprietorship

2. Partnerships:

   a. General partnership;

   b. Limited partnership;

   c. Limited liability partnership;

   d. Limited liability limited partnership;

3. Limited Liability Companies:

4. Corporations:

   a. C Corporation;

   b. S Corporation.

SOLE PROPRIETORSHIP

A sole proprietorship is the most straightforward form of business entity—simply an individual taxpayer operating a business. For that reason, many small businesses start out as sole proprietorships. The owner operates in his or her capacity as an individual, and since there is no separate legal entity, there is nothing necessary to operate a sole proprietorship other than to be "in business." (Though there may be state or local business licensing requirements.) Self-employed individuals (such as freelance writers or photographers) are treated as sole proprietors. Because there is no separate legal entity, sole proprietors are personally and fully liable for the debts and obligations of the business.

A sole proprietorship may be appropriate as an entity choice for a business owner who desires a less complicated tax structure and does not want to incur the expense and formalities of forming a business under state law. Moreover, for a single individual operating a business without significant liability concerns, a sole proprietorship may be appropriate.

Advantages

A sole proprietorship is the simplest form of business entity to start and requires no formal steps for formation.

It is also the easiest form of business in which to operate. Because there is a single owner, there are no complications regarding management decisions or the division of profits. Although a sole proprietor must keep separate business records, the taxpayer need only file a single tax return, Form 1040 with Schedules C and SE.

A sole proprietorship avoids the double taxation that occurs with C Corporations. A sole proprietor may even be able to deduct losses from the business on the individual tax return to offset income received from other sources.

Disadvantages

A sole proprietorship provides no liability protection, leaving the business owner liable for all business debts and expenses. In the event of a judgment against the business, the personal assets of the business owner may be available to the creditor. For this reason, it is typically difficult to raise cash for such businesses since few investors will want to place their funds at risk.

A sole proprietorship is unique to the business owner. A sole proprietor cannot admit another owner without legally ending the sole proprietorship and forming a new business such as a partnership.

The sole proprietorship generally dies (or becomes "disabled") at the death (or disability) of its owner. Thus, in most cases, very little of the value of a sole proprietorship can be transferred upon the owner's death. Additionally, the sole proprietorship is a poor estate planning tool since it is impossible to fractionalize or create layers of interests that can be transferred during lifetime or at death to others.

What are the Requirements?

There is nothing required to start a business as a sole proprietorship except to start the business. A single-owner business that is not incorporated or organized as a limited liability company is automatically a sole proprietorship. There may, however, be state and local requirements for permits or business licenses. Most states require a filing and a formal public notification when a business is operated under a name other than the owner's name.

A sole proprietor must keep records for business income and expenses separate from records for personal income and expenses. The business income and expenses must be reported on Schedule C and filed with the taxpayer's Form 1040. The net income on Schedule C is reported on the Form 1040 and is taxed to the taxpayer along with the taxpayer's other income.

Sole proprietors must also pay *self-employment taxes* (see below) to fund the Social Security and Medicare systems. The self-employment taxes are the equivalent of the payroll taxes deducted from employee paychecks and matched by their employers. Sole proprietors must pay the entire amount themselves. The self-employment tax is calculated on Schedule SE and filed with the taxpayer's Form 1040.

Tax Implications

For tax purposes, a sole proprietorship is not a separate entity from the taxpayer. At the federal level, all business income or losses are reported on Form 1040 with Schedule C attached. Sole proprietors generally must also pay the self-employment tax and file Schedule SE with their Form 1040. Moreover, the disposition (i.e. sale) of a sole proprietorship is not treated as the disposition of an entity. Therefore, the gain and loss on the disposition is determined on an asset-by-asset basis.

Income of a sole proprietorship is reported on the owner's federal income tax return and combined with other income for the year. The individual's combined income is subject to the ordinary income tax rates. Individuals having net earnings of $400 or more from self-employment are required to complete Schedule SE and compute the self-employment tax due.[1] For a detailed discussion of the tax implications of self-employment income, see Chapter 10.

PARTNERSHIP

A partnership is an unincorporated association of two or more persons as co-owners to carry on a business for profit. The four main types of partnerships are:

1. *General Partnerships*: This is the traditional type of partnership. Each partner is a principal, fully active in the business with a voice in its management, each partner is an agent of the other with full legal authority to act for the firm within the scope of its business activities, each is fully liable for firm debts, and each shares in the profits.

2. *Limited Partnerships*: A limited partnership receives its power to operate under state law such as the Uniform Limited Partnership Act. It is defined as a partnership having one or more general partners and one or more limited partners. A limited partner's financial liability is essentially limited to his investment in the

firm. A limited partnership must have at least one general partner with full personal liability.

3. *Limited Liability Partnerships (LLP)*: An LLP follows the structure of a general partnership, with the main difference that an LLP allows for the partners to benefit from partial liability. The partners remain liable for their own wrongful acts, but their personal assets are shielded from the wrongdoing of other partners. LLPs are a function of state law and some states limit what types of business can function as an LLP.

4. *Limited Liability Limited Partnerships (LLLP)*: an LLLP follows the same rules as a limited partnership with the exception that LLLP general partners are afforded limited liability. It is important to note that the LLLP form of business is not available in all states, and as such, general partners may still be subject to liability in a jurisdiction that does not recognize this form of partnership.

Further, Code Section 761 states that the term "partnership" includes a syndicate, group, pool, joint venture, or other unincorporated organization through or by means of which any business, financial operation, or venture is carried on, and which is not, within the meaning of federal tax laws, a corporation or a trust or estate. There are some differences, but limited partnerships, general partnerships, limited liability partnerships, and limited liability limited partnerships are treated in essentially the same manner for federal income tax purposes.

Advantages

For federal income tax purposes, the income, deductions, capital gains and losses, charitable contributions, stock dividends, and other tax attributes of a partnership pass through to the partners' separate income tax returns. This pass-through treatment avoids the double taxation of income applicable to C Corporations. Partners are taxed individually on partnership profits whether distributed or not.

Partners may be able to deduct partnership losses on their individual returns, subject to the passive activity loss and at-risk rules, discussed in Chapter 17.

A general partnership may be formed with few, if any, formalities. A general partnership may even be formed on the basis of an oral agreement between two or more parties to jointly operate a business for profit.

A partnership agreement may be carefully tailored to meet the goals of the partners. Profits and losses may be allocated among partners as desired, subject to the requirements for *substantial economic effect*. (See "What Are the Requirements?" below for a more detailed discussion of substantial economic effect.)

Disadvantages

General partners are personally liable for the liabilities and debts of the partnership. The risk is not even limited to a partner's pro rata share of the liabilities. If other partners are insolvent, a single partner can be personally liable for the entire amount owed by the partnership. This means that a general partner could be personally liable for another partner's actions with respect to the partnership, even if the general partner did not approve or have knowledge of the other partner's actions.

Terminating or exiting partnerships can be difficult. Without a carefully crafted partnership agreement, a partnership may automatically terminate if a partner dies, becomes incompetent, or decides to leave. Personal or management conflicts between partners can be difficult to resolve without a clear management structure governed by a partnership agreement with comprehensive provisions addressing such matters.

What are the Requirements?

While the agreement between partners may be either oral or written, most partnerships have a basic set of written rules on which the partners have all agreed. These rules, called the partnership agreement, govern the conduct of the business. They usually set forth the property contributed to the partnership by each partner, the time to be devoted to the business by each, and the share of the profits or losses from the operation of the business to which each partner is entitled.

The partnership agreement may also set forth an agreement between the partners whereby, upon the death or withdrawal of one of the partners, the remaining partners have the right to purchase his interest. The agreement may set the dollar price to be paid for such interest, or may set out a formula under which the price can be computed.

Each partner of a general partnership is subject to unlimited personal liability for firm debts if partnership assets are not sufficient. Unless the partnership agreement provides otherwise, most state statutes provide that:

- All partners share equally in profits and losses irrespective of the proportionate value of the capital or services each has contributed.

- All partners have equal rights in the management and conduct of the partnership business.

- No partner is entitled to remuneration for acting in the partnership business, except that a surviving partner is entitled to reasonable compensation for his services in winding up the partnership affairs.

- No person can become a member of a partnership without the consent of all the partners.

Each general partner becomes an agent of the others and may transact business on behalf of the firm, and bind all other partners, so long as the transaction is within the scope of the partnership business, and not otherwise restricted in the partnership agreement. Within these limits, each general partner is bound by the acts, contracts, and even the frauds of his partners, and is responsible for such acts just as fully and completely as if the transaction had been carried through by him personally. Such power does not, however, extend to the sale of the stock in trade, or of the entire assets, or of the fixtures of the firm, since such a complete transaction would tend to put the partnership out of business.

As a general rule, individual partners do not have the right to propose, and bind their associates in, the following acts:

1. to confess judgments;

2. to dispose of the goodwill of the business;

3. to make an assignment of the partnership property to a creditor, or to a trustee, for the benefit of a creditor, or of all creditors;

4. to do any act that would make it impossible to carry on the ordinary business of the partnership; or

5. to submit partnership claims to arbitration.

Each partner has three property rights concerning the partnership: (a) his rights in specific partnership property; (b) his interest in the partnership; and (c) his right to participate in the management. All partners are co-owners of property held in the name of the partnership, and all have the right to possess the property for partnership purposes. No partner has the right, without the consent of the other partners, to possess partnership property for any non-partnership purpose, or to assign his rights in specific partnership property.

A partner's interest in the partnership is his share of the profits and surplus. This interest may be assigned without dissolving the partnership. In the absence of a contrary provision in the partnership agreement, each partner has an equal voice in the management of partnership affairs, irrespective of his proportionate contributions of capital or services.

The partnership relationship is a highly personal one; any one of a number of occurrences may cause dissolution. Dissolution is not the same as liquidation or termination. Dissolution is simply a change in the relation of the partners caused by any partner's ceasing to be associated with the carrying on as distinguished from the winding up, of the business.

On the dissolution, the partnership is not terminated, but continues until the winding up of partnership affairs is completed. The business may continue after dissolution, or it may be liquidated, depending upon what arrangements have been made in advance and upon what agreement is reached among retiring, remaining or surviving partners, creditors and successors in interest of deceased partners. In general, dissolution terminates the authority of partners to act for the partnership, except as is necessary to wind up affairs or to complete transactions begun before dissolution.

Example: Max, Aaron, Charlene, and Kevin each contribute $25,000 to form the new 4J General Partnership. Under the partnership agreement, they are each required to work full time for the partnership and are each entitled to one quarter of the profits and losses of the partnership. At the end of the first year, the partnership has gross income of $1,000,000; ordinary business expenses of $500,000; capital gains of $25,000; charitable contributions of $5,000; and $10,000 in dividends received by the partnership from its stock holdings.

The partnership files an information return (Form 1065) separately listing the income, expenses, capital gains, charitable contributions, and stock dividends. Each partner receives a Schedule K-1 showing ordinary income from the partnership of:

- $125,000 (one-quarter of the net income of $500,000);

- capital gains of $6,250 (25 percent of $25,000);

- charitable contributions of $1,250 (25 percent of $5,000); and

- stock dividends of $2,500 (25 percent of $10,000).

Each partner will report those items individually on his or her federal income tax return.

Partnership agreements may specify a particular distribution of profits and losses among partners. The regulations under Code section 704(b) regarding such distributions are quite extensive. In order for an allocation to be respected for tax purposes, the Code provides a two-part test to determine if an allocation has substantial economic effect.

First, an allocation must have "economic effect," generally meaning that the allocation must be consistent with the business arrangement of the partners.[2] The economic effect test is objective and consists merely of complying with the mechanical requirements. Generally speaking, the partnership agreement and the allocations must be reflected in properly maintained and respected capital accounts.

The second test is for "substantiality."[3] For an allocation to be substantial, there must be a reasonable possibility that the allocation will substantially impact the dollar amounts to be received by the partners apart from the tax consequences. An allocation is not substantial if the economic effect of the allocation is likely to be reversed by a contemporaneous or subsequent allocation and the overall tax liability of the partnership is reduced.[4]

Partnership capital accounts are used to track a partnership's accounting. Upon the formation of a partnership, partners typically contribute start-up capital to the business. Under IRC Section 721, this contribution of start-up capital is tax-free. So, even appreciated assets can be contributed without triggering a tax. Upon the formation, the partnership holds the assets with an adjusted basis transferred from each contributing partner.

Each partner has a capital account with the partnership representing the fair market value of the contributed property. These capital accounts are used to track allocations of gains and losses to individual partners as well as to account for distributions and contributions. Liquidation of a partnership will generally be made in accordance with the capital accounts.

Example: Three partners contribute property to a new partnership. Alan contributes $25,000 in cash. Bob buys a piece of property for $50,000 and contributes it to the partnership. Carl contributes securities worth $75,000 to the partnership. Carl had an adjusted basis in the securities of $50,000. At the time of formation, the partnership has no liabilities and accounts as listed below:

Assets		
	Adjusted Basis	Book Value
Cash:	$25,000	$25,000
Property:	$50,000	$50,000
Securities:	$50,000	$75,000
Total:	$125,000	$150,000

Partners' Capital		
	Adjusted Basis	Book Value
Alan	$25,000	$25,000
Bob	$50,000	$50,000
Carl	$50,000	$75,000
Total:	$125,000	$150,000

In its first year, the new partnership had net income of $300,000, all in cash. Under the partnership agreement, Alan was entitled to one-sixth of the net profits, Bob was entitled to one-third of the net profits, and Carl was entitled to one-half of the net profits, in proportion to their original financial contributions. Each partner reported and paid taxes on their distributive share: $50,000 for Alan, $100,000 for Bob, and $150,000 for Carl. Each partner also took a distribution of $50,000 in cash. After this activity, the partnership accounts look as follows:

Assets

	Adjusted Basis	Book Value
Cash:	$175,000	$175,000
Property:	$50,000	$50,000
Securities:	$50,000	$75,000
Total:	$275,000	$300,000

Partners' Capital

	Adjusted Basis	Book Value
Alan	$25,000	$25,000
Bob	$100,000	$100,000
Carl	$150,000	$175,000
Total:	$275,000	$300,000

Tax Implications

A partnership is not taxable entity. Each partner must report his share of partnership profits, whether or not distributed, on his individual income tax return. However, the partnership must file an informational income tax return (Form 1065) with the IRS. The business expenses of the partnership are allocated to the partners and reported on Schedule K-1. To the extent not otherwise restricted, the partners may then deduct their allocated losses on their personal income tax returns.

A partnership interest is a capital asset. Therefore, a sale of a partnership interest generally results in a capital gain if the purchase price exceeds the partner's basis in the partnership interest sold.

The partnership tax rules dictate that if a partner contributes property with built-in gain (i.e., the income tax basis is less than the fair market value at time of contribution), the contributing partner bears the income tax consequences associated with the built-in gain. As such, if the partnership later sells the contributed property, the built-in gain is reported by the contributing partner, and any gain in excess of the built-in gain is shared among the partners according to the partnership agreement.[5]

Example: Allison, Barb, and Carol create a partnership in 2010. As part of her capital contribution to the new partnership, Allison contributes stock with a current value of $25,000. Allison had purchased the stock in 2008 for $15,000, so at the time of its contribution to the partnership it has $10,000 in "built-in" gain.

In 2014, the partnership sells the stock for $40,000. The $15,000 gain that occurred since the stock was contributed to the partnership is divided among the partners in accordance with the partnership agreement. The $10,000 built-in gain must be reported by Allison alone.

Partners are restricted from contributing property that is then distributed to another partner. If property that is contributed by one partner is distributed to another partner within seven years of its contribution, the contributing partner must recognize gain or loss on the property as if it had been sold for fair market value at time of its contribution.[6]

The partnership tax rules also prevent partners from transferring tax losses through the contribution of property with built-in loss (where the property's basis exceeded its fair market value at time of its contribution), by requiring that only the contributing partner may realize the built-in loss from the contributed property.[7]

Partnership Distributions

As mentioned previously, partners are required to report income regardless of whether distributions are received in the current year. As such, when a partnership makes a cash distribution to the partners, partners do not pay an additional tax so long as the distribution does not exceed their basis in the partnership.[8] Furthermore, it follows that cash distribution to partners will reduce their basis in the partnership by the amount distributed.[9]

If the partnership distributes property to partners, the partnership does not recognize any gain or loss as a result of such distribution, and the partner does not recognize any gain or loss unless the property distributed qualifies as account receivables or inventory with a basis less than the partner's basis in the partnership.[10] Moreover, the distributed property's basis will have a transferred basis in the hands of the partner, and the partner that receives the property will reduce his/her basis in the partnership by the amount of the distributed property's basis.[11]

The recipient partner also gets to tack the partnership's holding period on to his holding period for the distributed property.[12]

Sale of Partnership Interests

If a partner sells his or her interest in the partnership, the sale is treated as a sale or exchange of a capital asset. Any resulting gain is treated as a capital gain with the exception of any ordinary income that is required to be recognized under Code section 751.[13]

The gain or loss attributable to unrealized receivables and inventory is determined by looking through the partner's ownership interest in the partnership to his or her share of those items. The most common items that generate ordinary gain or loss to a selling partner include:

- Assets held for sale to customers.

- Rights to payments for goods or services already delivered or to be delivered. The most common application of this is the unrealized accounts receivable of a partnership on the cash basis method of accounting.

- The recaptured portion of real and personal property that is subject to depreciation under code sections 1245 and 1250.

Any gain from activities that the selling partner did not materially participate in would qualify as investment income. The capital gain from the sale of the interest in the partnership qualifies as investment income and, depending on the selling partner's other investment income activities, may be subject to the 3.8 percent net investment income tax (NIIT). (See Chapter 11 for more details on the NIIT.)

A selling partner could reduce their net investment income tax liability by materially participating in the trade or business of the partnership, or by electing to group all of the partnership's activity to make it easier to meet the requirement of material participation in all of the partnership's activities.

LIMITED LIABILITY COMPANY

Limited Liability Companies (LLCs) are hybrid business entities created under state law. They typically combine the limited liability normally associated with corporations and the pass-through tax treatment of partnerships. All states allow the formation and operation of LLCs but the requirements, operating rules, and tax treatment vary widely among the states. For instance, some states impose a state income tax on LLCs as an entity while others do not.

Advantages

The liability of members in an LLC is generally limited to the amount of their investment in the LLC. Members of an LLC are not personally liable for the debts of the LLC or the acts of its other members – except to the extent they specifically agree to personal liability.

LLCs allow a great deal of flexibility in ownership and management structure. They may any number of members, including one (a "single-member LCC"). LLC members can be individuals (including non-resident aliens), partnerships, trusts, corporations, or other LLCs. Members may collectively manage an LLC or may elect or hire a management group to do so. Unlike a limited partnership, members may be actively involved in managing the business, while still enjoying limited liability.

An LLC has fewer required formalities under state law than a corporation. For example, a corporation is generally required to have a board of directors and to hold annual meetings. LLCs usually do not have to adhere to these formalities.

Under the "Check-the-Box" regulations,[14] the members of an LLC—other than those LLCs automatically classified as corporations—may choose the tax regime under which the entity (or its owners) will be taxed. See "Tax Implications" below.

Disadvantages

LLC requirements vary from state to state. This can make multi-state transactions complicated where state laws conflict.

Some states tax LLCs that are treated as partnerships for federal income tax purposes as separate tax paying entities, or assess a fee for conducting business in this form.

The conversion of an existing business into an LLC may result in the recognition of income tax.

What are the Requirements?

To form an LLC, articles of organization must typically be filed with the state's office of the secretary of state. The articles of organization contain basic information about the LLC, such as its name, principal place of business, purpose, agent, etc. Some states also require that an operating agreement be filed along with the articles of organization. Even if not required, an operating agreement is important to set out the rules for the management of the LLC. An operating agreement serves the same purposes for an LLC as a partnership agreement or corporate bylaws do for their respective entities.

Most states require an LLC to have an address for service of process within that state. Some states mandate public disclosure of an LLC's ownership interests and/or the identity of its officers.

LLCs must also renew their registrations with the state annually. Often, a short annual report is required to be filed with the renewal state. Many times this can be done inexpensively and entirely online with the Secretary of State's office. Failure to properly renew an LLC may result in the LLC being administratively disbanded, which can have liability consequences.

In order for an LLC to have its own bank account and file its own tax documents, it is often necessary to obtain an Employer Identification Number for the LLC from the IRS.

Tax Implications

By default, most LLCs with two or more members are taxed as a partnership. This means that the income, deductions, capital gains and losses, charitable contributions, stock dividends, and other tax attributes of the business pass through to the members' individual income tax returns. Single-member LLCs are generally taxed as sole proprietorships. LLCs may file Form 8832 and elect to be treated as an "association" taxable as a C Corporation.[15]

Example: John, Jane, James, and Jill each contribute $25,000 to form the new 4J Enterprises, LLC. They file articles of organization with the secretary of state and hire an attorney to draft an operating agreement. Under the operating agreement, they will each have defined management responsibilities and will each be entitled to one-quarter of the business profits.

If the members of 4J Enterprises, LLC, do nothing to change their tax status, the LLC will be treated as a partnership for federal income tax purposes, and the income, deductions, capital gains and losses, charitable contributions, stock dividends, and other tax attributes of the business pass through to the members' individual income tax returns. If they want to be taxed as a C Corporation (or potentially an S corporation), the LLC must file Form 8832, *Entity Classification Election*, and elect that treatment.

Federal tax laws automatically classify and tax certain LLC business entities as corporations:[16]

- A business entity formed under a federal or state statute or under a statute of a federally recognized Indian tribe if the statute describes or refers to the entity as incorporated or as a corporation, body corporate, or body politic.

- A business entity formed under a federal or state statute if the statute describes or refers to the entity as a joint stock association.

- A state-chartered business entity conducting banking activities, if any of its deposits are insured by the FDIC.

- A business entity wholly owned by a state of political subdivision thereof, or a business entity wholly owned by a foreign government.

- An insurance company.

- A business entity taxable as a corporation under a provision of the code other than Code section 7701(a)(3).

- Certain named foreign entities equivalent to corporations.

An LLC may change a classification election by filing Form 8832 with the IRS. The change may be from a prior election or the LLC's default tax treatment. A change may be effective no more than seventy-five days before, or no more than twelve months after the election is filed. Once a change of classification election has been filed, another change may not be made for sixty months.[17] An initial election for a newly-formed entity does not count as a change; therefore, a change of election may be filed within sixty months of the initial election.

Changing a classification election is treated as a termination of the first entity for tax purposes and a transfer of the assets and liabilities to the new entity or the owners thereof.[18] More specifically, the results are as follows:

- *Partnership to Corporation*: The partnership contributes all of its assets and liabilities to the corporation in exchange for stock. Immediately thereafter, the partnership liquidates and transfers the stock to the partners.

- *Corporation to Partnership*: The corporation liquidates and distributes all of its assets and liabilities to its shareholders. Immediately thereafter, the shareholders contribute the assets and liabilities to the newly-formed partnership.

- *Sole Proprietorship to Corporation*: The sole proprietor contributes all of the assets and liabilities of the business to the newly-formed corporation in exchange for the corporation's stock.

- *Corporation to Sole Proprietorship*: The corporation liquidates and distributes all of its assets and liabilities to its single owner.

An LLC classified as a partnership becomes a sole proprietorship if the LLC's membership is reduced to one member. A single-member LLC taxed as a sole proprietorship becomes a partnership when the LLC gains a second member. If an elective classification change under the "Check-the-Box" regulations becomes effective at the same time as a membership change, the elective change takes precedence over the change in membership.[19]

C CORPORATION

A subchapter "C" corporation (a "corporation") is a business entity that limits the liability of its owners. Legally, a corporation is a separate entity from its owners and employees. A corporation can own property in its own name, enter into contracts in its own name, and can sue and be sued in its own name.

Advantages

A corporation offers limited liability to the owners of the business. However, business owners who are also employees of the corporation cannot limit their liability for actions that they themselves commit. For example, if a doctor incorporates his medical practice, he will be personally liable for any medical malpractice that he might commit (and his corporation may also be liable as his employer). Also, for a small corporation, limited liability may not be fully realized because creditors may require personal guarantees from the shareholders of the corporation.

Shares in a corporation can be easily transferred by sale, gift, or bequest. Note, however, that this can also be considered a disadvantage as someone who is undesirable to the other shareholders may come into ownership of some of the corporation's shares. This is why many closely-held corporations place restrictions through "first offer" agreements or even mandatory buy-sell agreements that limit the shareholders' rights to give away, sell, or otherwise transfer their shares. (A "first offer" agreement provides that the stock must first be offered for purchase to the corporation or current shareholders before it can be purchased by an outsider.)

A corporation has continuity. It will continue its separate legal existence even if the identity of its shareholders changes. Sole proprietorships and partnerships generally end as a legal entity if an owner dies, retires, or sells his/her interest in the business. With a non-corporate business, any remaining partners who wish to continue to operate must do so by forming a new legal entity.

C corporation employees have access to certain benefit plans that are allowed by the federal income tax laws that may not be available to owners of non-C corporation businesses. However, owners of non-C corporations can generally take advantage of most qualified and non-qualified retirement planning vehicles.

Disadvantages

One of the primary disadvantages of the corporate entity is the potential double taxation of corporate profits. Profits of a corporation are taxed at the corporate level. Then, if the profits are distributed as dividends to shareholders, they are taxed again at the shareholder level. The negative impact of double taxa-tion has been relieved somewhat by the current income tax rules, which lowered the federal income tax rate on most dividends to 15 percent for taxpayers below the 39.6 percent tax bracket. However, for taxpayers in the 39.6 percent tax bracket the tax on dividends is 20 percent. This disadvantage can be mitigated if the corporation retains its earnings; but, as discussed below, there are limitations on a corporation's ability to do so.

The fact that shares in a corporation can be easily transferred by sale, gift, or bequest can be a disadvan-tage if the owners of the corporation want to ensure that the ownership will stay within the circle of current own-ers. Many closely-held corporations have shareholder agreements that strictly limit the ability of shareholders to transfer their shares freely.

More formalities may be required in the operation of a corporation than in a partnership, limited liability company, or sole proprietorship. These formalities include formal elections of directors, meetings of the board of directors, and shareholder meetings. Many owners of small corporations may find these require-ments to be a waste of time or, thinking they are unim-portant, ignore them. However, if these formalities are not observed, local courts may disregard the corporate existence. As a result, the owners may not be consid-ered shareholders protected by limited liability, but may instead be considered partners or (in corporations with only one shareholder) sole proprietors. This loss of corporate status can have significant tax and non-tax implications.

What are the Requirements?

Almost all states require a corporation to file certain papers with the state. These papers (commonly called articles of incorporation or certificates of formation) will include at least the corporation's legal name, its purpose, and the name and address of an agent located in the state who can be served should the corporation be sued. Some states may also require a corporate charter and the corporate bylaws to be filed.

Depending on the law of a particular state, a corpora-tion generally must hold a shareholder meeting once a year and periodic meetings of the board of directors. There generally must be formal elections of directors and records must be kept of the minutes of shareholder meetings and meetings of the board of directors.

Tax Implications

Income Tax Rates

The taxable income of a corporation is calculated in much the same way as for an individual. Gener-ally, a corporation may take the same deductions as an individual, except those of a personal nature (such as deductions for medical expenses and the personal exemptions). Employee benefits provided for employees are, generally, deductible as ordinary and necessary business expenses, even for those employees who are also owners of the corporation. A corporation is not allowed a standard deduction. The exhibit below lists the corporate income tax rates.[20]

Taxable Income	Tax	Tax Rate on Excess
0	0	15%
$50,000	$7,500	25%
$75,000	$13,750	34%
$100,000	$22,250	39%
$335,000	$113,900	34%
$10,000,000	$3,400,000	35%
$15,000,000	$5,150,000	38%
$18,333,333	$6,416,667	35%

Note that the 39 percent marginal rate and the 38 percent marginal rate are designed to phase out the graduated tax rates available at lower income levels. The highest percentage a corporation will pay on its total income under the regular income tax is 35 percent.

There are a few special deductions for corporations, including a deduction equal to 70 percent of dividends received from other domestic corporations, 80 percent of dividends received from a 20-percent-owned company, and 100 percent for dividends received from affiliated corporations.[21] A corporation may deduct contributions to charitable organizations to the extent of 10 percent of taxable income (with certain adjustments). Generally, charitable contributions in excess of the 10 percent limit may be carried forward for five years.[22]

Personal Service Corporations

Certain personal service corporations are taxed at a flat rate of 35 percent so that the graduated corporate income tax rates are not available.[23] A personal service corporation is a corporation that substantially all of its activities involve the performance of services in the fields of health, law, engineering, architecture, accounting, actuarial science, performing arts, or consulting. Also, substantially all the stock must be owned directly by employees, retired employees, or their estates, or indirectly through partnerships, S corporations, or qualified personal service corporations.[24]

Distributions from the Corporation

When a corporation distributes money or property to its shareholders the distribution will be treated in one of three ways: as either (1) dividend; (2) reduction in basis; or (3) gain from the sale or exchange of property.[25] Under the first method, the money or property may be considered a dividend to the extent the corporation has earnings and profits. Earnings and profits is a technical concept that generally is defined as retained earnings, and will also generally include tax-exempt income such as death benefits from a life insurance contract. Under the second characterization, if and to the extent the distribution exceeds the corporation's earnings and profits, the shareholder's basis in the corporation's stock will be reduced by the amount the distribution exceeds earnings and profits. Finally, amounts that are distributed that are not dividends and that exceed the basis the shareholder has will be treated as a capital gain. Note that none of these types of distributions is deductible to the corporation.

Capital Gains of a Corporation

Capital gains and losses are netted in the same manner as for an individual (see Chapter, Capital Gains and Losses). If the net short-term capital gain exceeds net long-term capital loss, this excess is added to the corporation's other income and taxed at the corporation's regular tax rates. A corporation reporting a "net capital gain" (net long-term capital gain exceeds net short-term capital loss) is taxed under one of two methods, depending upon which produces the lower tax:[26]

1. *Regular method*. Net capital gain is included in gross income and taxed at the corporation's regular tax rates.

2. *Alternative method*. First, a tax on the corporation's taxable income, exclusive of the net capital gain, is calculated at the corporation's regular tax rates. Then, a second tax on the net capital gain (or, if less, taxable income) for the year is calculated at the rate of 35 percent.

The tax on income exclusive of net capital gain and the tax on net capital gain are added to arrive at the corporation's total tax.

The alternative method will be used only if Congress raises the top corporate marginal tax rate above 35 percent.

Alternative Minimum Tax

In addition to the "regular" corporate income tax, a corporation may also be liable for the alternative minimum tax (AMT). A corporation calculates its liability under the regular income tax and also calculates its "tentative minimum tax," then adds the tentative minimum tax that exceeds its regular income tax to its regular tax. The amount that is added is the AMT.[27]

To calculate its AMT, a corporation first calculates its "alternative minimum taxable income" (AMTI). Also, the corporation calculates its "adjusted current earnings" (ACE), increasing its AMTI by 75 percent of the amount by which ACE exceeds AMTI (or possibly reducing its AMTI by 75 percent of the amount by which AMTI exceeds ACE).[28]

The tentative minimum tax is a flat 20 percent of AMTI.[29] Each corporation receives a $40,000 exemption to reduce AMTI; however, this exemption is reduced by 25 percent of the amount by which AMTI exceeds $150,000, with the exemption completely phased-out at an AMTI of $310,000.[30]

A corporation's AMTI is its regular taxable income determined with certain adjustments and then increased by certain tax preferences. Adjustments to a corporation's income include the following:[31]

- property is generally depreciated under a less accelerated or a straight line method over a longer period, however, a longer period is not required for property placed in service after 1998;

- mining exploration and development costs are amortized over ten years;

- a percentage of completion method is required for long-term contracts;

- net operating loss deductions are generally limited to 90 percent of AMTI;

- certified pollution control facilities are depreciated under the alternative depreciation system except those that are placed in service after 1998, which use the straight line method; and

- the adjustment based on the corporation's ACE.

Tax preferences for corporate taxpayers are the same as for other taxpayers, which are discussed in more detail in a previous section.

One of the most important corporate AMT adjustments is the ACE adjustment.[32] To calculate a corporation's ACE, it begins with its AMTI and makes additional adjustments. These adjustments include adding certain amounts of income that are includable in earnings and profits, but not in AMTI (including income on life insurance policies and the receipt of life insurance death proceeds).

The amount of income that is added to the AMTI is reduced by any deductions that would have been allowed in calculating AMTI if the item had been included in gross income. The corporation is generally not allowed a deduction for ACE purposes that are not allowed for earnings and profits purposes. However, certain dividends received by a corporation are allowed to be deducted. For property placed into service after 1989 but before 1994, the corporation must recalculate depreciation according to specified methods for ACE purposes. Earnings and profits are adjusted further for certain purposes such as the treatment of intangible drilling costs, amortization of certain expenses, installment sales, and depletion.

A corporation subject to the AMT in one year may be allowed a tax credit against regular tax liability in subsequent years.[33] The credit is generally equal to the amount of AMT paid in prior years minus the amount of AMT tax credits allowable in prior years. However, the amount of the credit cannot be greater than the amount the corporation's regular tax liability exceeds its tentative minimum tax amount. Thus, the AMT credit cannot cause a corporation's tax liability to go below its tentative minimum tax.

Certain "small corporations" are exempt from the AMT.[34] To qualify for the exemption, the corporation must meet a gross receipts test for the previous three years. The corporation's average annual gross receipts for the previous three years must be less than $7.5 million.

To initially qualify for the exemption, the corporation must meet the three-year gross receipts test, but the average receipts must be less than $5 million instead of $7.5 million. A corporation is exempt from the AMT in its first year of existence.

Accumulated Earnings Tax (AET)

The accumulated earnings tax is a penalty tax against a corporation that holds profits beyond its normal business needs, thus keeping the profits from taxation upon distribution.[35] The amount of this tax is the product of 15 percent and the corporation's accumulated taxable income. Accumulated taxable income is generally taxable income for the year adjusted for the federal income tax and minus dividends paid to shareholders and the accumulated earnings credit.[36]

The tax is imposed only on amounts that are accumulated beyond the amount that is required to meet the reasonable needs of the business. This is because there is an accumulated earnings credit that is equal to the amount that is reasonably needed for the business to operate. For example, if the corporation can show that it needs $2 million in retained earnings to run its business, its accumulated earnings credit will be $2 million. For most corporations, the minimum accumulated earnings credit is the amount by which $250,000 exceeds the accumulated earnings and profits of the corporation at the end of the previous year. This amount is reduced to $150,000 for service corporations in the fields of health, law, engineering, architecture, accounting, actuarial science, performing arts, or consulting. Because of these amounts, a corporation can accumulate up to $250,000 ($150,000 for service corporations) regardless of the needs of the business.

Personal Holding Company Tax

The personal holding company (PHC) tax is another penalty tax that can be imposed on a corporation.[37] The PHC tax is designed to keep shareholders from avoiding the individual income tax on income-producing property that is held inside a corporate entity. A corporation is subject to the PHC tax if it meets both a stock ownership test and a PHC income test.[38]

The stock ownership test is met if more than 50 percent of the value of the stock is owned, directly or indirectly, by no more than five shareholders. The PHC income test is met if 60 percent or more of the corporation's adjusted ordinary gross income is PHC income.

PHC income is generally defined to include:

- dividends, interest, royalties, and annuities;

- rents;

- mineral, oil, and gas royalties;

- copyright royalties;

- film rents;

- compensation from the use of corporate property by shareholders;

- personal service contracts; and

- income from estates and trusts.[39]

The rate for the PHC tax, like the rate for the AET, is 20 percent. This rate is imposed on the corporation's undistributed PHC income, which is generally PHC income of the corporation minus dividends paid to the shareholders.[40]

S CORPORATION

A subchapter "S" corporation (an "S corporation") is a corporation that has elected to have its income, deductions, capital gains and losses, charitable contributions, and credits passed through to its shareholders. For federal income tax purposes, an S corporation is treated similar to a partnership. For almost all other purposes, an S corporation is treated as a "regular" corporation.

Advantages

As in a regular corporation, an S corporation allows its owners to limit their liability for the debts and obligation of the S corporation. However, like C corporations, S corporation owners who are also employees of the S corporation cannot limit their liability for actions that they themselves commit.

The profits of an S corporation are taxed only once. Income of an S corporation is pro-ratably "passed-through" to its shareholders based on their ownership

interests. For instance, if an S corporation has two shareholders who own 70 and 30 percent of the stock respectively, then the first shareholder is entitled to (and will report as income) 70 percent of the corporation's profits, while the second shareholder will receive 30 percent.

Disadvantages

There are requirements on the number and type of shareholders an S corporation may have. There are also other potential "traps" that an S corporation must be aware of so that it does not unexpectedly lose its S status. For example, if an S corporation has retained earnings from when it was a C corporation, its S-election may be terminated if it derives too much income from "passive" investments. Also, if stock is sold or given to someone who is an ineligible shareholder, such as a nonresident alien or a C corporation, the election will be terminated, with possible adverse tax consequences for all of the shareholders.

Owners who own more than two percent of an S corporation are treated as partners for fringe benefit purposes. This severely limits the ability of owners to take advantage of tax-favored fringe benefits. However, S corporation shareholders have almost all of the qualified retirement opportunities that non-shareholder employees can use.

If the shareholders are in the highest marginal income tax bracket, the income from an S corporation may be taxed at a higher rate than if it was a C corporation.

Example: An S corporation with one shareholder earns $50,000, and the shareholder is in the 39.6 percent marginal tax bracket and subject to the 3.8 percent net investment income tax (NIIT). Here, the shareholder will pay $21,700 in federal income tax on the S corporation's income.

If the corporation was a C corporation, it would pay corporate income tax of $7,500 as a result of the lower tax bracket structure for corporate taxable income, leaving $42,500 to distribute to the shareholder as a dividend. If the $42,500 dividend is taxed at 23.8 percent (20 percent capital gain tax plus the 3.8 percent NIIT), the tax liability will be $10,115, for a total tax liability of $17,615. Here, taxation as a C corporation would result in a savings of $4,085 compared to an S corporation.

What are the Requirements?

An S corporation is formed in the same manner as a C Corporation: by filing organizing documents with the state of domicile. An S corporation must be a domestic corporation. It must have been organized under the laws of the United States or one of the individual states.[41] To obtain S status for federal tax purposes, the corporation files IRS Form 2553.

Certain types of entities are not eligible to elect S corporation treatment:

- a financial institution that uses the reserve method of accounting;

- an insurance company;

- corporations that elect to have credits for certain income from non-U.S. sources; and

- a current or former domestic international sales corporation.[42]

An S corporation may have no more than one hundred shareholders.[43] Members of a family, as well as married couples, are considered one shareholder.[44] Nonresident aliens may not be shareholders of an S corporation.[45] S corporation shareholders must be individuals, estates, or certain trusts. The types of trusts that may be shareholders of an S corporation include:

- a grantor trust whose owner is a U.S. citizen or resident;

- a trust that was a grantor trust before the owner's death may be a shareholder for two years after the death of the owner;

- a trust that has S corporation stock transferred to it may be a shareholder for two years after the transfer;

- a voting trust; or

- a qualified subchapter S trust (QSST) and (6) an electing small business trust (ESBT).[46]

A QSST must have only one current income beneficiary (who must be a citizen or resident of the United States). It must distribute all income in the year it is earned and its assets may not be distributed to anyone else during the life of the beneficiary. The income interest must terminate upon the earlier of the beneficiary's death or the termination of the trust, and if the trust terminates during the lifetime of the income beneficiary, all the trust's assets must be distributed to that beneficiary. The beneficiary must make an election for the trust to be treated as a QSST.[47]

An ESBT is a trust in which all of the beneficiaries are individuals, estates, or certain charitable organizations, and each potential current beneficiary of an ESBT is treated as a shareholder. A potential current beneficiary is generally someone who is entitled to, or in the discretion of any person, may receive a distribution of principal or interest of the trust. Trusts that are exempt from income tax (e.g., QSSTs, charitable remainder annuity trusts, and charitable remainder unitrusts) may not be ESBTs. An interest in an ESBT may not be obtained by purchase.

An S corporation may only have one class of stock,[48] and each share must have equal distribution and liquidation rights. However, different shares may have different voting rights.[49] For example, shares could be issued that have no voting rights, or some shares may have twice (or three times) the number of votes as other shares. Generally, bona fide buy/sell agreements, agreements to restrict the transferability of shares, and redemption agreements do not create a second class of stock.[50] Generally, providing a shareholder with reasonable employee benefits such as split-dollar life insurance or nonqualified deferred compensation will also not be considered as creating a second class of stock.

In order for a C corporation to elect to be treated as an S corporation all shareholders of the corporation must consent to the change.[51] The election can be effective for the next taxable year, or for the current year if the election is made before the fifteenth day of the third month of the taxable year.[52] For example, an election made on February 28, 2014, could be effective for 2014 or 2015, but an election made on March 30, 2014, could be effective for only 2015.

An S corporation election may terminate in a number of ways.[53] First, shareholders holding more than 50 percent of the S corporation may elect to terminate the S election. A "consent" termination will be effective for the following tax year unless it is made before the fifteenth day of the third month of the year, in which case the termination is effective for that tax year. For example, a termination election made on March 1, 2014, will be effective for 2014, but a termination election effective on March 30, 2014, will not be effective until 2015.

Another way an S corporation can have its S election terminate is if it no longer meets the requirements to be an S corporation, such as having more than one hundred shareholders, or having an ineligible shareholder. A termination because of failure to meet the S corporation requirements will be effective on the date the requirements are not met.

Finally, a corporation can have its S election terminate if it fails the excess passive income for three years and it has earnings and profits from when it was a C corporation or due to a corporate acquisition. Excess passive income is passive income (e.g. rents, interest, dividends) that exceeds 25 percent of the gross receipts of the S corporation for three consecutive years. The termination will be effective the first day of the year following the three consecutive years of excessive passive income.

If an S election is terminated, the corporation generally cannot elect S status again for five years without the consent of the IRS.[54] The IRS may waive an inadvertent termination if the corporation corrects the event that caused the termination and agrees to treat the corporation as an S corporation during the period of time the election was terminated.[55]

An S corporation may own stock in another corporation if it owns 100 percent of the shares of the other corporation. The S corporation can make an election to treat the wholly-owned corporation as a qualified subchapter S subsidiary (QSub). A QSub is a corporation that could generally elect S corporation status except for the fact that its stock is owned by the parent S corporation, if 100 percent of its stock is owned by the parent S corporation, and the parent S corporation elects to treat the subsidiary as a QSub. A QSub is generally not treated as a separate corporation for tax purposes and its assets, liabilities, and items of income, deductions, and credit are treated as those of the parent S corporation.[21]

Example: Assume there are four equal shareholders of The Widget Corporation, which earns corporate taxable income of $100,000 per year. If Widget is a C corporation, the federal corporate

income tax on this $100,000 is $22,250, which leaves $77,750 to be distributed to the four shareholders. If the corporation distributes all the profits to the shareholders, they will each receive $19,437.50. Assuming the shareholders are taxed on dividends at the 15 percent rate, they will each pay $2,915.63 in taxes on the dividends. Thus, in total, the C corporation and its shareholders will pay $33,912.52 in federal corporate and individual income taxes, nearly 34 percent of the taxable income of the corporation.

If Widget is an S corporation, the entire $100,000 in taxable income will be "passed-through" to the shareholders and taxed on their individual tax returns. Each shareholder will include $25,000 of the S corporation's earnings in income. Assuming the shareholders are in the 28 percent marginal tax bracket, the shareholders will each pay $7,000 in federal income taxes. Together the shareholders will pay a total of $28,000 in federal income taxes. Therefore, in this example, an S election will save $5,912.52 ($33,912.52 - $28,000) annually.

Tax Implications

Much like a partnership, an S corporation is generally not subject to tax at the entity (corporate) level.[56] Whether the S corporation's profits are distributed to shareholders or not, they are taxed on the S corporation's taxable income. Shareholders take into account their shares of income, loss, deductions, and credit on a per-share, per-day basis.[57]

S corporation income that could directly affect the tax liability of the shareholder is passed directly through the corporation to the shareholder. Also, any loss or deduction that the S corporation takes that could directly affect the liability of the shareholder is also passed directly through to the shareholder. An example of this "separately stated" income is the treatment of capital gain income, which is taxed at a different rate than ordinary income. Another example is the treatment of charitable deductions of an S corporation, which are passed directly through to the shareholder.[58]

The basis of each shareholder's stock is increased by his share of income (including tax-exempt income) and any excess of deductions for depletion over the basis of property subject to depletion.

The basis of each shareholder's stock is decreased (but not below zero) by (a) his share of any loss the corporation suffers; (b) any expense of the corporation that is not deductible and is not a capital expense; and (c) depletion deductions to the extent the deduction does not exceed the shareholder's share of the basis in the property subject to depletion.

If the shareholder's basis would be reduced to less than zero, any excess reductions are used to reduce his basis in any loans made by that shareholder to the S corporation. A shareholder may not take deductions that exceed his basis in the stock and debt of the S corporation that he holds. These disallowed deductions and losses may be carried forward to future tax years indefinitely. Therefore, a shareholder may not deduct any more than he has "at risk" with the S corporation. Basis in a shareholder's stock is also reduced by distributions from the S corporation that are not included in the shareholder's income.[59]

Example: A shareholder of an S corporation has a basis of $100 in the stock he owns. He also holds debt of the corporation in which he has a basis of $50. The S corporation has income in year one and the shareholder's share of the income is $20. In that same year, the S corporation distributes $10 to the shareholder. His basis in the stock is now $110 ($100 + $20 - $10). The next year, the corporation has a loss and the shareholder's share of the loss is $65. The shareholder's basis in his stock is now $45 ($110 - $65). The following year, the S corporation has another loss and the shareholder's share of the loss is $55. The basis in his stock goes to $0, and the basis in the debt he holds is reduced to $40.

Distributions from an S corporation that do not exceed a shareholder's basis will not result in income to the shareholder. They are tax-free recovered income. Any distributions from an S corporation that are not from the corporation's earnings and profits and that are in excess of a shareholder's basis in his stock will be treated as a capital gain.

If an S corporation has earnings and profits, distributions to shareholders are treated as a distribution by an S corporation without earnings and profits, to the extent of an account called the accumulated adjustment account (AAA). If an S corporation has earnings and

profits, it will likely be because it had earnings and profits from when it was a C corporation, or as the result of a corporate acquisition. The AAA is an account of the S corporation that generally tracks how much of the S corporation's income was taxed to the shareholders minus any amounts that have been distributed to the shareholders. The AAA is designed to ensure that shareholders of an S corporation are not taxed twice on S corporation income.

Distributions from S corporations that have earnings and profits that are in excess of the AAA will be treated as a distribution under the normal corporate tax rules. This will generally result in a dividend up to the amount of earnings and profits, then a reduction of basis in the S corporation stock, and then finally a capital gain. If all shareholders who receive distributions agree, an S corporation with an AAA may elect to have distributions treated as if there was no AAA, which has the effect of reducing earnings and profits. An S corporation may do this because there can be negative tax consequences to an S corporation with earnings and profits and too much passive income.[60]

An S corporation is generally not subject to tax at the corporate level. However, a tax is imposed at the corporate level on certain gains. For S elections made after 1986 where the corporation had previously been a C corporation, if an S corporation disposes of property within ten years after an election has been made, it may be required to pay tax on part of the gain. The gain attributable to pre-election appreciation of the property (built in gain) is taxed at the corporate level to the extent the gain does not exceed the amount of taxable income imposed on the corporation if it were not an S corporation.[61]

Note that for tax years beginning in 2009 through 2013, the recognition period for built in gains was reduced from the normal ten year period. For 2009 and 2010, the recognition period was seven years and for 2011 through 2013, it was five years.[62]

A tax is imposed at the corporate level on excess "net passive income" of an S corporation but only if the corporation, at the end of the tax year, has accumulated earnings and profits and if passive investment income exceeds 25 percent of gross receipts. The rate is the highest corporate rate (currently 35 percent). Passive investment income for this purpose is rents, royalties, dividends, interest, annuities, and proceeds from sales or exchanges of stock or securities.

However, passive investment income does not include rents for the use of corporate property if the corporation:

- also provides substantial services in connection with the property (such as maid service in a hotel);

- has an interest in the property that was derived in the corporation's ordinary course of business; or

- has an interest on obligations related to the property that were acquired in the ordinary course of business (such as interest earned on accounts receivable).

Passive investment income also does not include gross receipts derived in the ordinary course of business of lending or financing; dealing in property; purchasing or discounting accounts receivable, notes, or installment obligations; or servicing mortgages. Passive investment income does not include certain dividends from C corporations where the S corporation owns 80 percent or more of the C corporation.[63]

Similar to the treatment of a partner in a partnership, for the purpose of calculating the AMT tax, items of preference arising at the corporate level are allocated to each shareholder in proportion to his/her ownership interest in an S Corporation. Therefore, each shareholder is required to combine those tax preference items with such items from the shareholder's other sources in determining his/her AMT liability.

When an S Corporation makes a distribution of appreciated property to its shareholders, the corporation is treated as having sold the property to its shareholders, and the gain is taxed at the shareholder's level.[64] However, when an S Corporation distributes a property with built-in loss, no loss is passed through to the shareholders.[65] The recipient shareholder is treated as receiving a distribution in the amount of the fair market value of the distributed property.[66]

WHERE CAN I FIND OUT MORE?

Sole Proprietorships

1. IRS Publication 334, *Tax Guide for Small Businesses* (revised annually).

2. IRS Publication 535, *Business Expenses* (revised annually).

Partnerships

1. Lind, Schwarz, Lathrope and Rosenberg, *Fundamentals of Partnership Taxation*, 8th Edition (West Publishing, 2008).

2. IRS Publication 541, *Partnerships* (revised December 2013).

Limited Liability Companies

1. Leimberg, Stephan R., *The Cutting Edge in Financial Services* (National Underwriter Co., 2003).

2. Ribstein, Larry E. and Robert R. Keatinge, *Ribstein and Keatinge on Limited Liability Companies*, 2nd Edition (West Group, 2005-2008).

3. Instructions for IRS Form 8832, *Entity Classification Election* (revised December 2013).

C Corporations

1. Bittker, Boris and James Eustice, *Federal Income Taxation of Corporations and Shareholders*, 7th Edition (Warren, Gorham & Lamont, 2002).

2. Cavitch, Zolman, *Tax Planning for Corporations and Shareholders*, 3rd Edition (Matthew Bender, 2006).

S Corporations

1. Bittker, Boris, and James Eustice, *Federal Income Taxation of Corporations and Shareholders*, 7th ed., (Warren, Gorham & Lamont, 2002).

FREQUENTLY ASKED QUESTIONS

Partnership

Question – What happens if a partner contributes property with a built-in loss to a partnership?

Answer – Under the American Jobs Creation Act of 2004, a partner may not shift a loss to other partners by contributing property with a built-in loss to a partnership. Only the partner contributing property with a built-in loss may take the loss. As far as the non-contributing partners are concerned, the partnership takes a basis in the property equal to the property's fair market value at the time of the contribution.

Example: Albemarle contributes to a partnership property worth $25,000 with an adjusted basis in his hands of $50,000. The partnership takes an adjusted basis of $25,000 in the property with respect to every partner other than Albemarle. If the property is ultimately sold for $25,000, the entire $25,000 loss is allocated to Albemarle.

By contrast, under the pre-October 22, 2004 rule, the partnership would have taken an adjusted basis of $50,000 in the property. When sold, the loss would have been allocated to the partners under the partnership's general allocation rules.

Question – How are distributions from a partnership to a partner taxed if they exceed the partner's adjusted basis in the partnership?

Answer – A partner normally recognizes gain on a partnership distribution to the extent any money (or marketable securities treated as money) included in the distribution exceeds the adjusted basis of the partner's interest in the partnership.[67] The gain is generally treated as capital gain from the sale of the partnership interest on the date of the distribution. If property other than money (or marketable securities treated as money) is distributed to a partner, the partner generally does not recognize gain until he sells or otherwise disposes of the property.

Special rules apply where a partnership distributes a partner's debt back to that partner, where a partner has contributed appreciated property to the partnership within the seven-year period before the distribution, or where a partner has contributed unrealized receivables or inventory items to the partnership.[68]

Question – What are guaranteed payments and how are they treated for tax purposes?

Answer – Guaranteed payments are payments made by a partnership to a partner for services rendered to the partnership determined without regard to the income of the partnership. For example, a partner in a law firm might be guaranteed a base salary from the firm irrespective of the firm's profits, or a general partner in a real estate partnership might be guaranteed an annual management fee, regardless of the partnership's profits. A guaranteed payment is treated as a hybrid. For some purposes it is treated as a payment made to a non-partner; for other purposes it is treated similarly to a partner's distributive share. A guaranteed payment is taxable to a partner as ordinary income, regardless of the amount or character of the partnership's overall taxable income. Furthermore, the payment is deductible to the partners as an ordinary business expense under Code section 162.[69]

Question – How is health insurance coverage for partners taxed?

Answer – Generally, partners are treated as self-employed individuals, not employees, and the rules for personal health insurance apply. This means that partners can generally deduct 100 percent of amounts paid during a taxable year for insurance that provides medical care for the partner, his spouse, and dependents during the tax year. The deduction is, however, limited to the amount of income earned from the partnership.[70] In addition, the deduction is not available to a partner for any calendar month in which he is eligible to participate in any subsidized health plan maintained by any employer of the partner or his spouse.[71] This rule applies separately to traditional health insurance policies and long-term care insurance policies.

If a partnership pays health insurance premiums for a partner for services rendered by the partner in his capacity as a partner—and not as an employee—then the premium payments are considered to be "guaranteed payments" (see question above).[72] The partner is then taxable on the premium payments, and may or may not be able to deduct them on his personal return.

Limited Liability Companies

Question – What is an association, and how is it taxed under the "Check-the-Box" regulations?

Answer – Under the "Check-the-Box" regulations an association is an entity other than a corporation that is taxed as a C Corporation.[73] Some entities, such as LLCs or sole proprietorships, are classified as associations only as the result of an election. Other entities, such as "eligible foreign entities"—foreign entities that are not on the list of corporate equivalents in the regulations—in which all the members have limited liability, are classified as associations by default.

The term association is also used loosely to describe a variety of organizations, both incorporated and unincorporated. In this broader context, "association" does not imply any specific legal structure or tax status.

Corporations

Question – What are the income tax consequences that result from the creation of a corporation?

Answer – Corporations can generally be formed on a tax-free basis. The corporation will not recognize any gain (or loss) when it receives money or property in exchange for its own stock, whether the stock is newly issued or treasury stock.[74]

Also, generally, a party who transfers money or property to a corporation will not recognize gain or loss when property is transferred to a corporation in exchange for the corporation's stock.[75] But this ability to transfer even appreciated assets in return for corporate stock tax free applies only if all the parties who contribute property and receive the stock control 80 percent or more of the stock after the transaction.[76] If the persons who contribute property to the corporation receive additional property or money in the transaction (i.e., "boot"), gain will be recognized, but the gain will not exceed the amount of any money received plus the fair market value of the property that is received.[77]

This tax-free treatment is not available for a corporation that is an investment company.[78] Whether or not a corporation is an investment company is beyond the scope of this text, but note that this issue may come up if a large percentage of the corporation's assets consist of passive investments including stocks, bonds, and real estate investment trusts.[79]

Property that is transferred to a corporation in a tax-free transaction described above will retain its basis in the corporation. In other words, the corporation will carry over the transferor's basis. Also, stock received in this transaction by the parties transferring assets to the corporation will have the same basis as the property that was transferred to the corporation for stock.[80]

Question – What are the income tax consequences when a corporation is liquidated?

Answer – Generally upon the complete liquidation of a corporation, the shareholders will receive money or property from the corporation in exchange for the stock that they own. If they receive more than the basis they have in their stock, they will have a capital gain. If they receive less than the basis in their stock, they will incur a capital loss. These gains and losses are subject to the rules discussed in Chapter, Capital Gains and Losses.

At the corporate level, if the corporation distributes property that has appreciated, the corporation will recognize gain on the distribution and be subject to income tax on that gain. Thus, upon a corporate liquidation, the corporation could be subject to tax at the corporate level on any appreciated property, and then the shareholders would be subject to tax upon the distribution of the property in exchange for their shares.[81]

However, if a corporation is liquidated into a parent corporation that owns more than 80 percent of the subsidiary's stock, there generally will be no gain or loss to either the parent corporation or the liquidating subsidiary corporation.[82]

CHAPTER ENDNOTES

1.   I.R.C. §1402(b)(2).
2.   Treas. Reg. §1.701-1(b)(2)(ii)(a).
3.   Treas. Reg. §1.701-1(b)(2)(iii)(a).
4.   Treas. Reg. §1.701-1(b)(2)(iii)(a).
5.   I.R.C. §704(c)(1)(A).
6.   I.R.C. §704(c)(1)(B).
7.   I.R.C. §704(c)(1)(C).
8.   I.R.C. §702(a).
9.   I.R.C. §705(a).
10. I.R.C. §731(a)(2).
11. I.R.C. §§732, 733.

12. I.R.C. §735.
13. IRC Sec. 741.
14. Treas. Reg. §301.7701-3.
15. The election form must be signed by each member of the LLC or by an officer, manager, or member authorized to sign on behalf of the LLC. The election form must state an effective date for the classification no more than seventy-five days before or no more than twelve months after the election is filed. Treas. Reg. §301.7701-3(c).
16. Treas. Reg. §301.7701-2(b).
17. Treas. Reg. §301.7701-3(c)(1)(iv).
18. Treas. Reg. §301.7701-3(g)(1).
19. Treas. Reg. §301.7701-3(f)(2).
20. I.R.C. §11(b)(1).
21. I.R.C. §243.
22. I.R.C. §170.
23. I.R.C. §11(b)(2).
24. I.R.C. §448(d)(2).
25. I.R.C. §301(c).
26. I.R.C. §1201(a).
27. I.R.C. §55(a).
28. I.R.C. §56(g).
29. I.R.C. §55(b)(1)(B).
30. I.R.C. §55(d).
31. I.R.C. §56.
32. I.R.C. §56(g).
33. I.R.C. §53.
34. I.R.C. §55(e).
35. I.R.C. §531.
36. I.R.C. §535.
37. I.R.C. §541.
38. I.R.C. §542(a).
39. I.R.C. §543(a).
40. I.R.C. §545(a).
41. I.R.C. §1361(b)(1).
42. I.R.C. §1361(b)(2).
43. I.R.C. §1361(b)(1)(A).
44. I.R.C. §1361(c)(1).
45. I.R.C. §1361(b)(1).
46. I.R.C. §1361(c)(2).
47. I.R.C. §1361(d).
48. I.R.C. §1361(b)(1)(D).
49. I.R.C. §1361(c)(4).
50. Treas. Reg. §1.1361-1(l)(2).
51. I.R.C. §1362(a)(2).
52. I.R.C. §1362(b).
53. I.R.C. §1362(d).
54. I.R.C. §1362(g).
55. I.R.C. §1362(f).
56. I.R.C. §1363(a).
57. I.R.C. §1366(a).
58. I.R.C. §1366(a)(1).
59. I.R.C. §1367.
60. I.R.C. §1368.
61. I.R.C. §1374.
62. IRC Sec. 1374(d)(7).
63. I.R.C. §1375.
64. IRC Sec 311(a).
65. IRC Sec. 311(a).
66. IRC Sec. 301(b)(1).
67. I.R.C. §731(a).
68. I.R.C. §§704(c)(1)(B), 751.
69. I.R.C. §707(c).
70. I.R.C. §162(l).
71. I.R.C. §162(l)(2)(B).
72. Rev. Rul. 91-26, 1991-1 CB 184.
73. Treas. Regs. §§301.7701-2(b)(2), 301.7701-3.
74. I.R.C. §1032(a).
75. I.R.C. §351(e).
76. I.R.C. §351(a).
77. I.R.C. §368(c).
78. I.R.C. §351(b).
79. See I.R.C. §351(e); Treas. Reg. §1.351-1(c).
80. I.R.C. §§358, 362.
81. I.R.C. §336(a).
82. I.R.C. §§332(a), 337(a).

COST RECOVERY CONCEPTS

CHAPTER 18

INTRODUCTION

Cost recovery is a term that refers to methods used by taxpayers to deduct the costs of business assets that generally must be deducted over a period of time, and not in the year that the assets were purchased. Cost recovery can also refer to amortization, which generally refers to deductions allowed for the acquisition of intangible property that has a limited useful life, but may be used in other situations.

WHEN IS IT INDICATED?

Depreciation is used when a taxpayer purchases certain capital assets. Generally, a taxpayer may not treat as an expense amounts that are paid for capital assets.[1] However, a taxpayer is allowed to take a deduction for the exhaustion, wear and tear, and obsolescence of property used in a trade or business or property held for the production of income.[2]

Only property with a limited useful life is subject to a deduction for depreciation. For that reason, land itself is not depreciable, although improvements to land can be depreciated. Also, inventory may not be depreciated.

TAX IMPLICATIONS

There are different methods that are used to depreciate property. The method that must be used depends on when the property was placed into service and the type of property it is, such as personal property or real estate.

Property is "placed into service" when it is first placed in a condition or state of readiness and availability for a specifically assigned function for use in a trade or business, for the production of income, or in a tax-exempt or personal activity.

Property Placed in Service Before 1981

Depreciable property that was placed in service before 1981 must be depreciated using the useful life of the property and its salvage value. The property, depending on its character (whether it is tangible or intangible, personal property, or residential or non-residential real estate), may be depreciated using the straight line, 200, 150, or 125 percent declining balance, the sum of the years' digits, or any reasonable, consistently used method.

Accelerated Cost Recovery System

Generally, tangible property placed in service after 1980 must be depreciated using the Accelerated Cost Recovery System (ACRS). The ACRS was modified for property placed in service after 1986 (see Modified Accelerated Cost Recovery System below). The pre-1987 ACRS rules apply generally to property placed in service after 1980 and before 1987.

The pre-1987 ACRS deduction is determined by multiplying the taxpayer's unadjusted basis in the property by a prescribed recovery percentage. A taxpayer's unadjusted basis in an asset is the basis of the asset for purposes of determining gain. Basis is usually the cost of the asset, but the basis may be reduced by amounts elected for amortization or for expensing. Because land may not be depreciated, the basis of improved land must be allocated between the land and its improvements.

If property is used in an individual's trade or business as well as in a personal or tax-exempt activity during a taxable year, the depreciable basis is determined by multiplying the unadjusted basis, as figured above, by the percentage of time the property was used in the trade or business. For example, the unadjusted basis of a car driven 20,000 miles in a year, of which 15,000 miles were for business purposes, would be multiplied by 75 percent.

Each year, the property's basis is reduced by the amount of the depreciation deduction taken so that the adjusted basis of the property reflects accumulated depreciation deductions. If depreciation is not deducted, the basis must still be reduced by the amount of allowable depreciation, but this "missed" deduction may not be taken in a subsequent year.

Property is classified as three, five, ten, fifteen, eighteen, or nineteen-year property, and recovery percentages are prescribed for each classification. The following is the classification of property by recovery period:

3 years	autos, light trucks, research and development equipment
5 years	heavy-duty trucks, production line equipment, most office furniture, most other equipment except long-life public utility property and certain single purpose agricultural structures and facilities used for petroleum storage
10 years	certain intermediate-life public utility property, railroad tank cars, theme park structures, coal utilization property, manufactured residential homes, depreciable real estate with an average asset depreciation range guideline life of 12.5 years or less
15 years	certain long-life public utility property, low-income housing, and most real estate placed in service before March 16, 1984
18 years	most real estate placed in service after March 15, 1984 and before May 9, 1985
19 years	most real estate placed in service after May 8, 1985

In computing depreciation on personal property, salvage value is ignored and in the first year a full year's deduction is taken regardless of the month the property is placed in service. However, no ACRS deduction is allowed in the year of an early disposition of the property.

An alternative method of calculating depreciation is available under the ACRS. The taxpayer could have elected to calculate the ACRS deductions according to the straight line method using one of the recovery periods, below, for each class of recovery property. The election must have been made by the due date (including extensions) of the income tax return for the taxable year the property is placed in service. Once this alternative method has been elected, permission of the IRS is needed in order to change to the regular ACRS method.

Straight-Line Recovery Periods by Class of Property

In the case of:	The individual may have elected a recovery period of:
3-year property	3, 5, or 12 years
5-year property	5, 12, or 25 years
10-year property	10, 25, or 35 years
15-year public utility property and low-income housing	15, 35, or 45 years
19-year property	19, 35, or 45 years

Note that during any taxable year, all personal property in a particular class which was placed in service during a particular year must have been depreciated using the same method. For real estate, however, the election may have been made on a property-by-property basis.

Modified Accelerated Cost Recovery System

Generally, the Accelerated Cost Recovery System (ACRS) was replaced with the Modified Accelerated Cost Recovery System (MACRS) for property placed in service after 1986. Faster depreciation than under ACRS was provided for certain property, new seven and twenty-year classes were created, and real estate was required to generally be depreciated over a much longer period than under the ACRS.[3]

The initial basis of the property is usually the cost of the property, which is then reduced by any available amortization or Section 179 expensing deductions (see below) and certain tax credits. The basis is then reduced each year by the amount of depreciation that is allowable. It is important to remember that even if depreciation is not claimed on depreciable property by a taxpayer, the basis is still reduced by the amount that could have been claimed.

The classification of property by recovery period and depreciation method is as follows:[4]

3 years 200% DB	class life of 4 years or less, certain horses, qualified rent-to-own property
5 years 200% DB	class life of more than 4 but less than 10 years, heavy trucks, buses, offshore drilling equipment, most computer and data handling equipment, cattle, helicopters and noncommercial aircraft, automobiles and light trucks
7 years 200% DB	class life of 10 or more but less than 16 years, most office furnishings, most agricultural machinery and equipment, theme park structures, most railroad machinery, equipment and track, commercial aircraft, property without a class life
10 years 200% DB	class life of 16 or more but less than 20 years, vessels, barges and similar water transportation equipment, petroleum refining equipment
15 years 150% DB	class life of 20 or more but less than 25 years, industrial steam and electric generation/distribution systems, cement manufacturing equipment, commercial water transportation equipment (freight or passenger), nuclear power production plants, certain real property that is a retail motor fuels outlet
20 years 150% DB	class life of 25 years or more, certain farm buildings, railroad structures and improvements, telephone central office buildings, gas utility production plants and distribution facilities, but excluding real property with class life of 27.5 years or more
25 years straight line	water utility property
27.5 years straight line	residential rental property
39 years straight line	nonresidential real property (class life of 27.5 years or more)
50 years straight line	railroad grading or tunnel bore

DB stands for declining balance method switching to the straight line method at a time to maximize the deduction.

150 percent DB is substituted for 200 percent DB if three-, five-, seven-, or ten-year property is used in a farming business. An election can be made to use the straight line method instead of the declining balance method. Also, a taxpayer may elect to use the 150 percent declining balance method for three, five, seven, and ten-year property.

The IRS has assigned "class lives" to most types of depreciable property, and Congress has also provided legislatively what class lives will be for certain property.

For certain property acquired after September 11, 2001, and before January 1, 2005, a depreciation "bonus" of 30 percent could be taken in the year the property was placed in service. Taxpayers could elect to not take this bonus depreciation. Also, for certain property acquired after May 5, 2003, and before January 1, 2005, bonus depreciation of 50 percent could be taken. For eligible property, taxpayers could elect 50 percent bonus depreciation, 30 percent bonus depreciation, or no bonus depreciation. Bonus depreciation is also allowed for property placed in service in 2008.[5]

In the year that depreciable property is acquired, the depreciation is limited to the portion of the year the property is held by the owner according to the following conventions. Residential rental property, nonresidential real property, and railroad grading or tunnel bore are treated as placed in service on the mid-point of the month in which the property is placed in service. Any other property is generally treated as placed in service on the mid-point of the year in which it was placed in service. There are similar rules regarding when property is considered to be disposed of by the taxpayer.[6]

The mid-quarter convention applies to property placed in service during the taxable year if the aggregate bases of property placed in service by the taxpayer during the last three months of the taxable year exceeds 40 percent of the aggregate bases of property placed in service during the taxable year. This is called "the 40 percent test." Regardless of whether the mid-year convention or the mid-quarter convention applies, no depreciation deduction is available for property placed in service and disposed of in the same year.

Property subject to the mid-month convention is treated as placed in service on the mid-point of the month without regard to whether the taxpayer has a short taxable year. The mid-quarter 40 percent test is also made without regard to the length of the taxable year. Thus, generally if property is placed in service in a taxable year that is three months or less, the mid-quarter convention applies regardless of when the property was placed in service, because 100 percent of property will have been placed in service in the last three months.[7]

In the case of a short taxable year and with respect to property to which the mid-year or mid-quarter convention applies, the recovery allowance is determined by multiplying the deduction that would have been allowable if the recovery year were not a short taxable year by a fraction, with the numerator equal to the number of months in the short taxable year and the denominator equal to twelve.

Alternative Depreciation System

An alternative depreciation system must be used for:

- tangible property that is used predominately outside the United States;

- tax-exempt use property;

- tax-exempt bond financed property;

- certain imported property covered by an executive order regarding countries engaging in unfair trade practices; and

- property for which the taxpayer makes an election to use the alternative system.

The election may be made with respect to each property in the case of nonresidential real property and residential rental property. For all other property, the election is made with respect to all property placed in service within a recovery class during a taxable year.[8]

The alternative depreciation deduction is determined using the straight line method and the applicable convention (mid-month, mid-quarter, or mid-year), over the following periods:

tax-exempt use property subject to a lease	longer of 125% of the lease term or period below
residential rental property and nonresidential real property	40 years
personal property with no class life	12 years
railroad grading or tunnel bore	50 years
all other property	the class life

Other Limitations

Depreciation deductions are also generally limited for certain property placed in service after June 18, 1984 if the business use of the property does not exceed 50 percent of its total use during the taxable year. This "listed property" includes any passenger automobile or certain other property used for transportation; any property of a type used for entertainment, recreation or amusement; certain computers, any cellular telephone; or other property specified by the IRS.[9]

If the business use of the listed property does not exceed 50 percent, depreciation under the pre-1987 ACRS and post-1986 MACRS is not allowed. For property placed in service after 1986, the amount of the depreciation is limited to the amount determined using the alternative depreciation system (described above).[10]

The depreciation of passenger automobiles that are purchased and leased is also subject to other limitations on the amount that can be taken as a depreciation deduction.

Depreciation Recapture

When depreciable property is sold, the seller often will realize more than his basis because of depreciation deductions that have been taken. Generally, this gain will be treated as a capital gain that may be subject to favorable tax rates while the gain is, at least in part, attributable to depreciation. To prevent a double benefit, the IRC requires that some of the gain that would otherwise generally be capital gain must be treated as ordinary income. In effect, it requires the seller to "recapture" some of the ordinary income that was offset in previous years by depreciation.[11] With respect to depreciable property other than real estate, the total amount of depreciation claimed is generally subject to the recapture rule under current law. With respect to real estate, the general rule under current law provides that property that has been depreciated under an accelerated method will be subject to recapture, while property that has been depreciated under the straight-line method will not. For residential real estate, the amount recaptured is the amount of depreciation claimed that is in excess of the amount that would have been allowable under the straight-line method. For nonresidential real estate that has been depreciated under an accelerated method, the entire amount of depreciation claimed is generally subject to recapture.

Cost Recovery for Intangible Assets

Generally, taxpayers are permitted depreciation deductions for certain intangible property. A depreciation deduction is allowed for certain computer software readily available to the general public, business interests and rights, and mortgage servicing rights.[12] Computer software eligible for this deduction is depreciated over a thirty-six-month period using the straight-line method. Other assets are depreciated under different schedules. The deduction generally is allowable for depreciable intangible property acquired after August 10, 1993, unless the taxpayer elects to take the deduction for such property acquired after July 25, 1991.

Intangible property for which a depreciation deduction is allowed includes

(1) computer programs available for purchase by the general public that are designed to cause a computer to perform a desired function,

(2) a right under a contract or granted by a government entity that entitles the taxpayer to receive tangible property or services,

(3) a right under a contract or granted by a government agency if such right has a fixed duration of less than fifteen years, or if such right is fixed as to amount and would otherwise be recoverable under a method similar to a unit-of-production method,

(4) any interest in a patent or copyright, and

(5) any right to service indebtedness that is secured by residential real property.

Certain other intangible assets held for business or the production of income are eligible for amortization deductions over a 180-month period, in lieu of depreciation, under IRC Section 197. Assets that are eligible for 180-month amortization are not eligible for any other depreciation or amortization deduction. The taxpayer, must, of course, have a tax basis in such assets in order to amortize them. These assets include (among others) goodwill and going concern value, business books and records, operating systems, proprietary databases, and patents, copyrights, formulas, and similar items. Computer software eligible for thirty-six-month depreciation as described above cannot be amortized. The rules for amortization apply to intangible assets acquired by

the taxpayer pursuant to a written contract that was in effect after August 10, 1993.

Section 179 Expensing

A taxpayer may elect to treat the cost of certain property as an expense in the year the property is placed in service. To qualify, the property must be eligible for depreciation or certain amortization provisions, it must generally be personal property (in other words, real estate is not eligible), and must have been acquired by purchase (from an unrelated person) for use in the active conduct of a trade or business. The property may not be an air conditioning or heating unit or "ineligible property." Ineligible property is generally property used outside the U.S., for lodging, by tax-exempt organizations, or by governments or foreign persons or entities. This election is not available to a trust or estate, and it may not be used for property held for the production of income.[13]

The aggregate cost that can be expensed when making this election is $25,000 for purchases made after 2010. These amounts are reduced by one dollar for each dollar of the cost of the above described property placed in service during the taxable year that exceeds $500,000 as indexed in 2007 through 2010, or $200,000 after 2010.[14]

The amount expensed is limited to the aggregate amount of income derived from the active conduct of any trade or business of the taxpayer. An amount that is not deductible because it exceeds the aggregate taxable income from any trade or business may be carried over and taken in a subsequent year.

The amount that may be carried over and taken in a subsequent year is the lesser of

(1) the amounts disallowed because of the taxable income limitation in all prior taxable years (reduced by any carryover deductions in previous taxable years); or

(2) the amount of unused expense allowance for such year. The amount of unused expense allowance is the excess of (1) the maximum cost of property that may be expensed taking into account the dollar and income limitations; or (2) the amount the taxpayer elects to expense. Married individuals filing separately are treated as one taxpayer for purposes of determining the amount that may be expensed and the total amount of the cost of all property eligible for expensing.

REPAIR REGULATIONS

On September 13, 2013, the IRS issued more than 200 pages of regulations that are intended to quell the controversy over the deduction/capitalization issue by providing a general framework for distinguishing capital expenditures from supplies, repairs, maintenance, and other deductible business expenses.[15]

The determination whether a particular expense is a deductible repair or maintenance expense or a depreciable capital expenditure generally requires an examination of the taxpayer's particular facts and circumstances. The subjective nature of the existing standards governing the determination—based on case law, the differing interpretations of various courts and on a number of IRS rulings—has resulted in considerable controversy between taxpayers and the IRS over many years.

The new rules—known as the "repair regulations"—also cover the retirement of depreciable property under Code section 167 (occurring when a depreciable asset is taken out of service with no salvage value) and provide accounting rules for property under the Modified Accelerated Cost Recovery System (MACRS) required by Code section 168. However, the repair regulations do not finalize the rules that address the definition of "disposition" for property subject to the section 168 MACRS.[16] Instead, revised regulations under section 168 were proposed with the final regulations.

Under Code section 263(a), certain business expenditures related to improving property must be capitalized and depreciated over the property's prescribed depreciable life. These expenditures include any amount:

1. paid out for new buildings or permanent improvements, or betterments made to increase the value of any property; or

2. expended in restoring property or in making good its exhaustion through a reserve for depreciation allowance

Previous final rules issued under section 263(a) defined capital expenditures as including amounts paid to either (1) add to the value, or substantially prolong the useful life, of a taxpayer's property, or (2) adapt the property to a new or different use. However, those regulations also specified that amounts paid or incurred for incidental repairs and maintenance of property are not capital expenditures and may be currently deducted. Thus, there was confusion about how to classify many types of expenditures: was a taxpayer paying for something that "substantially prolonged the useful life" of the property, or undertaking "incidental repairs and maintenance"?

The final repair rules retain and modify many of the provisions contained in temporary and proposed regulations issued in 2011, and apply to taxable years beginning on or after January 1, 2014. However, taxpayers can choose to apply the final regs to taxable years beginning on or after January 1, 2012. The rules are divided into five basic parts:

*   Regulation 1.162-3 provides rules for materials and supplies

*   Regulation 1.162-4 addresses repairs and maintenance

*   Regulation 1.263(a)-1 provides general rules for capital expenditures

*   Regulation 1.263(a)-2 provides rules for amounts paid for the acquisition or production of tangible property

*   Regulation 1.263(a)-3 provides rules for amounts paid for the improvement of tangible property

Materials and Supplies

While retaining the framework and many of the rules contained in the 2011 temporary regs, the final regulations expand the definition of materials and supplies to include property that has an acquisition or production cost of $200 or less (increased from $100 or less), clarify application of the optional method of accounting for rotable and temporary spare parts, and simplify the application of the *de minimis* safe harbor of Reg. §1.263(a)-1(f) to materials and supplies. The final regs also define standby emergency spare parts and limit the application of the election to capitalize materials and supplies to only rotable, temporary, and standby emergency spare parts.

De minimis safe harbor. A taxpayer with an applicable financial statement may rely on the *de minimis* safe harbor and elect to currently deduct the cost of tangible property and materials and supplies only if the amount paid for the property does not exceed $5,000 per invoice, or per item as substantiated by the invoice.[17] An "applicable financial statement" is a statement filed with the SEC, audited by an independent CPA that is used for certain purposes, or a statement other than a tax return that required to be provided to an agency of the federal or a state government (other than the IRS or the SEC).

The safe harbor also applies to a financial accounting procedure that expenses amounts paid for property with an economic useful life of twelve months or less as long as the amount per invoice (or item) does not exceed $5,000. Such amounts are deductible under the *de minimis* rule whether this financial accounting procedure applies in isolation or in combination with a financial accounting procedure for expensing amounts paid for property that does not exceed a specified dollar amount. Under either procedure, if the cost exceeds $5,000 per invoice (or item), then the amounts paid for the property will not fall within the *de minimis* safe harbor.

In addition, an anti-abuse rule is provided to aggregate costs that are improperly split among multiple invoices. The final regulations provide the IRS and the Treasury Department with the authority to change the safe harbor amount through published guidance.

The final regulations also include a *de minimis* rule for taxpayers without an applicable financial statement. Such taxpayers may rely on the *de minimis* safe harbor only if the amount paid for property does not exceed $500 per invoice (or item) as substantiated by the invoice.

Note that if a taxpayer meets the requirements for the safe harbor, which requires, in part, having written accounting procedures in place at the beginning of the taxable year and treating amounts paid for property as an expense in accordance with those procedures, then a change in the procedures, by itself, is not a change in accounting method.

However, the regulations specify that the *de minimis* safe harbor does not apply to:

1. amounts paid for property that is, or is intended to be included in inventory property;

2. amounts paid for land; or

3. amounts paid for rotable, temporary, and standby emergency spare parts that the taxpayer elects to capitalize and depreciate, or accounts for under the optional method of accounting for rotable parts pursuant to Reg. §1.162-3(e).[18]

Repairs and Maintenance

The final regulations retain the rule from the 2011 temporary regulations providing that amounts paid for repairs and maintenance to tangible property are deductible if the amounts paid are not otherwise required to be capitalized under Reg. §1.263(a)-3.

Routine maintenance safe harbor expanded. Under the 2011 temporary regs, the costs of performing certain routine maintenance activities for property other than a building or the structural components of a building were not required to be capitalized as an improvement. The final regulations extend the safe harbor to apply to buildings, provided the taxpayer reasonably expects to perform the relevant activities more than once during a ten-year period.

General Rules for Capital Expenditures

The new rules provide for the coordination with other provisions of the Internal Revenue Code, and state that nothing in the repair regulations changes the treatment of amounts that are specifically provided for in other Code provisions (other than Sections 162(a) and 212).[19] The Unicap rules under Code section 263A are cited as an example.

In addition to amounts paid to acquire, produce, or improve units of real or personal tangible property, the regulations cite examples of capital expenditures, including:

- amounts paid to facilitate the acquisition of a business or change the capital structure of a business entity; and

- amounts paid to acquire or create interests in land (such as easements, life estates, mineral interests, timber rights, or zoning variances).

Amounts Paid to Acquire or Produce Tangible Property

In general, the final regulations retain the rules from the 2011 temporary regulations with regard to expenses related to acquiring or producing tangible property. The new regulations continue the requirements to capitalize amounts paid to acquire or produce a unit of real or personal property, or to defend or perfect title to real or personal property. They also include rules for determining the extent to which taxpayers must capitalize transaction costs related to the acquisition of property.

The new rules also include the requirement from the 2011 regulations that taxpayers capitalize amounts paid to facilitate the acquisition or production of real or personal property and retain the list of "inherently facilitative costs" that generally must be capitalized as transaction costs.[20]

The final rules also clarify the meaning of "finders' fee" and "brokers' commission," and provide that if a real estate broker's commission is contingent on the successful closing of the acquisition of real property, the amount paid as the commission inherently facilitates the acquisition of the property acquired and, therefore, must be capitalized as part of the basis of such property.

Amounts Paid to Improve Property

For purposes of determining whether an amount improves, betters, or restores a unit of property and must be capitalized, the final repair rules generally define a "unit of property" as consisting of all the components of property that are functionally interdependent. Special rules are provided in the repair regs for determining the unit of property for buildings, plant property, and network assets and for determining the units of property for condominiums, cooperatives, and leased property, and the treatment of improvements (including leasehold improvements).

Restorations

The 2011 temporary regulations provided that an amount paid to restore (and therefore improve) a unit of property generally must be capitalized, if it meets one of six tests:

1. it is for the replacement of a component of a unit of property and the taxpayer has properly deducted a loss for that component (other than a casualty loss);

2. it is for the replacement of a component of a unit of property and the taxpayer has properly taken into account the adjusted basis of the component in realizing gain or loss resulting from the sale or exchange of the component;

3. it is for the repair of damage to a unit of property for which the taxpayer has properly taken a basis adjustment as a result of a casualty loss under Code section 165, or relating to a casualty event described in section 165 ("casualty loss rule");

4. it returns the unit of property to its ordinarily efficient operating condition if the property has deteriorated to a state of disrepair and is no longer functional for its intended use;

5. it results in the rebuilding of the unit of property to a like-new condition after the end of its class life; or

6. it is for the replacement of a major component or a substantial structural part of the unit of property ("major component rule").

The repair regulations retain this basic rule, but clarify the definition of major component, and, more significantly, add a new definition for major components and substantial structural parts of buildings. The final regulations define a "major component" as a part or combination of parts that performs a discrete and critical function in the operation of the unit of property, and a "substantial structural part" as a part or combination of parts that comprises a large portion of the physical structure of the unit of property.

WHERE CAN I FIND OUT MORE?

IRS Publication 946, "How to Depreciate Property" has information about both depreciation and Section 179 expensing. It contains tables providing the appropriate percentages to calculate the depreciate property and has tables that list the appropriate class lives and recovery periods for property. It also provides a comprehensive example of a hypothetical business and how the business would calculate and report its depreciation.

FREQUENTLY ASKED QUESTIONS

Question – How do repairs to depreciable property affect the property's basis and therefore its depreciation deductions?

Answer – If a taxpayer creates depreciable property, the expense of creating the property may not be taken as a business expense, but instead the cost must be recovered using depreciation. In the same way, if improvements are made to depreciable property that slow down deterioration or prolong the life of the property, these improvements must also be depreciated and cannot be expensed. However, the cost of "incidental" repairs which do not materially add to the value of the property nor prolong the life of the property may be taken as a business expense in the year the expense is incurred.[21]

Question – What is depletion?

Answer – Depletion is another cost recovery method that excludes (by way of income tax deductions) from the proceeds of mineral operations the part of the proceeds that represents a tax-free return of an investor's capital. Depletion deductions compensate the owner of wasting mineral assets "for the part exhausted in production, so that when the minerals are gone, the owner's capital and his capital assets remain unimpaired."[22] There are two different types of depletion: cost depletion and percentage depletion. If a taxpayer is eligible to take both percentage depletion and cost depletion, the amount that results in the larger deduction must be taken.

Cost depletion is calculated under the following formula:[23]

$$\text{Cost Depletion} = \frac{\text{Basis of Property}}{\text{Units Remaining as of Tax Year}} \times \text{Units sold during year}$$

The basis is the adjusted basis (including adjustments for previous depreciation) that would be used to determine the gain on the sale of the property. The Units Remaining is the units remaining at the end of the year plus the number of units sold during the year.

Percentage depletion is not based on the adjusted basis in the property, but instead uses a method where a specified percentage is multiplied by the investor's gross income from the property for that year.[18] The percentage rate will vary depending on the type of mineral or natural resource that is extracted. Certain taxpayers are not permitted to use percentage depletion, depending on the extracted natural resource and the classification of the taxpayer.

CHAPTER ENDNOTES

1. I.R.C. §263(a).
2. I.R.C. §167(a).
3. I.R.C. §168.
4. I.R.C. §§168(c), 168(e); Rev. Proc. 87-56, 1987-2 CB 674.
5. I.R.C. §168(k).
6. I.R.C. §168(d).
7. Rev. Proc. 89-15, 1989-1 CB 816.
8. I.R.C. §168(g).
9. I.R.C. §280F.
10. I.R.C. Secs. 1245, 1250.
11. I.R.C. §167(f).
12. I.R.C. §179.
13. Rev. Proc. 2008-66, 2008-45 IRB ___.
14. Treas. Reg. §1.162-4.
15. 78 Fed. Reg. 182 (September 19, 2013)
16. Treas. Regs. §§1.168(i)-1T to 1.168(i)-8T.
17. Teas. Reg. §1.263(a)-1(f).
18. Treas. Reg. §1.263(a)-1.
19. Treas. Reg. §1.263(a)-1.
20. Treas. Reg. §1.263(a)-2(f)(2)(ii).
21. *Paragon Jewel Coal Co., Inc. v. Comm'r.*, 380 U.S. 624 (1965).
22. Treas. Reg. §1.611-2(a).
23. I.R.C. §613.

BASIS

CHAPTER 19

INTRODUCTION

The concept of basis is an extremely important one in the current tax law. It is one of only a very small number of items that carries over from one year to the next when determining tax liability. For example, basis is used in determining:

1. gain or loss on the sale of an asset,

2. depreciation or amortization expense, and

3. deductibility of certain losses.

Basis is most commonly interpreted as the amount one pays for an asset. When that asset is sold, basis is subtracted from the amount received to determine the overall gain or loss realized. In this case, basis is the portion of the gross proceeds that is recovered income tax free upon the sale of an asset.

_____

Example: Mark buys a plot of land for $10,000 using funds that he saved from working in a local restaurant. The $10,000 Mark paid for the land represents his basis in the land. A few months later, John offers to purchase the land from Mark for $25,000. To compute his report-able gain, Mark may subtract his basis from the amount he realizes in the sale. So Mark's gain would be $15,000, the $25,000 realized minus Mark's $10,000 basis. Without the basis rules, Mark would be taxed not only on the appreciation of the land, but also on his purchase price which came from savings which were already taxed when it was earned. So basis is a means by which the tax law prevents double taxation.

_____

Because basis carries over from one year to the next and may be adjusted every year, it is one of the more complex and cumbersome burdens for taxpayers to comply with when preparing and filing their income tax returns. It is also an area that the Internal Revenue Service is likely to challenge upon the examination of a return. Maintaining complete, meticulous, and easily retrievable records of purchase payments and capital outlays is the best means of substantiating basis.

A STARTING POINT

As mentioned above, the starting point for determining basis is the amount that is paid in cash or other property for a particular asset. For example, Aaron Sterling, an investor, buys 100 shares of LISI, an information and analysis provider. Aaron's basis for his 100 shares of LISI will be the total price he paid. This includes any fees and commissions incurred as a result of the transaction. If the per share price at the time of purchase of the 100 shares is $50 and a $30 commission was paid on the transaction, Aaron's original basis is $5,030 (the total of the $5,000 cumulative share price plus the $30 commission).

When property other than (or in addition to) cash is used to acquire an asset, and the transaction does not qualify as a tax-free exchange, the basis of the property acquired is the sum of (a) any cash paid *plus* (b) the fair market value of any property transferred by the buyer. For instance, if Max Sterling purchased rental property for $10,000 in cash plus IBM stock worth $90,000, Max's original basis in the rental property would be $100,000 (the sum of the $10,000 cash he paid plus the $90,000 fair market value of the stock he transferred to the seller).

Typically, when an investor exchanges one property for another in an arm's length transaction, the market value of the property given up and the market value of the property received will be approximately equal. The fair market value of both properties will, as a practical matter, usually be ascertained by reference to the property whose value is most easily determined. In the example in the previous paragraph, it is easy to determine Max's basis in the rental property since Max paid for the property with cash ($10,000) and publicly traded IBM stock ($90,000), the value of which can easily be found.

When property is acquired subject to a mortgage or other debt, the basis of the property is not merely the amount of the investor's equity in the property. The basis is the total of the cash *and* the value of other property paid *plus* the amount of the debt assumed or incurred. For example, if Charlie Ratner buys a $1,000,000 apartment house, paying $250,000 in cash and borrowing the remaining $750,000, his basis in the property is the sum of the cash he's paid plus the debt he has assumed, (i.e., the full $1,000,000).

Basis is also used in depreciation calculations. The owner of property used in a trade or business that is subject to depreciation will use basis to determine the annual amount of expense. In the above example, Charlie's depreciable basis in the apartment house is $1,000,000 minus the amount of cost allocable to the land on which the building sits.

BASIS VARIATIONS

What complicates matters is the number of variations that exist for basis. Simply adding a word before "basis" changes the meaning within the tax law. What follows are examples of variations of the term "basis" and a short description of when the variation might be used.

Cost basis: "Cost basis" refers to the basis of property acquired by purchase. The cost of property includes amounts paid in cash, debt obligations assumed, or other property transferred by the buyer to the seller as part of the purchase price.[1]

Carry-over (or" transferred") basis: The donee (recipient) of a gift has a cost basis even though he or she may have paid nothing (see "transferred basis" and "stepped-up" basis, below).

Adjusted basis: The tax impact of certain transactions that occur after the initial purchase of a property may create the need for adjustments to the basis. Positive (upward) adjustments are made—and therefore basis is increased—when the owner makes additional investments or improvements with respect to the original property.[2] Downward adjustments are made—and therefore basis is reduced—when depreciation is claimed on property used in a trade or business.[3]

Unadjusted basis: "Unadjusted basis" is the amount of basis that can be claimed as cost recovery deductions (depreciation) over the duration of the recovery period (depreciable life) of the asset.[4] This term is used almost interchangeably with "depreciable basis" and is also used to identify a property's original cost basis.

Exchanged basis: "Exchanged basis" is basis that is determined in whole or in part by reference to other property held at any time by the taxpayer.[5] The most common application of this term is in the situation of a taxpayer who acquired property in what is called a "like-kind exchange" under Code section 1031. Prior to the enactment of Code section 7701(a)(42), "substituted basis" was used to describe what is now called "exchanged basis." In the context of a like-kind exchange, the exchanged basis starts with the taxpayer's adjusted basis in the relinquished property, and then (1) increases it by any gain recognized by the taxpayer in the exchange, and (2) decreases it by the value of any boot received.[6]

Transferred basis: As described more completely later in this chapter, "transferred basis" is basis that is determined in whole or in part by reference to the basis in the hands of the donor, grantor, or other transferor of property.[7] Prior to the enactment of Code section 7701(a)(43), this was usually referred to as "carryover basis." Many practitioners, and even some Code sections, continue to refer to transferred basis as carryover basis.

Stepped-up basis: Property received as an inheritance may obtain a "stepped-up" basis. If the decedent's property had a fair market value that exceeded its adjusted basis on the date of death, the property in the hands of the beneficiary receives a basis equal to the fair market value—that is, the basis gets a "step up" from the level it was at before the death occurred. For instance, if Dr. Rob Sterling purchased a home in Baltimore for $600,000 and it was worth $900,000 at the date of his death, Rob's heirs would compute any gain on a later sale using the stepped up $900,000 basis. (It is also possible for basis to be "stepped-down). These concepts will be explained more completely later in this chapter.

Negative basis: As a general rule, a taxpayer's basis is not permitted to be adjusted below zero. If negative basis were permitted, taxpayers could receive benefits for funds that were not actually spent on the asset. "Negative basis" is often used, even incorrectly, to describe situations in which a taxpayer's investment in a partnership or S corporation is reduced by losses in excess of their initial amount of capital. The impact of basis adjustments on flow-through entities will be discussed more completely later in this chapter.

BASIS FOR ALTERNATIVE MINIMUM TAX PURPOSES

The alternative minimum tax (AMT) is determined under a separate set of rules (See Chapter 18, Alternative Minimum Tax). Because certain items are treated differently for the purpose of computing a taxpayer's exposure to the AMT, there are times when it is possible for a taxpayer to have two or more adjusted basis figures for the same property.[8]

The most common difference in basis between the two tax systems is with adjusted basis for determining depreciation. Depreciation for certain property placed in service before January 1, 1999 was computed for AMT using different recovery methods and potentially longer lives. For assets placed in service after 1998, taxpayers must recompute depreciation using the same recovery period that they use for regular tax purposes but potentially a different recovery method.[9] As a result, upon the disposition of such an asset, the gain or loss for regular tax purposes will be different than what will be reported for the AMT. This disparity is due to the difference in the adjusted basis at the time of disposition.[10]

Corporate taxpayers that are subject to recomputing their depreciation using the allowable methods and lives for adjusted current earnings (ACE) may find that they have yet another set of adjusted basis numbers to track.[11]

Another area in which a taxpayer may have a different adjusted basis for regular tax and AMT purposes is with incentive stock options (ISOs). Although there is an exclusion from gross income for stock acquired by the exercise of ISOs, the exclusion is not permitted for the AMT.[12] As a result, the adjusted basis of the stock will be different.[13] This adjustment is more fully explained in Chapter 9, Alternative Minimum Tax and Chapter 26, Stock Option Planning.

USING BASIS TO DETERMINE DEDUCTIBLE LOSSES

The concept of basis is also applied to a taxpayer's investment in a pass-through entity, such as a partnership, limited liability company (LLC), or S corporation, to determine if losses from an entity are deductible. In a similar manner, individuals and certain C corporations must apply the at-risk limitation rules to activities that generate losses.[14] The at-risk rules are covered in detail in Chapter 20, Passive Activity and At-Risk Rules.

Partnerships (or LLCs Taxed as Partnerships)

A partner or LLC member (hereinafter referred to as "partner") typically determines his or her basis in their partnership interest (also known as the partner's "outside basis") starting with their initial investment in the partnership.[15] The starting point may be different if the partner acquired the partnership interest in any way other than as a direct purchase or contribution upon formation.

After the original cost basis is determined, the following adjustments are made each year to the partner's basis:

- increases for the partner's distributive share of the partnership's taxable income,[16]

- increases for the partner's distributive share of the partnership's tax-exempt income,[17]

- increases for the partner's distributive share of the partnership's excess of depletion deductions over the basis of the depletable property,[18]

- reductions for distributions,[19]

- reductions for the partner's distributive share of partnership losses,[20]

- reductions for the partner's distributive share of partnership expenditures that are not capitalized and not deducted,[21] and

- reductions for the partner's depletion deduction for partnership oil and gas property to the extent it does not exceed the proportionate share of the adjusted basis of the property allocated to such partner under Code section 613A(c)(7)(D).[22]

As previously mentioned, in no situation is a partner's adjusted basis reduced below zero.[23] In the event that any of the above adjustments, if made in full, would decrease the partner's basis below zero, the adjustment is limited to the amount of available basis. In addition, the tax impact to the partner is also limited.

Example: John McFadden contributes $5,000 to a newly formed partnership. In the first year, John's distributive share of the partnership's taxable loss is $6,400. Under the basis rules, only $5,000 of that loss would be deductible by John. The remaining $1,400 loss is suspended. John could use that suspended loss to offset future income or it could become deductible if John's basis is otherwise increased in a future tax year.

Each partner's share of the partnership's liabilities is treated as additional basis for the partner's interest in the partnership. An increase in a partner's share of the partnership's liabilities is treated as if that partner had made an additional contribution to the partnership.[24] Any decrease in a partner's share of the partnership's liabilities is treated as a distribution made to the partner from the partnership.[25]

Example: Assume the same facts as above, except that John's share of the partnership's liabilities is $2,000. This would be treated as a contribution made by John to the firm for purposes of determining his basis. His basis would then be $7,000 ($5,000 plus $2,000) before the adjustment for the current year's loss. Since the adjustment for the current year loss is less than the available basis, all of the current year's loss would be deductible. John's adjusted basis at the end of the year is $600 ($7,000 minus $6,400).

One year later, John's partnership breaks even but is able to pay off all of its liabilities. John must adjust his basis for his share of the decrease in partnership liabilities. However, the $2,000 reduction of John's liabilities, which is treated as a distribution to John, exceeds his $600 adjusted basis by $1,400 ($600 - $2,000). Since John is not permitted to reduce his adjusted basis below zero and because he already received the tax benefit in the prior year for the additional $1,400 of losses supported by the liabilities, John would be required to report the $1,400 ($2,000 deemed distribution less $600 adjusted basis) as currently reportable income.

Shareholders in S Corporations

Determining a shareholder's basis in an S corporation is somewhat different from calculating a partner's basis. An S corporation shareholder may have two different adjusted basis numbers to track, one for his stock basis and one for his debt basis. Unlike a partner of a partnership, an S corporation shareholder does not adjust his basis for the partner's share of the S corporation's liabilities.

Typically, an S corporation shareholder's stock basis begins with the amount the shareholder paid for his stock. The stock basis is then increased or decreased by the following adjustments:

- increases for the shareholder's share of the S corporation's separately stated items of income,[26]

- increases for the shareholder's share of the S corporation's non-separately stated items of income,[27]

- increases for the shareholder's share of the S corporation's excess of depletion deductions over the basis of the depletable property,[28]

- reductions for distributions not included in the shareholder's gross income,[29]

- reductions for the shareholder's share of the S corporation's separately stated items of loss and deduction,[30]

- reductions for the shareholder's share of the S corporation's non-separately computed loss,[31]

- reductions for the shareholder's share of the S corporation's expenditures that are not capitalized and not deducted,[32] and

- reductions for the shareholder's depletion deduction for S corporation oil and gas property to the extent it does not exceed the proportionate share of the adjusted basis of the property allocated to such shareholder under Code section 613A(c)(11)(B).[33]

As was the case with partnership basis, a shareholder's adjusted stock basis cannot be reduced below zero.[34] If a shareholder's stock basis is reduced to zero by losses and other adjustments of the S corporation, the shareholder may still be able to deduct the losses allocated to the shareholder assuming the shareholder has sufficient debt basis.

A shareholder may create debt basis by making a direct, bona fide loan to the S corporation. Note, however, that guarantees of S corporation debt or other indirect loans do not give a shareholder debt basis. Any unused portion of the reductions applicable to the shareholder's stock basis may be used to reduce the shareholder's debt basis.[35] Again, in no case can the shareholder's adjusted debt basis fall below zero.[36]

Once a shareholder reduces stock basis to zero and begins to reduce debt basis, any subsequent basis increases are first applied to restore the debt basis to the full amount of the outstanding loan.[37] Once the debt basis is fully restored, stock basis is increased from zero.

Example: Art Werner purchases a 50 percent interest in XYZ, Inc., an S corporation, for $10,000. In the first year, the company passes through a loss of $8,000 to Art. The $8,000 is deductible by Art because he has sufficient basis in his stock (subject to other limitations such as the passive activity rules). At the end of the first year, Art's adjusted stock basis is $2,000 ($10,000 original basis minus $8,000).

During the second year, Art directly loaned XYZ, Inc. $20,000 and guaranteed another loan of the S corporation for $50,000. Art's share of the second year loss was $27,000. Art will be able to deduct $22,000 of the $27,000 loss. First, Art's stock basis is reduced from $2,000 to zero. Second, Art reduces his debt basis from $20,000 to zero. Note that the guarantee of the S corporation loan does not give Mark any additional debt basis. The remaining $5,000 loss is suspended until Art has sufficient increases to his basis to cover it.

In the third year, XYZ, Inc. earned $150,000. Art's share is $75,000. Of the $75,000, $5,000 is offset by the suspended loss from the second year and is not reported by Art as income. The next $20,000 restores Art's debt basis and is reported as taxable income. The remaining $50,000 is also reported as income and increases Art's stock basis by this amount.

It is important to remember that an investor's ability to create basis through the use of debt is limited by the "at-risk" rules. These rules provide that losses are deductible only to the extent the investor is personally "at-risk." The at-risk rules are more fully covered in Chapter 20, Passive Activity and At-Risk Rules.

The at-risk rules limit deductions for borrowing that attempt to be characterized as "at-risk" for tax purposes when there is no actual economic risk to the investor. For instance, assume Janet Werner, a corporate executive, wants to purchase a $100,000 interest in an oil drilling venture. She intends to invest $20,000 of her own funds while borrowing the $80,000 balance. The bank providing the loan to Janet has agreed to make a "nonrecourse" loan to her. In other words, the bank will rely solely on the value of the property as its collateral for the debt. In the event Janet cannot repay the loan, the bank cannot look to Janet's other assets to cover the unpaid balance. Since the most Janet can lose on her investment is $20,000 in cash, her deductions will be limited to that $20,000 (plus the amount of income generated from the investment).

The at-risk rules cover essentially all investment activities except for real estate acquired before 1987. With respect to real estate subject to the at-risk rules, "qualified nonrecourse financing" is treated as an additional amount at-risk.

An investor is considered at-risk to the extent of:

1. Cash invested, *plus*

2. The basis of property invested, *plus*

3. Amounts borrowed for use in the investment that are secured by the investor's assets (other than the property used in the investment activity), *plus*

4. Amounts borrowed to the extent the investor is personally liable for its repayment, *plus*

When the investment is made in partnership form:

1. The investor-partner's undistributed share of partnership income, *plus*

2. The investor-partner's proportionate share of partnership debt, to the extent he is personally liable for its repayment.

An investor is not considered "at-risk" with respect to nonrecourse debt (other than qualified nonrecourse financing, see above) used to finance the activity, or to finance the acquisition of property used in the activity.

Furthermore, an investor will not be considered "at risk" with respect to any other arrangement for the compensation or reimbursement of any economic loss.

———

Example: If Janet, in the example above, is able to obtain commercial insurance against the risk that the oil drilling fund will not return her original $20,000 cash investment, she would not even be considered "at-risk" on that amount.

———

Losses limited by the at-risk provisions are not lost; instead, these amounts may be carried over and deducted in subsequent years (but only if the investor's at-risk amount is sufficiently increased).

The benefit of previously deducted losses must be recaptured when the investor's at-risk amount is reduced below zero.

———

Example: Assume Tania's loss deductions from her interest in an oil drilling venture total $5,000 through the end of last year. Her basis in the venture at the end of last year (after the deductions) was $1,000. In the current year, Tania received $3,000 in cash distributions. Without any limitations for negative basis, that distribution would reduce Tania's basis by $3,000 to a figure of *minus* $2,000. But since an investor cannot have a negative basis in an investment for tax purposes, Tania must recapture the $2,000 of prior year deductible losses in order to bring her basis up to zero. In addition, Tania will not be able to deduct any losses from the venture in the current year because she has a zero basis.

———

BASIS OF PROPERTY ACQUIRED FROM A DECEDENT

Under current law, when an investor dies, the beneficiary of his property does not "carry over" the decedent's basis. Instead, the basis of property acquired from or passing from a decedent is the fair market value of the property as of the date of (a) the investor's death, or (b) the federal estate tax alternate valuation date if that date (typically six months after the date of death) is elected by the estate's executor.[38]

Therefore, if the value of an investment held until death increases from the date of its acquisition, the potential gain (or loss in the case of a decrease in value) is never recognized for income tax purposes.

An increase in the property's basis to its federal estate tax value is called a "step-up" in basis. Note that this "stepped-up basis" is obtained by the recipients of the property after the prior owner's death even though no one pays income tax on the intervening appreciation.

———

Example: Susan Smith purchased stock that cost $10,000. At the time of her death, the stock had a fair market value of $50,000. Her beneficiary would receive a $50,000 basis for the stock. The $40,000 appreciation in the value of the stock would never be subject to income taxes. If the beneficiary then sold the property for $65,000, his taxable gain would be only $15,000.

———

The alternate valuation method may be elected by an executor or administrator only if the election will decrease (a) the value of the gross estate and also (b) the amount of the federal estate tax imposed.[39] Generally, an election to use the alternate valuation date means that property will be included in the gross estate at its fair market value as of six months after the decedent's death.[40] However, if any property is distributed, sold, exchanged, or otherwise disposed of within six months after the decedent's death, the value of the property at that disposition date becomes the "alternate value."[41]

———

Example: Assume Les Brun, a widower, buys property for $10,000 and it is worth $50,000 at his death. Assume that his executor sells the asset for $45,000 three months after his death. If the alternate valuation date is elected, the valuation date for this property would be the date of its sale. Its basis becomes $45,000. The estate realizes no tax gain or loss because the $45,000 amount realized on the sale is equal to the property's $45,000 basis.

———

Due to the one-year repeal of the estate tax in 2010, special rules applied to the determination of basis for inherited property acquired from a 2010 decedent. Depending on how the decedent's estate elected to be treated in 2010, the recipient of the inherited property may have carryover basis instead of the typical stepped-up basis.

BASIS OF PROPERTY ACQUIRED BY GIFT

When property is acquired by lifetime gift and there is a gain on the sale by the donee, the general rule is that the property in the hands of the donee has the same basis (subject to an adjustment discussed below) it had in the hands of the donor.[42] The donee of the gift—the new owner—computes his basis by referring to the basis in the hands of the donor. In other words, the donor's basis is "transferred" and "carried over" to the donee so that gain will not escape tax but merely be deferred. Note that this is now technically defined as "transferred basis" under Code section 7701(a)(43) (although many practitioners continue to refer to this as "carry-over basis"). The gain remains deferred only until the donee disposes of the property in a taxable transaction.

Example: Assume that Jared purchases stock for $3,000. After it appreciates in value to $9,000, he gives it to Maria. The basis of the stock in Maria's hands for determining gain on a later sale by Maria is still $3,000. Therefore, if she sells it for $10,000, she has a $7,000 gain.

When the donor's basis is used, it is subject to an adjustment for any gift taxes paid on the net appreciation in the value of the gift (but not above the amount of the gift tax paid).[43] For instance, in the example in the paragraph above, if the gift tax were $1,500, the donee's basis would be the $3,000 carryover basis plus $1,000 adjustment, a total of $4,000.

The addition to basis is computed according to the following formula:

Filing status	2009	2008
Married filing jointly	$250,200	$239,950
Head of household	$208,500	$199,950
Unmarried	$166,800	$159,950
Married filing separately	$125,100	$119,975

In our example, the computation would be:

Married filing jointly	$110,000
Married filing separately	$55,000
All others	$75,000

The basis rule for determining loss on the sale of property acquired by gift is different from the rule for determining the amount of the gain on the sale. For purposes of determining the amount of a loss, the basis of the property in the hands of the donee is the lesser of (a) the donor's basis or (b) the fair market value of the property at the time of the gift.[44] The purpose of this special provision is to prevent investors from gaining a tax benefit by transferring property with a built-in loss to persons who could take advantage of tax losses.

Assume, for instance, that in the example above the value of the stock at the time of the gift was only $1,000. If Jared sold the stock, he would have a capital loss of $2,000 ($3,000 basis – $1,000 amount realized). If Jared had other capital losses of at least $3,000 but no capital gains, the additional $2,000 loss would be treated as a capital loss carryover for the year and would provide no immediate tax benefit to him. Were it not for the special provision, Jared might give the stock to his father who had capital gains. If his father were allowed to use Jared's $3,000 basis, his father could sell the stock, take a $2,000 loss, and obtain a current tax benefit from the loss that Jared himself could not have used. For this reason, the father, in determining his loss on the sale, must use as his basis the $1,000 fair market value of the property at the time of the gift since that is lower than Jared's $3,000 basis. If Jared's father sold the property for $900, he would only recognize a $100 loss on the sale ($900 proceeds less $1,000 basis). If Jared's father sold the property at a time when it was worth only $1,200 (or any other amount between the $1,000 fair market value at the date of the gift or the $3,000 transferred basis), no gain or loss would be recognized.

ALLOCATION OF BASIS

When the assets of a trade or business are acquired, the purchase price must be allocated among the acquired tangible and intangible assets using what is called the "residual allocation" method.[45] This process is extremely important to the acquiring taxpayer since the amounts allocated to each asset create the basis by which future depreciation and amortization expenses are determined.

The residual method uses a "class" system to identify the amount of the purchase price that is to be allocated to each asset. The purchase price is applied to the assets of each class in proportion to their relative fair market values. The asset classes are:[46]

Class I: Cash and general deposit accounts, including savings and checking accounts, but excluding certificates of deposit held in banks, savings and loan association and other depository institutions

Class II: Actively traded personal property, certificates of deposit and foreign currency

Class III: Accounts receivable and assets that the taxpayer marks-to-market at least annually

Class IV: Inventory or other property held primarily for sale to customers in the ordinary course of its trade or business

Class V: Assets not covered by any other class (typically the fixed assets of the business)

Class VI: Section 197 intangibles, except goodwill and going concern value

Class VII: Goodwill and going concern value

An independent appraisal of each asset being purchased is a recommended process in order to substantiate and document the allocation of the purchase price. Each of the amounts that are allocated may result in a potentially different tax treatment in the future for the acquirer. For instance, amounts allocated to fixed assets may be depreciable in the hands of the acquirer. In most cases, the taxpayer would then benefit from a relatively short recovery period (depending on the asset involved) and recoup a portion of the investment soon. Conversely, if more of the purchase price falls to goodwill, the acquirer may be faced with a much longer recovery period, if at all.

Example: ABC buys the assets of XYZ for $1,000,000. ABC acquires XYZ's accounts receivable valued at $200,000, inventory valued at $50,000, and fixed assets valued at $400,000. $200,000 of the purchase price is allocated to the accounts receivable and that amount becomes the basis for the receivables. Likewise, the inventory is allocated $50,000 of the purchase price and the fixed assets are allocated $400,000. The remaining amount of the purchase price, $350,000, is allocated to goodwill.

An allocation of basis is also required in circumstances when a taxpayer receives multiple types of property in a single transaction. The best example of this is improved real estate. The building, if used in a business or rental operation, would be eligible for depreciation, while the underlying land is not depreciable. Further, taxpayers may undergo a cost segregation study in order to determine if there are parts of a property that may be classified as depreciable property with a shorter life, thereby increasing the annual depreciation expense.

FREQUENTLY ASKED QUESTIONS

Question – How is a taxpayer's basis determined when selling a stock investment?

Answer – As previously discussed, the basis of one's stock investment is determined by the cost of the stock, plus any commissions paid. When a stock is sold and the investor sold less than their entire position in a given security, the stock is deemed to be sold using a first-in, first-out method (FIFO). FIFO is used whenever the investor does not or cannot specifically identify which shares of stock were sold.[47]

An investor may specifically identify the shares that were sold by delivering the shares to be sold to the broker. If the shares are held in street name by the broker, (1) the investor must identify to the broker at the time of the sale which shares are to be sold, and (2) the broker must confirm the share identification to the investor within a reasonable time after the sale.[48]

Beginning in 2011, brokers were required to comply with new cost basis reporting rules for their investors. Prior to this date, the only reporting requirement was for sales proceeds on the sale of securities. Following the schedule below, the information reports provided by brokers must also include the cost basis of the asset sold.

- **Beginning January 1, 2011**, brokers must report information on any common or preferred stock, exchange-traded funds (ETFs), American Depositary Receipts (ADRs) and Real Estate Investment Trusts (REITs).

- **Beginning January 1, 2012**, information about mutual funds and dividend reinvestment plans must also be recorded and reported.

- **Beginning January 1, 2013**, options, fixed income, and any other security otherwise not included in the previous tax years must be recorded by the brokerage and reported to the IRS.

The basis of security purchases prior to the above dates are not required to be reported by the brokers. So, for instance, the basis of a mutual fund purchased in June 2011 does not need to be reported by the broker when sold since the purchase occurred prior to the date of implementation.

Question – How is a taxpayer's basis determined when selling a mutual fund investment?

Answer – An investor's basis in a mutual fund starts with the original cost of the mutual fund shares, plus any commissions or fees paid. Basis is then increased by any amounts of reinvested income (typically taxable and tax-exempt dividend income and capital gain distributions). Basis may be reduced by distributions treated as return of capital. The sources of these basis adjustments are normally found on Form 1099-DIV or Form 2439, so it is imperative that these forms be maintained to properly maintain accurate basis records.

When less than the full amount of a mutual fund investment is sold, an investor has three choices for allocating basis to determine the capital gain or loss. The three methods are (1) FIFO, (2) specific identification, or (3) average basis. Like the rules for stocks, if the average basis method is not elected or specific identification is not used, basis should be determined on a FIFO basis.

An investor may elect to use the average basis method on a fund by fund basis. The election must be made in the first year that mutual fund shares from a given fund are sold. Every year after the election is made, a taxpayer is required to disclose the continued use of the method on all future sales of the same fund.

There are two average basis methods – single category and double category. The single category method is simply determined by the total basis of the mutual fund shares on the date of the sale divided by the total shares held immediately prior to the sale.[49] The holding period is determined on a FIFO basis. Note that many mutual fund companies provide single category average basis information to their shareholders each year along with their tax information statements.

When double category method is elected, a taxpayer is required to divide his mutual fund holding into short and long-term shares and the average basis for each of these lots are determined. From this point, the taxpayer may opt to sell out of the short or long-term position and use the appropriate average cost basis for those shares.[50] The use of the double category method is not widely used.

With the cost basis reporting requirements placed on the brokers (beginning in 2012 for mutual fund purchases), care must be taken to ensure that the correct cost basis is disclosed to the IRS on the Form 1099-B. Most brokers allow investors to select a cost basis method to be used in lieu of the broker's default method, which in most cases is single category average cost for purchases after the beginning reporting date.

Question – How is basis determined for a bond issued or purchased at a discount?

Answer – A bond issued at less than its stated redemption price is treated as a discounted bond. The amount of the discount is simply the difference between the redemption price and the issue price and is referred to as the original issue discount (OID). Over time, the holder of the bond is required to report the OID in their income and increase their basis in the bond by the same amount. If the bond is held to maturity, the full value of the bond will be paid and there will be no gain or loss (ignoring transaction costs) since the recognition of the full amount of the OID would have increased the taxpayer's basis to equal the face value of the bond.

If an OID bond is sold before its maturity, the bond's basis is determined by its original cost plus any OID previously recognized as income.[51]

A bond purchased at a discount on the secondary market is referred to as a market discount bond, and different rules apply. The amount of the market discount may be recognized in the bond holder's income on an annual basis by making an election on the bond holder's tax return in the year of the purchase.[52] If an election is not made, the market discount is recognized when the bond matures or is otherwise disposed of by the taxpayer (including via gift). Any gain on the bond is treated as ordinary income to the extent of the market discount.[53] The market discount rules do not apply to: (1) short-term obligations (such as T-bills) with fixed maturity dates one year or less from the date of issue; (2) tax-exempt obligations purchased before May 1, 1993; and (3) U.S. savings bonds.[54]

Question – How is basis determined for a bond issued or purchased at a premium?

Answer – If a debt instrument is purchased or issued at a price that is greater than the stated maturity amount, the bond holder is paying a premium. The amount of the premium paid on a taxable bond remains as part of the holder's basis of the bond until it is sold or redeemed unless an election is made to amortize the premium amount.[55] Tax-exempt bond holders are required to amortize the bond premium, even though no corresponding tax deduction results from the amortization. As amortization of a taxable or tax-exempt bond occurs, a bond holder's basis is reduced accordingly.[56]

Amortization of a taxable bond issued after September 28, 1987 is determined using the constant yield to maturity method and is reported as a reduction to the taxpayer's interest income each year (bond issued prior to that date may be amortized using any reasonable method).[57] However, the amount of the bond amortization may not be greater than the amount of interest being reported on that particular bond in any given year.[58]

Essentially, the election to amortize the premium paid on a taxable bond results in a tax deduction against a taxpayer's ordinary income through the reduction of taxable interest. If the election is not made, the taxpayer will report the bond premium by using a higher basis when the bond matures or is otherwise disposed of, resulting in an offset to their capital gain income and, usually, less of a tax benefit.

Note that for bonds with a call feature, the call date and amount must be used for the amortization calculation.[59]

Question – What is the basis of property converted from a nonbusiness use to a business use?

Answer – When property that is used personally is converted to business use, the property's basis is the lower of (1) the basis of the property when it was acquired for personal use, or (2) its fair market value at the time of the conversion.[60]

CHAPTER ENDNOTES

1. Treas. Reg. §1.1012-1(a).
2. I.R.C. §1016(a)(1).
3. I.R.C. §1016(a)(2).
4. I.R.C. §168(b)(1).
5. I.R.C. §7701(a)(42).
6. I.R.C. §1031(d).
7. I.R.C. §7701(a)(43).
8. Since so many states have decoupled from the federal tax depreciation system, especially with respect to the concept of "bonus" depreciation, many taxpayers are forced to maintain adjusted basis calculations for their fixed assets for state tax purposes.
9. I.R.C. §56(a)(1).
10. I.R.C. §56(a)(6).
11. I.R.C. §56(g)(4)(A).
12. I.R.C. §56(b)(3).
13. *Ibid.*
14. I.R.C. §465(a)(1).
15. A partner's outside basis is defined as the partner's adjusted basis in the partnership interest. A partner's inside basis is defined as the partner's share of the partnership's adjusted basis in its assets.
16. I.R.C. §705(a)(1)(A).
17. I.R.C. §705(a)(1)(B).
18. I.R.C. §705(a)(1)(C).
19. I.R.C. §705(a)(2).
20. I.R.C. §705(a)(2)(A).
21. I.R.C. §705(a)(2)(B).
22. I.R.C. §705(a)(3).
23. I.R.C. §§705(a)(2), 705(a)(3).
24. I.R.C. §752(a).
25. I.R.C. §752(b).
26. I.R.C. §1367(a)(1)(A).
27. I.R.C. §1367(a)(1)(B).
28. I.R.C. §1367(a)(1)(C).
29. I.R.C. §1367(a)(2)(A).
30. I.R.C. §1367(a)(2)(B).
31. I.R.C. §1367(a)(2)(C).
32. I.R.C. §1367(a)(2)(D).
33. I.R.C. §1367(a)(2)(E).
34. I.R.C. §1367(a)(2).
35. I.R.C. §1367(b)(2)(A).
36. *Ibid.*
37. I.R.C. §1367(b)(2)(B).
38. I.R.C. §1014(a).
39. I.R.C. §2032(c).
40. I.R.C. §2032(a)(1).
41. I.R.C. §2032(a)(2).
42. I.R.C. §1015(a).

43. I.R.C. §1015(a).
44. I.R.C. §1015(a).
45. I.R.C. §1060(a).
46. Treas. Reg. §1.1060-1(c)(2).
47. Treas. Reg. §1.1012-1(c)(1).
48. Treas. Reg. §1.1012-1(c)(3).
49. Treas. Reg. §1.1012-1(e)(4).
50. Treas. Reg. §1.1012-1(e)(3).
51. I.R.C. §1272(d)(2).
52. I.R.C. §1278(b).
53. I.R.C. §1276(a)(1).
54. I.R.C. §1278(a)(1).
55. I.R.C. §171(c).
56. I.R.C. §1016(a)(5).
57. I.R.C. §171(b)(3).
58. Treas. Reg. §1.171-2(a)(4).
59. I.R.C. §171(b)(1)(B).
60. Treas. Reg. §1.165-9(b)(2) and §1.167(g)-1.

PASSIVE ACTIVITIES AND AT-RISK RULES

CHAPTER 20

INTRODUCTION

The passive activities and at-risk rules provide hurdles that taxpayers must overcome in order for certain losses to offset other sources of income in a given year. The at-risk rules are applied after the basis limitation provisions that are discussed further in Chapter 19. If a taxpayer's loss passes the basis and at-risk limitation tests, the passive activity rules are applied. The at-risk rules focus on the taxpayer's investment (risk) in the venture, while the passive rules focus on the nature of the taxpayer's involvement in the venture. Losses may be suspended (i.e., can't be utilized in the current year but are not lost and may be used at a future date) at any or all of these levels.

Taxpayers often invest substantial amounts of money into ventures without being aware of the potential tax impact of these limitations. If a taxpayer expects losses from an investment to automatically offset their other sources of income, they may be in for a bad surprise.

This situation comes up very often with an investment in real estate. Since the depreciation on a property often outpaces the amortized principal in the early years, a property may throw off a positive cash flow but report a taxable loss. That taxable loss must meet the tests of each of the three limitation rules before the taxpayer can claim any of the loss as an offset to their taxable income.

Starting in 2013, the passive activity rules are also used to determine when trade or business and rental activities are subject to the Net Investment Income ("NII") tax. This determination now puts a greater importance on these rules in situations regardless of whether an activity is generating income or losses.

AT-RISK LIMITATION RULES

The at-risk limitation rules were added to the Internal Revenue Code with the Tax Reform Act of 1976. Prior to the addition of these rules, taxpayers were allowed to deduct losses from investment activities to the extent of their basis, which is determined by adding the taxpayer's:

1. actual cash investment;

2. adjustments from the results of operations;

3. liabilities the taxpayer is obligated to pay (recourse); and

4. costs financed through nonrecourse loans that the taxpayer will not be obligated to pay personally.

The enactment of the at-risk rules was the first major attempt by Congress to deal with the growing number of tax shelters. Tax shelters were a popular way for investors to take advantage of their ability to deduct losses up to their basis in the investment. The taxpayer's basis, however, was often increased by liabilities that the investor would never be called upon to pay in the event the business failed.

Initially, the at-risk rules were applied only to investments in five activities that were perceived to be the most abusive tax shelters. The five original activities subject to the at-risk limitation rules were:[1]

1. farming;

2. exploring for or exploiting oil and gas resources;

3. holding, producing, or distributing motion picture films or videotapes;

4. equipment leasing; and

5. exploring for or exploiting geothermal deposits.

In 1978, the at-risk limitation rules were extended to all other investment activities except real estate. Finally, in 1986, the at-risk rules added real estate activities to the scope of activities covered by Code section 465.[2] The at-risk rules continue to apply under today's law and cover all investment activities.

INTRODUCTION TO THE PASSIVE ACTIVITY LOSS LIMITATION RULES

In a further effort to curb perceived abuses with the growing use of tax shelters, Congress enacted the passive activity loss (PAL) rules with the Tax Reform Act of 1986. At the time, tax shelters were being marketed to investors with the purpose of generating losses to offset high-income taxpayers' salaries and wages. Back in 1986, the highest marginal tax rate was 50 percent, so a great deal of tax savings was at stake.

Although the number of abusive tax shelters may have been reduced, in part, by these rules, they have cast a much wider net and many taxpayers who have not invested in tax shelters still have to deal with the PAL limitations each year when they file their tax return. The PAL rules are contained in Code section 469 and the corresponding regulations.

The PAL rules apply to any individual, estate, trust, certain closely held C corporations, and personal service corporations.[3] A passive activity can be practically any business or rental activity owned by a taxpayer directly or held by a taxpayer in a flow-through entity such as a partnership, limited liability company, or S corporation.

TAX IMPLICATIONS

At-Risk Rules

The at-risk limitations are applied to individual taxpayers and closely held corporations. Closely held corporations are defined as one having five or fewer shareholders owning more than 50 percent of the corporation's stock during the last half of the tax year.[4] For flow-through entities, such as partnerships, certain limited liability companies, and S corporations, these limitations are applied at the individual partner, member, or shareholder level.

The at-risk rules limit deductions for borrowing that attempt to be characterized as "at-risk" for tax purposes when there is no actual economic risk to the investor. For instance, assume Georgia wants to purchase a $100,000 interest in an oil drilling venture. She intends to invest $20,000 of her own funds while borrowing the $80,000 balance. The bank providing the loan to Georgia has agreed to make a "nonrecourse" loan to her. In other words, the bank will rely solely on the value of the property as its collateral for the debt. In the event Georgia cannot repay the loan, the bank cannot look to Georgia's other assets to cover the unpaid balance. Since the most Georgia can lose on her investment is $20,000 in cash, her deductions will be limited to that $20,000 (plus the amount of income generated from the investment).

The amount at-risk for a given activity is the combined total amount of money and the adjusted basis of other property contributed with respect to the activity and amounts borrowed with respect to the activity.[5] However, in order for an individual to be treated as at-risk for amounts borrowed by the entity owning the activity, the individual must be personally liable for the repayment of the borrowed amounts or pledge property outside the investment as security.[6] The courts have interpreted this to mean that the individual must have the ultimate liability for the repayment of the debt.

The at-risk rules cover essentially all investment activities (except for real estate acquired before 1987). With respect to real estate subject to the at-risk rules, "qualified nonrecourse financing" is treated as an additional amount at-risk. Qualified nonrecourse financing is any debt incurred that:

1. Is borrowed for the holding of real property;

2. Is borrowed from a "qualified person" (one in the business of lending money, such as a bank or savings and loan institution) or represents a loan from any federal, state, or local government or instrumentality thereof, or is guaranteed by any federal, state, or local government;

3. Holds no person personally liable for repayment; and

4. Is not convertible debt.[7]

An investor is considered at-risk to the extent of:

1. Cash invested, *plus*

2. The basis of property invested, *plus*

3. Amounts borrowed for use in the investment that are secured by the investor's assets (other than the property used in the investment activity), *plus*

4. Amounts borrowed to the extent the investor is personally liable for its repayment (including qualified nonrecourse financing), *plus*

When the investment is made in partnership form —

1. The investor-partner's undistributed share of partnership income, *plus*

2. The investor-partner's proportionate share of partnership debt, to the extent he is personally liable for its repayment.

An investor is not considered "at-risk" with respect to nonrecourse debt (other than qualified nonrecourse financing, see above) used to finance the activity, or to finance the acquisition of property used in the activity, or with respect to any other arrangement for the compensation or reimbursement of any economic loss. For example, if Georgia is able to obtain commercial insurance against the risk that the oil drilling fund will not return her original $20,000 cash investment, she would not even be considered "at-risk" on that amount.

If a taxpayer does not have sufficient amounts at-risk in a given activity, the deductibility of the losses from that activity are limited to the amount at-risk. Any excess losses are carried forward to future years and may be utilized to offset future income from the activity or be deducted when the taxpayer adds amounts to the activity for which the taxpayer is deemed to be at-risk.

A taxpayer who previously deducted losses from an activity based upon amounts that were at-risk in a prior year may be required to recapture those losses if the amount that a taxpayer has at-risk falls in a future year.[8] This can happen if the taxpayer used a certain amount of liabilities as an amount at-risk to deduct losses to the full extent of the amount at-risk. If the subsequent principal repayments of the liability reduce the amount at-risk below zero, they would need to be recaptured in that year.

Taxpayers with losses from activities with amounts not at-risk are required by the IRS to complete and file with their tax return Form 6198, *At Risk Limitations*.[9]

Passive Activity Rules

In general, losses from passive activities are deductible in a given year to the extent the passive activity income exceeds the losses from passive activities. Passive activity losses in excess of passive activity income are suspended. Suspended passive activity losses are carried forward indefinitely to future years to offset future income from passive activities. PALs may not be used to offset other nonpassive income such as salaries, investment income, or capital gains. However, passive losses from one activity can generally be offset with passive income from a different activity.

Credits from passive activities are also disallowed unless there is net passive income in a given year. Like PALs, these credits are carried forward indefinitely to future years. There is no carryback provision for either PALs or passive activity credits.

Suspended losses, but not credits, may be utilized in the year in which an activity is completely or substantially disposed.

The IRS requires that taxpayers with passive activities complete and file with their tax return Form 8582, *Passive Activity Loss Limitations*. If credits from passive activities are being reported by a taxpayer in any year, Form 8582-CR, *Passive Activity Credit Limitations* should be used.

DETERMINING THE "ACTIVITY"

As you can see from the short introduction above, both the at-risk and passive loss rules use the term "activity." Unfortunately, what an activity is for purposes of the at-risk rules does not necessarily carry over to the PAL rules.

At-Risk Activities

The definition of an activity for the purposes of the at-risk limitation rules begins with the five original activities defined under Code section 465(c)(1). Each of the original five activities must be treated as a separate activity.[10] This has been interpreted to mean that any project that is covered under one of these activities must be accounted for separately under the at-risk rules. The only exception is for the leasing of tangible personal property by a partnership or S corporation. All leased assets placed in service in a single tax year are treated as a single activity.[11]

For activities other than the five original activities under Code section 465(c)(1), if the activities constitute a single trade or business, all the activities of that trade or business are aggregated if:[12]

1. the taxpayer actively participates in the management of the trade or business; or

2. the trade or business is carried on by a partnership or S corporation, and 65 percent or more of the losses for the tax year are allocable to persons who actively participate in the management of the trade or business.

The determination of an activity for purposes of the at-risk rules is very important since the losses of one activity that are limited by the at-risk rules may not be deducted using available at-risk amounts in another activity.

Passive Activities

A passive activity is (1) any activity that involves the conduct of a trade or business in which the taxpayer does not "materially participate" or (2) any rental activity.[13]

Since the definition of a "passive activity" includes the term "activity," one would expect to find a definition of "activity" somewhere. Unfortunately, taxpayers are not so lucky. An activity is based on a case by case "facts and circumstances" evaluation. The IRS has allowed any "reasonable method" to determine whether one or more trade or business activities constitute an appropriate "economic unit." Therefore, one or more trade or business activities may be grouped to represent an economic unit.

In order to group activities for the purpose of determining an appropriate economic unit, taxpayers must evaluate:[14]

1. the similarities and differences in types of business;

2. the extent of common control and ownership;

3. geographic location; and

4. interdependencies between or among the activities.

For example, taxpayers are generally allowed to aggregate activities in the same line of business into one activity without considering geographic location if the activities are commonly controlled by the same owners.

Example: A taxpayer owns an ice cream store and a shoe store in Pittsburgh, and an ice cream store and a shoe store in a Philadelphia shopping mall. There are four different possible combinations of the activities based on all the facts and circumstances:

1. one activity aggregating all four businesses;

2. two separate activities – a Pittsburgh activity and a Philadelphia activity;

3. two separate activities – an ice cream store activity and a shoe store activity; or

4. four separate activities – one for each business.

Certain activities may not be grouped. A rental activity that leases real property may not be grouped with a rental activity that leases personal property, unless the rentals are provided together.[15] Also, a rental activity may not be grouped with a trade or business activity unless the combination of the two activities represent an appropriate economic unit and:[16]

1. the rental activity is "insubstantial" in relation to the trade or business activity;

2. the business activity is "insubstantial" in relation to the rental activity; or

3. each owner of the trade or business activity has the same proportionate ownership in the rental activity.

Although "insubstantial" is not defined in the current regulations, prior temporary regulations accepted up to 20 percent of the total gross receipts of the combined activities to be considered insubstantial. However, this test is not valid under current rules which favor a stricter facts and circumstances test. As a result, the Service can challenge groupings even if the receipts of one of the activities are well below the 20 percent "insubstantial" level.

Example: A owns a building in which he operates a card store. The card store has two rental spaces. Gross receipts from the rental spaces are 15 percent of the total receipts of the combined activities. The rental activity may be insubstantial in relation to the combined activity, so the rental activity and business activity may possibly be grouped based on other subjective facts.

––––––––––––

What is critically important is that the taxpayer makes a proper grouping election in the first year they wish to group activities. The regulations specifically exclude the ability to use the grouping rules solely to avoid a PAL problem.[17] In 2010, a revenue procedure was issued which describes how a grouping election should be made and what information needs to be included in the election.[18]

Married couples are considered as one taxpayer when applying the grouping rules. Therefore, if B owns a rental property and B's spouse, C, owns a retail store, the rental property and retail store may be grouped into one activity for the application of the PAL rules.

An activity is the unit of measurement for the PAL rules. Once the activity is determined, several tests are applied to determine whether the taxpayer's participation in the activity is passive or nonpassive. These tests include:

1. material participation (defined below);

2. active participation for rental real estate; and

3. when suspended losses of passive activities become available upon the complete disposition of an activity.

Once an activity group is created, the taxpayer may not change the groupings unless the combination of the activities is clearly inappropriate or a material change has occurred from when the initial grouping was made. Starting in 2013, there is an exception to this rule in which an individual or trust subject to NII tax is allowed a one-time "fresh start" regrouping which doesn't require a previous grouping to be inappropriate.[19] If the grouping is broken, disclosure must be made to the IRS.[20]

The IRS may regroup a taxpayer's activities if:[21]

1. the taxpayer's aggregation fail to reflect one or more appropriate economic units; and

2. one of the primary purposes of the taxpayer's grouping is to circumvent the PAL rules.

Since a group of activities is considered as one activity for the application of the PAL rules, suspended losses are only deductible upon the complete (or substantially complete) disposition of the group of activities.[22] This provision suggests that the taxpayer should group activities in the smallest possible units unless the goal of the grouped activities is to obtain a level of material participation.

FREQUENTLY ASKED QUESTIONS

At-Risk Limitations

Question – Do guarantees by a taxpayer of a partnership's debt increase the amount at-risk?

Answer –A guarantee of partnership debt does not increase the guarantor partner's amount at-risk unless the partner is actually required to make payments to the creditor.[23] The guarantor must have no right of action against any other party should payment be required under the terms of the guarantees.

Question – How are suspended at-risk losses carried forward?

Answer – If the at-risk rules prevent a taxpayer from deducting the full amount of a loss, the losses may be carried forward indefinitely. The losses may then be used to offset income in a future year from the same activity or when the taxpayer increases the amount at-risk in the activity. If the taxpayer recognizes a gain on the disposition of the activity, the gain could be offset by the suspended losses. However, unlike the passive rules, there is no automatic "freeing-up" of the losses on disposition.

Losses that are limited retain their character from year-to-year. That is, if a long-term capital loss is limited, the carryover will continue to be a long-term capital loss to be used when sufficient at-risk basis is generated. There are many instances where a taxpayer may have more than one type of loss limited by the at-risk rules. Although there is no formal ordering rule for deducting losses subject to the at-risk rules, the instructions to Form 6198 require a pro rata share of each type of loss limited by the at-risk rules be carried forward. Note that there was an ordering rule established by a proposed regulation in 1979.[24] However, the regulation has never been finalized. In fact, the instructions to Form 6198 contradict the proposed regulation.

Passive Activity Loss Limitations

Question – How does a taxpayer's participation in an activity impact the application of the PAL rules?

Answer – A taxpayer's participation determines whether the activity is treated as a passive activity or a nonpassive activity. To be a nonpassive activity, the taxpayer must "materially" participate in the activity.

Question – What is "material" participation?

Answer – Material participation is defined as a taxpayer's participation on a regular, continuous, and substantial basis.[25] The regulations under Code section 469 provide seven tests for material participation. A taxpayer that meets any one of the seven tests is deemed to be a material participant for that year. The tests must be applied on an annual basis to each activity of a taxpayer.

If a taxpayer materially participates in an activity that generates a loss in a given year, the loss may be used in that year to offset passive, portfolio, or nonpassive income. If a taxpayer is deemed not to be a material participant, any losses are generally treated as passive and are not deductible against any other source of income except income from other passive activities.

The seven tests for material participation are:[26]

1. The taxpayer participates in the activity for more than 500 hours during the year.

2. The taxpayer's participation in the activity constitutes substantially all of the participation by all individuals in the activity, including nonowners.

3. The taxpayer's participation is more than 100 hours during the year, and no other individual, including nonowners, participates more hours than the taxpayer.

4. The activity is a significant participation activity (the taxpayer participates more than 100 hours during the year) and the taxpayer's annual participation in all significant participation activities is more than 500 hours.

5. The taxpayer materially participated in the activity for any five tax years during the ten immediately preceding tax years.

6. If the activity is a personal service activity (one in the fields of health, law, engineering, architecture, accounting, actuarial science, performing arts, consulting, or any other trade or business in which capital is not a material income-producing factor), the taxpayer materially participated in the activity for any three tax years preceding the current year.

7. Based on all the facts and circumstances, the taxpayer participates on a regular, continuous and substantial basis during the year.[27]

There is reciprocity to the application of the material participation tests. If a taxpayer's spouse materially participates in an activity, the taxpayer is also considered to materially participate. In addition, participation of both spouses is combined to determine if the material participation tests are met regardless of whether a joint return is filed.

A close reading of the above tests show that the focus is on the quantity of hours, not the quality of the work performed. Any work performed by the taxpayer is considered participation for the purpose of these tests – unless (1) the work is not customarily done by the owner of an activity and (2) avoidance of PAL rules is a principal purpose.

Taxpayers must be able to substantiate their participation by reasonable means according to Treas. Reg. section 1.469-5T(f)(4). Under examination, the Internal Revenue Service tends to focus on contemporaneous documentation of hours spent in an activity in order to determine the level of participation. However, contemporaneous documentation is not required if the taxpayer can reasonably establish their participation by other means. Auditors will consider it difficult for someone who earns a salary reported on a Form W-2 to also have enough time to also spend 500 hours in a separate activity.

Taxpayers commonly use calendars, appointment books, phone records, e-mail logs, and automobile mileage logs to help support the level of participation. Some types of work do not count towards the required number of hours, including:

(1) Investor-type activities (unless the taxpayer is involved in the day-to-day management or operations), such as:

   a. Studying or reviewing financial statements or reports;

   b. Preparing or compiling summaries or analyses for the individual's own use; or

   c. Monitoring finances or operations in a non-managerial capacity.

(2) Work not customarily done by an owner. This is asserted where the work is normally assigned to an employee, but was done by an owner in order to avoid the disallowance of losses under section 469.

(3) Services not integral to operations. The most common example of this limitation is travel time.

Question – Can a limited partner materially participate?

Answer – A limited partner cannot materially participate in an activity unless:[28]

1. the limited partner is also a general partner;

2. the limited partner participates more than 500 hours in the activity;

3. the limited partner materially participated for any five of the ten preceding years; or

4. the activity is a personal service activity and the limited partner participated for any three preceding years.

Note that limited liability company members are generally treated by the IRS as limited partners for the purpose of applying the material participation rules. However, as of this edition, no formal guidance has been issued by the IRS.

Question – How are the PAL rules applied to different types of income?

Answer – Income from a passive activity is divided into passive income and portfolio income. Portfolio income includes interest, dividends, and investment capital gains or losses and is fully reportable by a taxpayer without the application of the PAL rules. This split between passive and portfolio income is not found in most other areas of the tax law such as in the case of foreign income categorization in which most types of portfolio income are considered passive. Congress realized that such a split was necessary in the case of the passive rules to prevent taxpayers from creating passive (portfolio) investment companies whose income could be shielded by other types of passive income.

Passive losses are aggregated and applied against passive income in a given year. If the passive losses exceed the passive income for the year, the excess losses are allocated to the loss activities and are carried forward indefinitely.

Losses from publicly traded partnerships (PTPs) may only be used against income from that specific partnership. No grouping of PTPs is permitted, even if they operate in the same industry, such as oil and gas. As a result, losses from PTPs generally accumulate over time. Unless the PTP passes income through to the investors, a PTP may need to be disposed of in order to release the suspended losses and be used to offset other income.

Question – How are rental real estate activities treated under the PAL rules?

Answer – A rental real estate activity with active participation is separately categorized under the PAL rules. Up to $25,000 of losses from such activities (which are limited to those activities of natural persons) with active participation may be used to offset other nonpassive income.[29] This special loss allowance begins to be phased-out for joint filers with modified adjusted gross income (MAGI) over $100,000. The allowance is reduced 50 cents for every dollar of MAGI over $100,000.[30] Therefore, the special loss allowance is fully phased-out for married taxpayers in excess of $150,000.

Active participation is determined separately from material participation. In order to be considered an active participant, a taxpayer must make management decisions, such as approving tenants or setting policies, or arrange or perform other services, such as making repairs.[31] In addition, an active participant must be a 10 percent owner of the activity, by value, not including interests as a limited partner.[32]

Certain rental real estate activities are not considered as such under the PAL rules. These include rentals in which:[33]

1. the average period of use is seven days or less (e.g. a motel);

2. the average period of use is thirty days or less and significant personal services are provided (e.g. a hotel);

3. extraordinary personal services are provided;

4. rentals are incidental to nonrental activity;

5. the property is available for nonexclusive use (e.g. a golf course); or

6. the property is provided for use in a related entity with a nonrental activity.

Example: Roger owns a vacation property in New Jersey and rents it to individuals and families for an average of less than seven days (see number 1 above). As a result, the property is not automatically treated as a passive activity because it is not classified as a real estate activity. If Roger meets one or more of the material participation tests, the income or loss from the rental of the vacation property will not be treated as passive. Any loss from the rental will be fully deductible against his ordinary income.

Note, however, that since the activity is not treated as a rental real estate activity, the special "active" loss allowance described above is not available. Therefore, if Roger is not able to substantiate his material participation in the property, the loss would be passive with no offset from the special loss allowance. Ordinarily, this will occur in situations where the owner of

the property uses a management company for the day-to-day rental operations. Since most of the material participation tests are based on hours devoted to the activity, the delegation of the management of the property will make it difficult, if not impossible, for a taxpayer to materially participate in such an activity.

Question – When do suspended losses for an activity become fully deductible?

Answer – Suspended losses of a passive activity become fully deductible in a complete, fully taxable disposition of the activity to an unrelated party.[34] The activity may also be considered as fully disposed if "substantially all" of the assets held by the activity are disposed. A discontinuation of operations or the retaining of the underlying assets is insufficient to be treated as a disposition.

Current year income or loss is then combined with the suspended losses of the activity. If the activity has a net loss in the year of disposition, the loss is treated as nonpassive if it exceeds income and gains from other passive activities. If the activity has net income in the year of disposition, the income is treated as passive and may be used to offset losses from other passive activities.

Question – What happens to suspended losses when there is not a complete, fully taxable disposition?

Answer – If an activity is disposed in a nontaxable or tax-deferred event, the suspended losses remain suspended and attach to the newly acquired property.

If an activity is sold through the use of an installment sale, the suspended loss is recognized each year in the same percentage as the gain on the sale.[35]

For dispositions of passive activities by gift, suspended losses are added to the donee's basis of the property. However, if the passive activity is subsequently sold at a loss by the donee, the basis for the loss is the lessor of the donee's basis including the suspended PAL or the fair market value on the date of the gift.[36] The result is that it may be better to dispose of the activity through a taxable transaction rather than by gift.

If a taxpayer dies with suspended PAL losses, the losses may be deducted on the decedent's final income tax return after being reduced by any step-up in the basis of the passive activity property.[37]

Question – In what circumstances are activities that are deemed to be passive recharacterized as nonpassive (NOPA rules)?

Answer –If property is rented to a nonpassive activity (the "self-rental" rules), if property is rented incidental to development activity, if a taxpayer significantly participates in an activity.

A taxpayer may not use net income from a property to offset other passive losses if the property is rented for use in a trade or business in which the taxpayer materially participates. Any income from self-rented property is treated as nonpassive. However, if the self-rented property generates a net loss, the loss is treated as passive since the rental activity would be deemed passive absent any other provisions.[38] Self-rentals, therefore, represent an area in which appropriately grouping the activities may be effective. However, since the regulations state income or loss is determined at each item of property (not necessarily the activity), a grouping that would still otherwise be considered passive, would not be effective for self-rented property purposes. Rental income from a property that which was rented less than twelve months before the disposition, and the taxpayer materially or significantly participated in the performance of services of enhancing the value of the property would be considered as nonpassive.[39]

An activity is considered a significant participation activity for a taxable year if it is a trade or business activity (not a rental activity) and the taxpayer participates in the activity for more than one hundred hours during the year. The income from all significant participation activities would be considered nonpassive to the extent it exceeds significant participation losses.[40]

Question – What are the special rules available to real estate professionals?

Answer – Real estate professionals treat otherwise passive rental real estate activities as nonpassive.[41] This provision, which was introduced in the early-1990s, gives such professionals the ability to convert passive rental real estate losses that they materially

participate in and would otherwise be suspended into nonpassive losses that can be used to offset other sources of income.

In order to qualify as a real estate profession a taxpayer must meet the following requirements:

1. more than 50 percent of the personal services performed by the taxpayer are performed in real property trade or businesses in which the taxpayer materially participates, and

2. the taxpayer must perform more than 750 hours in real property trade or businesses.[42]

A real property trade or business is one that involves real estate in one of the following activities:[43]

1. development;
2. redevelopment;
3. construction;
4. reconstruction;
5. acquisition;
6. conversion;
7. rental;
8. operation;
9. management;
10. leasing; or
11. brokerage.

If a taxpayer meets these qualifications then they can make an election to treat all rental real estate activities as a single activity.[43] By making this affirmative election to combine rental real estate activities, the taxpayer treats all rental real estate interests as a single activity, including those held as a limited partner. Material participation is then determined for the activity as a whole. Absent this election, all rental activities are treated as separate activities and the taxpayer may be saddled with large suspended losses. Once the election to combine the rental real estate activities is made, it is irrevocable unless the facts and circumstances of the taxpayer materially change.

Question – How are losses from former passive activities handled?

Answer – Situations occur in which a taxpayer owns an activity that is properly classified as passive and, at some point in the future, the taxpayer is deemed to materially participate in the activity. Any suspended losses of the activity from the years in which the taxpayer treated the activity as passive are first deducted to the extent the taxpayer recognizes income form the same activity. Any remaining suspended losses from the former passive activity are treated as a normal PAL carryforward and may be used to offset passive income from other activities.

Question – Are there any specific rules for investments in hedge funds?

Answer – Certain taxpayers invest in partnerships that are not treated as a passive activity even though the taxpayer does not materially participate or invested as limited partner. Many hedge fund or other partnership Schedule K-1s report that the income or loss from the activity is neither passive nor portfolio under Treasury Regulation section 1.469-2T(d)(2). A partnership interest carrying this footnote on its Schedule K-1 is identifying the partnership as one that trades in stocks, bonds and securities for its own account (and those of its partners). Losses from such an activity should not be treated as being from a passive activity and, therefore, be deducted in full. Likewise, the income from such an activity cannot be used to offset other passive activity losses.

CHAPTER ENDNOTES

1.   I.R.C. §465(c)(1).
2.   I.R.C. §465(c)(3).
3.   I.R.C. §469(a)(2).
4.   I.R.C. §465(a)(1).
5.   I.R.C. §465(b)(1).
6.   I.R.C. §465(b)(2).
7.   I.R.C. §465(b)(6).
8.   I.R.C. §465(e).
9.   IRS Ann. 84-14, 1984-6 IRB 22.
10. I.R.C. §465(c)(2).
11. I.R.C. §465(c)(2)(B)(i).
12. I.R.C. §465(c)(3)(B).
13. I.R.C. §§469(c)(1)-(2).
14. Treas. Reg. §1.469-4.
15. Treas. Reg. §1.469-4(d)(2).
16. Treas. Reg. §1.469-4(d)(1).
17. Treas. Reg. §1.469-4.
18. Rev. Proc. 2010-13, 2010-4 IRB 329.
19. Treas. Reg. §1.469-11(b)(3)(iv).
20. Treas. Reg. §1.469-4(f).
21. Treas. Reg. §1.469-4(g).
22. Prop. Treas. Reg. §1.465-6(d).
23. Prop. Treas. Reg. §1.465-38.
24. I.R.C. §469(h).
25. Temp. Treas. Reg. §1.469-5T(a).
26. Treas. Reg. §1.469-5; Temp. Treas. Reg. §1.469-5T(a).
27. Temp. Treas. Reg. §1.469-5T(e).
28. I.R.C. §469(i).
29. I.R.C. §469(i)(3)(A).
30. Committee Report P.L. 99-514 (1986).
31. I.R.C. §469(i)(6).
32. Treas. Reg. §1.469-1T(e)(3).
33. I.R.C. §469(g).
34. I.R.C. §469(g)(3).
35. I.R.C. §469(j)(6).
36. I.R.C. §469(g)(2).
37. Treas. Reg. §1.469-2(f)(6).
38. Treas. Reg. §1.469-2(f)(5).
39. Treas. Reg. §1.469-2T(f)(2).
40. I.R.C. §469(c)(7)(A).
41. Treas. Reg. §1.469-9(g)(1).
42. I.R.C. §469(c)(7)(B).
43. I.R.C. §469(c)(7)(C).

MARRIAGE AND DIVORCE

CHAPTER 21

WHAT IS THE MARRIAGE PENALTY?

The "marriage penalty" is the anomaly of a married couple owing more tax than the combined total tax of two single individuals with the same amount of income. Although the marriage penalty manifests itself in many ways, from a historical perspective, for most married taxpayers, the brunt of the penalty is attributable to the fact that tax rate brackets and standard deduction for married couples were far less than twice what they were for single filers. Although since 2001, legislative changes to tax law has provided some relief, higher tax rates for some married couples as well as the phase-out of certain tax benefits at much lower income levels continue to perpetuate the marriage penalty for many taxpayers.

Tax Rates

For lower income taxpayers, one significant change that provided marriage penalty relief was to make the taxable income range of the 10 percent and 15 percent tax brackets for married couples filing jointly exactly twice the amount as the taxable income range of a single filer. For example, for tax year 2014, the 10 percent tax bracket for a married couple filing jointly is taxable income up to $18,150 or twice the taxable income of $9,075 for a single filer in that same tax bracket. Similarly, the 15 percent bracket for a married couple filing jointly is taxable income over $18,150 but not over $73,600 or twice the taxable income range for a single filer of over $9,075 but not over $36,900.[1] Thus, for married taxpayers in those tax brackets, there is no marriage penalty.

However, for married taxpayers in the 25 percent tax bracket and beyond, the marriage penalty becomes increasingly severe. This is because the taxable income ranges of those higher tax brackets for joint filers are far less than double the combined incomes of two single taxpayers. For example, for the 25 percent tax bracket of a single taxpayer, the taxable income range is taxable income over $36,900 but not over $89,350. Thus, two unmarried taxpayers with combined taxable income of up to $178,700 (or $89,350 for each taxpayer) would be in the 25 percent bracket. Conversely, if those same taxpayers were married, the 28 percent tax bracket for joint filers would begin once their combined taxable income exceeds $148,850. As a result, the married couple filing jointly would $29,850 worth of income that was taxed at 28 percent. Where the nonmarried coupe pays $7,463 of tax on that portion of their incomes (25 percent of $29,850), the married couple pays $8,358 (28 percent of $29,850). See Figure 21.1.

Finally, the most severe manifestation of the marriage penalty occurs with regard to the 39.6 percent tax bracket. To this point, for tax year 2014, the 39.6 percent tax bracket for a single filer begins with taxable income over $406,750 and for joint filers with taxable income over $457,600. So, as illustrated by Figure 21.2, two unmarried individuals with combined taxable income of $813,500 ($406,750 each) would not be in the 39.6 percent tax bracket. On the other hand, for joint filers with the same combined taxable income, however, a total of $355,900 of the $813,500 would be taxed at the 39.6 percent bracket ($813,500 minus $457,600 the beginning of the 39.6 percent tax bracket for joint filers). As a result, in this instance, there would be a marriage penalty of $32,661 of tax (the difference between $268,899, the tax for joint filers and $236,238, the combined tax of two single filers).

Phase-outs

Simply stated, a "phase-out" occurs when a tax benefit is gradually reduced until it is significantly

Figure 21.1

"MARRIAGE PENALTY" EXAMPLE 1			
Single Taxpayers			
	Taxable Income	Highest Tax Bracket	Tax
Taxpayer A	$89,350	25%	$18,194
Taxpayer B	$89,350	25%	$18,194
Combined	$178,700	25%	$36,388
Married Taxpayers			
	Taxable Income	Highest Tax Bracket	Tax
Taxpayer A	$89,350	28%	N/A
Taxpayer B	$89,350	28%	N/A
Combined	$178,700	28%	$37,283

Figure 21.2

"MARRIAGE PENALTY" EXAMPLE 2			
Single Taxpayers			
	Taxable Income	Highest Tax Bracket	Tax
Taxpayer A	$406.750	35%	$118,119
Taxpayer B	$406,750	35%	$118,119
Combined	$813,500	35%	$236,238
Married Taxpayers			
	Taxable Income	Highest Tax Bracket	Tax
Taxpayer A	$406,750	39.6%	N/A
Taxpayer B	$406,750	39.6%	N/A
Combined	$813,500	39.6%	$268,899

decreased and, in some instances, totally eliminated. For example, tax deductions such as itemized deductions and exemptions Phase-out incrementally to the extent that a taxpayer's adjusted gross income exceeds an "applicable amount."

Phase-out of Itemized Deductions

In tax year 2014, for single taxpayers, the phase-out of certain itemized deductions begins with adjusted gross income in excess of the "applicable amount" of $254,200 as compared to adjusted gross income in excess of $305,050 for joint filers.[2] The phase-out reduces the amount of those itemized deductions by the lesser of 3 percent of the excess of adjusted gross income over the applicable amount or 80 percent of those deductions.[3]

Two unmarried individuals with a combined adjusted gross income of $508,400 ($254,200 each) would not be subject to any reduction of itemized deductions because neither taxpayer's adjusted gross income exceeded the applicable amount. On the other hand, if the same taxpayers were married, their combined adjusted gross income of $508,400 would exceed the applicable amount for joint filers of $305,050 by $203,350. As a result, in contrast to the single taxpayers who would suffer no loss of itemized deductions, the married couple could potentially lose up to $6,100 of itemized deductions (three percent of $203,350).

Phase-out of Exemptions

Similar to the phase-out of itemized deductions, the marriage penalty also affects the phase-out of personal and dependency exemptions. For tax year 2014, the exemption amount is $3,950. The exemption is subject to being reduced by 2 percent for each $2,500 (or part thereof) above a certain threshold amount of adjusted gross income.[4] For a single filer, the threshold is adjusted gross income in excess of $254,200 as compared to $305,050 for a married joint filers.[5]

For example, if two single filers each have adjusted gross income of $200,000, neither taxpayer would be subject to a phase-out because his or her adjusted gross income is below the threshold of $254,200. On the other hand, if those same taxpayers were married and filed a joint return, the aggregate amount of their adjusted gross incomes would exceed the $305,050 threshold by $94,950 ($400,000 minus $305,050). As a result, the married taxpayers would be subject to a phase-out of approximately 76 percent of the exemption amount claimed.

Figure 21.3 outlines the phase-out ranges for exemptions.[5]

Phase-out of child tax credit. Subject to special qualification rules, there is a child tax credit for every child under the age of seventeen.[5] There is, however, a phase-out of the credit in the amount of $50 for each $1,000 of adjusted gross income over a threshold amount. The threshold amounts are:

- $55,000 of adjusted gross income for married filing separately;

- $75,000 of adjusted gross income for single, head of household and qualifying widow(er); and

- $110,000 of adjusted gross income for joint filers.

Thus, similar to the other phase-outs discussed above, the phase-out of the child credit for joint filers begins at adjusted gross income amounts that are significantly less than twice the amount applicable to single filers. Therefore, the phase-out of this tax benefit for joint filers would occur at relatively low adjusted gross income amounts.

Standard Deduction

For 2014, the basic standard deduction for married taxpayers filing jointly is $12,400 or twice as much as $6,200 the standard deduction for a single taxpayer.[7] Thus,

although the doubling of the standard deduction for joint filers would appear to mitigate the marriage penalty, the accelerated phase-out of itemized deductions (should they itemize rather than take the standard deduction) discussed above exacerbates the marriage penalty.

MARRIAGE BONUS

In spite of the onerous effects of the marriage penalty, there are some positive tax advantages for married couples filing jointly. Figure 21.4 lists some of those tax advantages.

TAX IMPLICATIONS OF SAME-SEX MARRIAGE

As a result of the Supreme Court's decision in *Windsor*,[8] the Federal government must recognize the validity of same-sex marriages in any state in which they are legal. This means that the IRS must apply the tax laws to married same-sex couples in the same way they are applied to heterosexual married couples. In light of the marriage penalty and marriage bonus discussed above, a same-sex couple should take into account the same tax and financial considerations that a heterosexual couple weighs in deciding whether to get married or remain single. Moreover, as discussed below, similar to heterosexual married couples, same-sex married couples should also consider whether it is prudent to file married separately rather than jointly.

Finally, state income tax returns can present significant complications for couples in same-sex marriages. At the time of publication, some states have legally recognize same-sex marriages, and allow a same-sex married couple to file a joint state tax return in the same manner that they file a joint federal return. However, a majority of states have not recognized the legality of same-sex marriages, and do not permit same-sex couples to file joint tax returns.[9] The result is that same-sex couples who work, live, or have property or

Figure 21.3

EXEMPTION PHASE-OUT RANGES[6]		
Filing Status	*Phase-out Beginning AGI*	*AGI for Complete Phase-out*
Married Joint and Surviving Spouse	$305,050	$427,550
Head of Household	$279,650	$402,150
Unmarried Individuals	$254,200	$376,700
Married Separate	$152,525	$213,775

Figure 21.4

"MARRIAGE BONUS"		
Tax Benefit	*Single*	*Married Filing Jointly*
Exclusion of gain from sale of principal residence	Up to $250,000 of gain excluded	Up to $500,000 of gain excluded
Exclusion from gross income of employer provided health insurance	Exclusion does not extend to unmarried partner	Exclusion also includes health insurance provided to employee's spouse
"Averaging" high income of one spouse with lower income of other spouse	Unavailable	By filing a joint return, adding the lower income of one spouse to the higher income of the other spouse causes their combined income to be taxed at a lower overall rate than two unmarried single filers.
Earned Income Credit	A single non-working parent would not qualify for the credit due to the lack of earned income.	A non-working parent who is married to a spouse with low income would likely qualify for the credit.

income interests in those states face a more complicated tax planning problems. Unfortunately, in many of these states, same-sex couples may need to "mock-up" separate federal returns in order to complete the obligatory separate state returns. Advisors should stay abreast of developments in the states in which they operate to plan the best strategies for dealing with these hurdles.

Tax Implications of Filing Married Separately vs. Jointly

Married couples have the option of filing jointly or separately. Subject to the possible application of innocent spouse relief, married individuals are jointly and individually obligated to pay the tax, interest and penalties due on a joint return. The scope of responsibility can extend to an obligation to pay the tax for a spouse who did not properly report his or her income and/or additional assessments of tax made by the IRS. For that reason, a spouse may choose to file a "separate" return if:

- he or she believes the other spouse is not reporting all of his or her income; or

- he or she does not want to be responsible for additional tax attributable to the lack of adequate withholding and/or sufficient estimated payments on the part of the other spouse.

On the flip side, there are many disadvantages inherent if filing married separately. Generally, there are many tax benefits that are either limited or simply not available for married individuals filing separately that

will result in a much higher overall tax than would be owed if filing jointly.

Example: Samantha and Michelle are a married couple. In 2014, Samantha has a net capital loss of $3,000. Michelle, however, has no capital losses. If Samantha and Michelle file jointly, they will be able to deduct the entire $3,000 capital loss even though it is all attributable to Samantha. Conversely, if they file separately, Samantha will be able to deduct only $1,500 of the capital loss on her separate return and Michelle will not be able to deduct any part of the capital loss on her separate return.

Figure 21.5 sets forth a list of many of those limited or disallowed tax benefits:

Example: Asher and Ashley are a married couple. In 2014, the standard deduction for a married couple filing separately is $6,200 for each spouse. Asher has $10,000 of itemized deductions and Ashley has only $500 of itemized deductions. If Asher and Ashley each take the standard deduction, they would deduct $6,200 on their separate returns. On the other hand, if instead of taking the standard deduction, Asher chooses to itemize to take advantage of the $10,000 of itemized deductions. Because Asher itemized, Ashley will not be allowed to claim the $6,200 standard deduction. Instead, Ashley must also itemize limiting her deduction to $500.

Figure 21.5

MARRIED FILING SEPARATELY VS. JOINTLY		
Tax Benefit	*Married Filing Jointly*	*Married Filing Separately*
Exclusion from Income of Employer's Dependent Care Assistance Program	$5,000	$2,500[10]
Deduction for Student Loan Interest or Tuition and Fees Deduction	Available	Not Allowed[11]
Income from Qualified U.S. Savings Bonds Used to Pay Higher Education Costs	Available	Not Allowed[12]
Exclusion of Social Security Benefit Payments	Some or All Excluded Based on Adjusted Gross Income	More Likely to be Taxed Up to 85 percent of the Benefits[13]
Rolling a Traditional IRA into a Roth IRA	Available	Not Allowed[14]
Child Care Credit Retirement Savings Contributions Itemized Deduction Personal Exemptions	Phase-out Do Not Begin Until Reach Higher Adjusted Gross Income Threshold	Phase-out Thresholds Are Half of Those for Married Filing Jointly
Credit for Expenses for Household and Dependent Care Services	Available	Not Allowed[15]
Earned Income Credit	Available	Not Allowed[16]
Standard Deduction or Itemized Deductions	One or the Other is Available. Joint filers generally deduct the higher of itemized deductions or standard deduction.	If one spouse itemizes the other spouse must itemize. See example below.[17]

TAX IMPLICATIONS OF DIVORCE

As discussed below, the tax consequences with regard to child support and alimony are significant. Whereas the payment and receipt of child support from one spouse to the other has no tax consequences; the payor of alimony is entitled to a deduction and the payee must include it in income. There may also be significant tax consequences from the division of property that is part of every divorce decree.

Alimony

As stated above, alimony is deductible by the payor and includible in the gross income of the payee. However, simply labeling a payment as "alimony" does not mean it will be treated that way for tax purposes. Regardless of its designation or by court order or agreement between divorcing spouses, to be treated as alimony for tax purposes, the requirements of Code section 71(b) must be met. Alimony is any payment in cash if:

- The payment is made to or on behalf of a spouse under a divorce or separation decree.

- The divorce decree is silent as to whether the payment as is not includible in gross income or allowable as a deduction. This means that if the parties do not want a payment to be treated as alimony, language in the instrument that states that it is not includible or deductible will negate its tax status as alimony.

- The payee spouse and the payor spouse are not members of the same household at the time of payment.

- There is no liability to make this payment after the death of the payee spouse.

The requirement that alimony be paid in cash means it can only be made in cash, check or money order. Because of this limitation, a transfer of property or services to the payee spouse is not considered an alimony payment for tax purposes.[18]

The significance of payment not being treated as alimony has profound tax consequences.

Example: Pursuant to divorce decree, Asher is to pay Ashley $5,000 a month for five years as alimony. In the event of Ashley's death prior to the end of the term, Asher is obligated to continue to make those payments to Ashley's estate for the remaining duration. Under those circumstances, the payments would not be treated as alimony because Asher's obligation to make those payments continues following Ashley's death. As a result, for none of the years (including the years in which Ashley was alive), Asher will not be entitled to a deduction and Ashley will not be required to include those payments in gross income. Instead, the payments will treated as a non-taxable "property settlement" with no tax consequences to either spouse.[19]

Front Loading Alimony

Because alimony payments are deductible to the payor spouse, there is the temptation on his or her part to "front load" or make excessive payments in the early years of the alimony term to maximize deductions in those years. Then in later years, the payments are much less. So as a negotiation tactic, it is possible that in exchange for a larger up front deduction generated by a substantial initial payment, the payor spouse might agree to pay the payee spouse an overall larger amount of alimony. Conceptually, however, alimony is a mechanism to provide support to a spouse which means the payments should be relatively level over the payment period. So this type of front loading appears to be more like a disguised property settlement than an alimony arrangement.

In order to curb potential abuse, Code section 71(f) essentially recharacterizes "excessive payments" as non-alimony. Generally, excessive payments are the amounts that are disproportionate to amounts that would have been paid as alimony in a relatively level flow. Based on a formula beyond the scope of this chapter, all payments (including excessive payments) made in the first two years of the payment period are treated the same way as any alimony payments (i.e., deduction for payor and income for payee). In the third year, however, the Code reverses the deduction the payor received for the year one and year two excessive payments by requiring he or she to include those payments in gross income. Similarly, the Code reverses the inclusion by the payee spouse of excessive payment he or she included in gross income by allowing a deduction for such payments. By doing so, the adjustment effectively converts the excessive payments into non-taxable non-deductible property settlement payments. Figure 21.6 provides an over-simplified table demonstrating the application of the front loading rules.

Child Support

Unlike alimony, child support is not taxable to the recipient and not deductible by the payor.[20] This is because the paying of child support is the discharge of legal obligation inherent in parenthood. Similarly, the recipient spouse does not have income because he or she is obligated to use the payment for the support of the children. Consequently, with some planning, by increasing the amount of alimony payments and decreasing

Figure 21.6

	FRONT LOADING ALIMONY					
	Year 1	Tax Consequences	Year 2	Tax Consequences	Year 3	Tax Consequences
Payor	Non-Excessive Alimony plus Excessive Alimony	Deduction	Non-Excessive Alimony plus Excessive Alimony	Deduction	Non-Excessive Alimony	Deduction
					Year 1 and Year 2 Excessive Alimony	Include in Gross Income
Payee	Non-Excessive Alimony plus Excessive Alimony	Include in Gross Income	Non-Excessive Alimony plus Excessive Alimony	Include in Gross Income	Non-Excessive Alimony	Include in Gross Income
					Year 1 and Year 2 Excessive Alimony	Deduction

child support payments income can be shifted from a high income payor spouse to a low income payee spouse.

Example: Sam is in the 33 percent tax rate bracket and is willing to pay $9,000 of child support. His spouse, Jennifer, is in the 15 percent tax rate bracket and wants $11,000. Both can stay close to their goals and perhaps reach a compromise by treating the payments as alimony. Because Sam can deduct alimony payments, but not child support, he should be indifferent between paying $9,000 in child support and $13,433 ($9,000/(1-.33)) in alimony. If Jennifer receives $13,433 in alimony, she will have $11,418 ($13,433 x (1-.15)) cash after paying taxes. Reclassifying the payments from child support to alimony accomplishes both spouses' goals.

However, caution should be exercised with regard to alimony payments that appear to be "disguised" as child support. Pursuant to Code section 71(c), if part of a payment otherwise qualifying as alimony would be reduced on the happening of an event specified in the decree relating to a child attaining a certain age, marrying, dying, leaving school or the like, such part would be treated as child support rather than alimony. As these contingencies suggest, a reduction of "alimony" by a certain amount due to a child attaining the age of eighteen is more likely child support wrapped into an alimony payment. Not surprisingly, under those circumstances, the payor would not be entitled to a deduction and the payee would not be required to include in gross income that portion of the payment.

Example: Pursuant to their divorce decree, Asher is pay Ashley $5,000 a month as alimony until their son Ben attains the age of eighteen. At that time, the alimony payment is to be reduced to $4,000 a month. Under those circumstances, only $4,000 of the $5,000 payment would be treated as alimony (deductible by Asher and included in gross income by Ashley). The other $1,000 payment that is to terminate when Ben attains the age eighteen would be treated as child support.

Property Division

The division of property between divorcing spouses has no tax consequences. In other words, just as property flows freely between spouses during marriage without tax consequence, its division pursuant to a divorce is also tax free.[21] In fact, no gain or loss is recognized on the transfer of property from an individual to a spouse or a former spouse if the transfer is incident to the divorce. The transfer of property must occur within one year after the date on which the marriage ceases or must be related to the cessation of the marriage. In addition, the basis of property transferred from one spouse to another does not change.[22]

Example: Pursuant to the divorce decree, Jim transfers stock he owns to his spouse, Mary. The stock has a basis of $60,000 and a fair market value of $100,000. Jim recognizes no gain as a result of the transfer, and Mary takes his $60,000 basis in the property. If Mary sells the stock shortly after the divorce for $101,000, she will have $41,000 ($101,000 - 60,000) of taxable gain.

For negotiation purposes, any division of property should also take into consideration bases. This is because a property's basis as compared to the fair market value will determine whether the sale of the property would generate a taxable gain or loss. As illustrated by the example below, a division of property of equal value may be inequitable if there is a large disparity in the bases of the property.

Example: Asher and Ashley who are in the process of getting divorced have two properties with equal value. There is an antique car that Asher purchased for $100,000 which now has a fair market value of $200,000. In addition, there is a stock portfolio with a basis of $250,000 and a fair market value of $200,000. Although the values of the property are equal, the spouse who receives the antique care would recognize a $100,000 capital gain upon its sale to a third party. Thus, the amount of the after tax proceeds he or she receives would be less than $200,000. On the other hand, the spouse who receives the stock would recognize a $50,000 loss upon its sale to a third party. As a result, that spouse would receive the entire $200,000 tax-free as well as a potentially deductible loss that may reduce other taxable income. So if the parties intended a true equal split of property, they should also have taken into account the tax consequences of a subsequent sale.

Retirement Plans

Retirement plans such as pension and profit-sharing plans, Keogh plans of a self-employed individual, 401(k) plans, SIMPLE plans, and tax-deferred annuities are also available for tax-free division between spouses. Routinely, a negotiated or court ordered portion of a retirement plan is transferred into the name of the other spouse or child through a qualified domestic relations order (QDRO) issued by the family court.[23] QDROs provide an income stream from a qualified retirement plan to a spouse or child recipient.

If the beneficiary of the QDRO is the spouse, he or she is allowed to roll over the QDRO into an IRA.[24] Although distributions are subject to regular income tax, distributions from the QDRO prior to attaining the age of 59½ are not subject to the 10 percent early withdrawal penalty.[25]

Example: Ashley, who is forty years old, receives a distribution from the portion of her ex-spouse's retirement plan that was allocated to her through a QDRO. Although the distribution will be taxable to her, she is not subject to the 10 percent early withdrawal penalty. Thus, the benefits derived from a QDRO are (1) having access to funds allocated to her from in an ex-spouse's retirement account, and (2) receiving distributions without being subject to the 10 percent early withdrawal penalty.

Distributions from QDROs to children are treated differently. For example, distributions to a child are taxed to the participant rather than the child. Consequently, a QDRO to a child may not be rolled over into an IRA established for the child. However, distributions to or for the benefit of a child from the QDRO are not subject to the 10 percent early withdrawal penalty.

Finally, although individual retirement accounts can be divided tax-free, QDROs cannot be used as a division vehicle.[26] Usually, a portion of the IRA designated for the other spouse is rolled over to his or her existing or newly created IRA.

POST-DIVORCE TAX ISSUES

Filing as Head of Household

After a divorce, each spouse becomes a single filer. If there are children, however, it may be possible for one or both spouses to file as a head of household (HOH). Filing as a HOH is usually much more advantageous to filing as a single unmarried individual. In order to qualify, the taxpayer must meet the following requirements:

- be considered unmarried on the last day of the tax year;

- pay more than half of the cost of maintaining the home; and

- have a qualifying person (generally a minor child) live with the taxpayer for more than half the year.[27]

The benefits of filing as HOH include:

- a higher standard deduction (in 2014, the standard deduction for HOH is $9,100 as compared to $6,200 for a single filer);[28]

- an extra personal exemption for each qualifying person;

- lower tax rates (for example, in 2014, the 33 percent tax bracket for HOH begins at $208,800 as compared to $186,350 for a single filer);[29] and

- greater likelihood of qualifying for the earned income credit.

Claiming a Child as a Dependent

Generally, the custodial parent is entitled to the exemption deduction for the child. By virtue of claiming the exemption, there are a whole host of other tax benefits potentially available to the claiming parent including:

- child tax credit;

- HOPE Scholarship credit;

- Lifetime Learning Credit;

- Head of Household filing status (discussed above);

- dependent care credit; and

- Earned Income Credit.

However, the custodial parent can essentially transfer the exemption to the noncustodial spouse by executing a Form 8332, *Release of Claim to Exemption for Child of Divorced or Separated Parents.*[30] If there are two or more children, the divorce decree may specify that one parent has custody of one child and the other parent has custody of the other. Under these circumstances, both parents may be able to file as HOH, claim a dependency exemption for the child as well as other child related tax credits.

PAYMENTS FOR TAX-RELATED DIVORCE LEGAL ADVICE

Each Spouse Pays His or Her Own Legal Fees

Generally, the legal expenses arising from a divorce are nondeductible, personal expenses. An exception to this rule allows a deduction for the portion of the legal fees that relates to tax advice or the production of income that may be part of the legal representation.[31] Tax-related issues encountered during divorce include gain from the property division, the taxability of alimony and child support, and distributions from retirement plans. Production of income issues includes attempts to obtain alimony or distributions from a qualified retirement plan. To take this deduction, however, the attorney must provide documentation that shows the portion of the legal fees related to tax advice or the production of income.

Example: Sue's legal fees from her divorce total $5,000. On his fee statement, there are tax advice related entries of $2,000. Legal fees related to tax advice are deductible as miscellaneous itemized deductions on Schedule A of Form 1040. The utility of the deduction, however, may be limited as miscellaneous itemized deductions are deductible to the extent that all of her miscellaneous itemized deductions exceed 2 percent of her adjusted gross income.

One Spouse Pays Legal Fees of Other Spouse

As stated above, legal fees related to divorce are generally considered to be personal non-deductible expenses. For that reason, one spouse who pays the legal fees of another spouse may not claim a deduction for those fees as a business expense. However, assuming it meets the requirements of Code section 71(b) discussed above, the payment of the fees on behalf of the other spouse could qualify as deductible alimony. In that case, the payee spouse would be required to include such fee payment in gross income. On the other hand,

if the payee spouse is in a relatively low income bracket and the payor spouse is in a relatively high income tax bracket, the spouse who pays the other spouse's legal fees as an alimony payment could receive the benefit of the deduction with little or no tax detriment to the low tax bracket spouse who must include it in income.

FREQUENTLY ASKED QUESTIONS

Question – Why does a provision in the divorce decree that requires the payor spouse to continue to make payments to the payee's estate in the event of his or her death prior to the end of the payment term disqualify its treatment as alimony?

Answer – Alimony is intended to provide spousal support. This means the payments are intended to cover living expenses. Once a spouse dies, the need for support comes to an end. For this reason, payments required after the death of a spouse are more indicative of a property settlement rather than alimony support payments.

Question – How can the IRS ascertain whether the alimony deduction claimed by the payor spouse matches the amount included in the payee spouse's gross income?

Answer – Obviously, a payor spouse would like every payment made to a payee spouse to be deductible alimony. Conversely, a payee spouse would like every payment received to be non-taxable child support or a property settlement. With that temptation, a payor spouse might be inclined to overstate the alimony and a payee spouse might be inclined to understate the alimony. Under those circumstances, from the IRS perspective, this would create an unfavorable mismatch of over deduction and under inclusion. For that reason, it would behoove the IRS to have a means to ascertain that the payee and payor are at least imputing the same amount. This can be accomplished by cross referencing. On line 31a of Form 1040, the payor spouses enters the amount of alimony paid as an above-the-line deduction; and, on line 31b enters the social security number of the payee spouse. So by searching through the tax return data base, the IRS can cross check the return of the payee spouse to ascertain whether the amount deducted on line 31a of the payor's Form 1040 matches the amount of alimony income reported by payee spouse on line 11 of his or her Form 1040.

Question – Do payments to third parties, such as paying off an ex-spouse's credit cards, making the mortgage payment, or paying premiums for life insurance qualify as taxable/deductible alimony?

Answer – Yes, as long as the payments are in cash and on behalf of a spouse, they can be made to third parties instead of directly to the spouse. The key is that the payment cannot be for an item for which the payor has any personal liability. In other words, there is no alimony deduction for:

1. credit card payments with respect to a joint account;

2. mortgage payments on a home the payor owns even if he or she does live there; or

3. premium payments on life insurance if which the payor has an ownership interest in the policy.

Question – Should spouses who file separately coordinate their returns before filing?

Answer – Yes. Although in most instances married couples will pay less overall tax filing jointly, there are a number of couples who file separately. The reason may be lack of trust or a desire not to be responsible for the other spouse's tax deficiency. Or it can be that the couple just does not get along.

Example: The standard deduction for each spouse is $6,200. However, if one spouse itemizes the other spouse must also itemize. So if spouse A has $11,000 of itemized deductions and itemizes and spouse B has only $1,500 of itemized deductions, he or she must also itemize. So in this case, spouse B's deduction shrinks from $6,200 to $1,500.

What if spouse B does not know that spouse A is itemizing or is unaware that if one spouse itemizes the other must as well? If in that case, spouse B claims the $6,200 standard deduction, if could result in an unwelcomed and unexpected notice from the IRS disallowing the standard deduction.

Also, if the spouses intend to split certain itemized deductions, each should be aware of what the other spouse intends to claim. The most common item is likely to be mortgage interest. It would be prudent for each spouse to include a statement with

their returns indicating how much of the mortgage interest he or she is claiming of the total amount. However, in spite of this precaution, if the Form 1098 lists one spouse as the payor, it is certainly possible that the IRS will send the other spouse a notice proposing to disallow the mortgage interest deduction claimed on his or her return.

The bottom line is that married spouses who file separately may have a contentious relationship. That relationship will probably get worse if the return filed by one spouse causes IRS grief for the other spouse. Therefore, coordinating returns before filling is highly recommended.

CHAPTER ENDNOTES

1. Rev. Proc. 2013-35, 2013-47 IRB 537.
2. Rev. Proc. 2013-35, 2013-47 IRB 537.
3. I.R.C. §68(a).
4. I.R.C. §24(a).
5. Rev. Proc. 2013-35, 2013-47 IRB 537.
6. Rev. Proc. 2013-35, 2013-47 IRB 537.
7. Rev. Proc. 2013-35, 2013-47 IRB 537.
8. *Windsor v. United States*, 113 S. Ct. 2884 (2013).
9. This situation is currently the subject of litigation in nearly every state that does not recognize same-sex marriages. The results of the litigation will almost certainly have an impact on tax planning issues for couples who are obligated to file returns in those states.
10. I.R.C. §129(a)(2).
11. I.R.C. §222(d)(4)..
12. I.R.C. §135(d)(3).
13. I.R.C. §86(c)(1)(C).
14. IRS Publication 590.
15. I.R.C. §21(e)(2).
16. I.R.C. §32(d).
17. I.R.C. §63(c)(6).
18. Treas. Reg. §1.71-1T.
19. I.R.C. §1041.
20. I.R.C. §71(c).
21. I.R.C. §1041.
22. I.R.C. §1041(b)(2).
23. I.R.C. §414(p).
24. I.R.C. §402(e)(1)(B).
25. I.R.C. §72(t)(2)(C).
26. I.R.C. §408(d)(6).
27. I.R.C. §2(b).
28. Rev. Proc. 2013-35, 2013-47 IRB 537.
29. Rev. Proc. 2013-35, 2013-47 IRB 537.
30. I.R.C. §152(e)(2).
31. I.R.C. §212.

INCOME IN RESPECT OF A DECEDENT AND RELATED DEDUCTIONS

CHAPTER 22

INTRODUCTION

Just as no good deed goes unpunished, essentially no taxable income goes untaxed. Even death does not stop the inevitability of income taxes. "Income in Respect of a Decedent" (IRD) is the device the Internal Revenue Code uses to tax income earned by an individual prior to his/her death, but received by someone else at a later time.

Example: Sam Stone was a long-time agent for XYZ Insurance Company. Just weeks before his death, Sam had closed one of the largest sales of his career, earning him a first year commission of $50,000. The commission was paid to Sam's estate two months after he died. Sam was a cash basis taxpayer (as are most individuals). Consequently, the commission was not includable in Sam's final lifetime income tax return. But under the IRD rules,[1] the commission is taxable income to his estate upon receipt.

Consistent with the requirement that IRD be included in income by the post-death recipient, allowable expenses incurred but not deductible on the final life time return may be deducted by the ultimate payor.[2] These expenses (or losses) are commonly referred to as "Deductions in Respect of a Decedent" (DRD).

Example: In earning the $50,000 commission, Sam incurred $6,000 of business expenses which were not paid prior to his death. These expenses were not deductible by Sam, but can be deducted by his estate when paid.

The inclusion of IRD as taxable income to the ultimate recipient does not remove the value of the right to receive the income from the decedent's estate for federal estate tax purposes. Thus, there is a potential for some double taxation on IRD.

Example: Sam's $50,000 commission, earned but not received by him prior to his death, must be reflected on his estate tax return as a taxable asset (receivable). Similarly, the $6,000 of business expenses incurred by Sam, but not paid before his death, would be an estate tax deductible liability. Consequently, Sam's estate may have to pay both an estate tax and an income tax on the same net $44,000.

DEDUCTION FOR INCOME IN RESPECT OF A DECEDENT

To mitigate the double taxation on IRD, the law does allow a deduction by the person who pays the income taxes on the IRD to the extent of the estate taxes attributable to that income.[3] If the estate is not large enough to be subject to an estate tax, there is obviously no deduction permitted on the income tax return of the recipient. If the estate does pay a federal estate tax, only a proportionate amount of the estate tax is deductible when the income is subject to income taxes.

Example: Of the federal estate tax paid by Sam's estate, $19,800 was attributable to the commission receivable, net of related unpaid business expenses. The income tax return of the estate, for the year in which the commission was

223

received and the expenses were paid, would reflect the $44,000 of net commission income and the $19,800 deduction for estate taxes paid on that income.

There is some logic in the "double" taxation of IRD. If, in our example, Sam had received the commission income prior to his death, he would have paid the income taxes. But only the net after tax amount of the commission, what Sam had left after paying his income taxes, would be included in his taxable estate. The income tax deduction allowed for IRD subject to estate tax is intended to yield the same net tax result. But, the equality is not always there.

Example: Assume the marginal estate tax bracket imposed on Sam's estate was 45 percent, the marginal income tax bracket for Sam was 28 percent, and the marginal income tax rate for the estate was 35 percent.

If Sam had received the commission and paid the expenses before dying, the income tax would have been $12,320 (28 percent of $44,000). Only $31,680 would have been included in his estate ($44,000 net commission - $12,320 income tax). The estate tax on the net $31,680 would have been $14,256 (45 percent of $31,680). The combined income and estate taxes would have been $26,576, leaving $17,424 net to the estate.

If Sam died before the commission/IRD was received and the related business expenses were paid, the estate tax would have been $19,800 (45 percent of $44,000). The estate would pay an income tax of $8,470 (35 percent of $24,200, representing $44,000 of net commission income less a $19,800 deduction for estate taxes on the IRD). The combined income and estate taxes would have been $28,270, leaving $15,730 net to the estate.

If Sam and the estate were both in the 35 percent marginal income tax bracket, the net to the estate should normally be the same, whether the income tax or the estate tax is paid first. But in addition to income tax rate differentials, other factors, such as the calculation of the estate taxes attributable to the IRD eligible for the deduction or limitations on itemized deductions, may lead to unexpected results.

The increase in the estate tax exclusion amount ($5,340,000 per person in 2014), together with the "portability" of the unused exclusion amount from a deceased spouse to a surviving spouse, has substantially limited the double tax (estate tax and income tax) on IRD by eliminating the estate tax implications for most individuals. However, a decedent's estate or beneficiaries must still recognize and pay income taxes on the decedent's IRD.

IRD DEFINED

Income in respect of a decedent (IRD) is not specifically defined in the Internal Revenue Code. But IRD is generally considered to be income earned by an individual prior to death, which the decedent was entitled to receive at death, but was not included in his/her final lifetime income tax return under his regular method of accounting.[4]

Since most individuals are cash basis taxpayers, the IRD rules will generally apply when cash or property earned by the decedent is received by the decedent's estate or other beneficiaries. Since IRD in essence represents all amounts that would have been taxed to the decedent if it was received prior to his death, IRD generally includes:

1. Unreceived balance of accrued income of a cash basis individual as of date of death,

2. Income which become receivable or accrues solely by reason of the decedent's death by an accrual basis taxpayer, and

3. Income to which the decedent taxpayer had a contingent claim at the time of his death.

Common examples of income which may fall within the "trap" of IRD include:

1. Salary, bonuses, commissions, and payments for work in progress earned but not received by a cash basis taxpayer prior to death,

2. Interest or dividends earned but not received by a cash basis taxpayer prior to death, including U.S. Treasury EE Savings Bonds,

3. Zero-basis accounts receivable,

4. Qualified retirement plan balances as of date of death, including pension, profit sharing, 401(k)

and 403(b) plans, and individual retirement accounts (IRAs),

5. Deferred gain from installment sales,

6. Unrealized appreciation in employee stock options exercised by decedent's estate or beneficiaries, and

7. Income from certain pass-through entities.

DOUBLE TAXATION OF IRD

As noted above, the IRD income subject to income taxes to the ultimate recipient is not excluded from the federal taxable estate of the decedent. It may also be subject to generation-skipping transfer (GST) tax. The estate and GST taxes are imposed on the value of the receivable at the date of death (or alternate valuation date). The income taxability is due to the denial of a basis step up of the unrealized income receivable.[5] Since the decedent had a zero basis in these income receivable items, the zero basis carries over to the recipient. The result is taxable income when the cash or property is received.

WHO PAYS THE TAX ON IRD?

The usual recipients of income which may be treated as IRD include:

1. Decedent's probate estate,

2. Intervivos trust – Trust established by decedent during his lifetime to hold assets during lifetime and to receive assets (including the right to income) after death. In effect, such an intervivos trust takes the place of the decedent's probate estate with respect to the assets and income it holds or receives,

3. A testamentary trust – Trust established under the terms of the decedent's will,

4. An individual beneficiary of the probate estate or intervivos or testamentary trust that acquires the right to the IRD before payment was made,

5. A named beneficiary of a qualified retirement plan or IRA, and

6. A person who obtains the right to income by "operation of law" – For example, if an individual was the joint owner with right of survivorship in a Series EE bond, by operation of the joint tenancy laws, he would own the entire bond at the decedent's death. All of the bond interest earned, but not received by the decedent prior to death would be taxable to the joint owner upon receipt.

In summary, here is how the IRD rules would apply to the different types of recipients:

Probate Estate – If the decedent's probate estate obtains the right to receive the decedent's IRD under the terms of the will—or applicable probate laws if there is no will—the estate will report the income in the year received. Note that estates have the flexibility of choosing the end of their taxable year during the year following the date of death. This year end option for the estate can provide income tax planning opportunities in many cases.

Example: Joe Miller died on November 28, 2013. In December 2013 his estate received a $20,000 bonus check from Joe's employer for services performed prior to his death. The $20,000 is IRD taxable to the estate. If the estate choses a December year end, the $10,000 is taxable in 2013. However, if the estate elects a November 31 year end, there would be minimal income taxable to the estate in its first taxable year (two days in the month of November, 2013) and the $20,000 bonus would not be taxable until the year ended November 30, 2014 (subject to withholding requirements on the bonus).

Distributee from Probate Estate – If the right to receive the IRD is distributed by the estate to another person (individual, trust, etc.) in satisfaction of an inheritance, bequest, or devise, the distributee steps in the shoes of the estate and is taxable upon receipt of the IRD funds.[6]

Recipient of IRD upon death of successor-in-interest – If an individual receives a transfer of IRD as an inheritance or bequest, no income tax is due until cash or property is received. What if that beneficiary dies prior to the receipt of the IRD payment? The IRD will retain its tax treatment, with no income recognition until the ultimate receipt of cash or property, as long as

1. The right to receive the IRD was acquired from the original decedent by a bequest, devise, or inheritance, and

2. The amount of gross income in respect to the original decedent was never included in computing taxable income of the original decedent or first successor.[7]

Person acquiring right to IRD by reason of decedent's death (e.g., named beneficiary of an IRA) – The IRD is taxable to the recipient upon receipt of the cash or property.[8]

Person receiving IRD in satisfaction of a pecuniary (fixed-dollar amount) bequest – Income recognition is accelerated to the time of the pecuniary bequest, even if the IRD itself is not yet received. The transferor recognizes income based on the present value of the IRD, in other words the actuarial value of the right to receive future income, as of the time of the transfer. The transferee would increase his basis in the receivable by the amount of income recognized by the transferor.[9] But the income recognized by the transferor, and consequently the basis increase to the transferee, is reduced by any distribution deduction allowed by the estate or trust transferor with respect to the distributed IRD.

Example: Harry Henshaw was a beneficiary of the estate of his uncle, Melvin. Under Melvin's will Harry was left a specific bequest of $10,000. At his death, Melvin was entitled to a $10,000 commission which was payable within six months of Melvin's death. The commission was IRD. Harry, who worked for the same company as his uncle, agreed to accept a distribution of the $10,000 commission receivable in fulfillment of his pecuniary bequest. The parties agreed that $9,750 was the present value of the future receivable.

Upon transferring the commission receivable to Harry, the estate was required to recognize $9,750 of ordinary income. Since the $10,000 bequest to Harry was a fixed and determinable amount as of the date of Harry's death, the transfer of the IRD receivable is considered

a specific distribution of principal under the terms of the will, and would not give rise to an allowable distribution deduction for the estate. If the estate was subject to federal estate tax, an income tax deduction would be permitted on the income tax return of the estate for the estate taxes attributable to the $9,750 of IRD, in the year the income was recognized.

Harry would recognize no income upon the receipt of the IRD receivable and would be entitled to a basis adjustment for the $9,750 income recognized by the estate Harry would have $250 of taxable income upon receiving the $10,000 commission, since he would only have a $9,750 basis in the receivable.

If an estate or trust transfers IRD to a nonspecific or non-residuary legatee, for any reason other than as a consequence of the decedent's death, the transferor entity must recognize the IRD as income at the time of the transfer, based on the fair market value (FMV) of the right to the income as of the date of the transfer plus any amount received by the estate or trust in excess of the FMV of the transferred IRD.[10] For this purpose a transfer would include a:

1. Sale or exchange,

2. Gift, and

3. Other disposition, including the satisfaction of an installment obligation having IRD, at less than FMV.

Example: At the time of his death, Joe Moran held an outstanding receivable for commissions earned of $10,000. The estate, needing funds to pay certain debts of the decedent, sold the receivable to Joe's partner, Jake, for $9,500. The estate must recognize $9,500 of income upon the sale of the receivable to Jake.

NOTE – It is clear under Code Section 691 that IRD is not recognized as taxable income until the income is actually or constructively received in the form of cash or property. In effect, IRD is always cash basis income, even to an otherwise accrual basis taxpayer.

CHARACTER OF IRD

Generally, the character of income in the hands of a decedent is retained by the recipient of that income as IRD.[11] Therefore, qualified dividends and long term capital gains retain their character and are subject to a maximum federal tax rate of 23.8 percent (20 percent regular tax plus the Net Investment Income Tax of 3.8 percent). Tax-exempt interest and other forms of income excluded from taxable income if received by the decedent are not IRD and are not taxable to the ultimate recipient.[12] But IRD that would be self employment income if received by the decedent is not self employment income if received by an estate, trust, or beneficiary.[13]

SPECIAL ISSUES OF INCOME COMMONLY SUBJECT TO IRD RULES

Employee Compensation and Business Income

Legal Obligation vs. Voluntary Payment – It is clear under the regulations that if an employee or self employed contractor has a contractual right to receive income at the time of his death, such income will be IRD.[14] The courts have expanded the inclusion of compensation amounts in the definition of IRD to include voluntary payments by an employer to a deceased employee's estate or spouse. The courts have concluded that the amounts paid, even if paid because of a moral obligation or custom or policy of the payor, without legal obligation, are still compensation income which would have been taxable if received by the decedent.[15]

In certain cases the courts have also held that such discretionary payments are IRD, even though they are not taxable assets in the decedent's estate, since the decedent had no enforceable right to receive the payment.[16]

Employee Stock Options – There are two standard forms of employee stock options: (1) Incentive Stock Options (ISOs), and (2) Nonqualified Stock Options (NQSOs). [Note - ISOs may only be granted to employees, while NQSOs may also be granted to non-employee consultants or members of the Board of Directors.] Both types of stock options grant the recipient the right to purchase company stock at a price established at the time the option is granted, with the option price generally measured by the fair market value of the stock at the time of grant. ISOs are eligible for special advantageous tax treatment, if certain requirements are met.

The critical dates applicable to both forms of stock option and the normal tax treatment at those dates can be summarized in Figure 22.1 (See Chapter 26 for a complete discussion of employee stock options.)

Figure 22.1

CRITICAL DATE	NQSOs	ISOs
Grant or issuance of option	Not taxable	Not taxable
Expiration of option unexercised	Not taxable	Not taxable
Exercise of option	Taxable as compensation (ordinary income) to the extent the FMV of stock exceeds the exercise price.	Not subject to regular tax, but results in Alternative Minimum Taxable Income (AMTI) for Alternative Minimum Tax (AMT) purposes to the extent the FMV of stock exceeds exercise price.
Sale of Option shares	Capital gain or loss measured by the difference between FMV at exercise and proceeds of sale. Must hold stock for over one year from exercise to qualify for long term capital gain rates.	Ordinary compensation income if sold within two years from grant of option <u>and</u> one year of exercise. For regular tax purposes, long term capital gain if sold after the 2yr/1yr holding period. Amount of gain is the excess of the proceeds of sale over the exercise price. For AMT purposes, gain or loss on sale equals the difference between FMV at exercise and proceeds of sale.

If the owner of either ISOs or NQSOs dies before the exercise of his options, and the options survive his death, no income is recognized by the decedent with respect to unexercised options. In addition, there is no IRD associated with unexercised options.

But most employee stock options permit a decedent's estate to exercise surviving options within defined periods. (Three months is statutory maximum for ISOs.) The exercise or sale of employee stock options may be subject to IRD treatment, as summarized in Figure 22.2.

Dividend Income

The treatment as IRD of a decedent's dividend income received by his estate or beneficiaries will depend on the interplay of (1) the decedent's date of death, (2) the date of dividend declaration, (3) the dividend record date, and (4) the dividend payment date:

- Decedent dies after the dividends are declared, but before the date of record, ordinary income to recipient, but not IRD.

- Decedent dies after the record date, but before the payment date, IRD to recipient.

- If no record date is fixed, declaration date is used instead of record date. Therefore,

  – If the decedent dies before the declaration date, no IRD, but ordinary income when dividend received.

  – If decedent dies after declaration date (with no fixed record date), but before the payment date, IRD to recipient.

Figure 22.2

CRITICAL DATE	NQSOs	ISOs
Exercise of Option	Taxable as <u>IRD</u> (ordinary income) to the exercising estate or beneficiary to the extent the FMV of stock at <u>date of death</u> exceeds exercise the price. Any additional appreciation between the <u>date of death</u> and the exercise date is ordinary income, but is not IRD.	<u>Not IRD</u> and not subject to regular tax, but results in Alternative Minimum Taxable Income (AMTI) for Alternative Minimum Tax (AMT) purposes to the extent the FMV of stock exceeds the exercise price.
Sale of Option shares – *NQSOs*	<u>No IRD</u> - Capital gain or loss measured by the difference between FMV at exercise and proceeds of sale. Must hold stock for over one year from exercise to qualify for long term capital gain rates.	
Sale of *ISOs* before the end of the 2yr/1yr holding period		Ordinary <u>IRD</u> income, at least in part, if sold within two years from grant of option <u>and</u> one year of exercise. IRD amount is the excess of the FMV at <u>date of death</u> over exercise price. Any additional appreciation between the date of death and the exercise date is ordinary income, but is not IRD.
Sale of *ISOs* after the 2yr/1yr holding period		<u>No IRD</u> - For regular tax purposes, long term capital gain if sold after the 2yr/1yr holding period. Amount of gain is the excess of the proceeds of sale over the exercise price. For AMT purposes, gain or loss on sale equals the difference between FMV at exercise and proceeds of sale.

Interest Income

Original Issue Discount - Since interest income is generally earned or accrued on a daily basis, interest earned but not received by a cash basis taxpayer as of the date of death will be IRD. But the tax code provides for special income tax recognition for so called "original issue discount" bonds and other debt instruments.[17]

The most common example of an OID instrument is a "zero coupon" bond. No interest is paid to the owner of the bond while it is outstanding. Instead, the bond is issued at a "discount," with payment of the full face value of the bond upon maturity. The difference between the discount purchase price and the maturity value is in effect the interest earned, but not payable until the bond is cashed in. For example, a zero coupon bond issued at a price of $800 with a face value of $1,000, is paying $200 of interest at maturity.

The tax law does not permit a cash basis taxpayer to defer the recognition of accrued interest income on OID instruments until maturity. The tax code requires that the taxpayer recognize income as it is earned, on a daily basis, over the life of the bond.[18] In effect, the taxpayer is treated as an accrual basis taxpayer with respect to OID. Consequently, a deceased taxpayer would not have any earned but untaxed income from an OID instrument as of the date of death, and there cannot be any IRD related to that asset.

U.S. Savings Bonds – Although many U. S. Savings bonds, such as Series EE bonds, do not pay interest until the bonds are cashed in, such instruments are not subject to the OID rules of Code Section 1272.[19] A cash basis taxpayer may elect to recognize the income on such bonds as is accrues.[20] Such an election can be made at any time, resulting in income recognition for all interest accrued up to the date of the election in the year of the election. This permits an estate executor to make the election, if advantageous, effective with the final lifetime return of the decedent.

If the election is made by the decedent during his lifetime, or by the executor with respect to the final lifetime return, all interest accrued on the bond would be taxed as earned, and there would be no IRD.

If no election is made, then the estate or other beneficiary would recognize the income after the decedent's death (either when received or upon a post-death accrual election made by the estate or beneficiary that is not applicable back to the final return of the decedent).

To the extent of the interest income that has accrued up to the date of death, the estate or beneficiary will have IRD income. Interest earned on the bond after the date of death would not be IRD, but would be ordinary interest income.

Life Insurance Proceeds and the Transfer for Value Rules

Generally, death benefits from life insurance are not subject to income tax.[21] But a major exception to this tax-free treatment is the "transfer for value" rules.[22] The following is a simple example of the application of the transfer for value rules.

Example: Ninety-five year old Mabel Jacobs owned a $500,000 life insurance policy on her life with a cash value of $275,000. Needing cash to pay medical bills, and trying to maximize the cash she could receive, Mabel sold the insurance policy to her friend, Sally Jones, for $300,000. Over the years Mabel had paid insurance premiums on the policy totaling $260,000. Mabel would therefore recognize $40,000 of ordinary income upon the sale of the policy to Sally ($300,000 sale proceeds - $260,000 basis).

Unfortunately, Mabel died two months after the sale. Sally had not paid any additional insurance premiums after the purchase of the policy. Upon receiving the $500,000 of death benefits, Sally would be required to recognize $200,000 of taxable income, resulting from the application of the transfer for value rules ($500,000 death benefit - $300,000 purchase price of the policy). The transfer for value rules would subject the death benefit to income tax because ownership of the policy had been transferred to Sally for valuable consideration ($300,000 purchase price), and none of the exceptions to the transfer for value rules apply.

The IRD rules come into play if the purchaser of a life insurance policy, which is subject to the transfer for value rules, dies before the insured's death.

Example: Assume in the above example, Sally died one month after purchasing the life insurance policy from Mabel, and Mabel died one month later. Sally's estate would be entitled to receive the $500,000 death benefit upon Mabel's death. Assume further that the life insurance policy on Mabel's life was valued at $350,000 upon Sally's unexpected death. Standing in Sally's place, the estate would be required to recognize the $200,000 of taxable income resulting from the application of the transfer for value rules. But $50,000 of the income would be treated as IRD ($350,000 value of the policy at Sally's death - $300,000 purchase price). The remaining income would be taxable to the estate, but not as IRD.

Income from Pass-through Entities

A pass-through entity is a legal organization which "passes through" all or part of its taxable income to other persons who are either owners or beneficiaries of the entity. The typical forms of pass-through entities are partnerships, S Corporations, Limited Liability Companies (typically taxed as partnerships), estates, and trusts. The tax treatment of a decedent's estate with respect to income earned within such an entity and when the income is passed through to the estate or beneficiary, will vary among the entity types.

Partnerships – If an individual is a partner in a partnership as of his date of death, his interest in the partnership effectively terminates on that date. Accordingly, a partnership K-1 will be issued in the name of the decedent for the portion of the taxable year ending on that date, to be included in the final lifetime return, and the estate, or other successor in interest, will receive a separate K-1 for the income earned for the balance of the year. There is no IRD with respect to these amounts.

When a successor in interest to a decedent receives distributions in liquidation of that partner's interest in the partnership, the nature of that distribution will dictate whether there is any IRD.

1. If the amount received is considered a distributive share of the partnership income,[23] the recipient beneficiary, estate, or trust would have IRD.[24] For example, this treatment applies if a partnership agreement states that upon the death of a partner,

the estate or beneficiaries of the deceased are entitled to what would have been that partner's share of income for the next three years.

2. If the estate or beneficiary receives a guaranteed payment[25] due to but not paid to the decedent prior to death, the recipient would have IRD.[26]

3. Payments in exchange for the deceased partner's interest in partnership property,[27] no IRD results unless:

    a. The payments are attributable to certain so-called "hot assets," such as unrealized receivables, or

    b. The payments are in exchange for goodwill, unless the partnership agreement provides for such payments, but only if:

    i. Capital is not a material income-producing factor (e.g., a law firm partnership or other personal service partnership), and

    ii. The deceased partner was a general partner.[28]

When the estate or beneficiary receives payments from the sale of the decedent's partnership interest (rather than a distribution from the partnership), IRD is recognized to the extent of the partner's share of hot assets, including unrealized receivables and inventory.[29]

The fair market value of the partnership interest as of the date of death, and consequently the successor's basis, must be reduced by the amount treated as IRD.

S Corporations – The death of a shareholder of an S Corp terminates that individual's interest in the entity. The S Corporation will issue a K-1 in the name of the decedent representing his share of the company's income up to the date of death. The estate or other successor in interest will receive a K-1 for the balance of the year.

There is no IRD with respect to the amounts reflected on the K-1s. However a person obtaining a deceased shareholder's stock in an S Corporation must recognize as IRD the deceased shareholder's share of items which would have been IRD if such items were obtained directly from the decedent.[30] For example, unrealized receivables of a cash basis S Corporation will result in IRD to the person acquiring the stock just as if that person had obtained the receivables directly.

Estates and Trusts – In the year of his death, an individual beneficiary of an estate or trust only recognizes income from the estate or trust to the extent income distributions are actually received by him. This is so even if the trust agreement requires all income to be distributed. To the extent income required to be distributed is not distributed until after the decedent's death, the ultimate recipient (successor in interest) must treat such income as IRD.[31]

Retirement Plan Distributions

Generally, all amounts received by an estate or beneficiary with respect to a decedent's qualified retirement plans are treated as IRD, except to the extent of contributions made to the plans of after-tax dollars. Such retirement plans would include employer or union pension and profit sharing plans, 401(k) and 403(b) plans, self-employed Keogh plans, and individual retirement accounts (IRAs).[32]

The *unrealized appreciation in employer securities* held in a retirement plan that are distributed as a lump sum, either to the original owner of the retirement account or to his beneficiaries after death, are eligible for special tax treatment. Only the cost basis of the securities to the plan (the value of the securities as of the date placed in the account), plus the value of other assets or amounts received, is taxable at the time of distribution. Any appreciation in the employer securities after they are contributed to the plan is not taxed until the securities are sold or otherwise disposed of by the distributee.

If the employer securities are distributed to the beneficiaries of an estate, the unrealized appreciation as of the date of death is IRD to the beneficiary when the securities are sold. Any appreciation from the date of death to the date of distribution would be treated as capital gain when the securities are sold, and eligible for long term treatment at a 23.8 percent maximum rate (20 percent regular tax plus the Net Investment Income Tax of 3.8 percent) if the securities are held for more than one year from distribution from the plan.

DEDUCTIONS IN RESPECT OF A DECEDENT

When an individual dies with unpaid expenses which would have been deductible by him if paid before death,

such expenses are allowed by the successor in interest (estate or beneficiary) who pays those expenses of the decedent. The allowed deductions are called "deductions in respect of a decedent" (DRD).[33]

Just as IRD may be subject to a double tax (income tax and federal estate tax), DRD expenses provide a potential for a double deduction. In addition, DRD expenses are netted against IRD in computing the income tax deduction for estate taxes paid on IRD.

The expenses that may be deducted as DRD are specifically listed in Code Section 691(b). These expenses include:

1. Ordinary and necessary business expenses,[34]
2. Interest expense,[35]
3. Taxes,[36]
4. Investment expenses,[37] and
5. Depletion.[38]

DRD expenses are generally deductible in the year the expenses are paid. Consequently, the cash method of accounting applies to DRD (as it does to IRD), regardless of the accounting method of the payor. If a decedent's property is passed to the estate or beneficiary subject to a liability that represent DRD, the recipient of the property is entitled to the DRD deduction in the year the liability is paid.[39] The payor does not need to receive any IRD related to the property to claim the DRD deduction.

HOW IT IS DONE

When IRD is received, and therefore subject to income tax by the recipient, the taxpayer is allowed a deduction for any federal estate taxes attributable to the IRD recognized in that year.[40] This deduction may only be claimed by the taxpayer who pays the income tax on the IRD, even if some other taxpayer is responsible for the estate tax.

In computing the allowable deduction for estate taxes, the amount of IRD is reduced by any DRD deductions.

The amount of Code Section 691(c) deduction for estate taxes paid is computed by calculating the estate tax both "with and without" the IRD.

Example: Murray Lang died with a significant taxable estate. Included in the value of the estate was a $50,000 bonus receivable. The bonus, which was IRD, was collected by his son, Ron. The total federal estate tax paid by Murray's estate was $125,000. To compute the section 691(c) deduction, the estate tax was recomputed without the $50,000 bonus receivable. With a marginal estate tax bracket of 40 percent applicable to the entire $50,000 bonus, the recomputed estate tax was only $105,000, a difference of $20,000. The section 691(c) deduction on Ron's income tax return in the year he received the $50,000 would be $20,000.

Individuals entitled to claim the section 691(c) deduction must include the amount as an "Other Miscellaneous Deduction" on Schedule A of form 1040. The deduction is not subject to the 2 percent adjusted gross income (AGI) limitation applicable to most other miscellaneous deductions, but is subject to the overall itemized deduction limitation based on a taxpayer's AGI. Of course, if an individual taxpayer does not itemize deductions for a year in which the section 691(c) deduction applies, the deduction will go unused. Therefore, a taxpayer who knows he will have such a deduction should attempt to manage his income and other deductions in such a manner to ensure that the maximum benefit is achieved.

Trusts and estates are also entitled to claim the section 691(c) deduction. If the trust or estate is including an item of IRD in income and it is taxed within that entity, the section 691(c) deduction is a direct offset to the trust or estate's taxable income for that year since such entities do not itemize deductions. But since the IRD is a component of a trust or estate's income, it also becomes part of their "distributable net income," or DNI. If any portion of a trust or estate's DNI is distributed to one or more beneficiaries, some or all of the IRD will be passed out to the beneficiaries. The beneficiaries are then responsible for reporting the distributed portion of the IRD in their income. It logically follows that an section 691(c) deduction also is passed out to the beneficiaries in proportion to the amount of IRD they are required to report.

The deduction for estate taxes is based on the estate taxes attributable to the lesser of (1) the value of the IRD included on the estate tax return, or (2) the amount of the IRD actually collected. Any income received in excess of the value of the IRD does not generate a section 691(c) deduction for estate taxes paid.

Example: At the time of Al Porter's death, the value of his IRA account, as reflected on his estate tax return was $100,000. The IRA was fully funded with pre-tax contributions, so that if Al had withdrawn the funds before dying, it would all be subject to income tax. By the time the account was distributed to his son, Mark, in a lump sum, the value of the IRA was $120,000. Only $100,000 would be treated as IRD, although the entire $120,000 would be taxable to Mark. The section 691(c) deduction for estate taxes paid would be computed using the $100,000 IRD value.

If, by the time the distribution was made to Mark, the value of the IRA account was only $90,000, the section 691(c) deduction would be computed using the $90,000 IRD value.

CHAPTER ENDNOTES

1. I.R.C. §691.
2. I.R.C. §691(b).
3. I.R.C. §691(c).
4. Treas. Reg. §1.691(a)-1(b).
5. I.R.C. §1014(c).
6. Treas. Reg. §1.691(a)-4(b)(3).
7. Treas. Reg. §1.691-(a)-1(c).
8. I.R.C. §691(a)(1).
9. Treas. Reg. §1.1014-4(a)(3).
10. I.R.C. §691(a)(2).
11. I.R.C. §691(a)(3).
12. Treas. Reg. §1.691(a)-1(d).
13. Rev. Rul. 59-162, 1959-1 CB 224.
14. Treas. Reg. §1.691(a)1-(b).
15. See e.g. *Rollert v. Comm'r.*, 752 F.2d 1128 (6th Cir. 1985), aff'g 80 TC 619 (1983).
16. See e.g. *Kramer v. U.S.*, 406 F.2d 1363 (6th Cir. 1969).
17. I.R.C. §1272.
18. I.R.C. §1272(a).
19. I.R.C. §1272(a)(2)(B).
20. I.R.C. §454(a).
21. I.R.C. §101(a)(1).
22. I.R.C. §101(a)(2).

23. I.R.C. §736(a)(1).
24. I.R.C. §753.
25. I.R.C. §736(a)(2).
26. I.R.C. §753.
27. I.R.C. §736(b).
28. I.R.C. §§736(b)(2), 736(b) (3).
29. I.R.C. §751(a)(2).
30. I.R.C. §1367(b)(4).
31. Treas. Reg. §1.662(c)-2.
32. I.R.C. §691(a)(1).
33. I.R.C. §691(b).
34. I.R.C. §162.
35. I.R.C. §163.
36. I.R.C. §164.
37. I.R.C. §212.
38. I.R.C. §611.
39. I.R.C. §691(b)(1)(B).
40. I.R.C. §691(c).

TIMING OF INCOME AND DEDUCTIONS

CHAPTER 23

INTRODUCTION

A person who can control the timing of income and deductions may be able to save taxes or take advantage of the time value of money. The timing of income or deductions is generally done by shifting income or deductions to an earlier year or later year as needed. Some special tax provisions permit the shifting of income or deductions. In other instances, the ability to shift income or deductions is limited. Income and deductions are discussed in some detail in Chapters 3 and 6.

Taxes may be saved when income is shifted to a year in which tax rates are lower. Taxes may also be saved when deductions are shifted to a year in which tax rates are higher. Tax rates may be higher or lower based on changes in tax laws from year to year. They may also be higher or lower based on the amount of the individual's taxable income.

An individual can save taxes by controlling the amount of income or deductions in a year so that certain tax benefits can be achieved. For example, medical deductions are generally limited to the amount of medical expenses in excess of 7.5 percent of adjusted gross income. A person might be able to increase the amount of deductible medical expenses by shifting medical expenses and other deductions into a year while shifting income out of that same year.

If tax rates remain level, the time value of money can be used by accelerating deductions into an earlier year and deferring income into a later year. Paying taxes later rather than sooner allows the taxpayer to invest the deferred taxes and earn additional income. If tax rates are lower later, then taxes may also be saved. If tax rates are higher later, the value of deferring taxes must be weighed against the value of the increased taxes.

WHEN IS THE USE OF SUCH A DEVICE INDICATED?

1. When Congress changes tax rates. If tax rates go up, consider accelerating income and deferring deductions before the changes take full effect. If tax rates go down, consider deferring income and accelerating deductions before the changes take full effect.

2. If the amount of a taxpayer's income fluctuates. Income might fluctuate for a number of reasons or at certain times: because of a loss of a job or a change in jobs, because of the nature of the job (e.g., commissions are not level), because of general economic conditions (e.g., an upturn or a downturn), when a spouse starts or stops working, on account of disability, or at retirement. When income is high in a particular year, consider moving income out of and deductions into that year. When income is low in a particular year, consider moving income into and deductions out of that year.

3. Even if the taxpayer's tax rates stay the same. Consider deferring income and accelerating deductions to take advantage of the time value of money.

4. When tax benefits are dependent on the amount of adjusted gross income. Shifting income or deductions into or out of a year may save the benefit. For example, prior to 2015, a traditional IRA could be converted to a Roth IRA only if adjusted gross income does not exceed $100,000 for the year (see Chapter 30). Also, various tax provisions provide for a phaseout of a tax benefit based on adjusted gross income, such as itemized deductions that are phased out at higher levels of income (see Chapter 4).

5. When the taxpayer has high current income. Retirement plans (see Chapter 30) permit income to be deferred to later in life, possibly when income and tax rates are lower. Installment sales (see Chapter 3) and like-kind exchanges (see Chapter 28) also permit income to be deferred to a later date. To some extent, tax shelters, such as real estate or oil and gas, permit deductions to be accelerated into earlier years.

WHAT ARE THE REQUIREMENTS?

1. A taxpayer who is using the accrual method of accounting (see Chapter 16) generally accrues income and deductions as economic performance occurs. For example, wages are generally treated as taxable when the work for which wages are paid is performed rather than when payment is made. And property taxes may be deductible in the year for which the taxes are owed rather than when paid. The ability to shift income is not as great as for a taxpayer using the cash method of accounting.

2. A taxpayer who is using the cash method of accounting (see Chapter 16) generally recognizes income as it is received and deductions as they are paid. Through control of when income is received or when deductions are paid, some flexibility to shift income or deductions is obtained. Certain taxpayers, including C corporations, partnerships with a C corporation as partner, and tax shelters, cannot use the cash method of accounting.

Accelerating or deferring income or deductions is often simply a matter of moving the income or deduction from one year to the next year, or vice versa. It can be as simple as shifting income or deductions from January of one year to December of the preceding year, or from December of one year to January of the following year. For example, stock could be sold in December 2014 or January 2015, depending on whether the taxpayer would like to include the capital gain in income in 2014 or 2015. Similarly, a year-end bonus could be paid in either December of one year or January of the next year. Real estate taxes or medical expenses could be paid in December 2014 or January 2015, depending on whether the taxpayer would like to take the deduction in 2014 or 2015. Similarly, charitable contributions could be made in either December of one year or January of the next year.

3. The requirements for a number of special provisions for deferring income are discussed elsewhere in this book. These provisions generally provide deferral for a number of years. Retirement plans, including individual retirement accounts and qualified plans, may be used to defer income (see Chapter 30). Installment sales may be used to spread out income from the sale of assets over the years in which payments are received (see Chapter 3). A like-kind exchange of property can be used to postpone recognition of gain until the replacement property is sold (see Chapter 28). Sale of property to a charity in return for a charitable annuity or contribution of appreciated property to a charitable remainder trust can be used to obtain a current income tax charitable deduction while deferring recognition of gain from the property until later years (see Chapter 27). Nonqualified deferred compensation, discussed in *The Tools & Techniques of Employee Benefit and Retirement Planning*, is another way to defer income until a later year. Annuities, discussed in *The Tools & Techniques of Life Insurance Planning*, allow income to be deferred until annuity payments are received.

HOW IT IS DONE

Example 1. Robin expects to be in the 25 percent marginal tax rate bracket in 2014 and 2015. She will pay $2,500 of federal income tax on her $10,000 bonus whether it is paid on December 31, 2014 or January 2, 2015. By taking the bonus in January 2015, she has the use of the money for over a year before she pays tax on the income in April 2016. If she can earn 3 percent after-tax on the $2,500 in tax owed, the present value of the tax if paid in in April 2015 would be $2,481. The present value of the tax if paid in fifteen months in April 2016 would be $2,408. From a time value of money perspective, postponing the tax disbursement on the deferred income is advantageous.

If Robin's tax rate for 2015 will drop to 20 percent, as it might for someone who is retiring, the tax is reduced to $2,000 and the present value of the April 2016 payment is $1,926. Robin benefits from the reduced tax rate as well as the time value of money on the deferral.

On the contrary, if Robin's tax rate will increase to 39.6 percent because of an increase in compensation, the present value of the $3,960 of income tax owed in April 2016 would be $3,814. In this case, Robin should not defer the income to January 2015. The time value of money benefit from postponing the tax payment is less than the additional cost of paying tax at a higher rate.

Example 2. Sam expects to be in the 25 percent marginal tax rate bracket in 2014 and 2015. He will save $5,000 of federal income tax on a $20,000 charitable contribution whether it is paid on December 31, 2014 or January 2, 2015. By making the contribution in December 2014, he reduces his tax in April 2015 and has the use of the tax savings for over a year compared to making the contribution in January 2015. If he can earn 3 percent after-tax on the $5,000 in tax saved, the present value of saving the tax in three months in April 2014 is $4,963. The present value of reducing the tax in fifteen months in April 2016 is $4,816. From a time value of money perspective, accelerating the tax savings from a charitable contribution is advantageous.

If Sam's tax rate for 2015 drops to 20 percent, lowering the tax savings from the contribution to $4,000, the present value of making the charitable contribution in January 2015 and saving taxes in April 2016 drops to $3,853. In other words, the benefit of making the contribution in December 2014 is even greater because the tax savings are received sooner and at a higher marginal tax rate.

On the contrary, if Sam's tax rate will increase to 39.6 percent because of an increase in compensation, the present value of the $7,920 of income tax saved in April 2016 is $7,629. In this case, Sam should make the charitable contribution in January 2015. The additional benefit from saving tax at the higher marginal tax rate exceeds the benefit of making the contribution sooner.

TAX IMPLICATIONS

1. In general, income deferred to a later year reduces taxable income in the earlier year and increases taxable income in the year to which deferred. Income accelerated to an earlier year increases taxable income in such year and reduces taxable income in the later year.

2. In general, deductions accelerated to an earlier year reduce taxable income in such year and increase taxable income in the later year. Deductions deferred to a later year increase taxable income in the earlier year and decrease taxable income in the year to which deferred.

3. Certain tax provisions encourage the deferral of income. These include: annuities, retirement plans, installment sales, like-kind exchanges, and non-qualified deferred compensation.

4. Certain tax provisions encourage the acceleration of deductions. For example, accelerated depreciation is often permitted and a certain amount of otherwise depreciable property placed in service in a trade or business can be expensed in the year of purchase (see Chapter 18).

5. Various tax provisions restrict the acceleration of deductions. For example, prepaid interest or rent generally cannot be deducted until the expense is accrued or incurred. Investment interest expense is not deductible unless there is investment income to offset the deduction (see Chapter 6). Passive losses may not be deducted until there is passive income (see Chapter 20). A taxpayer may deduct losses with respect to certain activities only to the extent the taxpayer is at risk (see Chapter 20). Only a limited amount of net capital losses are deductible in any year; otherwise such losses must be offset by capital gains or carried over to another year (see Chapter 4).

6. The alternative minimum tax should also be considered when shifting income or deductions between years. This is discussed in detail in Chapter 9.

FREQUENTLY ASKED QUESTIONS

Question – What tax rate should be used to evaluate the benefit of deferring income to future years, the effective rate of tax to be paid on income for the year or the marginal rate of tax?

Answer – Either rate can be used, but the marginal tax rate approach is used more frequently. The effective rate of tax is equal to the amount of tax owed divided by the total income received during the year. The marginal rate of tax is the tax rate that will apply to the next dollar of taxable income to be received.

Assume a taxpayer is married with $125,000 of income in 2014. Taxable income after deductions is approximately $100,000. With $100,000 of taxable income, the marginal rate of tax is 25%, but tax owed is approximately $17,400, meaning an effective rate of tax of about 14 percent ($17,400/$125,000).

Marginal tax rates are used more frequently in planning because for a given level of income a planner can quickly project the amount of tax savings. For example, if a taxpayer is in the 25 percent marginal income tax rate bracket and contributes $12,000 to a 401(k) plan, the planner can readily predict that the 401(k) deferral will reduce income tax by $3,000.

The effective rate is useful for comparing the success of tax strategies from one year to the next. In a year a taxpayer contributes to a 401(k) plan, the effective rate of tax will decrease although the marginal rate may not. To illustrate, assume the above taxpayer with $125,000 of income contributed $12,000 of compensation to a 401(k). He would lower his taxable income to $88,000 ($100,000 – $12,000) and reduce his tax to about $14,400. His effective tax rate decreases from about 14 percent to about 11.5 percent ($14,400/125,000), but his marginal rate of tax remains 25 percent.

Question – When calculating the present value of tax savings, what investment rate should be used?

Answer – Excellent question for which there is no single correct answer. The investment rate differs from taxpayer to taxpayer. Conceptually, the taxpayer would use the after-tax rate of return of investments the taxpayer is investing in because the tax savings represents money that may be added to, or at least not withdrawn from, those investments to pay the government. For some investors, this rate may be the rate of return earned on risk-free investments, such as Treasury securities and certificates of deposit. For others, such as the owners of closely held businesses, the rate of return may far exceed investment returns available in the securities markets.

CONVERSION OF INCOME

CHAPTER 24

WHAT IS CONVERSION OF INCOME?

The federal income tax system is based upon two primary classifications of income: (1) ordinary and (2) capital. The technique of converting income from ordinary to capital can allow taxpayers to benefit from the reduced tax rates that capital income enjoys.

Long-term gains on the sale of capital assets have historically been granted preferential treatment in the rate applied to determine a taxpayer's liability. This is true under the current law even after the passage of the American Taxpayer Relief Act of 2012 (ATRA)[1] and the Health Care and Education Reconciliation Act of 2010 (Reconciliation Act of 2010),[2] both of which increased taxes for some taxpayers as of January 1, 2013.

ATRA introduced a new top tax rate for higher-income taxpayers and also a higher tax rate on capital gains for those taxpayers in the top tax bracket. The Reconciliation Act of 2010 added and a new "net investment income tax (NIIT)" on investment income, which includes gain on the sale of certain capital assets for higher-income taxpayers.[3]

Under the current tax law in 2014, the highest ordinary income tax bracket is 39.6 percent. For most taxpayers, long-term capital gains are taxed at the capital gains tax rate of 15 percent (and for lower income taxpayers, the rate may be as low as 0 percent). For those taxpayers in the new 39.6 percent highest income tax bracket, the capital gains rate increased from 15 to 20 percent. Additionally, the NIIT, is 3.8 percent on long-term capital gains (such as on the sale of stock, bonds and mutual funds) for taxpayers who have modified adjusted gross income above certain thresholds (for example, in 2013, the threshold is $200,000 for single taxpayers and $250,000 married taxpayers filing a joint return). For higher-income taxpayers, the higher capital gains tax and the NIIT result in an overall tax rate of 23.8 percent.

Although somewhat diminished by recent tax increases, the preferential treatment for long-term capital gains persists and equates to a 19.6 percent differential in the maximum tax rates between ordinary income and certain capital gain income assuming that the NIIT is neutral regardless on the income classification. The rate differential generates a great incentive for taxpayers to convert ordinary income into long-term capital gain.

However, there are times when proper planning dictates that ordinary, rather than capital, treatment is preferable. For example, due to the long-term capital loss limitations discussed in Chapter 4, there is an incentive for taxpayers to report losses, not as capital losses but, as a direct reduction to their ordinary income. Even if the capital loss limitations do not apply, a capital loss could be worth as little as 15 cents on the dollar for taxpayers not in the highest income tax bracket compared with the 39.6 cents a taxpayer could potentially save if the transaction can properly be reported as an ordinary loss. Overall, taxpayers tend to focus on finding ways to treat gains as long-term capital and losses in a manner that will directly offset ordinary income.

In addition, taxpayers often focus on other ways to have certain forms of income treated in a manner that will result in lower taxation. Under current law, qualifying dividends are taxed at the same preferential rates applicable to long-term capital gains: a reduced rate of 15 percent for most taxpayers and possibly 0 percent for lower income taxpayers in 2014. For higher-income taxpayers, the rate is 20 percent plus the NIIT of 3.8 percent.

The combined rate of 23.8 percent is still below the top tax rate of 39.6 percent. Consequently, it may be beneficial for a taxpayer to ensure that any dividends received will be eligible for treatment as qualifying dividends and taxed at lower rates.

CONVERTING ORDINARY INCOME INTO CAPITAL GAIN INCOME

With long-term capital gains and qualifying dividends being taxed at a rate of 15 percent for most taxpayers and 23.8 percent for higher-income taxpayers, it is easy to identify converting ordinary income into capital gain income as a beneficial tax planning strategy. The question then becomes – How can it be done?

First, start with the understanding that most people will be unable to convert their salary or wages into capital gain. It just does not and cannot happen for most employees.

There are situations, however, in which executives may be able to structure a more complex compensation package that will result – at least partially – in long-term capital gain treatment.

That being said, the following is a list of techniques which will be addressed in this chapter for converting ordinary income to be eligible for long-term capital gains tax rates or maximizing the use of these lower tax rates:

1. Holding securities for the required period to qualify as long-term capital gains;

2. Using retirement plans to hold ordinary income or tax inefficient investments;

3. Converting interest income into qualifying dividends; and

4. Structuring compensation packages.

Holding Securities for the Required Period to Qualify as Long-Term Capital Gains

With capital gains tax rates currently at 15 percent for most taxpayers and 23.8 percent for higher-income earners, the easiest way to take advantage of these favorable tax rates is to ensure that capital assets are held for enough time to qualify for the long-term holding period. As discussed more completely in Chapter 4, Capital Gains and Losses, an asset must be a capital asset to be eligible for potential long-term capital gains treatment. A capital asset is any property except:

1. Inventory;

2. Depreciable or real property used in a taxpayer's trade or business;

3. Specified literary or artistic property;

4. Business accounts or notes receivable;

5. Certain U.S. publications;

6. Any hedging transaction clearly identified as such when acquired, originated, or entered into;

7. Supplies of a type regularly used or consumed by the taxpayer in the ordinary course of a trade or business of the taxpayer; and

8. Certain commodities derivative financial instruments held by a commodities derivatives dealer.[4]

Capital assets that are held for *more* than one year are treated as long-term. Any gain or loss on the sale of a capital asset held for more than one year is then a long-term capital gain or loss.[5] Unfortunately, in the quest for a lower tax rate, many taxpayers forget the inherent financial risks in holding certain capital assets, especially volatile equity investments, too long.

In the late 1990s, the stock prices of many companies (especially internet-based technology companies that had been recently offered to the public) rose dramatically. Many taxpayers saw their wealth on paper soar to levels that they had not ever imagined. It was almost commonplace to see investments double or even quadruple in value in just a matter of months. With a large unrealized gain staring at them in the face and realizing that a tax would need to be paid on the gain when realized and recognized, a large portion of the taxpayers decided to wait until they met the one-year holding period to sell their stock. In early 2000, this would allow taxpayers to receive treatment under the maximum capital gains tax rate of 20 percent, compared to the highest marginal income tax rate of 39.6 percent.

With the bursting of the "Internet Bubble" in the early part of 2000, taxpayers saw their one-time wealth drop precipitously (or in some cases, practically vanish). Instead of generating a large short-term capital gain, on which ordinary income taxes would need to be paid, they often found themselves in a far worse position.

Example: Doug Davis bought 1,000 shares of NuTech, Inc. on April 15, 1999 (the date of its initial public offering) for $15,000. By late-December 1999, NuTech was trading above $95 per share. Since Doug is in the highest tax bracket (39.6 percent), he decides not to sell and recognize the $80,000 gain since the ordinary tax on the gain would wipe out approximately $32,000 of the value, leaving him with a "mere" $63,000. Instead, Doug holds onto the stock into 2000 in order to reach the long-term holding period. The stock price tumbles during March of 2000 and Doug finally sells the stock in May 2000 for $3,000. Doug now has a $12,000 long-term capital loss that can only be used to reduce ordinary income by $3,000 (with the remainder carried forward for future years) unless he has other capital gains to offset. In retrospect, Doug would probably have preferred to keep his "mere" $63,000 after paying a $32,000 tax bill, rather than finishing with only $3,000 of stock proceeds and a $12,000 long-term capital loss.

There is a substantial tax benefit for holding a capital asset with an unrealized gain for the required period, particularly for individuals in higher marginal income tax brackets. However, this benefit must be weighed against the financial risks associated with the (potentially extreme) possible decline in the value of the asset during the time needed to meet the required holding period. This was evidenced once again with the drastic market declines in 2008.

As discussed in Chapter 4, Capital Gains and Losses, taxpayers may also control the taxation of their investment gains and losses by using the specific identification method when selling an investment. When multiple lots of the same asset are purchased, it may be beneficial to the taxpayer to treat something other than the first shares purchased as having been sold, to target shares eligible for long-term capital gains treatment or *non*-long-term capital loss (or ordinary loss) treatment.[6]

Using Retirement Plans to Hold Ordinary Income or Tax Inefficient Investments

Most qualified retirement plans allow for investments to grow on a tax deferred basis until amounts are withdrawn from the plan. Any interest, dividends, capital gains, or other sources of income earned within the retirement plan escape current taxation.[7]

When amounts generated by money that was never taxed are withdrawn from a retirement plan, the amount withdrawn is normally treated as ordinary income, regardless of the type of income that had been earned during the years.[8] For this reason, it is prudent for a taxpayer with an overall portfolio of retirement and non-retirement accounts to hold the income-producing assets within the retirement plan. Conversely, assets that will generate capital gain (or qualifying dividends subject to the 15 percent or 23.8 percent maximum tax rates) typically should be held outside of a retirement plan. By structuring assets in this manner, capital assets that will be eligible for long-term treatment once the holding period requirement is satisfied will enjoy the preferential tax rates and not be subject to ordinary income as retirement plan withdrawals, while income-producing assets (that would have been treated as ordinary income anyway) will continue to be treated as ordinary income when withdrawn from retirement accounts.

Example: Fred Bartons has $100,000 in his traditional individual retirement account (IRA) and $100,000 in a taxable brokerage account. No nondeductible contributions have been made to the traditional IRA. He owns two investments – a bond paying an uncompounded rate of 6 percent interest and a technology stock that increases in value by $10,000 each of the next five years. At the end of five years, Fred withdraws all of the funds from his IRA and sells all of his assets in the taxable brokerage account. His ordinary income tax rate is 35 percent and his capital gains tax rate is 15 percent. By holding the bond inside the IRA and the stock in his taxable account, he has $227,000, an additional $10,000, of wealth after taxes at the end of five years, as compared to holding the stock inside the IRA and the bond in his taxable account and having $217,000. (NOTE: Total taxes are calculated at the end of the period, although, in fact, tax on the bond interest would have been paid year by year; the result is the same in either case because the bond interest is assumed to be non-compounding.)

	IRA – Bond	Taxable – Stock	IRA – Stock	Taxable – Bond
Year 0	$100,000	$100,000	$100,000	$100,000
Year 1	$106,000	$110,000	$110,000	$106,000
Year 2	$112,000	$120,000	$120,000	$112,000
Year 3	$118,000	$130,000	$130,000	$118,000
Year 4	$124,000	$140,000	$140,000	$124,000
Year 5	$130,000	$150,000	$150,000	$130,000
Tax	($45,500)	($7,500)	($52,500)	($10,500)
Net	$84,500	$142,500	$97,500	$119,500
Total		$227,000		$217,000

Retirement plans are also an excellent choice for holding inefficient tax investments, such as many mutual funds. Mutual funds are required to distribute all of their interest and dividend earnings, as well as their recognized capital gains and losses each year. Therefore, unlike holding individual equity investments, mutual fund investors are often unable to control the timing of the recognition of various types of income from their investments. This is particularly applicable for capital gains and losses; an individual investor would likely have recognized interest and dividends paid even if held directly and not within a mutual fund.

This problem regarding the inability to control recognition of gains may be exacerbated if the mutual fund already has "nested" capital gains when acquired (capital gains recognized and pending distribution before the taxpayer purchases the fund). In this case, gains will be distributed to the taxpayer and consequently recognized, even though they are attributable to increases in the value of investments held before the taxpayer even owned the asset! On the other hand, some mutual funds may have nested capital *losses* and a taxpayer may be able to avoid recognition of gains after the fund is purchased because the gains will be offset by recognized but not used or distributed capital losses incurred before the taxpayer acquired the fund. This "nested" gains and losses effect can be further compounded if the underlying fund has substantial *unrealized* gains or losses on the underlying assets.

Many mutual funds are now being touted as "tax efficient" or "tax aware." Those who are considering investing in mutual funds outside of a retirement plan may benefit by reviewing these types of mutual funds since they typically will pay out less income that must be recognized and often completely avoid making any capital gain distributions each year. Alternatively, exchange traded funds, or "ETFs," may be a more tax efficient way to invest in certain market indices. Prior to the advent of ETFs, investors were commonly purchasing mutual funds that were tied to a given index. ETFs give investors the same basket of underlying investments, but trade like a stock, so they are better able to control the timing of the capital gains.

Converting Interest Income into Qualifying Dividends

Although qualifying dividends are taxed at a rate of 15 percent for most taxpayers and 23.8 percent for taxpayers in the top marginal tax bracket, interest and all other (non-qualifying) dividends are still taxed as ordinary income (subject to a maximum tax rate under current law of 39.6 percent plus the 3.8 percent NIIT for 2014).

Generally, qualifying dividends are dividends paid by domestic corporations and qualified foreign corporations (a foreign corporation's dividends would normally qualify provided the corporation was not in a country designated as a "tax haven").[9]

The focus of the current tax law is to reduce the impact of dividend double taxation by granting qualifying dividend treatment to any dividends paid out by entities that pay tax on income at the entity level (although the entity is not actually required to have *paid* tax on the specific income or dollars distributed for the dividend to receive preferential treatment). Certain types of payments or specific entities that make distributions do not receive qualifying dividend status. Dividends which do not qualify for the lower tax rate include:

1. dividends paid by credit unions, mutual insurance companies, tax-exempt organizations, real estate investment trusts (REITs) (unless the REIT does not deduct distributions but instead pays tax at the REIT entity level), and employee stock ownership programs;[10]

2. dividends paid on stock that was not held for more than 60 days during the 120-day period beginning 60 days before the ex-dividend date (i.e., stock not purchased before the ex-dividend date will not be held on the record date – on

which the corporation finalizes the list of share-holders who will receive the dividend. The ex-dividend date marks the deadline by which the investor must purchase the stock to receive the dividend. The ex-dividend date is usually two days before the record date, but may be as late as the day after the record date, depending upon the method of purchase and the brokerage account settlement requirements);[11]

3. dividends paid on preferred stock that was not held for more than 90 days during the 180-day period beginning 90 days before the ex-dividend date; and

3. dividends that cause an obligation to make payments of property that is substantially similar to the stock or property that is paid as a dividend (e.g., a reciprocal dividend arrangement).[12]

Investors usually look to the expected after-tax yield on a prospective investment to determine whether it is worth the risk. With the lower tax rates on qualifying dividends, many solid blue-chip companies which have paid dividends on a consistent basis will provide, with the same dividend, a higher after-tax yield than they have in the past. This increased yield may justify the added risk of fluctuation in the stock price. Investors might consider shifting some of their funds from a lower-yielding fixed income investment into a dividend paying stock. This may be particularly applicable to the higher dividend payments often received from preferred stocks. However, it is *vital* to properly evaluate the (potentially *substantial*) increased risk of holding various types of dividend-paying equities instead of fixed income or guaranteed investments.

One potential downside to increasing one's qualified dividends is the impact on investment income for the purpose of deducting investment interest expense. Investment interest expense may be claimed as an itemized deduction to the extent the taxpayer has sufficient investment income. The tax law excludes dividends and capital gains that are subject to a tax rate that is other than a taxpayer's ordinary income tax rate from investment income. Therefore, qualified dividends are not considered to be investment income and certain margin interest may not be immediately deductible as a result.

Taxpayers may elect to treat some or all of their qualified dividends or long-term capital gains as investment income. The election essentially treats the specified amount as not subject to the preferential tax rate, but, rather, to the taxpayer's ordinary income tax rate. The

investment interest expense then becomes deductible. The net result of the election is an acceleration of the deduction at a cost of forgoing the preferential tax rate. This election becomes economically feasible if the taxpayer would not otherwise generate sufficient investment income in the coming years.

Example: John Charrard incurs interest on his margin loan in the amount of $5,000. He has $100 of interest income and $10,000 of qualified dividends. Assuming he itemizes his deductions, he would be entitled to deduct $100 of his margin loan interest. The remaining $4,900 would be carried forward to future years until it can be utilized.

Alternatively, John could elect to treat $4,900 of his qualified dividends as investment income. The remaining $5,100 would still be taxed at 15 percent, but the elected amount would be taxed at his ordinary income tax rate. But the full $5,000 of margin loan interest could be deducted in the current year.

Structuring Compensation Packages

Certain highly paid executives may be able to structure compensation packages with their companies to convert compensation income that would otherwise be taxed as ordinary income into capital gain. Two of the more common compensation package items that foster potential capital gains treatment are restricted stock plans and incentive stock option awards. Incentive stock options are covered in detail in Chapter 26, and consequently will not be further discussed here.

A company may grant stock to an employee subject to various restrictions. The granting of this stock is usually done at little or no cost to the employee. If the restrictions meet certain requirements, the employee may forgo recognizing compensation when the stock is received. Once the restrictions lapse, the employee would be taxed at that time based on the fair market value of the stock at that time as compensation received.

Stock that is issued to an employee is restricted stock only if the following two conditions are met:

1. the stock is subject to a substantial risk of forfeiture;[13] and

2. the stock is not transferable.[14]

The stock is subject to a substantial risk of forfeiture only if there is a realistic expectation and requirement of future performance (or condition of refraining from a specified action or performance) of substantial services by the employee. For example, a requirement that stock is forfeited unless there is continued employment for X years would be a substantial risk of forfeiture; stock that is forfeited only upon being convicted of a crime does not meet the guidelines.[15] The non-transferability rule simply states that if the stock is allowed to be transferred to anyone other than the employer, the receiver of the stock would be forced to return the stock should the employee forfeit the right to the stock. The transferee must be subject to the same risk of forfeiture as the transferor.[16]

Once the stock, or any portion thereof, is no longer subject to restrictions, the stock award that is no longer restricted is recognized as compensation and taxed as ordinary income. The compensation is based on the excess of the stock's value on the date the restrictions lapse over the amount the executive paid for the stock.[17] The employee's holding period for the unrestricted stock would begin on this date (the date restrictions lapse) and any future appreciation after the restrictions lapse would be taxed as capital gain.

Example: Supurflous, Inc. issues 10,000 shares of stock to its new Chief Financial Officer, Gayle Conn, at no cost to her. The stock will vest in 2,000 share increments over the next five years. The vesting will only continue as long as Gayle remains employed by the Company. Under the terms of the stock agreement, she is not permitted to transfer the stock to anyone else. The stock would qualify as restricted stock and Gayle would not report any income upon receiving the shares from the Company. Once each fifth vests, the fair market value of that portion of the stock on that date would be treated as compensation to Gayle. If the stock price is $20 per share on the date that the first 20 percent of stock vests, Gayle would have taxable compensation of $40,000 (2,000 shares at $20 per share). Note that if Gayle was required to pay some portion of the cost of the stock as part of the transaction, only the excess of the stock's fair market value over the amount paid by Gayle would be considered taxable compensation.

Section 83(b) Elections

A planning opportunity exists for an employee to consider making an election under Code section 83(b) (an "83(b) election") to recognize income on the date the restricted stock is received, instead of waiting until the restrictions lapse. If an 83(b) election is made, the income element of the stock award is equal to the fair market value on the date of the award less the employee's cost. If an 83(b) election is made, the employee's holding period begins immediately and any future appreciation would be taxed as capital gain. The employee's basis in the stock under an 83(b) election is the fair market value of the stock when received (which would also equal the employee's cost plus the amount of compensation recognized under the 83(b) election).

Example: Gayle Conn decides to make an 83(b) election at the time the restricted stock is issued to her. At that time the stock is trading at $2 per share. Her 10,000 shares would generate compensation of $20,000 in the year of receipt. When the first 2,000 shares vest, the unrestricted stock would still be worth $40,000, as in the previous example, but, if she were to sell the shares, she would recognize a capital gain of $36,000 ($40,000 less 2,000 shares with a cost basis of $2 per share).

An 83(b) election must be made no later than thirty days (the "deadline" date) after the transfer of shares from the company to the employee.[18] Three copies of the election are required. One copy of the election must be filed with the Internal Revenue Service by the deadline date. A second copy must be attached to the employee's tax return for the year the stock is received. A third copy must be provided to the employer with an acknowledgement in writing being received in return.

There are a number of important considerations when evaluating whether an 83(b) election should be made. These include:

1. the employee does not receive any cash at the time of the stock award to pay the tax on the compensation recognized under an 83(b) election (unless separately provided by the employer as additional compensation);

2. if the restricted stock is forfeited after making an 83(b) election, only the amount of cash paid outright for the stock would be deductible by the employee. The compensation recognized and tax paid by making the 83(b) election is not deductible. Thus, in the example above, if Gayle made an 83(b) election and subsequently quit eleven months later, she would receive no stock whatsoever and would have no loss deduction available despite the fact that taxes had to be paid on the $20,000 of compensation ($7,000 of taxes paid at a 35 percent Federal tax rate) recognized because of the election. Consequently, the employee should be fairly comfortable that he or she will continue his/her performance of services through the date the restrictions on the stock will lapse;

3. if the stock price declines after an 83(b) election is made, the employee may actually recognize more income (the fair market value at issue) than he or she would have if an election were not made (the reduced fair market value when restrictions lapse);

4. if the stock has no value (or only a nominal value) at the time of the award, there is little or no downside to the employee by making an 83(b) election;

5. if the out-of-pocket cost to the employee is the fair market value of the stock at the time of the issuance (i.e., the employee pays the entire purchase price of the stock), no income is recognized by making an 83(b) election. This is because income recognition is only required to the extent that the fair market value of the stock granted exceeds the cost. However, by making the 83(b) election at no tax cost, all subsequent appreciation would be capital gain. Furthermore, even if the employee does in fact forfeit the stock, the loss will be deductible to the extent that the employee paid for the stock at issue; and

6. if the stock price is expected to rise dramatically between the issuance date and when the restrictions are set to lapse, a large amount of income can be converted into capital gain by making an 83(b) election. This difference

could potentially be so substantial (although stock price increases can never be certain) that the employee is willing to make an 83(b) election even when there is a high risk of forfeiture (without the subsequent loss deduction).

Example: Joseph Gantman paid $3 per share for the 15,000 shares of restricted stock issued by his employer. The restrictions on the stock were set to lapse in ten years as long as Joseph remained employed with the company. At the time of the transfer, the employer's stock was trading at $4 per share. Since Joseph believed the company's stock price would rise, he made an 83(b) election and recognized $15,000 of compensation in the year the restricted stock was issued. Five years later, Joseph is fired from his position with the company and the restricted stock is returned. Joseph may recognize a capital loss of $45,000 (15,000 shares at $3 per share cash paid at issue). Despite the fact that Joseph recognized $15,000 of compensation and paid taxes on it at the time the 83(b) election was made, no deduction is permitted for that portion of his loss.

Because some restricted stock grants extend out for many years, the employee is often virtually certain that the stock price of a solid and growing company will be higher in the future and that an 83(b) election would be beneficial. The primary issue becomes a determination by the employee about the likelihood of potential stock forfeiture.

CONVERTING CAPITAL LOSSES INTO ORDINARY LOSSES

While much of the focus of planning for the conversion of income revolves around making ordinary income eligible for long-term capital gains tax rates, there is some prudent planning that should be considered for converting capital losses into ordinary losses. Since certain losses may offset other sources of ordinary income on a dollar-for-dollar basis, the realization and recognition of these losses may save the taxpayer 39.6 percent or more of the amount of the taxpayer's loss on his/her tax bill.

ORDINARY LOSSES FOR SMALL BUSINESS STOCK

When stock (a capital asset) is sold at a loss or becomes worthless, the general rule is that the loss is a capital loss and is available to offset other capital gains in that year. If the capital losses exceed the capital gains, up to $3,000 of the net capital loss may be deducted against ordinary income in the current year. The balance is carried over to future years to offset capital gains in those years (also taking into account future capital losses). If there is a remaining net capital loss after including the loss carryforward and the future year's capital gains and losses, $3,000 of the net capital loss may again be deducted against ordinary income. This process may continue each year until the capital loss carryover is fully utilized.

Certain stock that is issued by a "small business corporation" as defined under Code section 1244 ("section 1244 stock") may receive preferential treatment in the event a loss is realized upon a sale or due to worthlessness. Specifically, a loss on section 1244 stock may be treated as an ordinary loss (instead of a capital loss). Section 1244 exists to encourage investors to put money into small businesses, despite the added risk associated with such investments, by providing more beneficial loss treatment in the event the business is not successful.

Only losses from the disposition of section 1244 stock are treated as ordinary. Gains from the sale of section 1244 stock continue to receive capital gain treatment (a rare "Heads I win, tails you lose" for the taxpayer).

The section 1244 stock loss ordinary income deduction is limited to $50,000 per year ($100,000 for taxpayers filing a joint return).[19] If the loss from the sale or worthlessness of section 1244 stock exceeds this amount, the excess loss is still treated as a capital loss. Once the loss is characterized as a capital loss due to the imposition of the limitation, it remains a capital loss and is subject to the capital loss carryover rules. Consequently, taxpayers with section 1244 losses in excess of the annual limitations should consider selling the stock in multiple years to maximize the amount of losses that may be claimed as an ordinary deduction.

Section 1244 stock is identified as such (or determined later based upon available facts) at the time of issuance and must meet all of the following requirements:

1. The corporation is a "small business corporation."[20] A small business corporation is defined as one in which the amount of money and property received by the corporation for stock or as a contribution to capital does not exceed $1 million.[21] Once the corporation receives more than $1 million of capital, no additional section 1244 stock can be issued. However, the stock that was issued prior to the first million of capital was received will continue to be section 1244 stock. Special rules exist to designate which stock qualifies as section 1244 stock in the year the corporation's receipt of capital exceeds $1 million.[22]

2. The stock was issued to the taxpayer in exchange for cash or other property (excluding stock and securities).[23] Stock issued for services rendered by the taxpayer does not qualify. However, the taxpayer could receive the compensation in cash and pay for the stock with the cash received for the services provided.

3. The stock must have been issued directly to the owner of the stock. No person other than the person to whom the stock was issued may claim a loss under section 1244. In addition, the owner of the stock must be an individual or a partnership.[24] In the case of a partnership, a section 1244 loss is available only to those who were partners in the partnership on the date the stock was issued.

4. Stock must be either common stock or preferred stock issued after November 6, 1978. Securities convertible into common stock or common stock convertible into other securities does not qualify.[25]

In the year a loss is claimed, more than 50 percent of the corporation's gross receipts during the five most recent tax years must from be from sources other than royalties, rents, dividends, interest, annuities, and sales or exchanges of stocks or securities.[26] In addition, the corporation must be an operating company during this period.[27] Corporations with cumulative deductions in excess of cumulative gross income during the previous five years are not subject to this gross receipts test.[28] If the corporation has not been in existence for at least five years, only the full years that the corporation has existed are considered. If the company existence is less than one year, the entire corporate life of the entity is considered.[29]

Example: Jackie Rhoads invests $150,000 into Qualford, Inc. Qualford's stock qualifies as section 1244 stock for Jackie. Six years after her investment, Qualford ceases operations, declares bankruptcy, and declares the stock to be worthless. If Jackie files a joint return, she and her husband may deduct $100,000 as an ordinary loss in the year the stock becomes worthless. The remaining $50,000 is a long-term capital loss available to offset their other capital gains.

Stock of an S corporation will usually be section 1244 stock in the hands of its owners. However, basis increases as a result of future contributions or reported flow-through income do not qualify as potential section 1244 losses.[30] The ratio of the original contributions to the total stock basis determines the portion that may be treated as a section 1244 loss.[31]

Example: Harry Townsend put $10,000 into his S corporation. He recognized $5,000 of income and put an additional $15,000 into the company over the years. His total basis is now $30,000. He sells his stock for $18,000, realizing a loss of $12,000 ($18,000 proceeds less $30,000 basis). Of this $12,000 loss, $4,000 is deductible as an ordinary loss from section 1244 stock ($10,000 ÷ $30,000 x $12,000). The remaining $8,000 is treated as a capital loss.

INVESTOR VS. TRADER STATUS

There is a segment of the population that spends so much time and effort investing in the stock market that their activity could be considered a profession. These individuals often attempt to profit from short-term swings in the market price of equities. The rise in the stock market in the late 90s coupled with the creation of "discount" brokers and online trading support made "day trading" a legitimate (although possibly short-lived) profession.

Taxpayers who trade securities for their own account will qualify either as an investor or trader for tax purposes. While the majority of people will be treated as investors, there are potentially large tax saving benefits for those who can qualify as a trader for tax purposes.

Investors typically buy securities and hold them for long-term appreciation. The time commitment involved, while it may be more than insignificant, does not rise to the level of being their main profession. When the securities are sold, the gain or loss is treated as a capital gain or loss. Expenses associated with their investing activity (excluding commissions which decrease the realized gain or loss[32]) are deductible as a miscellaneous itemized deduction subject to the 2 percent of adjusted gross income limitation,[33] and are not deductible at all for purposes of AMT calculations.[34] As a result, most, if not all, of an investor's expenses do not generate any substantial income tax savings. The reinstatement of the "Pease" limitation as part of the American Taxpayer Act of 2012, which limits certain itemized deductions including miscellaneous itemized deductions for higher-income earners, make this conclusion all but certain.[35] In contrast to investors, traders are treated as participating in the active conduct of a trade or business. As a result, the expenses of traders are treated as business expenses and are fully deductible from the trader's income in reporting his/her trading-business profits or losses. The expenses of a trader are reported on Schedule C of Form 1040, and the net income from the business on Schedule C is reported as an above-the-line item of income or loss when computing AGI. As a result, the expenses of a trader are typically transformed from an itemized deduction that rarely benefits many taxpayers to a bona fide offset to income (either directly reducing the trading-business income or flowing through as an above-the-line loss in computing AGI).

On the income side, the realized gain or loss of a trader still maintains its capital nature. Because the securities still generate capital gain or loss, traders remain subject to the $3,000 annual capital loss limitation and the wash sale rules under Code section 1091. Traders will often run afoul of the wash sale rules (even unintentionally or unknowingly) due to the high volume of trades that are made – often in the same security.

Maintaining capital gain or loss treatment is not usually valuable to taxpayers who want to qualify as a trader. Most, if not all of their trades will be either short-term gains or losses which, if taxed as a gain, will be subject to their marginal ordinary income tax rate. No benefit will be obtained from the more favorable long-term capital gain rate. So, traders have none of the upside where capital gains are involved, but still remain subject to the detriments to capital transactions (the annual loss limitation and the wash sale rules).

Traders may wish to consider making an election to "mark their security holdings to the market value" as of the end of the tax year.[36] The mark-to-market election forces the tax recognition of unrealized gains in the hands of a trader even though the security has not actually been sold. Since many traders operate as day traders, most open security positions are closed by the end of the trading day. As a result, traders do not generally have an inventory of securities that must be marked-to-market at the end of the year.

If the election is made, all gains and losses from the trading activity are treated as ordinary income or loss,[37] and are reported on Form 4797 instead of Form 1040, Schedule D. This applies even if the securities are not actually held on the last day of the year, as long as they would have qualified if they were still held.[38] Therefore, the annual $3,000 capital loss limitation and wash sale rules do not apply. The election is binding in the year it is made *and for all future years for the trader's business* and may not be revoked without the consent of the Internal Revenue Service.[39]

It is important to bear in mind that if the trader is generally very successful and most trades result in gains, then the mark-to-market election will guarantee that no security held for the trading business will *ever* be eligible for long-term capital gains treatment, even if the trader attempts to maintain particular securities with gains for the requisite holding period. Nonetheless, to the extent that most securities traders do not maintain positions for extended periods of time, the benefit of obtaining ordinary (rather than capital) loss treatment for all losses sustained throughout the taxable year generally weighs in favor of the mark-to-market election.

Traders fared well under the final regulations promulgated for the new net investment income tax (NIIT) regime under Code section 1411. As discussed fully in Chapter 11, the NIIT is a 3.8 percent surcharge on "net investment income" for taxpayers with modified adjusted gross income above certain levels. Net investment income includes (but is not limited to) interest, dividends, and capital gains. For NIIT purposes, interest and dividends for both investors and traders are treated the same: both are included in the calculation of net investment income. Regarding capital gains, the tax treatment is favorable for traders. The final regulations treat all trading gains and trading losses as capital gains and losses from the sale of property not used in an active trade or business.[40] That means that trading business gains and losses are able to offset investment capital gains and losses. Furthermore, the final regulations permit a section 475 trader to deduct excess losses from the trading business from other categories of income.[41]

Taxpayers may not simply declare themselves to be traders and avail themselves of the potentially more favorable rules. The tax court has ruled that "in determining whether an individual who manages his own investments is a trader, we consider the following nonexclusive factors: (a) the taxpayer's investment intent; (b) the nature of the income to be derived from the activity; and (c) the frequency, extent, and regularity of the taxpayer's securities transactions."[42]

Thus, a taxpayer is engaged in carrying on a trade or business as a securities trader only where both of the following are true: (a) the taxpayer's trading activity is substantial (must be frequent, regular, and continuous); and (b) the taxpayer seeks to catch the swings in the daily market movements, and profit from investments.[43] Factors such as the number of trades, the amount of time spent trading and researching potential trades, and the amount of time the securities are held all help to substantiate a taxpayer's classification as a trader.

Example: Bill Burns, a retired executive, lives on a $400,000 per year pension. To fill his time, he began trading stocks on a regular and frequent basis. In the first year, he incurred $20,000 of expenses and generated total losses of $50,000. His adjusted gross income for the year is expected to be approximately $500,000 (including other sources of income such as interest and dividends). The tax treatment of his "activity" will be dependent on whether he is an investor, trader, or a trader with a mark-to-market election. See Figure 24.1 for a summary of how his expenses and loss would be treated under each situation.

Figure 24.1

		INVESTOR	TRADER	MARK-TO-MARKET TRADER
Expenses		Itemized deduction subject to 2% of AGI limitation. With $500,000 of AGI, the first $10,000 of Bill's expenses would not be deductible (assuming no other itemized deductions). Further, the itemized deductions would be subject to the high income phase-out.	The full amount of expenses would be deductible on Form 1040, Schedule C as a business expense.	The full amount of expenses would be deductible on Form 1040, Schedule C as a business expense.
Loss		The $50,000 loss would be a capital loss available to offset other capital gains. If the losses are greater than the gains, $3,000 of the losses may be deducted from Bill's gross income. The remainder would be carried forward for future years.	The $50,000 loss would be a capital loss available to offset other capital gains. If the losses are greater than the gains, $3,000 of the losses may be deducted from Bill's gross income. The remainder would be carried forward for future years.	The full amount of the losses would be deductible from Bill's gross income as an ordinary loss.

CHAPTER ENDNOTES

1. P.L. 112-240 (2012).

2. P.L. 111-152 (2010).

3. I.R.C. §1411. See Chapter 11 for more information about the NIIT.

4. I.R.C. §1221.

5. I.R.C. §1222(3).

6. Treas. Reg. §1.1223-1(i).

7. See I.R.C. §408(e)(1).

8. See I.R.C. §408(d)(1).

9. I.R.C. §1(h)(11)(B)(i).

10. I.R.C. §1(h)(11)(B)(ii).

11. I.R.C. §1(h)(11)(B)(iii)(I).

12. I.R.C. §1(h)(11)(B)(iii)(II).

13. I.R.C. §83(c)(1).

14. I.R.C. §83(c)(2).

15. Treas. Reg. §1.83-3(c)(2).

16. Treas. Reg. §1.83-3(a)(3).

17. I.R.C. §83(a).

18. I.R.C. §83(b)(2).

19. I.R.C. §1244(b).

20. I.R.C. §1244(c)(1)(A).

21. I.R.C. §1244(c)(3)(A).

22. Treas. Reg. §1.1244(c)-2.

23. I.R.C. §§1244(c)(1)(B).

24. Treas. Reg. §1.1244(a)-1(b).

25. Treas. Reg. §1.1244(c)-1.

26. I.R.C. §1244(c)(1)(C).

27. Treas. Reg. §1.1244(c)-1(e)(2).

28. I.R.C. §1244(c)(2)(C).

29. I.R.C. §1244(c)(2)(A).

30. I.R.C. §1244(d)(1)(B).

31. Treas. Reg. §1.244(d)-2(a).

32. Treas. Reg. §1.263(a)-2(e).

33. I.R.C. §67.

34. I.R.C. §56(b)(1)(A)(i).

35. P.L. 112-240 (2012).

36. I.R.C. §475(f).

37. I.R.C. §475(d)(3)(A)(i).

38. I.R.C. §475(d)(3)(A)(ii).

39. I.R.C. §475(f)(3).

40. Treas. Reg. §1.1411–4(c).

41. Treas. Reg. §1.1411–4(f).

42. *Moller v. U.S.*, 52 AFTR2d 83-6333 (Nov. 18, 1983).

43. *Mayer, Frederick R.*, 32 Fed. Cl. 149, 74 AFTR 2d 94-6402 (Ct. Fed. Cl., 1994).

ALTERNATIVE MINIMUM TAX PLANNING

CHAPTER 25

INTRODUCTION

As discussed in Chapter 9, the alternative minimum tax (AMT) system is a second income tax system that is imposed on most taxpayers. A taxpayer must compare his or her income tax liability under the regular tax system to the AMT system and essentially pay the higher of the two amounts.

Income tax planning in general is difficult. With all of the various code sections, regulations, interpretations, explanations, rulings, etc., professionals in the area spend a lifetime just trying to understand one aspect well enough to be considered an expert. By adding a second layer of potential tax to consider, the planning becomes that much more difficult, but also, that much more important.

To make matters more complex, the AMT potentially generates a minimum tax credit (MTC) in certain situations where the extra tax is caused by timing adjustments or preferences.

AMT planning is not for the faint of heart. At a minimum, proper planning involves multiple year tax projections that must consider the interaction of the AMT and regular income tax systems along with any potential benefits created by the MTC.[1]

BRIEF OVERVIEW OF THE AMT

Recall from Chapter 9 that the tentative minimum tax for individuals is assessed at a rate of 26 percent of alternative minimum taxable income (AMTI) in excess of the AMT exclusion amount, up to $182,500 ($91,250 for married taxpayers filing separately) and 28 percent of AMTI exceeding that amount.[2] Preferential tax rates used to determine regular tax liabilities for long-term capital gains and qualifying dividends are also used in determining an individual's tentative minimum tax.[3]

AMTI is computed as follows:

1. Taxable income (before subtracting personal exemptions) as computed on Form 1040[4]

    PLUS OR MINUS

2. Adjustments to taxable income (alternative methods, discussed below, to calculate certain gains, losses, and deductions)[5]

    PLUS

3. The amount of "preference items" (specified items, discussed below, on which the taxpayer is receiving preferential tax treatment)[6]

    EQUALS

4. Alternative Minimum Taxable Income

The tentative minimum tax is calculated by applying the AMT system tax rates to the AMTI in excess of the exemption amount (up to $52,800 for a single taxpayer, $82,100 for a married couple filing jointly, or $41,050 for a married couple filing separately).[7] With the 2012 Tax Relief Act these exemption amounts will be indexed annually for inflation[8]

The allowable exemption is reduced by 25 percent of the amount by which AMTI exceeds $156,500 for married taxpayers filing jointly, $117,300 for single taxpayers, and $78,100 for married taxpayers filing separately.[9] Thus, the exemption is completely phased out for joint filers with AMTI in excess of $484,900. The complete phase-out amount for single filers is AMTI over $328,500 and for married couples filing separately is $242,300.

If the tentative minimum tax computed under this formula does not exceed the taxpayer's regular tax, the AMT does not apply. If the computed tentative minimum tax exceeds the taxpayer's regular tax, the excess of the tentative minimum tax over the regular tax is the AMT that is added to the regular tax liability.

For a more detailed discussion of the AMT and the related adjustments and preferences, please refer to Chapter 9.

IDENTIFYING THE AMT TRAPS

Before any AMT planning can be effectively started, an understanding of what items of AMT adjustment or preference might be creating the AMT in the taxpayer's situation is essential.

As covered in Chapter 9, most individual taxpayers who itemize deductions (whether they know it or not) are required to add back certain of these deductions when determining their AMTI. Deductions for charitable contributions, casualty losses, and wagering losses to the extent of reportable winnings are allowed in full for both regular tax and AMT purposes. For all other itemized deductions, the taxpayer must be diligent to ensure that he/she correctly follows the rules to determine what adjustments are applied in computing AMTI. Figure 25.1 describes some of the issues that can arise based on itemized deductions.

As covered in Chapter 9, most individual taxpayers who itemize deductions (whether they know it or not) are required to add back certain of these deductions when determining their AMTI. Deductions for charitable contributions, casualty losses, and wagering losses to the extent of reportable winnings are allowed in full for both regular tax and AMT purposes. For all other itemized deductions, the taxpayer must be diligent to ensure that he/she correctly follows the rules to determine what adjustments are applied in computing AMTI. Figure 25.1 describes some of the issues that can arise based on itemized deductions.

Of course, AMT traps are not limited to itemized deductions alone. There are also income-based adjustment and preference items that have traps for the unwary. These are discussed in Figure 25.2.

Certain deductions are also impacted by the AMT. There are some solutions to minimizing the impact of the AMT, although most involve making annual elections to slow down the deduction that is creating the problem. These issues are discussed in Figure 25.3

The last set of traps to be aware of relate to the utilization of credits. There are a number of credits that are available to reduce a taxpayer's regular tax liability. However, a taxpayer may be limited in the amount of credits that may be used to offset his/her regular tax liability based on the AMT for the year.

A individual taxpayer's nonrefundable personal tax credits are allowed to offset both regular tax and AMT.[11] Nonrefundable personal credits are those that are defined under Internal Revenue Code sections 21 through 26, which include:

1. Child tax credit

2. Education credits (Hope and Lifetime Learning Credits)

3. Child and dependent care credit

4. Adoption credit

5. Credit for interest paid on certain home mortgages

6. Retirement savings contribution credit

7. Residential energy efficient property credit

A taxpayer that has business tax credits may not use the credits to offset his/her AMT in a given year. The general business credit of a taxpayer is limited to the taxpayer's net regular tax (net of nonrefundable personal credits, foreign tax credit, and certain other rarely used credits) plus AMT, less the larger of (1) tentative minimum tax or (2) 25 percent of the amount by which the net regular tax exceeds $25,000.[12]

Example: Jessica Nelson's net regular tax liability for 2014 was $50,000. Her tentative minimum tax was $47,000. She also received a $5,000 general business credit from one of her partnership investments. She is permitted to claim $3,000 of the credit against her 2014 tax

Figure 25.1

ITEMIZED DEDUCTION-BASED AMT TRAPS AND ESCAPES[10]		
Itemized Deduction	*AMT Treatment (Trap)*	*Planning Idea (Escape)*
Medical	Deductible for AMT only to extent the expenses exceed 10% of AGI.	Utilize employer provided pre-tax medical deduction or Cafeteria plan. Funds are set aside from paycheck on a pre-tax basis and recovered in full with substantiated medical receipts.
Taxes (Real estate, state, Local, etc.)	Must be added to AMTI in year of payment.	Determine if real estate taxes can be claimed as a business expense (e.g. home office or rental property), which is not added back for AMT purposes. Also, see "Moving Deductions Into a Non-AMT Year" below.
Mortgage Interest	Not deductible for AMT unless used to acquire, construct, or substantially improve a principal residence or qualified dwelling (not a boat treated as a second home).	Watch the use of home equity loans to finance non-home expenditures (consider other financing alternatives for car purchases, tuition, etc.). If the expenditure is for business property, determine if the interest should be Claimed as other than an itemized deduction for mortgage interest (e.g. home office, rental property, interest expense on business property, investment interest).
Investment Interest	Recalculate deduction using interest from private activity bonds as an addition to investment income and excluding all investment expenses.	Determine the impact investments in private activity bonds and investment expenses is having on after-tax yield and consider investment alternatives, if appropriate.
Miscellaneous Itemized Deductions	Must be added to AMTI. Typically created by large unreimbursed business expenses or investment- related expenses.	Always try to have expenses fully reimbursed by employer through an accountable plan (one in which expenses are substantiated). Alternatively, negotiate a Reduction of salary and a payment of your expenses.

liability and thereby reduce her regular tax to $47,000. The remaining $2,000 may be carried forward to future years subject to carry-forward limitations.

AMT PLANNING TECHNIQUES

Rarely can the impact of the AMT system be considered by analyzing only one particular year. Even when a taxpayer is expecting an unusually high amount of income that creates an AMT liability for that year, the planning ideas will typically include an analysis of accelerating or deferring income or deductions which will force a multiple year projection of the taxpayer's liabilities.

Once a taxpayer is subject to the AMT under the current rules, it is likely the taxpayer will continue to be caught in that trap if the taxpayer's income, deductions, adjustments and preferences in future years continue at the same level or increase.

Unfortunately, there is no overall planning strategy that can be implemented in order to avoid the imposition of the AMT. Each taxpayer's situation is very different – the items creating an AMT liability need to be identified before any planning can begin. For example, a married couple may have an AMT liability because they have six children and the AMT does not allow personal exemptions, while another couple with the same amount of income may be paying the AMT because of high medical expenses or investment expenses (a miscellaneous itemized deduction).

In order to create a complete AMT planning analysis, it is imperative to begin with a multiple year projection of the taxpayer's regular tax liability, AMT liability and expected MTC. From this point there are a number of general planning strategies that can be considered, including:

1.   Moving income into an AMT year;

2.   Moving deductions into a non-AMT year;

Figure 25.2

INCOME-BASED AMT TRAPS AND ESCAPES		
Income	*AMT Treatment (Trap)*	*Planning Idea (Escape)*
State/Local Tax Refunds	Although refunds may be taxable for regular tax purposes, these refunds are always excluded from AMTI.	Since taxpayers are not allowed to deduct state and local taxes when computing AMTI, it is only fair that taxpayers are not required to report the corresponding refunds.
Tax-Exempt Interest	Tax-exempt interest from private activity bonds must be included in the determination of AMT. Interest from bonds issued during 2009 and 2010 is not included.	Determine the impact of investments in private activity bonds (including the adjusted rules regarding investment expenses) on after-tax yield. Consider investment alternatives, if appropriate. See "Timing of Adjustments and Preferences" below.
Section 1202 Gain	7% of the excluded gain on qualified small business stock must be included in AMTI. (Prior to the 2003 Tax Act, the applicable percentage to be added to AMTI was 42% of the excluded gain.	With the enactment of JGTRRA 2003, this preference item is not as damaging as it was before. Consider deferring other deductions which may cause the imposition of the AMT in the year of the gain. See " Timing of Adjustments and Preferences" below.
Incentive Stock Options(ISOs)	The excess of the fair market value of the stock over the exercise cost of the option is an adjustment for AMT.	The timing of the exercise of ISO is essential in maximizing the after-tax return to the taxpayer. This adjustment item can single-handedly create a taxpayer's AMT liability, but will also typically create a MTC for the future. Also, do not forget that negative adjustments are allowed, so when the stock acquired by ISO is sold, a large portion of the MTC may be realized against regular tax. See "Timing of Adjustments and Preferences" below.
Adjusted Gain Or Loss	The difference between an asset's regular tax and AMT basis. This adjustment can be sizeable depending on the nature of the asset.	Maintain meticulous records detailing not only the regular tax basis of assets but also the AMT basis. (For example, as mentioned above, the exercise of ISOs could create a large difference between the tax basis for regular tax and AMT.)
Capital Gains	Although capital gains continue to receive preferential treatment under the AMT system, the increase in AMTI can trigger an AMT liability and cause other income to be taxed under the higher AMT rates.	Evaluate the potential impact of large capital gains on the total tax bill under both tax systems, and consider moving a portion of capital gains into a non-AMT year to avoid increased taxes on non-capital-gains income.

3. Timing the recognition of adjustment or preference items;

4. Making elections to minimize the AMT; and

5. Utilizing alternative tax net operating losses (ATNOL).

A multiple year projection is essential to completing the AMT planning process. Most (if not all) of the general planning strategies listed above involve issues of timing. For example, deductions for real estate taxes and income (or sales) taxes must be added back when taxpayers determines their AMTI. It is not a matter of whether taxpayers are going to pay these taxes, it is simply a matter of when. If taxpayers are able to control when certain items of income are earned or when certain (deductible) expenses are paid, much more flexibility exists for creative AMT planning.

Figure 25.3

DEDUCTION-BASED AMT TRAPS AND ESCAPES		
Deductions	*AMT Treatment (Trap)*	*Planning Idea (Escape)*
Standard Deduction	If taxpayer does not itemize, this must be added back to AMTI.	Most taxpayers who claim the standard deduction are not paying the AMT because of this adjustment alone.
Personal Exemptions	The deduction for personal exemptions is not permitted for AMT purposes. Large families are sometimes subject to the AMT just because of the number of dependents (e.g., children).	Carefully determine if all of the individuals being claimed as dependent qualify as such. It may be more beneficial for dependents to claim themselves on their own tax returns if they somehow fail the dependency rules. Consider the family's overall tax liability in this case.
Depletion, Depreciation, Passive Activities, Circulation, Expenditures, and Research and Development Expenditures	All of these items are business related deductions with are more accelerated for regular tax purposes than they are for AMT purposes.	Each of these items have a corresponding election which may be made in order to treat the deduction for regular tax purposes identically as the treatment for AMT purposes. See "Making Elections to Minimize the AMT" below.
Alternative Tax Net Operating Loss (ATNOL)	A taxpayer's ATNOL will almost always be different than their regular NOL. Depending on the year of the loss and the current tax year, the ATNOL may only e allowed to offset 90% of a taxpayer's AMTI.	In the year an ANTOL is created, carefully consider the impact of carrying the NOLs back to previous years instead of forward to future years. There may be more regular income tax saved by carrying the loss back, but more AMT savings (and thus total tax savings) by carrying the NOLSs forward.

Moving Income into an AMT Year

Timing the recognition of income can be advantageous to a taxpayer who may be subject to the AMT in one year but not another. Accelerating income into an AMT year works best for a taxpayer when the following conditions exist:

1. the AMT is primarily due to the add-back of exclusion-type adjustments or preferences; and

2. the taxpayer's marginal tax bracket in future years will exceed 28 percent, the top tax bracket of the AMT system.

To the extent the AMT is generated by exclusion items, there is no MTC involved and the AMT represents a pure permanent tax increase under the AMT system. As a result, any additional income that is recognized in the AMT year is taxed at a maximum marginal rate of 28 percent instead of a potentially higher marginal tax rate under the regular tax system (e.g., 33, 35, or 39.6 percent).

However, due to the nature of the AMT system, taxpayers in this situation will not be able to accelerate an unlimited amount of income into the AMT year at a 28 percent tax rate. Since the AMT system is a parallel tax system, as one adds income subject to the AMT, the regular tax liability will also increase – and eventually it will increase at a faster rate (as the marginal tax rate under the regular tax system exceeds 28 percent). Therefore, there will sooner or later be some point at which the regular tax liability will equal the AMT liability, any future increases in income will increase the total tax liability at the higher regular tax system marginal rate, and the marginal tax savings will have been completely absorbed.

Recall from Chapter 9 that adjustment and preference items that are treated as exclusions include:[13]

1. Taxes;

2. Medical expenses;

3. Certain residential interest expense;

4. Miscellaneous itemized deductions;

5. Standard deduction;

6. Personal exemptions;

7. Excess depletion;

8. Tax-exempt interest from private activity bonds; and

9. Applicable add back for the section 1202 exclusion for gain from the sale of small business stock.

Moving Deductions into a Non-AMT Year

Since itemized deductions such as taxes, medical expenses and investment expenses increase a taxpayer's exposure to the AMT without the generation of a corresponding MTC, it would be prudent for a taxpayer to attempt to pay these expenses in a year in which the AMT does not apply. Otherwise, no tax benefit would be generated from the payment of these expenses due to the imposition of the AMT.

Example. Nicholas and Amanda Wright earn compensation of $100,000 per year and have no children. They always give $5,000 per year to charities, spend $6,000 on real estate taxes and pay $20,000 in mortgage interest. Five percent of their compensation is withheld for state income tax purposes. In 2013, the Wrights sold some of their stock holdings and recognized a long-term capital gain of $400,000 gain. They immediately set aside $20,000 to cover the state income tax on the gain (they live in a 5 percent flat tax state) but are unsure if they should pay the amount before the end of 2013 to claim the deduction or wait until April 15, 2014. A multiple-year analysis would show that they would save $1,000 by paying their state tax liability in 2013.

	Pay State Tax in 2013		Pay State Tax in 2014	
	2013	2014	2013	2014
Regular Tax	63,236	7,508	70,236	4,508
AMT	12,753	-0-	9,753	-0-
Total Tax	75,989	7,508	79,989	4,508

Timing of Adjustments and Preferences

A certain degree of planning can be undertaken with respect to adjustment and preference items that are in the complete control of the taxpayer and only impact the AMT. This section of the chapter will discuss two items in particular: Incentive Stock Options (ISOs) and tax-exempt interest from private activity bonds

Incentive Stock Options

Chapter 26 is dedicated to planning with stock options. The adjustment for AMT purposes of the excess of the fair market value over the exercise cost for ISOs is one of the more common adjustments that has been creating a great deal of anguish for taxpayers.

Taxpayers may defer regular tax on income resulting from the exercise of an ISO as defined in Code section 422.[14] Unlike nonqualified stock options ("NQSO"), which are taxed to the extent of the value of the stock over the exercise cost, the taxation of an ISO occurs only when the stock acquired by exercise of the ISO is sold or otherwise disposed. At that time, the difference between the selling price and the amount paid for the stock when the ISO was exercised is taxed as a capital gain.

The capital gains treatment at the time of the exercise of the ISO does not apply if the taxpayer disposes of the stock within two years from the grant date of the ISO or within one year of the exercise date of the option.[15] If the taxpayer makes a disqualifying disposition, he/she realizes gain as ordinary income in the taxable year of the disposition.

For AMT purposes, the ISO does not receive the deferral treatment at the time of exercise. Instead the ISO is treated like a NQSO.[16] This means that the value of the stock acquired at the time of exercise in excess of the exercise cost creates a positive AMT adjustment in that year.

Taxpayers who exercise ISOs must keep accurate dual records of the basis of their stock. For regular tax purposes, the basis will equal their exercise cost plus any transaction costs. For AMT purposes, the basis will equal the value of the stock on the date of exercise plus any transaction costs. When the stock acquired by ISO is ultimately sold, the taxpayer will reduce the AMTI in that year by the amount of the basis difference.

Taxpayers with stock options can manage the exercise and sale of such options by using such timing techniques as:

1. Exercising only the amount of ISOs that can be done without triggering the AMT in a given year;

2. Coordinating the timing of the sale or exchange of stock acquired by ISO with the exercise of newer ISOs; and

3. Accelerating the exercise of NQSOs to a year in which the AMT applies to benefit from the lower marginal tax rate (see "Moving Income into an AMT year" above).

Each of these planning techniques is fully discussed in Chapter 26.

Example 1: Kevin Peterson is an unmarried executive for a major corporation. He lives in Florida (no state income tax) and has not yet left the apartment that he rents in South Beach. In 2014, he expects to earn $500,000 in compensation. He has no other source of earnings and does not itemize deductions. He has 10,000 incentive stock options with an exercise price of $10. The stock is currently trading at $30 per share. Since he expects to hold the stock for some time into the future and believes he will likely receive more ISOs in the future, he wants to exercise as many ISOs as possible without triggering the AMT in 2014.

	No ISO Exercises	Exercise 2,888 ISOs
Taxable Income	$493,750	$493,750
Standard Deduction/ Personal Exemptions	6,250	6,250
ISO AMT Adjustment	0	58,000
AMTI	$500,000	$558,000
Tentative Minimum Tax	$136,500	$152,591
Regular Tax	$152,591	$152,591
AMT	0	0
Total Tax	$152,591	$152,591

By exercising 2,900 ISOs at an exercise purchase cost of $29,000, Kevin will generate an

AMT adjustment of $58,000 ([$30 - $10] x 2,900). At $558,000 of AMTI, Kevin's regular tax (where ISO excess gain is deferred) and tentative minimum tax (where ISO excess gain is recognized) are both $152,591.

Example 2: Kevin then decides he wants to know the impact of exercising all of the ISOs this year. The results are summarized as follows:

	No ISO Exercises	Exercise 10,000 ISOs
Taxable Income	$493,750	$493,750
Standard Deduction	6,250	6,250
ISO AMT Adjustment	0	200,000
AMTI	$500,000	$700,000
Tentative Minimum Tax	$136,500	$192,500
Regular Tax	$152,591	$152,591
AMT	0	$ 39,759
Total Tax	$152,591	$192,500

By exercising all 10,000 ISOs at an exercise purchase cost of $100,000, Kevin will generate an AMT adjustment of $200,000 ([$30 - $10] x 10,000). At $700,000 of AMTI, Kevin's regular tentative minimum tax exceeds his regular tax by $39,759 – which becomes the additional amount of tax he must pay under this scenario.

Note: Since all of Kevin's 2014 alternative minimum tax is generated by a deferral adjustment, the entire amount of his AMT becomes a minimum tax credit, eligible to offset regular tax in future years.

Example 3: In 2015, Kevin has the same amount of income but did not exercise any ISOs or sell any of the stock he acquired in 2013. He calculates his regular tax liability to be $152,591. The MTC is available to offset his regular tax liability dollar for dollar down to his tentative minimum tax. His tentative minimum tax liability is $136,350, allowing him to utilize $16,241 of the MTC generated in 2014.

His remaining unused minimum tax credit is carried forward to future tax years.

———————

Most municipal bond issues that are tax-exempt for federal income tax purposes are also tax-exempt for the AMT. However, the interest earned on "specified private activity bonds" must be added to AMTI. The amount of interest to be added back is reduced by any deductions (e.g., investment interest or other investment expense attributable to the bonds) which would have been allowable if the tax-exempt interest was includible in gross income for regular tax purposes.[17]

A specified private activity bond is any private activity bond which is issued after August 7, 1986.[18] Private activity bonds are covered by Code section 141 and include any bonds that meet either (1) the "private business use" test and the "private security or payment" test or (2) the "private loan financing" test.

A bond is identified as a private activity bond at the time of its issue. Because the inclusion of the interest paid on such bonds in the AMTI of its holders makes them undesirable (or at least less desirable), the market for these municipal bonds is slightly smaller and issuers must offer a slightly higher yield to successfully issue the bonds. It is notable that the increased yield on these bonds is almost never enough to make the (AMTI-based) after-tax yield on the bonds as high as municipal bonds not subject to AMT. Thus, for investors subject to the AMT, private activity bonds are generally not optimal investments on an after-tax basis. However, for taxpayers not subject to the AMT, this offers an opportunity to benefit from the extra yield available when purchasing and/or holding a private activity bond instead of a normal tax-free municipal bond. The extra amount of income, if it does not trigger the AMT, could be significant to a number of taxpayers.

———————

Example: Early-retirees Sam and Lydia Costello receive $100,000 of pension income per year and have a $1,000,000 portfolio of municipal bonds. The municipal bonds have a coupon yield of 4.25 percent ($42,500 of tax-exempt income per year). They understand that similarly-rated private activity municipal bonds are yielding 4.50 percent ($45,000 of regular tax-exempt income per year). Should Sam and Lydia invest in the AMT bonds, or will they generate an AMT liability that completely offsets (or even exceeds) their increased yield?

	Without AMT Bonds	With AMT Bonds
Taxable Income	$83,100	$83,100
Standard Deduction	10,300	10,300
Personal Exemptions	6,600	6,600
Private Activity Bond Int.	0	42,500
AMTI	$100,000	$142,500
Tentative Minimum Tax	$ 9,737	$18,606
Regular Tax	$13,890	$13,890
AMT	0	4,716
Total Tax	$13,890	$18,606

By converting all of their municipal bonds to private activity bonds, the Costellos create a $4,716 AMT liability, but enjoy only an extra $2,500 of bond interest income. Consequently, their after-tax yield would decrease from 4.25 to 4.03 percent ([$45,000 - $4,716] ÷ $1,000,000). They should not invest in the private activity bonds unless they could get a higher spread than 0.25 percent between the regular municipal bonds and the private activity bonds.

———————

Making Elections to Minimize the AMT

There are certain elections that can be made by a taxpayer or a taxpayer's business to help mitigate the potential impact of the AMT. However, these elections typically serve to slow down deductible items for regular tax purposes as well. Consequently, it can be particularly important to create multiple year projections of tax liabilities to properly evaluate the potential costs or benefits of these elections. In addition, it is important to bear in mind that if these elections are not made and the taxpayer is subject to alternative minimum tax, a minimum tax credit may be created.

Please note that some of these elections may need to be made by the taxpayer that owns the asset, as opposed to an individual investor who holds a partnership or shareholder interest.

Depreciation of Property Placed in Service After 1986 – Recall from Chapter 9, Alternative Minimum Tax, that property placed in service after 1986 is depreciated using MACRS, which is typically the 200-percent declining balance method over a specified life, depending on the type of asset. For assets placed in service prior to 1999, taxpayers were required to re-compute depreciation for AMT purposes using the 150-percent declining balance method with a longer recovery period. Taxpayers could elect either of the following two methods for regular tax purposes on the assets placed in service for that year to avoid future AMT depreciation adjustment(s):

- Code section 168(g)(7) – Straight-line depreciation method using the AMT recovery period. This is an annual election that is made by the entity that purchased and used the asset. With this election, no AMT adjustment is required.

- Code section 168(b)(2) – 150-percent declining balance method using the AMT recovery period. This is also an annual election that is made by the asset purchasing entity. However, since the depreciation method is still somewhat accelerated (150-percent versus straight-line), higher depreciation deductions will be realized for regular tax purposes in the earlier years (and lower depreciation deductions will be realized in the later years) than would be generated using the Code section 168(g)(7) election. Again, with this election no AMT adjustment is required.

After 1998, taxpayers could use the same recovery period that is used for determining their regular tax depreciation. However, the depreciation method still may be no faster than the 150 percent declining balance method.[19] Thus, the elections that may currently be used to reduce the impact of the AMT depreciation adjustments are:

- Code section 168(b)(3) – Straight-line depreciation method with no adjustment to the recovery period. Note that this annual election needs only to be made on personal property since real property is already being depreciated using the straight-line method and the recovery periods are the same for regular tax and AMT purposes. No AMT adjustment is required.

- Code section 168(b)(2) - 150-percent declining balance method using the same recovery period as would be used for regular tax purposes. This is also an annual election that is made by the asset purchasing entity. However, since the depreciation method is still somewhat

accelerated (150-percent versus straight-line), higher depreciation deductions will be realized for regular tax purposes in the earlier years (and lower depreciation deductions will be realized in the later years) than would be generated using the Code section 168(b)(3) election. Again, with this election no AMT adjustment is required.

Although the size and number of AMT depreciation adjustments has been reduced after 1998 due to the change in recovery period requirements, assets placed in service prior to 1999 can still have sizeable and/or important AMT adjustments to consider – especially given the fact that we are getting to the point when some of the depreciation adjustments will turn around (become negative) and begin to reduce the taxpayers' AMTI.

Research and Experimental Expenditures Paid or Incurred After 1986 – Code section 174(a) allows taxpayers to deduct research and experimental expenses incurred in connection with a trade or business. Alternatively, the taxpayer may elect to capitalize and amortize such expenditures over sixty months for regular tax purposes.[20]

For AMT purposes, if research and experimental expenditures are deducted, an adjustment must be made in computing a non-corporate taxpayer's AMTI. The amount of the adjustment is equal to the difference between the current year expense and the amount that would have been deducted had the expenditures been capitalized and amortized over ten years.[21] However, if the taxpayer materially participates (as defined in the passive activity rules) in the business activities of the entity than incurred the expenditures, no AMT adjustment is required if the expenditures are deducted under Code section 174(a).[22]

An election may be made under Code section 59(e) to capitalize and amortize research and experimental expenditures over ten years for regular tax purposes. If this election is made, no AMT adjustment is required. This election can be made in any year expenditures are incurred. The taxpayer may elect to capitalize all, or any portion, of the research and experimental expenditures. Again, it is notable that if the election is not made and an AMT liability is created, a minimum tax credit may be available.

Intangible Drilling Costs – Most taxpayers will only see *intangible drilling costs* (IDC) as an investor in an oil and gas venture. In general, these costs must be capitalized and depleted over the life of the mineral property. However, there is the opportunity to deduct such expenditures when paid or incurred.[23]

If the taxpayer makes the election to expense IDC, an AMT preference item may be created. The preference is equal to the amount by which the "excess IDC" exceeds 65 percent of the taxpayer's net income from oil, gas and geothermal properties for the year.[24] Excess IDC is the IDC deduction amount from productive wells less the amount that would have been deductible if the productive IDC were capitalized and either (a) amortized over ten years beginning in the first month of production, or (b) depleted using cost depletion.

A taxpayer may make an election under Code section 59(e) to capitalize IDC and amortize it over sixty months beginning in the month the expenditure is paid or incurred. Like the election for research and experimental expenditures, this election can be made for all, or any portion, of current year IDC expenditures. If the election is made, no AMT preference item should be reported by the taxpayer.

These elections must be used with caution. If the elections are being considered because the taxpayer is currently paying the AMT due to deferral or timing adjustments, the AMT will likely be generating a MTC that can offset tax in future years. Increasing current income by slowing down depreciation or amortization and giving up the credit may not be a wise decision. If, on the other hand, the taxpayer is paying the AMT due to permanent adjustments, these elections could preserve deductions for use in future years when the AMT does not apply to the taxpayer. Either way, the need for multiple year projections of tax liability should be clear.

For non-AMT reasons, the elections may also be beneficial if the taxpayer has expiring net operating losses in the near future.

Utilizing Alternative Tax Net Operating Losses

A taxpayer that has a net operating loss (NOL) in a year may also, but not necessarily, have an alternative tax net operating loss (ATNOL). For this reason, a separate calculation must be performed to determine a taxpayer's ATNOL. This is done by starting with the NOL for regular tax purposes and increasing or decreasing this amount by the AMT adjustments and preferences in the year of the loss.[25]

Example: Jack Sprat determined that he had a NOL of $175,000 as a result of his business falling on hard times. His only AMT adjustment in that year was a $15,000 positive depreciation adjustment. Since the positive depreciation adjustment increases his AMTI, it reduces his NOL by that amount to yield an ATNOL of $160,000.

The ATNOL must be carried to the same tax year as the NOL.[26] Therefore, care must be taken before a decision is made whether to use the automatic carryback period, or instead elect to carry forward the regular NOL. The ATNOL is used to offset AMTI in the carryover year even if the taxpayer did not have an AMT liability for that year. In general, taxpayers may carryback NOLs and ATNOLs two years and forward twenty years.[27]

The amount of ATNOL that can be claimed as a reduction to AMTI is limited to 90 percent of the taxpayers AMTI determined without regard to the ATNOL.[28]

Example: Using the facts from the example above, Jack carries back the loss two years to a year in which his AMTI was $100,000 but did not have an AMT liability. Jack could utilize $90,000 of his ATNOL in that year and carry forward the remaining $70,000 to the next year.

Since the regular tax NOL is permitted to offset 100 percent of a taxpayer's income in a carryover year and the ATNOL is limited to 90 percent of the taxpayer's AMTI, the carry back of a loss to a prior year may actually trigger an AMT liability for the taxpayer. The NOL may wipe out all of the taxpayer's income but leave a sufficient amount of AMTI for some AMT to be assessed. Therefore, taxpayers must compute the benefit of carrying back the NOL and ATNOL to prior years by reviewing the impact under both tax systems.

FREQUNTLY ASKED QUESTIONS

Question – Do individual states have their own version of an AMT?

Answer – Some do. For 2014, eight states have some form of alternative minimum tax system, including California, Colorado, Connecticut, Iowa, Maryland,

Minnesota, New York, and Wisconsin. The specifics of the state-level AMT system vary by state, but most are not indexed for inflation like the Federal system, and thus will increasingly affect taxpayers in their states in the coming years. Taxpayers in the above states should carefully review if they may be affected by their state-level AMT in addition to the Federal system.

CHAPTER ENDNOTES

1. Urban-Brookings Tax Policy Center, Burman, Gale, & Rohaly. "The AMT: Projections and Problems", July 7, 2003; Available at: www.brook.edu/views/articles/gale/20030707.htm.

2. I.R.C. §55(b)(1)(A). Amounts are for 2014 and will be increased annually for inflation as prescribed under I.R.C. §55(d)(4).

3. I.R.C. §55(b)(3).

4. I.R.C. §55(b)(2); line 43 of Form 1040 (2006), or line 38 of Form 1040 (2006) if the standard deduction was used.

5. I.R.C. §55(b)(2)(A).

6. I.R.C. §55(b)(2)(B).

7. I.R.C. §55(d)(1).

8. I.R.C. §55(d)(4).

9. I.R.C. §55(d)(3).

10. Note: This planning idea will save both regular tax and AMT. A reimbursed expense is always better than a deductible one.

11. I.R.C. §26(a)(2).

12. I.R.C. §38(c).

13. I.R.C. §53(d)(1)(B)(ii).

14. I.R.C. §421(a).

15. I.R.C. §422(a)(1).

16. I.R.C. §56(b)(3).

17. I.R.C. §57(a)(5)(A).

18. I.R.C. §57(a)(5)(C)(i).

19. I.R.C. §56(a)(1)(A).

20. I.R.C. §174(b).

21. I.R.C. §56(b)(2).

22. I.R.C. §56(b)(2)(D).

23. I.R.C. §263(c).

24. I.R.C. §57(a)(2).

25. I.R.C. §56(d)(2).

26. Rev. Rul. 87-44, 1987-1 CB 3.

27. NOLs incurred prior to 1998 were permitted to be carried back three years and forward fifteen years.

28. I.R.C. §56(d)(1)(A).

EQUITY BASED COMPENSATION PLANNING

CHAPTER 26

INTRODUCTION

Stock options are typically given to executives of publicly traded companies as an award for past performance or an incentive for future results. But they are also commonly granted to non-executive employees and used as incentive tools by larger non-publicly traded businesses as well.

A stock option is a right to purchase one share of stock at a specified price. Usually, stock options can be converted to stock only after a specified period of time has elapsed. Then, the exercise of the option must occur before the expiration of period of time specified in the option.

There are a number of key terms that need to be defined before the discussion about how stock options are taxed can begin:

Grant – The transfer of the stock option by the company to the option holder. The date on which the employee receives the option is called the "grant date."

Strike Price – Also referred to as the "exercise price" or "option price," this is the predetermined price at which the option can be converted to stock.

Exercise – The transaction that converts the stock option into stock. The date on which the transaction occurs is known as the "exercise date."

Spread – The difference between the fair market value of the stock and the strike price of the stock option on the date of exercise. The spread also represents the potential compensation element of stock options that could be subject to taxation. The spread is sometimes referred to as the "bargain element."

Vesting – Some stock options may not be exercised immediately upon grant. Instead, the absolute and unconditional right to exercise the options may accrue or "vest" over a specified period of time. It is not uncommon, for example, for stock options to vest in equal amounts over four years. In that case, 25 percent of the stock options would become exercisable on each anniversary of the grant.

Vested – Refers to stock options that are currently exercisable.

In-the-money – Stock options with a strike price that is less than the current fair market value of the stock. If the reverse is true, an option is said to be "out-of-the-money" or "underwater."

For tax purposes, stock options are divided into two possible types. The type of stock option is determined as of the grant date and controls how the options will be taxed upon their exercise.

Nonqualified stock options (NQSOs). Although the rules surrounding NQSOs are much less stringent than ISOs, taxation of these options occurs as of the exercise date. The spread between the exercise price and the stock price on the exercise date is taxed as additional compensation, subject to the taxpayer's ordinary income tax rate.

Incentive Stock Options (ISOs). Also referred to as statutory stock options, ISOs are covered by Code section 422. There are a number of stringent rules that must be adhered to, both by the company granting the options and the employee who receives the options. In general, the taxation of ISOs is deferred until the employee actually sells the stock. At that time, the employee is taxable at long-term capital gain rates on the difference between the selling price and the exercise price. But there are rules for alternative minimum tax ("AMT") purposes that could cause an acceleration, or pre-payment, of tax in the year of exercise.

NONQUALIFIED STOCK OPTIONS

NQSOs are options that do not meet the requirements of Code Section 422, either intentionally or otherwise. There are generally no tax implications to the recipient of an NQSO on the grant date. The only exception is for publicly traded stock options. But it is extremely rare to find nonqualified employee stock options that trade in the public market. Note that employee stock options are different than puts and calls that commonly trade on publicly held companies.

NQSOs are a convenient and flexible way to award or encourage employees. There are no limits as to how many NQSOs may be granted, how the exercise price is determined, or the time limitation for expiration of the option. In fact, NQSOs are sometimes granted at an exercise price that is less than the fair market value of the stock on the grant date. These are referred to as "discounted stock options." But the deferred compensation rules of Code section 409A may cause such discounted stock options to be subject to tax upon grant (see further discussion of Code section 409A below).

The taxation of NQSOs typically occurs on the exercise date. At that point, the difference between the fair market value of the stock and the exercise price is recognized as additional compensation unless the stock is restricted (i.e. the stock is subject to a substantial risk of forfeiture and is not transferable). Payroll taxes must be withheld upon the exercise of NQSOs (federal, state, and local withholding, FICA, and FUTA). The spread is also included on the employee's Form W-2 wages in the year of exercise.

Employers benefit in two ways from the exercise of NQSOs. First, the company receives the gross exercise cost of the options. Second, the company is entitled to a tax deduction for the compensation element that is taxed to the employee.

Example: Balloons, Inc., Drew Freeney's employer, granted Drew an NQSO for 1,000 shares of stock of Balloons, Inc. The NQSO was exercisable immediately but was not publicly traded. The exercise price was $20 per share.

When the stock hit $50 per share, Drew exercised the NQSO for all of the stock by paying Balloons, Inc. $20,000 (1,000 shares at $20 per share). As a result, he will recognize $30,000 of compensation (1,000 shares at $50 per share less his exercise cost of $20,000). Balloons, Inc. will report this $30,000 of compensation one Drew's Form W-2 for the year of exercise and will also claim a tax deduction for the same amount in the year of exercise. In addition, Drew must pay Balloons an amount sufficient to cover any required employee payroll taxes.

If, at the time a NQSO is exercised, the stock is deemed to be restricted, the taxation of the stock may be deferred until the restrictions lapse. As covered more fully in Chapter 25, Conversion of Income, if the stock is subject to a substantial risk of forfeiture and is not freely transferable by the employee, the stock is considered to be restricted stock.

Example: Using the same facts in the previous example, assume the stock option plan for Balloons, Inc. states that, although the NQSOs may be exercised at any time after grant, the stock will be forfeited if the employee leaves within five years of the date of grant and the stock is not transferable during that time. In that case, the taxation of the stock (and the company's deduction) would not occur until the restrictions lapse. On the fifth anniversary, if the stock is valued at $70 per share, Drew would be forced to recognize $50,000 of compensation income at that time ([$70 − $20] × 1,000). Drew's holding period for capital gain purposes begins on the date the restrictions lapse.

The employee does have the option to make a so called "Section 83(b) election." This would subject the stock to taxation at the time of exercise but enable the gain from that point to be capital gain. The mechanics of making Section 83(b) elections is covered in Chapter 24 Conversion of Income.

Example: Continuing with the same fact pattern, Drew feels very optimistic about both the growth potential of the stock and that he will be able to meet the terms of the restrictions. So he decides to make an 83(b) election despite the fact that the restrictions will not lapse for some time. The resulting compensation at the time of exercise will be subject to tax as a result of the 83(b) election. The holding period for the stock begins at the date of exercise, so all future appreciation will qualify for capital gain treatment once the stock becomes transferable.

Strategies for Exercising Nonqualified Stock Options

Exercising nonqualified stock options generates taxable income to the extent of the difference between (a) the stock's fair market value and (b) the exercise cost. Therefore, it is equivalent to the employee receiving a cash bonus from the company and then the employee immediately using the bonus to purchase company stock. From this point, the taxpayer can opt to sell the stock or hold onto the resulting shares.

There are four common methods of funding the exercise cost of NQSOs:

1. *The employee pays the exercise cost and holds the stock.* If the employee believes that the stock has the potential to rise in the future, exercising NQSOs and holding the stock will begin the clock for long-term capital gain treatment. The exercise cost and resulting payroll taxes would need to be paid by the employee. The employee uses her own cash or other investments to pay the exercise price.

2. *Funds are borrowed to exercise NQSOs.* Borrowing money to cover the exercise cost and related payroll taxes may be a sound way to convert options to stock. The interest paid on such a loan will usually qualify as an investment interest expense that is potentially deductible by the employee.

3. *"Cashless" exercise.* NQSOs may be exercised and immediately sold for the fair market value of the stock. If the employee sells all of the stock, the exercise is the equivalent of a cash bonus. But in a sense, it is better than a real cash bonus since the timing of the taxable event is within the employee's control. A cashless exercise also occurs in situations where the employee sells only a sufficient number of shares to cover the exercise cost and the required payroll taxes.

Example: Mary Marsh exercises 1,000 NQSOs with an exercise cost of $10 per share at a time when the stock is trading at $40 per share. As a result, Mary will recognize $30,000 of taxable income ([$40 – $10] × 1,000). In order to cover the exercise cost, Mary immediately sells 250 shares (250 shares at $40 per share = $10,000). She may also decide to sell extra shares to cover the payroll taxes on the $30,000 of taxable income.

Note that since options are exercised at an average fair market value, a cashless exercise may create a gain or loss since the sale of the stock would occur on the open market at the prevailing stock price.

4. *Exchanging existing shares to exercise NQSOs.* Instead of coming up with cash or borrowing funds to exercise NQSOs that the employee wishes to hold, existing shares of the company stock may be exchanged to cover the exercise cost and related payroll taxes. The exchange of existing shares for new shares in the same company is not taxable under Code section 1036.

Example: John Simms owns 100 shares of Palmer Corp. with a basis of $10 per share. He decides to exercise 500 NQSOs he received from Palmer with an exercise cost of $20 per share. At the time of the exercise, the stock is trading at $100. Since the value of his existing shares equals his exercise cost of the NQSOs ($10,000), he uses the existing shares to fund this cost. John will report compensation of $40,000 ([$100 – $20] × 500). Ignoring the payroll tax cost, which John will need to pay from separate funds, John will have 500 shares of Palmer Corp. 100 of these shares will continue to have a cost of $10 per share—representing a carryover of the basis and holding period of the shares that were exchanged and not taxed. The remaining 400 shares will have a cost basis of $40,000, the taxable income recognized on the exercise of the 500 NQSOs.

INCENTIVE STOCK OPTIONS

A stock option can qualify as an ISO only if all of the requirements of Code section 422 are satisfied. As a general rule, the employee will not recognize any taxable income upon the grant or the exercise of an ISO. Instead, taxation will occur upon the ultimate sale of the stock acquired through the exercise of the ISO. So the timing of the taxable event is within the control of the employee. At that point, the resulting gain is normally taxed as a long-term capital gain.

Although no taxable income is recognized at the exercise of an ISO, the spread does create an adjustment item for alternative minimum tax (AMT) purposes. Since the AMT is often an unexpected (and costly) result of exercising ISOs, proper planning must be done to determine the amount and timing of ISO exercises.

There are six requirements for an option to qualify as an ISO:

1. *Option plan must be approved by shareholders.* The stock option must be granted as part of a plan approved by the shareholders of the company. The number of shares available under the option plan and the eligible employees must be identified.[1]

2. *Expiration of options.* The options must be granted within ten years of the earlier of shareholder approval or adoption and exercised within ten years of the grant date.[2]

3. *Exercise price.* The exercise price of the option must equal or exceed the fair market value of the stock on the grant date.[3]

4. *Restrictions on transferability.* The options may not be transferred except upon the death of the employee. The employee can be the only eligible person to exercise an ISO.[4]

5. *Shareholder restrictions.* If an employee owns more than 10 percent of the company at the time the option is granted, the option price must be at least 110 percent of the stock's fair market value and the option must be exercised within five years of the grant date.[5]

6. *Limitation on grant.* The fair market value of the stock that can be obtained through the exercise of ISOs is limited to $100,000 per calendar year. The fair market value is determined as of the grant date. The applicable year is determined by the year in which the ISO is first exercisable. Any ISOs granted that exceed this limit are treated as NQSOs.[6] Note that this limitation

is determined as of the grant date. It makes no difference when the options are ultimately exercised.

Example: Jones, Inc. grants Ted Johnson 10,000 ISOs with an exercise price of $50 per share. One-quarter of the ISOs vest over each of the next four years. Therefore, 2,500 ISOs with a total fair market value of $125,000 would be exercisable for the first time in each of the next four years. Only 2,000 of the options would qualify as ISOs (2,000 × $50 = $100,000). The remaining 500 options would be treated as NQSOs.

As previously mentioned, there is generally no income to be recognized by an employee upon the exercise of an ISO.[7] The exercise price of the ISO becomes the employee's basis in the stock and the holding period begins upon the exercise. Upon the sale of the stock in a "qualifying disposition," the taxpayer recognizes a long-term capital gain which is taxed at the more favorable capital gain rates. Unlike the rules for NQSOs, the issuing company does not receive a compensation deduction upon the exercise or ultimate sale of ISO stock in a qualifying disposition.

A qualifying disposition is one that occurs more than two years from the date of grant and more than one year from the date of exercise. In addition, the employee must have been continuously employed by the company that granted the ISO from the grant date up to three months before the exercise date (except in the case of death or disability).[8] Exchanges, gifts, and transfers of legal title are all considered dispositions for the purpose of this rule.

Example: Andy Williams is granted 1,000 ISOs on March 15, 2012. He exercises the options on July 6, 2013. He must hold the ISO stock until July 7, 2014 in order to sell the shares in a qualifying disposition.

Any disposition that is not a qualifying disposition is automatically considered to be a disqualifying disposition. If a disqualifying disposition of stock acquired by the exercise of an ISO occurs, the gain from the disposition is determined as follows:

1. Capital gain is recognized to the extent the selling price exceeds the fair market value on the date of exercise.

2. Ordinary income (treated as compensation) is recognized to the extent of the difference between the fair market value on the exercise date and the exercise cost. If the fair market value on the disposition date is less than the fair market value on the exercise date, the ordinary income is limited to the gain on the sale of the stock.

3. A capital loss is recognized only if the selling price is less than the exercise cost.

If a disqualifying disposition occurs, the ISO is essentially treated like a NQSO and the corporation would be entitled to a deduction for the ordinary income recognized by the employee.[9] Federal payroll taxes (FICA, FUTA, and federal income tax withholding) are not assessed on disqualifying dispositions.[10]

ISOs and the AMT

Although there is no income to be reported as a result of an exercise of ISOs for regular tax purposes, there are potential AMT implications. Generally, the spread that would be reported as compensation if the ISO were a NQSO is an addition to the employee's AMT income in the year of exercise.[11]

Since the spread is reported as income for AMT purposes, the employee has two different tax bases—one for regular taxes (equal to the exercise cost) and one for AMT (equal to the fair market value on the exercise date).

___

Example: Maria Shaunessy exercised 100 ISOs at a total cost of $5,000 in July. On the exercise date, the stock price was $75 per share. The total value of $7,500 (100 shares at $75 per share) less the exercise cost of $5,000 represents the spread that must be added to Maria's AMT income ($2,500). Maria's regular cost basis is the $5,000 exercise cost and her AMT cost basis is the $7,500 fair market value on the exercise date.

___

If the stock acquired through an ISO exercise is sold in a disqualifying disposition in the same year, no AMT adjustment is reported.[12]

___

Example: Using the same facts from the previous example, if Maria sells the stock for $8,500

in November of the same year, she would recognize a gain of $3,500. Of this amount $2,500 would be ordinary income ($7,500 – $5,000) and $1,000 would be a short-term capital gain. No AMT adjustment would be required.

___

Since the regular tax basis and AMT basis are different, the sale of stock acquired through ISOs in any other year represents an adjusted gain or loss for AMT purposes in the future year.

___

Example: Instead of selling the stock in November, Maria waits until January of the following year. The AMT adjustment of $2,500 would be reported in the year of exercise. In the year the ISO stock is sold, she would adjust her AMT income down by the $2,500 difference in the tax basis of the stock.

___

Warning: The $3,000 capital loss rules apply for AMT as well as for regular tax purposes. If the stock price declined from the date of the ISO exercise, it is possible that the amount of the negative adjustment will be limited to account for the $3,000 capital loss limitation.

___

Example: Jack Brown exercised 5,000 ISOs when the stock was trading at $100 per share. His total exercise cost was $10,000 and he reported a positive AMT adjustment of $490,000 and paid a large amount of AMT as a result. The stock price tumbled and Jack sold the stock in a qualifying disposition when it was trading at $40 per share. For regular tax purposes, Jack recognizes a long-term capital gain of $190,000 ([$40 × 5,000] – $10,000). For AMT purposes, Jack recognized a loss of $300,000 ($500,000 – $200,000). Since he has no other capital gains, his AMT loss is limited to $3,000. He will report an adjusted gain or loss of a negative $193,000 and carryover an AMT capital loss of $297,000 to future years.

___

Because of the potential AMT due in the year of exercise, combined with the capital loss limitations in future years, it may be wise to sell ISO stock that has declined since the exercise date in a disqualifying disposition in the same year as the year of exercise. It was not uncommon during the stock market's "Internet Bubble" to have an employee's AMT liability exceed the value of the stock when the tax was due. By selling stock in a disqualifying disposition, no AMT adjustment would need to be reported and the AMT can be minimized, if not eliminated. The net proceeds would then be used to pay the ordinary income tax due upon the disqualifying disposition.

The AMT adjustment created by the exercise of ISOs is a deferral item. As a result, any AMT that is paid may be recovered through the minimum tax credit ("MTC"). To the extent the AMT was generated by deferral items, a MTC is created. The MTC may generally be used in future years to offset a regular tax liability that exceeds the taxpayer's tentative minimum tax.

AMT paid as a result of ISO exercises is generally a prepayment of tax due to this MTC and will be recovered when the ISO stock is sold or as time passes and the MTC is utilized. The MTC is covered more fully in Chapter 9, Alternative Minimum Tax.

STRATEGIES FOR EXERCISING INCENTIVE STOCK OPTIONS

The interplay of the AMT, MTC, and regular tax implications creates the need for long-term multi-year planning to determine the most tax efficient way to exercise ISOs. Of course the fluctuation in the stock price makes obtaining absolute tax efficiency impossible.

In addition to the strategies outlined earlier in this chapter for funding the exercise of NQSOs, which also apply to ISOs, the following are ISO strategies which should be considered:

Staggering ISO exercises. Many employees wait to exercise their ISOs until the expiration date is approaching under the assumption that they are deferring taxes. But it may be wise to exercise a certain number of ISOs each year to reduce the overall AMT impact.

Since the AMT is usually less the regular tax liability for most taxpayers, there is a certain amount of ISO "spread" that can be absorbed each year without the imposition of the AMT. As a result, the employee (1) obtains ISO stock without paying any additional tax and (2) starts the clock running on the holding period needed for a qualifying disposition. After ISO stock is held for the requisite amount of time, the sale creates a negative adjustment, which then creates more room for additional ISOs to be exercised in the later years.

Example: Howard Washington projects that he is able to absorb $25,000 worth of AMT adjustments from the exercise of ISOs. He exercises 1,000 ISOs with cost of $10 per share when the stock price is $35 per share. He reports the $25,000 adjustment but pays no AMT. Howard projects in the next year that he once again is able to absorb $25,000 of AMT adjustments. He also decides to sell the stock he acquired from the ISO exercise in the prior year (more than one year from the exercise date and two years from the grant date). The negative AMT adjustment of $25,000 will allow him to absorb a larger amount of positive AMT adjustments from current year ISO exercises. Note that due to capital gains tax rate differences, the amount that can be absorbed may be less than $50,000, the otherwise available AMT adjustment room and the negative AMT adjustment created by the sale.

Planning for restricted stock. If the stock that is acquired by an ISO is restricted, the AMT adjustment is not reported until the year in which the restrictions lapse. If the stock price rises between the exercise date and when the restrictions lapse, a larger AMT adjustment must be reported at that time.

As is the case for restricted stock acquired by the exercise of NQSOs, the employee has the option to make a Section 83(b) election at the time of exercise. The AMT adjustment would then be locked in based on the fair market value on the exercise date. The mechanics of making Section 83(b) elections is covered in Chapter 24, Conversion of Income.

Use of leverage to buy dividend paying stocks. Until ISOs are exercised and converted to stock, the employee has no right to any dividends. While there is a preferential tax rate for qualified dividends, it may make sense to exercise ISOs sooner, even if a loan were necessary to support the exercise cost.

Example: Six years ago, Nina Walsh was granted 10,000 ISOs with an exercise cost of $5 per share. The stock is now trading at $30 per share and pays an annual dividend of $1 per share. In order to exercise the ISOs, she would need to pay $50,000 (assume that she does not pay any AMT as a result of this exercise). Using an interest rate of 8 percent, her total interest on the loan would be $4,000 per year. The interest could be fully deductible against ordinary income as investment interest expense depending on Nina's investment income and other itemized deductions. Assuming her marginal tax bracket is 35 percent and the interest can be fully deducted, her total interest cost is $2,600, after taxes. Since she now owns the stock, she will receive $10,000 per year of dividends. Assuming her tax rate on qualified dividends is 15 percent, she will net $8,500 of dividend income, after taxes. As a result of this strategy, she is ahead $5,900 per year after taxes.

Exchanging stock for stock. A common practice is to use existing ISO stock to exercise more ISOs. Since ISO stock usually has an unrealized gain associated with the shares, this stock would achieve the maximum gain deferral. In order for the technique to work, the ISO stock that is being exchanged must have been held for the requisite amount of time to avoid the disqualifying disposition rules.

As mentioned earlier for the NQSO strategies, the number of shares used in the exchange retain the basis (for regular and AMT purposes) and holding period they had before the exchange. The additional shares acquired would have a regular tax cost equal to amount of funds needed for the ISO exercise in excess of the value of the shares used in the exchange. The AMT basis for the new shares would be the fair market value of the new shares plus any additional amounts needed to fund the exercise cost.

Example: Mike Simms owns 100 shares of Palmer Corp. (acquired by ISO) with a regular tax basis of $10 per share and an AMT basis of $40 per share. He decides to exercise 500 ISOs he received from Palmer with an exercise cost of $20 per share. At the time of the exercise, the stock is trading at $100. Since the value of his existing shares equals his exercise cost of the ISOs ($10,000), he uses the existing shares to fund this cost. John will report an AMT adjustment of $40,000 ([$100 – $20] × 500). John will then have 500 shares of Palmer Corp. 100 of these shares will continue to have a cost of $10 per share for regular tax purposes and $40 per share for AMT purposes—representing a carryover of the basis and holding period of the shares that were exchanged and not taxed. The remaining 400 shares will have a cost basis

of zero (John paid nothing for them) and an AMT basis of $40,000, the total fair market value of the additional shares acquired by the ISO exercise.

FREQUENTLY ASKED QUESTIONS

Question – How are commissions and fees incurred upon the sale of stock acquired by an option exercise treated?

Answer – Commissions and fees are added to the cost of the stock acquired. Therefore, even in the case of an option exercise and immediate sale of the stock, the employee may report a small capital loss as a result of these expenses.

Question – Do the states follow the federal rules for ISOs?

Answer – Certain states follow the federal rules and others do not. The laws of state of residency and the state in which the options were earned (if different) should be reviewed to determine how the options are treated. States which do not follow the federal ISO rules typically treat the options as NQSOs and subject them to tax in the year of exercise.

Question – How do the deferred compensation rules of Code section 409A apply to typical stock option plans?

Answer – Code section 409A was structured to tax certain plans that provide for the deferral of compensation into future years unless certain requirements were met. The requirements centered on the timing of the elections by the employee to defer compensation, how the deferred compensation plan was funded, and the ultimate distribution options to the employee.

NQSO plans are not subject to the 409A rules if the terms of the plan meet certain safe harbor guidelines as contained in the final 409A regulations:

1. The exercise price must not be less that the value of the stock on the date of the grant *and* the number of shares must be fixed on the original date of the grant.

2. The stock received on exercise is subject to tax under Code section 83.

3. The option does not include any feature for the deferral of compensation other than the deferral of income until the later of (a) the date of exercise or the disposition of the option, or (b) the time the stock first becomes substantially vested.[13]

If the plan fails to meet any one of these three provisions, the entire plan is tainted and taxation of the options would occur upon grant and potentially subject the employee to a 20 percent penalty on the deferred compensation.[14]

ISO plans are excluded from the Code section 409A rules.[15]

CHAPTER ENDNOTES

1. I.R.C. §422(b)(1).
2. I.R.C. §§422(b)(2) and (3).
3. I.R.C. §422(b)(4).
4. I.R.C. §422(b)(5).
5. I.R.C. §422(b)(6).
6. I.R.C. §422(d).
7. I.R.C. §422(a)(1).
8. I.R.C. §422(a)(1).
9. I.R.C. §421(b).
10. I.R.C. §§421(b), 3306(b)(19), and 3121(a)(22).
11. I.R.C. §56(b)(3).
12. I.R.C. §56(b)(3).
13. Treas. Reg. §1.409A-1(b)(5)(i)(A).
14. I.R.C. §409A(a)(B).
15. Treas. Reg. §1.409A-1(b)(5)(ii).

Figure 26.1

COMPARISON OF NQSOs AND ISOs		
	Nonqualified Stock Options	**Incentive Stock Options**
Taxation at Grant	No tax consequences unless the option is publicly traded	No tax consequences
Number of Options	Unlimited	Only options on stock with an underlying value of $100,000, determined as of the grant date, may first be exercisable by an employee in any given calendar year.
Exercise Price	Can be set at any amount.	Cannot be lower than the fair market value of the stock on the grant date. If the employee is a 10% or greater shareholder, the exercise price must be at least 110% of the stock's fair market value on the grant date.
Taxation at Exercise	Difference between fair market value and exercise cost is taxable as ordinary income and is subject to payroll taxes. If the stock is restricted, taxation is deferred until restrictions lapse unless an 83(b) election is made by the employee.	No tax consequences for regular tax purposes. The difference between the fair market value and exercise cost is a positive AMT adjustment in the year of exercise unless the stock is sold in a disqualifying disposition in the same year.
Payroll Taxes	Must be collected upon exercise	Federal payroll taxes are not required upon the exercise or disqualifying disposition. Review state and local requirements.
Taxation at Disposition	Gain or loss on sale is recognized. Basis of stock is equal to the exercise cost and the amount of ordinary income reported on the exercise.	If the sale is a qualifying disposition, any gain is taxed as a long-term capital gain. The difference between the basis of the stock for regular tax and AMT purposes is a negative adjustment for determining AMT in the year of disposition. If the sale is a disqualifying disposition, the gain on the sale is ordinary income to the extent of the spread at the time of exercise. Any excess gain is capital gain.

CHARITABLE CONTRIBUTION PLANNING

CHAPTER 27

INTRODUCTION

An individual may deduct certain amounts for contributions made to, or for the use of, qualified charitable organizations.[1] Such tax-deductible contributions may be in the form of cash, property, or certain partial interests in property. Although the act of donating money or property to a charity may be relatively easy, claiming a valid deduction for a charitable contribution involves more work. A donor and/or his tax advisor must know or confirm:

- which organizations are qualified to receive charitable contributions;

- what types of contributions are deductible;

- how much is deductible;

- what records to acquire from the charity or appraiser and keep for the files;

- when those records must be obtained; and

- how to report the charitable contribution.

This chapter explores the various types of charitable giving strategies that exist for taxpayers and the rules affecting the income tax charitable deduction. For the rules affecting the gift tax and estate tax charitable deductions, see the sidebar "Comparing the Income, Gift, and Estate Tax Charitable Deductions." For an overview of the advantages and disadvantages of the various types of charitable gifts, see Figure 27.1.

COMPARING THE INCOME, GIFT, AND ESTATE TAX CHARITABLE DEDUCTIONS

For the most part, charitable deductions under the gift tax and estate tax rules are similar to those under the income tax rules, but subtle distinctions do exist. In some instances, charitable contributions to certain organizations are allowed only for income tax purposes. For example, gifts to certain cemetery companies provide a donor with a current income tax charitable deduction, but such organizations are not mentioned by the gift tax or the estate tax rules.[2] In addition, although gifts to or for the use of possessions of the United States made exclusively for public purposes are deductible under Internal Revenue Code section 170(c), such gifts are not provided for in similar provisions of the gift and estate tax rules.

In certain cases, the estate and gift tax rules are more flexible than the income tax rules. For instance, contributions to or for the use of any corporation organized and operated exclusively for religious, charitable, scientific, literary, or educational purposes do not have to be used within the United States to be deductible. Furthermore, the estate and gift tax rules allow deductions for contributions to or for the use of a fraternal society, order, or association without the requirement found in the income tax rules that such organizations be domestic. For gift tax purposes, nonresidents are subject to a separate set of rules that generally require that gifts be used within the United States or made to qualifying domestic corporations to be deductible. The distinctions noted above should be considered and the income, estate, and gift tax rules should each be examined to generally determine what types of organizations may receive charitable contributions.

Figure 27.1

TYPES OF CHARITABLE GIFTS		
TYPE OF GIFT	**ADVANTAGES**	**DISADVANTAGES**
Outright gifts	Donor receives a current income tax deduction.	Amount of income tax deduction is limited to certain percentages of the donor's contribution base.[2]
	Assets are removed from gross estate if gift is not made within three years of the donor's death.[1]	Gift must be of an absolute interest in most cases.[3]
	Gift may be given to charity immediately.	Funds or assets are no longer available for use by donor during lifetime.
Charitable bequests	Charitable gift is revocable during lifetime.	No current tax benefits.
		A bequest may become a liability of the estate.
	A bequest is relatively inexpensive to set up.	Assets may need to be liquidated at less than fair market value to meet the charitable obligation.
	A bequest provides a charitable gift painlessly.	
	Gift can be made with anonymity during lifetime.	The estate may experience "shrinkage" due to the charitable obligation.
	Unlimited charitable deduction for the estate.	Charitable bequests must be probated, adding cost and time.
	Creates the potential for a smaller estate and, thus, a possibly lower estate tax.	
Charitable gift annuities	Charitable gift annuities are relatively simple and easy to understand.	The charitable gift is irrevocable.
		The annuity income will remain fixed and will not compensate for inflation.
	The charity receives a current gift.	
	The annuitant will receive a predictable income for life.	Charity needs to be financially sound, or reinsure the payout.
	Capital gain is distributed over the life of the annuity.	
	The donor will receive a tax-free return of principal.	
	The donor will receive a current income tax charitable deduction.	
	Charitable gift annuity can be funded with relatively small amounts of money.	

1. I.R.C. §. 2035.
2. I.R.C. §. 170(b).
3. See I.R.C. §. 170(f).

Figure 27.1 (cont'd)

TYPES OF CHARITABLE GIFTS		
TYPE OF GIFT	**ADVANTAGES**	**DISADVANTAGES**
Charitable remainder trusts: • Charitable remainder annuity trusts (CRATs) • Charitable remainder unitrusts (CRUTs)	Donor receives a current income tax deduction.[1] Donor can contribute highly appreciated property and not have to recognize the gain. Donor can reduce future estate taxes. Assets placed in the trust can be sold or converted to increase income. The trust can invest in tax-exempt vehicles.	Complex creation and administration. Assets are irrevocably donated to the trust. Accounting and trustee fees are required. A qualified appraisal of the assets will generally have to be made.[2]
Charitable lead trusts: • Charitable lead annuity trusts (CLATs) • Charitable lead unitrusts (CLUTs)	Allows the donor to pass on assets to heirs in the future at a discount. The donor gives a current gift to charity. A current income tax deduction can be utilized by the donor. The donor can transfer highly appreciated property without recognizing the gain. The donor can maximize the effectiveness of the generation-skipping tax exemption.	If the donor receives a current income tax deduction, all the future income from the trust will be considered taxable income to him.[3] Charitable lead trusts are somewhat complex and difficult to draft and administer. The donor and heirs give up use of the income for the life of the trust. The transfer of assets to a charitable lead trust is irrevocable.
Supporting organizations, community foundations	Gives the donor greater flexibility in structuring their charitable wishes. Relatively easy to set up and administer for the donor. Relatively inexpensive to use. Higher deductibility limits than private foundations. Enables the donor and his descendants to participate in charitable giving in the community for generations.	Donor has very little control over investments and distributions. Gifts are irrevocable. Donor may disagree with the policies of the community foundation. Most grants from the community foundation go to the surrounding community and not to national charities.

1. I.R.C. §. 170(f)(2)(A).
2. Treas. Reg. §1.170A-13(c)(1).
3. I.R.C. §. 170(f)(2)(B).

Figure 27.1 (cont'd)

TYPES OF CHARITABLE GIFTS		
TYPE OF GIFT	**ADVANTAGES**	**DISADVANTAGES**
Pooled income funds	Donor receives current income tax deduction.	Fund cannot receive or invest in tax-exempt securities.[1]
	Non-income producing assets can be converted into income-producing assets.	Income is unpredictable from year to year.
	Donating highly appreciated assets does not cause recognition of gain.	All income received is taxed as ordinary income.
	Income will be paid to income beneficiaries for life.	Remainder interest will generally go to only one charity.[2]
	Pooled income fund will pay out the actual income earned.	Pooled income fund cannot easily accept hard to value or illiquid assets.
Donor advised funds[3]	Donor receives an immediate charitable deduction, even if grants are spread out for years.	Gift is irrevocable.
		Annual fees and charges are usually imposed by the sponsoring charity.
	Compared to private foundations, donations made to a donor advised fund receive favorable tax treatment. If cash is donated, the donor's deduction can be applied to 50% of his AGI. If highly appreciated assets are donated, the deduction is limited to 30% of AGI.	Some charities put restriction on grants immediately after the fund is established (e.g., disallowing grants exceeding a fixed percentage of the fund, or requiring that a high minimum amount be paid out).
		Donor's rights to control the management and distribution of the fund assets are limited.
	Donor has ability to recommend a number of charitable grantees. As long as the sponsoring charity approves the distribution and ensures that no private benefit is inuring to the donor, the fund can benefit numerous charitable causes.	
	Generally very simple to understand and easy to use.	
	Can be established relatively quickly, which can be very useful in year-end tax planning.	

1. I.R.C. §. 642(c)(5)(C).
2. I.R.C. §. 642(c) (5)(E); Treas. Reg. §1.642(c)-5(b)(5).
3. *Tools & Techniques of Charitable Planning* (2nd Edition), pp. 176-177 (National Underwriter Company, 2007).

Figure 27.1 (cont'd)

TYPES OF CHARITABLE GIFTS		
TYPE OF GIFT	**ADVANTAGES**	**DISADVANTAGES**
Private foundations	Provides donor with a current income tax charitable deduction.[1]	Smaller percentage limits on a donor's adjusted gross income reduce the amount the donor can potentially deduct.
	Donor has more control over distributions.	Income tax deduction for some gifts of appreciated property may be limited to basis.[2]
	Donor can memorialize his name or the family name.	
	Allows the donor to create a lasting charitable vehicle.	Complex to establish and maintain.
		Must apply to IRS for recognition of tax exempt status.[3]
	Donor can prefund future gifts to charity.	Minimum payout required annually.[4]
	Creates an entity where the donor and his family can work together for a common charitable goal.	Tax returns open to the public.[5]
		Subject to excise taxes.[76]

1. I.R.C. §. 170(b)(1)(B), 170(b)(1)(D).
2. I.R.C. §. 170(e)(1).
3. See I.R.C. §. 508(a)(1).
4. See I.R.C. §. 508(e).
5. I.R.C. §. 6104.
6. See I.R.C. §. 4940–4945.

WHAT IS A "QUALIFIED CHARITY"?

It is critical to determine to what type of organization a donor may make a contribution *and* also receive a charitable deduction for income tax purposes.[3] Charitable contributions to nonqualified organizations (i.e., organizations that do *not* fall within the categories listed in the Internal Revenue Code) will *not* be deductible by the donor.

There is an important distinction between an *exempt* organization and a *charitable* organization. An *exempt* organization is an organization that is exempt from federal income tax under Code Section 501.[4] Exempt organizations are commonly referred to as "501(c)(3)" organizations because this is where the types of organizations eligible for exemption are listed in the Internal Revenue Code.[5] However, contributions to *exempt* organizations are *not* necessarily tax deductible.

A *charitable* organization, on the other hand, is an exempt organization that is qualified to receive charitable contributions that are deductible for income tax purposes. For purposes of the income tax charitable deduction, there are five types of organizations to which a charitable contribution can be made:

(1) **Charitable organizations.** A corporation, trust, community chest or fund, or foundation that satisfies all of the following requirements:

  a.   Organized or created in (or under the laws of) the United States, any state, the District of Columbia, or a U.S. possession;

  b.   Organized and operated *exclusively* for one or more of the following purposes:

  •   religious, charitable, scientific, literary, or educational purposes,

- to foster national or international amateur sports competition (so long as the organization's activities does not involve the provision of athletic facilities or equipment), *or*

- for the prevention of cruelty to children or animals;

c. No part of the organization's net earnings inure to the benefit of any private shareholder or individual; *and*

d. The organization is not disqualified from tax exempt status due to its attempting to influence legislation, and the organization does not participate in activities considered a part of a political campaign on behalf of or against any candidate for public office.

(2) **Governmental units**. The United States, a state, a U.S. possession, a political subdivision of a state or possession, or the District of Columbia *if* the gift is made *exclusively* for public purposes.

(3) **War veterans' organizations**. If the gift is made to a domestic fraternal society, order or association organized in the U.S or a possession *if* no part of the organization's net earnings inures to the benefit of a private shareholder or individual.

(4) **Fraternal associations**. To qualify, the gift must be:

a. made by an individual;

b. made to a domestic fraternity society, order, or association operating under the lodge system; *and*

c. used exclusively for religious, charitable, scientific, literary, or educational purposes, or for the prevention of cruelty to children or animals.

(5) Certain nonprofit cemetery companies.[6]

The organizations listed above are all "qualified" charitable organizations; however, the amount that may be deducted by a donor varies according to the rules explained below. The IRS maintains the "Exempt Organizations Select Check," a publically available database of qualified charities (as well as charities

that have been automatically revoked for failure to file a Form 990 or 990-N for three consecutive years).[7]

WHAT TYPES OF GIFT TECHNIQUES ARE AVAILABLE?

Although cash is one of the most commonly used gifts, it is not necessarily the most advantageous or convenient gift for a donor to make – and in fact, over the long run, it may not be the donor's best option. For this reason, many advisors have encouraged their clients to look at different gift techniques, including:

- Outright Gifts
- Charitable Bequests
- Charitable Gift Annuities
- "Split Interest" Gifts (typically in the form of a trust)
- Private Foundations
- Supporting Organizations
- Community Organizations
- Donor Advised Funds
- Pooled Income Funds
- Charitable Gifts of Life Insurance

Each technique is explained in detail below.

Outright Gifts

Outright gifts are the type of charitable gifts with which people are most familiar. The simplest type of outright gift is a contribution of cash to charity. Determining the value of a cash gift is inherently easy, and proof of payment can be established without a large amount of documentation.

Outright gifts create the most immediate economic benefit to the charity because the gift is made either in cash or property in which the charity assumes an absolute interest. But while a donor retains absolutely no interest in an asset that is donated outright, he can still attach restrictions on the charity's use of the donated asset. For instance, a donor can designate that a cash gift be used for building a new facility for the charity or be placed in a university scholarship fund.

Aside from the satisfaction of making a charitable gift, the donor also can benefit by:

- taking an immediate income tax deduction, generally for the fair market value of the gift, and

- removing assets from his gross estate (and, thus, reducing the amount of estate tax due).[8]

However, the donor should be aware of the income tax rules that limit the donor's income tax charitable deduction to certain percentages of adjusted gross income.[9] When making gifts other than cash, the most significant tax benefit comes from a contribution of highly appreciated property; assuming that the gift is deductible at its fair market value, such a contribution generally does not result in a taxable gain (or loss) to the donor.[10]

Charitable Bequests

More charitable gifts are made by bequest than any other method of giving. A *charitable bequest* is a charitable gift that is made by will, revocable during the life of the donor, and operable only upon the donor's death. A bequest can be made of any of the following:

- a specific amount;

- a specific asset; or

- a percentage of the estate.

When a will is probated, the charity is provided with the assets or amount designated.[11] Charitable bequests can also be part of a donor's estate planning as the donor's estate will generally receive a deduction for the amount equal to the bequest.[12] The estate may deduct the entire value, since there is no income or estate tax limitation on the deductible amount of a charitable bequest.[13] Furthermore, reducing the assets in the estate through charitable bequests can result in "bracket slippage," thereby compounding the saving of estate taxes, as illustrated by the following example.

Example: Lisa died in 2013 with a gross estate of $7.7 million, but made a charitable bequest of $700,000. Without the charitable bequest (and assuming she did not use any of her unified credit), her estate would have owed federal estate taxes of $980,000. Because of her bequest of $700,000, the value of her estate was lowered for estate tax purposes from $7.7 million to $7.0 million, which lowered her federal estate tax bill to $700,000, a savings of $280,000 (40 percent).

Charitable Gift Annuities

A *charitable gift annuity* agreement is a contract entered into between a charity and a donor in which the charity agrees to pay an annuity to the individual donor in return for an amount transferred by the individual to the charity. The result is that the charity receives a current gift and the donor/annuitant is provided with a predictable income stream for life.

A charitable gift annuity is basically the same as a commercial annuity since the person who receives the annual income is the annuitant and the income is paid to the annuitant for over a period of one or two lives. The main difference is that a commercial annuity will pay a higher income and the charitable annuity will pay a lower rate, which reflects the "gift" element of the arrangement. Many charities use the annuity rates recommended by the American Council on Gift Annuities in determining payment amounts to annuitants (see Appendix B). These rates are designed to provide a residual amount for the charity of 50 percent of the initial amount of the contribution, if the donor lives to life expectancy.

The charitable gift annuity is comprised of two components. The first component is the annuity part of the transaction and is very similar to a commercial annuity in concept and in income tax treatment. Each payment that the annuitant receives is made up of a taxable interest portion and a tax-free return of principal.

The second component consists of the gift amount, which is viewed as an outright gift to charity. The amount of the charitable contribution is equal to the amount by which the assets transferred to the charity exceed the value of the annuity.[14] To calculate the current income tax deduction, subtract the present value of the gift annuity from the fair market value of the property transferred. The present value of the gift annuity is determined by reference to the tables contained in the estate tax regulations.[15]

Figure 27.2

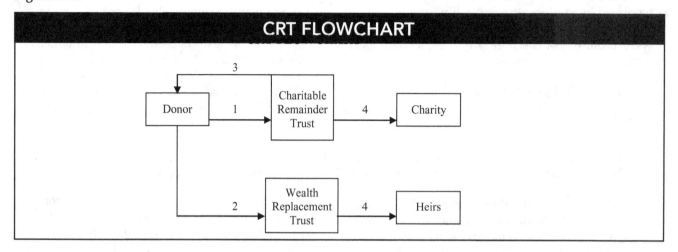

"Split Interest" Gifts

The term *split interest* refers to gifts where an interest in the property benefits a charitable and a noncharitable beneficiary. The donor can transfer an immediate benefit to the charitable beneficiary with the remainder interest going to a noncharitable beneficiary later, or employ the reverse strategy where a noncharitable beneficiary receives the immediate economic benefit with the remainder interest eventually going to charity. When the donor makes the charity the remainder beneficiary, the split interest gift is commonly referred to as a "deferred gift." A split interest gift may be made in trust or property; however, charitable split interest trusts include many of the more popular methods of charitable giving such as charitable remainder trusts and charitable lead trusts (both discussed below).

Charitable Remainder Trusts

A *charitable remainder trust* (CRT) is a trust instrument that provides for specified payments to one or more individuals, with an irrevocable remainder in the trust property to be paid to or held for a charity.[16] The trust has three associated entities:

(1) the **donor**, who contributes an asset to the trust;

(2) a **lead annuity or unitrust beneficiary**; and

(3) a **charitable beneficiary** of the remainder interest.

The donor and the lead beneficiary can be the same person.

CRTs have become very popular as a charitable giving technique because of the many tax advantages they offer to the charity and donor. The charity receives what frequently turns out to be a sizable gift while the donor receives an income tax deduction and reduces his future estate tax. CRTs are also popular because they give the donor the opportunity to donate highly appreciated property to the CRT and potentially avoid recognizing the capital gains.

Charitable remainder trusts are typically used in conjunction with *wealth replacement trusts*. The basic concept of a *wealth replacement trust* is to replace the assets given to charity for the benefit of the donor's heirs. Wealth replacement trusts generally take the form of an irrevocable trust and are generally funded with life insurance in an amount equal to, or greater than, the value of the property transferred to the CRT. The charitable planning design of a typical CRT can be summarized in four steps:

Step 1: The donor contributes assets to the CRT. The donor receives a charitable deduction equal to the present value of the remainder interest.[17]

Step 2: The donor sets up a "wealth replacement trust" (see below).

Step 3: The lead beneficiary, often the donor, receives annuity or unitrust payments from the CRT for a term of years (not in excess of twenty years) or for the life of the donor.[18]

Step 4: At death or the end of a term of years, the heirs receive the proceeds of the wealth replacement trust, and the charity receives the remaining assets in the CRT as the holder of the remainder interest in the trust.

Figure 27.3

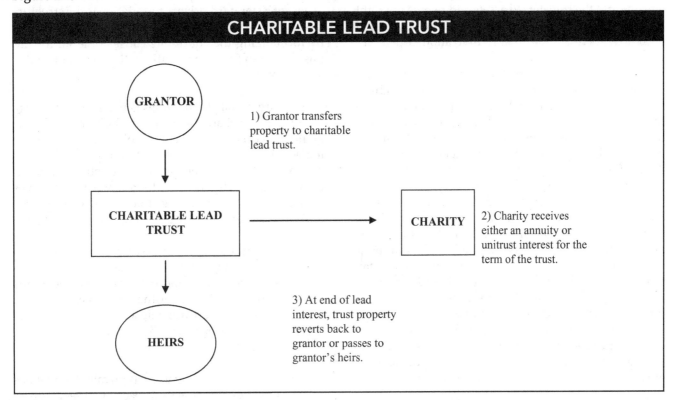

Charitable remainder trusts are designed in one of two basic variations, as explained below:

- charitable remainder annuity trusts (CRATs); and

- charitable remainder unitrusts (CRUTs).

Charitable Remainder Annuity Trusts

A *charitable remainder annuity trust* (CRAT) provides to a noncharitable beneficiary a fixed payment at least annually of not less than 5 percent or more than 50 percent of the initial net fair market value of the trust, with an irrevocable remainder interest to be paid to or held for charity.[19] The value of the remainder interest must be at least 10 percent of the initial net fair market value of all property placed in the trust.[20] The assets in a CRAT are valued at the inception of the trust, and the donor can contribute to the CRAT only at the time the trust is created. Furthermore, the fixed payment amount cannot be limited to the net income of the trust.

Charitable Remainder Unitrusts

A *charitable remainder unitrust* (CRUT) is similar to a CRAT, but with a few important differences. The lead interest in a CRUT usually takes one of three basic forms:

(1) **Standard CRUT:** The payout of the trust is a fixed percentage of not less than 5 percent or more than 50 percent of the net fair market value of the trust assets calculated at least annually.[21]

(2) **Net income unitrust:** The payout is the *lesser* of (1) the fixed percentage or (2) the actual income for the trust in that year (this type is also known as an "income only" unitrust).[22]

(3) **Net income with makeup unitrust:** Commonly known as a "NIMCRUT," the trust is an income-only trust that provides for any income deficiencies in past years to be *made up* to the extent trust income exceeds the amount of the specified percentage in later years.[23]

In addition, with respect to each contribution to the trust, the value of the remainder interest generally must be at least 10 percent of the net fair market value of the property as of the date it was contributed.[24]

Charitable Lead Trusts

A *charitable lead trust* (CLT) is essentially the reverse of a charitable remainder trust. In a CLT, the donor gives the charity the current economic benefit or payment stream from the transferred assets and retains the right to receive the assets back at the end of the designated term of years or transfer that right to another person.

As in the case of a charitable remainder trust, a CLT can be either an annuity trust or a unitrust. A charitable lead annuity trust (CLAT) will pay the charity a fixed amount each year regardless of the income that the assets generate, whereas a charitable lead unitrust (CLUT) will pay the charity a fixed percentage of the value of the assets of the trust calculated annually.[25]

In general, the CLT gives the donor the opportunity to pass on assets to heirs in the future at a discount while also providing beneficial tax treatment to the donor and his estate. If the CLT is structured as a grantor trust (see Chapter 13) taxable to the grantor for income tax purposes, the grantor/donor may be allowed an upfront income tax charitable deduction in the amount of the present value of the charity's annuity or unitrust interest.[26] If the CLT is not structured as a grantor trust, no upfront income tax charitable deduction is available, but the trust may be able to deduct amounts as they are distributed from the trust to charity.

Note that the income tax deduction for the charitable contribution determined upon the creation of the CLT is subject to a 30 percent of adjusted gross income limitation. Any unused excess charitable contribution may be carried forward for up to five years.

Another reason for using a CLT is the reduction of transfer costs to future heirs as it can be instrumental in maximizing the generation-skipping transfer tax exemption. The Section 7520 rate represents the "hurdle" rate over which cumulative earnings and appreciation will be transferred to the beneficiaries of the trust free of gift tax. Accordingly, a CLT provides more significant advantages when the Section 7520 rate is low.

Private Foundations

Standard private foundation

A *private foundation* (also referred to as a "family foundation") is a charitable organization generally established by an individual donor or a family who wishes to control, as much as possible, the use of their contributions for charitable purposes. Standard private foundations are the most common type of private foundation. This type of organization allows the donor to memorialize his name or the name of

a family member in perpetuity. Another attractive aspect of a standard private foundation is the structure that it can give to the charitable activities of a family by formalizing the charitable causes of a family and passing on to future generations the charitable value system of its founders.

Standard private foundations generally don't engage in any type of charitable activity, don't apply for any grants, and generally don't get involved in any fundraising activities. They are designed simply to hold funds from which contributions are made to other charitable organizations. (This type of foundation is sometimes referred to as a "nonoperating" foundation to distinguish it from a private "operating" foundation – see below.)

A private foundation can assist a donor who has a high-income-year to fund several years' worth of donations in one year. The foundation can then give grants to the donor's charities over the next several years. A private foundation can also help a donor make a gift to several different charities with an asset that is difficult to divide and donate (e.g., real estate).

Note, however, that standard private foundations are the most restrictive with respect to current income tax charitable deductions; they are also subject to all of the excise tax rules. In general, cash given to a private foundation is currently deductible up to 30 percent of the donor's contribution base. Gifts of long-term capital gain property to a private foundation generally are deductible up to the donor's basis and limited to 20 percent of the donor's adjusted gross income.[27] In addition, private foundations are subject to a 2 percent excise tax on investment income (which may be lowered to 1 percent depending on the foundation's level of giving relative to its asset base), and may be subject to other excise taxes as well.[28]

Private Operating Foundations

A private "operating" foundation is a foundation that must participate in charitable activities, rather than just making contributions to other charitable organizations.[29] Traditionally, these types of private foundations operate institutions such as museums, libraries, and historic preservation sites.

A private operating foundation has a distinct benefit over the standard private foundation in that donors have a more liberal income tax deduction. A donor can contribute cash and deduct up to 50 percent of his adjusted gross income rather than 30 percent. However, the private operating foundation is still subject to most of the excise tax regulations that apply to standard private foundations.

Another benefit of private operating foundations is that donors may contribute highly appreciated property and use the full fair market value in determining the charitable income tax deduction. Alternatively, with a standard private foundation the deduction is generally limited to the donor's adjusted cost basis in the property and the contribution is deductible only up to 20 percent of the donor's adjusted gross income.

Supporting Organizations

Supporting organizations and community foundations provide a great deal of flexibility for donors in structuring their charitable wishes. A *supporting organization* is a subcategory of public charity that, as its name implies, gives its founders and their descendants the opportunity to "support" favorite charitable causes by way of grants and distributions to public charities. One of the more common public charities supported are community foundations (see below). In general, these charitable giving vehicles allow the donor and his descendants to charitably participate in the community for generations. Supporting organizations and community foundations work well together since the supporting organization can benefit from the community foundation's staff and accounting systems for their distribution and financial reporting needs.

Contributions to a supporting organization are generally treated just like contributions to any other public charity and, thus, qualify for the 50 percent contribution base limits.[30] Gifts of appreciated property to a supporting organization are generally deductible up to 30 percent of the donor's contribution base.[31]

Community Foundations

A *community foundation* is a 501(c)(3) grant-making organization that is treated as a public charity for federal tax purposes. In order to attain this status, the foundation must qualify as a "publicly supported" organization and satisfy one of two public support tests.

The community foundation has a board of directors or trustees whose main duty is to distribute funds for the use of charities in the community. A community foundation maintains separate trusts or funds for the contributions that it receives, but these funds must be under the ultimate control of the governing body and must be treated as a single entity. Donors who contribute to a community foundation generally have two basic options for their funds. The first is to make a contribution to an unrestricted fund, which will be used for community needs as determined by the board members. The second option for contributions is for a donor to contribute through one of several types of restricted accounts. These types of restricted accounts may include several different categories of funds, such as a designated fund, a field of interest fund, a scholarship fund, an agency endowment fund, or a donor advised fund (see below).

Gifts of cash to a community foundation qualify for a current income tax charitable deduction up to 50 percent of the donor's contribution base.[32] Furthermore, capital gain property is deductible up to 30 percent of the donor's contribution base.[33]

Donor Advised Funds

A *donor advised fund* provides a means by which a donor can make a deductible charitable contribution to a pool of assets, offer recommendations about the direction of his contribution, and yet avoid the expense of starting a private foundation or supporting organization himself. As long as the donor does not have final say or legal control over the distributions, the contributions will be complete and qualify for a charitable deduction.[34] The basic types of donor funds are:

- **Donor Advised Funds:** This type of fund is one of the fastest growing charitable tools. In brief, a donor enters into a written agreement with a sponsoring charity to establish an account to benefit the donor's causes. He then transfers cash or other assets to the account, receives an immediate charitable deduction, and over the next days, months, or years, requests that the sponsoring charity make grants to the donor's chosen charities. (Donor advised funds differ from pooled income funds in that they do not provide for a lifetime income stream to the donor or other beneficiary.) The donor receives regular statements from the sponsoring charity and, in some cases, may nominate an investment advisor or choose between a small number of investment funds.

    The sponsoring charity usually receives a small annual fee for managing the account and may provide services, ranging from performing due diligence on the donor's selected grants, to providing a list of worthy grant recipients which match the donor's goals and criteria.

- **Component Funds**: With this type of fund, a foundation establishes separate funds or trusts to receive and manage donors' contributions. If a donor's fund can qualify as a component fund, there are significant advantages. Even though the community foundation does not generally hold title to these component funds or trusts, a completed gift by the donor to such a trust is considered a donation to the community foundation; therefore, it is subject to the 50 percent deduction limits for cash gifts.

Gifts of cash to a donor advised fund qualify for a current income tax charitable deduction up to 50 percent of the donor's adjusted gross income.[35] Furthermore, capital gain property is deductible up to 30 percent of the donor's adjusted gross income.

Donor advised funds are specifically defined as funds which:

1. are separately identified by reference to contributions of a donor or donors;

2. are owned and controlled by a sponsoring organization; and

3. allow the donor, or any person designated by the donor, advisory privileges with respect to the distribution or investment of amounts held in the fund by reason of the donor's status as a donor.[36]

A donor advised fund will not be treated as such if it makes distributions to only a single identified organization or governmental entity.[37] In addition, a donor advised fund may not make grants to individuals for travel, study, or similar purposes if certain conditions exist.[38]

Pooled Income Funds

A *pooled income fund* is a trust maintained by a charity into which each donor transfers property and from which each named beneficiary receives an income interest from the charity in the form of shares. The simplest analogy for a pooled income fund is that of a mutual fund, since contributions to the fund from the different donors must be commingled. Each time a donor transfers property to the pooled income fund,

he will receive shares or units of participation in the fund equal to the value of the property. The fair market value of the shares or units at the time of the transfer is determined by dividing the fair market value of all the property in the fund at such time by the number of shares or units in the fund.

The shares generate income that is payable to the donor or someone the donor designates to receive the income. The amount of income attributed to each share of a pooled income fund is calculated by dividing the income of the fund by the outstanding number of units in the fund at the end of the year.[39] The income received by a noncharitable beneficiary will be taxed similar to that of income received from any other complex trust. In the case of a pooled income fund this will generally result in all of the distributions being taxed as ordinary income in the year received.[40]

The donor receives a current charitable deduction for the value of the remainder interest.[41] The charity benefits from this arrangement by receiving an irrevocable remainder interest in the donated property.[42]

Charitable Gifts of Life Insurance

Making a charitable gift of life insurance is one of the easiest ways to make a significant gift to charity, and it can be done in one of several different ways. A donor can simply make a charity the beneficiary of a policy owned by the donor, donate a current policy to a charity, or finally, have a charity purchase a new policy on the donor's life. The tax advantages of a charitable gift of life insurance will depend upon how the life insurance gift is structured. For instance, a donor may be able to receive a deduction for the value of premiums paid to maintain an existing or newly purchased policy, or for the value of a fully paid policy equal to the amount an insurance company would charge for a single premium policy on a person the same age as the donor Regardless, charitable gifts of life insurance typically allow a donor to make a large gift in the future for a relatively small contribution.

WHEN ARE CHARITABLE CONTRIBUTIONS DEDUCTIBLE?

For a charitable contribution to be deductible, the charity must receive some benefit from the donated property.[43] Here is a list of which contributions are *not* deductible.

Figure 27.4

CHARITABLE INCOME TAX DEDUCTION LIMITS FOR GIFTS OF LIFE INSURANCE
• **Recently Issued Policy:** The deduction is equal to the lesser of   ○ the cost basis, or   ○ the fair market value of the contract. This is defined as the first premium paid.
• **Existing Life Policy in Premium Paying Mode:** The deduction is equal to the lesser of   ○ the cost basis, or   ° the fair market value of the contract. This is defined as the interpolated terminal reserve plus unearned premium. This latter number is roughly equal to the cash surrender value but that is an approximation only.
• **Paid Up Life Insurance Policy:** The deduction is equal to the lesser of   ○ the cost basis, or   ° the fair market value of the contract. This is defined as the replacement value of the contract. This latter number is equal to what the donor would have to pay for a new single premium policy with the same death benefit at his or her current age.
• **Definition of Cost Basis:** In general, the cost basis is the sum of all premiums paid to date less 1) amounts surrendered or 2) dividends received in cash.
• **Policy Valuation:** If requested, the insurance company will provide free of charge either 1) the interpolated terminal reserve plus unearned premium, or 2) the replacement cost for the policy on Form 712.
Source: *The Tools & Techniques of Charitable Planning* (2nd Edition), p. 100 (National Underwriter Company, 2007).

- A contribution to a nonqualified organization (see "What is a Qualified Charity?")

- A contribution to a specific individual

- The portion of a contribution from which the donor receives, or expects to receive, a benefit (see "Contributions from which the donor benefits")

- The *value* of the donor's time or services

- The donor's personal expenses (however, nonpersonal, unreimbursed out-of-pocket expenses that are directly related to, and incurred in furtherance of, the services provided by the charitable organization are deductible as an additional charitable gift)

- Appraisal fees (although the fees may be deductible as a miscellaneous itemized deduction subject to the 2 percent of adjusted gross income (AGI) limitation)

- Certain contributions of partial interests in property

In general, a charitable contribution is made voluntarily and without receiving, or expecting to receive, anything of equal value.

If the donor pays more than "fair market value" (generally, the price at which property would change hands between a willing buyer and willing seller) to a qualified charitable organization for merchandise, goods, or services, the amount paid that is more than the value of the item can be a charitable contribution. In order for the excess amount to qualify, the donor must pay it with the intent of making a charitable contribution. A *quid pro quo* contribution is a payment made partly in consideration for goods or services. To determine whether such a payment qualifies as a charitable deduction, the IRS has adopted a 2-part test. To satisfy the test, a taxpayer must:

(1) intend to make a payment in excess of the fair market value of the goods or services received; *and*

(2) actually make a payment in an amount that exceeds the fair market value of the goods or services.[44]

If a donor receives a benefit as a result of making a contribution to a qualified organization, he can deduct only the amount of his contribution that is more than the value of the benefit he receives. The deduction must not exceed the *excess* of (1) the fair market value of the goods and services *over* (2) the fair market value of any goods or services provided in return.[45]

Example: Sally Smith pays $65 for a ticket to a charity dinner-dance, but the ticket itself has a fair market value of only $25. All of the proceeds will go to the charity and Sally knows that the value of the ticket is less than her payment. Sally's charitable contribution would be $40 – that is, the total payment ($65) minus the value of the benefit received by Sally ($25).

If a donor makes a payment to, or for the benefit of, a college or university and, as a result, he receives the right to buy tickets to an athletic event in the athletic stadium of the college or university, he can deduct 80 percent of the payment as a charitable contribution.[46] However, if any part of the donor's payment is for tickets (rather than the right to buy tickets), that part is not deductible. In that case, the donor must subtract the price of the tickets from his payment. As a result, 80 percent of the remaining amount is a charitable contribution.

Example: Jack Jones pays $300 a year for membership in an athletic scholarship program maintained by State University. The only benefit of membership is that John has the right to buy one season ticket for a seat in a designated area of the stadium at the university's home football games. John can deduct $240 (80 percent of $300) as a charitable contribution.

Certain goods and services received in return for a charitable contribution may be *disregarded* for purposes of determining: (1) whether a taxpayer has made a charitable contribution; (2) the amount of any charitable contribution; and (3) whether any goods or services have been provided that must be substantiated or disclosed. These include:

- goods or services that have an insubstantial value under IRS guidelines (e.g., token items);

- certain membership benefits received for an annual payment of $75 or less (e.g., free or discounted admission to the organization's facilities or events; free or discounted parking; preferred access to goods or services; and discounts on the purchase of goods and services); *and*

- certain admission to events (i.e., admission, while the donor is a member, to events that are open only to members of the organization if the organization reasonably projects that the cost per person is not more than a specified amount).[47]

DEDUCTION LIMITS

The amount of an individual's income tax charitable deduction may be limited to 50, 30, or 20 percent of the donor's *contribution base* (i.e., adjusted gross income) depending on such factors as:

- the type of charity;

- whether the gift is made "to" or "for the use of" the charity; *and*

- the type of property donated.[48]

For a chart summarizing the various deduction limitations, see Figure 27.5. For an explanation of the order in which charitable deductions must be taken into account and the "carryover rule," see Figure 27.6.

Example: Alice Johnson had $50,000 of AGI last year. She donated $2,000 in cash to the American Red Cross. She also gave $5,000 in cash to a private family foundation (i.e., a 30% charity). Her third charitable contribution for the year was a piece of real estate purchased in 1998 with a cost basis of $22,000 and a fair market value of $28,000, which she gave to the American Heart Association. Alice did not choose the special election for long-term capital gain property. Therefore, she may deduct the fair market value of the property up to 30% of her AGI.

First, the $2,000 cash donation to the American Red Cross is fully deductible up to 50% of her AGI (50% × $50,000 = $25,000). Since $2,000 is less than $25,000, $2,000 of the cash gift is fully deductible to Alice.

Figure 27.5

INCOME PERCENTAGE LIMITS FOR LIFETIME CHARITABLE GIFTS

TYPE OF GIFT:	"50% CHARITIES"	"30% CHARITIES"
	Public Charities, Private Operating Foundations, Pass-through Private Foundations, Pooled Fund Private Foundations, Certain Supporting Organizations	Private Non-Operating Foundations ("Family Foundations"), Other Qualified Non-50% type Charities (veterans' associations, fraternal groups)
Cash or cash equivalents	Up to 50% of AGI	Up to 30% of AGI
Ordinary income property or short-term capital gain property	Generally, cost basis up to 50% of AGI	Generally, cost basis up to 30% of AGI
Long-term capital gain property	FMV up to 30% of AGI. (Under a special election, the taxpayer may choose to deduct the cost basis up to 50% of AGI.)	Generally, cost basis up to 20% of AGI
"Qualified Stock" (long-term capital gain stock with readily ascertainable market quotes)	Not Applicable	FMV up to 20% of AGI (The stock cannot be more than 10% of the value of the corporation's shares.)
Tangible personal property (held long-term)	Related to the charity's use: FMV up to 30% of AGI (or, the cost basis is deductible up to 50% of AGI) Unrelated to Use: Generally, cost basis up to 50% of AGI	Related or Unrelated to the Charity's Use: Generally, cost basis up to 20% AGI
Gifts "for the use of" the charity instead of "to" the charity (e.g., contribution of remainder interest held in trust for benefit of charity)	Up to 30% of AGI	Up to 30% of AGI
• Life insurance premiums paid directly "to" the charity on policies owned by the charity	Up to 50% of AGI	Up to 30% of AGI
• Life insurance premiums paid to the life insurance company, or "for the use of" the charity on a policy owned by the charity	Up to 30% of AGI	Up to 30% of AGI

Source: *The Tools & Techniques of Charitable Planning* (2nd Ed.), Appendix D, p. 263.

In the pecking order of deductions, the gift to the private foundation is considered before the gift of long-term capital gain property to the 50% organization. Alice's total contributions to the 50% charities equal $30,000 ($28,000 + $2,000). But 50% of her AGI is equal to $25,000, so her total contributions exceed the amount she can deduct for the year. Therefore, the $5,000 gift to the 30% charity is not deductible for the year. However, it can be carried forward to future years.

The gift of land is considered next and is deductible up to 30% of her AGI, or $15,000 (30% × $50,000 = $15,000). Alice's carryover for the year is determined by subtracting the deductible amount from the fair market value of the land ($28,000 − $15,000 = $13,000).

Alice's total charitable deductions for the tax year are $17,000 ($2,000 + $15,000). Her carryover generated from this tax year is equal to $18,000 ($5,000 + $13,000)

Figure 27.6

ORDER OF CHARITABLE DEDUCTIONS ALLOWED*

The percentage limitations are not "stacked." In other words, each level is reduced by contributions deducted (or carried over) at the next higher level. In general, a donor's charitable deductions must be accounted for in the following order for income tax purposes:**

(1) Gifts subject to the 50% limitation, *only*, up to 50% of the donor's adjusted gross income (AGI);

(2) Gifts subject to the 30% limitation, up to the *lesser* of:

- 0% of the donor's AGI, or

- the *excess* of:

  - 50% of the donor's AGI, *over*

  - the amount of the allowable contributions made to 50% organizations.

Caution: Contributions of long-term capital gain property to 50% organizations, which ordinarily would be subject to the 30% limitation, must nevertheless be included in the latter amount.

(3) Gifts of long-term capital gain property subject to the 30% limitation, up to 30% of the donor's AGI.

(4) Contributions subject to the 20% limitation, up to the *lesser* of:

- 20% of the donor's AGI, or

- the *excess* of:

  - 30% of the donor's AGI, *over*

  - the amount of contributions of long-term capital gain property to 50% organizations to which the 30% limitation applies.

Carryover rule. If the donor's contributions exceed any of the limits that apply, the excess may be carried over. Charitable contributions that exceed the 50% or 30% limitations can generally be carried forward up to five additional tax years to the extent the limit is not used up in those years. Amounts carried forward retain their character as 50%, 30%, or 20%-type deductions.

The following example illustrates the order of deduction rules:

Effect of the special election. If Alice had chosen the special election for long-term capital gain property, she could have deducted the cost basis of the real property, which was $22,000. Recall that Alice's AGI was $50,000. Because she had a cash gift of $2,000 to the American Red Cross, her total contributions of the real property and the cash gift totaled $24,000 ($2,000 + $22,000). Since 50% of her AGI is $25,000, she could have deducted both contributions in full. So far she has deducted only $24,000. Consequently, $1,000 of the $5,000 cash gift to the private family foundation would be deductible in the current tax year. Her total charitable deductions for the tax year would be $25,000 ($2,000 + $22,000 + $1,000), and her carryover generated from this tax year would be $4,000 ($5,000 − $1,000).

* *The Tools & Techniques of Charitable Planning* (2nd Ed.), pp. 22-23.

** See I.R.C. § 170(b)(1).

Limits Based on Type of Charity

Public Charities

The charities listed below are frequently referred to as *public* charities because they receive the majority of their funding from the general public. A 50 percent limit applies to the total of all charitable contributions that a donor makes during the tax year *to* public charities. (For the limit applicable to gifts made *for the use of* public charities, see below.) This means that the donor's deduction for

charitable contributions cannot be more than 50 percent of the donor's adjusted gross income for the year.[49] The following organizations are 50 percent limit charities:

- **Churches** and conventions and associations of churches;

- **Educational organizations** must be organizations with a regular faculty, curriculum, and student body);

- **Hospitals** and organizations that provide hospital or medical care, along with medical research organizations associated with those hospitals;

- **Organizations that benefit public colleges and universities** including organizations that are operated only to receive, hold, invest, and administer property and to make expenditures to or for the benefit of state and municipal colleges and universities, *and* that normally receive substantial support from the United States, or any state or their political subdivisions, or from the general public;

- **Governmental units** of federal, state, and local governments;[50]

- **Publicly-supported charities** can include corporations, trusts, community chests, funds, or foundations that normally receive a substantial part of their support from direct or indirect contributions from the general public, or from the federal state or local government;

- **Supporting organizations** that are organized and operated exclusively for the benefit of, to perform the functions of, or to carry out the purposes of one or more public charities);[51]

- **Donor advised funds** including a fund that has legal ownership and control of the donated assets immediately after the contribution. Donors may contribute to the fund and make nonbinding recommendations with regard to the ultimate distribution of the assets or how the assets are invested;[52] and

- **Certain private foundations.**[53]

Gifts made "for the use of" public charities. The 50 percent limit explained above applies to gifts made "to" public charities. Gifts are "to" a charitable organization if made directly to the organization. For purposes of the deduction limits, even though the gift may be intended to be used by the charity, and the charity may use it, if it is given directly to the charity, it is a gift "to" the charity and not "for the use of" the charity.

Conversely, gifts made "for the use of" public charities are deductible only up to 30 percent of the donor's adjusted gross income. "For the use of" applies to

indirect contributions to a charitable organization. The term does *not* refer to a gift of the right to use property; such gifts are generally nondeductible because they are donations of less than the donor's entire interest in the property (see "Partial Interests," below).[54]

Private Charities

Gifts made to or for the use of private charities (known as "30 percent charities") are limited to 30 percent of the donor's adjusted gross income. Unlike the public (50 percent) charities, the 30 percent charities are generally nonpublic in nature. The 30 percent (private) charities are:

- **Private family foundations** Included in this group are standard private foundations, all of which are "non-operating." This group is primarily composed of private family foundations; and

- **Other qualified non-50 percent-type charities.** This group includes veterans' groups, fraternal societies, and nonprofit cemeteries.[55]

To be deductible, a contribution "to" or "for the use of" a 30 percent-type charity cannot exceed the *lesser* of (1) 30 percent of the donor's adjusted gross income, or (2) 50 percent of the donor's adjusted gross income *minus* the amount of charitable contributions allowable for 50 percent-type charities.[56]

20 percent Limit The deduction for contributions of long-term capital gain property to most private foundations (i.e., family foundations) is limited to the *lesser* of (1) 20 percent of the donor's adjusted gross income; or (2) the 30 percent of adjusted gross income *minus* the amount of charitable contributions allowed for contributions to the 30 percent charities.[57]

Contributions that a taxpayer is unable to deduct in the current year due to an AGI limitation may be carried forward for up to five years.[58] After the fifth carryover year, any remaining carryover is lost.

The ordering of deductible charitable contributions is very important since current year contributions are considered against and AGI limitation before carryovers. The utilization of carryovers within a given percentage limitation is made on a first-in, first-out basis. Therefore, taxpayers that are approaching the end of a carryover period should consider deferring current year contributions if AGI is not sufficient to absorb all contributions.

A taxpayer that does not itemize deductions in a year in which a carryover is available must, nonetheless, reduce their allowable carryover by the amount that would have been deducted had the taxpayer itemized their deductions.[59]

Limits Based on Type of Property

If a donor contributes property to a charitable organization, the amount of the donor's contribution is generally the fair market value of the property at the time of the contribution. "Fair market value" is defined as the price at which the property would exchange hands between a willing buyer and a willing seller, with neither party being under any compulsion to buy or sell, and both having reasonable knowledge of the facts.[60]

However, if a donor contributes property with a fair market value that is more than his adjusted (cost) basis in it, he may have to *reduce* the fair market value by the amount of "appreciation" (i.e., increase in value) when calculating his deduction. Different rules apply depending on whether the property is *long-term capital gain property* (see below) or *ordinary income property* (see below).

Long-Term Capital Gain Property

Special limitations apply with respect to charitable contributions of property that would generate long-term capital gain (LTCG) if sold at the time of the contribution. The term *capital gain property* means any capital asset whose sale at fair market value would have resulted in long-term capital gain.[61] Long-term capital gain property is any "capital asset" held for more than one year. "Capital assets" include stocks, Treasury bonds, and corporate bonds.[62]

The percentage limits affecting contributions of long-term capital gain property to public and private charities are as follows:

LTCG property donated to public charities: The deduction for contributions of long-term capital gain property to public charities is limited to the *lesser* of:

- 30 percent of the donor's adjusted gross income, *or*

- the unused portion of the 50 percent limitation.[63]

Although the deduction is generally limited to 30 percent, the donor has the benefit of deducting the full fair market value of the gift. The deduction for such gifts can be *increased* to the 50 percent limit if the donor elects to limit the amount of the deduction to his adjusted (cost) basis.[64]

LTCG property donated to private charities: Contributions of long-term capital gain property made to private charities (i.e., most private foundations) are subject to a different set of limitations. A donor's deduction to such organizations is limited to the *lesser* of:

- 20 percent of his adjusted gross income, or

- the unused portion of the 30 percent limitation described above.[65]

Ordinary Income Property

In the case of a charitable contribution of *ordinary income property* (i.e., property which, if sold, would result in ordinary income or short-term capital gain), the amount of the contribution is *reduced* by the amount of gain that would *not* have been long-term capital gain if the property had been sold at its fair market value at the time of contribution.[66] In other words, assuming the donor would not recognize any long-term capital gain if the property were sold, the donor's charitable deduction would be limited to his adjusted basis in the ordinary income property contributed.

Ordinary income property includes items such as:

- a work of art or manuscript created by the donor;

- letters or memorandums prepared by or for the donor;

- any capital asset held by the donor for one year or less (i.e., short-term capital gain property – see below); *and*

- Section 306 stock to the extent gain is treated as ordinary income on disposition.[67]

Short-term capital gain property is defined as any capital asset held by a donor for one year or less and can include such assets as Treasury bills, short-term corporate bonds, and stocks held for one year or less.[68]

Other Property Requiring Reduction in Value

Prior to the application of the percentage limitations, the value of two other types of gifts must be *reduced* by the amount of gain that would have been long-term capital gain if the property had been sold by the taxpayer at its fair market value as determined at the time of contribution. Simply put, the deduction is generally limited to the donor's adjusted (cost) basis in the property if:

- the donated property is appreciated *tangible personal property* that is put to an *unrelated* use by the charity; or[69]

- the appreciated property is contributed to, or for the use of, certain private non-operating foundations.[70]

Tangible personal property essentially means any property (other than land or buildings) that can be seen or touched. It includes furniture, books, jewelry, paintings, and cars.

In general, an item of donated property is considered to be a "related use" gift if it will be used in a manner that is consistent with the charity's charitable purpose(s). The term *unrelated use* means a use that is unrelated to the exempt purpose(s) or function(s) of the charitable organization.[71] For example, a donation of a valuable book collection to a library, which will display the collection in its archives and make the books available for reading by scholars and researchers, would fall into the "related use" category. A donation of office furniture to a charity that will use the gift to furnish its offices would also be a "related use" gift. On the other hand, a donation of a rare medieval manuscript to a modern art museum that sells the manuscript and uses the proceeds to purchase modern art would be an "unrelated use" gift.[72]

Special Rules for Donated Property

Publicly traded stock contributed to certain private foundations. Contributions to private nonoperating foundations (i.e., family foundations) of *qualified appreciated stock* can be accounted for at its full fair market value instead of being reduced to the property's adjusted basis. *Qualified appreciated stock* is defined as corporate stock (1) for which market quotations are readily available, and (2) that would produce long-term capital gain for the donor if sold at the time of contribution. But note that the stock cannot be more than 10 percent of the value of the corporation's shares. A donation of publicly traded stock donated to a private family foundation (i.e., a 30 percent limit organization) is deductible up to 20 percent of the donor's adjusted gross income.[73]

Property that has decreased in value. If a donor contributes property that has *decreased* in value, the donor's deduction is limited to the property's fair market value.[74] A donor may not claim a deduction for the difference between the property's cost basis and its fair market value. In general, it is recommended that donors sell such property first, and then donate the cash to the intended charity.

Property subject to a debt. If the donor donates property subject to a debt (e.g., a mortgage), he must reduce the fair market value by any allowable deduction for the interest that he paid (or will pay) attributable to any period after the contribution.[75]

Future interests in tangible personal property. A donor cannot deduct the value of a contribution of a "future interest" in tangible personal property until all intervening interests in, and right to, the actual possession or enjoyment of the property have either expired or have been turned over to someone other than (1) the donor, (2) a related person, or (3) a related organization. A "future interest" is any interest that is to begin at some future time, regardless of whether it is designated as a future interest under state law.[76]

PARTIAL INTERESTS

A *partial interest gift* is a contribution of less than a donor's entire interest in an asset to a charity. With limited exceptions, a charitable deduction is generally *not* allowed for partial interest gifts.[77] This applies not only for income tax purposes, but for gift and estate tax purposes as well.[78] However, there are several exceptions to the partial interest rule that will allow a donor to contribute less than his entire interest and still receive a charitable income tax deduction. These exceptions are:

(1) A contribution of an undivided portion of the donor's entire interest in property;

(2) A contribution of a remainder interest in a personal residence or farm; and

(3) A qualified conservation contribution.[79]

A deduction for a gift of a partial interest will also be allowed to the extent that a deduction would be allowed if the interest had been transferred in trust.[80] Specifically, a donor may receive a deduction for conveying a remainder or income interest by way of a split-interest trust.

It should be noted that giving a charity the "right to use" an asset is less than the donor's entire interest in the asset and generally does *not* qualify for a charitable deduction.[81]

A donor may be eligible to take a charitable deduction for a partial interest in property if he donates an "undivided portion of his entire interest in the property."[82] An "undivided portion" must consist of a "fraction or percentage of each and every substantial interest or right owned by the donor in such property and must extend over the entire term of the donor's interest in such property and in other property into which such property is converted."[83] However, if the donor divides his property in order to create a partial interest and avoid the partial interest rule, the donor's charitable deduction will not be allowed.[84]

Example: John was given a life estate in an office building for the life of his mother in 2011. He has no other interest in the building. In 2014, John decides to donate a one-half interest in his life estate to a local charity (in a transfer that is not made in trust). As a result, he is allowed a deduction for his contribution because the gift is considered a contribution of an undivided portion of the donor's entire interest in the property.[85]

The amount of the deduction for most gifts of a partial interest is the fair market value of the partial interest at the time of contribution; however, the deduction for certain gifts of appreciated property must be reduced in the same manner as if the gift were not of a partial interest.[86]

CORPORATE CHARITABLE CONTRIBUTIONS

A corporation's total deductions for its charitable contributions may not exceed 10 percent of the corporation's taxable income.[87] The corporation's taxable income, for this purpose, is computed without regard to charitable contributions, any capital or net loss carrybacks, and most of the special deductions for corporations.[88]

RECORDKEEPING, APPRAISALS, AND REPORTING

Generally, the deduction for a contribution is taken in the year the gift is made.[89] In order to deduct a charitable contribution, an individual donor must file Form 1040 *and* must itemize deductions on Schedule A. A charitable contribution will be allowed as a deduction only if *substantiated* (i.e., proven) in accordance with the regulations.[90]

Contributions of Less than $250

Prior to the enactment of the Pension Protection Act of 2006, the minimum substantiation requirements for contributions of less than $250 could be met by maintaining a cancelled check, a receipt from the charitable organization or some other reliable written records showing the name of the charity, the amount of the contribution, and the date of the contribution. Under the new law, no deduction is allowed (no matter how small) for any contribution (not just cash, check, or other monetary gift) *unless* the donor maintains as a record of the contribution (1) a bank record, (2) a written communication from the donee showing the name of the donee organization, the date of the contribution, and the amount of the contribution, or (3) other reliable written records (including small tokens or buttons received) showing the name of the charity and the date and amount of the contribution.[91] Therefore, a cash gift to the Salvation Army made by dropping money into the jar hosted by a volunteer with a bell standing outside a mall during the holiday season will no longer be deductible unless properly substantiated, nor would a twenty dollar bill dropped into the basket at church.

Contributions of $250 or More

Charitable contributions of $250 or more (whether in cash or property) must be substantiated by a contemporaneous written acknowledgment of the contribution supplied by the charitable organization.[92] The acknowledgment must include the following information:

(1) the amount of cash contributed and a description (excluding value) of any property contributed;

(2) a statement of whether the charitable organization provided any goods or services in consideration for the contribution;

(3) a description and good faith estimate of the value of any such goods or services; and

(4) a statement to the effect that the goods or services provided consisted solely of intangible religious benefits.[93]

The acknowledgment is considered to be "contemporaneous" if it is obtained by the taxpayer on or before the earlier of:

- the date the taxpayer files his return for the year; or

- the due date (including extensions) for filing the return.[94]

Substantiation is not required if the information is reported on a return filed by the charitable organization.[95]

For contributions of property other than money, the taxpayer is generally required to maintain a receipt from the charitable organization showing the name of the charity, the date and location of the contribution, and a description of the property, including the value of it.[96]

Noncash Contributions Exceeding $500

If the claimed value of a noncash contribution exceeds $500, the taxpayer must complete and attach to his tax return Form 8283 ("Noncash Charitable Contributions"), which includes a description of the property and an acknowledgment by the organization of the amount and value of the gift.

In any event, the Pension Protection Act of 2006 limits the types and quality of clothing and household items that may be claimed as a charitable deduction. No deduction is allowed for any clothing or household item unless it "is in good used condition or better."[97] Further, the IRS may institute regulations that deny deductions for any contribution of clothing or a household item that has minimal monetary value, such as used socks or undergarments.[98] Household items subject to this rule include furniture, furnishings, electronics, appliances, linens and other similar items.[99]

Contributions Exceeding $5,000

In addition to the requirements described above, individuals who claim a deduction for a charitable gift of property (except publicly traded securities) valued in excess of $5,000 ($10,000 for non-publicly traded stock) are required to do all of the following:

(1) obtain a qualified appraisal report;

(2) attach an appraisal summary (containing the information specified in regulations) to their return for the year in which the deduction is claimed; *and*

(3) maintain records of certain information related to the contribution.[100]

A qualified appraiser may *not* be any of the following:

- the taxpayer;

- a party to the transaction in which the taxpayer acquired the property;

- the charity;

- an employee of any of the above; or

- any other person who might appear not to be totally independent.[101]

The appraiser cannot base his fee on a percentage of the appraisal value, unless the fee is based on a sliding scale that is paid to a generally recognized association regulating appraisers.[102]

If the donor gives similar items of property (such as books, stamps, paintings, etc.) to the same charity during the taxable year, only one appraisal and summary is required. If similar items of property are given during the same taxable year to several charities, and the aggregate value of the donations exceeds $5,000, a separate appraisal and summary must be made for each donation.[103] The appraisal summary must be signed and dated by the charity as an acknowledgement of the donation.[104]

Taxpayers need not obtain a qualified appraisal of securities whose claimed value exceeds $5,000 if the donated property meets the definition of *publicly traded securities*, which are securities that are:

- listed on a stock exchange in which quotations are published on a daily basis; or

- regularly traded in a national or regional over-the-counter market for which published quotations are available.[105]

Penalties for Overvaluing Donated Property

If a taxpayer underpays his tax because of a *substantial valuation misstatement* of property donated to charity, he may be subject to a penalty of 20 percent of the underpayment attributable to the misstatement.[106] However, this penalty applies only if the underpayment attributable to the misstatement exceeds $5,000.[107] A "substantial valuation misstatement" exists if the value claimed is 150 percent or more of the amount determined to be correct.[108] If the value claimed is 200 percent or more of the amount determined to be correct, there is a "gross valuation misstatement," which is subject to a 40 percent underpayment penalty.[109]

The Pension Protection Act of 2006 also added penalties on any appraiser who "knows, or reasonably should have known" that an appraisal would be used as part of a tax return and the appraisal results in a substantial valuation misstatement for income tax purposes or a gross valuation misstatement.[110] The amount of the penalty is the *lesser* of:

1.   The greater of 10 percent of the amount of the underpayment attributable to the misstatement or $1,000; *or*

2.   125 percent of the gross income received by the appraiser from the preparation of the appraisal.[111]

A limited exception to the penalty exists if the value established in the appraisal by the appraiser was "more likely than not the proper value."[112]

WHERE CAN I FIND OUT MORE?

1.   Leimberg, et al, *The Tools & Techniques of Charitable Planning*, 3rd Edition, The National Underwriter Company, 2014.

2.   *Tax Facts on Investments*, The National Underwriter Company (updated annually).

FREQUENTLY ASKED QUESTIONS

Question – What factors should be considered when deciding between a charitable remainder annuity trust (CRAT) and a charitable remainder unitrust (CRUT)?

Answer – A CRAT offers the primary benefits of simplicity and certainty. With a CRAT, the retained interest is a fixed dollar amount. Therefore, since the amount is fixed, there is no need for an annual revaluation as with a CRUT. For that reason (i.e., no annual revaluation requirement), a CRAT will be considerably easier, and less expensive to administer than a CRUT, especially when there are hard-to-value assets being contributed to the trust.

A second consideration is the need (or desire) for a fixed return. With a CRAT, the annual payout is fixed. The annuity payment will not be reduced if the value of the trust decreases, unless the trust is completed liquidated by distributions.

A third consideration is the need for a hedge against inflation. While a CRAT offers the promise of a fixed annual return, this fixed annual payout can be a significant detriment in the event of inflation. For this reason, younger donors often prefer the flexible unitrust payment that is available with a CRUT, as opposed to the fixed payment guaranteed by a CRAT.

With a CRAT or a CRUT, the cash flow created from the trustee's investment of the entire amount of the proceeds from the tax-free sale of the contributed asset will be significantly more than the cash flow that would have been earned by the donor from the net after-tax proceeds had the contributed asset been sold. Furthermore, selling the contributed asset inside the CRAT or the CRUT and allowing the trustee to invest the proceeds in a diversified portfolio can diversify the donor's source of income.

Another consideration is whether additional contributions to the trust are contemplated. A donor can make multiple contributions to a single CRUT, but the *initial* contribution is the *only* contribution that can be made to a CRAT.[113]

Question – How is a charitable lead trust different from a charitable remainder trust?

Answer – While both are split-interest charitable trusts, there are significant differences between charitable lead trusts and charitable remainder trusts. The most obvious difference is that the lead and remainder beneficiary roles are reversed. In a lead trust, a charity is entitled to the annuity or unitrust interest and a noncharitable beneficiary is entitled to the remainder. Conversely, in a charitable remainder trust, the noncharitable beneficiary is entitled to the annuity or unitrust interest with a charitable beneficiary receiving the remainder interest.

Aside from the reversed trust interest roles, there are other differences. For example, charitable remainder trusts are tax-exempt entities, whereas charitable lead trusts are not. Additionally, charitable remainder trusts have minimum and maximum payout rates, as well as maximum term limits. Charitable lead trusts do not have these same requirements.[114]

Question – A taxpayer owns an asset that has appreciated rapidly since its acquisition. What are the implications if the asset has not been held for at least one year?

Answer – Donors of appreciated property are permitted to receive a charitable deduction equal to the fair market value of the asset provided that it has been held for at least one year (i.e. it qualifies for a long-term holding period). Consideration should be given to delaying the contribution of an asset that has significantly appreciated, but not met the long-term holding period requirement. If an asset is donated that has not been held for at least one year, the charitable contribution is limited to the taxpayer's basis in the asset.

Question – A taxpayer owns an asset that could be used by a charity, but is worth more than what the taxpayer would be willing to give. Can the taxpayer engage in a part-sale, part-gift transaction with a charity?

Answer – The part-sale, part-gift of property is covered by the bargain sale rules.[115] A bargain sale is split into transactions – one sale and one charitable contribution. The sale portion is subject to tax, generally as a capital gain. As a result, the tax basis of the property must be allocated between the two components of the transaction.

The tax basis allocated to the sale is determined by the proportion of the sales proceeds received in the transaction over the property's fair market value. This proportion is applied to the tax basis of the asset. The net sales proceeds

in excess of the allocated tax basis represents the taxable gain.[116]

The difference between the fair market value of the property and the sales proceeds received is the charitable contribution amount.

Question – What are the special rules involving charitable donations from individual retirement accounts (IRAs)?

Answer – Under the Pension Protection Act of 2006, IRA owners may make distributions from their IRA directly to a qualified charity. Prior to this law, such a distribution would constitute a taxable IRA withdrawal followed by a charitable contribution. Because of the itemized deduction rules and the charitable contribution limits, a taxpayer may not be able to fully offset the tax on the income they are required to report with the tax benefit from the charitable deduction.

The IRA charitable rollover provision contained in this law is somewhat limited. Transfers may not be made to private nonoperating foundations, donor advised funds, or any supporting organization. In addition, the provision only applies to individuals who are over age 70½ and is capped at $100,000 per year.

For IRA owners over age 70½, the rules allow up to $100,000 to be distributed directly to a qualified charity. The amount of the distribution is not reportable as income to the taxpayer, and the taxpayer is not entitled to a deduction for the amount given to the charity. The amount of the distribution may also be used to satisfy any portion of the taxpayer's required minimum distribution for that year. As a result, a taxpayer may be able to distribute their entire required minimum distribution to a qualified charity and not be subject to any tax.

Only IRA distributions are eligible for this special treatment. Simplified employee plans (SEPs), SIMPLE plans, 401(k) and 403(b) plans, profit sharing and pension plans do not qualify. As a result, a taxpayer who wishes to avail themselves of this provision will need to either use amounts from their IRA or roll over amounts from an ineligible plan into an IRA before making the charitable distribution.

The law has been part of the annual "extenders" legislation and last expired at the end of 2013. As of the writing of this edition, this provision is not available for 2014 or future years.

Question – What are the special rules for conservation easements?

Answer – A conservation easement is a restriction placed on the use of a piece of real property. The land owner does not give up ownership or control of the land. Common conservation easements involve the saving of open space or a natural habitat, protecting historical value, or preserving property for outdoor recreation.

The amount of the deduction for a qualified conservation easement is normally determined by an appraiser, who ascertains the diminution of the property's fair market value as a result of the restrictions placed on the property. Since the land will normally constitute a donation of capital gain property, a conservation easement that is given to a public charity (a 50 percent charity) is limited to 30 percent of a taxpayer's AGI. For qualified conservation easements made during 2006 through 2009, higher AGI limits and longer carryover periods may have applied.

Question – How are donations of cars, boats, and airplanes treated?

Answer – For charitable donations of cars, boats, and airplanes exceeding $500 in value, the charitable deduction is determined, in part, by how the donated car, boat, or airplane is used by the charity.

If the charity sells the property without significantly using it or making material improvements, the deduction is limited to the proceeds received by the charity from the sale. The charity reports the proceeds received on a Form 1098-C, which is provided to the IRS and the donor of the property.

If the charity does significantly use the property or makes material improvements before ultimately selling it, the donor's deduction is determined by the fair market value of the property as of the date of the donation. The same rule would apply if the charity transfers the property to a needy individual. The charity will indicate such use, improvements, or transfer on Form 1098-C.

The taxpayer cannot deduct any amount for a donated car, boat, or airplane above $500 unless the charity provides acknowledgement on Form 1098-C. The charity is required to issue the form within thirty days of the sale or thirty days of meeting one of the other exceptions described above. The donor/taxpayer must attach Form 1098-C to his or her tax return for the year of the donation.

Question – When are donations made by credit card deductible?

Answer – The date of the charitable contribution is determined by when the charge is incurred. Therefore, if a taxpayer is looking to give money to a charity before the end of a particular taxable year, he or she may charge the donation to their favorite credit card (and get their frequent flyer miles!) even though the charge will not be paid until the following year.[117] However, if the taxpayer incurs interest or any other related charges as a result of using the credit card to fund the charitable gift, that amount is not deductible.

Question – What are the deduction rules for property that has declined in value?

Answer – If at all possible, taxpayers should not donate property used in a trade or business or held for investment that has declined in value. The charitable deduction is limited to the property's fair market value. The unrealized loss in the property is not considered to be an additional deduction either as a charitable contribution or as a capital loss.

Instead, the loss should be realized by selling the property for cash and, thereby, realizing the loss. Then, the taxpayer can donate the cash to the charity. The charity will realize the same amount as a donation, but the taxpayer will have a potentially deductible loss against their other sources of income.

Note that a loss on property held for personal use, such as the family car, is not deductible. So, all things being equal, nothing is lost by a taxpayer donating the family car instead of selling it first and donating the cash.

CHAPTER ENDNOTES

1.   I.R.C. §170(a).

2.   I.R.C. §§2055(a), 2522(a).

3.   Other charitable deductions include the gift tax charitable deduction and the estate tax charitable deduction. See the sidebar, above.

4.   I.R.C. §501(a).

5. I.R.C. §501(c)(3).

6. I.R.C. §170(c).

7. Available at: http://apps.irs.gov/app/eos/ePostSearch.do?sea rchChoice=revoked&dispatchMethod=selectSearch.

8. Treas. Reg. §1.170A-1(c).

9. See I.R.C. §170(b).

10. Rev. Rul. 55-410, 1955-1 CB 297.

11. In some cases, the charity may be the first in line to receive assets before any of the heirs. This can sometimes cause problems from the standpoint of the estate having to liquidate assets to meet the charitable obligation, which can result in "shrinkage" of the estate greater than the amount of the charitable gift.

12. I.R.C. §2055.

13. I.R.C. §§642(c), 2055(d).

14. Treas. Reg. §1.170A-1(d).

15. Treas. Reg. §1.170A-1(d)(2). For gift annuities, the Section 7520 interest rate and the most current mortality tables are used to determine the value of the gift annuity. I.R.C. §7520(a). The use of the Section 7520 rate for the month in which the gift was completed, or in either of the previous two months, is required. It is important to calculate the present values using the highest of these three Section 7520 rates. Generally speaking, the higher the Section 7520 rate, the lower is the value of the annuity and, consequently, the higher is the charitable deduction.

16. Treas. Reg. §1.664-1(a)(1)(i).

17. Treas. Regs. §§1.664-2(c), 1.664-4(a).

18. See I.R.C. §664(d).

19. I.R.C. §664(d)(1)(A).

20. I.R.C. §664(d)(1)(D).

21. I.R.C. §664(d)(2)(A).

22. I.R.C. §664(d)(3)(A).

23. I.R.C. §664(d)(3)(B).

24. I.R.C. §664(d)(2)(D).

25. I.R.C. §170(f)(2)(b).

26. I.R.C. §2522(c)(2). See also Treas. Regs. §§1.170A-6(c)(3), 20.2055-2(f)(2)(iv), 20.2055-2(f)(2)(v).

27. I.R.C. §§170(b)(1)(B), 170(b)(1)(D), 170(e)(5).

28. I.R.C. §4940.

29. See I.R.C. §4942(j)(3).

30. I.R.C. §170(b)(1)(A).

31. I.R.C. §170(b)(1)(C).

32. I.R.C. §170(b)(1)(A).

33. I.R.C. §170(b)(1)(C).

34. See Treas. Reg. §1.507-2(a)(8).

35. I.R.C. §170(b)(1)(A).

36. I.R.C. §4966(d)(2).

37. I.R.C. §4966(d)(2)(B)(i).

38. I.R.C. §4966(d)(2)(B)(ii).

39. Treas. Reg. §1.642(c)-5(c)(2)(i).

40. Treas. Reg. §1.642(c)-5(a)(4).

41. In determining the amount of a charitable contribution to a pooled income fund for purpose of determining the allowable

deduction, the value of the remainder interest is generally determined on the basis of the highest rate of return by the fund for any of the three taxable years immediately preceding the taxable year of the fund in which the transfer is made. If the fund has been in existence less than three years, the rate of return is deemed to be equal to the interest rate that is 1 percent less than the highest annual average of the monthly Section 7520 interest rates for the three years preceding the transfer. Generally, the higher the rate of return for the fund, the lower the present value of the charity's remainder interest, and the lower the current charitable deduction.

42. I.R.C. §642(c)(5).

43. See *Winthrop v. Meisels*, 180 F.Supp. 29 (DC NY 1959), *aff'd*, 281 F.2d 694 (2nd Cir. 1960).

44. Treas. Reg. §1.170A-1(h)(1); *United States v. American Bar Endowment*, 477 U.S. 105 (1986).

45. Treas. Reg. §1.170A-1(h)(2).

46. I.R.C. §170(l).

47. Treas. Regs. §§1.170A-1(h), 1.170A-13(f)(8); Rev. Proc. 2002-70, 2001-2 CB 845.

48. I.R.C. §170(b).

49. See "30 percent limit" below for the exception that applies to gifts of capital gain property for which the donor calculates his deduction using the fair market value without reduction for appreciation. Another exception to the 50 percent rule applies to gifts of capital gain property to public charities, which are limited instead to 30 percent.

50. Note that the gift must be made for *exclusively public purposes*.

51. I.R.C. §§170(b)(1), 170(c)(1), 170(c)(3), 509(a)(2), 509(a)(3).

52. Donor advised funds are specifically defined under I.R.C. Section 4966(c)(2) as a result of the Pension Protection Act of 2006.

53. Private foundations included in this group include private operating foundations, distributing (or conduit) foundations, and pooled fund foundations. A private operating foundation differs from a standard private foundation (i.e., family foundation) in that it must participate in charitable activities instead of just making contributions to other charitable organizations. Traditionally, these types of private foundations operate institutions such as museums, libraries, and historic preservation sites. Distributing foundations, like private operating foundations, must make a certain amount of distributions each year.

54. See Treas. Reg. §1.170A-8(a)(2); *Davis v. United States*, 495 US 472 (1990).

55. I.R.C. §170(b)(1)(E).

56. I.R.C. §170(b)(1)(B).

57. I.R.C. §170(b)(1)(D).

58. I.R.C. §170(d)(1); Treas. Reg. §1.170A-10.

59. Treas. Reg. §1.170A-10(a)(2).

60. Treas. Reg. §1.170A-1(c).

61. I.R.C. §170(b)(1)(C)(iv).

62. I.R.C. §1222(2).

63. I.R.C. §170(b)(1)(C)(i).

64. I.R.C. §170(b)(1)(C)(iii). This reduction must be made *before* the percentage limitations (explained above) are applied.

65. I.R.C. §170(b)(1)(D).

66. I.R.C. §170(e)(1)(A); Treas. Reg. §1.170A-4(a)(1).

67. Treas. Reg. § 1.170A-4(b)(1).
68. I.R.C. §1222(1).
69. I.R.C. §170(e)(1).
70. I.R.C. §170(e)(1).
71. I.R.C. §170(e)(1)(B).
72. See Treas. Reg. §1.170A-4(b)(3)(i).
73. I.R.C. §170(e)(5).
74. Treas. Reg. §1.170A-1(c)(1).
75. Treas. Reg. §1.1011-2(a)(3); Rev. Rul. 81-163, 1981-1 CB 433.
76. Treas. Reg. §1.170A-5(a)(1).
77. I.R.C. §§170(f)(3)(A), 2055(e)(2), 2522(c)(2).
78. I.R.C. §§170(f)(3)(A), 2055(e)(2), 2522(c)(2).
79. I.R.C. §170(f)(3)(B).
80. I.R.C. §170(f)(2).
81. I.R.C. §170(f)(3)(A).
82. I.R.C. §170(f)(3)(B)(ii).
83. Treas. Reg. §1.170A-7(b)(1).
84. Treas. Reg. §1.170A-7(a)(2)(i).
85. Treas. Regs. §§1.170A-7(b)(1)(i), 1.170A-7(a)(2)(i).
86. Treas. Reg. §1.170A-7(c).
87. I.R.C. §170(b)(2).
88. I.R.C. §170(b)(2)(B).
89. I.R.C. §170(a)(1). Different rules apply for future interests in tangible personal property, gifts of undivided present interest, and gifts of future interests in real property or intangible personal property. See I.R.C. §170(a)(3); Treas. Reg. §1.170A-5.
90. I.R.C. §170(a)(1).
91. I.R.C. §170(f)(17); Treas. Reg §1.170A-13(a)(1).
92. I.R.C. §170(f)(8)(A).
93. I.R.C. §170(f)(8)(B); Treas. Reg. §1.170A-13(f)(2).
94. I.R.C. §170(f)(8)(C); Treas. Reg. §1.170A-13(f)(3).
95. I.R.C. §170(f)(8)(D).
96. Treas. Reg. §1.170A-13(b)(1).
97. I.R.C. §170(f)(16).
98. I.R.C. §170(f)(16)(B).
99. I.R.C. §170(f)(16)(D)(i).
100. Treas. Reg. §1.170A-13(c)(2).
101. Treas. Reg. §1.170A-13(c)(5)(iv).
102. Treas. Reg. §1.170A-13(c)(6).
103. Treas. Reg. §1.170A-13(c)(4)(iv)(B).
104. Treas. Reg. §1.170A-13(c)(4)(iii).
105. Treas. Reg. §1.170A-13(c)(7)(ix)(A).
106. I.R.C. §§6662(a), 6662(b)(3).
107. See I.R.C. §6662(d).
108. I.R.C. §6662(e)(1)(A).
109. I.R.C. §6662(h)(2)(A)(i).
110. I.R.C. §6659A(a)(1).
111. I.R.C. §6659A(b).
112. I.R.C. §6659A(c).
113. *The Tools & Techniques of Charitable Planning* (3rd Edition), p. 155 (National Underwriter Company, 2007).
114. *Ibid.*
115. Treas. Reg. §1.170A-4(c)(2)(ii).
116. I.R.C. §1011(b).
117. Rev. Rul. 78-38.

LIKE-KIND EXCHANGES

CHAPTER 28

WHAT ARE LIKE-KIND EXCHANGES?

In general, when a taxpayer transfers property in exchange for cash or other property, the taxpayer must recognize gain or loss on the transfer.[1] However, there are several areas of the tax law that permit (or require) non-recognition of gains or losses in certain circumstances.

One of the more well-known non-recognition provisions of the tax law is for like-kind exchanges. When a taxpayer transfers property to another party and, in exchange, receives property that is similar to what was given up, the taxpayer is essentially in the same economic position that he or she was in prior to the exchange. It is viewed as a continuation of the same investment. For that reason, the tax law requires that no gain or loss be recognized on property exchanged for other property that is of "like-kind."

As a result of the non-recognition of the gain or loss, the taxpayer's basis in the new property carries the basis of the transferred property, with certain adjustments. Therefore, the unreported gain or loss is not extinguished or forgotten but merely deferred into the future until the property received in the exchange is finally sold in a taxable transaction. The holding period of like-kind property relinquished in the exchange generally carries over (tacks on) to the holding period of the property that was received.

Transactions involving like-kind property may also include property not of a like-kind. The taxpayer not only receives the similar property but something else "to boot". This so-called "boot" may force the recognition of some or all of the otherwise deferred gain or loss.

Like-kind exchanges only apply to property held for productive use in a trade or business or for investment. Such exchanges are most commonly seen in transfers of real estate, automobiles, and business equipment (machines, computers, furniture, etc.).

As a result of the popularity of the non-recognition rule for like-kind exchanges, different techniques have emerged over the years to allow more taxpayers to participate in a variety of exchanges and meet the like-kind exchange requirements, such as:

- Multiparty exchanges – Like-kind exchanges involving more than two parties to the exchange;

- Deferred (forward) exchanges – Like-kind exchanges involving the relinquishment of property prior to the receipt of replacement property; and

- Reverse exchanges – Like-kind exchanges involving the purchase of replacement property prior to the sale of the relinquished property.

Realizing that it is sometimes impossible to complete a like-kind exchange of properties at the exact same time, the like-kind exchange rules contain specific time periods during which like-kind property must be identified and obtained by the taxpayer.

GENERAL RULE FOR LIKE-KIND EXCHANGES

Code section 1031 sets forth the rules for like-kind exchanges of property. The general rule, contained in Code section 1031(a), carries a number of requirements, each of which must be defined and followed in order to ensure the applicability of the non-recognition provision. Code section 1031(a)(1) states:

"No gain or loss shall be recognized on the exchange of property held for productive use in a trade or business or for investment if the property is exchanged for property of like kind which is to be held either for productive use in a trade or business or for investment."[2]

This general rule requiring non-recognition is mandatory, not elective. Therefore, taxpayers with losses built in to the property that will be exchanged would be wise to use the rules in reverse – that is, to ensure that the provisions of this tax law are *not* met.

Example: Stephanie Pressman owns an acre of land in the Philadelphia suburbs that she has held for investment purposes. She originally purchased the land for $50,000 and it is now worth $200,000. Jennifer Lansing owns an investment in five acres of land in rural West Virginia. Jennifer paid $250,000 for the land and it has a fair market value of $200,000. Stephanie and Jennifer agree to exchange their holdings. Stephanie's realized gain of $150,000 is deferred as part of the like-kind exchange, as is Jennifer's realized loss of $50,000. Stephanie will take the West Virginia property with a basis of $50,000 and Jennifer will receive the Philadelphia suburb property with a basis of $250,000. Jennifer could have recognized the $50,000 loss by ensuring that she did not meet the provisions of Code section 1031.

Non-Qualifying Property

The like-kind exchange provisions do not apply to certain types of property. Qualifying property does not include:

1. stock in trade or other property held primarily for sale,[3]

2. stocks, bonds or notes,[4]

3. other securities or evidences of indebtedness or interest,[5]

4. interests in a partnership[6] (unless the partnership has a valid election under Code

section 761(a) in effect to be excluded from the application of the partnership rules of Subchapter K),[7]

5. certificates of trust or beneficial interests, or[8]

6. choses in action[9] (choses in action are defined by the Supreme Court as the "infinite variety of contracts, covenants, and promises, which confer on one party a right to recover a personal chattel or a sum of money from another.")[10]

Each party involved in an exchange does not need to treat the transaction as a like-kind exchange. One party could be required to treat the transaction as a like-kind exchange while another falls outside the rules for mandatory application.[11]

Example: Car Lot, Inc. is a dealer in passenger automobiles. Sebro, Inc. is a service business that is looking for a new car for its sole owner, John Sebro. Sebro purchases a new car from Car Lot, Inc. for $30,000. In exchange, Sebro trades-in a five-year old car that has an adjusted basis on Sebro's books of $5,000. Car Lot gives Sebro $8,000 on the trade and credits that amount against the $30,000 purchase price. Sebro pays $22,000 cash for the car. Since Car Lot is a dealer in passenger automobiles, the property is not qualifying property under Code section 1031(a)(2)(A). However, Sebro is trading business property for business property and since the business has met the like-kind exchange rules, it is required to apply the like-kind exchange provisions and defer recognition of gain.

Property received will also not be considered as property of a like-kind if it is not identified on or before the day which is forty-five days after the date on which the taxpayer transfers the property relinquished in the exchange.[12] Furthermore, the replacement property must be received by the earlier of:

- the day which is 180 days after the date on which the taxpayer transferred the property relinquished in the exchange, or[13]

- the due date (including extensions) for the transferor's tax return for the taxable year in which the transfer of the relinquished property occurs.[14]

The regulations provide that the identification and replacement periods end at midnight of the 45th and 180th days following the relinquishment of the property, respectively.[15]

Example: On December 30, 2013, Highway Realty Partnership, a calendar year partnership, transfers an apartment building to Suburban Properties with the anticipation of having the transfer be treated as a like-kind exchange. In order to comply with the like-kind exchange time requirements, Highway Realty must identify the replacement property no later than midnight on February 14, 2014. The replacement property must be received no later than April 15, 2014, the due date of Highway Realty Partnership's tax return, unless the taxpayer requests an extension of time to file their 2013 tax return. In that case, Highway Realty has until midnight on June 29, 2014, to acquire the replacement property.

Like-Kind Property

So, what exactly is like-kind property? In general, property of a like-kind refers to the nature or character of the property and not to its grade or quality.[16] For example, a used car and a new car are like-kind property.

For the purposes of determining whether the like-kind requirement is satisfied, property can be categorized in three ways:

1. depreciable tangible personal property

2. other personal property

3. real property

Depreciable Tangible Personal Property – Tangible personal property subject to depreciation is considered of a like-kind if the property in question is either of a like class or a like kind.[17] The regulations provide a safe harbor test for determining if property is of a like class. The test involves reviewing if the exchanged properties are in the same "General Asset Class" or the same "Product Class."

The General Asset Classes are defined in Revenue Procedure 87-56[18] and contain a number of common

properties that are used by businesses. The regulations provide that exchanged assets within one of the asset classes 00.11 through 00.28 and 00.4 of Rev. Proc. 87-56 are treated as like-kind property.[19] The following is a list of the General Asset Classes:

- Office furniture, fixtures, and equipment (asset class 00.11);

- Information systems (computers and peripheral equipment) (asset class 00.12);

- Data handling equipment, except computers (asset class 00.13);

- Airplanes (airframes and engines), except those used in commercial or contract carrying of passengers or freight, and all helicopters (airframes and engines) (asset class 00.21);

- Automobiles, taxis (asset class 00.22);

- Buses (asset class 00.23);

- Light general purpose trucks (asset class 00.241);

- Heavy general purpose trucks (asset class 00.242);

- Railroad cars and locomotives, except those owned by railroad transportation companies (asset class 00.25);

- Tractor units for use over-the-road (asset class 00.26);

- Trailers and trailer-mounted containers (asset class 00.27);

- Vessels, barges, tugs, and similar water-transportation equipment, except those used in marine construction (asset class 00.28); and

- Industrial steam and electric generation and/or distribution systems (asset class 00.4).[20]

Exchanged property may alternatively be considered of a like-kind if it is in the same Product Class. The Product Class is a four-digit numerical code (the "SIC Code") contained within Division D of the Standard Industrial Classification Manual (the "SIC Manual"). If a property is listed in more than one product class, the property is treated as being listed in any one of those product classes. Note that four digit codes ending in "9" (miscellaneous categories) are not considered a product class for purposes of Code section 1031.[21]

A property may not be classified within more than one General Asset Class or one Product Class. The General Asset Class safe harbor is applied first. If a property is classified within a General Asset Class, it may not also be classified within a Product Class.[22]

Example: Barnum, Inc. trades-in a used BMW passenger car for a brand new Ford pick-up truck. The BMW is considered to be in General Asset Class 00.22 (automobiles) while the Ford is classified as General Asset Class 00.241 (light general purpose trucks). Since the two vehicles are classified within a General Asset Class, they may not also be classified within a Product Class.[23]

Other Personal Property – Since most properties that are exchanged are defined as depreciable tangible personal property or real estate, this is the least used of the three categories. Property that falls into this category includes primarily:

- intangibles, such as patents or copyrights; and

- collectibles, such as stamps, gems, antiques or coins.

No like classes are provided for intangible personal property. The determination of whether intangible personal property is of a like-kind to other intangible personal property depends on the nature or character of the rights involved and also on the nature or character of the underlying property to which the intangible personal property relates.[24] The goodwill or going concern value of one business is not intangible personal property of a like-kind to the goodwill or going concern value of another business.[25]

Example: Bruce Mailer exchanges the copyright on one novel for the copyright on another novel. These properties are of a like-kind. However, exchanging a copyright on a novel for a copyright on a song is not an exchange of properties of a like-kind.[26]

Real Estate – Real estate is generally considered to be property of a like-kind with any other real estate property.

The regulations even provide an example of a like-kind exchange of real property in the city with a ranch or farm.[27] Also, unimproved real estate is of a like-kind with improved real estate.[28]

Example: Philadelphia Realty Partnership would like to exchange a suburban strip mall complex for an apartment building in the city. Since both properties qualify as real estate, they will be treated as properties of a like-kind.

A leasehold interest represents a lesser ownership than a fee interest in real estate. However, if the lease will exist for a sufficiently long enough period of time, it may be considered to be like-kind property with a fee simple interest. In order to meet the safe-harbor, the lease must last for at least thirty years (including all potential options to extend the term of the lease) to be considered as qualifying like-kind property.[29] A leasehold interest of less than thirty years may only be exchanged for another leasehold interest that extends less than thirty years.

An important point to consider is how international properties are treated under the like-kind exchange rules. Unfortunately for many taxpayers, real estate located in the United States is not considered to be property of a like-kind with property located outside the United States.[30]

Property Held for Productive Use in Trade or Business or for Investment

"Held for productive use in a trade or business or for investment" is not defined in the Code or in the regulations. However, in the past, the IRS has applied the definition of "property used in the trade or business" under Code section 1231(b) for purposes of the like-kind exchange rules. The taxpayer shoulders the burden of proving the property is held for use in a trade or business or for investment. The determination is made at the time of the exchange.

The inclusion of the words "held for" within the general rule for like-kind exchanges implies that there is a time element that may need to be satisfied in order for the like-kind exchange rules to apply. Although there is no holding period outlined in the law, it is clear that property acquired solely for the purpose of executing an exchange is not "held for productive use in a trade or business or for investment."[31]

Example: Phyllis owns a parcel of land (held for investment) that she contracts to sell to Joan. Phyllis agreed that if Joan could find suitable property of a like-kind, Phyllis would exchange her property for Joan's. Joan finds a property that Phyllis agrees to exchange for her land. Phyllis will recognize like-kind exchange treatment on the transaction, but Joan will not. Joan's acquisition of the property was done solely for the purpose of executing an exchange.

RECEIPT OF BOOT

Code section 1031 only applies to the like-kind property received in an exchange for other like-kind property. If the taxpayer, in addition to receiving like-kind property, receives money or other dissimilar property in the exchange ("boot", i.e., the taxpayer received the like-kind property and cash 'to boot'), gain will be recognized to the extent of (a) any money received plus (b) the fair market value of the boot received in the exchange.[32] However, in a classic "heads I win – tails you lose" ploy, the Code provides that if the transaction results in a loss to the taxpayer and boot is received in the exchange, the loss is not recognized.[33]

Like-kind exchanges rarely involve only property of a like-kind. The values of the exchanged properties will most likely not be identical, causing one party to "make-up" the difference by paying some cash, assuming some liabilities, or providing some other form of non-qualifying property (i.e., property that is not of a like-kind).

Example: Highpoint, Inc. and Crosstown, Inc. each own a piece of machinery (of a like-kind) used in their respective businesses. Highpoint's machine has an adjusted basis of $50,000 and a fair market value of $90,000. Crosstown's machine has an adjusted basis of $40,000 and a fair market value of $80,000. Highpoint agrees to accept Crosstown's machine plus $10,000 cash in exchange for their machine. Highpoint realizes a gain of $40,000 on the exchange ($80,000 value of Crosstown's machine plus $10,000 cash less the $50,000 adjusted basis of the relinquished machine). Highpoint must recognize $10,000 of

the $40,000 realized gain because they received $10,000 of cash (boot). Crosstown realizes a gain of $40,000, but recognizes no gain – the gain is deferred since they met the like-kind exchange requirements and did not receive any non-qualifying property to boot.

When a liability is assumed (or property is taken subject to a liability) in an exchange, the liability is treated as boot received by the original debtor.[34] This is because, in the IRS view, the assumption of the original debtor's liability is equivalent to the new owner providing the original owner cash in the exchange to pay off the loan while simultaneously financing this cash by establishing a loan against the property received. This "implied cash transfer" is treated as boot received by the original debtor/owner.

Example: Longpoint Apartments owns a building with an adjusted basis of $500,000 that is valued at $1,700,000. The property currently has a mortgage of $1,000,000, leaving the owner with a net equity of $700,000. Longpoint exchanges the property with Shortfall Apartments, which owns an unencumbered building with a value of $700,000. The amount realized by Longpoint in the exchange is $1,700,000 ($700,000 value of property received plus $1,000,000 of liabilities assumed by Shortfall). The gain realized by Longpoint is $1,200,000 ($1,700,000 amount realized less $500,000 adjusted basis), of which the boot of $1,000,000 must be recognized as gain in the year of the transfer.

If an exchange involves the reciprocal assumption of liabilities, the amount of debt relief may be offset by the amount of liabilities assumed.[35] The amount of debt relief may also be offset by other forms of boot transferred in the exchange (e.g. cash).[36] However, other boot received may not offset boot given in the exchange.[37] Furthermore, it is notable that when the taxpayer *receives* boot, he/she cannot reduce the amount treated as boot in acknowledgment of any liabilities that were assumed, even though he/she would have received no boot if the cash were simply used to pay down the liability before the transfer.[38]

Example 1: LKE, Inc. transfers property subject to a $500,000 mortgage in exchange for property subject to a $400,000 mortgage. Since the liability transferred exceeds the liability assumed, the LKE would be in receipt of $100,000 of boot.

Example 2: Same facts as above except that LKE also transfers $100,000 of cash in the exchange. LKE's debt relief is completely offset by the liability assumed plus the cash transferred. Therefore, no boot is received in the transfer and LKE will not be required to report any gain.

Example 3: The other party to the transfer in the above example, ONO, Inc., has relinquished property subject to a $400,000 mortgage and received property subject to a $500,000 mortgage plus $100,000 of cash. ONO can fully offset the $400,000 of debt relief with the $500,000 of liabilities assumed. However, the $100,000 of cash received will still be treated as boot and may force ONO to recognize gain up to this amount on the exchange. Note that this treatment could be avoided by having LKE take the $100,000 of cash and pay down that amount of the liability immediately prior to the transfer. LKE and ONO would then each be assuming $400,000 of liabilities and no boot would be transferred to/from either party.

BASIS RULES

The basis of properties acquired in a like-kind exchange is identical to the basis of the property exchanged with the following adjustments:

- Decreased by the amount of money received,

- Increased by the amount of gain recognized on the like-kind property,

- Increased by the amount of boot transferred (money paid or the basis of the property transferred if other non-qualifying property besides cash was transferred),

- Increased by the amount of gain recognized on non-qualifying property transferred, and

- Decreased by the amount of loss recognized on non-qualifying property transferred.[39]

Example: Using the facts included in the Highpoint/Crosstown example, Highpoint's

basis in the new machine is $50,000 ($50,000 adjusted basis of relinquished property, reduced by $10,000 cash received, increased by $10,000 gain recognized). Therefore, if Highpoint sells the machine tomorrow for its $80,000 fair market value, the remaining $30,000 of deferred gain would be recognized.

A loss may be recognized in a like-kind exchange where the property transferred in the exchange includes property that is not like-kind.[40]

Example: Again using the previous example, instead of using cash in the transaction Crosstown gives up a car with a fair market value of $10,000 and an adjusted basis of $30,000. Crosstown will recognize the $20,000 on the transfer of the car since it is not like-kind property. Crosstown's basis in the machinery will now be $50,000 ($40,000 adjusted basis in relinquished property, increased by the $30,000 basis of boot transferred, decreased by the $20,000 of loss recognized on non-qualifying boot transferred). Note that, for the purposes of the machinery, this is equivalent to the result if Crosstown simply transferred cash to achieve a basis of $50,000 ($40,000 adjusted basis in relinquished property, increased by $10,000 of boot transferred). However, in this situation Crosstown has been able to recognize the unrealized loss on the car as a part of the exchange.

If a taxpayer receives both like-kind property and property that is not like-kind, the basis is allocated first to the non-like-kind property to the extent of its fair market value, and then to the property that is of a like-kind, to the extent of the aggregate basis – the adjusted basis of the relinquished property, decreased by any money received or liabilities assumed, and increased (decreased) by any gain (loss) recognized on the exchange.[41]

Example: Continuing our Highpoint/Crosstown example, if Highpoint receives the car instead of cash, Highpoint will still realize a $40,000 gain on the exchange. Of this amount, $10,000 will be recognized as gain due to the receipt of the car as property not of a like-kind. The aggregate basis of the machine and the car is $60,000 ($50,000 adjusted basis of relinquished property, reduced by $0 cash received, increased by $10,000 gain recognized). The basis is then allocated first to the car, up to its fair market value of $10,000. The remaining $50,000 of basis is allocated to the machine, the like-kind property received in the exchange.

Expenses related to an exchange, such as brokerage fees and commissions, are treated the following way:

1. deducted from the amount of gain or loss realized in the like-kind exchange;

2. offset against cash payments (boot) received; and

3. included in the basis of the property received.[42]

EXCHANGES BETWEEN RELATED PERSONS

The like-kind exchange rules provide a limitation on the application of the non-recognition provision in the situation where the parties to an exchange are related. The intention of Congress was to discourage such exchanges where the intent was to reduce or avoid gain recognition on subsequent sales, and to restrict "basis shifting."[43]

Under section 1031(f), if a taxpayer exchanges property with a related person in a transaction to which section 1031 originally applies and within two years of the date of the exchange, the taxpayer or the related party dispose of the property acquired in the exchange, the original gain or loss deferred from the original exchange must be recognized.[44] The gain or loss recognized is taken into account as of the date of the disposition of the property.[45]

Example: William Barson owns an apartment building with an adjusted basis of $300,000. His sister, Flora also owns an apartment building that was left to her by her late uncle. Her adjusted basis in the apartment building is $1,900,000. Both properties are valued at $2,000,000. Flora decides that she does not want to own and manage the property. William thinks that Flora's property has much more upside potential than his but if he were to sell his property, he would realize a $1,700,000 gain. The two decide to exchange properties. One year later, Flora

realizes she can't take the stress of being a landlord anymore and sells her property for $2,000,000 and recognizes her $100,000 gain ($2,000,000 proceeds less $1,900,000 basis). By selling the property within two years of the exchange, she automatically triggers the gain to her brother, William, by application of Code section 1031(f). As a result, William will recognize the gain of $1,700,000 that was originally deferred under the like-kind exchange rules.

Of primary importance in the application of these related-party rules is the question of who is considered to be a related person. For purposes of this rule, a related person is defined in the same way as it is under Code section 267(b) and Code section 707(b)(1).[46] The most common application of the related person rule is where members of a family are involved in a transaction.[47] Members of a family include brothers, sisters (whether by the whole or half blood), spouse, ancestors (parents and grandparents) and lineal descendants (children and grandchildren).[48] However, nieces, nephews, aunts, uncles, in-laws, step-parents, step-children and step-grandchildren are not considered members of a family for this purpose.

Example: If William was Flora's nephew, the related party rules would not apply. Flora would recognize the gain on the sale of her property but would not trigger the gain recognition on William's property.

In addition, related parties under sections 267(b) and 707(b)(1) also include:

- A corporation and an individual that owns, directly or indirectly, by or for himself/herself, more than 50 percent of the value of the outstanding stock;

- Two corporations which are members of the same controlled group;

- A grantor and a fiduciary of any trust;

- A fiduciary of a trust and a fiduciary of another trust, if the same person is a grantor of both trusts;

- A fiduciary of a trust and a beneficiary of such trust;

- A fiduciary of a trust and a beneficiary of another trust, if the same person is a grantor of both trusts;

- A corporation and a fiduciary, if more than 50 percent of the value of the outstanding stock is owned, directly or indirectly, by or for the trust or by or for a person who is a grantor of the trust;

- A personal and an organization to which section 501 applies and which is controlled directly or indirectly by such person or by members of the family of such individual;

- A corporation and a partnership if the same persons own more than 50 percent in value of the outstanding stock of the corporation, and more than 50 percent of the capital interest, or the profits interest, in the partnership;

- A partnership and a person owning more than 50 percent of the capital interest, or the profits interest, in such partnership;

- Two partnerships in which the same person owns, directly or indirectly, more than 50 percent of the capital interests or profit interests;

- An S corporation and another S corporation if the same persons own more than 50 percent in value of the outstanding stock of each corporation;

- An S corporation and a C corporation, if the same persons own more than 50 percent in value of the outstanding stock of each corporation; and

- Except in the case of a sale or exchange in satisfaction of a pecuniary bequest, an executor of an estate and a beneficiary of such estate;

MULTIPARTY EXCHANGES

Like-kind exchanges frequently will involve more than two parties. Three and four parties to an exchange are not an uncommon occurrence.

Example: Lisa owns a building that Matt would like to purchase for cash. Lisa intends to use the proceeds to purchase another building and would prefer to structure the transaction as a like-kind exchange. Nate owns a building that Lisa would like to acquire. A like-kind exchange can be accomplished for Lisa in the following manner:

1. Matt purchases Nate's property for cash

2. Matt and Lisa exchange their buildings in a transaction that qualifies as a like-kind exchange for Lisa. Note that Matt would not receive like-kind exchange treatment on the transaction with Lisa since the property was acquired solely for the purpose of the exchange.

Although ultimately, in the final step, this transaction was structured as a basic like-kind exchange, if multiparty exchange structures like this were not permitted, the like-kind exchange rules would have much less applicability. The transferor of a property would be forced to not only find a person who would like to receive the property but also have property of a like-kind that the transferor wants in return.

FORWARD (DEFERRED) EXCHANGES

A forward (or deferred) exchange is one in which the taxpayer transfers the property now and receives replacement property at a later date. Section 1031 may still apply to such a transaction provided:

1. replacement property is identified within forty-five days of the transfer of the relinquished property ("the identification period"), and

2. replacement property is received by the earlier of the due date of the tax return (including extensions) for the year of the transfer or within 180 days of the transfer of the relinquished property ("the replacement period").

There are no extensions (aside from the tax return due date exception) available to these time constraints. If the replacement property is either identified or received after the applicable respective time periods, the like-kind rules will not apply and gain or loss must be recognized on the transaction.[49]

Replacement property must be identified as such in either:

1. a written agreement covering the exchange that is signed by all parties before the end of the identification period; or

2. a written document signed by the taxpayer and hand delivered, mailed, telecopied, or otherwise sent before the end of the identification period to:

   - a person involved in the exchange (such as an intermediary, escrow agent or title company) other than the taxpayer, a related party, or the agent of the taxpayer; or to

   - the person obligated to transfer the replacement property to the taxpayer (regardless of whether that person is a related party or an agent of the taxpayer).[50]

More than one property may be identified as replacement property. However, the maximum number of properties that may be identified is (1) three properties of any fair market value or (2) any number of properties as long as the aggregate fair market value of the properties does not exceed 200 percent of the fair market value of the relinquished properties as of the date of the transfer.[51]

If more than the allowable number of properties is identified (i.e., neither of the prior paragraph requirements are satisfied), then no replacement properties will be treated as identified unless the replacement property is (1) acquired before the end of the identification period or (2) identified before the end of the identification period and obtained before the end of the replacement period, the value of such property being at least 95 percent of the aggregate fair market value of all identified properties.[52]

The identification of a property as replacement property may be revoked before the end of the identification period in a written amendment to the original agreement delivered, mailed, telecopied or otherwise sent to all parties to the agreement, or in an additional written document of revocation delivered, mailed, telecopied, or otherwise sent to the person to whom the original identification was sent.[53]

Replacement property will meet the time limitations if it is received before the end of the replacement period and is substantially similar to the identified property.[54]

Due to the complexities of transferring property before replacement property is identified, forward exchanges (as well as reverse exchanges, which will be discussed later) often involve more than two parties in the exchange. Taxpayers will frequently rely on "intermediaries" to ensure like-kind exchange treatment.

An intermediary will typically arrange to sell the taxpayer's property and purchase replacement property to exchange with the taxpayer. This arrangement will be treated as a like-kind exchange if the intermediary is a "qualified intermediary[55] and the taxpayer is not in constructive receipt of the proceeds on the sale of the relinquished property.

It is important in a deferred exchange that the taxpayer not be in constructive receipt of the proceeds of the sale during the process (i.e., after the sale but before the subsequent purchase).[56] A taxpayer is in constructive receipt of money or other property at the time that he/she receives the economic benefit from it, such as when it is credited to the taxpayer's account, set apart for the taxpayer, or otherwise made available so that the taxpayer may draw upon it at any time or may draw upon it at any time if notice of intention to draw is given.[57] The taxpayer avoids the constructive receipt rules as long as substantial restrictions must be placed on the taxpayer's control of the receipt of the funds or property, and continues to *not* be in constructive receipt unless and until the restrictions lapse, expire or are waived.[58]

Usually, an escrow account will be established to hold the proceeds from the sale of the relinquished property to meet the prior paragraph requirements for avoiding constructive receipt. If the escrow account is a "qualified escrow account," the taxpayer will not be in constructive receipt of the proceeds. A qualified escrow account is an escrow account wherein:

1. The escrow holder is not the taxpayer, a related party, or an agent of the taxpayer, and

2. The escrow agreement expressly limits the taxpayer's rights to receive, pledge, borrow, or otherwise obtain the benefits of the cash or cash equivalent held in the escrow account.[59]

A qualified trust may be used in place of a qualified escrow account provided the trust agreement expressly limits the taxpayer's rights to receive, pledge, borrow or otherwise obtain the benefits of the cash or cash equivalent held by the trustee, and the trustee is not the taxpayer, a related party, or an agent of the taxpayer.[60]

A qualified intermediary (QI) is not considered to be an agent of the taxpayer.[61] A QI is a person who:

1. is not the taxpayer, a related party, or already an agent of the taxpayer; and

2. enters into a written agreement with the taxpayer (the "exchange agreement") and, as required by the exchange agreement, acquires the relinquished property from the taxpayer, transfers the relinquished property, acquires the replacement property and transfers the replacement property to the taxpayer.[62]

Example: Albert Trammell wants to sell his office building. The adjusted basis of the building is $600,000 and it is worth $1,100,000. Lee Sheffield wants to buy Albert's office building. Linda Gomez wants to sell her apartment complex for $900,000. QI, Inc. is a qualified intermediary who is not a disqualified person (a related party or an agent of the taxpayer). The following steps fulfill the requirements necessary to ensure that Albert Trammell receives like-kind exchange treatment on the transaction:

Step 1 – On April 1, Albert enters into an agreement to sell his office building to Lee for $1,100,000. The closing is set for May 5. (Note: Lee does not care to or want to participate in a like-kind exchange).

Step 2 – On April 29, Albert enters into an exchange agreement with QI, Inc. The exchange agreement expressly limits his rights to receive, pledge, borrow or otherwise obtain the benefits of money or other property held by QI in a qualified escrow account. In the exchange agreement, Albert assigns to QI all of his rights in the agreement with Lee. Albert notifies Lee of the assignment to QI.

Step 3 – On May 5, Albert executes and delivers to Lee a deed conveying the office building to him. In return, Lee pays $1,100,000 to QI, Inc., which is placed into the qualified escrow account.

Step 4 – On June 10, Albert identifies Linda's apartment building as replacement property and delivers to QI, Inc. a written document that states the identification.

Step 5 – On July 17, Albert enters into an agreement with Linda to purchase the apartment building from Linda for $900,000. Albert then assigns his rights to QI and notifies Linda of the assignment in writing.

Step 6 – On August 21, QI pays $900,000 from the qualified escrow account to Linda who then transfers the deed conveying the apartment building to Albert. QI disburses the remaining $200,000 to Albert.

Result – Albert receives like-kind exchange treatment on the transfer of his office building to Lee in exchange for Linda's apartment building. His realized gain on the transfer is $500,000 ($1,100,000 amount realized less $600,000 adjusted basis). Since Albert received $200,000 of cash (boot), he will recognize $200,000 of the realized gain. His basis in the apartment building will be $600,000 (thus deferring the remaining $300,000 of gain while acquiring the replacement building worth $900,000).

REVERSE EXCHANGES

Forward or deferred exchanges refer to a transaction where a taxpayer relinquishes a property and subsequently identifies and receives replacement property. A reverse exchange, on the other hand, occurs in 'reverse' order - the replacement property is obtained before the relinquished property is transferred. Unfortunately, the regulations do not specifically cover this type of transaction.

Revenue Procedure 2000-37 added certain safe harbor procedures for reverse exchanges. In particular, a taxpayer who wishes to use a reverse exchange can employ an intermediary (similar to a qualified intermediary) in the form of an "exchange accommodation titleholder" (EAT). The EAT will not be treated as the taxpayer's agent.

In general, for a like-kind exchange to be effective, the taxpayer may not receive the replacement property before the relinquished property is transferred. However, if properly structured, an EAT, and not the taxpayer, will be considered the owner of the replacement property. The transfer of title by the EAT to the taxpayer will then be postponed until after the taxpayer transfers the relinquished property, completing the exchange.

The IRS will treat an EAT as the beneficial owner of the relinquished and replacement property if the property is held in a "Qualified Exchange Accommodation Arrangement" (QEAA). Property is held in a QEAA when each of the following five requirements are met:

Ownership Requirement – The EAT must possess qualified indicia of ownership of the transferred property during the time it is held by the EAT. The EAT must be a person other than the taxpayer or a disqualified person (a related party or an agent of the taxpayer). The EAT must be subject to federal income tax or be a partnership or S corporation owned more than 90 percent by persons subject to income tax.[63]

Qualified indicia of ownership must be held by the EAT at all times from acquisition until ultimate transfer. Qualified indicia of ownership are either (1) legal title; (2) beneficial ownership under applicable principles of commercial law (e.g. a contract for deed); or (3) ownership of an interest in an entity that is disregarded as separate from its owner for federal income tax purposes, if the entity is the property's legal or beneficial owner.[64]

Intent Requirement – At the time the ownership is transferred to the EAT, the taxpayer must have a bona fide intent that the transferred property be held by the EAT as either replacement or relinquished property in an exchange that is intended to qualify for non-recognition of gain or loss under section 1031.[65]

QEAA Requirement – The taxpayer must enter into a written qualified exchange accommodation agreement with the EAT within five days following the transfer of property to the EAT. The terms of the agreement must specify that the EAT is holding the property for the benefit of the taxpayer in order to facilitate an exchange under section 1031 and Revenue Procedure 2000-37, that the EAT will be treated as the beneficial owner of the property for all federal income purposes, and that the income tax attributes of the property will be reported on the income tax returns of the taxpayer and the EAT as appropriate.[66]

Identification of Relinquished Property Requirement – Within the forty-five days following the transfer of qualified indicia of ownership of replacement property to the EAT, the taxpayer must identify relinquished property in a manner similar to the identification requirement under the rules for deferred exchanges.[67]

Time of Transfer Requirement – There are two separate 180 day time limits for the completion of the exchange. The first is that the length of time any one piece of property may be held in a QEAA by an EAT is 180 days regardless of whether it is the relinquished or replacement property.[68] Therefore, the longest time period that any relinquished or replacement property can be owned by the EAT is 180 days.

The second time limit is a 180-day "combined time period" that the EAT may hold both replacement and relinquished property.[69]

Example: Oceanside, Inc. enters into a reverse exchange by relinquishing property to an EAT. The EAT holds qualified indicia of ownership for 30 days during which time Oceanside identifies a like-kind replacement property and has the EAT obtain the property. The EAT transfers the replacement property to Oceanside (ostensibly completing the exchange for Oceanside), and now holds only the relinquished property. The EAT may continue to hold such property for up to 150 days before the relinquished property must be transferred to a new owner.

FREQUENTLY ASKED QUESTIONS

Question – How are like-kind exchanges reported for tax purposes?

Answer – Taxpayers involved in a like-kind exchange must complete and file Form 8824 in the year of the exchange.

Question – If a taxpayer acquires a property in a like-kind exchange and subsequently dies, is the deferred gain required to be recognized in the year of death?

Answer – No. The deferred gain would escape income tax just as if the taxpayer had held the relinquished property at the time of his death. Further, the property held at death would be entitled to a step-up in basis to its fair market value as of the date of the taxpayer's death.

Question – If a taxpayer acquires a property in a like-kind exchange and subsequently uses the property as a personal residence, can the gain exclusion rules of section 121 be used to effectively remove the deferred gain from taxation?

Answer – Yes, but with special rules. Ordinarily, a taxpayer must use and occupy a property as a personal residence for two of the last five years in order to avail themselves of the section 121 gain exclusion rules. However, a property that was acquired by a taxpayer who did not recognize gain under the like-kind exchange rules must hold the property for five years (in addition to meeting all of the other requirements of section 121) in order to qualify for the gain exclusion on the sale of a personal residence.[70]

Question – When should the like-kind exchange rules be avoided?

Answer – Taxpayers may want to avoid the mandatory application of the like-kind exchange rules under the following circumstances:

- The property has an unrealized loss that would benefit the taxpayer by realizing the loss (this is normally the case with automobiles used in a trade or business).

- The taxpayer has losses in the current year (or carryovers into the current year) that can be utilized to absorb the gain on the sale of the property.

- The gain is passive under Section 469 and would be offset by current and suspended passive activity losses.

- The taxpayer anticipates that their personal tax rate will increase in future years and the payment of the tax on the gain in the current year would be more beneficial than if the gain were deferred.

Question – How might a taxpayer avoid the application of the like-kind exchange rules?

Answer – A desire to avoid the like-kind exchange rules often occurs with automobiles that are subject to luxury auto limitations. The luxury auto limitations slow down depreciation to a point that the actual value of the car may be declining more rapidly than the taxpayer can claim depreciation. As a result, a taxpayer who wants to purchase a new car would be wise to sell the used car to a third party and recognize the loss instead of trading in the used car in a transaction with the dealer of the new car.

There are many requirements for a like-kind exchange to occur. Willfully failing any of the requirements will create the opportunity to recognize gain or loss on the transaction.

Question – Do states follow the like-kind exchange rules?

Answer – Taxpayers need to review their individual state tax laws to determine if their state allows for the non-recognition of gain and loss on transactions involving like-kind property. While many do, some only classify transactions involving like-kind property in their state as a valid non-recognition event. For example, real estate in one state transferred for real estate in a neighboring state will generally qualify for like-kind treatment for federal purposes but may fail the state requirement since the new property is in a different state.

See Figures 28.1 and 28.2 for worksheets for single asset like-kind exchanges.

CHAPTER ENDNOTES

1. I.R.C. §1001.
2. I.R.C. §1031(a)(1).
3. I.R.C. §1031(a)(2)(A).
4. I.R.C. §1031(a)(2)(B).
5. I.R.C. §1031(a)(2)(C).
6. I.R.C. §1031(a)(2)(D).
7. I.R.C. §1031(a)(2).
8. I.R.C. §1031(a)(2)(E).
9. I.R.C. §1031(a)(2)(F).
10. *Sheldon v. Sill*, 49 U.S. 441 (1850).
11. Rev. Rul. 75-292, 1975-2 CB 333.
12. I.R.C. §1031(a)(3)(A).
13. I.R.C. §1031(a)(3)(B)(i).
14. I.R.C. §1031(a)(3)(B)(ii).
15. Treas. Reg. §1.1031(a)-2(b)(1).

16. 1987-2 CB 674.

17. Treas. Reg. §1.1031(a)-2(b)(2).

18. Treas. Reg. §1.1031(a)-2(b)(2)(i) through (xiii).

19. Treas. Reg. §1.1031(a)-2(b)(3).

20. Treas. Reg. §1.1031(a)-2(b)(1).

21. See Priv. Ltr. Rul. 200241013.

22. Treas. Reg. §1.1031(a)-2(c)(1).

23. Treas. Reg. §1.1031(a)-2(c)(2).

24. Treas. Reg. §1.1031(a)-2(c)(3) Examples (1) and (2).

25. Treas. Reg. §1.1031(a)-1(c).

26. Treas. Reg. §1.1031(a)-1(b).

27. Treas. Reg. §§1.1031(a)-1(c).

28. I.R.C. §1031(h)(1).

29. Rev. Rul. 75-291, 1975-2 C.B. 332.

30. I.R.C. §1031(b).

31. I.R.C. §1031(c).

32. Treas. Reg. §1.1031(d)-2.

33. Treas. Reg. §1.1031(b)-1(c).

34. Treas. Reg. §1.1031(d)-2.

35. Treas. Reg. §1.1031(d)-2.

36. Treas. Reg. §1.031(d)-2 Example (2)(b).

37. I.R.C. §1031(d).

38. Treas. Reg. §1.1031(d)-1(e).

39. I.R.C. §1031(d).

40. Rev. Rul. 72-456, 1972-2 CB 468.

41. Senate Committee Print and Conference Committee Report to P.L. 101-239.

42. I.R.C. §1031(f)(1).

43. *Id*.

44. I.R.C. §1031(f)(3).

45. I.R.C. §267(b)(1).

46. I.R.C. §267(c)(4).

47. I.R.C. §1031(a)(3).

48. Treas. Reg. §1.1031(k)-1(c).

49. Treas. Reg. §1.1031(k)-1(c)(4)(i).

50. Treas. Reg. §1.1031(k)-1(c)(4)(ii).

51. Treas. Reg. §1.1031(k)-1(c)(6).

52. Treas. Reg. §1.1031(k)-1(d).

53. Treas. Reg. §1.1031(k)-1(g)(4).

54. Treas. Reg. §1.1031(k)-1(f)(1).

55. Treas. Reg. §1.1031(k)-1(f)(2).

56. *Id*.

57. Treas. Reg. §1.1031(k)-1(g)(3)(ii).

58. Treas. Reg. §1.1031(k)-1(g)(3)(iii).

59. Treas. Reg. §1.1031(k)-1(g)(4)(i).

60. Treas. Reg. §1.1031(k)-1(g)(4)(iii).

61. Rev. Proc. 2000-37 §4.02(1).

62. *Id*.

63. Rev. Proc. 2000-37 §4.02(2).

64. Rev. Proc. 2000-37 §4.02(3).

65. Rev. Proc. 2000-37 §4.02(4).

66. Rev. Proc. 2000-37 §4.02(5).

67. Rev. Proc. 2000-37 §4.02(6).

68. I.R.C. §121(d)(10).

Figure 28.1

DETERMINING GAIN OR LOSS		
1. Fair market value of qualifying property received	_____	
2. Fair market value of other property (boot) received	+_____	
3. Cash (boot) received	+_____	
4. Net indebtedness relief associated with properties exchanged (net debt relief/boot)	+_____	
5. Total consideration received (sum of lines 1 through 4)		_____
6. Original cost or other basis of properties surrendered	_____	
7. Accumulated depreciation of property surrendered	−_____	
8. Adjusted basis (line 6 less line 7)		−_____
9. Lesser of cash surrendered or line 4		−_____
10. Gain or loss realized (line 5 less lines 8 and 9 – if a loss, skip next section)		−_____
DETERMINING BOOT RECEIVED		
11. Indebtedness associated with property transferred (debt relief/boot)	_____	
12. Indebtedness associated with property received	−_____	
13. Cash surrendered	−_____	
14. Fair market value of other property (boot) surrendered	−_____	
15. Net boot received (line 11 less lines 12 through 14 but not less than zero)		_____
16. Fair market value of other property (boot) received		+_____
17. Cash received		+_____
18. Boot received (sum of lines 15 through 17)		_____
DETERMINING GAIN RECOGNIZED		
19. Gain recognized (Lesser of line 10 or 18)		_____

Figure 28.2

DETERMINING BASIS OF PROPERTY RECEIVED			
1. Adjusted basis of qualifying property surrendered	_____		
2. Adjusted basis of other property (boot) surrendered	+_____		
3. Total adjusted basis of property surrendered (sum of lines 1 and 2)		_____	
4. Cash surrendered and notes given		+_____	
5. Indebtedness associated with property received		+_____	
6. Gain recognized (line 19 from Figure 30.1)		+_____	
7. Gain recognized on other property (boot) surrendered		+_____	
8. (sum of lines 3 through 7)			_____
9. Cash received			−_____
10. Indebtedness associated with property surrendered			−_____
11. Loss recognized on other property (boot) surrendered			−_____
12. Aggregate basis of all properties received (line 8 less lines 9 through 11)			_____
DETERMINING BASIS OF NON-RECOGNITION PROPERTY RECEIVED			
13. Aggregate basis of all properties received (from line 12)		_____	
14. Fair market value of other property (boot) received		−_____	
15. Basis of non-recognition property received (line 13 less line 14)		_____	

PLANNING FOR THE SALE OR EXCHANGE OF ASSETS

CHAPTER 29

INTRODUCTION

When a taxpayer sells an asset, it could very well represent one of the single biggest sources of income he or she will ever report in a lifetime. On the flip side, sales of assets often yield losses that—for income tax purposes—may be available to offset other sources of income the taxpayer will have to report. The planning techniques for the sale or exchange of assets can be summarized into three broad categories:

1. Planning for gain deferral;

2. Planning for gain exclusion; and

3. Planning for loss recognition.

As mentioned in Chapter 4, the appreciation (or depreciation) of an asset is not reportable in a taxpayer's income until the asset is sold. This ability to time and defer taxation of the asset's appreciation is a powerful tool. If a taxpayer were required to report a stock's (or any other appreciating asset's) growth in value each year and pay tax on the appreciation, the ultimate value of the taxpayer's asset would be markedly diminished and the taxpayer could suffer liquidity problems because he'd be taxed before actually receiving income to pay the tax.

Example: John Harrington bought 1,000 shares of LISI stock for $10 per share. His $10,000 investment appreciates 10 percent each of the next five years. If John had to pay a 15 percent tax on the appreciation each year (as opposed to paying tax on his gain when the property was ultimately sold), he might be forced to sell a portion of his investment. On the other

hand, his investment would be worth $372.38 (approximately 2.5 percent) more at the end of the five years, if he could defer the taxation of the appreciation until the asset is sold.

Pay Tax on Appreciation

	Beginning	Appreciation	Tax	Ending
Year 1	10,000.00	1,000.00	(150.00)	10,850.00
Year 2	10,850.00	1,085.00	(162.75)	11,772.25
Year 3	11,772.25	1,177.23	(176.58)	12,772.89
Year 4	12,772.89	1,277.29	(191.59)	13,858.59
Year 5	13,858.59	1,385.86	(207.88)	15,036.57

Defer Tax on Appreciation

	Beginning	Appreciation	Tax	Ending
Year 1	10,000.00	1,000.00	–	11,000.00
Year 2	11,000.00	1,100.00	–	12,100.00
Year 3	12,100.00	1,210.00	–	13,310.00
Year 4	13,310.00	1,331.00	–	14,641.00
Year 5	14,641.00	1,464.10	(696.15)	15,408.95

Most of the time, taxpayers have control over when a taxable event such as a sale or exchange will occur and, therefore, also can time when gain or loss will be reported.

But there are situations in which a taxpayer has no such control and must report a gain or loss regardless of any action, or lack of action on his/her part:

- Capital gain distributions by mutual funds;

- Certain corporate acquisitions or mergers;

- Cash received in lieu of fractional shares; and

- Gains or losses reported by flow-through entities such as S corporations, partnerships, or limited liability companies

In situations where the taxpayer does control the recognition of the gain or loss, there are a host of income tax planning techniques that can be implemented to possibly defer the gain into future years or possibly even exclude all or part of the gain from taxation altogether.

PLANNING FOR GAIN DEFERRAL

As noted in the previous example, deferring gain from one year to the next is a powerful income tax and financial planning tool. The ability to defer the payment of tax is in essence an interest free loan from Congress. The "magic" of compounding allows for much more wealth to be built by deferring the ultimate payment of taxes. But along with gain deferral come the risks associated with being in the market after a particular security or other asset has appreciated in value. For instance, when Internet stocks were booming in the late 1990s, many investors failed to sell at or near the market peak simply because of the tax consequences they would face. Unfortunately, too many investors rode the wave of Internet stocks up to the crest only to see their paper fortunes vanish.

There are a number of ways planners can help clients achieve a deferral of tax on appreciation:

- Specifically identifying the security being sold

- Electing to use one of the average cost methods for selling mutual funds

- Selling short against the box

- Buying or selling put and call options

- Negotiating an installment sale

- Entering into a like-kind exchange

- Electing involuntary conversion treatment

- Investing in a specialized small business investment company (SSBIC)

- Reinvesting the proceeds from the sale of qualified small business stock into another qualified small business stock

Identifying shares involved in a transaction – In many cases, a taxpayer may have purchased multiple lots of the same stock at different times. Each lot carries with it a different cost basis and beginning date for the holding period. When less than a taxpayer's entire investment is sold, the identification of which securities were sold can hold a great deal of significance in determining the amount of the gain or loss.

If the lot from which the shares were sold cannot be adequately identified, the earliest shares are deemed to be sold first.[1] This is the so-called first-in, first-out method (FIFO). But if the shares sold are adequately identified, the FIFO rule does not apply.[2]

Sometimes using the FIFO method will generate the smallest tax bill for the taxpayer. But it is more likely that the FIFO method will create the largest possible gain. When the FIFO method does not generate the smallest gain (or the largest loss), the taxpayer may benefit from specifically identifying the shares that were sold.

A common misconception is that taxpayers are permitted to use an average cost when stock acquired at different times are sold. This is not true. The average cost method is only available to sellers of mutual funds (as discussed later in this chapter). Sellers of stock or other securities may only use the FIFO or specific identification methods.

Note that brokers and investment firms are required to report to report to the Internal Revenue Service, not only the proceeds derived from the sale of securities, but also the cost basis and indicate whether the sale is short or long-term. This reporting requirement began for certain types of securities in the 2011 tax year. See Chapter 19 (Basis) for further information.

For those investors who hold the stock certificate that they intend to sell, adequate identification is achieved by delivering the certificate that represents the shares being sold.[3]

If the shares being sold are held by a brokerage, bank or other investment company, the taxpayer must do two things in order to adequately identify the shares that are being sold:

1. At the time of the sale, the taxpayer specifies to the broker or other investment professional the specific security to be sold.

2. Within a reasonable time after the sale, the taxpayer receives written confirmation of the identification of the security that was sold.[4]

Example: Barbara Penney owns two lots of Weber Machines, Inc. stock. The first lot of one hundred shares was purchased twenty years ago for $500. The second lot of one hundred shares was purchased two years ago for $15,000. She wants to sell fifty shares and expects to receive $10,000. If she fails to specifically identify that she is selling fifty shares out of the second lot, she will recognize a gain of $9,750 (proceeds less half of the $500 basis). If she specifically identifies the shares from the second lot, her taxable gain will be only $2,500 (proceeds less half of the $15,000 basis).

In order to satisfy the first requirement, the taxpayer must give specific instructions as to which shares are being sold. This instruction is not required to be in writing. The shares being identified can be referred to by

- the date of purchase,

- the purchase price, or

- the lot itself (e.g. the shares purchased most recently).

This information will mean very little to the broker. He or she will simply sell the number of shares as requested. But this information is precisely what must be confirmed in writing to the taxpayer in order to satisfy the second requirement of adequate identification.

If lots of an identical security are held in separate accounts, the identification of the shares sold is achieved by selling the shares out of the desired account.

Example: The older of Barbara Penney's two lots is held at AAA Financial while the newer lot is held at I-Trade. If she sells the fifty shares out of her I-Trade account, that should constitute adequate identification of the shares that are being sold. No written confirmation would be required.

Special rules for sales of mutual funds – Like sales of stock and other securities, the basis and holding period is applied to mutual funds on a FIFO basis. Taxpayers may achieve a more tax favored result by specifically identifying the shares of the mutual fund to be sold. The rules for specific identification of mutual fund shares are the same as for stock and securities.

In addition to the FIFO and specific identification methods, mutual fund owners can avail themselves of two other methods for determining cost basis and holding period. Both methods must be elected by the taxpayer on a fund-by-fund basis. Once an election is made with respect to a particular mutual fund, it is irrevocable without the consent of the IRS. The two methods are

- single category average cost method; and

- double category average cost method.

Many mutual fund companies automatically calculate a mutual fund holder's gain or loss on the disposition of a portion of the mutual fund using the single category average cost method. This relieves the taxpayer of much of the burden of keeping track of all of the periodic investments as well as the dividend reinvestments that typically occur on a regular basis.

Taxpayers that elect to use the single category average cost method add the cost basis of all the shares held in the mutual fund and divide that total by the number of shares held. The average number is then used as the basis for the shares that were sold.[5]

For purposes of determining the taxpayer's holding period, mutual fund shares are deemed to be sold on a FIFO basis.[6] A quick way to determine if any of the shares that were sold during the year were short-term is to look at the number of shares that remain after the sale. If that number is greater than the number of shares acquired in the previous twelve months (the cut off for long-term holding period), then all of the shares sold should be considered as long-term. Otherwise, some of the shares sold may have a short-term holding period.

Example: Lisa Ramos bought shares in a mutual fund two years ago for $10,000. She has also added $500 per month for the last twenty-four months. Last year, she also received a $500 dividend from the mutual fund which was reinvested. During the last two years, the mutual fund has done quite well and substantially increased in value. If Lisa uses the FIFO method of allocating basis to the shares that were sold, she would be using her lowest cost shares and generating the highest possible long-term capital gain. If she specifically identifies the more recent purchases as the shares that were sold, her gain would be minimized, but it would be treated as a short-term capital gain. By electing to use the single-category average cost method, Lisa receives the benefit of the mutual fund shares that have been purchased at a higher price by the corresponding increase in the overall average cost. She also treats the entire gain as a long-term capital gain since the holding period is determined on a FIFO basis.

The double category average cost method is an extension of the single category method. Taxpayers who elect to use the double category average cost method will need to calculate two averages. The first average cost is determined for all of the shares that meet the one-year holding period requirement for long-term treatment. Once that average cost number is obtained, the cost basis of the remaining shares is aggregated to determine the average cost for the short-term mutual fund shares.[7]

The second step to the double category average cost method is to identify whether the short-term or long-term shares are being sold. Since two average costs are calculated, it is possible to reduce the gain or report a loss if the short-term shares are sold first. In order to treat the short-term shares as being sold, the

taxpayer must specifically identify (using the procedures described in the previous section) that the mutual fund shares being sold are the ones acquired within the last twelve months. Failure to specifically identify the shares being sold as from the short-term group will cause the shares to be treated as sold out of the long-term group first.[8]

Note that there are some flaws with the double category average cost method. First, it must be elected by the taxpayer with the filing of his or her tax return. This is generally long after the sale occurred. Second, in order to take advantage of selling out of the short-term group, the specific identification rules must be followed, which includes provisions for instructing the broker or mutual fund company *at the time of the sale*. Finally, if the election is made and the shares are not specifically identified as being sold out of the short-term group, the shares will be treated as sold out of the long-term group. The average cost of the long-term group will be less using the double category method than the average cost using the single category method in a rising market environment since the short-term shares will have a higher cost basis.

In order to elect an average cost method, a statement must be attached to the tax return for the first year in which the election is to apply. Once the election is made with respect to a particular mutual fund, it continues to apply until the mutual fund is completely disposed of.

Selling short against the box – A short sale is a transaction where an investor sells a stock that they do not

Figure 29.1

SINGLE-CATEGORY AVERAGING WORKSHEET	
1. Beginning Basis	_____
2. Cost of mutual fund share purchases	_____
3. Reinvested dividends and distributions	_____
4. Basis adjustments	_____
5. Total basis (sum of lines 1 through 5)	_____
6. Number of shares owned before sale	_____
7. Average basis per share (divide line 5 by line 6)	_____
8. Number of shares sold	_____
9. Basis of shares sold (multiply line 7 by line 8)	_____
10. Total basis before sale (from line 5)	_____
11. Basis of shares sold (from line 11)	_____
12. Ending basis	_____

Figure 29.2

DOUBLE-CATEGORY AVERAGING WORKSHEET	
1. Beginning Basis	_____
2. Cost of mutual fund share purchases	_____
3. Reinvested dividends and distributions	_____
4. Basis adjustments	_____
5. Total basis (sum of lines 1 through 5)	_____
6. Number of shares owned before sale	_____
7. Basis of short-term shares owned before sale	_____
8. Number of short-term shares owned before sale	_____
9. Basis per short-term share (divide line 7 by line 8)	_____
10. Basis of long-term shares owned before sale	_____
11. Number of long-term shares owned before sale	_____
12. Basis per long-term share (divide line 10 by line 11)	_____
13. Number of shares sold	_____
14. Basis of shares sold (multiply line 13 by 9 or 12)	_____
15. Total basis before sale (from line 5)	_____
16. Basis of shares sold (from line 14)	_____
17. Ending basis	_____

own. Essentially what occurs is this: The investor "borrows" the shares from another investor and promises to "repay" the shares at a later time.

A short sale is opened at the time the investor receives the cash for the sale. The short position remains open until the investor closes the position by purchasing or delivering shares of the same stock to cover the short position. An investor who purchases shares to cover the open short position will realize a gain if the price of the stock has decreased and a loss if the price has increased—the exact opposite of traditional investing (buying "long").

If the investor currently owns a stock and opens a short position in the same security, the investor is "selling short against the box." The offsetting positions will ensure that the value of the investor's positions will remain constant. But if the long position has been held for less than one year at the time the short position is opened, or if a long position is acquired while a short position is opened:

1. any gain on the short sale will be treated as a short-term gain and;

2. the holding period for the long position begins when the short position is closed or when the stock is sold.[9]

Example: Ethan Dillworth owns 1,000 shares of Rose Petals, Inc. He initially purchased the shares for $15,000 and they have since grown in value to $60,000 (a $45,000 increase). In order to protect his gain, he decides to sell 1,000 shares short against the box. He opens the short position and receives $60,000 for the short sale. While both the long and short positions are open, his total gain of $45,000 is protected. If the stock falls to $40 per share, he would still have a $45,000 gain—$25,000 on the long position and $20,000 on the short position.

In the above example, the investor was able to protect his overall profit without having to recognize the inherent gain at the time the protective transaction, the short sale, was opened. However, the Taxpayer Relief Act of 1997 created the constructive sale rule to force the recognition of gain on certain transactions that have the effect of neutralizing an investor's potential for further fluctuations in value.

The constructive sale rule applies to transactions involving "appreciated financial positions" that remain open beyond a statutorily determined time. An appreciated financial position is any position with respect to any stock, debt instrument, or partnership interest if there would be gain were such position sold, assigned or otherwise terminated at its fair market value.[10] Therefore, if a short against the box position is opened at a time when the fair market value is less than the investor's basis, the constructive sale rules will not apply.

If the transaction does involve an appreciated financial position, the second test is to determine whether the open position was closed soon enough to avoid the application of the constructive sale rule. A constructive sale will not occur if:

1. the transaction is closed before the end of the thirtieth day after the close of the taxable year;

2. the taxpayer continues to hold the appreciated financial position throughout a sixty-day period beginning on the date the transaction was closed; and

3. the taxpayer does not, at any time during the sixty-day period, reduce his or her risk of loss with respect to the appreciated financial position (such as enter into another short against the box transaction).[11]

Example: Michelle Grattia opened a short against the box transaction on March 15 in order to protect a gain she has in her stock. She closes the short position by purchasing identical shares on January 20 of the following year. As long as she does not limit her risk of loss by opening another protective transaction, no constructive sale exists.

If a constructive sale occurs as a result of not complying with the three above requirements, the taxpayer will recognize the gain as if the position were sold at its fair market value on the date the protective transaction was opened.[12] This is true even though the taxpayer will not know that a constructive sale occurred in the prior year until as late as the end of March of the following year.

A constructive sale results in a deemed sale and immediate repurchase of the appreciated financial position.[13] In addition, the holding period of the appreciated financial position restarts as of the date of the constructive sale.[14] But since the short position is still open, the holding period will only restart upon the closing of the short position that created the constructive sale.[15]

Example: Linda Wellington owns 2,000 shares of stock in Dual Sound, Inc. with a cost basis of $10,000. She has held the stock for over two years. The stock is worth $30,000 when she opens a 2,000-share short position on December 12. On February 10 of the following year, she closes the short position by purchasing 2,000 shares on the open market. Since she failed to close the open short position by January 30, she is deemed to have made a constructive sale as of December 12. She must recognize the $20,000 long-term gain on her tax return. Her basis in the stock becomes $30,000 and the holding period will restart on February 10 when the short position is closed.

Buying or selling put and call options – Options give investors the right to purchase or sell a certain number of shares of a particular stock at a stated price within a defined time period. A call option permits the option holder to buy the stock. A put option gives the option holder the right to sell the stock. Options trade on the open market and should not be confused with stock options that are granted by an employer to an employee. These types of stock options are covered in Chapter 26, Equity Based Compensation Planning.

Of course for every option holder, there must be an option writer. The option writer is the one who will deliver the stock to the call holder if the call option is exercised or, in the case of a put option, will have the stock delivered to them if the put option is exercised by the put holder.

Each option controls 100 shares of the underlying stock. An investor who purchases an option will pay a certain price or "premium" to acquire the right to buy or sell stock at a specified or "strike" price within a given time period.

Example: Alan Weiss purchases five call options on TripMaker, Inc. for $1,000 with a strike price of $50. The option expires one month later on August 21. If the company's stock price increases beyond $50 per share, the option is said to be "in the money" and may be exercised by Alan by paying $25,000 (five option contracts at $50 each multiplied by one hundred shares per contract). His total cost to acquire the shares would then be $26,000 ($25,000 stock cost plus $1,000 option cost).

If the option is not exercised by the end of the option contract period, the option is said to expire. The holder is treated as having sold the option as of the expiration date for no proceeds. The loss will be reported as short or long-term depending on the length of time the option was held.

The option may also be sold by the option holder to another party. Any gain or loss must be recognized on the transaction in accordance with the normal capital gain and loss rules.

Writers of put and call options receive the premiums that are paid by the option purchasers (after the various fees and commissions, of course). But no gain or loss is recognized by the option writer until the option is exercised, expires, or is otherwise closed.

Options have the effect of hedging against further gains or losses in a particular stock. For this reason, it is possible to combine puts and call options to "collar" an open stock position and protect the inherent gain without having to sell the stock. Again, the constructive sale rules may apply.

It is clear that an investor who acquires only one-way protection is not treated as having made a constructive sale. For instance, an investor holding an appreciated financial position may purchase a put option to protect against a decline in the stock price. But the investor still may benefit from a further rise in the stock price and, in that case, would simply let the put option expire unexercised or sell the put option before the expiration date. Since only the downside is

Figure 29.3

TAX TREATMENT OF PUT AND CALL OPTIONS

Transaction	Option Holder	Option Writer
Call option is exercised	Basis of call option is added to the cost of the stock. Holding period for the stock begins on the date the option was exercised.	No gain or loss reported on option. Sales proceeds from sale of the stock combined with the proceeds on the sale of the option. Gain or loss from the sale of stock recognized on the date of the exercise.
Call option expires	Option treated as sold for $0 on the expiration date. Short or long-term loss recognized based on holding period of the option.	Short-term gain equal to the proceeds received from the writing of the option recognized on the expiration date. Gain cannot be long-term.
Call option position closed	Proceeds received less the premium paid are treated as a capital gain or loss. Holding period determines whether the gain or loss is long or short-term.	Short-term capital gain or loss recognized based on the difference between the initial amount received and the amount paid to close the transaction. Holding period of option cannot create a long-term gain or loss.
Put option exercised	No gain or loss reported on option. Amount received from the sale of the stock is reduced by the cost of the put option. Holding period of the stock determines long or short-term gain or loss.	No gain or loss reported on option. Basis of stock acquired reduced by the amount received for the put option.
Put option expires	Option treated as sold for $0 on the expiration date. Short or long-term loss recognized based on holding period of the option.	Short-term gain equal to the proceeds received from the writing of the option recognized on the expiration date. Gain cannot be long-term.
Put option position closed	Proceeds received less the premium paid are treated as a capital gain or loss. Holding period determines whether the gain or loss is long or short-term.	Short-term capital gain or loss recognized based on the difference between the initial amount received and the amount paid to close the transaction. Holding period of option cannot create a long-term gain or loss.

protected, a constructive sale is not deemed to have occurred.

Although regulations have not been issued on the use of stock options in the area of constructive sales, it is widely believed that buying a put option or writing a call option that is "deep in the money" may be equivalent to selling the stock short. For instance, if a put option is purchased with a strike price of $100 when the stock is trading at $60, the transaction may be treated like a short sale against the box, thereby forcing the application of the constructive sale rule.

If an investor combines put and call options and effectively limits the range of potential gain or loss, the "collar" will likely cause a constructive sale.

Example: Barry Hastings owns 1,000 shares of Kids World, Inc. with a value of $470,000 ($47 per share). Barry purchases ten put options with a strike price of $45 and writes ten call options with a strike price of $50. A collar this tight would be equivalent to a short sale and would likely be treated as a constructive sale.

The United States Treasury is expected to issue regulations dealing with just such a transaction. Commentators believe that a collar that has a spread of at least 20 percent around the current price should not cause a constructive sale. The length of time the collar may exist is also expected to be addressed by future regulations.

Example: If the Treasury does adopt a 20 percent spread rule, Barry (from the previous example) would be able to place a collar on his stock by using a spread of approximately $10. He could accomplish this by adjusting the strike price of the call option up to $55 or the put option down to $40.

Negotiating an installment sale – If the terms of the sale of real or personal property call for at least one payment to be made in a tax year later than the year of disposition, the installment sale rules may allow for a deferral of the taxation of the gain until the payment or payments are received.[16]

The taxation of an installment sale is determined by computing a gross profit percentage and applying this percentage to the payments that are received. The gross profit percentage will equal the total of all of the principal payments to be made by the buyer over the term of the installment sale, plus any liabilities assumed by the buyer, less the seller's adjusted basis in the property that was sold.

Each payment received under an installment sale agreement will typically consist of three parts: (1) non-taxable recovery of basis; (2) capital gain; and (3) interest. Interest is involved in any installment sale whether it is stated in the sales agreement or not. Agreements that fail to provide for interest (or do not provide for a rate of interest which is at least as high as the applicable federal rate) on the deferred payments will have imputed interest. Interest income is reportable by the seller of the property and thereby reduces the amount that is taxed at the more favorable capital gains rates. Likewise, the purchaser reports interest expense and should properly account for the true purchase price of the property.

When property is sold subject to an installment sale, and the parties to the contract later agree to change the stated purchase price, only the gross profit on remaining payments is recomputed.[17]

Example: 122 Downtown Associates contracts to sell a building on December 12, 2013. Under the terms of the agreement, half of the purchase price is to be paid at the closing and the remaining half in June 2014. 122 Downtown Associates will realize a $100,000 gain upon the disposition. Without considering the application of other rules dealing with depreciation recapture or imputed interest, the taxpayer would recognize $50,000 of gain in 2013 and $50,000 of gain in 2014.

The application of the installment sale rules is automatic. Taxpayers who wish to recognize the entire gain in the year of disposition may elect out of the installment sale method of reporting by making such election on a timely filed return (including extensions) in the year of disposition.[18]

Installment sale reporting is not permitted for dispositions of:

1. real or personal property by dealers;[19]

2. personal property considered inventory;[20]

3. personal property under a revolving credit plan;[21] or

4. stock or securities traded on an established securities market.[22]

The installment sale method may not be used if the transaction generates a loss. Also, any portion of a sale which generates ordinary income due to the recapture of depreciation may not be deferred.[23] Installment sales are also covered in Chapter 3, Income.

Entering into a like-kind exchange – When a taxpayer transfers property to another party and, in exchange, receives property that is similar to what was given up, the taxpayer is essentially in the same position that he or she was in prior to the exchange. It is viewed as a continuation of the same investment. For that reason, the tax law requires that no gain or loss be recognized on property exchanged for other property that is of "like-kind."

Like the rule for installment sales, the rule requiring non-recognition on like-kind exchanges is mandatory, not elective. Therefore, taxpayers with losses built in to the property that will be exchanged would be wise to use the rules in reverse—that is, to ensure that the provisions of this tax law are *not* met. Like-kind exchanges are fully covered in Chapter 28, Like-Kind Exchanges.

Electing involuntary conversion treatment – When a taxpayer's property is destroyed, stolen, seized, condemned, or is under a threat of condemnation, an election is available under Code section 1033 that allows for gain deferral. In order to fully defer the gain, a taxpayer must purchase replacement property (or restore the original property) within a given time period. The replacement property must be similar or related in service or use to the original property that was subject to the involuntary conversion. In addition, the full amount realized must be reinvested in the replacement property. This amount usually is based on the insurance or condemnation proceeds received.

Gain must be recognized to the extent that the taxpayer receives unlike property or retains any portion of the amount realized, unless the replacement property was financed with new debt at the time of purchase.

The period of time permitted to restore or replace the original property begins on the date the property is disposed or the date of the threat or imminence of requisition or condemnation of the property, whichever is earlier.[24] The replacement period ends two years from the end of the tax year in which a gain is realized.[25] Longer replacement periods are in place for condemned real estate (three years), livestock (four years), a principal residence (four years), and property destroyed in the New York Liberty Zone (five years). An application for extension of time to replace property may be filed with the IRS based on reasonable cause.[26]

The taxpayer's basis in the new property will be the identical to the basis in the old property if all of the gain is deferred under these rules. Note that the involuntary conversion rules only apply to the deferral of gains. Losses are immediately recognized.

A taxpayer may replace involuntarily converted property with corporate stock that owns qualifying property.[27] Though rarely used, it is important to note that both the taxpayer's basis in the corporate stock and the corporation's basis in the assets must be reduced by the amount of gain deferred (cost of stock or fixed asset less gain deferral). This ensures the continued potential for double taxation which exists in a corporate environment.

Involuntary conversions stemming from presidentially declared disaster areas are granted additional relief under these rules. Replacement property may be any tangible property held for productive use in a trade or business.[28] It need not be similar in use or of a like-kind.

Investing in a Specialized Small Business Investment Company – As a general rule, when an investor sells stock of a publicly traded company, gain must be recognized in the year of the sale. In 1993, an exception was created if taxpayer elects to rollover the sales proceeds into the purchase of common stock or a partnership interest in a specialized small business investment company (SSBIC) within a sixty-day period beginning on the date of the sale of the publicly traded securities. If the taxpayer fails to reinvest the entire amount of sales proceeds, gain is required to be recognized on any un-reinvested portion.[29]

A SSBIC is any partnership or corporation which is licensed by the Small Business Administration under Section 301(d) of the Small Business Investment Company Act of 1958.[30] SSBICs are few in number, often require large investments, and are typically very risky investments. A list of SSBICs can be found at www.sba.gov/inv/. But the lists include small business investment companies (SBIC) as well as *specialized* small business investment companies. Only those companies that are treated as SSBICs qualify for the rollover.

Only individuals and C corporations may defer gain by investing in a SSBIC. The rollover provisions are not available to estates, trusts, partnerships, LLCs, or S corporations.[31]

Individuals may defer up to $50,000 of gain per year not to exceed a lifetime maximum of $500,000.[32] For C corporations, the annual limit is $250,000 of gain, not to exceed $1,000,000 in all preceding years.[33]

The cost basis of an investment in a SSBIC must be reduced by any gain not recognized as a result of the election to rollover the gain.[34] But since 50 percent of the gain on the sale of an SSBIC investment may be excluded under Code section 1202, the basis is not reduced for the purpose of determining the gain eligible for exclusion.[35] That is, only the increase in value associated with the SSBIC is eligible for the exclusion, not the gain deferred under this election.

The election to defer recognition of the gain on the sale of publicly traded security must be made on Form 1040, Schedule D on or before the due date of the tax return for the year of the sale. The taxpayer must also attach a statement showing:

1. how the non-recognition was calculated;

2. the SSBIC in which the sales proceeds were invested;

3. the date the SSBIC stock or partnership interest was purchased; and

4. the basis of the SSBIC interest.[36]

Reinvesting the Proceeds from the Sale of Qualified Small Business Stock into another qualified small business Stock – All non-corporate taxpayers may elect to roll over a gain from the sale of "qualified small business stock" (QSBS) if:

1. the QSBS was held for more than six months; and;

2. another QSBS is acquired during a sixty-day period following the date of sale.[37]

Like the rule for SSBIC rollovers, gain is only recognized to the extent that the amount realized on the initial sale exceeds the cost of the replacement QSBS.[38]

Qualified small business stock is stock originally issued after August 10, 1993 by a C corporation with aggregate gross assets of less than $50 million at any time from August 10, 1993 through the issuance of the stock.[39]

The business must also meet an active business requirement.[40] This requirement states that 80 percent or more of the business assets are used in one or more businesses other than certain excluded businesses.[41] Excluded businesses include certain personal service activities, banking and other financial services, farming, mineral extraction businesses, and hotels and restaurants.[42]

If a rollover occurs and the taxpayer elects the gain deferral treatment, the basis in the newly acquired QSBS is reduced by the amount of deferred gain.[43] The holding period for the newly acquired QSBS will include the holding period of the stock sold. But the newly acquired QSBS must be held for six months before another gain deferral may be elected.

Note that the definition of QSBS for purposes of the rollover of gain is identical to the definition of QSBS for purposes of the 50 percent gain exclusion, discussed below.

Example: Michael Rice invests $250,000 into Falcon Manufacturing Corp. on January 10, 2008. He sells the stock for $400,000 on July 26, 2008 realizing a $150,000 gain. On September 7, 2008 he purchases stock in Hale Manufacturing Corp. for $350,000. Both investments in Falcon and Hale qualify as QSBS. Michael must recognize $50,000 of the $150,000 gain since only $350,000 of the total sales proceeds was reinvested. He may elect to defer the remaining $100,000. If he does so, his basis in Hale would be $250,000. His holding period for determining long-term gain or loss on Hale will begin on January 10, 2008. But for the purpose of a further rollover under Code section 1045 or an exclusion of gain under Code section 1202, his holding period beings on September 7, 2008.

PLANNING FOR GAIN EXCLUSION

What is even better than deferring a gain into a future year? The answer is simple—excluding the gain from income forever. Obviously there are many fewer options that allow a taxpayer to perpetually exclude a gain from tax, but the following do exist and will be discussed in detail later in this chapter:

- Selling a personal residence

- Selling qualified small business stock held for more than five years (50 percent exclusion)

- Contributing appreciated property to charity

Selling a personal residence – The sale of a personal residence will often represent the single largest transaction a taxpayer will ever have. Since housing values have traditionally increased over time, the transaction is likely to result in a capital gain. Much of that gain may escape federal income taxation due to the special rules under Code section 121. The current rules are:

- A taxpayer may exclude up to $250,000 of realized gain from the sale of a principal residence.[44]

- Married taxpayers filing a joint return may exclude up to $500,000 of realized gain.[45]

- The realized gain is determined by subtracting the taxpayer's adjusted basis (defined below) from the net selling price of the property.

- If the transaction results in a net loss, the loss is not deductible.[46]

A principal residence is determined by all facts and circumstances available.[47] A residence may be a house, condominium, houseboat, trailer, cooperative apartment, etc.

If a taxpayer owns more than one residence, the determination of which residence is the principal residence is also made based on facts and circumstances.[48] The property used the majority of the time will generally be considered the principal residence. But other factors that are considered include:

- the taxpayer's place of employment;

- the principal place of abode of the taxpayer's family members;

- the address listed on the taxpayer's federal and state tax returns, driver's license, automobile registration, and voter's registration card;

- the taxpayer's mailing address for bills and correspondence;

- the location of the taxpayer's banks; and

- the location of religious organizations and recreational clubs with which the taxpayer is affiliated.[49]

In order to qualify for the gain exclusion, a taxpayer must meet the following three tests:

- *Ownership test* – the taxpayer must have owned the residence for at least two of the five years before the sale or exchange.[50]

- *Use test* – the taxpayer must have occupied the residence as a principal residence for periods adding up to two years within the five-year period ending on the date of the sale.[51]

- *One sale in two years test* – the taxpayer must not have used the exclusion for any residence sold or exchanged during the two-year period ending on the date of the current sale.[52]

For purposes of the use test, a short, temporary absence is generally counted as a period of use.[53] But a one-year sabbatical leave is not considered a short, temporary absence.[54]

The calculation of a taxpayer's adjusted basis in a principal residence requires an analysis of the previous settlement sheet from the purchase of the principal residence that has now been sold. Certain items such as real estate taxes and points represent items of deduction in the year of purchase and should not be included in basis.

Any improvements that were made to the property during the period of ownership should also be added to the taxpayer's adjusted basis. But failure to maintain appropriate records could result in a larger gain being reported than necessary.

Example: Stacy Whitten, a single taxpayer, purchased her first home in 1996 for $200,000. A review of her settlement sheet from the purchase of that home shows closing costs of $4,000 that could be capitalized into the basis of her home. In 2000, she finished her basement at a cost of $10,000. Her total adjusted basis in her home is $214,000 when she sells her home in 2008. She receives $420,000 for her home and pays $16,000 of closing costs, including the sales commission. Her realized gain is $190,000. Since she qualifies for gain exclusion of up to $250,000, the entire gain is not taxed for federal income tax purposes.

Prior to May 7, 1997, gains were not excluded from income. Rather, there was a gain deferral subject to certain limitations. The gain deferral only applied if the proceeds were reinvested into a new residence. Note that there is no longer a requirement for the proceeds from the sale of a principal residence to be reinvested. This creates a potential windfall for taxpayers who decide to "trade down" into a smaller home.

Married taxpayers may exclude up to $500,000 of gain if:

1. either spouse owned the home for periods aggregating two years or more during the five-year period ending on the date of the sale;

2. both spouses used the home as a principal residence for periods totaling two years or more during the five–year period ending on the date of sale (including use before a marriage); and

3. neither spouse is ineligible for the exclusion because he or she had sold another home within the two-year period ending on the date of the sale to which the exclusion applied.[55]

If only one of the spouses, but not both, meet the second or third test, that spouse may still exclude up to $250,000 of gain on the joint return.

Taxpayers who fail to meet the ownership and use tests or the one sale in two years test may be eligible for a partial gain exclusion if the primary reason for selling the principal residence is due to:

1. a change of place of employment;

2. health; or

3. unforeseen circumstances.[56]

The partial exclusion is determined multiplying the maximum exclusion amount by a fraction. The denominator of which is 730 days or twenty-four months. The numerator of the fraction is the shorter of:

1. the lesser of the aggregate amount of time during the five-year period ending on the date of the sale that the taxpayer either (a) owned the

residence or (b) used it as the principal residence; or

2. the amount of time elapsed since the taxpayer last used the maximum exclusion amount[57]

Example: Wayne and Wendy Right sold their home on October 1, 2007 and excluded $350,000 of gain. They bought a new house for $400,000 on the same date. As a result of a job transfer, Wayne and Wendy moved out of the house on February 1, 2008. They sold the house on June 1, 2008 for $450,000, realizing a $50,000 gain. Wayne and Wendy are entitled to a partial gain exclusion since the move was caused by a change in employment. They moved out of the house after 123 days. Based on the number of days between the sale of the former home and the sale of the home in question, the amount of time elapsed since the exclusion was last used is 243 days. The shorter of these two periods becomes the numerator of the fraction (123). Therefore, partial gain exclusion is $84,247 ($500,000 x 123 ÷ 730). Since the partial gain exclusion is greater than the gain realized, the entire gain is excluded from the Rights' income.

In order to qualify for the partial gain exclusion using the change of place of employment for a qualified individual, the change in place of employment must occur while the taxpayer owns and is using the property as a principal residence and the new place of employment is at least fifty miles farther from the residence sold than the former place of employment.[58] A qualified individual is the taxpayer, taxpayer's spouse, a co-owner of the property or other person whose principal place of abode is the same household as the taxpayer.[59]

If the move occurs for health reasons, the primary reason for the sale must be to obtain, provide, or facilitate the diagnosis, cure, mitigation, or treatment of a disease, illness or injury to a qualified individual.[60] A qualified individual includes those listed above as well as any of those individual's dependents and descendants of the taxpayer's grandparents.[61] A change in residence that is recommended by a physician qualifies as a health reason.[62]

An unforeseen circumstance is an event that the taxpayer does not anticipate before purchasing and occupying the residence.[63] The following events are deemed to be unforeseen circumstances under the temporary regulations:

1. the involuntary conversion of the property (e.g. destroyed by fire);

2. natural or man-made disasters or acts of war or terrorism resulting in a casualty to the residence;

3. a qualifying individual's (as defined under the change of employment test)

   a. death,

   b. cessation of employment resulting in unemployment compensation,

   c. change in employment status that results in the taxpayer's in ability to pay housing costs and reasonable basic living expenses for the taxpayer's household,

   d. divorce or legal separation, or

   e. multiple births from the same pregnancy; or

4. an event determined by the IRS to qualify as an unforeseen circumstance published in guidance of general applicability or in a ruling to a specific taxpayer.[64]

Example: Lucy Swanson purchased her home and lived there three months before selling the property. Her major reason for selling the home was due to a neighbor who was extremely noisy and rude. Despite every attempt to improve the situation, she could not continue living in the house. The noisy neighbor is not an unforeseen circumstance that would qualify for a partial gain exclusion.

Beginning in 2009, gain from the sale of a principal residence may not be excluded for any period of time (hereinafter called "nonqualified use") where the taxpayer, the taxpayer's spouse, or the taxpayer's former spouse did not use the property as their principal residence. Gain is allocated between periods of qualified and nonqualified use based on the amount of time the property is used for each purpose. The amount of gain must be allocated to periods of nonqualified use based on the ratio of aggregate periods of nonqualified use

over the total period of time the property was owned by the taxpayer.

This law change closes a well-known and regularly used loophole. Before the Housing Assistance Tax Act of 2008, taxpayers who owned a property as a vacation home could move into that property, use it as their primary residence for two years, and exclude up to $250,000 (or $500,000) of gain.

The new law does not apply to non-qualifying use prior to 2009. There are several exceptions to the definition of nonqualified use including leaving the home vacant and temporary absences due to change in employment, health, or unforeseen circumstances. In addition, the law allows a taxpayer a five-year period to sell the principal residence after having moved out of it, without having to count this time as nonqualified use.

Example 1: Matt Beregson bought a vacation home on January 1, 2005 and moved into it as his principal residence on January 1, 2011. On January 1, 2013, Matt sells the property. He meets the two-out-of-five-year requirement, but two years (2009 and 2010) are periods of nonqualified use. Therefore two-eighths (1/4) of the gain is not eligible for the exclusion.

Example 2: Jack Robinson buys a property on January 1, 2009 for $400,000 and uses it as a rental property for two years, claiming $20,000 of depreciation deductions. On January 1, 2011, Jack converts the property into his principal residence. Jack moves out of the property on January 13, 2013 and sells the property on January 1, 2014 for $700,000 for a gain of $320,000 ($700,000 less adjusted basis of $380,000). The $20,000 of gain attributable to the depreciation deductions is included in Jack's income regardless of the application of this rule. Of the remaining $300,000 gain, 40 percent (two of the five years the property is owned), or $120,000, is allocated to nonqualified use and is not eligible for the exclusion. Since the remaining gain of $180,000 is less than the maximum gain exclusion of $250,000 (assuming Jack is single), the remaining gain of $180,000 is excluded from income.

Selling qualified small business stock held for more than five years (50 percent exclusion) – As mentioned above, the sale of QSBS may be deferred if the proceeds are rolled over into another investment in QSBS. If QSBS is held for more than five years, a noncorporate taxpayer may exclude 50 percent of the gain from the sale of the stock.[65] The remaining half of the gain is taxed at a rate of 28 percent.[66] This generates an effective rate of 14 percent.

For alternative minimum tax purposes, 7 percent of the excluded gain must be added back to income in computing alternative minimum taxable income.[67] Special provisions have been added over the years that incorporate the following, higher, exclusion amounts:

- 75 percent gain exclusion for QSBS acquired after February 17, 2009 and on or before September 27, 2010.[68]

- 100 percent gain exclusion for QSBS acquired after September 27, 2010 and on or before January 1, 2014.[69]

The amount of gain eligible for the exclusion is limited on a per issuer basis. The excluded gain cannot exceed the greater of:

1. $10 million reduced by the taxpayer's aggregate prior year gains from stock of the same issuer; or

2. Ten times the taxpayer's basis in his QSBS from such corporation disposed of during the year.[70]

Contributing appreciated property to charity – Taxpayers often contribute various types of property to charity. Certain contributions of appreciated property may allow taxpayers to receive a double benefit—exclusion of capital gain coupled with a deduction for the fair market value of the property contributed. Note that this topic is covered more fully in Chapter 27, Charitable Contribution Planning and in the book, *Tools & Techniques of Charitable Planning* (National Underwriter Co.).

The most well documented technique involves the contribution of appreciated stock or securities to a public charity, donor advised fund, or private charity. If the stock or securities (or any other type of intangible personal property and real property) have been held for more than one year, the fair market value of the stock or securities on the date of the charitable contribution is allowed as a deduction. Since technically, the property has not been sold, no capital gain is recognized even though the donor receives a tax deduction.

Example: Donald McTish donates 100 shares of Abacab, Inc. when it is valued at $5,000. His basis in the stock is $3,000. Donald will report a charitable deduction (subject to adjusted gross income limitations) of $5,000. The $2,000 of appreciation is excluded from his income since the stock was not sold.

Had Donald sold the stock first and contributed the proceeds, the $2,000 would be taxed as a capital gain. Using a 15 percent capital gains tax rate, he would pay $300 of tax. If he contributed the full $5,000 of proceeds, his tax bill would still be $300 higher than it would have been had he contributed the stock directly to the charity.

If the property is used in a trade or business (Section 1231 property), the value of the donation must be reduced by the amount of ordinary income that would have been recaptured if the property were sold for its fair market value.[71]

Tangible personal property that has been held for more than one year may also receive a fair market value deduction. Again, the fair market value is reduced by any amount that would have been recaptured as ordinary income if the property were sold at its fair market value. But in order to receive the deduction for the fair market value, the donee's use of the property must be determined. If the property is used by the donee for anything other than its exempt purpose, the taxpayer's deduction is limited to the adjusted basis.

Example: A painting donated to a museum for public display is related to the museum's exempt purpose. If the painting were contributed to a school that sold the painting and used the proceeds for educational purposes, the donation would not be considered as used for the school's exempt purpose and would, thereby, limit the taxpayer's deduction.

Donations of capital gain property to public charities and donor advised funds ("50 percent charities") are limited to 30 percent of a taxpayer's adjusted gross income.[72] Donations of capital gain property to private foundations ("non-50 percent charities") are limited to 20 percent of a taxpayer's adjusted gross income.[73]

At the election of the taxpayer, a donation of capital gain property to a 50 percent charity may be limited to the taxpayer's adjusted basis. If the election is made, the donation may use the 50 percent of adjusted gross income limitation in place of the special 30 percent limitation.[74]

A taxpayer's deduction for donations of ordinary income and short-term capital gain property is limited to the taxpayer's basis in the property.[75]

Property that has decreased in value is still limited to its fair market value at the time of contribution.[76] Any loss is not deductible. Therefore, a taxpayer would generally be in better situation if the property were sold at a loss with a subsequent donation of the proceeds.

PLANNING FOR LOSS RECOGNITION

Almost as important as the planning that taxpayers should do for deferring or excluding the recognition of a gain is protecting the deductibility of a loss. As discussed in Chapter 4, if a taxpayer's losses exceed their gains in a given year, only $3,000 of the excess may be claimed currently against other sources of income. The balance of the net capital loss is carried over to future tax years to offset capital gains in those years. Therefore, large capital losses may take many years to recoup.

Example: Morris Branson was involved in an automobile accident in 1997. He received a lump sum disability payment of $100,000 in 1998. Against the advice of his team of financial planners, he invested the entire amount into a single Internet company stock. By the end of 1999, the investment was worth $500,000. Partly because he believed the stock would continue to rise and partly because he didn't want to pay approximately $80,000 in taxes, he held onto the stock into 2000. The value of Morris' stock dropped to $10,000 by the end of 2000. Morris

sold the stock at that time. Morris has no other assets and does not anticipate recognizing any future capital gains. Under the current tax laws, Morris' $90,000 capital loss will take thirty years to recover by claiming $3,000 of the capital loss each year.

Although not much can be done given Morris' facts, there are planning opportunities—and one big trap—when losses are realized on an investment.

- Claiming a loss on worthless securities

- Deducting a loss from the sale of small business stock

- Planning around the wash sale rules (the trap)

Claiming a loss on worthless securities – If a stock owned by an investor becomes worthless, a capital loss may be claimed as if the stock were sold on the last day of the year in which the stock became worthless.[77]

In order to support a claim that the investment has become worthless, it is necessary to show that there is no current value to the stock and no potential future value. This is often very difficult since, even though a company may halt the trading of its stock, declare bankruptcy, etc., the company may still have some value. This problem is further compounded by the requirement that the loss be claimed in the year the stock became worthless. It is often difficult to ascertain if a company has any value prior to the due date of a taxpayer's return. For this reason, taxpayers are given a seven-year period (four years longer than normal) to file an amended return in order to claim a loss on a worthless security.[78]

The best approach to deal with a security that is believed to be worthless is to enter into a transaction to sell the security. Some brokerage houses would be happy to purchase the stock for a nominal price simply to assist in the documentation of the sale. Note that a sale to a family member or other "related party" will not allow for the loss to be deductible by the taxpayer.

Example: Quincy Harris owns stock in Cool Technologies Corp. In November 2013, the company's stock is delisted. In January 2014, the company files for bankruptcy and subsequently ceases operations in April 2014. In June 2014,

Cool Tech sends a letter to shareholders stating that the business has sold all of its assets and paid as much of their outstanding liabilities as they could in compliance with the bankruptcy court. No further payments to the shareholders will be made. Quincy can deduct the loss on the stock as of December 31, 2014, the last day of the year in which the company became completely worthless.

***

Deducting a loss from the sale of small business stock – Taxpayers with losses in certain small business stock may benefit from the rules under Code section 1244. Losses on "1244 stock" may be deducted against the ordinary income up to an annual dollar limitation.[79] The loss may be triggered by a sale or exchange of the Section 1244 stock or by the worthlessness of the stock.

Section 1244 stock must meet the following requirements:

1. It must be common or preferred stock of a domestic corporation.

2. At the time of issuance the company must be a "small business corporation."

3. The stock must be issued in exchange for money or other property, but not stock or securities.

4. For the five years prior to the year of the loss (or since inception if in existence for less than five years), more than 50 percent of the corporation's aggregate gross receipts must have been derived from sources other than royalties, rents, dividends, interests, annuities, and sales or exchanges of stocks or securities.[80] This requirement does not apply if the corporation's allowable deductions exceed the gross income for the five-year period.[81]

A small business corporation is defined as one that has received less than $1 million of cash or other property in exchange for its stock.[82] Once the corporation has received $1 million, the corporation may identify which shares qualify as Section 1244 shares.

The ordinary loss for Section 1244 stock may only be claimed by an individual to whom the stock was originally issued. Shareholders that acquire otherwise qualifying Section 1244 stock through gift, inheritance or purchase are not eligible for Section 1244 treatment.[83]

The maximum amount a taxpayer may claim as a loss from the disposition or worthlessness of Section 1244 stock is limited to $50,000 per year for a single taxpayer or $100,000 for a married couple filing a joint return.[84] Section 1244 losses in excess of these annual limits are treated as capital losses.

***

Example: Bill Coleman started as business with his close friend Jack Haggarty. Each put $125,000 into the corporation. The business operated for a few years and then wound up operations. Both shareholders walked away with nothing. Assuming the stock qualifies as Section 1244 stock, Bill, who is married, may deduct $100,000 of the $125,000 loss as an ordinary loss. The remaining $25,000 is treated as a capital loss. Jack, who is single, is limited to a $50,000 ordinary loss and will treat the $75,000 balance as a capital loss.

***

An often overlooked situation involving Section 1244 stock involves stock of closely held S corporations. If a loss is sustained by an initial shareholder upon the disposition of the stock, the loss may qualify as an ordinary loss if the stock meets all of the Section 1244 requirements.

Planning around the wash sale rules – One area that can trap many taxpayers is the often misunderstood or forgotten wash sale rules. If a taxpayer sells stock or securities at a loss and, within a period beginning thirty days before the sale and ending thirty days after the sale, the taxpayer acquires or enters into a contract to acquire substantially identical stock or securities, the loss will not be allowed.[85] The "wash sale period" is therefore a sixty-one-day period covering thirty days before and after the sale. Note that the wash sale period covers sixty-one calendar days, not trading days.

In order for the wash sale rules to apply, there must be an investment in substantially identical securities. It has been widely accepted that stock of different companies are not substantially identical, even if they are in the same industry. So, a taxpayer could sell AT&T at a loss and purchase Verizon within the wash sale period. In fact, this is a technique that many financial planners tout to their clients. If the client does not want to be out of a particular investment because of a belief that a particular sector will increase in value, the wash sale rule may be avoided by simply investing in a similar company in the same industry.

Investors in mutual funds often run into wash sale issues where less than the entire mutual fund is sold. Dividend reinvestments are treated as purchases that may reduce the deductibility of a loss if they occur within the wash sale period. Like the theory for stocks, if a mutual fund investor wants to recognize a tax loss but still wants to be invested in the same asset class served by the mutual fund being sold, an investment in a similar mutual fund that has similar goals should not be deemed to be substantially identical. An exception may exist for index funds. Although there is no guidance one way or the other, it seems reasonable that an S&P 500 index fund from one mutual fund company is substantially identical to an S&P 500 index fund from another mutual fund company.

If the amount of stock or securities acquired within the wash sale period is less than the amount sold, then the loss is disallowed only with respect to the amount of the stock or securities acquired.[86]

Losses subject to the wash sale rules are added to the basis of the investment acquired during the wash sale period.[87] The holding period for the replacement investment includes the holding period of the original investment.

Example: Brian Mitchellson sold 500 shares of DotCom, Inc. at a loss of $10,000 on July 15. On August 10, Brian purchased another 500 shares of DotCom, Inc. for $40,000. Since Brian purchased substantially identical securities within 30 days after the sale, the loss is not deductible. Brian's basis for the new shares must be adjusted by the disallowed loss. His basis in the 500 shares purchased on August 10 becomes $50,000 and his holding period will include the holding period of the first sale.

Now that brokers are required to report basis on the sale of securities, they are also charged with identifying wash sales from transactions within the same account. While this does help taxpayers and the IRS report wash sales properly, these transactions have become much more difficult to find where the purchases or sales occur within different brokerage accounts.

FREQUENTLY ASKED QUESTIONS

Question – What is a taxpayer has a sale of a stock at a loss, followed by a repurchase of the same stock within the taxpayer's IRA, 401(k) or other retirement plan?

Answer – After many years of uncertainty, the IRS released Revenue Ruling 2008-5, which simply states that the wash sale rule applies to a taxpayer who sold stock for a loss and caused his IRA or Roth IRA to purchase substantially identical stock within thirty days after the sale. In order to avoid the wash sale rules, consider the following planning techniques:

1. Sell the stock at a loss followed by a repurchase thirty-one or more days after the sale.

2. Purchase replacement stock at least thirty-one days prior to the sale of the stock at a loss. This doubles the taxpayer's exposure to the stock for those thirty-one days and could require an outlay of cash that is not available to the taxpayer.

3. Purchase another stock that is likely to move similarly to the stock being sold at a loss. Obviously there is no guarantee that the replacement stock will move exactly like the loss stock. But after thirty-one days, the replacement stock can be sold and the original stock may be repurchased.

CHAPTER ENDNOTES

1.   Treas. Reg. §1.1012-1(c)(1).
2.   *Ibid.*
3.   Treas. Reg. §1.1012-1(c)(2).
4.   Treas. Reg. §1.1012-1(c)(3).
5.   Treas. Reg. §1.1012-1(e)(4)(i).
6.   Treas. Reg. §1.1012-1(e)(4)(ii).
7.   Treas. Reg. §1.1012-1(e)(3)(i).
8.   Treas. Reg. §1.1012-1(e)(3)(ii).
9.   I.R.C. §1233(b).
10. I.R.C. §1259(b)(1).
11. I.R.C. §1259(c)(3)(A)
12. I.R.C. §1259(a)(1).

13. I.R.C. §1259(a)(2)(A)
14. I.R.C. §1259(a)(2)(B).
15. II.R.C. §1233(b).
16. I.R.C. §453(b)(1).
17. Rev. Rul. 72-570.
18. I.R.C. §453(d).
19. I.R.C. §453(b)(2)(A).
20. I.R.C. §452(b)(2)(B).
21. I.R.C. §453(k)(1).
22. I.R.C. §453(k)(2).
23. I.R.C. §453(i).
24. I.R.C. §1033(a)(2)(B).
25. I.R.C. §1033(a)(2)(B)(i).
26. Treas. Reg. §1.1033(a)-2(c)(3).
27. I.R.C. §1033(a)(2).
28. I.R.C. §1033(h)(2).
29. I.R.C. §1044(a).
30. I.R.C. §1044(c)(3).
31. I.R.C. §1044(c)(4).
32. I.R.C. §1044(b)(1).
33. I.R.C. §1044(b)(2).
34. I.R.C. §1044(d).
35. *Ibid.*
36. Treas. Reg. §1.1044(a)-1(b).
37. I.R.C. §1045(a).
38. *Ibid.*
39. I.R.C. §1202(d)(1).
40. I.R.C. §1202(c)(2)(A).
41. I.R.C. §1202(e)(1).
42. I.R.C. §1202(e)(3).
43. I.R.C. §1045(b)(3).
44. I.R.C. §121(b)(1).
45. I.R.C. §121(b)(2).
46. Treas. Reg. §1.165-9(a).
47. Treas. Reg. §1.121-1(b)(2).
48. *Ibid.*
49. *Ibid.*
50. I.R.C. §121(a).
51. *Ibid.*
52. I.R.C. §121(b)(3).
53. Treas. Reg. §1.121-1(c).
54. Treas. Reg. §1.121-1(c)(4), Example 4.
55. I.R.C. §121(b)(2).
56. I.R.C. §121(c).
57. I.R.C. §121(c)(1)(A).
58. Temp. Treas. Reg. §1.121-3T(c)(2).
59. Temp. Treas. Reg. §1.121-3T(f).
60. Temp. Treas. Reg. §1.121-3T(d)(1).
61. Temp. Treas. Reg. §1.121-3T(f).
62. Temp. Treas. Reg. §1.121-3T(d)(2).
63. Temp. Treas. Reg. §1.121-3T(e).
64. Temp. Treas. Reg. §1.121-3T(e)(2).
65. I.R.C. §1202(a)(1).
66. I.R.C. §1(h)(4) and (7).
67. I.R.C. §57(a)(7).
68. I.R.C. §1202(a)(3).
69. I.R.C. §1202(a)(4).
70. I.R.C. §1202(b)(1).
71. I.R.C. §170(b)(1)(C)(iv).
72. I.R.C. §170(b)(1)(C)(i).
73. I.R.C. §170(b)(1)(D).
74. I.R.C. §170(b)(1)(C)(iii).
75. I.R.C. §170(e)(1)(A).
76. Rev. Rul. 79-419.
77. I.R.C. §165(g)(1).
78. I.R.C. §6511(d)(1).
79. I.R.C. §1244(a).
80. I.R.C. §1244(c)(1).
81. I.R.C. §1244(c)(2)(C).
82. I.R.C. §1244(c)(3).
83. Treas. Reg. §1.1244(a)-1(b).
84. I.R.C. §1244(b).
85. I.R.C. §1091(a).
86. I.R.C. §1091(b) and Treas. Reg. §1.1091-1(c).
87. I.R.C. §1091(d).

RETIREMENT PLANNING

CHAPTER 30

INTRODUCTION

With the possible exception of an individual's home, qualified retirement plans, Section 403(b) arrangements, and individual retirement accounts may represent the single largest asset a person will ever have. Since these retirement account balances may have been built up over forty years or more, many employees with only moderate income levels may find that their retirement plan assets are worth several hundred thousand dollars. One of the biggest drawbacks of retirement plans is the myriad of highly complex rules and regulations that must be followed to avoid the imposition of what can be draconian penalties. These penalties may be imposed if distributions from retirement plans are too early, too late, or too small.

Most retirement plans must require that distributions begin shortly after age 70½ and penalize individuals who withdraw funds prior to age 59½. These two milestones are very important factors to consider when planning for retirement. When individuals decide to retire before age 59½, planning to avoid the penalties that are imposed for premature distributions from qualified retirement plans is an essential step in the planning process. Also, given that there is an onerous penalty for failing to make the minimum required distributions once an individual reaches her required beginning date, it is imperative to make sure that the minimum required distribution rules are strictly followed.

The general rules describing when contributions to and distributions from retirement plans may be made can be summarized as follows. (Of course, since there are so many types of retirement plans, it is important to review the rules for the plan in question to ensure that all requirements are met.)

Age of Participant	Contributions	Withdrawals
Before age 59½	Permitted	Generally permitted, but with penalty
Between age 59½ and 70½	Permitted	Unlimited without penalty
After age 70½	May be limited	Minimum amount required each year (special exception available for qualified plan participants who are less than 5% owners in the plan sponsor)

TYPES OF RETIREMENT PLANS

It seems as if the types of retirement plans in which an individual may participate are continually increasing. From individual retirement accounts ("IRAs") to plans that just refer to an Internal Revenue Code section like 401(k), 403(b) or 457 – the retirement plan landscape is confusing from the start.

This section of the chapter will provide a basic introduction to the types of retirement plans that will be discussed in the balance of the chapter. More detail on all types of retirement plans can be found in *Tools & Techniques of Employee Benefit and Retirement Planning*.

Individual Retirement Account ("IRA") – IRAs are probably the best-known of the retirement plan vehicles.

Of course, there are many different types of IRAs, each of which may have its own set of rules:

1. **Traditional IRA** – A traditional IRA is usually established by an individual with a bank or brokerage firm acting as trustee or custodian. For the 2014 tax year (and increasing with cost of living adjustments in $500 increments thereafter), individuals may deposit up to the lesser of their earned income (their "compensation") or $5,500 into a traditional IRA. Individuals over age fifty may also contribute an additional $1,000 towards a traditional IRA, for a combined total of $6,500.

   Contributions that are made to a traditional IRA may be deductible depending on whether the taxpayer (or the taxpayer's spouse) is a participant in an employer-sponsored retirement arrangement (e.g. a qualified retirement plan such as a "401(k) plan" or a tax-deferred Section 403(b) arrangement) and the taxpayer's adjusted gross income.

   Individuals who are not covered by an employer-sponsored retirement plan are permitted to make a fully deductible IRA contribution for a given tax year. If an individual is covered by a retirement plan, the ability to fund an IRA is phased out for individual taxpayers with income over $60,000 in 2014 and $96,000 for married taxpayers filing a joint return. The deductible IRA contributions are fully phased out at $70,000 and $116,000, respectively, for 2014.

   The income earned and appreciation inside traditional IRAs grows on a tax-deferred basis.

   Distributions from a traditional IRA are fully taxable and may not begin before age 59½ without penalty. Once a taxpayer reaches age 70½, a minimum amount must be distributed from the IRA each year.

2. **Spousal IRA** – A spousal IRA is one in which a taxpayer's nonworking spouse is permitted to contribute to an IRA based upon the compensation of the taxpayer. Therefore, in order to fully fund a traditional and spousal IRA, the total compensation received in that year must exceed $11,000 ($5,500 for each spouse). All other rules for traditional IRAs apply to spousal IRAs.

If the working spouse participates in an employer sponsored plan and the married couple files a joint tax return, the spouse is permitted to make a deductible IRA contribution provided their AGI is less than $181,000 for 2014. Once AGI reaches this level, the deduction is completely phased out at $191,000 of AGI. For married taxpayers who file separate returns, the phase-out begins at $0 of AGI and is fully phased out at $10,000 of AGI.

3. **Rollover IRA** – A rollover IRA (or "conduit IRA") is an IRA that has been established to accept a distribution from a qualified plan. Distributions from an IRA can be rolled over to a qualified plan to the extent that the distributions from the IRA would otherwise be included in the IRA owner's income if the distributions were not rolled over to the qualified plan.

4. **Nondeductible IRA** – Contributions of up to $5,500 (for 2014) per person may be made to an IRA provided the individual has earned income of at least that amount during the year for which the contribution is made. If the taxpayer is unable to deduct the IRA contribution either because of the adjusted gross income limitation or because the taxpayer or spouse is an active participant in an employer-sponsored retirement plan, the contribution may stay in the IRA. However, the contribution is not deductible. Nondeductible IRA contributions create "basis" for the IRA owner. When distributions are made from an IRA that holds nondeductible contributions, part of the distribution is not taxed.

5. **Roth IRA** – A Roth IRA accepts nondeductible contributions from individuals whose income falls within certain limits. Like traditional IRAs, the earnings within the Roth IRA are not taxed year by year as they accumulate.

   When distributions are made from the Roth IRA, the distributions are not taxable to the Roth IRA owner, provided that certain requirements are met.

   Unlike traditional IRAs, taxpayers may make contributions to Roth IRAs after reaching age 70½ and Roth IRAs do not require that minimum distributions be made during the lifetime of the account owner.

6. **SEP-IRA** – A simplified employee pension (SEP) IRA is an employer-sponsored arrangement that consists of a collection of traditional IRAs – one for each employee – with much higher contribution limits. For purposes of the annual contribution limit, a SEP-IRA is treated like a qualified profit sharing plan. An employer may contribute up to the lessor of (1) 25 percent of compensation or (2) $52,000 (for 2014). The compensation that may be counted for this purpose is limited by Code Section 401(a)(17) to $260,000 in 2014.

7. **SIMPLE IRA** – A SIMPLE IRA is available to employers with one hundred or fewer employees who earned at least $5,000 during any two preceding calendar years and is expected to receive at least that amount in the current year. Self-employed persons may also establish a SIMPLE IRA.

   SIMPLE IRAs are funded with elective deferrals by the employee and either matching or nonelective contributions by the employer. Although they are IRAs and are generally subject to the same rules as traditional IRAs, they have higher annual contribution limits and a higher penalty on withdrawals occurring within the first two years of participation.

   Employee elective deferrals or salary reduction contributions are limited to $12,000 in 2014 and may be combined with a $2,500 "catch-up" contribution for those employees age fifty or older.

   Employers must contribute to the each employee's SIMPLE IRA in one of the following ways:

   1. A nonelective contribution of 2 percent of each eligible employee's compensation regardless of the amount deferred by the employee in the plan year.

   2. A matching contribution of 3 percent of each employee's elective deferral amount. This matching contribution may be lowered (but not lower than 1 percent) for up to two calendar years out of the last five year period.

   The chosen contribution method is required to be disclosed to the employees during the election period for the plan year:

Qualified Pension and Profit Sharing Plans – A qualified plan is one that allows for (i) an immediate deduction by the employer for contributions the employer makes to the plan each year; (ii) tax-free growth of contributions while they are held by the plan; and (iii) deferral of income tax on each participant's interest in the plan until the he or she actually receives a distribution from the plan (and then only to the extent of the actual distribution).

There are two main types of qualified plans:

1. **Defined contribution plans** – In a defined contribution plan, the plan establishes an individual account for each participant. When the participant is eligible to receive benefits, the benefit amount is based upon the account balance at that time. These plans are called "defined contribution" plans because the plan defines how much the employer will contribute to the plan. The plan makes no guarantees as to the amount of the future *benefit* that an employee will ultimately receive.

   There are three principal types of defined contribution plan formulas

   a. **Profit sharing plan** – In a profit sharing plan, the employer decides how much to contribute each year. There is no requirement that the employer contribute something every year. Each year's employer contribution is then allocated among the accounts of participants; the formula for allocating the contribution can be in proportion to compensation and/or other facts (such as years of service – or age). A 401(k) plan is a type of profit sharing plan that combines the potential for employer contributions with elective salary deferrals made by the employee. "401(k)" refers to the Internal Revenue Code section that sanctions the ability of employees to defer the receipt of compensation and cause the deferrals to be contributed to their accounts in the plan.

   Employers are permitted to add a Roth 401(k) feature to their 401(k) plan. Employees would then be allowed to make either pre-tax salary deferrals to their regular 401(k) account or after-tax salary deferrals to their Roth 401(k) account. The total amount that may be deferred ($17,500 in 2014) does not change. The catch up contribution limits which apply to those participants over age fifty also apply ($5,500 additional in 2014). The amount that is earmarked for the Roth 401(k) does not reduce the employee's taxable income, but, like its Roth IRA counterpart, will grow and may be withdrawn free of federal income taxes.

b. **Money-purchase pension plan** – The employer must make annual contributions to the plan based upon the employees' compensation for the year. The aggregate deductible contribution an employer can make each year to a money purchase pension plan on behalf of all participants, expressed as a percentage of participants' aggregate compensation, can be as high as 25 percent. The amount of that contribution that can be allocated to a particular participant's account each year cannot exceed 100 percent of the participant's eligible compensation or $52,000 (for 2014, increased annually for cost of living). Note that these plans are less frequently used since amendments by EGTRRA 2001 permit profit sharing plans the same potential employer deduction without the mandatory funding requirement.

b. **Target-benefit pension plan** – A target benefit pension plan is a special type of money purchase pension plan. Instead of basing each year's contribution solely as a percentage of each participant's compensation, the employer's annual contributions use a formula based on the employee's compensation and the employee's age. The result is that older employees receive larger contributions than younger employees.

2. **Defined benefit plans** – Unlike a defined contribution plan, a "defined benefit" plan is one in which the plan promises a specific amount of benefit to an employee at normal retirement age. The plan may offer up to the lesser of 100 percent of the participant's average compensation in his high three years of service (usually at the end of the employee's career), or $210,000 (in 2014). The amount of the employer's contribution is determined actuarially and must be funded each year regardless of the employer's profitability. Since the employer must provide

adequate funding for the benefit that is promised, the risks (and rewards) of investment performance are borne by the employer.

Other arrangements that mimic qualified plans include Section 403(b) plans (for non-profit organizations and public school employees) and Section 457 plans (for government employees).

Deferred Annuities – A deferred annuity is another source of retirement income, but it is usually a personal investment and not typically associated with an employer/employee relationship. The investor makes a single large cash payment or a series of periodic payments to purchase the annuity. In return the annuity issuer agrees to pay a specified amount on a periodic basis to the investor at some point in the future. The annuity payout may be for the life of the annuitant, for the joint lives of the annuitant and spouse, or for a fixed term. It may be immediate (i.e., it starts as soon as the payment is made for the contract with the insurer) or deferred for many years.

Once the annuity is purchased, the subsequent earnings accumulate on a tax deferred basis. No income from the annuity is taxed until the annuity begins or is otherwise cashed in.

RETIREMENT PLAN DISTRIBUTION OPTIONS

Employer-sponsored retirement plans will typically provide for a number of different distribution options once an employee (or former employee) is eligible for and elects to begin to receive benefits.

Defined benefit plans and money purchase pension plans must pay benefits in the form of a qualified joint and survivor annuity (QJSA) to retiring employees and a qualified preretirement survivor annuity (QPSA) to employees who terminate prior to their normal retirement date, unless the employee and, if the employee is married, the employee's spouse, consent to a different benefit payment option. A QJSA is an annuity that is payable for the life of the plan participant with a survivor annuity for the life of the spouse, should the surviving spouse outlive the participant. The survivor annuity may not be less than 50 percent, nor more than 100 percent, of the annuity payable to the participant. In plan years beginning after December 31, 2007, plans must also offer a 75 percent qualified optional survivor annuity if the spouse waives the QJSA.

A QPSA is an annuity that is payable for life of the participant's spouse and is equal to the survivor annuity portion of the QJSA that would have been paid if the participant had retired and died.

Although an employee may select another form of annuity or a lump sum distribution, the waiver of the QJSA and/or QPSA usually requires the written consent of the employee and the employee's spouse.

Defined contribution plans that are not money purchase pension plans may offer annuity or installment forms of benefit distribution. But the single most common form they offer is a lump sum distribution Upon termination of service, an employee in a qualified plan who receives a lump sum distribution can roll over the distribution, tax-free, to the employee's own IRA or to a qualified plan maintained by the employee's new employer.

Other benefit payment options include an annuity with payments that are guaranteed for a specified minimum number of years (e.g. life annuity with ten years certain).

If the plan must offer a QJSA and QPSA, the employee and the employee's spouse must both agree to waive the QJSA and QPSA in order to receive any other benefit payment option the plan may offer.

All of the benefit payment options must have the same actuarially equivalent value.

IRAs are much more flexible.

- IRA owners do not have to obtain their spouse's consent to a form of distribution. IRAs are not subject to the QJSA/QPSA or QOSA requirement. The IRA owner can choose any benefit payment option he or she desires, without the need to secure a spouse's consent.

- IRAs can distribute benefits in any form, at any time, and in any amount the IRA owner desires. Unlike qualified retirement plans, which may offer a limited menu of benefit payment options that is controlled by the employer, IRA owners can craft their own benefit payment methods. (Wherever there is a general rule, there usually is an exception. And one applies here: IRAs, like qualified plans, must obey the minimum required distribution rules, discussed below).

A 10 percent penalty is usually assessed for distributions from IRAs and qualified plans that are made too soon (generally, before reaching age 59½). More onerous penalties apply if distributions begin too late (generally, soon after reaching age 70½) or are not enough to satisfy the minimum required distribution rules.

TAX IMPLICATIONS
Retirement Plan Distributions

Unless a retirement distribution is rolled over to another eligible retirement plan, (i.e., funneled directly into another qualified plan or IRA), a distribution is taxable as ordinary income in the taxable year in which it is received.[1]

If nondeductible contributions are made to a retirement plan (with the exception of Roth IRA and Roth 401(k) contributions), the taxpayer accumulates basis in the retirement plan that should be recovered when distributions are made.[2] The distributions will consist of both a taxable and nontaxable portion. The nontaxable portion cannot be recovered first.

The computation of the nontaxable portion of a distribution from an IRA that contains nondeductible contributions is calculated as follows:

$$Nontaxable\ Portion = C \times \left(\frac{X}{Y}\right)$$

Where:

X = Total nondeductible contributions made to all IRAs;

Y = The sum of all IRA account balances at year-end, plus any IRA amounts distributed during the year, plus any outstanding rollover that is completed in the following year; and

C = Total IRA distributions made during the year.

Example: Thomas Hewer withdrew $20,000 from one of his IRAs during the year. Over the years, he had funded this IRA with $20,000 of nondeductible contributions. As of the end of the year, he has three IRAs with an aggregate value of $180,000. He made no other nondeductible contributions. Of the $20,000 distribution, only $2,000 will be a tax-free recovery of basis.

$$\left[\frac{\$20,000}{(\$180,000 + \$20,000)}\right] \times \$20,000 = \$2,000$$

Qualified plans may also permit employees to make nondeductible, after-tax contributions. After-tax employee contributions have already been subject to income tax and are not taxed again to the employee when distributions begin from the qualified plan. However, like IRA distributions containing both taxable and nontaxable amounts, qualified plan distributions can carry taxable amounts (contributions that were originally made on a tax-deductible basis) and nontaxable amounts (a portion of those employee after-tax contributions).

The taxation of a non-lump sum distribution from a qualified plan depends on whether the distribution is received in the form an annuity. If the distribution is received as a periodic payment in a systematic liquidation of the participant's benefit, the annuity rules of Code section 72 are used to determine the taxability of the benefit.[3] If the distribution is not a lump sum distribution or an annuity, the non-annuity payment rules will apply.[4]

When annuity payments are made from a qualified plan, the tax-free portion of the distribution is spread evenly over a specified number of payments.

The annuity rules of section 72 apply to periodic plan distributions made over more than one taxable year of the employee in a systematic liquidation of the participant's benefit. Amounts distributed are taxable in the year received, except for a proportionate recovery of the cost basis. The method used for recovery of the cost basis depends on the participant's annuity starting date.

If the annuity starting date is after December 31, 1997 and the annuity is payable over two or more lives, the excludable portion of each monthly payment is determined by dividing the employee's cost basis by the number of payments shown in the table below:

If the combined ages of the annuitants are:	Number of Payments
Not more than 110	410
More than 110 but not more than 120	360
More than 120 but not more than 130	310
More than 130 but not more than 140	260
More than 140	210

If (a) the annuity starting date was after November 18, 1996 and before January 1, 1998 and the annuity is payable over two or more lives, *or* (b) the annuity starting date is after November 18, 1996 and the annuity is payable over one life, the excludable portion of each monthly payment is determined by dividing the employee's cost basis by the number of payments shown in the table below:

Age	Number of Payments
Not more than 55	360
More than 55 but not more than 60	310
More than 60 but not more than 65	260
More than 65 but not more than 70	210
More than 70	160

In the case of participants with an annuity starting date after July 1, 1986 and before November 19, 1996, the cost basis is recovered through the calculation of an exclusion ratio that is applied to each payment to determine the nontaxable amount.

The exclusion ratio is:

$$\frac{\text{Investment in the Contract}}{\text{Expected Return}}$$

Basically, the "investment in the contract" is the participant's cost basis. In the case of a life annuity, the "expected return" is determined by multiplying the total annual payment by the participant's life expectancy. Life expectancies are determined under tables found in Treasury Regulations for section 72.[5]

Example: Fred Retiree retired in 1995 at age sixty-five with a pension of $500 per month for his life. Fred's cost basis in the plan was $20,000. Using a life expectancy of twenty years, Fred's exclusion ratio was calculated as follows:

$$\frac{\$20,000}{\$120,000} = \frac{1}{6}$$

The numerator is Fred's cost basis; the denominator is Fred's annual pension of $6,000 multiplied by his life expectancy. Therefore, one-sixth of each payment Fred receives will be nontaxable. The remainder of each payment is taxable as ordinary income.

Once the exclusion ratio is determined it continues to apply until the cost basis is fully recovered. Payments made subsequently are taxable in full. If the participant dies before the cost basis is fully recovered, an income tax deduction for the unrecovered basis is allowed on the participant's final return. Special tables are used for joint life expectancies and separate computations may be necessary to determine expected return in some situations, such as where there is a period certain guarantee.

A simplified "safe harbor" method (for annuity starting dates after July 1, 1986 and before November 19, 1996) was provided by the IRS in Notice 88-118.[6] This alternative to the use of the exclusion ratio only applies to payments from a qualified plan—or section 403(b) tax-deferred annuity plan—which were to be paid for the life of the employee or the joint lives of the employee and a beneficiary. Under this method, the employee's investment in the contract was divided by the number of expected monthly payments set out in the IRS table below. The number of payments was based on the employee's age at the annuity starting date and the same table was used for both single life and joint and survivor annuity payments. The resulting dollar amount was excluded from each payment until the cost basis was fully recovered.

Age	Number of Payments
55 and under	300
55-60	260
61–65	240
66–70	170
71 and over	120

Taxation of Annuities

A client's investment in an annuity is returned in equal tax-free amounts during the payment period. Any additional amount received is taxed at ordinary income rates. This means that part of each payment is considered return of capital and is therefore nontaxable and part of each payment is considered return on capital (income) and is therefore taxable at ordinary rates.

The formula for determining the nontaxable portion of each year's payment is:[7]

$$\frac{\text{Investment in Contract}}{\text{Number of Years of Expected Return}}$$

This is called the "exclusion ratio." It is expressed as a percentage (rounded to three decimal places and applied to each annuity payment to find the portion of the payment that is excludable from gross income.[8] For instance, assume a seventy-year-old purchases an annuity. He pays (i.e., the investment in the contract is) $12,000 for the annuity. Assume his expected return is $19,200.

The exclusion ratio is 62.5 percent ($12,000 divided by $19,200). If the monthly payment he receives is $100, the portion that can be excluded from gross income is $62.50 (62.5 percent of $100). The $37.50 balance of each $100 monthly payment is ordinary income.[9]

The excludable portion of any annuity payment may not exceed the unrecovered investment in the contract (unless the annuity started before January 1, 1987). The "unrecovered investment in the contract" is the policy owner's premium cost (reduced by any dividends received in cash or used to reduce premiums and by the aggregate amount received under the contract on or after the annuity starting date to the extent it was excludable from income). This rule limits the total amount the policy owner can exclude from income to the total amount of his contribution. Once an annuitant actually lives longer than his or her actuarial life expectancy, 100 percent of each payment will be taxable.

Some annuities provide a refund if the annuitant dies before recovering his entire cost, or provide a "period-certain" guarantee (payments will be made for a specified period regardless of how long the annuitant lives). The value of the refund or period-certain guarantee must be ascertained by government tables and subtracted from the investment in the contract.[10]

The "expected return" is the total amount that the annuitant (or annuitants) should receive, given the payments specified multiplied by the life expectancy according to the government's tables (currently Table V for single lives and Table VI for joint and survivor annuities). For instance, under Table V, a seventy-year-old has a life expectancy of sixteen years. If he (or she, since the life expectancy tables are unisex) receives $100 a month, the expected return would be $19,200 (sixteen years at $1,200 per year).[11]

When an annuitant dies before receiving the full amount guaranteed under a refund or period certain life annuity, the beneficiary receiving the balance of the guaranteed amount will have no taxable income (unless the amount received by the beneficiary plus the amount that had been received tax free by the annuitant exceeds the investment in the contract).

If the refund or commuted (present) value of the remaining installments is applied by the beneficiary to purchase a new annuity, payments received will be taxed under the annuity rules to the beneficiary. The refund amount will be considered the beneficiary's investment in the new contract and a new exclusion ratio must be determined.

If the annuitant was receiving payments under a joint and survivor annuity, the survivor excludes from income the same percentage of each payment that was excludable by the first annuitant. An income tax deduction may be available to the survivor annuitant to the extent inclusion of the annuity in the estate of the first to die generated an estate tax. A similar deduction may be available if the annuity generated a generation skipping transfer tax.

When an annuitant makes a partial withdrawal from the contract and takes a reduced annuity for the same term, a portion of the amount withdrawn will be subject to income tax.

When an annuitant makes a partial withdrawal from the contract (allocable to an investment in the contract made after August 13, 1982) and chooses to take the same payments for a different term, to the extent the cash surrender value of the contract exceeds the investment in the contract, gain will be realized in the form of a taxable withdrawal of interest.

The purchase of a variable annuity is not taxed on income during the accumulation period. No tax will be payable until the earlier of (a) the surrender of the contract or (b) the time payments under the annuity begin (the "annuity starting date"). To obtain annuity treatment, however, the underlying investments of the segregated asset account must be "adequately diversified" according to IRS regulations.

Payments made as an annuity under a variable annuity are not subject to the same exclusion ratio as is a regular fixed annuity. This is because it is impossible to determine the expected return. Instead, the following formula is used:

$$\frac{\text{Investment in Contract}}{\text{Number of Years of Expected Return}}$$

If there is a period certain or refund guarantee, the investment in the contract is adjusted accordingly. If payments are made for a fixed number of years without regard to life expectancy, the divisor is that fixed number of years. If payments are made for a single life, IRS Table V is used; if payments are to be made on a joint and survivor basis Table VI is used.

The exclusion ratio no longer applies once an annuitant reaches his life expectancy. So if a person's actual life exceeds his actuarial expectancy as anticipated when benefits began, the total amount that can be excluded is limited to the total amount of his investment. For instance, assume a sixty-five-year-old paid $40,000 for his life annuity. Since his life expectancy is twenty years, his yearly exclusion is $2,000 ($40,000 divided by twenty). The $2,000 continues to be excludable until the annuitant has recovered the $40,000.

If payments drop below the excludable amount ($2,000 in this example) in any given year, the annuitant can elect to redetermine the excludable amount in the next tax year in which he receives an annuity payment. The loss in exclusions is divided by the number of years remaining (in the case of a fixed period annuity). In the case of a life annuity the loss is divided by the annuitant's life expectancy computed as of the first day of the first period for which an amount is received as an annuity.

Example: Bouillabaisse is a sixty-five-year-old taxpayer who purchased an annuity for $20,000. The contract provides variable monthly payments for life. Since his life expectancy is twenty years per Table V, he may exclude $1,000 of each annuity payment from income ($20,000 dived by twenty years of life expectancy). Assume on his seventieth birthday he receives only $200, $800 less than his excludable amount. At age seventy his life expectancy is sixteen years. He may elect to add $50 ($800 dived by sixteen years of life expectancy) to his $1,000 exclusion, a total of $1,050 which he may exclude that year and in subsequent years.

If an annuitant dies before the amount of payments received equals his or her cost, a loss deduction can be taken for the amount of the unrecovered investment, provided the annuity starting date was after July 1, 1986. This same result applies where one person purchases an annuity on the life of another who dies prematurely.

So if a wife purchases a single premium nonrefundable annuity on the life of her husband, and the husband dies before all costs have been recovered, a loss deduction will be allowed.

The deduction for the unrecovered investment in the contract is an itemized deduction, but not a miscellaneous deduction. Therefore, it is not subject to the two percent floor.

Amounts payable under a deferred annuity contract at the death of an annuitant (prior to the contract's maturity) will be taxed as ordinary income to the beneficiary. The excess of (a) the death benefit (plus aggregate dividends and other amounts that were received tax free) over (b) total gross premiums is taxable.

Beneficiaries can elect to delay reporting of the gain in the year of the annuitant's death if the beneficiary applies the death benefit under a life income or installment option within sixty days of the annuitant's death. The beneficiary will then report income according to an exclusion ratio. The beneficiary's investment in the contract will be the same as the annuitant's investment in the contract. The expected return is based on the income the beneficiary will receive and the beneficiary's life expectancy.

The owner of an annuity often takes dividends, makes cash withdrawals, or takes other amounts out of the annuity contract before the date the annuity is to start (the "annuity starting date"). Such amounts are taxable as income to the extent that the policy cash value exceeds the investment in the contract. (Different rules apply to contracts purchased on or before August 13, 1982.)

The so called "interest first" rule (i.e., amounts received are treated first as interest income, then as a recovery of cost) was imposed to discourage the use of annuity contracts as short term investment vehicles. Under this rule, a loan is considered a cash withdrawal.

Likewise, to the extent the contract is used as collateral for a loan, amounts borrowed will be taxable (to the extent the amount received equals or is less than any gain inherent in the contract). If the amount received exceeds the built-in gain, the excess of what was borrowed over potential gain is considered a tax free return of the contract owner's investment. With respect to contracts entered into after October 21, 1988, amounts borrowed increase investment in the contract on the extent they are includible in income under these rules.

In applying the interest first rule, all contracts entered into after October 21, 1988 and issued by the same company to the same policyholder during any twelve month period are treated as one contract.

"Premature" distributions (those made before certain dates listed below) are subject not only to the normal tax on ordinary income, but also to a penalty tax of 10 percent. Exceptions to this penalty exist and are discussed in more detail later in this chapter.

If an annuity owner dies before the starting date of the annuity payments, the cash value of the contract must either be distributed within five years of death or used within one year of death to provide a life annuity or installment payments payable over a period not longer than the beneficiary's life expectancy. However, if the surviving spouse if the beneficiary; the distribution requirements are applied by treating the spouse as the owner of the annuity contract.

If the annuity contract is transferred by gift, the tax deferral on the inside build up that was allowed to the original contract owner is terminated. The donor of the gift is treated as having received non-annuity income in an amount equal to the excess of the cash surrender value of the contract at the time of the transfer over the investment in the contract at that time.

Tax free build-up within the contract is allowed only to "natural persons." If an annuity contract is held other than by a natural person, then the annuity contract is not treated as an annuity and the income on the contract is treated as ordinary income received or accrued by the owner during that taxable year.

Corporations are not "natural persons." Neither is the typical trust although a trust acting as the agent for a natural person would itself be considered a natural person. But if an employer is the agent for its employees, the contract will be considered as if owned by the employer. The employer will therefore be taxed currently on the inside build-up. This means annuities are not appropriate tax advantaged investments for nonqualified deferred compensation agreements.

Exceptions from the "natural persons" rules allow tax-free buildup of the following annuities:

1. annuities received by the executor of a decedent at the decedent's death,

2. annuities held by a qualified retirement plan or IRA,

3. annuities considered "qualifying funding assets" (used to provide funding for structured settlements and by property and casualty insurance companies to fund periodic payments for damages),

4. annuities purchased by an employer on termination of a qualified plan and held until all amounts under the plan are distributed to the employee or his beneficiary,

5. annuities that are "immediate," (i.e., those that have a starting date no more than one year from the date the annuity was purchased and provide for a series of substantially equal periodic payments to be made at least annually over the annuity period).

Minimum Required Distributions

During Owner's Lifetime

Retirement accounts benefit from the tax deferral of earnings while amounts are being accumulated. The minimum required distribution (MRD) rules[12] force retirement account owners to receive distributions that will then be subject to income tax. MRDs must begin by the owner's required beginning date (RBD).

Note that the minimum distribution rules discussed in this section apply to qualified plans, 403(b) tax sheltered annuities, section 457 plans and traditional IRAs. The owners of Roth IRAs are not subject to the lifetime MRD rules. Minimum distributions from Roth IRAs are required only upon the death of the account owner.[13]

All participants in qualified plans, Section 403(b) arrangements, and Section 457 deferred compensation plans, and all traditional IRA owners, must begin to receive distributions no later than their required beginning date (RBD).[14] Once distributions begin, they must continue each year in minimum required amounts.

The RBD for qualified plan participants is April 1 of the year following the year in which the individual attains age 70½. But, employees who continue to work for the employer sponsoring the qualified plan after age 70½ and who own 5 percent or less of the employer may defer taking distributions until they retire (provided the plan permits it).[15]

The RBD for IRA owners and for qualified plan participants who own more than 5 percent of the business is April 1 of the year following the year in which they turn age 70½, even if they have not retired.

Section 403(b) plans generally follow the same rules as qualified plans, except that all participants who work beyond age 70½ may defer starting distributions until April 1 of the year after the year they retire. However, some 403(b) plan participants may be permitted to defer distributions of pre-1987 account balances until they reach age 75.

If a decedent's spouse is the sole beneficiary of the decedent's IRA, the surviving spouse can roll over that IRA into the surviving spouse's own IRA or the surviving spouse may elect to treat the decedent's IRA as the surviving spouse's own IRA. The surviving spouse is then treated as the new owner of the IRA and MRDs need not begin until April 1 of the year following the year the surviving spouse attains age 70½. If the surviving spouse is already 70½ when the IRA is inherited, MRDs must begin by December 31 of the year following the year of the rollover or election to treat the IRA as his or her own.

So, age 70½ is an important date for the application of the MRD rules. Since most people stop counting half birthdays around age ten, when exactly does a person become age 70½? The regulations state that an individual reaches age 70½ on the date that is exactly six months after his or her 70th birthday.[16]

The first MRD is payable for the year in which the owner reaches 70½. It is not required to be paid until April 1 of the following year. Each subsequent year, the MRD must be distributed by December 31 of that year.

Example: Gavin McCloone turned age 70½ on January 24, 2014. Therefore, his first MRD is payable for 2014 and must be distributed by April 1, 2015. The 2015 MRD must be distributed by December 31, 2015.

As noted in this example, the first and second MRDs are actually payable in the same year. (The first two MRDs are the only ones affected by this since all subsequent MRDs must be paid by December 31.) The doubling up of the MRDs may cause the taxpayer to pay more federal income tax on the two distributions in that year than if the MRDs had been paid in separate years.

In order to avoid this doubling up effect, taxpayers should consider receiving their first MRD by December 31 of the year in which they turn age 70½ instead of waiting until April 1 of the following year.

MRDs are calculated each year independently of any other year. For example, during 2014, a taxpayer takes out $5,000 more than her MRD for 2014. This taxpayer, may not apply that excess amount to reduce her MRD in any other year.[17]

The MRD for a year is determined by dividing the account balance, determined as of the last valuation date in the preceding year, by the owner's life expectancy.

- Determining the account balance. The account balance is determined as of the last valuation date in the preceding calendar year.[18] No adjustments are made to the account balance for contributions or distributions occurring after that date.

Example: Fred Lubert uses his account balance on December 31, 2013 to determine his first MRD, which is $20,000. Since he turned age 70½ in 2014, he must distribute that amount by April 1, 2015. As of December 31, 2014, he has not yet distributed his first MRD. His account balance as of December 31, 2014 is used to determine his 2014 MRD without adjusting the balance down for the undistributed MRD that is payable by April 1, 2015.

- Determining life expectancy.

Distributions during the life of a retirement account owner must begin no later than the owner's RBD and must be distributed over a period no longer than:

1. the owner's life expectancy,

2. the life expectancies of the owner and a designated beneficiary, or

3. a fixed period that does not extend beyond such life expectancies.[19]

The final regulations provide that these rules are satisfied by calculating the MRD using the factor found in the Uniform Lifetime Table based on the owner's age at the end of the applicable distribution calendar year.[20] This table may be used regardless of the age of the designated beneficiary as well as when there is no designated beneficiary.

The only exception to the use of the Uniform Lifetime Table is when the participant/owner's designated beneficiary is a spouse who is more than ten years younger than the participant/owner. In that case, the Joint and Last Survivor Table may be used.[21]

Example: Alex Weston is seventy-five years old. His wife Renee is sixty-two and his son Todd is forty. Alex has three IRAs. One names his wife as the designated beneficiary, the second names Todd and the third names his estate. During his lifetime, the applicable life expectancy factors to be used to determine Alex's MRDs are:

Beneficiary	Table Used	Account Balance	Life Expectancy	MRD
Renee	Joint and Last Survivor	$800,000	25.0	$32,000
Todd	Uniform Lifetime	$300,000	22.9	$13,100
Estate	Uniform Lifetime	$250,000	22.9	$10,917

MRDs must be determined separately for each qualified plan and IRA. The MRD for a qualified plan must be distributed from that qualified plan.[22] The MRDs for an owner's IRAs may be totaled and distributed from any one or more of the owner's IRAs.

Example: Adam Coultier is seventy-three years old. He determines that the MRD from his qualified plan is $8,000. He also owns two IRAs which have MRDs of $5,000 and $16,000. Adam must receive at least an $8,000 distribution from his qualified plan in order to satisfy the MRD rules. For the IRAs, he may pay the MRDs out of each of the IRAs or aggregate the two MRDs and pay the entire $21,000 out of one of the IRAs. As long as $21,000 is distributed from Adam's IRAs during the year, it makes does not make a difference how much comes from each of his IRAs.

MRDs are calculated each year through the year of the owner's death using the Uniform Lifetime Table (or the Joint and Last Survivor Table if the participant/owner is married to a spouse more than ten years younger than the participant/owner). This rule applies regardless of who is the beneficiary of the participant/owner's retirement arrangement.

Qualified Charitable Distributions

For 2006 through 2013, an IRA (traditional or Roth) participant over age 70½ may distribute up to $100,000 each year directly to a qualifying charitable organization.[23] The $100,000 annual limit may be made up of several smaller charitable distributions to one or more organizations. Although such "qualified charitable distributions" are not subject to income tax and will not generate a deductible charitable contribution, they do qualify as part of a participant's MRD for that year. This provision does not apply to distributions from a SEP-IRA or SIMPLE IRA.

Congress has a history of allowing this provision to expire from the law and then retroactively reinstating it as part of a broader piece of legislation. In one particular instance for 2012, the provision was not extended for that year until January 2013. As of the writing of this chapter, qualified charitable distributions are not part of the tax law for 2014.

In the absence of legislation, a taxpayer may still make a distribution directly to charity. However, the distributed amount would be additional gross income for the year and the taxpayer would be able to claim the amount contributed as a charitable donation if they are able to itemize their deductions for that year. With so many tax provisions now being determined based on a taxpayer's AGI, the real benefit to having the qualified charitable distribution in the Code is the ability to have a direct offset to income without having to needlessly increase gross income for the year. It is also beneficial in instances where the taxpayer otherwise does not itemize deductions.

Designated Beneficiaries

The "designated beneficiary" is an important factor in retirement plans because the life expectancy of the beneficiary is generally used to determine the MRD after the death of the account owner.

Only individuals and certain trusts may be "designated beneficiaries," *as that term is defined in the regulations.*

If a trust has been designated as the beneficiary of the retirement plan or account, then the beneficiaries of the trust can qualify as "designated beneficiaries" only if:

1. the trust is valid under state law,

2. the trust is irrevocable or will, by its terms, become irrevocable upon the death of the account owner,

3. the trust beneficiaries are identifiable from the trust document, and

4. a copy of the trust document is provided to the trustee or administrator, or the owner agrees to provide a copy of the trust instrument to the plan upon request.[24]

A charity cannot qualify as a "designated beneficiary." Neither can an estate. Only human beings can qualify as "designated beneficiaries" and, unless the special rule for qualifying trusts, described above, applies, human beings can qualify as "designated beneficiaries" only if (i) the participant/owner formally designated them as beneficiaries or (ii) the terms of the plan or account treat them as beneficiaries. If one of the named beneficiaries is not a *designated beneficiary*, all MRDs to all beneficiaries must be calculated as if there is no "designated beneficiary." This will dramatically reduce the period of time over which distributions could otherwise be made.[25]

This poor planning result occurs because of the mechanics the final regulations use to determine MRDs after the participant/owner's death. As described in more detail below, the final regulations employ these general rules to determine the MRDs that must occur after the participant/owner's death:

- The general rule: use the life expectancy of the designated beneficiary to calculate the MRD to the beneficiary.

- If there is more than one beneficiary, then – unless an exception applies – use the age of the oldest beneficiary to determine the MRDs that must be made for *all* of the beneficiaries.

- If the beneficiary does not qualify as a "designated beneficiary," or if there is more than one beneficiary and one of them does not qualify as a "designated beneficiary," then the plan/account is treated as if there are *no* "designated beneficiaries." If there are no designated beneficiaries, then the MRD must be calculated this way:

- If the participant/owner died *before* reaching his or her required beginning date, the plan or account must be completely distributed by the end of the fifth year following the year of the participant/owner's death.

- If the participant/owner died *after* reaching his or her required beginning date, then the MRD must be based on the deceased participant/owner's life expectancy, determined as of the date of the participant/owner's death.

The identity of the "designated beneficiaries" of a retirement plan, IRA, section 403(b) arrangement or section 457 arrangement is not actually determined until September 30 of the year following the year in which the participant/owner died. (The potential universe of "designated beneficiaries" cannot be expanded after the death of the account owner.) This allows for a certain degree of post-mortem planning; for example, disclaimers, cashing-out of benefits, or dividing the decedent's IRA into separate accounts, all in order to avoid the adverse effects of these rules.

For example, beneficiaries who are much older than the rest of the beneficiaries, or beneficiaries who cannot qualify as a "designated beneficiary" (e.g., a charity) can receive their share of the retirement plan or IRA balance prior to September 30 in the year following the year of the participant/owner's death. Since the universe of "designated beneficiaries" is not fixed until that September 30 date, and since the "undesirable" beneficiaries won't be beneficiaries as of that September 30 date, they are disregarded in determining MRDs, thereby preserving the ability of each of the qualifying beneficiaries to calculate the MRD based on his or her life expectancy. If there are multiple designated beneficiaries as of September 30 in the year after death, and the retirement account has not been divided into separate accounts for each beneficiary, the life expectancy of the oldest designated beneficiary must be used to determine the MRDs for all of the beneficiaries. It would be prudent in such a case to divide the deceased participant's account into separate accounts for each beneficiary prior to the September 30 determination date in order to preserve the ability for each designated

beneficiary to use his or her own life expectancy to calculate the MRD.[26]

___

Example: Jerry Martin dies on March 2, 2014 and leaves his $600,000 IRA equally to his three sons, Ross (age thirty-six), Andrew (age thirty-four) and Kyle (age twenty). If the IRA is segregated into three $200,000 IRAs for each son by September 30, 2015, the MRDs will be calculated based upon each son's single life expectancy. If the IRA is not segregated, each son's MRD will be determined using the oldest son's life expectancy.

___

After the Owner's Death

As noted above, lifetime MRDs are calculated each year through the year of the owner's death using the Uniform Lifetime Table, regardless of who is named as beneficiary (except that the Joint and Last Survivor Table is used if the participant/owner's spouse is the beneficiary and is more than ten years younger than the participant/owner). And, as noted above, upon the death of the participant/owner, the MRD rules change.

If an owner dies after his or her RBD, the MRD for the year of death must be calculated and distributed. Beginning with the year following the year of death, the Internal Revenue Code states that distributions must continue at least as rapidly as they were before the death of the account owner;[27] however, final regulations require payouts to be determined based upon the life expectancy of the "designated beneficiary" of the account. Under the final regulations, the designated beneficiary is determined as of September 30 of the year following the year of the owner's death. The required distribution periods are based on the type of beneficiary, as follows:

- *No designated beneficiary* – If no designated beneficiary is named (e.g., the account is payable to the owner's estate, a nonqualifying trust, or a charity), the account owner's single life expectancy as of his or her birthday in the year of death is determined by using the Single Life Table.[28] The life expectancy is the divisor for the purpose of calculating the MRD and is reduced by one in each subsequent year.

- *Nonspouse designated beneficiary* – The beneficiary's single life expectancy is determined in the year following the year of the owner's death by using the Single Life Table. However, if the owner's single life expectancy is longer (i.e. the owner was younger than the beneficiary), that life expectancy may be used. The life expectancy is the divisor for the purpose of calculating the MRD and is reduced by one in each subsequent year.

- *Spouse is sole designated beneficiary* – The spouse's life expectancy is determined using the Single Life Table based on the spouse's age at the end of the calendar year for each MRD. This life expectancy is determined each year, so the spouse's life expectancy will be reduced by something less than one each year. If the owner's single life expectancy is longer, that factor may be used and reduced by one each subsequent year. Upon the death of the spouse, MRDs can be made over his or her remaining single life expectancy determined in the year of death and reduced by one each year thereafter. If the spouse is not the sole beneficiary, the rules for no designated beneficiary or non-spousal beneficiaries applies depending on who the other beneficiary is.

If the account owner dies before his or her RBD or if the account is a Roth IRA, the general rule is that the entire account balance must be distributed on or before December 31 of the year which includes the fifth anniversary of the owner's death (the "five-year rule").[29] An exception to the five-year rule applies if there is a nonspouse designated beneficiary and distributions begin by December 31 of the year after the year in which the owner died. In this case, distributions may be made over the beneficiary's life expectancy.

Prior to the Pension Protection Act of 2006, nonspouse beneficiaries of employer sponsored plans (such as a 401(k) plan) had no choice but to withdraw the funds from the plan in a lump sum and pay tax in that year. Effective for distributions after December 31, 2006, nonspouse beneficiaries may elect to rollover the balance of an employer sponsored plan into an inherited IRA. The transaction must occur in a direct trustee-to-trustee transfer (i.e. the beneficiary must not take any possession of the funds). The nonspouse beneficiary must then withdraw the account balance under the rules described above.[30]

If the participant/owner's spouse is the sole beneficiary of the plan or account, the surviving spouse can defer distributions until the later of (a) the end of the calendar year after the year in which the owner died or (b) the end of the calendar year in which the owner would have reached age 70½.[31] If the surviving spouse dies before the later of these two dates, the life payout rule and five-year rule (if available) apply as if the surviving spouse were the owner of the account.[32]

A second option would be for the spouse to roll over the account balance and defer MRDs until April 1 of the year following the year the spouse attains age 70½. A third option allows the spouse to treat the decedent's IRA as his or her own. This also allows for a deferral of the MRDs until the spouse's RBD.

The election to treat the decedent's IRA as the spouse's own IRA may be made at any time after the owner's death. The election is deemed to have been made by the surviving spouse failing to make an MRD or if additional amounts are contributed to the account (excluding rollovers of other plan balances of the decedent).

The spousal rollover or election may not be a wise decision if the surviving spouse is the older spouse. In that case, the MRDs may be accelerated unless a new beneficiary is named. Another situation in which the spousal rollover or election might be a bad decision is when the surviving spouse is under age 59½ and may need to take distributions from the IRA to support his or her current lifestyle. Distributions made on account of death are an exception to the premature distribution rules. If the balances are rolled over or the election is made, distributions prior to age 59½ would be considered premature and would be subject to the penalty.

Example: John Ashworth died at the age of 47. He had accumulated $750,000 in his IRA and his wife Andrea (age 46) was named as the beneficiary. John and Andrea have no other assets and Andrea does not earn a salary. If Andrea rolls over the IRA into her name or elects to treat it as her own, it would be difficult for her to take distributions from the IRA without a penalty until she is age 59½. Instead, she should leave the IRA in John's name and take distributions as needed. Since the distributions are made to the beneficiary of a decedent's IRA, no premature distribution penalties will apply.

Penalty for Failure to Make Minimum Required Distributions

If any portion of an MRD is not made on a timely basis, a penalty equal to 50 percent of the unpaid amount is imposed.[33] The IRS may waive the penalty if it can be shown that the unpaid amount was due to reasonable error and steps are being taken to distribute the proper amount.[34]

Example: Aaron Hastings' MRD for the year was $25,000. Aaron failed to make the proper requests for distribution and, as a result, failed to distribute any amount from his retirement account. Aaron faces a $12,500 penalty (50 percent of $25,000) unless he can show that the lack of a distribution was due to a reasonable error.

Premature Distributions

A penalty tax is imposed in addition to the regular income tax on most distributions from qualified plans and IRAs if they are made before age 59½.[35] The penalty is equal to 10 percent of the taxable amount of the premature distribution.[36] The penalty is not imposed to the extent a distribution is a nontaxable return of basis or is rolled over into another IRA or qualified plan within the prescribed time periods.

Note: The penalty is increased to 25 percent for the first two years an employee participates in a SIMPLE IRA plan.[37]

Example 1: Sam Sneed, who is age thirty-five, withdraws $2,000 from his IRA to pay for damages to his car. None of the balance in his IRA has been previously taxed (no nondeductible contributions). Sam must include $2,000 in his taxable income in the year of distribution and pay an additional $200 penalty due to the early distribution.

Example 2: Assume that only $1,200 of the $2,000 is includible in Sam's income due to the recovery of previous nondeductible contributions. Sam would need to include $1,200 in his taxable income and would pay a penalty of $120.

There are a number of exceptions to the premature distribution penalty. The 10 percent penalty does not apply if the distribution is:

- made on or after the death of the owner,[38]

- made on account of the disability of the owner,[39]

- part of a series of substantially equal periodic payments over the life of the owner or the lives of the owner and a designated beneficiary.[40] For non-IRA type retirement accounts, this exception may be used only after the employee separates from service.[41] See further discussion below.

- used to pay medical expenses that exceed 7.5 percent of the taxpayer's adjusted gross income (without regard to whether the employee/owner itemizes deductions for that taxable year).[42]

- from a qualified plan and made to an employee following separation from service after reaching age fifty-five (does not apply to IRAs)

- from a qualified plan and paid to an alternate payee pursuant to a qualified domestic relations order (does not apply to IRAs)

- from an IRA and used to pay the health insurance premiums of an unemployed owner who has received unemployment compensation for at least twelve consecutive weeks in the year of the distribution or in the previous year (this exception does not apply to qualified plan distributions).[43]

- from an IRA and used to fund higher education expenses, which may include graduate school, for the taxpayer, spouse, children or grandchildren (this exception does not apply to qualified plan distributions).[44] Qualified higher education expenses include tuition, fees, books, supplies, required equipment and room and board.[45]

- from an IRA and used for a first-time home purchase, up to a $10,000 lifetime cap (this exception does not apply to qualified plan distributions).[46] In order to use this exception, a qualified first time homebuyer must use the distribution within 120 days to fund the costs of acquiring, constructing or reconstructing a residence, including any usual or reasonable settlement, financing or other closing costs.[47] An individual is a first time homebuyer if the individual, and, if married, his or her spouse had no present ownership interest in a principal residence during the two-year period ending on the date of acquisition of the principal residence.[48] The distribution may be used to fund the first time home purchase of the owner, the owner's spouse, or any child, grandchild or ancestor (including their spouses) of the owner.

Substantially Equal Periodic Payments

The premature distribution penalty exception for substantially equal periodic payments (SEPP) is very useful in situations where the taxpayer has a recurring annual need for funds prior to reaching age 59½. This situation is common in early retirements where the taxpayer is no longer working and virtually all of the taxpayer's wealth is tied up in retirement plan accounts.

To avoid the penalty, SEPPs must be made at least annually and must continue until *the later of*:

1. the date the individual turns age 59½, or

2. the close of the five-year period beginning with the date the initial payment was received.[49]

The amount of the SEPP cannot be altered before the later of the two above dates (except on account of death or disability). If payments are altered, all of the prior payments under the SEPP are retroactively taxed as if a SEPP did not exist. The tax is payable in the first year the modification is made. Interest will also be assessed beginning on the date the tax would have been paid had a SEPP not been in place and ending on the date the actual payment is made.[50]

SEPPs may be calculated using one of three methods:

Life Expectancy Method – The annual payment is determined in a manner similar to the MRD rules. The account balance as December 31 of the year prior to the distribution year is divided by a life expectancy factor using one of the following three tables:

1. Uniform Lifetime Table

2. Single Life Expectancy Table

3. Joint Life Expectancy Table, if there is a designated beneficiary

Since the account balance will change each year, the amount of the SEPP will vary from year to year. This is the only variation in the amount of the SEPP that is permitted. This method generally produces the smallest amount payable under a SEPP and offers the least amount of control since the investment performance of the retirement account will have a material impact on the future required distribution.

Fixed Amortization Method – The annual payment is determined by amortizing the account balance at the beginning of the SEPP over the life expectancy at a chosen interest rate. The owner's life expectancy or joint life expectancy of the owner and designated beneficiary is determined using one of the three tables listed in the life expectancy method. The interest rate factor must not exceed a "reasonable interest rate." Any interest rate that is not more than 120 percent of the federal mid-term rate for either of the two months immediately preceding the beginning of the SEPP is considered reasonable.[51] Once the amortized amount is determined, the SEPP is not recalculated. The same amount is distributed each period.

Fixed Annuitization Method – The annual payment is determined by dividing the account balance by an annuity factor using a mortality table and a reasonable interest rate, as defined above.[52] Like the fixed amortization method, the amount of the SEPP will not change from period to period.

For those taxpayers who start a SEPP and use either the fixed amortization or fixed annuitization methods, a one-time change is allowed to the life expectancy method, in any year after a SEPP begins.[53] Once the change is made to the life expectancy method, that SEPP may not be changed back to either of the other methods. No other modification to the SEPP is permitted.

There is some question as to whether the SEPP can incorporate a cost-of-living adjustment each year and not violate the SEPP. Revenue Ruling 2002-62 clearly states that, if a SEPP is modified prior to the time period at which a SEPP ends, "all payments in the series lose the shelter of the exemption, and the penalty applies, retroactively and with interest, to all pre-age 59½ distributions."

A *modification* occurs when there is (i) any addition to the account balance other than gains or losses, (ii) any nontaxable transfer of a portion of the account balance to another retirement plan, or (iii) a rollover by the taxpayer of the amount received, resulting in such amount not being taxable. Of course, a modification would also occur if the taxpayer took out more or less than the SEPP mandates. However, various letter rulings issued by the IRS (in years prior to the release of Revenue Ruling 2002-62) have allowed for cost of living adjustments and other modifications. Revenue Ruling 2002-62 does not specifically address modifications of this type.[54]

An important point to remember is that SEPPs apply to each retirement plan of the taxpayer, rather than the aggregate of all plans.[55] Therefore, if a taxpayer has a large IRA from which he would like to set up a SEPP, it may be better to divide the IRA into two or more IRAs before beginning the SEPP. Only one of the IRAs will pay the SEPP distributions. Thereafter, if additional funds are needed on an annual basis, one or more of the other IRAs can begin making SEPP distributions as well.

When determining how to set up a SEPP, it is best to work from the desired end result, backwards.

1. Determine how much is needed on an annual basis from the SEPP.

2. Perform calculations to determine how much of an account balance is needed to produce the desired level of distributions.

3. Separate the account into at least one SEPP account and one non-SEPP account.

When determining how to set up the SEPP, consider the following:

- The life expectancy method will generally produce smaller SEPP distributions and will not be known for the next year until the end of the current year.

- A higher reasonable interest rate will result in a larger payment under the annuitization and amortization methods.

- A smaller payment can be determined using a designated beneficiary and a joint life expectancy.

- The SEPP should be set up with only the amount of the account balance needed to support the desired distribution. Protect the

ability to have future SEPPs by dividing the account balance into more than one account.

———

Example: Harvey Wilson is 55 years old and recently retired. He would like to set up the largest SEPP possible using his $250,000 IRA. At the time the SEPP would begin, the reasonable interest rate is 4.50 percent and Harvey's single life expectancy is 29.6 years. Based on this information, the SEPP can be established using one of the following three methods:

a. Life expectancy method = $703.83 per month

b. Amortization method = $1,287.33 per month

c. Annuitization method = $1,277.42 per month

The amortization method provides the largest benefit to Harvey. If it is decided that Harvey needs something less than $1,287.33 per month, he may benefit from dividing his IRA account into two accounts. The account that will generate the SEPP will be large enough to meet his retirement need. For instance, if Harvey only needs $1,000 per month, he can set up two IRAs, one with $194,200 and the other with $55,800. The larger account will generate a $1,000 monthly distribution using the amortization method.

———

Lump Sum Distributions

Lump sum distributions (LSDs) are generally treated as taxable income in the year the distribution is received. Since LSDs may be rather large, care must be taken when making such an election so that the taxpayer is not driven into the highest income tax bracket unnecessarily. LSDs can be rolled over into an eligible retirement plan with a continuation of the tax deferral. In addition, certain LSDs from qualified plans may be eligible for special tax treatment.

The LSD is a distribution, or series of distributions, of a participant's entire balance in a qualified plan paid out in a single tax year. The taxable amount of the LSD is the total value of the distribution less any after-tax contributions and other items that make up the participant's cost basis.

For individuals who were age fifty or older before January 1, 1986 (born prior to 1936), LSDs may be taxed under a capital gain method and ten-year averaging provision. Since most individuals currently retiring were born after 1936, this benefit is rarely used.

The capital gain treatment allows a person born before 1936 and who participated in a qualifying plan prior to 1974 to treat a portion of an LSD as long-term capital gain. The portion treated as capital gain is determined by the number of months of participation in the qualifying plan prior to 1974 over the total months of participation times the LSD.

For the remaining portion, or the ordinary income portion of the LSD, an individual born prior to 1936 may be able to elect ten-year averaging, which essentially taxes the distribution based on 1986 tax rates. Generally, the higher the distribution amount, the less likely the taxpayer is to benefit from this special treatment. Since we are so far past the 1986 date, there are few taxpayers who would benefit from this provision.

For lump sum distributions received prior to January 1, 2000, a special one-time five-year averaging provision was available. This election became unavailable for years beginning after 1999.

The LSD may be an appropriate retirement plan distribution in situations where the taxpayer has a net operating loss or other credits or carryovers which may otherwise expire unutilized.

Rollovers

Tax-free rollovers of distributions from qualified plans, IRA and other retirement plans allow participants to continue to receive the tax deferred benefits of these plans. An "eligible rollover distribution" may be rolled over, in whole or in part, to an "eligible retirement plan."

The rollover must occur within sixty days after the funds are received.[56] The sixty-day period begins on the day after the distribution is received. If the sixtieth day falls on a weekend or legal holiday, the next business day will be considered the last day for the rollover to occur.[57]

An *eligible retirement plan* generally includes any of the following:

1. a traditional IRA,

2. a qualified pension, profit sharing or stock bonus plan,

3. an eligible Section 457 governmental plan (if certain separate accounting requirements are met), and

4. a Section 403(b) plan.[58]

An eligible rollover distribution is any distribution to a participant of all or part of his or her account balance in a qualified plan that is not:

1. part of a series of substantially equal periodic payments made at least annually over (a) the life or life expectancy of the participant or the joint life expectancies of the participant and designated beneficiary or (b) a specified period of ten years or more – the test is applied at the beginning of the payout period,

2. a minimum required distribution

3. the nontaxable portion of a distribution unless made to a traditional IRA or a qualified plan and certain requirements are met,

4. the return of excess 401(k) annual additions of elective deferrals that are returned due to Code Section 415 limitations,

5. corrective distributions of excess contributions, deferrals or aggregate contributions along with the income allocable to the corrective distributions under a 401(k) plan,

6. distributions to a beneficiary other than a surviving spouse or a current or former spouse under a qualified domestic relations order,

7. hardship distributions, or

8. deemed distributions of plan loans.[59]

An eligible rollover distribution that is paid directly to the participant is generally subject to a 20 percent withholding of federal taxes.[60] If the distribution is rolled over directly to the eligible retirement plan, no withholding is required. A direct rollover may be in the form of a trustee-to-trustee transfer accomplished through a wire transfer or a check made payable to the trustee.[61]

Withholding of more than 20 percent may be permitted by the plan administrator. State income tax withholding may also be required.

If the participant takes an eligible rollover distribution and does not directly roll the distribution over into an eligible retirement plan, the participant may find that he or she does not have sufficient funds to complete the rollover within the sixty-day period.

Example: Joanne Risler thought that it would be a smart idea to use her IRA to fund the purchase of a new car. She knew she would be getting a $30,000 bonus within the next two months, so she felt that she could repay the $30,000 IRA distribution by rolling the amount over into a new IRA within the sixty-day period. She received a check for $24,000 which she used to purchase the car. Income tax of 20 percent, or $6,000 was properly withheld by the trustee. When she received her $30,000 bonus, her net paycheck was only $20,000. She had to come up with another $10,000 from other sources in order to complete the full rollover. If she failed to redeposit the $10,000 that she was short, that amount would be taxable in the year of distribution and could be subject to a premature distribution penalty if Joanne is under age 59½.

The sixty-day rollover period may be waived when the taxpayer is affected by a casualty, disaster or other event beyond his or her reasonable control and when not waiving the sixty-day rule would be "against equity or good conscience."[62] Automatic waivers of the sixty-day rule are granted for failed rollovers caused by errors made by financial institutions.

Rollovers from qualified plans do not need to be converted to cash prior to completing the rollover. Stock, bonds, mutual fund shares or other noncash property may be rolled over without being sold.[63]

There are several good reasons for not rolling over a distribution from a qualified plan to an IRA:

1. Taxpayers may borrow from qualified plans (if the plan contains a loan provision), but not IRAs.

2. Life insurance can be purchased within a qualified plan, but not an IRA.

3. If the employee separates from service after age 55, distributions may be taken from a qualified plan and not be subject to a penalty for early withdrawal. An IRA owner must wait until age 59½ unless some other exception from the penalty is met.

4. Qualified retirement plans have broader federal creditor protection in the case of malpractice, bankruptcy, divorce, business, or creditor problems.

Only one rollover from an IRA may be made by an individual in any 365-day period.[64] The 365-day period begins on the date the first IRA withdrawal is made. Trustee-to-trustee transfers are excluded from the one-year rule.[65] The essence of this rule is to avoid having individuals take short-term loans from IRAs only to roll over the balance to another plan.

Example: Sarah Parker withdraws $10,000 from her IRA at ABC Bank on March 1. On April 29, she completes the rollover of $10,000 by depositing this amount into another IRA in her name at First National Bank. On July 3, she rolls over a qualified plan balance from her former employer into a rollover IRA at Finest Investments. Later that month, on July 29, Sarah directly transfers her rollover IRA balance from Finest Investments to Prudent Bank in a trustee-to-trustee transfer. On February 3 of the following year, Sarah withdraws $10,000 from her IRA at First National Bank. She completes this rollover by redepositing this amount into another IRA at Prudent Bank on February 20. All of the rollovers are permitted except for the one occurring on February 3. Therefore, the $10,000 withdrawal will be taxable in the year of distribution and should be withdrawn from the IRA or else the contribution will violate the allowable annual contribution limit.

The one rollover in a 365-day period rule for 2014 applies to each IRA separately. So an individual with two IRAs would be able to rollover both IRAs within a 365-day period at any point in time. However, beginning in 2015, the IRS has announced that only one rollover will be permitted in the 365-day period regardless of the number of IRAs that are owned.[66] This policy change does not impact the following transactions, which can be performed an unlimited number of times within a year:

1. Direct (trustee-to-trustee) transfers where the participant never has control of the funds[67]

2. Rollovers from employer plans to IRAs

3. Rollovers from IRAs to employer plans

4. Roth conversions

A rollover from a qualified plan into an IRA will preserve the ability to roll over the funds back into a qualified plan in the future. The future rollover into a qualified plan preserves the benefits listed above.

Example: Sally Rhodes receives a rollover distribution of $250,000 from her 401(k) plan at a former employer. She would like to retire at fifty-five, at which time she would need the funds from her retirement plans. Since she does not have a new job to which she can roll the qualified plan balance directly into a new qualified plan, she establishes an IRA to accept the rollover. When she starts her new job, she can roll over the amount invested in the IRA into her new employer's qualified plan and protect her ability to begin receiving payments at age fifty-five without penalty.

Distributions of Employer Securities

Large publicly traded corporations often use company stock to fund matching contributions to their employees' retirement plans. Employees are also often given the opportunity to buy company stock as one of their investment options. As a result participants may have a large position in the stock of their employer within their qualified plan.

Although it may go against prudent asset allocation judgment, the accumulation of company stock is given preferential treatment to employees when the stock is received as part of a lump sum distribution (LSD). Employees are not taxed on the net unrealized appreciation (NUA) of employer securities received as part of a LSD.[68] NUA is the excess of the fair market value of the employer securities received on the distribution date over the aggregate cost or other basis of such securities to the plan. Only the basis of the shares is included in the employee's gross income.

When the employer stock is sold after the distribution, the gain is treated as long-term capital gain subject to the maximum capital gains tax rate to the extent attributable to NUA not taxed at the time of receipt. Any additional gain is treated as long or short-term based on how long the stock was held after the distribution.[69]

If the employer securities are sold within the plan before the LSD occurs, the favorable tax treatment for the NUA is lost. Likewise, if the entire LSD, including the employer securities is rolled over into an IRA or other retirement plan, the opportunity to receive the special tax treatment is lost.

The 10 percent penalty for premature distributions will apply if the LSD is received before age 59½ and the employer securities are not rolled over. However, the tax and the penalty are determined only on the basis of the employer securities, not the fair market value.

Example: Rich Davidson leaves his job when he is age forty-five and receives an LSD from his employer's 401(k) plan. The distribution is made up of $300,000 of cash and $150,000 of employer securities. The cost basis of the distributed stock is $60,000. The NUA is $90,000. Rich rolls over the $300,000 cash portion of the LSD into an IRA and escapes taxation on that amount. He decides to keep the stock and pay the tax and 10 percent penalty on the $60,000 of basis. When Rich sells the stock, the first $90,000 of gain will be taxed as long-term capital gain. Any additional gains will be treated as long or short-term based upon his holding period from the date of distribution.

If a taxpayer receives employer securities that do not have NUA, but actually have built in losses or are even worthless, special rules may apply.

Worthless securities received in a LSD in which the taxpayer has basis (i.e. purchased with funds from non-deductible contributions) may be claimed as an ordinary loss in the year of distribution as a miscellaneous itemized deduction subject to the 2 percent floor.[70]

If the employee receives securities that have some fair market value but are worth less than the employee's nondeductible contributions, the loss may be recognized only if the securities are sold or exchanged.[71] The loss will be either long or short-term based upon the holding period beginning on the date of distribution.[72]

Roth IRAs

Contributions and Conversions

Roth IRAs are unlike any other type of retirement plan. As such, this section of the chapter is devoted solely to the special rules that cover this type of IRA. All rules applicable to traditional IRAs also apply to Roth IRAs unless the Internal Revenue Code provides otherwise – and there are a lot of them.

A Roth IRA is an IRA that is designated as a Roth IRA at the time it is established.[73] Unlike all other retirement plans, the contributions to a Roth IRA are not deductible,[74] but any "qualified distributions" are tax-free.

Contributions to a Roth IRA cannot exceed, on an annual basis, the excess of the maximum contribution permitted to an IRA over the aggregate amounts contributed to all other IRAs.[75] Therefore, the maximum amount that may be contributed to a Roth IRA is the regular IRA limit for the year, including catch-up contributions, reduced by any deductible or nondeductible contributions to any traditional IRAs. Unlike a traditional IRA, contributions to a Roth IRA may be made after reaching age 70½.[76]

The maximum contribution amount to a Roth IRA is phased out for individual filers with 2014 adjusted gross income (AGI) between $114,000 and $129,000 and for joint filers with 2014 AGI between $181,000 and $191,000. The AGI phase-out range for married couples filing separately is between $0 and $10,000.[77] The married filing separately limitations do not apply if the couple lived apart for the entire taxable year.[78]

For the purpose of the above limits, a taxpayer's AGI is determined with regard to the includable amount of Social Security benefits and passive loss limitations, but without regard to the exclusions for education savings bonds, adoption expenses, foreign housing or earned income. The deduction for IRA contributions is also not counted for this purpose.[79]

Prior to 2010, taxpayers with modified AGI of less than $100,000 in a given year were allowed to convert a non-Roth IRA balance into a Roth IRA provided it is a qualified rollover contribution. Beginning in 2010, which had a special, on-time two-year inclusion period for 2011 and 2012, the AGI limitations were eliminated. This allows any taxpayer to convert an eligible retirement plan to a Roth IRA.[80]

The regulations covering Roth conversions defines a qualified rollover contribution is one of the following:

1. a distribution from a traditional IRA rolled over to a Roth IRA within sixty days of the distribution,

2. a trustee-to-trustee transfer from a traditional IRA to a Roth IRA, and

3. a transfer of the amount in a traditional IRA to a Roth IRA maintained by the same trustee.[81]

Beginning after 2007 qualified rollover contributions to a Roth IRA were permitted from other types of retirement plans, including 401(k), 403(b) and 457 plans.[82]

Any amount that is converted from an eligible retirement plan to a Roth IRA must be included in the taxpayer's gross income in the year of the distribution from the traditional IRA.[83] Note that the 10 percent penalty for premature distributions does not apply to converted traditional IRA distributions.[84]

A taxpayer who converts all or part of an eligible retirement plan into a Roth IRA has a one-time opportunity to recharacterize (undo) the conversion. Provided the recharacterization is done by the due date of the taxpayer's return, including extensions, for the year of the conversion, the converted amount plus any earnings allocable to the converted amount may be sent back to the an eligible retirement plan in a trustee-to-trustee transfer.[85]

A recharacterization may be considered when the value of the investments substantially drop from the date of the conversion. Since the converted amount is reported in the taxpayer's income, a substantial decline in value diminishes the benefit of the conversion. It may be prudent to recharacterize the earlier conversion and reconvert the IRA balance in the current or later year at a reduced tax impact.

A taxpayer who converts an eligible retirement plan to a Roth IRA and then recharacterizes the conversion may not reconvert the eligible retirement plan balance until the later of:

1. the beginning of the tax year following the tax year the amount was converted to a Roth IRA, or

2. the end of the thirty-day period beginning on the day the original conversion is recharacterized.[86]

Distributions

Qualified distributions from a Roth IRA are not included in income; that is, they are entirely tax-free.[87] Qualified distributions are distributions that occur after the five-taxable-year nonexclusion period and are:

1. made on or after the date on which the individual reaches age 59½,[88]

2. made to a beneficiary on or after the death of the account owner,[89]

3. attributable to the account owner's disability,[90] or

4. for a "qualified special purpose" distribution (i.e. first-time homebuyer expenses up to $10,000).[91]

The Roth IRA nonexclusion period is defined as the five-taxable-year period beginning with the first taxable year for which a taxpayer made a contribution of any kind to a Roth IRA.[92]

Example: Chris Mattheson opened a Roth IRA on July 1, 2009 with a $2,000 contribution. He converted a traditional IRA balance worth over $150,000 into the Roth IRA on December 15, 2011. Chris may not make any qualifying distributions from his Roth IRAs until after 2013, the fifth taxable year following the first Roth IRA contribution.

If the distribution from a Roth IRA is not a qualifying distribution (for whatever reason), the distribution is includible in the taxpayer's income to the extent attributable to earnings. For nonqualifying distributions, all Roth IRAs are treated as a single Roth IRA and distributions are deemed to be made in the following order:

1. amounts contributed by the taxpayer, until all contributory assets are fully recovered,

2. amounts converted to a Roth IRA, chronologically by tax year of conversion, until all conversion assets are fully recovered, and

3. total earnings.[93]

Distributions attributable to amounts contributed by the taxpayer are tax-free and penalty-free regardless of whether they would otherwise be a qualifying distribution.

Example 1: Bud Wisler withdrew $5,000 from his Roth IRA in 2014. He has contributed $2,000 each year since 2009 and is over age 59½. Since he is receiving a return of contributions to the Roth IRA, the distribution will not be included in income.

Example 2: Bud's sister, Sharon heard what Bud had done and withdrew the same amount. However, she had contributed only $2,000 for each of the last two years and is under age 59½. She will recover her $4,000 of contributions as nontaxable and be taxed on the $1,000 that came from the earnings on her Roth IRA. In addition, the $1,000 will be subject to a 10 percent penalty as a premature distribution.

The premature distribution penalty will apply to the taxable portion of any nonqualified distributions before age 59½. In addition, converted amounts that are withdrawn within five years of the conversion are subject to the penalty unless one of the exceptions from the penalty under Code Section 72(t) applies to the converted amount as well as any earnings.[94]

Example: Jimmy Jones converted a $100,000 IRA to a Roth IRA two years ago. He withdraws $40,000 when he is fifty-five years old. He does not qualify for any exceptions to the 72(t) penalty for premature distributions. The $40,000 is not taxable income but is subject to the 10 percent premature distribution penalty.

Roth IRAs are not subject to the lifetime minimum distribution requirements.[95] Thus, distributions from a Roth IRA are not required during the lifetime of the account owner.

If the Roth IRA passes to the spouse upon the death of the owner, the surviving spouse may treat the Roth IRA as his or her own (by rollover or otherwise) and thereby defer the application of the lifetime mandatory distribution rules until death. If the successor to the Roth IRA is not a designated beneficiary or a surviving spouse, the balance of the Roth IRA must be distributed within five years of the year of the owner's death.[96] However, if the owner has named a designated beneficiary, the balance of the Roth IRA may be distributed, beginning within one year of the death of the account owner, over the lifetime or a period not in excess of the life expectancy of the designated beneficiary.[97]

Beneficiaries of Roth IRAs may benefit from deferring the distributions by taking them out over their life expectancy. This allows for the Roth IRA balance to continue growing on a tax-free basis.

FREQUENTLY ASKED QUESTIONS

Question – When are contributions to retirement plans required to be funded?

Answer – The funding deadline for IRAs (including Roth IRAs) is April 15 of the year following the year for which the contribution is intended. Qualified plan funding (other than salary deferrals which must be deposited within thirty days by the employer) must be completed by the extended due date of the tax return on which the deduction will be claimed, generally October 15.

Question – Are amounts rolled over or converted from a traditional IRA to a Roth IRA subject to a 10 percent penalty tax if the owner is less than 59½ years of age at the time of the rollover?

Answer – Although a conversion is not subject to the 10 percent early withdrawal penalty when the conversion occurs, it may be subject to the penalty if withdrawals from the Roth IRA occur within five years of the conversion and the reason for the withdrawal does not qualify as one of the exceptions to the Section 72(t) 10 percent penalty tax.

If a portion of the distribution is categorized as a taxable conversion asset under the ordering rules and the distribution occurs within five taxable years of the taxable year of the conversion, the portion of the distribution attributable to amounts that were includable in income due to the conversion is subject to the 10 percent penalty tax. If the distribution occurs after the five-year period, the penalty tax does not apply.

Question – Who benefits from an eligible retirement plan to Roth IRA conversion?

Answer – Roth IRAs have their greatest attraction to those people who do not need to withdraw any funds from their retirement plans during life, especially those individuals who expect to live well beyond the average life expectancy due to their sex, genetic heritage and/or health. A retirement plan participant approaching age 70½ is generally required to take distributions that will substantially diminish, if not eliminate, the account over a long life span.

Converting to a Roth IRA just before death should be considered when benefits will otherwise have to be paid out just after death since such conversion may permit the longer post-death deferral of distributions.

For estate planning purposes, if retirement plan must be used to fund the credit shelter trust, part of the advantage of escaping estate taxes is mitigated by the necessity of the trust to pay income taxes out of its principal; in many cases the tax rate on such taxable income will be higher for the trust than for any of the beneficiaries. While this can be corrected by a withdrawal from the retirement plan of a sufficient amount (grossed-up by the income tax), this requires the loss of continued deferral inside the retirement plan. With the Roth IRA conversion, the income taxes are removed from the estate but the deferral of taxes continues and the credit shelter pays no income taxes on the receipt of distributions from the Roth IRA.

Question – Can the owner of a Roth IRA change his designated beneficiary after reaching the age of 70½?

Answer – The Roth IRA participant is permitted to change his "designated beneficiary" after age 70½, and have that change be effective for determining minimum required distributions after his death. The new designated beneficiary's life expectancy at the date of the owner's death will be used for determining the amount of the required distributions.

Figure 30.1

IMPACT OF RETIREMENT PLAN BENEFICIARY DESIGNATIONS		
Designated Beneficiary	**Owner Dies Before RBD**	**Owner Dies After RBD**

Spouse	1. MRDs must begin at the latest of:
	  a. Year following owner's death
	  b. Year owner would have reached age 70½
	  c. End of the fifth year after the owner's death, if the plan permits and the surviving spouse elects
	2. MRDs made over the spouse's life expectancy, unless five-year rule is used.
	3. Spousal rollover defers MRDs until surviving spouse reaches age 70½.
		1. Distributions can be made over the surviving spouse's single life expectancy, recalculated each year or the owner's life expectancy as of the year of death, reduced by one each year.
		2. Spousal rollover defers MRDs until surviving spouse reaches age 70½.

Nonspouse Individual	MRDs must be made over the single life expectancy of the designated beneficiary beginning in the year following the year of death. If this first distribution is not made, the entire account must be distributed by the end of the fifth year following death.	MRDs must be made over the longer of the single life expectancy of the designated beneficiary or the owner's remaining life expectancy beginning in the year following the year of death. Life expectancies are reduced by one each year.
Trust	MRDs are determined using the life expectancy of the oldest trust beneficiary. Distributions must begin in the year following the year of death if the trust qualifies as a designated beneficiary. If the trust does not qualify as a designated beneficiary, the entire account must be distributed by the end of the fifth year following the owner's death. Spouse may rollover the account balance and defer MRDs if the spouse is the sole trust beneficiary.	MRDs must be made over the longer of the single life expectancy of the oldest trust beneficiary or the owner's remaining life expectancy beginning in the year following the year of death if the trust qualifies as a designated beneficiary. If the trust does not qualify as a designated beneficiary, MRDs must be made over the owner's life expectancy, reduced by one each year. Spouse may rollover the account balance and defer MRDs if the spouse is the sole trust beneficiary.
No Designated Beneficiary (Estate or Charity)	Distribution of the entire account balance must be made by the end of the fifth year following in the owner's death. Spouse may rollover the account balance and defer MRDs if the spouse is the sole and defer MRDs if the spouse is the sole beneficiary of the estate.	MRDs must be made over the owner's life expectancy, reduced by one each year. Spouse may rollover the account balance and defer MRDs if the spouse is the sole beneficiary of the estate.

CHAPTER ENDNOTES

1. I.R.C. §§72 and 408(d)(1).
2. I.R.C. §§72(e) and 408(d).
3. I.R.C. §§402(a) and 403(a)(1).
4. I.R.C. §72(e).
5. Treas. Reg. §1.72-9.
6. 1988-2 CB 450.
7. I.R.C. §72(b)(1).
8. Treas. Reg. §1.72-4(a)(2).

9. Treas. Reg. §1.72-4(d)(2). Note, however, that if the annuity starting date is after December 31, 1986, the excludable amount is limited to the investment in the contract. Once that amount is recovered, all future annuity payments are fully subject to ordinary income tax. I.R.C. §72(b)(2).
10. I.R.C. §72(c)(2).
11. Annuity tax calculations can be performed on Steve Leimberg's Financial Analyzer Software (Leimberg.com or (610) 924-0515).
12. MRD computations can be performed on Steve Leimberg's MRD Calculator (Leimberg.com or (610) 924-0515).
13. I.R.C. §408A(c)(5).

14. I.R.C. §401(a)(9)(A).

15. I.R.C. §401(a)(9)(C).

16. Treas. Reg. §1.401(a)(9)-2.

17. Treas. Reg. §1.401(a)(9)-5, Q&A-2.

18. Treas. Reg. §1.401(a)(9)-5, Q&A-3.

19. I.R.C. §401(a)(9)(A).

20. Treas. Reg. §1.401(a)(9)-5, Q&A-4.

21. The Joint and Last Survivor Table can be found in Treas. Reg. §1.401(a)(9)-9.

22. Treas. Reg. §1.401(a)(9)-8, Q&A-1.

23. I.R.C. §408(d)(8)(A).

24. Treas. Reg. §1.401(a)(9)-4, Q&A-3 and 5.

25. Treas. Reg. §1.401(a)(9)-4, Q&A-3.

26. Treas. Reg. §1.401(a)(9)-8, Q&A-2.

27. I.R.C. §401(a)(9)(B).

28. The Single Life Table can be found in Treas. Reg. §1.401(a)(9)-9.

29. I.R.C. §401(a)(9)(B)(ii).

30. See I.R.C. §402(c)(11).

31. Treas. Reg. §1.401(a)(9)-3, Q&A-3(b).

32. Treas. Reg. §1.401(a)(9)-3, Q&A-5.

33. I.R.C. §4974.

34. Treas. Reg. §54.4974-2, Q&A-7.

35. I.R.C. §72(t)(2)(A)(i).

36. I.R.C. §72(t)(1).

37. I.R.C. §72(t)(6).

38. I.R.C. §72(t)(2)(A)(ii).

39. I.R.C. §72(t)(2)(A)(iii).

40. I.R.C. §72(t)(2)(A)(iv).

41. I.R.C. §72(t)(3)(B).

42. I.R.C. §72(t)(2)(B).

43. I.R.C. §72(t)(2)(D).

44. I.R.C. §§72(t)(2)(E), 72(t)(7)(A).

45. I.R.C. §529(e)(3).

46. I.R.C. §72(t)(2)(F).

47. I.R.C. §72(t)(8)(C).

48. I.R.C. §72(t)(8)(D)(i) A longer period is provided in the event the individual had owned a principal residence outside the United States or was a member of the Armed Forces.

49. I.R.C. §72(t)(4).

50. I.R.C. §72(t)(4)(A)(ii)(II).

51. Rev. Rul. 2002-62, 2002-42 IRB 710.

52. Rev. Rul. 2002-62, 2002-42 IRB 710. The mortality table appears in Appendix B of the Revenue Ruling.

53. Rev. Rul. 2002-62, 2002-42 IRB 710.

54. The IRS interprets Revenue Ruling 2002-62 to permit a one-time modification in the method used. See "Retirement Plans FAQs Regarding Substantially Equal Periodic Payments," Question 8, available at: http://www.irs.gov/Retirement-Plans/Retirement-Plans-FAQs-regarding-Substantially-Equal-Periodic-Payments.

55. Let. Rul. 9050030.

56. I.R.C. §402(c)(3).

57. I.R.C. §7503.

58. I.R.C. §402(c)(8)(B).

59. I.R.C. §402(c)(4).

60. I.R.C. §3405(c).

61. Treas. Reg. §1.401(a)(31)-1, Q-3.

62. I.R.C. §402(c)(3)(B).

63. I.R.C. §402(c).

64. I.R.C. §408(d)(3)(B).

65. Rev. Rul. 78-406, 1978-2 CB 157.

66. Announcement 2014-15 referencing the decision in *Bobrow v. Comm'r.*, T.C. Memo. 2014-21.

67. Rev. Rul. 78-406, 1978-2 CB 157.

68. I.R.C. §402(e)(4)(B).

69. Treas. Reg. §1.402(a)-1(b)(1)(i)(b).

70. Rev. Rul. 72-328, 1972-2 CB 224.

71. Rev. Rul. 72-15, 1972-1 CB 114.

72. Let. Rul. 8724049.

73. I.R.C. §§408A(b), 7701(a)(37).

74. I.R.C. §408A(c)(1).

75. I.R.C. §408A(c)(2).

76. I.R.C. §408A(c)(4).

77. Treas. Reg. §1.408A-3, Q&A-3(b).

78. I.R.C. §408A(c)(3)(C).

79. I.R.C. §408A(c)(3)(B)(i).

80. I.R.C. §408(d)(3)(C).

81. Treas. Reg. §1.408A-4, Q&A-1.

82. I.R.C. §408A(e).

83. I.R.C. §408A(d)(3)(A)(i).

84. I.R.C. §408A(d)(3)(A)(ii).

85. I.R.C. §408A(d)(6) and (7). As long as the tax return is timely filed, the taxpayer has until October 15 to recharacterize a conversion regardless of whether extensions were actually filed (Reg. §301.9100-2(b)).

86. Treas. Reg. §1.408A-5, Q&A-9(a)(1).

87. I.R.C. §408A(d)(1).

88. I.R.C. §408A(d)(2)(A)(i).

89. I.R.C. §408A(d)(2)(A)(ii).

90. I.R.C. §408A(d)(2)(A)(iii).

91. I.R.C. §408A(d)(2)(A)(iv).

92. I.R.C. §408A(d)(2)(B)

93. I.R.C. §408A(d)(4)(B).

94. I.R.C. §408A(d)(3)(F).

95. I.R.C. §408A(c)(5)(A).

96. I.R.C. §401(a)(9)(B)(ii).

97. I.R.C. §401(a)(9)(B)(iii).

INCOME TAX ISSUES IN WEALTH TRANSFER PLANNING

CHAPTER 31

INTRODUCTION

Individuals who have accumulated resources beyond what they believe they may need for the rest of their lives will often transfer assets to other family members during their lifetime, rather than waiting until an ultimate bequest at death. The most common beneficiaries of such lifetime transferals are the donor's children and grandchildren.

Lifetime gifts generally do not generate income tax consequences in themselves. In addition, with the current level of the gift tax annual exclusion, plus the lifetime transfer tax (gift and estate) exclusions, most donors do not have to deal with transfer taxes upon making such gifts.

OUTRIGHT GIFTS

The simplest way to transfer accumulated resources to a family member—or anyone else—is to provide them with an outright gift. Such transfers are immediate, irrevocable, and typically have no income tax consequences for the transferor or recipient. However, there are several factors that should be considered before a sizable outright gift is made.

Gift Tax Exclusion

Each taxpayer is permitted to give up to $14,000 per year (in 2014) to any other person (who is not a spouse), regardless of the relationship between the taxpayer and the gift recipient.[1] This exclusion adjusts annually for inflation, and applies to each spouse individually. For instance, a married couple could give up to $28,000 per year to each of their children with no income or gift tax consequences. If the anticipated planning window is long enough (and the intended recipients are numerous enough), this exclusion can provide significant flexibility to the planner dealing with long-term wealth transfer issues.

However, even gifts that fall under the annual gift tax exclusion are not completely free of tax consequences. Taxpayers must also consider the lifetime gift tax exclusion, which is tied to the estate tax exclusion. Essentially, any gifts given away during one's lifetime count cumulatively against the estate tax exclusion (currently $5,120,000). This can complicate estate planning efforts, particularly if significant gifts were made prior to the beginning of the estate planning process.

Example: Mr. and Mrs. Clean own a number of successful car wash operations, and have three children and ten grandchildren. Each year for the past ten years, they have given $10,000 to each child and grandchild ($5,000 from Mr. Clean, and $5,000 from Mrs. Clean). While these amounts have been small enough that they have not incurred any gift tax liability, the Cleans have used up $1,400,000 of their estate tax exclusion and are leaving their advisor a $3,720,000 estate tax exclusion to work with. Should they continue to give outrights gifts at this rate, the available exclusion will shrink even further.

Additionally, taxpayers and their advisors should be aware that outright gifts can jeopardize Medicaid eligibility, which can be an important consideration when facing chronic medical issues at the end of life.

Gift Basis

If the property transferred is cash, the donee will generally have no income tax consequences upon receiving a gift. However, the recipient of transferred property will more often than might be expected be faced with future income tax consequences. Quite simply, such income tax consequences are the result of the donor gifting assets which have appreciated since acquisition, or are anticipated to grow in value in a reasonably short period of time. These deferred income taxes are the result of the "basis rules," as applied to gifts.

Generally, when property is received as a gift, the donee inherits the donor's basis in the property for purposes of computing the gain upon a subsequent sale of the property. However, for purposes of computing a loss on the sale of the property, the donee's basis is the lower of the donor's basis or the fair market value at the time of the gift. The result is to reduce the amount of tax loss recognizable upon a subsequent sale of a gift.

Example: Gift of Appreciated Securities. Kris Miller received a gift from his grandparents of marketable stocks. The cost basis of the securities to his grandparents was $25,000. If Kris were to sell the stocks for $35,000 he would recognize a taxable gain of $10,000, using his grandparents' basis of $25,000 as his basis. If Kris were to sell the stocks for $19,000, the amount of loss he would recognize would depend upon the fair market value of the property at the time he received the gift.

If the fair market value at the time of the gift was $30,000, Kris would compute the loss using his grandparents' basis of $25,000, resulting in a $6,000 loss ($25,000 basis at time of gift – $19,000 sale price).

If the fair market value at the time of the gift was $22,000, Kris' tax loss on the sale of the securities would only be $3,000 ($22,000 fair market value at the time of the gift – $19,000 sale price).

With a carryover of basis from donor to donee upon gifts of appreciated property, the total gain in the gifted property at the time of the gift is shifted to a new taxpayer. The ultimate income tax consequences will consequently depend upon the relative marginal tax bracket of the donor and the donee. For example, if a retired parent with a marginal tax bracket of 15 percent gifts property to an adult, working child whose marginal tax bracket is 39.6 percent, the long term capital gain tax would increase from 0 percent to 20 percent. On the other hand, if the gift is made from a 39.6 percent high income individual to a twenty-four-year-old child (above the age of any possible application of the "Kiddie Tax") who is a full time graduate school student with no source of income, the gain on the sale would potentially avoid any income taxes.

Even with the donee basis rules generally result in income tax savings under limited circumstances, there are several tax planning techniques that can are available to minimize the overall income tax consequences to the family. This chapter discusses some of the most relevant options.

JOINT OWNERSHIP UPON PURCHASE

Although perhaps the most logical planning concept, establishing a vehicle for the joint ownership of property at the time it is purchased is often the most difficult to structure and implement. Depending on the type of property, joint ownership may be complicated by restrictions on title requirements. Also, if the property carries potential liability (such as real property or a business), joint ownership may expose the intended recipient to that liability, and require special insurance planning considerations.

Example: John Stone would like to purchase an investment property of undeveloped land. His ultimate goal is to transfer either the property or the proceeds from its sale, to his children (all minors). John does not want to wait until his death before the children could enjoy the proceeds and earning thereon, from the sale of the land at what John believes will be a significant appreciation in several years due to the location of the property. John does not need the proceeds from the ultimate sale to maintain his lifestyle, or that of his wife, for the balance of their lives.

Accordingly, with the advice of counsel, John establishes a limited liability company (LLC) in which he is a minor owner, but managing member. A trust for the children owns the majority of the (LLC). Income and losses are shared in proportion to ownership in the venture; however, John is entitled to a reasonable management fee (guaranteed payment) for his services. The financing of the purchase of the property will of course be complicated, but can be accomplished with third party debt, loans from John and contributed capital, primarily from John.

Upon the ultimate, profitable sale of the property, the majority of the proceeds will be distributed to the trust for the children. The gain from the sale may be taxed at a lower bracket, depending on the timing and the implications of the Kiddie Tax. Of greater value to John is the shift of the proceeds to the next generation, as cash, with possible transfer tax consequences.

EMPLOYING FAMILY MEMBERS

If significant assets are being generated by a family, business, one method transferring the benefits of that business is through the employment of family members. This income tax planning technique provides a perfect example of what may be the good, the bad and the ugly of tax planning.

The Good is the potential shift of income from higher to lower bracket individuals, or at least the transfer of funds from one generation to the next with minimal if any transfer tax consequences. The technique also provides the opportunity for including the employed family members under company employee benefit plans, such as pensions or 401(k) plans and group health or life insurance programs.

The Bad is the imposition of employment taxes, such as FICA and Medicare taxes (both employer and employee shares), and the potential inclusion in Workers Compensation insurance premiums. These costs are flat rate expenses. Consequently, the net result of this income tax planning concept requires some level of number crunching to see if it is worth it.

The Ugly comes from two directions. The first issue is that generally, the IRS looks closely at the "value" provided by employed family members. Are such employees receiving fair or excessive compensation for the services performed? Are they working

at all? If an IRS agent is uncomfortable with what he or she sees in the analysis of the family member's contribution compared to the compensation received, the agent is more likely to look more closely at other areas of the employer's tax records where abuse often occurs, such as meal and entertainment expenses.

The other aspect of the "ugly" is the effect of the family member's level of services and compensation on other employees, other family members, and even the employed family member himself. If the employed family member is not carrying his weight, other employees may become resentful. Other family members may ask "why aren't I getting such a deal?" And the employed family member may become complacent, losing any drive or incentive to create his own carrier. Additionally, if the business is one that provides the services of a specially licensed professional (such as a doctor or lawyer), state law may place restrictions on who can work at or manage the business.

All of this being said, under the right circumstances, and with proper monitoring and controls, employing family members can be extremely effective to shift family wealth to kindred in lower tax brackets. This approach can be used anywhere from weekend and summer jobs for children, to fulltime employment for retired parents to supplement their income (in lower brackets), and anywhere in between. Other examples would include full time work for adult children with disabilities or jobs to supplement income of siblings (or their spouses) to provide them with additional income.

In any event, what is clear is that the shifting of income by hiring family members is an excellent example of the importance of keeping tax planning in its proper place as secondary to the taxpayers personal and financial goals.

SECTION 529 PLANS (QUALIFIED TUITION PROGRAMS)

Parents (and grandparents) have been a major source of funding post-high school education (college, graduate school, trade schools) of the children for generations. These costs were generally funded with after-tax dollars of the parents. Then, in 1996, Code section 529, Qualified Tuition Programs, became law, enabling taxpayers to set aside after tax dollars to grow on what is now a tax free basis if the funds are used for qualified higher education expenses. The example below uses a simple fact pattern to explain how the rules of a 529 plan work.

Example: Justin Cross has been planning to fund the college education of his four-year-old daughter, Jennifer, for four years of undergraduate school. Jennifer is not anticipated to graduate from high school before the year 2028. Even at the state university, room, board, tuition and books, in current dollars, would be $25,000 per year. Assuming only a 6 percent increase in annual costs, the total projected cost of Jennifer's four year college education, beginning in 2028, would be nearly $250,000:

2028 – $56,523

2029 – $59,914

2030 – $63,509

2031 – $67,319)

GRATS

A *grantor retained annuity trust* (GRAT) is a trust into which the grantor transfers property, retaining "the right to receive fixed amounts payable not less frequently than annually[2] (a "qualified annuity interest") for a term of years. After the expiration of the term, the annuity ends, and what is left is used for the benefit of family members.

A qualified annuity interest is a species of qualified retained interest; thus, if a GRAT is used, the value of the gift to the remainder beneficiaries can be determined by subtracting the value of the annuity retained by the grantor from the value of the property transferred to the trust. The gift involved equals the theoretical value of the remainder, determined by using the discount rate (or rate of return) specified in Code section 7520.

Advantages of GRATs

A GRAT is an attractive estate planning technique for a number of reasons. The main reason is that although a GRAT is a gift, and is theoretically subject to gift tax, the gift is measured by the present value of the remainder interest.

If the remainder interest in a ten-year GRAT was expected to be $10 million, given current interest rate assumptions, the gift would not be $10 million; instead it would be the amount of money that would produce $10 million if invested (tax-free!) at the assumed interest rate. If the assumed rate of return was 3 percent, $7.4 million would produce $10 million at the end of ten years, and therefore, so would an up-front gift of that amount; except that, interestingly, an up-front gift would not grow tax free. This is an often overlooked point worth considering.

With a GRAT, we can gamble that the rate of return will exceed the Section 7520 rate. If it does, we win, and can potentially win big. If the rate of return does not exceed the Section 7520 rate, we lose the gift tax on the value of the remainder. But if we make the annuity rate high enough, the gift tax on the remainder will be negligible, meaning that if we lose, we lose little.

Disadvantages of GRATs

There are two primary theoretical advantages that an outright gift might be preferable to a gift of a remainder under a GRAT, but those advantageous are largely illusory when viewed from the grantor's perspective. The basic distinction is one of certainty verses uncertainty.

(1) There is the risk that the GRAT will fail to perform at the Section 7520 rate. However, under a zeroed out GRAT, there is little downside to the grantor in this event.

(2) There is the risk that the grantor will fail to live out the term. Again, if the GRAT is zeroed out, there is little downside to the grantor in this event. Moreover, it might be possible to "insure" against this contingency.

If a GRAT grew at precisely the Section 7520 rate, and the grantor outlives the term, the result of an outright gift of the gift tax value of the remainder ought to produce just about the same result as a GRAT, except for the virtually never noticed fact that the Section 7520 rate does not take income taxes into account, and an outright gift growing at the Section 7520 rate is treated for tax purposes as if it would grow tax free in a GRAT, in effect (i.e., as far as the remainder beneficiaries were concerned). An outright gift will presumably be subject to income taxes.

When Should a GRAT Be Used?

If there are limited assets to work with, the outright gift provides a certainty not available under a GRAT. There are two primary uncertainties with which the beneficiaries of a GRAT must contend:

1. The GRAT may under-perform the Section 7520 rate.

2. If the grantor fails to survive the term, the property is includible in the grantor's estate, and in that case the beneficiaries achieve nothing under the GRAT.

There is little to lose if the trust under-performs the Section 7520 growth rate, and everything to gain if it outperforms it. Hence, there is therefore little to lose if the trust under-performs the Section 7520 growth rate and if the gift is structured to be close to zero. There is everything to gain if it outperforms it.

The other principal risk with a GRAT is the risk of the grantor's premature death. If the grantor fails to survive the term, the property, or a portion of it, is includible in the grantor's estate, and the beneficiaries achieve little or nothing. The risk of a premature death can be offset by term insurance, but only if the grantor is healthy and of a reasonable age. In the case of a zeroed out GRAT, the risk of premature death has little other downside potential, and the upside is unlimited. This particular downside is perhaps more important if there are limited assets to work with.

In summary, the outright gift provides certainty, with a transfer tax cost, and the GRAT provides uncertainty, with little or no cost.

What Happens if the Grantor Dies Prior to the Expiration of the Term Interest?

Probably the single greatest downside to creating a GRAT is that, if the grantor fails to survive the term, either all of the GRAT corpus is includible in the estate of the grantor under Code section 2039, or a portion of it is includible under section 2036.[3]

The IRS believes that both Code sections 2036 and 2039 apply here.[4] Arguably, only section 2036 applies. If true, then less than the entire corpus would be includible. The amount includible would presumably be computed under the principles annunciated in Revenue Rulings 76-273 and 82-105,[5] meaning that the portion of the value of the trust includible in the grantor's gross estate at death would be the amount necessary to generate the annuity amount per year, determined using the §7520 rate in effect at the date of the grantor's death.

It is also possible that Code section 2038 would apply if a power of appointment were retained; and, of course, section 2033 would apply to the portion of the GRAT payable to the grantor's estate.

What Should Happen to the GRAT Upon the Settlor's Death?

Some GRAT forms provide that if the Settlor dies prior to the expiration of the term the amount includible in the Settlor's estate should be paid over to the Settlor's estate. This may be desirable, but not necessarily sufficient. A GRAT ought to at least provide that if the Settlor dies prior to the expiration of the Term, payments of the annuity amounts shall continue to be paid to the Settlor's personal representative (executor/administrator) as a part of the Settlor's general probate estate.

Whether or not the document should additionally provide that such payments shall be increased or augmented as necessary to cover any estate taxes attributable to the payments is another matter.

How Is a GRAT Taxed for Income Tax Purposes?

How a GRAT is taxed for income tax purposes may depend, in theory, on whether the GRAT is wholly (entirely) or partly a "grantor trust." Under the grantor trust rules, the grantor is taxed on the income of the trust, as if the trust did not exist.

A GRAT is probably a "grantor trust" under Subpart E of Subchapter J of the Internal Revenue Code,[6] at least with respect to the income of the GRAT, and probably for all purposes, since corpus must be used if necessary to satisfy the fixed annuity payments. Thus, the trust will not pay income taxes on the income; instead, the grantor will, because a "grantor trust" is ignored for income tax purposes.[7] If the annuity exceeds the income, then it will not make any difference whether the trust is a grantor trust or not, since income is generally carried out and taxed to the distributee under normal trust income tax rules. However, if ordinary income exceeds the annuity payment, the grantor would owe taxes on it if the trust is a grantor trust.

If the GRAT is a grantor trust as to ordinary income, then the grantor will be taxed on the ordinary income, whether it exceeds the annuity or not. In practice, the annuity will usually exceed the ordinary income. If an amount equal to all of the distributable net income (DNI) is distributed in cash each year, that income will be taxed to the grantor/annuitant whether the GRAT is a "grantor trust" or not. If the GRAT is a "grantor trust" as to corpus, then the grantor will be taxed on the capital gains too.

It is important to know whether a GRAT is a grantor trust or not, and if so, whether it is a grantor trust as to income or as to income and corpus (i.e., capital gains and loss purposes).

QPRT

A qualified personal residence trust (QPRT, or "House GRIT") is an arrangement under which the grantor transfers the home, usually to the children, retaining a life estate in the home (the right to live there) for a term of years. Unlike a GRAT, the grantor does not retain a fixed annuity; but, rather, retains only the income from the trust, which could be very low.

When is the Use of a QPRT Indicated?

A QPRT produces a better gift tax result if the Section 7520 rate is higher, the opposite of a GRAT. In a GRAT, the interest rate is fixed, so the value of the annuity (the retained interest) is inversely related to the Section 7520 rate. The higher the Section 7520 rate is relative to the annuity, the less valuable the retained interest and the more valuable the gift. A QPRT (or any GRIT for that matter) is also inversely related, but in reverse: the donor has retained the income interest (in effect), and if the income interest is high, what has been retained is worth more than if the prevailing interest rate is low.

Think of the theoretical rate of return being on an investment (in this case, it could be the rental value of a house). If interest rates are low, the return is low, and so is the value of what was retained. Like a GRAT, but in reverse, the value of the gift (the remainder interest) is inversely proportional to the value of the retained interest. So, the more valuable the retained interest (which is more valuable the higher the assumed rate of return or Section 7520 rate), the less the taxable value of the gift.

In point of fact, the kids get the house at the end of the term no matter what the Section 7520 rate was at the time the QPRT was established, and the parent(s) got to live in the house during the term with no obvious difference in the value of living there to them; so the whole economic analysis of true value is almost entirely theoretical. The real world value of living in the house is actually quite independent of the prevailing interest rates, unless selling, renting, or mortgaging the house and investing the proceeds is a real option. Therefore, all one really needs to know is that the higher the Section 7520 rate the lower the value of the remainder interest in a QPRT, which likewise means that the higher the Section 7520 rate the less size of the taxable gift.

GRITs were very popular for a while; so popular, in fact, that Congress responded by enacting the very complicated Chapter 14 of the Internal Revenue Code.[8] It is Code section 2702 that forces planners to use a GRAT or some other form of "qualified interest" instead of a GRIT, where the remainder beneficiary is a member of the family, except in the case of a QPRT.

Why Is a GRIT More Effective if the Actual Rate Of Return Is Low?

In a QPRT, the actual rate of return is zero (or maybe the rental value of the home). If interest rates are high, the value of a retained income interest is high, and the value of the remainder is commensurately lower. If the GRIT is investing in assets that produce growth at the expense of fiduciary accounting income, and if all that has been retained is the right to fiduciary accounting income, then, in effect, value is being shifted from the life tenant/grantor to the remainder beneficiaries. That is why GRITs were so popular, prior to the advent of Chapter 14, which effectively stopped this technique where applicable family members retained an interest and the remainder beneficiaries were "members of the transferor's family," except in the case of a QPRT. However, as will be mentioned again later (because it is worth repeating) GRITs are unaffected by Chapter 14 if none of the remainder beneficiaries is a member of the family. "Significant others" come readily to mind as potential beneficiaries, as well as nephews, nieces and cousins.

A GRIT, including a QPRT, is more beneficial if the prevailing interest rate (as reflected in section 7520) is high, but the actual return on the investment, as measured by fiduciary accounting income, rather than growth, is low. A typical example where growth potential is high, but fiduciary income is low would be a ranch, or a house GRIT (QPRT).

How Is a QPRT Taxed if a Beneficiary Is a Family Member?

Because the grantor's retained income interest under a QPRT is not a "qualified interest," it will be taxed for transfer tax purposes as if the grantor had retained nothing as long as at least one beneficiary of the trust is a "member of the family." The term "member of the family" means, with respect to any individual:

1. a spouse;

2. any ancestor or lineal descendant of such individual or such individual's spouse;

3. any sibling of the individual; or

4. the spouse of any of the above.[9]

What If None of the Beneficiaries of the Grit Is a Member of the Family?

If no member of the transferor's family is a beneficiary, then a gift under a GRIT is determined by measuring the value of the remainder using the current interest assumptions found in section 7520. A GRIT, therefore, is still a useful technique to consider if the beneficiary is not a "member of the family"; for example, if the beneficiary is a "significant other" to whom the grantor is not married, or a nephew, niece or cousin.

WHAT IS A GRUT, AND WHY IS IT NOT POPULAR?

A GRUT is like a GRAT except that the annuity is revalued every year as a fixed percentage of the then present value of the trust. The reason it is not popular,

and not discussed in this memo, is that the GRAT is more effective than a GRUT if the trust corpus appreciates. (If the trust does not appreciate, neither type of trust is effective.) If the trust appreciates, then under a GRUT, much of that appreciation is shifted back to the grantor, which is not exactly the point of the exercise. Thus, the remainder beneficiaries of the GRUT will almost always receive less than the remainder beneficiary of the GRAT, even if the value for transfer tax purposes is the same. If the estate planning point is to shift as much growth to the remainder beneficiaries without increasing the transfer tax, a GRAT is preferable to a GRUT.

WHERE CAN I FIND OUT MORE?

Leimberg, Stephan R., *The Tools & Techniques of Estate Planning*, 16th Edition (National Underwriter Company, 2013).

CHAPTER ENDNOTES

1. Spouses (including same-sex couples) enjoy an unlimited gift tax exclusion, and may even be co-owners of property depending on state property tax laws.

2. I.R.C. §2702(b).

3. FSA 200036012; TAM 200210009; Priv. Ltr. Ruls. 9451056 (Dec. 23, 1994) and 9345035 (Nov. 12, 1993); Treas. Reg. §20.2039-1(b)(2), Example 1.

4. Rev. Rul. 82-105, 1982-1 CB 133; Priv. Ltr. Ruls. 9345035 (Nov. 12, 1993) and 20021009 (May 24, 2002); FSA 200036012; TAM 200210009.

5. Rev. Rul. 76-273, 1976-2 CB 268 and Rev. Rul. 82-105, 1982-1 CB 133.

6. I.R.C. §§671-769.

7. Subpart E of Subchapter J was passed when trust income tax rates were lower than individual rates. At the moment, trust rates are higher, not lower, than the individual income tax rates, and so the grantor trust rules are more of a boon than an impediment for most taxpayers.

8. I.R.C. §§2701-2704.

9. I.R.C. §2704(c)(2).

DISCHARGE OF DEBT INCOME

CHAPTER 32

INTRODUCTION

Many taxpayers are astonished (and almost all are horrified) when they receive a Form 1099-C indicating that they must report on their tax return income from the discharge cancelation) of debt, be it because of a forgiven credit card balance or a bank loan discharged in the aftermath of a foreclosure or some other discharge of a debt. This shock and angst is typically heightened by the taxpayer's lack of cash to pay the tax. After all, how can an individual who has just lost her house through a foreclosure or short sale find the funds to pay a potentially large tax bill? Moreover, taxing such a financially devastated individual seems unfair and counterintuitive to the notion that items of gross income are "accessions to wealth, clearly realized."[1]

Yet, there is a sound reason to treat discharge of debt as taxable income. Lenders—including credit card companies and vendors—provide a borrower with an economic benefit. This benefit is not treated as currently taxable income because of the corresponding obligation to repay the benefit.[2] The cancellation of that repayment obligation essentially voids the tax-free characterization of the previously enjoyed economic benefit. Consequently, the discharge of the obligation to pay causes a previously non-taxable economic benefit to become taxable.

Whether it is apparent to the taxpayer or not, from an economic benefit perspective the discharge of an individual's debt is equivalent to that person receiving money. Any amount of money received by a taxpayer may—or may not—be taxable depending on the context in which it is received. For example, money received for services performed by the taxpayer is included in gross income as compensation,[3] and money received for the use of property is included in gross income as rent.[4]

On the other hand, money received as a gift is excluded from gross income.[5] The discharge of a taxpayer's debt is economically equivalent to receipt of money. So the tax treatment of a discharge of debt depends very much on the circumstances in which the discharge occurs.

Once the taxpayer is relieved of her obligation to repay the underlying debt, she must then include the forgiven amount in gross income. Under most circumstances, the Internal Revenue Code explicitly includes a discharge of debt in gross income. Code section 61(a)(12) includes a discharge of debt in the taxpayer's gross income if:

1. The taxpayer and the creditor have a pure debtor-creditor relationship; and,

2. a debtor's legally enforceable obligation to repay the debt is forgiven by the creditor for no consideration.

For example, if a bank forgives a customer's loan, the balance of the loan when it was forgiven is includible in the customer's gross income pursuant to section 61(a)(12) because the customer and the bank have a pure debtor-creditor relationship and the bank forgave her legally enforceable repayment obligation for no consideration. On the other hand, if the debtor and the creditor have some other relationship, that relationship may alter how the taxpayer is to include the discharged debt in gross income.

Example: Garry Gizmo borrows $10,000 from his employer to purchase a car. The loan is evidenced by a promissory note bearing market interest which is due and payable on the one year anniversary of the loan. On the maturity date, Gary's employer forgives the loan. In this case, unlike a borrower and a conventional lender, Gary and his boss have an employee-employer relationship. For this reason, rather than characterize the forgiven debt as section 61(a)(12) income, it is treated as compensation income under Code section 61(a)(1).[6]

We can think of the example above as if Gary's employer had actually paid him $10,000 in compensation that he in turn used to repay the loan. Obviously, if that had occurred, there would be no discharge because the loan would have been paid in full. The only difference between the two scenarios is whether any money changed hands. For tax purposes, regardless of how the transaction is structured, the employee is deemed to have received taxable wages and not discharge of debt income because of his employment relationship with the "lender."[7]

In addition to a pure debtor-creditor relationship between the parties, sections 61(a)(12) requires that the debt be discharged for no consideration. If the debt is satisfied by the transfer of money or some other valuable good, the transaction is not considered a discharge of the debt, and is not included as section 61(a)(12) income.

Example: Patty Portrait borrows $10,000 from Gene Gallery. When the loan becomes due, Patty lacks the funds to pay it. In lieu of payment, Gene agrees to accept a painting Patty purchased several years ago for $5,000, which is now worth $10,000. Although Patty and Gene have a pure debtor-creditor relationship, Patty is essentially selling the painting to Gene for an amount equal to the outstanding debt. In the alternative, Gene could purchase the painting from Patty for $10,000 that she in turn could pay to Gene to satisfy the loan.

Similar to the previous example, even though no money actually changed hands, there is no forgiven debt. Instead, the transaction is treated as a sale of the painting. Patty's income (likely capital gain) is the difference between the fair market value of the painting—$10,000, which also happens to be the loan balance—and her basis of $5,000. Here, Patty realizes a $5,000 gain that is included in gross income under Code section 61(a)(3), rather than section 61(a)(12).[8]

WHEN CAN A DISCHARGE OF DEBT BE EXCLUDED FROM GROSS INCOME?

Sometimes items that are normally included in gross income are nonetheless excluded by a specific section of the Code. Such is the case with respect to section 61(a)(12) discharge of debt income. Under certain circumstances, Code section 108 excludes a discharge of debt from a taxpayer's gross income. The exclusion can apply to any type of liability, including loans, lines of credit, and credit card debt. The discharge can occur as the result of a creditor write-off, foreclosure, short sale, deed in lieu of foreclosure, or abandonment. However, this exclusion only applies to a discharge of debt that is otherwise required to be included in gross income under section 61(a)(12).

Types of Indebtedness

There are two important—and related—ways to categorize any debt. First, all debt is either "secured" or "unsecured." The second distinction is between "recourse" versus "nonrecourse" indebtedness.

Secured versus Unsecured

Debt is "secured" if the borrower pledges specific property as collateral against the loan. As a hedge against a potential default, many lenders insist on securing a loan with specific property owned by the borrower that is pledged as collateral. By doing so, payment of a defaulted loan is assured to the extent of the value of the secured property. Common types of secured loans include home mortgages and car loans. If the borrower fails to repay the loan according to schedule, the lender may take possession of the collateral (the house or the car) and use the proceeds from its sale to repay the loan.

If no collateral is offered, then the loan is "unsecured."

Recourse versus Nonrecourse

In a "recourse" debt, the borrower's obligation to repay a recourse debt is unconditional. This means that in the event of default, the lender may legally pursue collection against not only the assets purchased by borrowed money but *all* of the borrower's assets, even if the loan is secured by collateral.[9] Recourse debt may be either secured or unsecured, depending on whether the borrower pledged any of his or her property as collateral against the loan.

The main difference between a recourse and "nonrecourse" debt is that in nonrecourse debt, the lender cannot attach other assets of the borrower. Stated another way, the borrower has no *personal* obligation to repay a defaulted loan, and the lender's only remedy is repossession of the collateral. To protect the lender, at the time that the loan is completed the value of the collateral property is usually at least equal to the amount of the nonrecourse loan. As long as the borrower conforms to the terms of the loan, he or she retains ownership of the secured property. Unlike recourse debt, nonrecourse debt is *always* secured by the borrower's property pledged as collateral.

Example: Barry Businessman borrows $200,000 from Second Bank. The loan is nonrecourse and secured by a warehouse with a fair market value of $200,000. Several years later, the value of the warehouse has decreased to $100,000. So instead of paying the $200,000 loan to retain the warehouse worth $100,000, Barry decides to default on the loan. In a foreclosure action, the warehouse is transferred to Second Bank extinguishing Barry's obligation to repay the remaining balance of $100,000 ($200,000 minus $100,000 the fair market value of the warehouse). As a result, Second Bank absorbs the $100,000 loss.

Which Types of Debt Can Be Excluded from a Taxpayer's Gross Income?

To qualify for the exclusion from a gross income under section 108, a discharged debt must satisfy two conditions: First, the discharge must be of "indebtedness of the taxpayer." While this sounds simple, the definition of the term is quite specific, mandating that the discharged debt must be either:

- recourse indebtedness of the taxpayer; or

- debt that is secured by the taxpayer's property.

Because recourse indebtedness can also be secured debt, it is not uncommon for the discharge of a recourse debt to satisfy the first condition of section 108 in both ways.

If the debt meets the first condition of section 108, the next step is to determine if the discharge falls into one of several categories that qualify for exclusion from the taxpayer's gross income. The categories are listed below:

1. *Bankruptcy exclusion*: Any discharge that occurs in a bankruptcy case—regardless of amount—is excluded from gross income.[10]

2. *Insolvency exclusion*: A discharge that occurs when the taxpayer is insolvent—defined as when the taxpayer's liabilities exceed the fair market value of his or her assets[11]—is excluded to the extent that the debtor was insolvent prior to the discharge.[12]

3. *Qualified farm indebtedness exclusion*: A discharge of "qualified farm indebtedness" (subject to certain limitations beyond the scope of this chapter) can be excluded from gross income. "Qualified farm indebtedness" is debt that is directly in connected with a business in which 50 percent or more of the aggregate gross receipts for the three years preceding the taxable year of the discharge is attributable to farming.[13]

4. *Qualified real property business indebtedness exclusion*: Discharged debt that is "qualified real property business indebtedness" can be excluded from gross income (subject to certain limitations discussed later in this chapter) if the debt was incurred for the purposes of acquiring, building, or substantially improving real property that is used in a trade or business.[14] This exclusion is not available to C corporations.

5. *Qualified principal residence indebtedness exclusion*: A discharge of debt related to a taxpayer's principal residence can be excluded (subject to certain limitations beyond the scope of this chapter) if the discharge occurred before January 1, 2014. The debt must have been incurred to acquire, build, or make substantial improvements or renovations to the taxpayer's principal residence.[15]

6. *Student loan exclusion*: A discharge of student loans that occurs because the borrower worked for a certain period of time for a particular type of employer (such as public interest work) can be excluded from gross income.[16]

7. *Discharged debt that would have been deductible if paid*: If a taxpayer could have deducted some

portion of the payments toward a debt (e.g. interest payments on a business loan), then the discharged debt will not be included in the taxpayer's gross income. This exclusion only applies to the amount of the debt that would have been tax deductible had it been paid.[17] This type of discharge still carries consequences for the taxpayer's gross income: rather than being included as income, the discharge means that the taxpayer will not enjoy the benefit of the deduction.

8. *Discharge of purchase money debt*: "Purchase money debt" is money that is lent by a seller to a buyer to facilitate a purchase. The code treats a discharge of this type of debt as a reduction in the purchase price, and it is therefore excluded from the buyer/borrower's gross income. This exclusion applies even when the buyer is not in bankruptcy or insolvent.[18]

In many instances, it is possible that the discharge of debt may qualify for more than one category of exclusion under section 108. For example, a debtor who files bankruptcy may also be insolvent. If a discharge of debt qualifies for more than one of the section 108 exclusion categories, Figure 32.1 sets forth which of the exclusions would take precedence.[19]

The following example contains a step-by-step analysis of whether and to what extent a discharge of debt section 61(a)(12) would be excluded from gross income under section 108.

Example: Molly Cule, a sole proprietor, takes out $100,000 in recourse debt from First Bank to fund working capital in her business. A year later when the loan becomes due, Molly defaults. Although Molly owns attachable assets, First Bank forgives the loan without pursuing a legal collection action against her. At the time of the discharge the amount of Molly's liabilities are $140,000 (including the $100,000 loan), and the fair market value of Molly's single asset—a construction crane used in her business—is $90,000. Thus, prior to the discharge, Molly is insolvent with a negative net worth of $50,000—the amount by which her liabilities ($140,000) exceeds the fair market value of her cumulative assets ($90,000).

Step 1 – Is there section 61(a)(12) discharge of debt income? Recall that section 108 exclusions only apply to discharges of debt that would otherwise be considered gross income under Code section 61(a)(12). Here, Molly's discharge meets the section 61(a)(12) requirements because:

1. Molly and First Bank have a pure debtor-creditor relationship; and

2. First Bank forgave a legally enforceable debt for no consideration.

Thus, Molly has $100,000 of discharge of debt income tentatively included in gross income under section 61(a)(12).

Figure 32.1

If a discharge of debt qualifies for all the following section 108(a)(1) exclusions:	The exclusion that takes precedence is:
• Bankruptcy exclusion • Insolvency exclusion • Qualified farm indebtedness exclusion • Qualified real property business indebtedness exclusion • Qualified principal residence indebtedness exclusion	Bankruptcy exclusion
• Insolvency exclusion • Qualified farm indebtedness exclusion • Qualified real property business indebtedness exclusion	Insolvency exclusion
• Insolvency exclusion • Qualified principal residence indebtedness exclusion	Qualified principal residence indebtedness exclusion

Step 2 – Is the discharged debt considered "indebtedness of the taxpayer?" Molly's loan is not secured by her property, but it is a recourse loan. Upon her default, First Bank decided to forgive the $100,000 loan balance rather than pursue a legal collection action against Molly to attach her assets. Because the bank could have pursued all of Molly's assets, the $100,000 discharged loan meets the first requirement of section 108 by being a recourse loan.

Step 3 – Does the discharge fall into one of the exclusion categories found in section 108? Recall that immediately before the discharge Molly was insolvent to the extent of $50,000. Thus, the insolvency exclusion applies to Molly's $100,000 loan discharge. Also, though Molly was insolvent at the time of discharge, there is no indication that the discharge occurred pursuant to a bankruptcy, and none of the other section 108(a)(1) exclusions are applicable. Thus, the only exclusion applicable is the insolvency exclusion.

Step 4 – How much of the discharged debt is excluded from gross income under the applicable section 108 exclusion? Not all of the section 108 exclusions exclude the entire discharge of debt from gross income. Here, the insolvency exclusion is limited to the extent the taxpayer was insolvent prior to the discharge. Prior to the discharge Molly was insolvent by $50,000. After the $100,000 discharge, however, Molly became solvent by $50,000 ($90,000 asset minus the remaining liabilities of $40,000).

Thus, Molly's insolvency exclusion is limited to $50,000 of the $100,000 in discharged debt— the amount by which she was insolvent prior to the discharge. The remaining $50,000 of discharged debt made her solvent and increased her net worth from zero to $50,000. After applying the insolvency exclusion, Molly would include $50,000 in gross income under section 61(a)(12) from the discharge of the First Bank loan.

DISCHARGES OF DEBT IN FORECLOSURE-TYPE TRANSACTIONS

By their very nature, foreclosures, short sales, and deeds in lieu of foreclosure (collectively known as "foreclosure-type transactions") often involve discharges of debt. The question is whether the discharge qualifies as gross income under section 61(a)(12) and is therefore potentially excludible under section 108. The answer to this question depends greatly on whether the discharged debt was recourse or nonrecourse. Most of this section will discuss discharges of debt in foreclosure-type transactions under the assumption that the discharge applies to recourse debt. The rules for nonrecourse debt in foreclosure transactions are more complicated, and will be discussed separately.

At the outset, it is important to note that the Code treats foreclosures,[20] short sales, and deeds in lieu of foreclosure[21] as sales for tax purposes. This treatment means that in addition to potentially reporting income from a discharge of debt, a taxpayer must also calculate the gain or loss from the sale.

If the sale price of the underlying property is equal to or greater than the taxpayer's cost basis, the difference between the sale price and the taxpayer's cost basis for the property is considered "gain" on the sale of property (even though the taxpayer may not actually see any of that money), and is included in gross income under Code section 61(a)(3), rather than section 61(a)(12). Recall that section 108 exclusions are only available for discharges of debt income that fall under section 61(a)(12). Accordingly, the amount of discharge of debt income that falls under section 61(a)(12)—and is therefore potentially excludable under section 108—is limited to the amount by which the debt on the property that is forgiven exceeds the sale price.

It is also possible for the sale price to be less than the taxpayer's cost basis in the property. In that case, the difference between the sale price and basis is realized as a loss under Code section 165. When realizing a loss on the sale of the property, the discharge of debt income is still limited to the amount by which the balance of the loan exceeds the sale price of the property.

An important issue that often arises in foreclosure-type transactions is that a discharge of the debt is not guaranteed. If the sale price of the underlying property is less than the amount of discharged debt, the creditor can either pursue a legal collection action against the debtor to satisfy the remaining balance of the debt, or simply forgive the remaining balance of the debt. The treatment of this remaining balance varies according to state law, and is often subject to the lender's discretion or an agreement that the borrower may have reached with the lender prior to the sale. Sometimes the debt left over after the sale is forgiven. But in other instances, the lender will continue to pursue the borrower (and all of his or her legal assets) for the balance of the loan.

Nonrecourse Debt

The most significant difference between recourse and nonrecourse debt is the absence of personal liability in the event of default. Unlike recourse liability discussed above, *all* gain realized from a foreclosure-type transaction involving a nonrecourse loan is treated as income under section 61(a)(3). This is because the discharge of the nonrecourse debt occurs through a transfer of the underlying secured property, which is treated as a sale. Although the resulting "gain" extinguishes the debtor's obligation to repay the balance of the loan, it is not considered discharge of debt income under section 61(a)(12). Regardless of whether the amount of the outstanding debt is more or less than the sale price of the underlying property, foreclosure-type transactions involving nonrecourse debt can *never* produce income under Code section 61(a)(12), and thus the income can *never* be excluded under Code section 108, even if the balance of the loan exceeds the sale price of the property.[22]

Example: Molly Cule purchases a commercial office building for $100,000. The purchase price is financed entirely with a $100,000 nonrecourse loan from First Bank secured by the building. Several years later, when the principal balance of the loan is still $100,000, Molly defaults. Consequently, First Bank forecloses on the property. At the time of the foreclosure, as a result of $40,000 of depreciation deductions, Molly's basis in the building is $60,000. The property sells for $80,000 at auction.

After the $80,000 in sale proceeds are applied to the loan, an unpaid balance of $20,000 remains. If the loan had been recourse, First Bank could have pursued a legal collection action against Molly to satisfy the balance. If First Bank chose not to do so, there would be $20,000 of discharge of debt income. Here, the remaining nonrecourse debt is simply extinguished upon the transfer of the secured property to the creditor.

In this transaction, Molly realizes $40,000 of section 61(a)(3) income. (It may be useful to think of this as $20,000 in "gain" from the sale, and $20,000 of income from the discharge of debt that falls under section 61(a)(3), rather than section 61(a)(12) because it is non-recourse debt.) Because Molly has no section 61(a)(12) income, none of the $40,000 is subject to exclusion under section 108.

Many may wonder how a nonrecourse debtor, such as Molly in the example above, can have "income" from the discharge of nonrecourse debt that she has no personal obligation to repay. The answer relates back to the economic benefit of the initial borrowing. By virtue of the nonrecourse loan, the borrower enjoyed the economic benefit of acquiring the property. The only reason the borrowed funds were not included in gross income was due to the obligation to repay the loan.[23] When the borrower defaults on the loan, the transfer of the property to the lender extinguishes that obligation and the previously enjoyed (but originally untaxed) economic benefit of the borrowed funds becomes taxable income.

REFINANCING TRANSACTIONS

The treatment of discharged debt in refinancing transactions (including refinancing, restructuring, and partial forgiveness of debt) is treated similarly to discharges in foreclosure-type transactions, with one important difference.

As discussed above, income realized from discharge of *nonrecourse* debt via a transfer of the underlying secured property to the creditor (as is deemed to occur in a foreclosure-type transaction) is never treated as section 61(a)(12) income. However, if a creditor forgives a portion of nonrecourse debt and allows the debtor to retain the secured property (as is the case in a refinancing transaction), the discharge is not treated as a sale. This means that income from the discharge is reported under section 61(a)(12) rather than 61(a)(3), and is potentially excludable from the taxpayer's gross income under section 108.[24] The analysis of discharged debt in refinancing transaction proceeds in much the same way is it does in a foreclosure-type transaction involving recourse debt.

Example: Molly Cule borrows $100,000 from First Bank through a nonrecourse note. The loan is secured by a parcel of undeveloped land with a fair market value of $100,000 held by Molly as an investment. Subsequently, the fair market value of the land decreases to $80,000. Because the loan is "upside down," Molly offers First Bank a deed in lieu of foreclosure. In response, First Bank offers to reduce the amount of loan from $100,000 to $80,000—allowing Molly to retain the property—and Molly agrees. As a result, Molly has $20,000 of section 61(a)(12) income because

1) Molly and First Bank have a pure debtor-creditor relationship; 2) First Bank forgave the debt for no economic consideration; and 3) in order to retain ownership of the land, Molly is obligated to repay the reduced loan balance of $80,000.

Unlike a foreclosure-type transaction involving nonrecourse debt in which the obligation to repay is extinguished, a reduction of nonrecourse debt on property retained by the debtor does not extinguish the liability. For that reason, a partial forgiveness of nonrecourse liability triggers discharge of debt income. Similar to the discharge of recourse debt, the reduction of nonrecourse debt is eligible for potential exclusion pursuant to Code section 108. Figure 32.2 summarizes the differences in how discharges of recourse and nonrecourse debt are treated under the Code.

QUALIFIED REAL PROPERTY BUSINESS INDEBTEDNESS EXCLUSION

Often, business owners obtain secured loans in order to acquire and/or substantially improve the real property used in their trade or business. Occasionally, some or all of the debt is forgiven, resulting in discharge of debt income that may be excluded from gross income pursuant to the qualified real property business indebtedness (QRPBI)

exclusion under Code section 108.[25] For a financially distressed business owner, taking advantage of this exclusion may be a less onerous alternative to filing bankruptcy.

QRPBI can be generated in a foreclosure-type transaction or in a refinancing transaction. As discussed above, in a foreclosure-type transaction, only the discharge of recourse indebtedness can qualify for the exclusion.[26] On the other hand, in a refinancing transaction in which the debtor retains the secured property, the discharge of both recourse and nonrecourse indebtedness can qualify for the exclusion.

For the most part, the QRPBI exclusion functions the same as the other types of section 108 exclusions discussed above. However, it is subject to two additional limitations.

First, the amount excluded cannot exceed the difference between the outstanding total balance of the loan (prior to the discharge) and the fair market value of the property, as reduced by any other qualified real property business indebtedness. In other words, start with the outstanding balance of the loan which is to be forgiven (in whole or in part). Subtract from that balance the fair market value of the property. Then subtract the outstanding balance of any other loans that qualify as "real property business indebtedness" and are secured by the same property. Whatever amount remains after the subtractions is the upper limit of the QRPBI exclusion.

Figure 32.2

FORECLOSURE-TYPE TRANSACTIONS		
Amount of Discharge	**Recourse Debt**	**Nonrecourse Debt**
Sale price of secured property equal or greater than outstanding balance of debt	Treated as a sale resulting in either section 61(a)(3) income or section 165 loss	Treated as a sale resulting in either section 61(a)(3) income or section 165 loss
Sale price of secured property is less than the outstanding balance of debt	Treated as two transactions: • a sale to the extent of the sale price of the secured property, resulting in either section 61(a)(3) income or section 165 loss • a discharge of debt to extent outstanding balance of debt exceeds the sale price of secured property	Treated as a sale resulting in either section 61(a)(3) income or section 165 loss regardless of the amount of the debt
Refinancing Transactions		
Amount of Discharge	**Recourse Debt**	**Nonrecourse Debt**
Any amount forgiven	Treated as discharge of debt income under section 61(a)(12)	Treated as discharge of debt income under section 61(a)(12)

The second limitation on the QRPBI exclusion is simpler, at least in concept: in addition to the first limitation, the QRPBI exclusion also cannot exceed the aggregate bases of the taxpayer's depreciable property.[27] Obviously, calculating this limit on the QRPBI exclusion can be more or less complicated depending on the amount of depreciable property owned by the taxpayer.

Finally, it should be noted that the requirement to reduce other tax attributes (discussed in more detail below) does not apply to the QRPBI exclusion. Instead, Code section 108(c)(1)(A) requires the taxpayer to reduce the basis of the qualified business real property by the amount of the QRPBI exclusion when it is taken. Importantly, if the QRPBI exclusion is taken in the context of a foreclosure-type transaction, the newly reduced basis is used when calculating the amount of gain or loss from the sale.

HOW DOES EXCLUDING DISCHARGE OF DEBT INCOME AFFECT OTHER DEDUCTIONS AND CREDITS?

Once the type and amount of section 108 exclusion has been determined, the exclusion is allowed unconditionally. However, taking advantage of the bankruptcy, insolvency, or qualified farm indebtedness exclusions may affect the taxpayer's other deductions and credits. If a taxpayer has certain "tax attributes," section 108(b) requires a reduction of those tax attributes in an amount equal to the excluded discharge of debt income. A "tax attribute" is an item that reduces a taxpayer's tax liability. In other words, although section 108 is an exclusion section (and, thus, a tax attribute in its own right), there is a mandatory trade-off of some of the taxpayer's other tax attributes. If a taxpayer has a significant amount of certain tax attributes at the time of the discharge, the immediate tax benefit of the section 108 exclusion of discharge of debt income may be offset by the loss of other tax benefits.

Examples of tax attributes that are subject to reduction include a net operating loss, capital loss carryover, certain tax credits, and basis. Tax attributes that relate to deductions are treated differently than those that area related to credits. Deduction-related attributes (including basis) are reduced by one dollar for each dollar of excluded discharge of debt income.[28] Attributes related to credits are reduced by 33.3 cents for each dollar of excluded discharge of debt income.[29]

The adjustment of other tax attributes is the last step in a complex analysis of whether income from a discharge of debt can—and should—be excluded from a taxpayer's gross income under section 108. Figure 32.3 summarizes the steps that need to be taken to complete that analysis.

FREQUENTLY ASKED QUESTIONS

Question – Does the bankruptcy exclusion or the insolvency exclusion provide greater tax advantages?

Answer – Obviously, the decision to file for bankruptcy should not be taken lightly. However, looking at the issue purely from a tax perspective, the bankruptcy exclusion provides far greater tax advantages for several reasons.

First, *all* debt discharged in a bankruptcy proceeding is excludible from gross income. The insolvency exclusion is limited to the extent of the taxpayer's pre-discharge insolvency, which is almost always less than the amount that would be discharged in a bankruptcy case. When using the insolvency exclusion, the amount of the discharge that creates positive net worth for the taxpayer is not excludable from gross income under section 108.

Example: Barry Businessman has liabilities totaling $550,000 and assets with an aggregate fair market value of $250,000. Thus, Barry is insolvent with a negative net worth of $300,000. A number of Barry's creditors decide to forgive a total of $340,000 of Barry's indebtedness.

If the discharge occurs outside of bankruptcy, the discharge would qualify for the insolvency exclusion. As a result, the exclusion would be limited to $300,000—the amount of Barry's pre-discharge insolvency. The rest of the discharged amount ($40,000) would be taxable as section 61(a)(12) income.

Conversely, if the discharge occurs through bankruptcy, the entire amount of discharged liability ($340,000) would be excluded from gross income pursuant to the Bankruptcy Exclusion. Thus, even though the discharge made Barry solvent, there is no limitation of the exclusion amount.

Figure 32.3

REQUIREMENTS FOR EXCLUSION OF DISCHARGE OF DEBT INCOME UNDER CODE SECTION 108	
Analysis	**Requirements**
Step 1: Is there section 61(a)(12) discharge of debt income?	• Pure debtor-creditor relationship • Debt discharged for no consideration
Step 2: Is debt discharged "indebtedness of the taxpayer?"	• All recourse debt • All debt secured by the taxpayer's property
Step 3: Is it the right kind of discharge?	• Bankruptcy • Insolvency • Qualified farm indebtedness • Qualified business real property indebtedness • Qualified principal residence indebtedness (prior to January 1, 2014 • Discharged debt that would have been deductible if actually paid • Certain student loan forgiveness • Purchased money price adjustment
Step 3A: If more than one of the exclusions apply, which takes precedence?	• Bankruptcy over all others • insolvency over all the others except bankruptcy and qualified principal residence
Step 4: How much of the discharge debt is excluded from gross income?	• Bankruptcy—no limitation • Insolvency—to the extent of taxpayer's pre-discharge insolvency • Qualified farm indebtedness—subject to certain limitations beyond the scope of this chapter • Qualified real property business indebtedness—subject to certain limitations discussed above • Qualified principal residence indebtedness—subject to certain limitations beyond the scope of this Chapter • Discharged debt would have been deductible if actually paid—no limitation • Certain student loan forgiveness—no limitation • Purchase money price adjustment—no limitation
Step 5: Is a reduction of other tax attributes required?	• Required for bankruptcy, insolvency and qualified farm indebtedness exclusions
Step 6: If a reduction of tax attributes are required, which method is most favorable?	• Can use reduction schedules in either section 108(b)(2) or 108(b)(5)

Second, establishing a taxpayer's insolvency may be problematic. This is because the value of all the taxpayer's assets—even those that would be exempt from creditors' claims in a bankruptcy proceeding—are included.[30] Examples of types of property that are exempt from creditors' claims in a bankruptcy proceeding, but are nonetheless considered in determining insolvency, include:[31]

• Qualified retirement accounts

• IRA accounts

• Whole life insurance policies

• Real property

Thus, the value of otherwise exempt assets may substantially reduce—if not totally eliminate—a taxpayer's insolvency, leaving little or no exclusion to apply to any discharge of debt income. To avoid potential taxation, it may be prudent for a taxpayer in that position to file bankruptcy (if he or she was inclined to do so) as a way to exclude the entire amount of discharged debt income pursuant to the bankruptcy exclusion.

Question – Section 108(f) provides a student loan exclusion with regard to the discharge of all or part of a student loan. Is a taxpayer who qualifies for that exclusion required to reduce his or her tax attributes pursuant to section 108(b)(2) or section 108(b)(5)?

Answer – No. The mandatory reduction of tax attributes specifically applies to the bankruptcy, insolvency, and qualified farm indebtedness exclusions,[32] but the not student loan exclusion in section 108(f).

CHAPTER ENDNOTES

1. *Comm'r. v. Glenshaw Glass*, 348 US 426, 431 (1955).
2. *Comm'r. v. Rail Joint Co.*, 61 F.2d 751 (2d Cir. 1932).
3. I.R.C. §61(a)(1).
4. I.R.C. §61(a)(5).
5. I.R.C. §102(a).
6. Treas. Reg. §1.61-12(a).
7. The employer would be entitled to a corresponding deduction pursuant to Code section 162.
8. For Gene, there would be no tax consequences since the repayment of the principal of a loan is not a taxable event to the lender. In essence, Gene has simply purchased a painting for $10,000. Had Gene also recovered interest, he would have to report that interest as income.
9. Though procedures vary by state, generally a lender must pursue the lender's property that was pledged as collateral first. If the sale of the repossessed collateral does not fully repay the balance of a recourse loan, the lender may then pursue the borrower's other property. There are also limits on which assets may be pursued by a creditor, and how much of those assets may be claimed. These limits also vary from state to state, as well.
10. I.R.C. §§108(a)(1)(A) and 108(d)(2).
11. I.R.C. §§108(a)(1)(B) and 108(d)(3).
12. I.R.C. §§108(a)(3).
13. I.R.C. §§108(a)(1)(C).
14. I.R.C. §§108(a)(1)(D) and 108(c).
15. I.R.C. §§108(a)(1)(E) and 108(h).
16. I.R.C. §108(f).
17. I.R.C. §108(e)(2).
18. I.R.C. §108(e)(5).
19. I.R.C. §108(a)(2).
20. *Helvering v. Hammel*, 311 U.S. 504 (1941).
21. *Freeland v. Comm'r.*, 74 T.C. 970 (1980).
22. Treas. Reg. §1.1001-2(c), Example 7; *Comm'r. v. Tufts*, 461 U.S. 300 (1983).
23. *Comm'r. v. Tufts*, 461 U.S. 300 (1983).
24. Rev. Rul. 91-31, 1991-1 C.B. 19.
25. I.R.C. §108(a)(1)(D).
26. Section 61(a)(12) income is a prerequisite for any section 108 exclusion since the discharge of nonrecourse indebtedness in a foreclosure-type transaction is treated as section 61(a)(3) income, the QRPBI exclusion would not apply.
27. I.R.C. §108(c)(2)(B).
28. I.R.C. §108(b)(3)(A).
29. I.R.C. §108(b)(3)(B).
30. *Carlson v. Comm'r.*, 116 T.C. 87 (2001).
31. The types—and the amounts of those types—of property that are exempt from creditors in a bankruptcy proceeding varies depending on the circumstances of the debtor and state law.
32. I.R.C. §108(b)(1).

AFTER-TAX EQUIVALENTS OF TAX-EXEMPT YIELDS

Bracket	5%	10%	15%	20%	25%	26%	28%	33%	34%	35%	38%	39%
4.00	4.21	4.44	4.71	5.00	5.33	5.41	5.56	5.97	6.06	6.15	6.45	6.56
4.10	4.32	4.56	4.82	5.13	5.47	5.54	5.69	6.12	6.21	6.31	6.61	6.72
4.20	4.42	4.67	4.94	5.25	5.60	5.68	5.83	6.27	6.36	6.46	6.77	6.89
4.30	4.53	4.78	5.06	5.38	5.73	5.81	5.97	6.42	6.52	6.62	6.94	7.05
4.40	4.63	4.89	5.18	5.50	5.87	5.95	6.11	6.57	6.67	6.77	7.10	7.21
4.50	4.74	5.00	5.29	5.63	6.00	6.08	6.25	6.72	6.82	6.92	7.26	7.38
4.60	4.84	5.11	5.41	5.75	6.13	6.22	6.39	6.87	6.97	7.08	7.42	7.54
4.70	4.95	5.22	5.53	5.88	6.27	6.35	6.53	7.01	7.12	7.23	7.58	7.70
4.80	5.05	5.33	5.65	6.00	6.40	6.49	6.67	7.16	7.27	7.38	7.74	7.87
4.90	5.16	5.44	5.76	6.13	6.53	6.62	6.81	7.31	7.42	7.54	7.90	8.03
5.00	5.26	5.56	5.88	6.25	6.67	6.76	6.94	7.46	7.58	7.69	8.06	8.20
5.10	5.37	5.67	6.00	6.37	6.80	6.89	7.08	7.61	7.73	7.85	8.23	8.36
5.20	5.47	5.78	6.12	6.50	6.93	7.03	7.22	7.76	7.88	8.00	8.39	8.52
5.30	5.58	5.89	6.24	6.62	7.07	7.16	7.36	7.91	8.03	8.15	8.55	8.69
5.40	5.68	6.00	6.35	6.75	7.20	7.30	7.50	8.06	8.18	8.31	8.71	8.85
5.50	5.79	6.11	6.47	6.87	7.33	7.43	7.64	8.21	8.33	8.46	8.87	9.02
5.60	5.89	6.22	6.59	7.00	7.47	7.57	7.78	8.36	8.48	8.62	9.03	9.18
5.70	6.00	6.33	6.71	7.12	7.60	7.70	7.92	8.51	8.64	8.77	9.19	9.34
5.80	6.11	6.44	6.82	7.25	7.73	7.84	8.06	8.66	8.79	8.92	9.35	9.51
5.90	6.21	6.56	6.94	7.37	7.87	7.97	8.19	8.81	8.94	9.08	9.52	9.67
6.00	6.32	6.67	7.06	7.50	8.00	8.11	8.33	8.96	9.09	9.23	9.68	9.84
6.10	6.42	6.78	7.18	7.62	8.13	8.24	8.47	9.10	9.24	9.38	9.84	10.00
6.20	6.53	6.89	7.29	7.75	8.27	8.38	8.61	9.25	9.39	9.54	10.00	10.16
6.30	6.63	7.00	7.41	7.87	8.40	8.51	8.75	9.40	9.55	9.69	10.16	10.33
6.40	6.74	7.11	7.53	8.00	8.53	8.65	8.89	9.55	9.70	9.85	10.32	10.49
6.50	6.84	7.22	7.65	8.12	8.67	8.78	9.03	9.70	9.85	10.00	10.48	10.66
6.60	6.95	7.33	7.76	8.25	8.80	8.92	9.17	9.85	10.00	10.15	10.65	10.82
6.70	7.05	7.44	7.88	8.37	8.93	9.05	9.31	10.00	10.15	10.31	10.81	10.98
6.80	7.16	7.56	8.00	8.50	9.07	9.19	9.44	10.15	10.30	10.46	10.97	11.15

T A X   E X E M P T   Y I E L D S

TAX EXEMPT YIELDS

Bracket	5%	10%	15%	20%	25%	26%	28%	33%	34%	35%	38%	39%
6.90	7.26	7.67	8.12	8.62	9.20	9.32	9.58	10.30	10.45	10.62	11.13	11.31
7.00	7.37	7.78	8.24	8.75	9.33	9.46	9.72	10.45	10.61	10.77	11.29	11.48
7.10	7.47	7.89	8.35	8.87	9.47	9.59	9.86	10.60	10.76	10.92	11.45	11.64
7.20	7.58	8.00	8.47	9.00	9.60	9.73	10.00	10.75	10.91	11.08	11.61	11.80
7.30	7.68	8.11	8.59	9.12	9.73	9.86	10.14	10.90	11.06	11.23	11.77	11.97
7.40	7.79	8.22	8.71	9.25	9.87	10.00	10.28	11.04	11.21	11.38	11.94	12.13
7.50	7.89	8.33	8.82	9.37	10.00	10.14	10.42	11.19	11.36	11.54	12.10	12.30
7.60	8.00	8.44	8.94	9.50	10.13	10.27	10.56	11.34	11.52	11.69	12.26	12.46
7.70	8.11	8.56	9.06	9.62	10.27	10.41	10.69	11.49	11.67	11.85	12.42	12.62
7.80	8.21	8.67	9.18	9.75	10.40	10.54	10.83	11.64	11.82	12.00	12.58	12.79
7.90	8.32	8.78	9.29	9.87	10.53	10.68	10.97	11.79	11.97	12.15	12.74	12.95
8.00	8.42	8.89	9.41	10.00	10.67	10.81	11.11	11.94	12.12	12.31	12.90	13.11
8.10	8.53	9.00	9.53	10.13	10.80	10.95	11.25	12.09	12.27	12.46	13.06	13.28
8.20	8.63	9.11	9.65	10.25	10.93	11.08	11.39	12.24	12.42	12.62	13.23	13.44
8.30	8.74	9.22	9.76	10.38	11.07	11.22	11.53	12.39	12.58	12.77	13.39	13.61
8.40	8.84	9.33	9.88	10.50	11.20	11.35	11.67	12.54	12.73	12.92	13.55	13.77
8.50	8.95	9.44	10.00	10.63	11.33	11.49	11.81	12.69	12.88	13.08	13.71	13.93
8.60	9.05	9.56	10.12	10.75	11.47	11.62	11.94	12.84	13.03	13.23	13.87	14.10
8.70	9.16	9.67	10.24	10.88	11.60	11.76	12.08	12.99	13.18	13.38	14.03	14.26
8.80	9.26	9.78	10.35	11.00	11.73	11.89	12.22	13.13	13.33	13.54	14.19	14.43
8.90	9.37	9.89	10.47	11.13	11.87	12.03	12.36	13.28	13.48	13.69	14.35	14.59
9.00	9.47	10.00	10.59	11.25	12.00	12.16	12.50	13.43	13.64	13.85	14.52	14.75
9.10	9.58	10.11	10.71	11.38	12.13	12.30	12.64	13.58	13.79	14.00	14.68	14.92
9.20	9.68	10.22	10.82	11.50	12.27	12.43	12.78	13.73	13.94	14.15	14.84	15.08
9.30	9.79	10.33	10.94	11.63	12.40	12.57	12.92	13.88	14.09	14.31	15.00	15.25
9.40	9.89	10.44	11.06	11.75	12.53	12.70	13.06	14.03	14.24	14.46	15.16	15.41
9.50	10.00	10.56	11.18	11.88	12.67	12.84	13.19	14.18	14.39	14.62	15.32	15.57
9.60	10.11	10.67	11.29	12.00	12.80	12.97	13.33	14.33	14.55	14.77	15.48	15.74
9.70	10.21	10.78	11.41	12.13	12.93	13.11	13.47	14.48	14.70	14.92	15.65	15.90
9.80	10.32	10.89	11.53	12.25	13.07	13.24	13.61	14.63	14.85	15.08	15.81	16.07
9.90	10.42	11.00	11.65	12.38	13.20	13.38	13.75	14.78	15.00	15.23	15.97	16.23
10.00	10.53	11.11	11.76	12.50	13.33	13.51	13.89	14.93	15.15	15.38	16.13	16.39
10.10	10.63	11.22	11.88	12.63	13.47	13.65	14.03	15.07	15.30	15.54	16.29	16.56
10.20	10.74	11.33	12.00	12.75	13.60	13.78	14.17	15.22	15.45	15.69	16.45	16.72
10.30	10.84	11.44	12.12	12.88	13.73	13.92	14.31	15.37	15.61	15.85	16.61	16.89
10.40	10.95	11.56	12.24	13.00	13.87	14.05	14.44	15.52	15.76	16.00	16.77	17.05
10.50	11.05	11.67	12.35	13.13	14.00	14.19	14.58	15.67	15.91	16.15	16.94	17.21
10.60	11.16	11.78	12.47	13.25	14.13	14.32	14.72	15.82	16.06	16.31	17.10	17.38
10.70	11.26	11.89	12.59	13.38	14.27	14.46	14.86	15.97	16.21	16.46	17.26	17.54
10.80	11.37	12.00	12.71	13.50	14.40	14.59	15.00	16.12	16.36	16.62	17.42	17.70
10.90	11.47	12.11	12.82	13.63	14.53	14.73	15.14	16.27	16.52	16.77	17.58	17.87
11.00	11.58	12.22	12.94	13.75	14.67	14.86	15.28	16.42	16.67	16.92	17.74	18.03

SUGGESTED CHARITABLE GIFT ANNUITY RATES– SINGLE LIFE

APPENDIX B

Approved by the American Council on Gift Annuities on November 7, 2011 Effective January 1, 2012			
Age	Rate	Age	Rate
5-10	2.0%	65	4.7%
11-15	2.1	66	4.8
16-19	2.2	67	4.8
20-23	2.3	68	4.9
24-26	2.4	69	5.0
27-29	2.5	70	5.1
30-32	2.6	71	5.3
33-34	2.7	72	5.4
35-36	2.8	73	5.5
37-38	2.9	74	5.7
39-40	3.0	75	5.8
41-42	3.1	76	6.0
43	3.2	77	6.2
44-45	3.3	78	6.4
46	3.4	79	6.6
47	3.5	80	6.8
48-49	3.6	81	7.0
50	3.7	82	7.2
51-52	3.8	83	7.4
53-54	3.9	84	7.6
55	4.0	85	7.8
56-57	4.1	86	8.0
58	4.2	87	8.2
59	4.3	88	8.4

Approved by the American Council on Gift Annuities on November 7, 2011
Effective January 1, 2012 (continued)

Age	Rate	Age	Rate
60-61	4.4	89	8.7
62-63	4.5	90 and over	9.0
64	4.6		

WARNING: These annuity rates, for both immediate and deferred annuities and for both single life and two lives, should not be used if the gift portion, based on IRS tables and the applicable discount rate, is not more than 10% of the amount paid for the annuity.

NOTES:

1. The rates are for ages at the nearest birthday.

2. For immediate gift annuities, these rates will result in a charitable deduction of more than 10%, if the CMFR (Section 7520 interest rate) is 1.4% or higher and a quarterly payment frequency is used. If the CMFR is less than 1.4%, the deduction will be less than 10% when annuitants are below certain ages.

3. For deferred gift annuities with longer deferral periods, the rates may not pass the 10% test when the CMFR is low.

4. To avoid adverse tax consequences, the charity should reduce the gift annuity rate to whatever level is necessary to generate a charitable deduction in excess of 10%.

Source: American Council on Gift Annuities http://www.acga-web.org/gift-annuity-rates

GROUP TERM LIFE INSURANCE

General. In general, the cost of up to $50,000 of group-term life insurance coverage provided to an employee by his employer is *not* includable in the employee's gross income. However, the employee must include in his income the cost of employer-provided insurance that exceeds $50,000 of coverage, and then reduce that amount by any amount the employee paid toward the purchase of the insurance.[1]

If the individual's employer provided *more than* $50,000 of coverage, the amount included in the employee's income is reported as part of his wages in Box 1 of Form W-2. It is also shown in Box 12 with code C.[2]

Group-term life insurance is term life insurance protection (i.e., insurance that covers the insured person for a fixed period of time) that:

1. provides a general death benefit that is excluded from gross income under Code section 101(a);

2. is provided to a group of employees;

3. is provided under a policy carried by the employer; and

4. provides an amount of insurance to each employee based on a formula that prevents individual selection.[3]

If a group-term life insurance policy includes "permanent" benefits (i.e., a paid-up or cash surrender value), the employee must include in his income, as wages, the cost of the permanent benefits *minus* the amount the employee paid for them. The employer should tell the employee the amount to include in his income.[4]

Entire cost excluded. Under the following exceptions to the general rule, an employee will *not* be taxed on

the cost of group-term life insurance over and above the $50,000 exclusion amount if:

- The employee is permanently and totally disabled and has ended his employment;[5]

- The individual's employer is the beneficiary (directly or indirectly) of the policy for the entire period the insurance is in force during the tax year;[6] or

- A charitable organization to which contributions are deductible is the only beneficiary of the policy for the entire period the insurance is in force during the tax year.[7]

Entire cost taxed. Under the following circumstances, the $50,000 exclusion amount will not apply, requiring the employee to be taxed on the entire cost of group-term life insurance. The $50,000 exclusion occurs if either of the following circumstances applies:

- The individual's employer through a qualified employees' trust, such as a pension trust or a qualified annuity plan, provides the insurance;[8] or

- The individual is a key employee and his employer's plan discriminates in favor of key employees.[9]

Calculating the cost. To figure the taxable cost for each month of coverage, the employee should multiply the number of thousands of dollars of insurance coverage for the month (less $50,000, figured to the nearest tenth) by the cost from the table below. The employee's age on the last day of the tax year should be used.[10] The employee should prorate the cost from the table if less than a full month of coverage is involved.[11]

Table I – Uniform premiums for $1,000 of group term life insurance protection* (effective for group term life insurance provided after June 30, 1999)

5-Year Age Bracket	Cost per $1,000 of protection for 1-month period
Under 25	$0.05
25 to 29	0.06
30 to 34	0.08
35 to 39	0.09
40 to 44	0.10
45 to 49	0.15
50 to 54	0.23
55 to 59	0.43
60 to 64	0.66
65 to 69	1.27
70 and above	2.06

* In using the above table, the age of the employee is his attained age on the last day of his taxable year. Reg. §1.79-3(d)(2).

If the employee pays any part of the cost of the insurance, his entire payment reduces, dollar-for-dollar, the amount the employee would otherwise include in his income. However, an employee *cannot* reduce the amount that is includable in his income by:

- Payments for coverage in a different tax year;

- Payments for coverage through a cafeteria plan (unless the payments are after-tax contributions); or

- Payments for coverage not taxed to him because of the exceptions discussed above.[12]

Example: For example, assume that an employee, age fifty-two, is provided with $150,000 of group term life insurance coverage in each month of the taxable year 2014. His employer pays the entire premium. As seen in the calculation below, the excess coverage for each month of the taxable year is $100,000 ($150,000 – $50,000). The cost of the group term insurance is $276, which is arrived at by multiplying the

Table I rate of $0.23 for age fifty-two by twelve months to obtain a yearly rate of $2.76, and then multiplying this rate by one hundred to obtain $276, the cost for $100,000 of coverage.

Cost of Group Term Life Insurance in Excess of $50,000

Employee's Date of Birth:	January 1, 1955 (Age: 52)
End Employer's Taxable Year:	Calendar
Employee's Contribution:	$0
Employee's Tax Bracket:	28.00%
Level Amount of Group Insurance:	$150,000
Cost of Group Term Insurance:	$276
Estimated Tax on Term Group Insurance:	$78

Assume further that the employee contributes $0.15 per month per $1,000 of insurance. The employee's total contribution for the year would amount to $180, which is calculated by multiply the $0.15 by twelve months and then by one hundred. The $180 is subtracted from the cost of $276 to arrive at a figure of $96, which the employee must include in income.

The "price" of excess coverage, as computed above, is not, of course, the tax payable but the amount to be included in the employee's gross income. Thus, in the first example, if the employee's marginal tax bracket is 28 percent, he is obtaining $150,000 of group term coverage for a price of $78 (28 percent of $276) for the taxable year.

ENDNOTES

1. I.R.C. §79(a).
2. See I.R.C. §6052(a); Treas. Regs. §§1.6052-1, 1.6052-2.
3. Treas. Reg. §1.79-1(a).
4. Treas. Reg. §1.79-1(d).
5. I.R.C. §§79(b)(1); 72(m)(7).
6. I.R.C. §79(b)(2)(A).
7. I.R.C. §79(b)(b)(2)(B).
8. I.R.C. §79(b)(3); Treas. Reg. §1.79-2(d)(1).
9. I.R.C. §79(d)(1).
10. Treas. Reg. §1.79-3(d)(2).
11. See I.R.C. §79(c); Treas. Reg. §1.79-3.
12. Treas. Reg. §1.79-3(f)(2).

INCOME TAX RATE SCHEDULES

TAXABLE YEARS BEGINNING IN 2014

SINGLE INDIVIDUALS				JOINT RETURNS AND SURVIVNG SPOUSES			
Taxable Income		Tax on Lower Amount	Tax Rate on Excess	Taxable Income		Tax on Lower Amount	Tax Rate on Excess
$ -0- to	$9,075	$ -0-	10%	$ -0- to	$18,150	$ -0-	10%
9,075 to	36,900	907.50	15%	18,150 to	73,800	1,815.00	15%
36,900 to	89,350	5,081.25	25%	73,800 to	148,850	10,162.50	25%
89,350 to	186,350	18,193.75	28%	148,850 to	226,850	28,925.00	28%
186,350 to	405,100	45,353.75	33%	226,850 to	405,100	50,765.00	33%
405,100 to	406,750	117,541.25	35%	405,100 to	457,600	109,587.50	35%
406,750 to	......	118,188.75	39.6%	457,600 to	......	127,962.50	39.6%

MARRIED FILING SEPARATELY				HEAD OF HOUSEHOLD			
Taxable Income		Tax on Lower Amount	Tax Rate on Excess	Taxable Income		Tax on Lower Amount	Tax Rate on Excess
$0 to	$9,075	$ -0-	10%	$ -0- to	$12,950	$ -0-	10%
9,075 to	36,900	907.50	15%	12,950 to	49,400	1,295.00	15%
36,900 to	74,425	5081.25	25%	49,400 to	127,550	6,762.50	25%
74,425 to	113,425	14,462.50	28%	127,550 to	206,600	26,300.00	28%
113,425 to	202,550	25,382.50	33%	206,601 to	405,100	48,434.00	33%
202,550 to	228,800	54,793.75	35%	405,100 to	432,200	113,939.00	35%
228,800	......	63,981.25	39.6%	432,200 to	......	123,424.00	39.6%

TAX RATE SCHEDULE FOR ESTATES AND TRUSTS		
Taxable Income	Tax on Lower Amount	Tax Rate on Excess
$ -0- to $2,500	$ -0-	15%
2,500 to 5,800	375.00	25%
5,800 to 8,900	1,200.00	28%
8,900 to 12,150	2,068.00	33%
12,150 to	3,140.50	39.6%

TAXABLE YEARS BEGINNING IN 2013

SINGLE INDIVIDUALS			JOINT RETURNS AND SURVIVNG SPOUSES		
Taxable Income	Tax on Lower Amount	Tax Rate on Excess	Taxable Income	Tax on Lower Amount	Tax Rate on Excess
$ -0- to 8,925	$ -0-	10%	$ -0- to $17,850	$ -0-	10%
8,925 to 36,250	892.50	15%	17,850 to 72,500	1,785.00	15%
36,250 to 87,850	4,991.25	25%	72,500 to 146,400	9,982.50	25%
87,850 to 183,250	17,891.25	28%	146,400 to 223,050	28,457.50	28%
183,250 to 398,350	44,603.25	33%	223,050 to 398,350	49,919.50	33%
398,350 to 400,000	115,586.25	35%	398,350 to 450,000	107,768.50	35%
400,000 to	116,163.75	39.6%	450,000 to	125,846.00	39.6%

MARRIED FILING SEPARATELY			HEAD OF HOUSEHOLD		
Taxable Income	Tax on Lower Amount	Tax Rate on Excess	Taxable Income	Tax on Lower Amount	Tax Rate on Excess
$ -0- to $8,9250	$ -0-	10%	$ -0- to $12,750	$ -0-	10%
8,925 to 36,250	892.50	15%	12,750 to 48,600	1,275.00	15%
36,250 to 73,200	4,991.25	25%	48,600 to 125,450	6,652.50	25%
73,200 to 111,525	14,228.75	28%	125,450 to 203,150	25,865.00	28%
111,526 to 199,175	24,959.25	33%	203,150 to 398,350	47,621.00	33%
199,176 to 225,000	53,884.25	35%	398,350 to 425,000	112,037.00	35%
225,000	62,923.00	39.6%	425,000 to	121,364.50	39.6%

TAX RATE SCHEDULE FOR ESTATES AND TRUSTS		
Taxable Income	Tax on Lower Amount	Tax Rate on Excess
$ -0- to $2,450	$ -0-	15%
2,450 to 5,700	367.50	25%
5,700 to 8,750	1,180.00	28%
8,750 to 11,950	2,034.00	33%
11,950 to	3,090.00	39.6%

INNOCENT SPOUSE RULES

Married taxpayers typically choose to file a joint tax return because this filing status provides certain benefits. If married taxpayers file a joint tax return, both are jointly and individually responsible for the tax and any interest or penalty due on the joint return even if they later divorce.[1] This is true even if a divorce decree states that a former spouse will be responsible for any amounts due on previously filed joint returns. One spouse may be held responsible for all the tax due even if the other spouse earned all the income.

However, in some cases, based on the innocent spouse rules, a spouse may be relieved of some or all of his or her joint and several liability for tax, interest, and penalties assessed on a joint tax return.[2] The three types of relief are as follows:

- *Innocent spouse relief* for additional tax owed by a spouse because his or her spouse (or former spouse) failed to report income or claimed improper deductions or credits;

- *Separation of liability relief* provides for the allocation of any item giving rise to a deficiency on a joint return to the spouse responsible for the deficiency as if the responsible spouse had reported such item on a separate return.[2] In other words, it shifts the joint liability for the deficiency to the responsible spouse;[3] and

- *Equitable relief* may apply when a spouse does not qualify for innocent spouse relief or separation of liability relief with regard to an unpaid tax or deficiency.[4]

INNOCENT SPOUSE RELIEF

A spouse must meet all of the following conditions to qualify for innocent spouse relief:

- The spouse must have filed a joint return that has an understatement of tax directly related to his or her spouse's erroneous items. Any income omitted from the joint return is an erroneous item. Deductions, credits, and property bases (for computing taxable gain or loss) are erroneous items if they are incorrectly reported on the joint return.

- The spouse establishes that at the time he or she signed the joint return, he or she did not know, and had no reason to know, that there was an understatement of tax.

- Taking into account all the facts and circumstances, it would be unfair to hold the spouse liable for the understatement of tax; and

- The spouse requests relief no later than two years after the date the IRS first attempted to collect the tax from him or her.[5]

SEPARATION OF LIABILITY RELIEF

To qualify for separation of liability relief, the following conditions must be satisfied:

- A joint return was filed;

- At the time of the election, the spouse requesting the relief was separated or divorced (or widowed) or had not been a member of the same household at any time during the twelve-month period ending on the date of the request for relief;

- The requesting spouse sought relief within two years of the first IRS collection activity; and

- At the time of the signing of the joint return, the requesting spouse had no actual knowledge of the non-requesting spouse's item giving rise to the deficiency.[6]

EQUITABLE RELIEF

A spouse who does not qualify for innocent spouse relief or separation of liability relief, may qualify for equitable relief from joint and several liability. Unlike the latter two forms of relief, equitable relief covers underpayment of tax attributable to the other spouse in addition to an income tax deficiency. Rev. Proc. 2013-34[7] sets forth a three-step procedure to determine whether equitable relief is warranted.

First, the following threshold requirements must be met:

1. The requesting spouse filed a join return for the tax year in question;

2. The requesting spouse does not qualify for innocent spouse relief or separation of liability relief;

3. The claim for relief is timely filed;[8]

4. There were no assets transferred between the spouses as part of a fraudulent scheme by the spouses;

5. The non-requesting spouse did not transfer disqualified assets to the requesting spouse;[9]

6. The requesting spouse did not knowingly participate in the filing of a fraudulent joint return; and

7. Absent certain exceptions, the tax liability from which the requesting spouse seeks relief is attributable to an item of the non-requesting spouse that resulted in a deficiency or an underpayment of tax.

Second, in order to qualify for streamlined relief, the following three conditions must be met:

1. The spouse requesting the relief was separated or divorced (or widowed) or had not been a member of the same household at any time during the twelve-month period ending on the date of the request for relief;

2. The spouse requesting relief would suffer economic hardship[10] is relief was not granted; and

3. The spouse requesting relief did not know and or have reason to know that there was a deficiency with regard to the originally filed return, or, in the case of an underpayment, did not know or have reason to know that the non-requesting spouse would or could not pay the tax liability reported on the joint return.

Finally, if the requesting spouse fails to qualify for streamlined relief, equitable relief may be available if taking into account all of the facts and circumstances, it would be inequitable to hold the requesting spouse responsible for the deficiency or underpayment. Rev. Proc. 2013-34 lists the following non-exclusive list of factors to be considered in determining whether equitable relief is warranted. In doing so, the IRS "grades" the factors as weighing in favor of relief, against relief or neutral:

1. Whether the requesting spouse was married to the non-requesting spouse at the time the IRS made its determination regarding the deficiency or underpayment.

2. Economic hardship, i.e., the ability of the requesting spouse to pay reasonable living expenses if relief is not granted.

3. Lack of actual knowledge or reason to know of deficiency or whether the non-requesting spouse would not or could not pay the tax liability (that was ultimately not paid) at the time or within a reasonable amount of time after filing the return.[11]

4. Legal obligation by the requesting or non-requesting spouse to pay the outstanding tax liability as evidenced by a divorce decree or other legally binding agreement.

5. Whether the requesting spouse received a significant benefit from the unpaid tax or deficiency. A significant benefit goes beyond normal support and encompasses a lavish lifestyle. The revenue procedure further provides that if the amount of the unpaid tax or deficiency is small so that neither spouse received a significant benefit, this factor is considered to be neutral. However, in a recent decision, the Tax Court rejected the revenue procedure's characterization of that factor being graded neutral — holding that the lack of a significant benefit from a relatively small deficiency should weigh in favor of relief for the requesting spouse.[12]

6. Whether the requesting spouse has made a good faith effort to comply with the income tax laws in the taxable years following the taxable year or years to which the relief relates.

7. The state of the requesting spouse's mental or physical health at the time the return or returns were filed.

HOW IT IS DONE

In order to request innocent spouse relief, separation of liability relief, or equitable relief, the requesting spouse must:

- File Form 8857 (Request for Innocent Spouse Relief) or a written statement containing the same information required on Form 8857, and

- Sign Form 8857, or the written statement, under penalties of perjury.[13]

If a spouse requests relief from joint liability, the IRS is required to notify the non-requesting spouse to allow him or her to oppose the request by providing the IRS with relevant information.[14] If the IRS denies the spouse's request for relief, he or she may challenge the denial by filing a petition for review by the Tax Court.[15] In that event, the Tax Court must provide the non-requesting spouse notice of the proceeding and allow him or her to become a party in opposition to the request for relief.[16]

Spouses living in community property states (Arizona, California, Idaho, Louisiana, Nevada, New Mexico, Texas, Washington and Wisconsin) who file separate returns are also eligible for innocent spouse relief.[17]

Finally, it is possible that as part of the relief granted, the requesting spouse may be entitled to refund or tax credit with respect to amounts he or she paid to the IRS. This relief, however, is not available to spouse's requesting separation of liability relief.[18]

INJURED SPOUSE RELIEF

The IRS has the authority to apply a taxpayer's income tax refund from one tax year against outstanding income tax liabilities from other tax years.[19] As a result, if one spouse has an outstanding tax liability that he or she is solely responsible to pay, it may create a dilemma if the couple files a joint return. If such a joint return generates a refund, the IRS will generally apply the entire refund to the outstanding tax liability of the responsible spouse[20]—thus depriving the non-responsible spouse of his or her share of the refund. However, if the non-responsible spouse files an "injured spouse" claim, the IRS is required to pay over his or her share of the refund.[21] In order to make the claim, the injured spouse files a Form 8379 either with the originally filed joint return or separately.

ENDNOTES

1. I.R.C. §6013(d)(3); IRS Publication 971.
2. *Howerter v. Comm'r.*, T.C. Summary Opinion 2014-15 (February 19, 2014).
3. I.R.C. §6015(c).
4. I.R.C. §6015(f).
5. I.R.C. §6015(b).
6. I.R.C. §6015(c), 6015(c)(3); Treas. Reg. §1.6015-3.
7. 2013-43 I.R.B. 397, superseding Rev. Proc. 2003-2 C.B. 296.
8. If the relief is of joint and several tax liability, the claim must be made within the ten-year collection statute of limitation period. Rev. Proc. 2013-34, §4.01(3)(a). If the relief is a claim for a tax credit or refund, the claim must be made by the later of three years from the date the return was filed or two years from the date of payment. Rev. Proc. 2013-34, §4.01(3)(b).
9. A "disqualifying asset" is an asset transferred from the non-requesting spouse (the one who purportedly should be responsible for the tax) to the requesting spouse for the principal purpose of tax avoidance. I.R.C. §6015(c)(4)(B).
10. Economic hardship such that the requesting spouse would lack the means necessary for basic living expenses.
11. With regard to knowledge of whether the tax liability could or would be paid, the revenue procedure provides that if the requesting spouse was abused by the non-requesting spouse or the non-requesting spouse maintained control of the household finances by restricting the requesting spouse's access to that information; and, because of the abuse or financial control,

the requesting spouse was not able to question the payment of the tax reported for fear of the non-requesting spouse's retaliation, this factor would weigh in favor of relief even if the requesting spouse knew or had reason to know of the non-requesting spouse's intent or ability to pay the taxes.

12. *Howerter v. Comm'r.*, T.C. Summary Opinion 2014-15 (February 19, 2014).

13. Treas. Reg. §1.6015-5.

14. I.R.C. §6015(h)(2); Treas. Reg. §1.6015-6.

15. I.R.C. §6015(e).

16. I.R.C. §6015(e)(4).

17. I.R.C. §66(c); Treas. Reg. §1.66-4, Rev. Proc. 2013-34, 2013-43 I.R.B. 397 superseding Rev. Proc. 2003-61, 2003-2 C.B. 296.

18. I.R.C. §6015(g)(3).

19. I.R.C. §6402(b).

20. Rev. Rul. 84-171, 1984-2 C.B. 310.

21. IRM 25.15.1.2.5; Treas. Reg. §§31.285.2(f) and (g).

INDEX